83370

VIETNAM
AT 24
FRAMES
A SECOND

Texas Film and Media Studies Series
Thomas Schatz, Editor

VIETNAM
AT 24
FRAMES
A SECOND
JEREMY M. DEVINE

A Critical and Thematic Analysis of Over 400 Films
about the Vietnam War

Foreword by Thomas Schatz

University of Texas Press, Austin

Dedicated to Nancy,
with love and appreciation,
and to Alex, Sam, and Rachel,
with the hope that their generation may know peace,
and to Anne & Lenny

Published by special arrangement with McFarland & Company, Inc., Publishers, Jefferson, North Carolina.

Copyright © 1995 Jeremy M. Devine

Foreword and Introduction to the Paperback Edition copyright © 1999 by the University of Texas Press

All rights reserved

Printed in the United States of America

First University of Texas Press edition, 1999

∞ The paper used in this book meets the minimum requirements of ANSI/NISO Z39.48-1992 (R1997) (Permanence of Paper).

Library of Congress
Cataloging-in-Publication Data

Devine, Jeremy M., 1958–
Vietnam at 24 frames a second : a critical and thematic analysis of over 400 films about the Vietnam war / Jeremy M. Devine.
p.   cm. — (Texas film and media studies series)
Originally published: Jefferson, NC : McFarland, © 1995. Includes bibliographical references and index. ISBN 0-292-71601-X (pbk. : alk. paper)
1. Vietnamese Conflict, 1961–1975—Motion pictures and the conflict.   2. Indochinese War, 1946–1954—Motion pictures and the war.   3. War films—United States—History and criticism.   I. title.   II. Title: Vietnam at twenty four frames a second.   III. Series.
DS557.73.D48   1999
791.43'658—dc21   98-51732

Contents

Foreword

The Vietnam War Film:
America's Post-Traumatic Stress Disorder

by Thomas Schatz

The war film is utterly unique among movie genres. No other film formula adheres so closely to "real" historical conditions and events. No other fictional form intermingles so freely with news, documentary, and other nonfiction depictions of those same conditions and events. No other form of popular entertainment is so patently political and ideological, underscoring Hollywood's role as a "national cinema" in representing the collective consciousness of a people—the tangle of beliefs, values, and attitudes that can compel a nation to wage war. Sometimes these articulations are celebratory and upbeat, sometimes dark and disturbing. At times they are deadly accurate and at other times patently fictitious, even dangerously false. In no other genre, in fact, are the nation's history and mythology so dynamically fused—not even in the Western, in which chronological distance and nostalgia tend to recast history as national mythology.

The Hollywood war film was effectively "invented" during World War II, when the movies were America's central form of cultural expression, and when Hollywood served (at Washington's behest) as an impromptu propaganda agency, devoting roughly one-quarter of its feature films (and 90 percent of its newsreels) to the "war effort." From 1942 through 1945, Hollywood cranked out hundreds of war-related features, most notably "combat films" depicting actual battles—films like *Wake Island, Bataan, Air Force,* and *Guadalcanal Diary* which, taken together, coalesced into a vast on-screen serialization of the war. Meanwhile, non-combat subgenres, from musicals and spy thrillers to home-front romances and melodramas, examined war-related issues and conditions from various other perspectives. But whatever the subgenre, the overall message of those war films was essentially the same: the nation was a social and cultural community with a shared history and destiny, and with a populace utterly unified in its commitment to the war effort.

While World War II was the defining event for the United States in the first half of the twentieth century, the signal event of the ensuing quarter-century was Vietnam. But whereas World War II marked the nation's coming of age as a global power and as a people able to overcome deep differences in the heroic pursuit of a shared objective, Vietnam marked something else entirely: America's loss of innocence, its abuse of power on a global scale, and social divisions that only grew worse in the face of a national crisis.

It is scarcely surprising, then, that the movie industry treated the Vietnam

War in vastly different terms than it did World War II—a fact that Jeremy Devine makes abundantly clear in *Vietnam at 24 Frames a Second*. In this exhaustive and incisive treatment of the Vietnam War film, easily the best study on the subject yet written, Devine charts the gradual emergence and complex development of an utterly unique cycle of war films—a cycle that was both indebted to and altogether distinct from the genre that spawned it. As Devine demonstrates via both close analysis of individual films and careful consideration of the "larger" social and industrial context, the Vietnam War film was a species unto itself, a remarkably vital process whereby the public— or movie audiences, anyway—came to terms with the Vietnam War as both a military and a cultural conflict. Devine's main focus throughout is on the films themselves—on plot and character, setting and theme, visual style and pro- duction values, and also on industrial factors, from the financing and film- making process to the distribution and reception of key films.

The vast majority of these films appeared after the fall of Saigon and the ignominious U.S. withdrawal in 1975. Indeed, Devine demonstrates that "post-traumatic stress syndrome" applies not only to the Vietnam veteran's lingering reaction to combat but also, if these films are any indication, to the nation's delayed psychic response to the war. There were rare on-screen depic- tions during the war itself, most notably John Wayne's 1968 jingoistic fantasy *The Green Berets*—a film released the year of the Tet Offensive, which not only nullified its propaganda value but confirmed an industry bias that war- related features were box-office poison. Thus Devine, like other critics and scholars, argues that the wartime films which were most effective in dealing with Vietnam did so "by indirection"—films like *The Wild Bunch*, *Ulzana's Raid*, and *Deliverance*, which examined the macho ethos, blood lust, and na- tionalistic fervor that paved the way to Vietnam.

Jeremy Devine considers these back-handed wartime (and immediate post- war) efforts, emphasizing the ten-year span from 1967 to 1977. But the bulk and real strength of *Vietnam at 24 Frames a Second* involves his exhaustive account of Hollywood's deferred response to—and effective reconstruction of—the Vietnam War itself. This began in earnest with the release of a half- dozen breakthrough films in the late 1970s, most notably *The Deer Hunter* and *Coming Home* in 1978 and *Apocalypse Now* in 1979, three popular and commercial hits that removed the stigma of Vietnam and opened the way for a veritable outpouring of war-related films over the next decade.

Vietnam war films would fall into essentially the same subgenres as the World War II antecedents—combat films, prisoner-of-war films, home-front melodramas, returning vet sagas, and so on—but as Devine aptly points out time and again, these films differed vastly from Hollywood's earlier depic- tions of the "good war." The Vietnam War films did not attempt to historicize the conflicts and articulate the consensus view of "why we fight" (as Frank Capra's legendary World War II documentary series put it), but worked in- stead to reveal the deep-seated social conflicts and irreconcilable cultural contradictions that led to the war in Vietnam and fueled the war-related hostilities at home. What coalesced in Hollywood's on-screen representation of the Vietnam War, whether on the "home front" or "in country," was a portrait of a nation at war not with a common enemy but with itself.

Devine demonstrates that the Vietnam War film during the 1980s was a genre at war with itself as well, best exemplified perhaps by the rift between the Rambo films, those fantasies of heroic retribution and blatant historical reconstruction ("Do we get to win this time?"), and the grim fatalism and hyperrealism of films like *Platoon* and *Full Metal Jacket*. Home-front dramas were equally split, particularly in depicting the Vietnam vet—ranging from the deranged psychopath of countless thrillers to the sympathetic protagonist in male weepies, victimized by forces beyond his understanding or control.

Devine demonstrates, too, that by the mid-1990s both the cycle and the cultural angst it invoked had begun to run their course. In terms of simple output as well as critical and popular impact, the Vietnam War film fell off dramatically in the course of the 1990s, as the conflicts of that era and the residue of the Cold War mentality that informed it steadily faded into cultural memory. Thus the value and the import of Jeremy Devine's *Vietnam at 24 Frames a Second*, which so expertly traces both the genealogy and the trajectory of a crucial, complex cycle of popular films.

Acknowledgments

This book would not have been possible without my dear wife, Nancy. Aside from her assistance in word processing and editing, she kept me going when the task seemed insurmountable. She always believed in me and "the project." Additional thanks are due to Judith Holz and Laura Nelson for their editing assistance and feedback.

Introduction

As far back as 1898, when motion pictures were in their infancy, a short film entitled *Tearing Down the Spanish Flag* rallied its viewers to the American cause in the Spanish-American War. The very first film to win the Oscar for Best Picture in 1927 was the war film *Wings*, a tale of World War I flying aces. During the course of World War II nearly 450 features were made about the conflagration (see Tessa Horan's "F.Y.I.," *Premiere*, May 1991, p. 15). Although the Korean conflict, America's "forgotten war," had only nine releases concomitant to the hostilities, throughout the history of film, a body of work known only since 1896, war has provided one of the most compelling subject areas. Inherent in it is a panoply of human emotion, tragedy, and spectacle that lend themselves to the salient medium.

Conventional wisdom correctly tells us that many of our images and opinions of war are shaped by what we have seen on television or in film. The written word recedes in the wake of the electronic media and instantaneous satellite imagery exemplified by the coverage of the Persian Gulf War. Especially for our youth, the unforgettable moments are not what was gleaned from an astute author on the op-ed page. Rather, indelibly marked on the collective conscious are CNN's reports from Baghdad under air assault, the pitiful surrender of Iraqi troops to allied forces and ABC cameramen, or the dramatic, live, all-network briefing by General Schwarzkopf.

When America went off to fight communism in the jungles of Vietnam, twenty years of glorious World War II imagery from films accompanied the troops and policymakers. But something went awry in Southeast Asia. For the first time the United States lost a war and with it a great deal of pride, innocence, and many lives. Only one film was made about the Vietnam War during the conflict itself. Most appropriately that was the very personalized work of a man who exemplified gung-ho Americana, John Wayne. His instantly dated and reviled film *The Green Berets* was released in 1968.

As the consensus about the Vietnam War unraveled, Hollywood reacted as any for-profit business would; it retreated from the unpalatable. No longer could it serve its traditional propaganda-boosting role or entertain in a conventional sense. Therefore it was not until two years after the fall of Saigon in 1975 that the now-familiar Vietnam War films such as *The Deerhunter* and *Coming Home* were released. Since that time the casual observer might be able to mention only a handful of films about the hated conflict. They probably include *Apocalypse Now, Platoon,* and *Born on the Fourth of July.* Upon reflection one might also call to mind *The Boys in Company C, Hamburger Hill,* or *Full Metal Jacket.* Perhaps the important *Rambo* and *MIA* movies might also be discerned.

Correcting the notion that there have been relatively few Vietnam War films is what fills the pages of this book. Critical commentary is offered on more than 400 feature-length motion pictures. In attempting to be comprehensive, I have included discussions of many films that admittedly make merely tangential reference to the war. However, as a unique and tragic chapter in American history, the Vietnam War had a rich historic base not just in the jungles of Southeast Asia but also in the domestic issues of conscription, protest, veteran reintegration, loss, and rebirth.

This work begins with the dawn of the cold war in 1948, a period reflecting the background basis for the belief systems that led us into the conflict. It continues through the 1950s and the war years of the 1960s and early 1970s, then the aftermath and beyond, even into the future of the 1990s. This represents nearly a half-century body of work. This book runs the gamut of genres. Surprising to some will be the fact that critical attention is paid to horror films, comedies, and even one musical, as well as the anticipated plethora of dramas, actioners, and adventure tales.

This book is necessarily limited primarily to English-language and fictional works. Therefore by self-imposed definition many fine documentaries and foreign films are not discussed. However, rules, particularly self-imposed ones, are made to be broken. Thus there are a few French, Vietnamese, and other foreign films examined in these pages. So, too, a limited number of documentaries that received the rare general release are also included.

An attempt is made to place each chapter's era in its historical context. This takes the form of brief introductory passages that describe what was happening in the war and the greater world stage at the time of the films' releases. Utilizing a chronological approach to the subject best allows this essential integration of the reel and real worlds. In addition, the evolution of imagery becomes more apparent and speaks in a subtly patterned totality to the changes in perspective toward the war as reflected and as created by the films.

One other matrix is laid over the progression of film discussions to help in understanding the images. That is the dynamics of the film industry itself. The production, exhibition, and distribution of feature-length films is a fascinating process that exemplifies the often uneasy coexistence of artistic and business concerns in the American society. Far from tending to eliminate Vietnam War films, the programming or software concerns of the industry have dictated a contextualization of the relevant films. Vietnam as a subject has been part of the evolution from double features to drive-in flicks to made-for-television movies to made-for-video and cable releases. Each of these facets of the medium has contributed to the ranks of films discussed in the following pages.

As a practical note, in the video age it is relatively easy to gain access to many of the titles in these pages, and the reader is strongly urged to view these motion pictures. In many instances in the context of production histories, plot synopses, or commentary, I have revealed the endings or dénouements. Therefore, the reader who does not want such information is forewarned. One can either preview the movie or consult the index to determine the latter pages of a discussion of a particular film and skip them until after viewing. For the busy student or more casual reader, the entries are designed to be informative and not necessitate frequent, costly, and time-consuming rentals. However, as clearly defined by the relative length of certain treatments, some films are more important than others to this study and deserve viewing.

Forest Gump (Photo by Phillip V. Caruso, 1994)

Introduction
to the Paperback Edition

Gump and Rapprochement, 1994–1998

Since the publication of the first edition, the United States and Vietnam have normalized relations. This reconciliation is reflective of our continued process of healing from the trauma of the Vietnam War. As might be expected, film treatments on the conflict have dropped off. With 400-plus films preceding, many stories have already been played out. More importantly, many of the therapeutic aspects of the 40-plus years of films which are the subject of this work have been achieved.

Normalization of relations with Hanoi were led by a bipartisan coalition of legislators which included veteran Senators Bob Kerrey (D-Neb.), John Kerry (D-Mass.), John McCain (R-Ariz.) and Representatives Sam Johnson (R-Tex.) and Pete Petersen (D-Fla.). The latter three had all been POWs, and Petersen was named the first ambassador to Vietnam. As always, closely following the political overtures were economic missions. These included film-makers scouting locations, the theater multiplexing of Vietnam, and the sale of American films to Vietnamese television. In the mid-90s one of the hottest nightspots in Ho Chi Minh City, the former Saigon, was the Apocalypse Now Bar.

Encapsulating the ten chapters of this book into types of films by era reveals the cathartic nature of the oeuvre. The "Early Years" typified our ignorance and naïveté in Southeast Asia. The years concomitant to the war itself had very few direct treatments of it. Films that did exist often recontextualized Vietnam via allegory or metaphor. Most often we just ignored the war. The pragmatic for-profit studios recoiled from the unpopular and lethal conflict, assuming that it was box office poison. However, by the late 1970s a huge delayed Hollywood reaction was unleashed with many important portrayals of the war. This intensity dissipated by the early 1980s to be replaced by a cinematic reworking of the conflict in order to afford us the opportunity to "win" via Ramboesque fantasy. The late 1980s films revealed a desire to embrace the individual veterans and move away from the divisive political arguments. The Gulf War and 1990s movies reinforced the realization that the veterans of Vietnam had been shortchanged.

According to many actual veterans of the Vietnam War, the films were a painful but necessary part of the passage. Marine vet Gerald A. Byrne stated:

> How appropriate that it was the movie business that began my healing process. It started with "The Deerhunter," the film that said the most, at least for me,

about the misery of war. It showed the anger, fear, frustration and confusion, that were the common denominators of the conflict. . . . Hollywood hit Vietnam from every direction. . . .

Vietnam was a personal affair. It was different for everyone. So every vet could point to a picture and say that was their Vietnam.[1]

The most notable of the Vietnam war films of the 1994–1998 period is the story of a simpleton whose life adventures so uniquely captured the 1960s zeitgeist that it became the fifth highest grossing film of all time. *Forrest Gump* (1994) transcended hawks, doves, and other political considerations via the omnipresent grace afforded a truly likable but largely oblivious character. He presides at and survives the historic events that stripped away our collective innocence: the Civil Rights movement, Vietnam, etc. His resilience is that of America.

This charming film starring Tom Hanks and chock-full of evocative 1960s tunes synthesized many of the elements of the Vietnam War film genres. It featured harrowing combat scenes computer enhanced for maximum effect. It chronicled the difficult readjustment to civilian life of Forrest's beloved Lt. Dan (Gary Sinise), confined to a wheelchair having lost his legs. It touched upon the anti-war movement via Gump's love interest Jenny (Robin Wright). She, unlike Forrest, succumbs to all of the sinister pitfalls and traumas of the era, a symbol of our confusion. Ultimately, the Academy Award–winning performance of Hanks works because the opaqueness of the politics is not only transcended but rendered moot by the clarity of the hero's goodness.

Other notable films from the 1994–1998 period include *The Walking Dead* (1995), directed by Preston A. Whitmore II, and *Dead Presidents* (1995) from Albert and Allen Hughes. All are young African American filmmakers. Their perspectives on the combat experience and its aftermath for the Black soldier reflected a disgust with the exploitation and lack of gratitude they perceived. Their dramatic themes mimic many of the late 1970s Blaxploitation films.

Disney provided a rare child-friendly entry in 1995 with *Operation Dumbo Drop*. Loosely based on a real life incident, it tells the tale of good-natured American servicemen trying to aid their Montagnard allies by procuring their village a new pachyderm. On a more serious note was the much-anticipated adaptation of Neil Sheehan's Pulitzer Prize–winning biography of Lt. Colonel John Paul Vann, *A Bright Shining Lie* (1998), starring Bill Paxton. Vann's "tour of duty" from 1962 to 1972 began with gung-ho optimism but turned to disillusionment over our compromised tactics, corrupt allies, and inflated body counts. HBO's $14 million production traces the arc of U.S. involvement through the fascinating experiences of its flawed hero. Many other films in the 1994–1998 period contained characters who were veterans, featured combat sequences, or examined the soldiers' readjustment to civilian life. While new treatments, they were very much informed by the preceding four-decade body of work to be examined in the pages to follow.

By the time of this paperback publication, a notable cultural phenomenon is the rebirth of the World War II film. Stephen Spielberg's powerful ode to the World War II fighting man and the sacrifice of his generation, *Saving Private Ryan*, has taken the country by storm. Anxiously awaited is director Terence Malick's take on that conflict, *The Thin Red Line*. Other theatrical and cable entries on that war represent a resurgence that has not been seen in film in 30 years. One of the many topics elicited by the powerful *Saving Private Ryan*, starring Tom Hanks, is the reaction of actual World War II vets, now men in their seventies, to the harrowing, realistic, and gruesome combat sequences such as the D-Day invasion. Never before has the chaos and carnage of combat been so powerfully evoked. Thanks to Spielberg's genius and modern technological advances in sound editing, as well as their graphic nature, the scenes are gut wrenching.

This re-examination of the "Good War" is long overdue. There is no question that these films are partially informed by and owe a debt to the Vietnam War films with which their creators are now quite familiar. Their graphic nature reflects a shift in mores as to what is depictable. Their uncomfortable veracity in American boys not always acting according to the "rules of war" are truths that would not be presentable without the preceding generation of Vietnam treatments. The very fact that World War II has a long-overdue cinematic resurgence demonstrates the manner in which the Vietnam War films have receded from the stage. Yet they will continue, albeit in diminished quantity. We have exorcised many of our Vietnam demons. How poignant and long overdue it is that we help do the same for a generation that is literally dying out. It is important that we acknowledge our collective debt of gratitude to this generation that sacrificed so much for us to be free. In so doing we bring additional honor on them and the generation of their sons, some of whom also fought and died in the jungles of Vietnam.

Reference

1. Gerald A. Byrne, "Hollywood Helped Heal the Wounds of War," *Daily Variety*, July 22, 1991, pp. 4–5.

Chapter 1

Viet Where?
The Early Years, 1948–1966

In 1950, as the United States was becoming embroiled in the Korean War, its long-term commitment to South Vietnam was also beginning. On June 27 of that year, President Harry S Truman ordered the air force and navy to Korea following the North's invasion of the South. On the same day, 35 U.S. military advisers were sent to South Vietnam to provide aid and training to the anticommunist government.

The post–World War II dissolution of the colonial empires rocked the entire region of Southeast Asia. Assessing the escalating involvement from the Truman to the Nixon administrations is now most instructive not as a source of blame attribution but as evidence of the continuity of U.S. foreign policy. The American role in Vietnam cannot be said to have started at any one point. Not in 1950 with Truman's order, nor in February 1955 when the United States agreed to train the South Vietnamese army, nor with the first combat fatality, nor on August 7, 1964, when Congress passed the Gulf of Tonkin Resolution.

Despite these tragic milestones, it is also incorrect to say that movies about the war began with *The Green Berets* in 1968 or the postwar releases from the major film companies in 1978. War films set in Vietnam became Vietnam War films and along the way became more meaningful as our experience became more tragic. Many people dismiss as irrelevant the early films that predate the heart of the actual conflict. They do not bear the imprint of time, perspective, history, revisionism, firsthand knowledge, or, in other words, hindsight. However, the very ignorance and naïveté of the early films set in Vietnam are the key to their meaningfulness. It is precisely because many of them are so unknowing, so traditionally rooted in a "gung-ho" World War II style, that we can begin to see just how little Americans knew about what they were getting themselves into.

The filmmakers were not clairvoyant, so the early Vietnam War films are fascinating because they offer an inkling as to how the United States became embroiled in fighting communism in Southeast Asia. It is amazing to see how different Vietnam looked to Americans then and now. Not just that country changed; the United States did too.

1

For the most part, these early Vietnam-related films were low-budget "B" movies. A "B" movie usually connotes lower production values and second-tier casts. It was designed to fill less discriminating programming needs, such as the lower half of a double bill. Some of the early Vietnam movies concerned the French involvement in Indochina as much as a nascent American presence. As products of the late 1940s, 1950s, and early 1960s, they all exhibited a strong anticommunism. Their politics thus reflected the preeminent theme of U.S. foreign policy since the end of World War II. Aside from mirroring the attitudes and beliefs that eventually led to American involvement in Vietnam, these films helped reinforce those same ideas in the minds of their viewers. With the actual bloody debacle yet to come, heroism and romanticism were the order of the day in most war films.

Of the 14 films to be examined in this chapter, 11 could be construed as action B movies, including *A Yank in Indochina* and *Five Gates to Hell*. All take place "in-country," a term used later by hundreds of thousands of U.S. troops as a way of designating Vietnam. Sometimes the setting is merely labeled as a generic Indochinese country. Just a few years after the actual French defeat, the United States was acknowledged as the logical successor in the struggle for and as the guardian of freedom.

Rounding out the films in this chapter are big-budget "A" pictures. Their lesser number reflects the reticence of producers to risk large sums of money on a difficult subject such as Vietnam. Each recontextualized relevant contemporary commentary. The controversial adaptation of Graham Greene's *The Quiet American* turned the novel's representative of the U.S. government into a private citizen on a naïve mission. *The Ugly American* examined the turmoil in Southeast Asia in a more generic manner using the fictitious Sarkhan as a setting for upheaval. *The Lost Command* dealt with anticolonial revolution but quickly shifted from the French role in Vietnam to the equally disastrous Algerian revolution. All the A films had underlying ideas and themes that offered a glimpse into the complexity of the political landscape that the B movies were not willing or able to address.

The evolution of the role of the American characters in these early films reflects the process of U.S. involvement in the real-world situation. The two 1940s entries and the earliest 1950s picture merely tell the tale of American soldiers left over from World War II who get caught up in local intrigue. The mid–1950s films deal with the French role in Vietnam but feature American characters beginning to take responsibility in the anticommunist cause. By 1964–1966, the American characters are actively involved in the conflict, some in uniform as advisers and others as clandestine operatives. By *To the Shores of Hell*, U.S. combat troops are depicted arriving in Da Nang.

This examination and reflection of real-world events and attitudes as exemplified by the early pictures is the correct starting point for a thorough examination of Vietnam War films. To begin in 1968 with the only combat film produced during the war, *The Green Berets*, is to ignore background events and depictions.

Alan Ladd (second from left) starred with Veronica Lake in *Saigon* (Paramount Pictures, 1948).

Also, examining only the postwar-informed treatments of the late 1970s onward infuses the discussion with the omniscient negativism borne of defeat. Films featuring romantic naïveté and profound ignorance are a much more appropriate starting point.

In 1948, Paramount Pictures released *Saigon,* starring Alan Ladd and Veronica Lake and costarring Douglas Dick. Leslie Fenton directed and P. J. Wolfson produced the melodrama. Of interest to us now is the incorporation of the Vietnamese civil war into the story as an important backdrop for the action and intrigue. Pilots left over from the triumphs of World War II's Flying Tigers must decide whether they will use their expertise for black-market smuggling or for legal but less lucrative forms of commerce. This first feature thus shares some similar story-line components with a film made 42 years later and one of the last to be discussed in this book, *Air America.*

Also in 1948 was the Universal release *Rogue's Regiment,* starring Dick Powell. In this action adventure he portrayed a World War II vet who enlists in the French Foreign Legion in Indochina. There he actually ends up in pursuit of a Nazi war criminal. This is an interesting, albeit contrived, integration of the preceding and imminent conflicts.

In 1952, Douglas Dick returned to the region in Columbia's *A Yank in Indochina,* directed by Wallace A. Grissell. It also concerned American pilots in Southeast Asia, this time involved in guerrilla warfare. The movie was produced by Sam Katzman, was written by Samuel Newman, and costarred John Archer, Jean Wiles, and Harold Fong.

In 1954, the French were defeated at Dien Bien Phu. This loss by a mighty industrialized power to a determined band of Third World insurgents temporarily ended the Indochinese War. The dissolution of France's colonial empire became the source of many French films. The English-language versions of French involvement in this early period were more limited and reflected the overall American misunderstanding of real-life events.

Jump into Hell, released in 1955 by Warner Bros., was an action adventure B movie. The title refers to French paratroopers' attempts to reinforce their besieged garrison at Dien Bien Phu. *Jump into Hell* was directed by David Butler from a screenplay by Irving Wallace. It starred Jacques (anglicized to Jack) Sernas, Arnold Moss, Peter Van Eyck, and Kurt Kazsner. Dramatic newsreel footage of the French defeat was interspersed with fictionalized recreated action sequences. (This same airborne assault in the last days of the siege also served as the setting for the dramatic introduction of Alain Delon and his team of paratroopers in the big budget feature *The Lost Command* ten years later.)

During World War II, Sam Fuller had been a GI in the First Infantry Division, which was known as the "Big Red One." Upon returning to civilian life, Fuller made his way to Hollywood and by 1957 was not only directing films but was also the producer and writer of *China Gate* for Twentieth Century Fox. This B feature concerned the French in Indochina. Fuller utilized a veteran's trained eye to recreate exciting combat sequences. He offered gung-ho patriotism tempered by a man-in-the-trenches cynicism.

China Gate—like the preceding *Jump into Hell*—viewed the French as heroes trying to preserve not only their empire but also the liberty jeopardized by communist hordes. The initial voiceover dedicates the film to the French who taught the people of their lost colony the "love of God and of fellow man and advanced this backward society to its place as the 'Rice Bowl of Asia'." The postcredit newsreel footage recites a few historic facts to familiarize the audience with this far-off land. The film's title refers to Vietnam's position as Red China's gate to Indochina and the rest of the countries (later "dominoes") of Southeast Asia. The necessity of closing that gate is the subject of this jingoistic, ethnocentric adventure and love story.

China Gate's cast included Gene Barry, Angie Dickinson, Lee Van Cleef, George Givot, and Nat King Cole. The wonderful singer was afforded one song, a mournful title rendition. He managed to make the drivel sound beautiful and introduced the romantic aspects of the story.

The casting of *China Gate* is a marvelous example of the efforts that are made to pass off a Caucasian actor as a member of another race. Beautiful Angie Dickinson is Lucky, the fallen woman, a Eurasian half-breed. Lee Van Cleef appears as an evil, black-marketing Viet Minh major, utilizing Ming the Magnificent type makeup to achieve his racial transformation. Both are constantly forced to explain why they do not really look Oriental.

China Gate **(20th Century–Fox, 1957). Gene Barry as the American fighting alongside the beleaguered French in Vietnam.**

Set in 1954, the story begins in a besieged town in the north of Vietnam as
newsreel footage shows an airdrop on behalf of the French and anticommunist
forces. A cute little street urchin scurries about concealing his puppy from the
murderous clutches of a local barbarian. The child eludes the barbarian by
jumping into a foxhole occupied by a French legionnaire. Amid the ruins, the
isolation of the besieged town is underscored by the nearby highway sign. One
way points to Hanoi and the other to a curiously named Phuc Yen, with the letter
n scrawled much like a *w*.

The adorable innocent, a symbol of the future, makes his way to Lucky's
Bar, where the sultry Dickinson meets with the local French major. The legion-

naire proposes a secret mission to the black marketeer. Given her knowledge of safe smuggling routes and her romantic liaison with Van Cleef, the legionnaire proposes that she lead a group of commandos through the countryside to the secret tunnel stockpiles of the Viet Minh (the precursor to the Viet Cong). She declines the cash offer, instead intent on seeing that her only reward be that her son, the little boy with the dog, is brought to America to live out his life.

Complicating the dangerous mission is the assignment of the head dynamiter, American Gene Barry, to the team. It turns out that he is the father of the child and had abandoned Dickinson when their offspring exhibited Oriental features that his mother barely possessed. The grizzled legionnaires cannot believe he left such a woman and child. Barry is an outcast, but they all have a mission to perform in fighting the communists. The melodrama is stale and heavy-handed, but the setting is fascinating and topical.

In preparing for their journey, the men get acquainted. Like Korean War vet Barry, American Nat King Cole enlisted in the famed legion because what was started in Korea he wanted to finish here in Vietnam. After all, there are still a lot of "live Commies around." The French veterans of the Indochina campaign tell Cole that America is their friend and that even though his countrymen are not in uniform here, they support the French effort with money and supplies. Also present is a Vietnamese ranger and interpreter who goes under cover behind enemy lines. He is played by James Hong (an actor who will constantly reappear in the present work).

This international force arrayed against the communists is a necessity given the coalition of Russian, Chinese, and Vietnamese in opposition to a free way of life. To underscore the barbarism of the enemy, a local French missionary tells how the Viet Minh cut his leg off and staked a message to his back with a knife. Worst of all, the perpetrators of such atrocities switch sides at night, creating a problem of identifying the enemy. They line the trail with deadly booby traps of the most barbarous nature.

Amid some ancient Buddhist ruins Dickinson distracts a sentry; when he is killed, she remarks, "It's nothing at all." Her cynicism born of hardship and abandonment makes the men admire her and detest her ex-lover, their comrade in arms. Her words predate a similar steely refrain recited later by American soldiers in Vietnam in response to hardship: "It don't mean nothin'; it don't mean nothin'."

Finally alone, Dickinson and Barry confront each other. In Korea he was captured, and the communists tried to brainwash him. He survived and came back because "soldiering is my business. Korea got cold and Indochina got hot. . . . I don't like Commies, and the French got left holding the bag." This is one American who is going to do something about the situation! This is all well and good, but she knows the truth. He came back for a little Chinese boy, and they still love each other despite what they say. In the background of an enemy sentry's isolated jungle hut, scene of such pathos, are portraits of Ho Chi Minh, Joseph Stalin, and Mao Zedong.

Subsequently, there is an exciting firefight in the jungle, and Barry heroically saves the group. Further along in the journey a civilian boy spots the group and reports it to the nearby Viet Minh patrol. The group eludes the enemy, but not before Cole steps on a booby trap of nails. As the Viet Minh pass close by in the thick jungle, he grimaces in silence.

Dickinson joins some enemy soldiers in a party, distracting them as the group proceeds toward its destination. With great irony, the drunken and lascivious enemies sing "La Marseillaise" in unison with a purloined phonograph record. Leaving the undisciplined lot, Dickinson catches up with her squad.

She goes to meet the enemy major, who oversees the tunnel operation and storage of bombs and supplies. He too is a half-breed, and he is determined to prove his worth to his superiors. In an effort to impress the beautiful heroine, Van Cleef shows her the entire guerrilla operation and tells her that he is on a fast track to general on the winning side of this war. He correctly points out that the difference between a revolutionary and the father of a country is the outcome of just this type of conflict.

Dickinson returns to her band of men and briefs them on the tunnel system. She distracts the guards as one by one they are ambushed. Then she is unexpectedly detained by the major as the team continues to wire the stockpile with dynamite. The major tells her that he has been accepted at the prestigious Moscow staff school for generals! He is convinced that this will cause her to bring her little boy and join him.

Meanwhile the men await Dickinson's return in order to blow up the tunnels. The French commander is forced to tell Barry to push the plunger and complete this important military mission. He pleads for more time for his lover to escape. Tension mounts as the Viet Minh major detains Dickinson in conversation. They are interrupted by a phone call: the guards have discovered the charges and cut the wire. He knows that she has betrayed him! However, Dickinson manages to push the large man over a balcony, and she escapes to the tunnel. There she connects the cut wires and bravely blows herself and the arsenal to bits. The men mourn her as they escape back to the outpost where the adventure started. Barry and his son lovingly go off, bound for America. Cole watches and sings the sad lyrics of the title song, "China Gate."

The movie is dated in style but prescient in regard to an expanded U.S. role in the conflict, something the filmmaker advocates in the void left by the French departure. *China Gate* vilifies the enemy and propagandistically questions its civilization and way of life. The B movie's politics is tempered by drama, while action and bloodletting are softened by romance. This melodramatic integration would be rendered impossible by the real-world forces about to envelop the United States in Southeast Asia. *China Gate* as a 1950s potboiler is fascinating in its early depiction of the conflict. In retrospect, the film is humorous and tragic at the same time, both qualities inadvertently defining their power in a modern context.

The film is typical of its era in its vehement anticommunism. The depiction of Orientals is similar to that of World War II anti–Japanese films. Some ten years later, amid the controversy surrounding the U.S. combat role in Vietnam, another conservative anticommunist filmmaker, John Wayne, would use an innocent little boy to similar effect to connote our society's responsibility to the youth of this embattled region in his movie *The Green Berets.*

Even at this early juncture in the late 1950s, before our direct combat involvement occurred, other films would offer up a more complex assessment of the struggle taking place in Indochina. The straightforward advocacy of a strong role for the United States in *China Gate* would give way to further film discussions of specific foreign and military aid that echoed the concomitant real-life debate.

Of the group of early Vietnam War films, perhaps the best known is 1958's *The Quiet American.* Its fame is attributable to the controversial best-selling novel by Graham Greene from which it was adapted and whose title it shares. Also noteworthy and ironic is the casting of Audie Murphy as the protagonist, Alden Pyle, "The American." As the most decorated U.S. fighting man in World War II, the still baby-faced Murphy became (along with John Wayne) Hollywood's most readily identifiable soldier. Whereas the Duke personified the actor-soldier, Audie Murphy truly was the soldier-actor.

In the film, Murphy goes to Saigon as a representative of a privately funded aid effort. He is "determined to do good," intent on helping end the French-Indochina War by supporting a so-called third force as a democratic alternative in the battle. Michael Redgrave played a British journalist, Fowler, who narrates the story. The cynical observer becomes our eyes and ears on the conflict. In so doing, Fowler is the first such media type among many to come who all attempt to distance themselves from bloody circumstances. He and the American become friends but also rivals for the affections of a beautiful young Vietnamese girl, Phuong. She becomes a symbol of the covetous fighting of the colonials for the affections of the locals.

The duplicitous Fowler is used by the communists in their murder of the American Murphy. The film, like the book, is politically and socially prescient and also functions as a mystery thriller. *The Quiet American* is told in flashbacks leading to the violent death of the naïve young American. Claude Dauphin portrayed the French police inspector Vigot. The rest of the cast included Bruce Cabot, Richard Loo, Peter Trent, and a number of Asian (including Vietnamese) actors. Joseph L. Mankiewicz did triple duty for United Artists as producer, director, and writer.

In presenting a story featuring both political intrigue and a love interest, the film introduced the strange Vietnamese dichotomy of bloody reality coexisting with beautiful unspoiled romanticism. In the years to come, films portrayed many young Americans catching their first glimpse of Vietnam: each was struck by the intense beauty of the land and its people and then was quickly oriented to the danger and death inherent in the environment.

Englishman Fowler as a representative of the Old World order is struck by the American's inability to understand the danger, shifting loyalties, and inap-

The Quiet American **(United Artists, 1958). Michael Redgrave as Fowler, Giorgia Moll as Phuong, and Audie Murphy as Pyle, "the quiet American."**

propriateness of conventional notions of democracy in this context. In trying to explain to the naïve American what is happening, Fowler says, "You've been seeing war films. We're not a couple of Marines, and you're not even going to get the girl at the end." Later, in referring to the American's attempts to aid a repressive general and additionally galled when his rival saves his life out in the countryside, Fowler states in voiceover, "He moved like a hero in a boy's adventure story, wearing his heroism like a scout's badge and quite unaware of the absurdity and improbability of his adventure." These words are a prophetic warning to America, with its policymakers' penchant for supporting anyone who could be construed as our "man against communism" and with its general application of simple curatives to complex situations.

The Quiet American introduces the viewer to soon-to-be-familiar elements of the conflict, including the Viet Minh, the French debacle, the guerrilla nature of the enemy, and the domino theory. What the film eliminates but the novel describes are further unpleasant realities, such as the "bowel-loosening" intensity of combat, the use of napalm, and the military's management of the news.

When the American is involved in a tragic, mistimed terrorist explosion at the Place Garnier in Saigon, he is attempting to help create the third force as a nationalist-based rival to the communists for the hearts and minds of the populace. But as Fowler remarks in reference to the prototypical American, "His innocence is a type of insanity."[1] From the time the novel was written and the film was produced, such incidents of urban terrorism became commonplace in Saigon. Murphy's support of the general approximates the real-life American backing up Ngo Dinh Diem.

Jay Robert Nash and Stanley Ralph Ross in their compendium *The Motion Picture Guide* sum up why the film was criticized:

> Greene's book was highly critical of the American political involvement in Vietnam. The film, however, portrays Murphy's character not as an official of the American government (as he is in the novel), but as a private citizen with his own naïve plan for solving Vietnam's internal problems, not one officially sanctioned by the U.S. government. The switch removes Greene's point of view . . . and thereby removes any power the film might have had. Another problem is the casting of Murphy . . . not an actor of great depth. . . . In a film of seriousness and complexity he flounders. The audience is left emotionally tied to the Redgrave character (due to his superior performance), though his character is also adversely affected by the tampering with the source material.[2]

Physically, the war hero fit the bill as Alden Pyle, the quiet American described as "unmistakably young. . . . With an unused face . . . gangly legs and crew cut and wide campus gaze he seemed incapable of harm."[3] Here was a role that Martha Bayles writing in the *New Republic* calls "a single representative character—a prototypical American—to embody the pros and cons of United States policy."[4]

Although not a great actor, Murphy, by virtue of his genuine wartime heroism, was able to convey a rightness of attitude beyond his abilities in his new profession and indeed beyond the articulation of most American heroes and their government's own confused or obfuscated policies. Certainly Murphy's real-life exploits were an added plus and source of irony to Mankiewicz. If the casting of the hero Murphy as a misguided American caught in the confused gray morass of South Vietnam was ironic in 1958, it is doubly so now with 35-plus years of hindsight and lost lives. Murphy's youthful and handsome presence was that of a winner. His likable persona but ultimately limited range seemed to echo subliminally his character's good intent but oversimplistic understanding of the situation. Using Murphy made resonant such lines as "Your motives are good but . . . how are your scruples away from the wide-screened world of romance?" Clearly, America's future role in the conflict itself was as a victim of this same naïve paradox. The country that had never lost a war, the country of self-assurance, technological and military superiority, political and economic might, and good intent, would fail. This failure of analysis and execution added to the poignancy and breadth of Greene's political novel. All of America's arrayed strengths were impotent in the situation confronted in the film and in the war itself.

Among the little boys who would be forever touched by Audie Murphy and the heroic American soldier he personified was a young Ronnie Kovic of Massapequa, Long Island. In his celebrated book, *Born on the Fourth of July*, adapted and discussed later in its film version, Kovic puts into context the common cultural portrayal of war through films in general and the power of Murphy in particular: "Every Saturday afternoon we'd go down to the movies in the shopping center and watch . . . war movies with John Wayne and Audie Murphy. I'll never forget Audie Murphy in *To Hell and Back*. At the end he jumps on top of a flaming tank that's just about to explode and grabs the machine gun blasting it into German lines. He was so brave I had chills running up and down my back, wishing it were me up there. There were gasoline flames roaring around his legs, but he just kept firing that machine gun. It was the greatest movie I ever saw in my life."[5] This is the same actor whose character lay dead in the beginning of *The Quiet American*. Such are the power of movies and the responsibility of war movies. Whether romanticized or repugnant and realistic, most noncombatants' conceptions of war are formed or at least reinforced by such fictional portrayals. Movies are integral in creating a mass cultural psyche surrounding combat and the people we ask to risk their lives in it.

The Quiet American may have been sanitized, but it was important because it opened a window onto a storm that was forming. The film was technically significant and historic for another reason—it featured actual Vietnamese location photography. United Artists, a major film distributor with A movie stars and crew, shot much of the two-hour release in Vietnam before location shooting was quite as common as it is today. The B movies previously discussed were lucky to get into realistic locales or have second units. *The Quiet American* was in Vietnam during a several-year lull in full-scale military hostilities. When fighting broke out anew, Hollywood filmmakers found shooting to be logistically impossible. For American filmmakers, with the exception of *A Yank in Vietnam* in 1964, *Operation CIA* in 1965 (both to be discussed), and a few exterior establishing shots, actual Vietnamese locales were not used. They were simply impractical or off limits. Even after the cease-fire and the end of the Vietnam War, such filmmaking was not feasible from a political point of view. Thailand and the Philippines have most often served as the jungle and paddied stand-ins, with Hawaii, southern California, and even South Africa as less-authentic-looking locations for films set in Vietnam. With today's efforts at rapproachement, it is only a matter of time before much-needed American hard currency and filmmakers' desires for maximum authenticity combine to reestablish this genuine source of location shooting for movies about the Vietnam War.

When Graham Greene died on April 2, 1991, he was eulogized and honored as a great author. At around this same time, America rejoiced in eschewing the "ghost of Vietnam" through the Gulf War victory. America was also attempting to make postconflict policy concerning the fallout from its actions (i.e., the Kurds). In commenting on the author's life, critics revivified debates over the extent to which the United States could and should be responsible on the world stage. The war and Greene's death managed to reintroduce a discussion of his themes in a current context. In the process, his prescient early Vietnam-themed work managed to resurface as a bridge to the present.[6]

In Malaysia in the early 1990s, filmmaker Sydney Pollack was readying a new version of *The Quiet American,* which he promised would be a more "faithful remake" of the novel,[7] informed by 35 years of painful history. However, back in 1958 America's role in Vietnam was just beginning to escalate. Not even Greene could have completely predicted just how unhappy and unsuccessful the result of this commitment would be. Like the object of desire in *The Quiet American,* Phuong, the American people liked "films with happy endings best."[8]

James Clavell is famous as the best-selling author of *Shogun* and *Tai-Pan.* However, a lesser-known Clavel effort took place in 1959 when he produced, directed, and wrote the screenplay of a B melodrama from Twentieth Century–Fox entitled *Five Gates to Hell.* In reference to the title, it can be noted that when General William Tecumseh Sherman said during the Civil War that "war is hell," he provided part of the name for many films that wished to instantly convey their combat themes. The *China Gate* fearfully left open in 1957 was now a gaping *Five Gates* in 1959.

Five Gates to Hell starred gravelly voiced Neville Brand, Patricia Owens, Shirley Knight, Nancy Kulp, Benson Fong, and John Morley. In a tradition that has persisted from silents through Charlie Chan to the present-day controversy over the lead actor for the hit Vietnam-themed play *Miss Saigon,* Caucasian Brand was cast as an Oriental. He was an Asian guerrilla warlord in French Indochina. The preponderance of female cast members in a war movie is attributable to the fact that they are Red Cross nurses captured and abused by the evil mercenaries employed by the Chinese communists. Most of the nurses are pretty; most of the action is pretty lame.

In the early 1960s, before the direct U.S. military involvement in Vietnam, the conflicts in Southeast Asia were mostly indistinguishable in the minds of many Americans. Films were thus able to present an almost generic yellow communist menace. We were conditioned by years of seeing the Japanese as the enemy to easily apply anti–Oriental stereotypes to the new Asian bad guys. Even though the Japanese in World War II were fascists and the Chinese were communists, this discrepancy did not really matter. Ideology was irrelevant once these forces were perceived as opposing our way of life and endangering our men in arms. To discuss the Vietnamese conflict as a war of nationalism or an internal civil war, as opposed to a cold war fight against godless communism, was difficult or years away.

The same year that brought the Cuban missile crisis also produced a film with precisely this type of generic enemy. Paramount Pictures released *Brushfire* in February 1962. It shows an indifference to details regarding time, place, and cause. All we know is that this B movie is set somewhere in Southeast Asia. Jack Warner, Jr., was the director and writer. The film starred John Ireland, Everett Sloane, Jo Morrow, and Al Avalon.

In the inhospitable Southeast Asian jungle, an American couple is kidnapped by a group of rebels. James Hong makes yet another appearance as the enemy leader. The Americans are ransomed in return for guns and ammunition. Sloane and Ireland play two American soldiers left over from World War II who organize a rescue party. In the meantime, to establish evil credentials, the rebels rape the woman. With the help of local plantation workers, a daring rescue mission succeeds in freeing the captives. Confronted by the rebels during the getaway, the husband and the rebel leader are killed. When the scoundrels see their fallen commander, they retreat in a cowardly, undisciplined manner. Ireland explains that the rescue effort was worth the cost because it kept the uprising from developing into a full-scale rebellion. Perhaps if the real-life opposition in Vietnam had been as disorganized, then a similar result would have transpired. But the opposite was true, the Viet Cong and North Vietnamese were seasoned by years of resistance against the French and, before them, other enemies, and this facile result was not possible.

A well-known early Vietnam War film was *The Ugly American*, released in 1962 and primarily exhibited in 1963. At the time, it was tepidly received both critically and commercially. Like *The Quiet American*, *The Ugly American* is a pithy phrase meant to connote an American stereotype. The phrase is now an established idiomatic expression for describing the propensity for obnoxious behavior and or ignorant ethnocentrism while abroad of a person from the United States.

Marlon Brando starred in this Universal Studios film adaptation of W. J. Lederer and Eugene Burdick's novel of the same name. The screenplay was written by Stewart Stern, and the movie was produced and directed by George Englund. It was set in another mythical Southeast Asian country, this time known as Sarkhan.

The film was an expensive, first-class, Technicolor production that ran two hours. A full second photography unit was sent to Thailand, where it captured the beautiful lush rural countryside as well as the bustling pace of Bangkok. The blend of Western-style institutional architecture with Asian temples and private homes created authentic settings in establishing shots for the Kingdom of Sarkhan. In addition, a 30-acre Asian village was constructetd on the studio backlot. Therefore, through great effort a blend of Bangkok and Universal City combined to double for Sarkhan's capital, which was already more or less doubling for Saigon.

The Lederer and Burdick novel had focused attention on the perplexing nature of the Third World's mistrust and hatred of the United States despite what Americans felt were their own good intentions and efforts. It was an expensive gamble to dramatize America's foreign policy in Southeast Asia. The casting of Marlon Brando was the key to getting the big-budget production rolling. George Englund was aware of Brando's interest in politics and the Orient and brought the screenplay to him. Brando was familiar with the source material and immediately agreed to portray the main character, the U.S. ambassador to Sarkhan, Harrison Carter MacWhite.

Four years earlier, Brando had taken a trip to Southeast Asia and during his travels had researched the ongoing efforts of the United Nations in providing various aid programs. Tony Thomas writing in *The Films of Marlon Brando* quotes the actor's observations at the time: "For all our incredible facilities for modern communication, we have communicated very little with the world. I think we are insulated. I've seen Westerners in Thailand, in Java, in Japan, and most of them make no effort to learn the language or participate. They have their air-conditioned offices and Scotch in their ice boxes. They bring in a little society of America to the place they live in."[9]

Sandra Church starred with Brando as his wife, Marian. Pat Hingle was chief engineer Homer Atkins, and the other acting Brando, Jocelyn, played Homer's wife, Emma Atkins, a professional nurse. Arthur Hill portrayed Grainger, the first aide de camp to the ambassador. Rebel leader Deong was played by Eiji Okada, a Japanese actor. As the prime minister of Sarkhan, Kurrit Pramoj was cast through unusual circumstances. Pramoj was a newspaper publisher acting as a technical consultant for Universal on the production. However, director Englund and star Brando felt that he would be perfect for the role of Prime Minister Kwen Sei.[10] In a curious instance of life imitating art, some dozen years later in 1974, Pramoj actually did become the prime minister of Thailand.

The Ugly American begins as construction of the "Sarkhan-USA Freedom Road" is altering verdant jungle. Despite the cooperation of hardworking American foremen and their yellow-skinned native workers, all is not well. Two Sakhanese communist extremists murder an American truck driver and douse his body with alcohol to feign drunkenness. They push his truck down an embankment into a group of laborers. The death of a local in this "accident" enrages the natives and provides opponents of the Freedom Road with a martyr with which to consolidate opposition to the development project and to outside intervention in the affairs of Sarkhan.

An an anti–American rally swirls outside the compound, the U.S. ambassador prepares to leave his post amid a worsening political (and at times military) crisis. Cutting to Washington, D.C., we join the Senate Foreign Relations Committee confirmation hearings on the new ambassador-designate for Sarkhan. The committee questions MacWhite, a former reporter in Southeast Asia and now a successful publisher. He uses great charm as he describes his partial knowledge of the Sarkhanese language and his service in that country during World War II. He fought with the local underground against the Japanese occupation forces and became a friend of the opposition leader, Deong. This relationship and Mac-White's intimate knowledge of the country should make him eminently qualified for the post. However, it is precisely the nature of his friendship with Deong that seems to most trouble the vociferously anticommunist members of the committee. They attempt to assess MacWhite's perspective on his lifelong friend's politics. Is he a "Red"? MacWhite insists that Deong is no such thing; he is a nationalist.

Back in Sarkhan, Deong leads a rally proclaiming his country's neutrality in the cold war conflict. He vouches to the crowd for the integrity of his old friend, the newly appointed ambassador. Deong then leads the masses in a chant proclaiming, "Sarkhan for the Sarkhanese!" At the airport the ambassador's official

The Ugly American (Universal Pictures, 1963). Marlon Brando as MacWhite, the newly arrived American ambassador to Sarkhan. Also pictured: Reiko Sato and Arthur Hill.

greeting is marred by well-organized crowds of young demonstrators yelling, "Yankee Go Home!" In a tensely staged, extras-filled scene, the protest degenerates into a full-scale riot on the tarmac. The ambassador and his wife are buffeted about in their car and escape only when government troops arrive to restore order. Wasting no time, MacWhite orders an immediate meeting of the embassy staff. There is great disagreement over the source of the violent protest and the various forces at work. MacWhite demands that the staff shape up. How could staff members not know there was going to be a riot with 600 people? Where is their intelligence information? When a senior staffer arrives late from a tennis match and another protests that it is Sunday, they are chastised by their new boss.

Returning from the meeting and a visit with his wife, MacWhite goes to Deong's home. They carry on and drink into the wee hours. After getting reacquainted, the two friends reveal their true perspectives on the perplexing political situation. Deong says that in 1945 everybody loved the Americans. Now a decade and a half later, everything has changed. He confesses that he sent the people to the airport, but as a greeting. There was not supposed to be a riot!

Deong is opposed to the building of the Freedom Road and considers the present government of Sarkhan to be a puppet of the United States. MacWhite is defensive about the American role. The Sarkhanese leader uses increasingly trenchant Maoist dogma in his anti–American harangue.

Exhausted and slightly drunk, the ambassador attempts to challenge his old friend's perspective. He fires off a series of questions: You actually think America is being militarily provocative? Are we not helping the economy by building a road to the northern provinces? And, finally, is not encouraging economic prosperity a way to ensure resolve against a North Sarkhanese threat?

Deong views the Freedom Road as a military project and accuses the United States of strengthening a right-wing dictator in its fear of communism. Finally, the already shrill disagreement degenerates into Deong's accusing America and MacWhite of practicing paternalism wrapped in the Stars and Stripes and of trying to buy loyalty with handouts. He says the American notion of democracy is a fraud for "white people" only. MacWhite accuses Deong of being a twisted ingrate, a "Judas," and storms out.

The next morning a troubled MacWhite is convinced that Deong is a communist. This conclusion is strongly supported by the party-line idiom of the night before. Perhaps MacWhite was wrong and the Red-baiting senator was right? MacWhite is determined not to lose Sarkhan to the communists on "his watch." Quickly, the ambassador, his wife, and top aides depart on a fact-finding tour of the countryside and the Freedom Road project.

Chief American project coordinator Homer Atkins and his wife, Emma, act as hosts to the new ambassador. While the wives tour Mrs. Atkins's children's health clinic, the two men visit a village elder. The ambassador begins to understand the strength of rebel communist forces in the hinterlands. They terrorize the populace at night and, like the real Viet Cong, disappear by day.

Leaving his fact-finding tour, MacWhite calls on the prime minister. MacWhite expects to meet a corrupt, dictatorial puppet but instead finds a prime minister who projects great intelligence and a delicate understanding of the counterveiling forces at work. MacWhite has more difficulty understanding the nuances of anti–American feeling and nonalignment ideals. The two men agree on the importance of the Freedom Road, and MacWhite reiterates the U.S. commitment to the present government. His word is buttressed by the presence of the U.S. Navy fleet not far from the coast of Sarkhan.

Several days later, Homer Atkins reveals that the young Sarkhanese man who had been his chief assistant on the project was murdered. The situation in the countryside is degenerating. MacWhite is ready to respond with security forces. Atkins is deeply troubled by the simplicity of the ambassador's response. Upon questioning, Atkins assures the ambassador that Deong is not a communist but rather a "neutralist." MacWhite remains unconvinced.

In the next scene, Deong clandestinely meets with Chinese representatives, North Sarkhanese envoys, and the Russian ambassador. Deong is mindful of the delicate balance he needs to strike in order to gain assistance but not be used.

He receives assurance of supplies for his independence movement. Fearful of a communist takeover of his neutralist cause, Deong defers final judgment about the aid.

Atkins had proposed that the Freedom Road be diverted to a less controversial route away from the northern border. Perhaps the hospital and more clearly humanitarian development projects should be the destination. However, MacWhite and the prime minister decide otherwise. At a gala ribbon-cutting ceremony, the Sarkhanese prime minister and his aides, the ambassador and his staff (some of whom are obnoxious sycophants), Buddhist priests, and aggressive reporters are all assembled. Guerrilla forces begin shelling and sniping the ceremony. Panic and casualties result as the ambassador and others barely escape. This is the beginning of an insurgent offensive throughout the country.

Now caught in a shooting war, MacWhite begins to evacuate American personnel and dependents. As the crisis mounts, he attempts to determine if any foreign troops are engaged in the offensive. If so, then by treaty with Sarkhan, U.S. forces are obligated to intervene.

In a number of brief action sequences, apolitical peasants working in their rice paddies are attacked by North Sarkhanese paratroopers. Bands of Deong loyalists, communist cadres, gangs, and so on roam the countryside terrorizing the populace. In these simultaneous surprise actions, the offensive is chillingly prophetic in some details of the real-life Tet Offensive yet to come in South Vietnam in 1968. Village chieftains and leaders are rounded up and murdered. In a tense scene, a truckload of kerchiefed, heavily armed rebels threaten Emma Atkins and her staff at the hospital. The clinic personnel join hands in a determined human barrier. The leader of the cadre calls his anxious band off, sparing the facility and its workers.

Advancing on the government palace, Deong is emboldened by the swiftness of events and the adulation of the crowds. He issues a deadline for the present government to transfer power or lose it by force. The prime minister confides to MacWhite that years ago he was saying very much the same thing from the outside. The volatile events and the muddled loyalties of the competing factions continue to confound the U.S. ambassador. The prime minister tells him that many of the Sarkhanese forces will not fight if ordered to do so against their own people.

Some observers feel that the prime minister has staged the rural paratroop landings as a pretext for full U.S. military intervention. The prime minister denies this and shows that the intervention by communist forces was a complete surprise to Deong as well. MacWhite is unconvinced and agitated. Exasperated by the American's thickheadedness, the prime minister reveals the source of his intelligence information. In an adjoining office, a captured North Sarkhanese colonel has succumbed to interrogation and detailed plans to land troops and assassinate Deong.

At last understanding more of the true nature of the conflict and concerned for Deong's life, a panicked MacWhite takes action. He orders the U.S.

Seventh Fleet to stand by for an invasion. He then goes to Deong's heavily guarded compound to warn him of the plot and seek a coalition government. The old friends' estrangement makes communication difficult. However, with evidence, MacWhite convinces Deong of the extent of North Sarkhanese intrusions. Deong checks with his trusted northern outposts and confirms the invasion by communist forces. MacWhite prepares to leave the compound, having impressed upon Deong the necessity of a coalition.

Deong tells a trusted protégé of his plans to travel to the government house and institute talks to form a reformist coalition government. He also proclaims the need to check the communist advance and maintain an independent struggle. In response, the aide shoots Deong at point-blank range. The betrayer, a long-time communist agent, escapes as MacWhite rushes back to his mortally wounded friend. Each man knows that the other is not his enemy. Deong uses a familiar nickname in his last words: "Good-bye, Mac."

The next scene, reminiscent of the crazed evacuation of Saigon in 1975, takes place in the U.S. Embassy. Chaos reigns as civilians try to fight their way onto the grounds and personnel destroy files. Marine guards scurry about in combat gear as shells explode nearby. Reporters ask a beleaguered Ambassador MacWhite, "Who killed Deong?" He replies, "Communists and misunderstanding." He is demoralized and sees that despite the best intentions, he has totally botched his assignment. He resigns his post.

He speaks contemplatively to the assembled reporters and to the cameras. To paraphrase, he asks rhetorically, How did misunderstanding kill Deong, a leader of his people and the ambassador's friend? Mac answers that Deong had a certain kind of passion, the type that revolutionaries have, whether it be George Washington, Thomas Jefferson, or Ho Chi Minh. Americans tend to misunderstand that passion. "Their fight for independence is part of our own. . . . We can't win the cold war unless we remember what we are for as well as what we are against. I've learned in a very personal way: [do not] sacrifice principles for expediency. . . . I've learned the only time we are hated is when we stop trying to be what we started out to be 200 years ago."

As the ambassador speaks, we begin to see a double exposure of him on the embassy steps and on the freeways of America. Then the camera zooms in on a typical suburban home and then further inward to a black-and-white television as a man watches the ambassador's news conference. Continuing, MacWhite says, "I'm not blaming my country. I'm blaming the indifference that some of us show to its promises. . . . If the cold war disappeared right now, the American people would be in this fight against ignorance, hunger, and disease because it's right; it's right. . . . And if I had one appeal to make to every American, it would be that. . . " The television is turned off, the unfinished sentence remains suspended in the air, and indifference triumphs. The end appears, complete with musical strains of "America," and the credits roll.

The film's issues and its ending are prophetic. America's traditional support of right-wing governments as a cold war defense against communism; the misinterpretation of factions that are largely non–Western, non–Christian, non–Caucasian; the extent of anti–American and anticolonial resentment; the need for self-determination; the tragedies of miscommunication; and the use of might rather than diplomacy all reflect many of the problems Americans failed to understand in the Vietnam conflict.

The film's core dilemma, and the basis of its drama, is an analytical, foreign policy one that is only briefly shown as a military struggle. The ending conveys the indifference of the general public and does so by means of television, the medium by which the eventual actual war's images were transmitted to the American public. Like the anonymous television viewer, Americans preferred to go about their business without regard to the conflict.

In November 1963, the assassination of South Vietnamese president Ngo Dinh Diem was quickly overshadowed by the murder of President John F. Kennedy in Dallas. By this time, there were 15,000 U.S. troops in South Vietnam, and American aid to the beleaguered country was more than a half-billion dollars a year. The war films of this time were mostly about far-off World War II.

In June 1964, General William C. Westmoreland became the commander of U.S. forces in South Vietnam. On August 7, Congress passed the Gulf of Tonkin Resolution giving President Lyndon B. Johnson broad powers in protecting American forces and preventing aggression against U.S. allies in South Vietnam. By the end of the year, U.S. forces in the South totaled 23,000. The escalation of United States involvement went relatively unopposed.

That same fateful year, Allied Artists released a film that went relatively unnoticed also, *A Yank in Vietnam*. Once again, a Yank was far from home, but in the intervening 12 years since Columbia's picture, Indochina had become more specifically Vietnam. The picture was originally known as *The Year of the Tiger*, in reference to the corresponding Chinese calendar, but that was too cryptic for the American public. The film starred and was directed by Marshall Thompson as Major Benson. It costarred Enrique Magalona, Urban Drew, Hoang Vinh Loc, and Kieu Chinh.

The action drama begins as Major Benson's helicopter is shot down and he is captured by the Viet Cong. Nearby, a South Vietnamese hospital is attacked, with the brutal loss of many civilian lives and the capture of its head doctor. The doctor's daughter and a small group of brave South Vietnamese guerrilla fighters attempt a rescue mission and along the way are able to free the U.S. major. He then joins them in a raid on the Viet Cong to free the doctor. During their adventure, he and the daughter fall in love.

The 80-minute, black-and-white low-budgeter was filmed in part on location in South Vietnam. Notable is the fact that the main character is a full-fledged U.S. marine stationed in Vietnam. He is not a French soldier or a U.S. civilian; he is an actual American soldier fighting the Viet Cong in a setting contemporaneous with the film.

The year 1965 was pivotal in Vietnam in the transition from a limited U.S. role to a full-blown military conflict. On February 7, the Viet Cong attacked the

U.S. base at Pleiku and three days later killed 23 American soldiers at Qui Nhan. Operation Rolling Thunder, the sustained bombing of North Vietnam, began in March. That same month, U.S. marine infantry battalions began arriving at Da Nang, South Vietnam. Late in the year, widespread antiwar demonstrations broke out in the United States. By year end, 181,000 U.S. soldiers were stationed in South Vietnam.

Again, most of the war films of 1965 dealt with World War II, now 20 years past. But there were two feature-length fictional films that year about the conflict in Vietnam. *To the Shores of Hell* was released by the independent company Crown International Pictures. It was produced, directed, and written by Will Zens. Robert McFadden cowrote the feature. It starred Marshall Thompson again as a U.S. marine, and Richard Arlen portrayed a brigadier general. In Zens's picture, Thompson infiltrates a Viet Cong encampment to rescue his brother, a doctor forced to treat the wounded. With assistance from a priest, some local natives, and another soldier, the two brothers are successfully evacuated by helicopter.

This film's title, story, and stars embody a long list of derivative elements of other war films and thus provide a degree of continuity for the genre. "Hell" is once again the readily applied metaphor for war. "To the Shores of" is a reference to the words of the Marine Corps hymn. The story line of a doctor in peril and Marshall Thompson's role are very similar to those of *A Yank in Vietnam*. The plot was used again with little success 23 years later in 1988 in Star Classics Video's *Charlie Bravo*, an independent almost direct-to-video release about the Vietnam War. The doctor forced to stay with the enemy and either by duress or in respect to his Hippocratic Oath to treat the wounded was also used on television in 1989 in the Vietnam-themed "China Beach."

While a traditional film, *To the Shores of Hell* is also paradoxically an important transitional document. Made in 1965, it was concurrent with a rising military conflict. By 1965, its B movie depiction of the evil enemy had become more than drama; it was part of the war effort itself, propaganda in its own right. The Viet Cong kidnap innocents, coerce peasants, and rape nurses. Their heinousness is opposed by brave Americans, and for this the indigenous populace is truly grateful.[11] The United States is able by virtue of its goodness and technical superiority to triumph in the end over the bad guy.

The newness of this particular "theater of war" is underscored by the fact that the marines actually landed in Da Nang in March 1965. Will Zens was able that same year to obtain actual Department of Defense footage for inclusion in this nondocumentary. It allows for a breadth of action beyond the budgetary means of the film to recreate. Also significant is the acknowledgment of early domestic opposition to the war. Major Donahue refers to those who do not support the marine role as "indoctrinated beatniks."

Aside from Americans' "virtue," the superiority of a modern industrialized society's means to conduct a war and ultimately win is inherent in the film's climax. The rescue scene involves the use of a helicopter, which began a process of incorporating into movies the role of this important weapon in the U.S. arsenal. Helicopters, along with jets, were the source of a continued U.S. superiority in the sky. As will be observed later within the body of many Vietnam War films, the helicopter that rescues and saves the heroes here becomes more than a nonhuman participant. The helicopter becomes a symbol—at times audio, at times visual—for the entire conflict itself.

Burt Reynolds received his first starring film role in 1965 in *Operation CIA* as an agent assigned to Saigon. The Hei Ra Matt Production was released by the now-defunct Allied Artists. The screenplay was written by Bill Ballinger and Peer J. Oppenheimer. Oppenheimer was also the executive producer, and Christian Nyby directed the movie. *Operation CIA* was a moderate-budget film that featured wonderful on-location photography of Saigon, with additional footage from Thailand. Reynolds, years later commenting on the movie and the tough Southeast Asian climate during the shoot, remarked, "The lobby poster said: The Hottest Spot on Earth! It was. The movie wasn't."[12]

Before the credits roll in *Operation CIA*, two Viet Cong saboteurs on bicycles assassinate a South Vietnamese official in broad daylight on a Saigon street. Entering into this whirlwind of political upheaval is Reynolds, an ex-marine and now, in the local English vernacular, a spook. He lands at Saigon's Tan Son Nhut airport under cover as a professor attending a scholarly conference. The communist opposition is aware of his true identity from the moment of his arrival.

The "professor" follows an informant's tip and goes to a massage parlor to ascertain details about a plot to assassinate other South Vietnamese politicians. There he is knocked unconscious and robbed. So far he could be like any other visiting American in Saigon, looking for a little R&R and getting rolled! However, this incident is all part of international intrigue and a warning to go away.

In his hotel, Reynolds meets with an English war correspondent who fills him in on the deteriorating local situation. Political factionalism is at a crisis pitch, and assassinations are threatening the government's stability. As if to underscore the accuracy of the journalist's assessment, a grenade attack occurs in the street outside the hotel. The apparent targets of the attack, two U.S. marines, are injured, and an innocent South Vietnamese family is killed. The scene is reminiscent of the Place Garnier bombing in *The Quiet American*.

Reynolds meets with his agent contact, a pretty blond French woman played by Danielle Aubry. She has lived in Indochina for many years and is proud of the beauty of her adopted country. Aubry leads her partner around the city in an attempt to acclimate him to the bustling town. This provides the viewer with the opportunity to see the exotic locales of this grand metropolis. In their travels they encounter a student protest over the U.S. role in Vietnam. Some of the Vietnamese communication is in the native tongue, with subtitles provided for translation. The French language and influence from the colonial days are felt throughout the city.

Reynolds proceeds alone via the river on his mission. He breaks into a university professor's house and finds a floor plan of the American Embassy. Before he can escape, he must fight off two assassins. During his retreat, communist agents in a motorboat make another attempt on his life. They fail but manage to kill another local innocent, a gondola cabby. With a coolness under duress worthy of James Bond, Reynolds successfully gets back to his hotel. Along the way he receives aid from a beautiful Vietnamese woman played by Kieu Chinh, the same actress from *A Yank in Vietnam*. The story meanders along, with Reynolds encountering both good and bad Vietnamese agents in a variety of violent action episodes.

Vic Diaz presents an interesting characterization of a communist agent and university professor. He is fat and strangely androgynous, with a high-pitched, maniacal laugh. At one point Reynolds is saved from Diaz and his henchman by a group of ARVN (South Vietnamese army) soldiers. American military personnel are often present in the background in the streets and cafés.

Finally, Reynolds determines that there is a plot to put cyanide gas into the air-conditioning unit of the U.S. Embassy on the Chinese New Year's Day. Racing against time, Reynolds must fight a Viet Cong assassin trained in martial arts and a vaguely Eastern European spy who is behind the plot. A long chase sequence through the Saigon streets, a beautiful Buddhist shrine, and the embassy compound leads to the climactic ending.

Operation CIA makes good use of its extensive location shooting, and it is interesting to see Reynolds establishing his persona in this early vehicle. The good guy CIA agent is a ladies' man, operating athletically and bravely with great aplomb in the face of danger. Within a few years, the very idea of a main movie character being a CIA operative stationed in Saigon would be out of the question. The war was to become too real and that agency's role too controversial for any such characterization to be attempted in a light entertainment film.

Like the other films discussed in this chapter, *Operation CIA* is a movie paradox in the middle of a gathering maelstrom. On the one hand, it is a simplistic and dated work of marginal dramatic quality. On the other hand, given that it was made concurrent with the actual violence it shows, the film has a certain degree of veracity in its depiction of a rapidly degenerating situation. The trade paper *Boxoffice* in its review of November 15, 1965, said, "Christian Nyby has directed forcefully, conveying the immediacy and impact of the international intrigue now very much part and parcel of the Vietnam scene."[13]

The picture superficially shows the depth of internal dissent and hostilities in the South Vietnamese capital. The difficulty of not necessarily knowing or recognizing the enemy is readily apparent. The politicization of the intelligentsia is touched upon by the intrigue surrounding the professor's loyalties and the student demonstrations. Also striking is the randomness of much of the violence, which punctuates the daily life of the people. Death and destruction are visited upon old people, women, and children as much as on any unfortunate combatants. This is a dirty civil war in which the United States is already extricably entwined.

In January 1966, the United States resumed the bombing of North Vietnam after a 37-day hiatus. In March communist forces captured the U.S. Special Forces base in the Ashau Valley, a valuable staging area for supply convoys into the South. By the end of the year, there were 385,000 U.S. troops stationed in South Vietnam.

In February 1966, *Marine Battleground* was released by the independent Manson Distributing Corporation. This B movie was directed by Manli Lee from a screenplay by Hen-chul Yu, Burton Moore, and Tom Morrison. Codirection, adaptation, and editing credits went to Milton Mann. Jock Mahoney starred as journalist Nick Rawlins. Pat Yi headed a largely Korean and Thai cast as Young Hi Park.

Correspondent Rawlins interviews Young Hi Park, a Korean nurse serving in an American medical unit in Vietnam. She recalls the communist siege of Inchon and the death of her mother. In flashbacks we see her as a child saved and adopted by a U.S. marine platoon. Many of her rescuers are killed in combat, and in their memory she has devoted her life to the medical profession. *Marine Battleground* synthesizes through Young Hi Park's experiences the two American anticommunist conflicts in Southeast Asia. The similarities between the two undeclared and costly wars are readily apparent, and the U.S. experiences commingle in the context of this action picture loosely based on true life.

It had been almost 13 years since the defeat of the French in Vietnam. France's loss of its Indochinese colonies was followed by a revolution for independence in Algeria. That war provided most of the context for 1966's *The Lost Command*. However, the film not only started in Vietnam, but also its foreign policy decisions were rooted there. The story was pertinent to the Vietnam conflict, but the altered context made the film palatable to an increasingly divided American public.

The A budget international production was released domestically by Columbia Pictures and produced and directed by Mark Robson. The director of photography was one of Hollywood's best, the late Robert Surtees, using a broad panavision process. The screenplay was written by Nelson Gidding based on Jean Larteguy's novel *The Centurions*.

The renowned international cast was headed by Anthony Quinn as Lieutenant Colonel Raspeguy. Alain Delon portrayed Captain Esclavier. George Segal, in an absurd amount of pancake makeup, portrayed Lieutenant Mahidi, an Algerian in the French Legion. The gorgeous Claudia Cardinale portrayed Segal's sister and Delon's love interest, and Michele Morgan was the Countess de Clairfons. Wisely, the English-speaking performers made no attempt at French accents. The film crew was as international as its cast, and the production received both logistical and technical support from the military forces of France and Spain. The film was shot mostly in Spain, which was fine for the Algerian sequences but lacked authenticity in the initial Vietnamese scenes.

The tale opens with the following quote: "After eight years of fighting between the proud French army and the rebellious Vietnamese guerrillas in Indo-China, the end is near. . . . Dien Bien Phu . . . May 7, 1954." The voiceover introduction pays homage to the French and establishes the historic context in a manner similar to the beginning of the mid–1950s film treatments of the French involvement. Dashing in a red beret, Quinn commands the besieged garrison. The combat-seasoned Frenchmen are barraged with propaganda messages broadcast over communist loudspeakers telling them that they are far outnumbered and that the end of the war is imminent. Nevertheless, each successive wave of Viet Minh attack is bravely repulsed in fierce hand-to-hand combat. A planeload of paratroopers make a last-ditch effort to reinforce the garrison. As they attempt to land, they are cut to pieces.

Despite some reinforcements, the garrison is forced to surrender. There are several instances of prisoners being shot. After a brutal march reminiscent of Bataan, the French are imprisoned in preparation for an armistice. The Viet Minh commander attempts to splinter the prisoners by favoring the dark-skinned Algerian officer, whom he sees as a fellow victim of colonial oppression and a brother in the struggle against the white man. (Instances of this type are reenacted in later Vietnam War films as attempts are made to demoralize black troops with similar appeals based on persecution and oppression in a "white man's war.") Loyal French officer Segal will have nothing to do with this attempted manipulation.

While in Viet Minh custody, the experienced professional officers discuss the conflict. Quinn attributes the loss to a failure of the military to commit itself to the conflict because of interference by politicians back home. Delon, a French officer attached to the more civilian-oriented information unit of the army, sees aspects of brave freedom-fighting arrayed against forces of change. He proclaims the historical significance of the defeat. "Coolies" beat a white man's army. (This defeat of the French in 1954 by the Vietnamese was a first, and had profound repercussions throughout the world.) Despite differing perspectives, the men agree on the tenacity and bravery of their well-disciplined vanquishers. Did those watching in 1966 realize that Americans now faced these same opponents?

After three months of incarceration, the armistice is signed and the prisoners are released. Only Quinn's leadership and spirit were able to maintain the men's morale. As they are a defeated force, the official military welcome is muted, and the civilian welcome home to France is nonexistent. As they now attempt to reintegrate into society, the men have great difficulty coming to grips with their loss of comradeship and the lack of understanding and gratitude they encounter. On returning to Algeria, Lieutenant Mahidi (Segal) finds that a nascent independence movement led by radicals and malcontents has evolved into a popular uprising greatly inspired by the Vietnamese victory. His loyalties are torn as he sees the racist manner in which the colonial power treats his native people. When his radical younger brother is shot for a curfew violation, Mahidi must choose sides.

In the meantime, Quinn has returned to France, where after his valiant military effort and commanding leadership of his men in detention, he is "rewarded" with a demotion and scapegoated for the notorious defeat at Dien Bien Phu. His options are very limited as a career soldier of Basque rural heritage. He lacks political connections and, like the Arab Mahidi or the Oriental Viet Minh, is considered a swarthy nonwhite. Eventually Quinn is offered the unwinnable command that no one else wants: the Algerian campaign. To escape a humdrum peacetime existence and in loyalty to this beloved commander, all the junior officers from the Vietnam days volunteer to serve with their leader. But first Delon demands to know what it is he will be fighting for. Quinn thinks Delon is too cerebral, but after a confrontation over his loyalty, he, too, joins his old comrades in arms.

The balance of the film takes place in Algiers and its environs and is most interesting in its parallels to the Vietnam conflict these men survived. Their ultimately unsuccessful effort is also akin to the conflict the Americans were facing in Vietnam at the time of the film's release. The enlisted men are largely unmotivated draftees, dubious about their role in suppressing the indigenous population. The modern French military, with all its technical superiority, had been defeated in an inhospitable jungle environment by highly motivated guerrillas on their own turf in Vietnam. Here the men find the desert environment and the strange Arab culture equally baffling. The inability to face a uniformed regular army present strong parallels with the Viet Cong guerrilla opposition. Only some of the officers recognize these analogous dangers.

Most American policymakers chose to ignore the similarities between the French conflict and their own in Vietnam. In *The Lost Command*, the French division attempts to suppress opposition and "pacify" the population using increasingly brutal tactics. Vicious incidents beget atrocities and revenge killings. In 1966, such an ugly reality of war perpetrated by the protagonists in a film was quite rare. Years before the revelations of My Lai, the thought of American boys doing this in their Third World campaign was to many Westerners almost unthinkable.

The officers' debate over tactics mirrors the French government's indecision and the public's lack of consensus. In the film's final battle scene in Algeria, the besieged French forces are pinned down in a canyon. However, through the deceptive use of a helicopter, they are saved. Actor Raymond St. Jacques, as a black French medic, is evacuating wounded troops from the battle zone. Rebel leader Segal allows the Red Cross helicopter to enter as a humanitarian gesture. A desperate Quinn commandeers the chopper and refits it with heavy guns while preserving its humanitarian insignia. Abrogating the "rules of war," the French troops are able to outflank their Algerian opponents and escape to fight another day. Delon is appalled at the price of victory.

In the film's final scene, Quinn is decorated and made a general. Many in the unit are cited for bravery and awarded smart-looking medals. Watching from the side in civilian dress is a distressed Delon. As he leaves the ceremony, he sees a detail of French soldiers washing away proindependence graffiti on a nearby wall. He turns the next corner and sees a young Algerian boy writing the same "Free Algeria" message on another stone wall. The irony and what it bodes for the future are unmistakable.

The Lost Command has elements of soap opera and romantic subplots but remains a very watchable film. The movie acknowledges the horrible and some- times dishonorable nature of modern warfare and the exploitation of native peoples. As with other films discussed in this chapter, it has gained poignancy in the intervening years.

Big-budget major studio films such as The Quiet American, The Ugly American, and The Lost Command contained thought-provoking references to the United States–Vietnam conflict. The first predated full U.S. involvement, the second fictionalized the setting to a more generic Sarkhan, and the third con- cerned French, not Americans. The more modest B movies from independent producers, such as A Yank in Vietnam and To the Shores of Hell, were action films set in Vietnam but were more concerned with adventure and entertainment than with ideas. These films largely confirm Roger Ebert's comment that "'A' movies are about war, but 'B' war movies are about soldiers."[14]

By 1967, as U.S. casualties mounted in Vietnam, the public consensus about the war was degenerating. With the exception of John Wayne's The Green Berets in 1968, it would be almost a decade before Vietnam could be directly portrayed in a fictional, full-length, theatrical film. The war was becoming too tragic and controversial for anyone to risk such an expensive project. History was in the making, as were future screenplays, but a head-on examination was taboo. What would suffice were related subjects such as the returning vet in America, protests at home, and other recontextualizations.

In 1978 (ten years after Tet and three years after the fall of Saigon), when Vietnam was thrust back into the American consciousness via the first spate of incoming combat films, one of the first and finest was Go Tell the Spartans. Before the credits roll, the film harks back to the period examined above: "In 1964, the war in Vietnam was still a little war–confused and far away." This is the context in which the early Vietnam War films were made and presented. Viet- nam was not yet a dirty word, and America had yet to experience a gut-wrench- ing loss of innocence. The most powerful nation on earth was yet to be defeated and traumatized. No one making films from 1948 to 1966 could have envisioned the future. Even now, with the healing passage of time, there is no consensus on the lessons of the Vietnam conflict.

References

1. Graham Greene, The Quiet American (New York: Viking Press, 1956), p. 215.
2. Jay Robert Nash and Stanley Ralph Ross, The Motion Picture Guide (Chicago: Cinebooks, 1986), p. 2512.

3. Greene, *The Quiet American,* p. 12.

4. Martha Bayles, *The New Republic* (July 1988), p. 30.

5. Ron Kovic, *Born on the Fourth of July* (New York: McGraw-Hill, 1976), p. 54.

6. William Pfaff, "Graham Greene and the Insanity of Innocence," *Chicago Tribune,* April 7, 1991, sect. 4, p. 3.

7. "The Quiet American Remake," *Daily Variety,* March 1, 1991, p. 10.

8. Greene, *The Quiet American,* p. 246.

9. Tony Thomas, *The Films of Marlon Brando* (Secaucus, N.J.: Citadel Press, 1973), p. 144.

10. *Ibid.,* p. 149.

11. Michael Paris, "The American Film Industry in Vietnam," *History Today* (April 1987), pp. 19–26.

12. Nancy Streebeck, *The Films of Burt Reynolds* (Secaucus, N.J.: Citadel Press, 1977), p. 111.

13. *Boxoffice,* as quoted *ibid.,* November 15, 1965.

14. Roger Ebert, *The Movie Home Companion* (Kansas City: Andrews McMeel and Parker, 1988), p. 53.

Chapter 2

Head-On Conflict and Refracted Images, 1967–1969

In the ten years between 1967 and 1977, the United States fought, lost, and began to recover from the Vietnam War. Almost 58,000 Americans died in the conflict, and approximately 155,000 others were wounded. The war's human and economic costs split the country apart. Perhaps at no other period since the Civil War had Americans so disagreed about a single issue.

In film, this turmoil was portrayed in four fluidly defined subgenres. Of varying size and quality, these subgenres helped reflect and create a consciousness concerning the war. The first group is the traditional war story, the combat film. It could be gung ho or antiwar, but it was always action and battle oriented. This direct portrait of combat in a patriotic, unquestioning fashion was largely discredited by real-world events. Combat films became rarer as consensus broke down and casualties mounted. The overriding business factor affecting production of Vietnam combat films was their perceived lack of commerciality because of the depressing nature of the war. As the studios are for-profit corporations, these types of films were fiscal gambles.

During the war, the traditional portrayal of combat was limited to the 1968 major studio release of John Wayne's *The Green Berets*. Even this hawkish treatment was forced to acknowledge, in the character of a liberal journalist, the opposing view of the U.S. role. Also contributing to the dearth of product was a lack of firsthand Vietnam accounts on which to base screenplays. Such accounts necessitated a civilian reintegration for their witness-authors. Therefore, there was a lag time for these source materials.

The second subgenre encompasses stories of returning veterans. Such portrayals in the period during and immediately after the Vietnam War were broad characterizations, and often the military background in the plot was secondary. Only later would in-depth and honest portrayals of veterans and their readjustment be the main subject. This second group is so dominated by negative portrayals that it could be known as the "loser vet" genre. This harsh label reflects the cynical nature of the films and conveys some of the anger of the veterans as they experienced betrayal and loss. However, some of the noncombatant public also felt anger toward the veterans. They were somehow held responsible for the war itself and one of its most despised aspects: its losing nature. The retreat of the American forces was unique and traumatizing to our collective psyche.

This B movie mayhem has been assimilated into the culture and represents a disservice to the nine million Americans who served on active duty between August 1964 and May 1975. Their reintegration into society was complicated by the controversial nature of the war, the lack of gratitude they received from the public and government, the tragedy of noncombatant casualties, the guerrilla nature of the opposition, the mixed-up justifications, and the militarily compromised conduct of the war. In an insidious way, contributing to vets' readjustment problems were the awful portraits afforded in popular film.

Films in the loser vet group were initially B movies that provided programming for the then-flourishing drive-in industry. Motorcycle and "Hell's Angels" movies became populated by wired vets in such films as the aptly titled *The Angry Breed* (1968) and *Satan's Sadists* (1969). Also contributing to this violence-prone veteran portrayal were the Blaxploitation urban caper films of the early 1970s. Just as Hollywood had exploited the youth market, so, too, did it capitalize on this minority audience. Black veterans became easy characters to incorporate into action features that involved drugs, organized crime, and other urban scourges. By the end of this period, the readily dismissed drive-in and inner-city-exhibited movies had created such a stereotype that the A movie productions could join in using this type of character as an instantly identifiable antisocial misfit.

The third subgenre of films concerns the counterculture of the late 1960s and early 1970s. This counterculture was in large part a reaction to the Vietnam conflict and draft issues. These films range from independent productions by radical "auteurs" to B movie exploitation from "square" establishment corporate sources. Also included are a few elephantine A budgeted major studio attempts to cash in on the youth audience. Many of these films are at best tangentially related to the conflict and reveal as much in what they exclude as in what they include.

The fourth subgenre of films comprises those set in different locales or time periods that are about or highly influenced by the Vietnam War. These are the allegorical or metaphorical references that utilize the tradition of exploring complex subjects in nonliteral ways. An example is *M*A*S*H*, which is as much about Vietnam as Korea, where it is set. Somewhat more tenuous perhaps as to the merits of including them in the present work are the films that critic Pauline Kael has referred to as the "America is guilty" movies, which reflect a self-flagellating exercise in collective guilt. References can become so numerous and cryptic as to become meaningless. Therefore, this group of films is only briefly, albeit carefully considered.

This fourth category is a loose field for organization. Many films overlap into one or more of the subgenres. The present chapter covers the films produced and distributed in the years 1967, 1968, and 1969, a time of very active military involvement in Vietnam. Many commentators on Vietnam films from this period examine them according to a subject or exploitation versus serious treatments. However, only a chronological examination accurately reflects the commingling of the movies' perspectives.

In January 1967, American and South Vietnamese forces began an offensive against the communists along the supply routes of the Ho Chi Minh Trail. As the year passed and United States involvement escalated, many antiwar demonstrations were held in the United States and all over the world. In the fall of 1967, Thai troops arrived to join U.S. and South Vietnamese forces. They followed combat contingents from four other countries: Australia, New Zealand, South Korea, and the Philippines. In October, the North Vietnamese siege of Con Thien was broken. By Christmas of 1967, there were 486,000 U.S. troops in South Vietnam.

In 1967, American production of features related to the war was practically nil in contrast to renewed interest in the previously involved nation, France. Although foreign-language films and documentaries are not the focus of this work, it is interesting to note that these movies received token domestic presentation in the vacuum created by a lack of domestic product on the subject. The eclectic French films reflected the divisions in world opinion concerning the conflict. *Far from Vietnam* was a collaborative hodgepodge from several of France's finest New Wave directors. This quasidocumentary, released as *Loin du Viet-Nam*, featured the work of Alain Resnais, Agnes Varda, Claude Lelouch, and Jean Luc Godard. It opposed the war and expressed support for the North Vietnamese and Viet Cong. Godard, the most left wing of the group, had featured a sequence set in Vietnam in his earlier 1965 film *Pierrot le Fou*.

The radical fringe of the counterculture was represented by an independently produced French-Canadian film from producer-director-writer Jean Pierre Lefebvre titled *Le Revolutionnaire*. Stars Louis St. Pierre and Louise Rasselet were revolutionaries training under an authoritarian leader in rural Quebec. Their antisocial behavior leads to the deaths of several innocent bystanders. With a mixture of pop antiwar drama and comedy, this film comments on violence and the sanctioning of it by governments in the conduct of war. Eventually the crazed revolutionary leader is decorated by the same central authority he opposed. (This predated a similar twist in *Taxi Driver*, with the lionizing of the trained killer.) In a fitting finale, the revolutionary leader is assassinated by the one other surviving member of his group.

Far more conventional was the French language film *Live for Life*, originally *Vivre pour Vivre*. This Franco-Italian coproduction was directed by Claude Lelouch. International leading man Yves Montand costarred with America's Candice Bergen. The cast and crew were sufficiently prestigious to warrant a major United States distributor pickup from United Artists. Actually set in many locales including Vietnam, the drama, despite pretensions, is soap opera.

Montand, a Parisian television reporter, has an affair with Bergen, an American model. Eventually he accepts a dangerous assignment in Vietnam. He is captured by the Viet Cong, but, unlike the early films, Marshall Thompson does not appear to save him. Rather, he is set free. The compassionate treatment he receives from his captors is in marked contrast to the brutal portraits afforded in American productions. Upon his return to France, he and Bergen go through a tempestuous reconciliation.

The paucity in 1967 of head-on considerations of the Vietnam War was matched by a similar decline in movies about any war. Perhaps the best-remembered World War II action picture of the year was *The Dirty Dozen.* Another noteworthy portrayal was Englishman Richard Lester's *How I Won the War.* This antiwar black comedy had an irreverent, countercultural tone reflective of current anti–Vietnam sentiment. It is an example of the different place, different time subgenre. Beatle John Lennon appears in a tragicomic role undoubtedly designed to raise the box office potential among the young audience.

An interesting slice-of-life film that touched on the war was Andy Warhol's late 1967 comedy drama *The Nude Restaurant.* The avant-garde artist was the producer, director, writer, editor, and cinematographer. His protégé and later film collaborator Paul Morrissey gained experience as a "production assistant." Warhol's oft-used female star Viva portrayed a Greenwich Village waitress, with Julian Burroughs as a draft dodger. After some strange conversation and some stranger sexual pairings, Burroughs discusses his antiwar sentiments. The filmmaker, the characters, and likely the audience were thoroughly stoned at the time.

Rounding out the films of 1967 was a soon-to-be-common veteran exploitation film. By title alone this film helped create and reinforce a stereotype. The film, *Born Losers,* was directed by and starred Tom Laughlin, better known as "Billy Jack." To mask some of the film's low-budget origins or perhaps deflect its anticipated panning, Laughlin used the pseudonym T. C. Frank for the director's credit. This tale of motorcycle maniacs did a lot of business and spawned three sequels, the better-known *Billy Jack, The Trial of Billy Jack,* and *Billy Jack Goes to Washington.* Laughlin as the Native American half-breed and Vietnam veteran is the underdog victimized by society and goaded by rednecks. His Green Beret special forces training gives him a martial arts fluency that sends the bad guys fleeing. This action-oriented biker tale uses vigilantism to combat violence. Only in the later installments is the oppressed minority status of the main character used in higher profile. Jane Russell appeared in a cameo role.

The prototypical outlaw biker was born back in 1954, in *The Wild One,* when Marlon Brando rode his motorcycle into a small California town. Directed by Laslo Benedek and produced by Stanley Kramer, the movie had as its lead character an alienated young man lost in polite society. This same vein was mined throughout the 1950s with films that portrayed JDs (juvenile delinquents) as unloved victims of circumstances who were misunderstood except in a core group of like-minded peers. James Dean in *Rebel Without a Cause* in 1955 portrayed a similar sense of alienation. The youth of the 1950s responded to these portrayals and flocked to the box office.

As America expanded to the suburbs, so did the number of drive-in screens.

Born Losers (American International, 1967). Lobby card for the first screen appearance of Tom Laughlin as Billy Jack, Vietnam veteran.

The need for cheap filler product for double features increased. Because drive-ins were a place to neck and hang out, the level of quality of the films did not have to be high. Responding to this demand, businesspeople and filmmakers such as James H. Nicholson and Samuel Z. Arkoff formed a company called American International Pictures. At AIP they honed the JD films into the motor-cycle milieu and created a new tradition of mindless B action flicks featuring plenty of formulaic violence.

By the summers (drive-in season) of 1967 and 1968, the genre had found a needed shot in the arm with the inclusion of the returning vet characters. Their antisocial behavior was a result of the traumas they had endured in the Vietnam War. Their anger was the result of the treatment they had received at the hands of an ungrateful government and populace. They were trained to be killing machines in war, and now back in "the world" (the phrase used to mean back home, out of Nam), they had no socially acceptable place to practice those skills. This cynical, lazy, uncreative milieu was to have many B movie incarnations.

Angels from Hell, released in June 1968, is an example of the mayhem from American International Pictures. Bruce Kessler directed Tom Stern, who played an ex-biker and returning Vietnam War hero. Unable to relate to his wife and a rigid household routine, he returns to his old lifestyle. He and his buddies form a gang and soon clash with a rival outlaw biker group. In a rumble the vet uses his combat training to great effect. New status is conferred upon him, and he is able to unite several gangs under his leadership. After a few scenes of sex orgies and drug usage, violence erupts anew, and the hero is killed by the police.

The Vietnam background is topical window dressing for a formulaic biker movie. Surviving Nam and dying in America are viewed as great irony. *Angels from Hell* features odd monikers for the motorcycle gang members, such as Speed and Tiny Tim, to convey a type of adolescent male bonding. Like many of the platoon movies to follow a decade later, the nicknames reflect a shared and exclusive tribal closeness. Jack Starrett has a small role as a biker known as Captain Bingham. The actor would go on to direct several films included in this book.

If 1967 seemed a bad year, it was nothing compared to America's depth of trouble and pain in 1968. As if to herald real-life hellishness, the year began with the 77-day siege of the marines at Khe Sanh. This battle and the accompanying Tet Offensive in January and February proved that no location in Vietnam was safe from Viet Cong attack. Carefully trained cadres waged offensives in all provincial capitals, carried out political assassinations, and even penetrated the inner confines of the U.S. Embassy in Saigon. In March, not to be discovered until later, the My Lai massacre took place. In April, Martin Luther King, Jr., was assassinated; Robert Kennedy's assassination followed in June. Race riots rocked the country's inner cities throughout the summer. The political conventions in America were disrupted by antiwar demonstrations that escalated into full-scale riots. The base at Khe Sanh was abandoned in June. Against this backdrop a faint glimmer of light appeared as American and North Vietnamese officials had their first formal meetings in Paris in May. In October, President Johnson, who had chosen not to run for reelection, announced the cessation of bombing of the North. In November, Richard Nixon was elected president and promised he had a secret plan to end the war. By this traumatic year's end, there were a peak 536,000 U.S. troops in South Vietnam.

In February 1968, the low-budget underground film *Windflowers* was released in New York. Adolfas Mekas wrote and directed the film, which starred John Kramer. Told in flashback, this is the story of a fugitive draft dodger. Symbolically, the protagonist falls in love at a Fourth of July picnic. But his participation in that joyful American celebration is cut short by the arrival of the FBI agents who have been tracking his whereabouts. He is forced to flee and along his journey meets "love it or leave it" working-class types as well as a reporter who tries to understand his antiwar actions. In the end, the police and FBI close in, and through a series of overreactions, a rookie police officer (basically a "cherry," an FNG [fucking new guy], to use the vernacular of the troops in Vietnam) shoots and kills the young man. His death, like so many others, seems unnecessary. As an antiwar drama, the messages of wasted youth, violence, and an unjust society were in and of themselves political in nature.

There is nowadays a tendency to try to equate the victimization of the soldier in Nam with the sacrifices of the protesters of the war at home. Although this is a very unbalanced equation, a film such as *Windflowers* does show a rare but plausible fatal consequence of the domestic upheaval on the life of a noncombatant.

Independent filmmaker Robert Kramer made three films about the Vietnam conflict. The first, *The Edge*, was released in March 1968. As with all of Kramer's films, he was producer, director, and writer. The avant-garde leftist's style often utilized in lieu of action or story a lot of boring poseurs discussing their views on the war in monotonous dialogues. The grainy, underlit, black-and-white, neorealist style reveals the shoestring budget of these projects. Some of these deficiencies are also designed to convey an aura of "underground" origin, the surreptitious documentation of life in a supposedly revolutionary setting.[1]

The Edge features a group of cultured radicals who have settled down after years of activism on behalf of the civil rights and antiwar movements. Each character has reached a personal crisis of inner frustration and powerlessness. They are energized by the arrival of a young radical, but they also distrust him as a possible FBI spy. Therefore, when one of them plans to assassinate the president in retribution for his conduct of the war, it remains a closely guarded secret. The group is severely split over this desperate plan. Eventually the assassination is thwarted, and suspicion falls on various members as to who betrayed the cause. At the end, several of the group leave for Chicago to help organize draft resistance activity. Of course, later that year in real life, the student demonstrations at the Democratic National Convention were epic in scope.

Less politicized lower-middle-class youth watched movies at the drive-ins. College-educated young adults ordinarily were not attracted to watching a returned vet bust heads for his motorcycle gang. The skewing of entertainment along age lines was followed by this further division along class lines. As the civil rights protests of the early 1960s coalesced into the antiwar movement, this division widened. The intellectualization of upper-class youth gave rise to a more urbane taste in film. This cinema inevitably touched upon antiwar activism. The lower economic strata of youth continued to partake of the more traditional linear type of film. They were the same young men who were most likely to fight in Vietnam because of a lack of deferments and social connections.

The art-house-destined release seemed far away from *Born Losers*. However, all relied on a younger audience for their support. The studios sought a way to unite these niche films and generate greater box office revenue through a major A title. By 1968, the unpopularity of the war had reached such a high that filmmaking corporations began to explore antiwar attitudes within the context of mass market vehicles. This was a departure from the conservative establishment support the industry had always given to the government and the military. For the most part, the Vietnam War itself remained off limits, but there was money to be made in packaging the antiwar movement, so the studios joined the avant-gardists, documentarians, and independents with "hip" antiestablishment films.

The European studios, not quite as terrified of the Vietnam conflict as the Americans, continued their occasional look at the war. In 1968, an Italian film, *The Wild Eye*, was imported and helped fill the transition from "art" to "entertainment" vis-à-vis the war. Its protagonist, an amoral documentary filmmaker, was a perfect example of the introspective 1960s fascination with the war and with the media. Yves Montand in *Live for Life* was a member of the visual arts, a filmmaker. Fowler, the reporter in *The Quiet American*, represented the written word of the 1950s. The documentarians were some of the few people producing meaningful works on the war itself, so why not use fictional characters from this same realm? Hence, there were the once-removed protagonists: the journalists, filmmakers, and broadcaster characters who acted as observers of the war on behalf of audiences. It was as if the conflict was a blinding eclipse that one could not look at head-on. But through a camera's eye, the movie, or the story within the movie, this conflict became more presentable.

Television had made Vietnam the first "television war," where the nightly news showed the action with great realism. As body counts were reported each evening, much of the American public became numbed by the bloody images. What had been previously horrific was a little less affecting now. This look at life and death through the camera's eye corresponded with developments in technology, such as the beginnings of satellite transmission and the widespread use of color television. They added vividness to the amalgam.

Director Paolo Cavara's *The Wild Eye* is packed with the late–1960s fascination with the war, the media, and the new morality. It contains a number of scenes actually filmed in North and South Vietnam in 1967. The story involves Phillipe Leroy as Paolo, the filmmaker within the film. He is interested in recording events but not in choosing sides or being affected. He and his crew travel throughout the world looking for provocative images that he recreates and then falsely represents as unstaged. In Vietnam, he is almost able to persuade a Buddhist priest to immolate himself in protest over the war and the government's suppression of his religion. This is a reference to the famous protests that culminated in the June 11, 1963, suicide by immolation of Buddhist monk Thich Quang Duc in Saigon. It was immortalized in Malcolm W. Browne's horrifying photo for the Associated Press.

In Saigon in *The Wild Eye*, actual events overtake the fictional filmmaking crew in ways it would not stage. Paolo is beaten up by the Viet Cong. His group also witnesses the execution of a young VC suspect by police. Finally, documentarian Paolo finds out about a Viet Cong plot to bomb a popular nightclub. Rather than tell either the authorities or the patrons, he sets his camera to record the events. He is ecstatic when the camera captures the devastation. However, as he and his cinematographer move in, they find the body of Paolo's lover. The despicable Paolo remains composed enough to demand that his crew record his reaction.

The Wild Eye is replete with the iconography of the 1960s antihero. The conventional John Wayne–type good proactive hero is an anachronism. On the other side of the spectrum is the immoral man of action, a Clyde Barrow–type murderer from Arthur Penn's 1967 classic *Bonnie and Clyde*. Paolo's antihero typifies the malevolence of passivity and manipulation. His status as bystander and voyeur to the carnage is a damning reference to the apathy of the general viewer vis-à-vis the events in Vietnam at the time of the film's making.

The symbolism is underscored by the direct use of imagery from the conflict itself. The monk dousing himself with gasoline is an image that is impossible to forget. When Paolo gets to Saigon, the summary street execution of a VC suspect echoes the vigilante chaos in the capital. When *The Wild Eye* was filmed in August of 1967, the Tet Offensive had not yet taken place. By the time the film was imported to New York a year later, the profound impact of that major Vietnam War development had been felt. In retrospect, the film's execution scene conjures up a similar real-life image. The maker of *The Wild Eye* could not have incorporated the famous February 1, 1968, photograph, "Vietnam Execution," by the Associated Press's Eddie Adams. That picture indelibly marked on our consciousness the exact moment when the Saigon police chief blew a Tet Offensive rebel's brains out. *The Wild Eye* and other productions of the 1967–1970 period used topical images that sometimes predated real-life events.

The end sequence's act of sabotage, the Viet Cong bombing of a location frequented by U.S. personnel, was also based on a recent incident and was reminiscent of a similar act depicted in *The Quiet American*. The execution and bombing were to be used in 1977 in *Good Morning, Vietnam* to gruesomely convey the brutal nature of the war in its urban incarnations. In the midst of such a bloody and unpopular conflict, such current-event-oriented films as *The Wild Eye* were inherently controversial and only marginally successful.

Returning to the exploitation vein, again with a media-oriented component, was Commonwealth United Entertainment's *The Angry Breed* in the summer of 1968. David Commons produced, directed, and wrote the film in the tradition of independent, budget-conscious credit sharing. James MacArthur costarred with Murray MacLeod, who portrayed Johnny Taylor, an aspiring actor and a Vietnam vet. When in doubt, the soldier is always the one named Johnny, an apparent tradition that goes back to our own Civil War's pop-cultural designations in song and legend.

While in Vietnam, Johnny saves the life of the son of a Hollywood producer. When Johnny "comes marching home" to California, he calls in his favor. After a long day at the studio, Johnny is once again thrust into the role of hero. He rescues a producer's daughter from motorcycle gang harassment. A grateful father agrees to cast Johnny in a new movie. An agent, played by Jan Murray, objects to this change as his favorite client MacArthur was set for the role. Believe it or not, the actor is also the leader of the aforementioned motorcycle gang!

In a sneering bit of movie insider cynicism, the agent and actor conspire to kill Johnny. At a Halloween party they spike the punch with LSD. After a series of absurd action sequences, the veteran and his new love go off to start a new life. It seems that joining the trauma of Vietnam is now the trauma of Hollywood!

Johnny manages to survive both with his finely honed skills. At least Johnny in *The Angry Breed* is a good guy, albeit a violent one . . . but only when provoked.

That same year, a major studio, Paramount Pictures, released *Targets,* a modest but stylish film with a much more dangerous Vietnam veteran main character. Independent film mogul Roger Corman was the uncredited executive producer. Corman protégé Peter Bogdanovich made his debut as the director, writer, and producer. Once again the picture was self-consciously (and budget-savingly) set in the southern California film community. True to life, Boris Karloff played a famous horror film star. Tim O'Kelly was the marine veteran who, despite other failures, is a crack shot. *Targets* begins as Karloff is leaving a private screening of his latest film. We see him from a subjective camera through the crosshairs of a rifle sight. Veteran O'Kelly is in the process of purchasing the weapon for his burgeoning arsenal. At home the vet goes berserk and kills his wife, his mother, and a delivery boy. Then he drives to a point overlooking the Los Angeles freeway and picks off innocent victims.

As nightfall approaches, the killer retreats from the police to a drive-in showing a Karloff film. Coincidentally, the star and his entourage show up on a personal appearance tour. Hiding behind the screen, the killer pokes a hole through and begins to randomly shoot people parked in their cars. Panic ensues and only the brave aging star remains calm. He confronts the crazed vet, who, upon seeing himself juxtaposed against Karloff's huge image on the screen, is distracted long enough for the police to catch him.

The real-life audience watching would chuckle at the self-conscious irony of the finale. After all, the killer is also firing out at them from behind the screen. The violence in Vietnam, the main character, and the concern over crime in America made the film provocative beyond its cleverly staged B movie conventions. After the April 1968 murder of Martin Luther King, Jr., *Targets* was pulled from release.

(As far as the sharpshooting skills displayed in *Targets,* some 20 years later iconoclastic Stanley Kubrick in *Full Metal Jacket* commented on assassin Lee Harvey Oswald's same marine-instilled expertise. In a sick but funny bit, the real-life drill sergeant and Viet vet-turned-actor R. Lee Ermey quizzes his young charges on how Oswald learned to hit a moving target with a single bullet from a long distance. The sharpshooting was courtesy of the corps, the sergeant proclaims with a sick sense of pride. This odd boasting is not lost on the basic training recruits, who as draftees in 1968 are about to be shipped to Vietnam and embroiled in the Tet Offensive.)

The painful topicality of the Vietnam War continued to manifest itself in fictional films in indirect ways. America's consciousness about the war was paradoxical. On the one hand, it pervaded our perceptions; on the other hand, people attempted to ignore it. Casual references in films managed to satisfy both. As a source of orientation to current events, countless mentions of the war were injected as mere asides to the main story. Often they took the form of an incidental overheard television or radio report on the conflict. Richard Lester used this technique in his 1968 look at the mod scene in San Francisco in *Petulia*, starring Julie Christie and George C. Scott. Andy Warhol's look at the equally hip London scene, *The Chelsea Girls*, featured a take-off on a "Hanoi Hannah" (North Vietnam's version of Tokyo Rose) broadcast.[2]

The level of our obsession with but inability to confront the war was typified by the inclusion of gruesome Vietnam atrocity footage in the context of a G-rated musical comedy! In November 1968, Columbia Pictures released *Head*, featuring the Monkees. This frenetically paced psychedelia was an amalgam of pop-cultural references. Director Bob Rafelson's collaborators were writer Jack Nicholson (still prestar status) and executive producer Bert Schneider (six years away from his Vietnam documentary, *Hearts and Minds*).

Annette Funicello and Victor Mature, in a parody of their own Hollywood personas, joined the Monkees in their musical fantasy. Obviously, lighthearted entertainment was the operating motif. The inclusion of Vietnam War footage and references illustrates the alluded-to paradox. Far from being harrowing, the images have been neutralized by a media-barraged public. The flattening of the register of emotion reflects the ubiquity of references to the conflict but the paucity of meaningful portrayals.

On one level it seems in poor taste to juxtapose lightweight films with the serious real-life events of the war contemporaneous to their release. Such ignorance of the painful realities was often expedient. But like the early Vietnam War movies, films in this period acquire meaning because of their naïveté and seeming clairvoyance in regard to real events. With our hindsight, some sequences seem amazingly knowledgeable; others, incredibly stupid. However, in an unprecedented fashion, omniscience in the context of Vietnam remains a contradiction in terms.

In the spring of 1965, Robin Moore's novel *The Green Berets* was published.[3] In 1966, the song "Ballad of the Green Berets," by Sergeant Barry Sadler, was released. The best-selling book and hit song helped inspire the movie *The Green Berets*. In 1968, Warner Bros. released what was to become one of the most controversial films ever made about the Vietnam War. John Wayne's film was the only A production, direct-combat portrayal of Vietnam made during the war itself!

John Wayne was the prototypical gung-ho action hero, so thoroughly associated through his westerns and war films with America that he was a cultural icon. To more than one generation this actor helped inculcate a patriotic value system. The previously quoted Ron Kovic in *Born on the Fourth of July* sums up his naive affection as follows: "Like Mickey Mantle and the fabulous New York Yankees, John Wayne . . . became one of my heroes."[4]

When antiestablishment protests began against the Vietnam War, Wayne felt compelled to respond. He began by taking trips to Vietnam in 1966 and 1967. He visited with troops in a morale-boosting tour and did research for the anticipated project. He was impressed by the positive attitude of the troops at this early juncture in the war. This was particularly the case with the elite special forces units. These troops, known by their unique uniforms as the Green Berets, were highly trained fighters who had served as advisers since the earliest days of the conflict.

Inspired by his visit, Wayne went right to the top! As Lawrence Suid reports in his excellent book on the Pentagon and Hollywood, *Guts and Glory*:

> Wayne . . . wrote to President Johnson setting forth his interest in making a film about the Green Berets. He explained that while he supported the administration's Vietnam policy, he knew the war was not popular. Consequently, he thought it was "extremely important that not only the people of the United States but those all over the world should know why it is necessary for us to be there. . . . The most effective way to accomplish this is through the motion picture medium." He told Johnson he could make "the kind of picture that will help our cause throughout the world." While still making money for his company, he could "tell the story of our fighting men in Vietnam with reason, emotion, characterization, and action. We want to do it in a manner that will inspire a patriotic attitude on the part of fellow Americans – a feeling which we have always had in this country in the past during times of stress and trouble." To make this film, Wayne explained he would need the cooperation of the Defense Department, and in support of this request, he cited his long film career and specifically his portrayal of the military with "integrity and dignity" in such films as *They Were Expendable, Sands of Iwo Jima,* and *The Longest Day.* He concluded that this film could be "extremely helpful to the Administration" and he asked Johnson to help "expedite" the project."[5]

Wayne's concern about competition from television further solidified his desire to provide a script that would garner government production assistance and ensure an epic theatrical scope to the project. The government advised the Duke that certain covert actions were "not [those] that the Green Berets would participate in."[6] The Pentagon also requested a ban on all references to a civil war in favor of a representation of the conflict as aggression on the part of one neighbor into the affairs of another. It also objected to any portrait of brutal treatment of prisoners at the hands of our South Vietnamese allies. The Pentagon had the helicopters and the extras, so those were the rules.

After long negotiations, Wayne was prepared to make the necessary compromises. Other filmmakers with differing perspectives were not. Herein lies one more reason for the dearth of head-on combat films. The ordnance providing the correct level of verisimilitude was in current use by the armed forces. To obtain them, a filmmaker had to garner government cooperation or wait several years for the jetsam of the war to make it to civilian sources. Even though this was no excuse for small-scale production, it did practically hamper any proposed epic presentations.

Wayne's production company, Batjac, had been in close negotiation for the final funding and distribution from Universal Pictures. But at this point, the studio had had enough and pulled out of the project. The Waynes proceeded undaunted with final location scouting. At the army's urging, they accepted as a stand-in for Vietnam the rugged terrain of Georgia surrounding Fort Benning.

The Green Berets (Warner Bros.–Seven Arts, 1968). John Wayne as Colonel Kirby selects crack Green Berets for Vietnam service.

In June 1967, Warner Bros. stepped in with the needed funds. Principal photography began in August on a $150,000 mock-up of a Vietnamese village constructed adjacent to Fort Benning. Upon the film's completion, it became a training ground for the Green Berets on their way to Vietnam.

When *The Green Berets* opened in New York in July 1968, it ran a whopping 141 minutes. The credit for director was shared by John Wayne and Ray Kellogg. Veteran director Mervyn LeRoy also lent unbilled assistance in this area. The final screenwriting credit went to ex-marine James Lee Barrett. Michael Wayne was the producer of record. Reflecting the cumbrous production and the intimate role of the military in it, the credits listed many technical advisers and liaison officers.

Wayne's leading character was known as Colonel Mike Kirby. Civilian journalist George Beckwith was played by David Janssen (who had been Marshall Thompson's old comrade in arms way back in *A Yank in Vietnam*). Jim Hutton brought a young lightheartedness to his all–American Sergeant Peterson. Aldo Ray was a salt-of-the-earth Irish-American career soldier, Sergeant Muldoon. Bruce Cabot as Colonel Morgan supervised field operations from the relative safety of Da Nang.

Raymond St. Jacques was the merciful Doc McGee, reprising his role as a medic in 1966's *The Lost Command*. Casting a black actor as the medical officer was the choice in several other Vietnam films. Doing so seemed to provide a certain self-conscious racial balancing to the Nam equation. The number of black soldiers functioning as grunts in the conflict was well in excess of that minority's percentage of the population. Criticism of the field command hierarchy involved the discriminatory use of African-American soldiers in hazardous duty or in menial chores. The increasingly cynical portraits of the war in the years to come featured these controversial roles. There were other black faces in the cast; in fact a young Richard Pryor made an exceedingly brief appearance as Collier.

Rounding out the cast were the Asians who either represented the heroic South Vietnamese allies, the faceless hordes of the Viet Cong, or the pampered North Vietnamese communists. The loyal and astute ARVN ally at command was played by the late Jack Soo. In the field, the brave native with a dashing ranger hat was played by George Takei. Chinese actress Irene Tsu took over the role that Kieu Chinh had occupied in the early Vietnam War films. Her comely Oriental beauty masked a cunning that made her an effective undercover operative for the United States and South Vietnam. Child actor Craig Jue did his part for the war effort by displaying resourcefulness as the orphan boy "Hamchunk." These positive portraits of U.S. allies were without precedent, as later depictions showed them to be corrupt and inept.

The Viet Cong troops that seemed too stupid to avoid being howitzer fodder were played by Hawaiian-American soldiers ordered by the U.S. Army to be extras. Also, a wealth of pancake makeup transformed a number of Caucasian performers into a sickly yellow enemy. It is no wonder that a few of these converted Viet Cong got caught up in the besieged camp's perimeter defenses. They probably could not see well because their helmets were pulled down over their faces to cover their round eyes.

The Green Berets begins as an all-male chorus sings *The Ballad of the Green Berets.* Soldiers in parade dress pass by as an army public affairs officer welcomes a group of journalists on a tour of Fort Bragg. The visitors hear Green Berets introduce themselves in multiple languages and explain their area of expertise. Then veteran master sergeant Aldo Ray and medical officer Raymond St. Jacques lead a question-and-answer session.

There is no mistaking the screenplay's acknowledgment of the controversial nature of the conflict. However, opposition is borne of ignorance, and those who have been there will set the record straight. A reporter queries, "You've been in Vietnam. . . . Why is the United States waging this ruthless war?" Muldoon replies, "Foreign policy decisions are not made by the military. A soldier goes where he is told to go and fights whoever he is told to fight."

George Beckwith of the *Chronicle Herald* jumps up with his question. David Janssen's character will be our eyes on the conflict, and his change of perspective will eventually reflect the conclusions that the filmmaker seeks to instill in the audience. Sergeant McGee continues, "As soldiers . . . we can understand the killing of the military but the . . . intentional murder and torture of innocent women and children . . . In spite of this, there's always some little fella out there willing to stand up and take the place of those who've been decimated. They need us and they want us!" The sergeant's answer was chilling only six months after the devastation of the real-life Tet Offensive. Beckwith, now a bit more agitated, says, "A lot of people . . . believe this is a war between the Vietnamese people. Why not let them handle it?" Muldoon is ready as he steps over to a board and shows the Chinese, Soviet, and Czech guns and ammunition captured from the enemy. "What's involved here is communist domination of the world."

The session ends and the Duke invites the skeptical journalist to see for himself. Several days later when the Green Berets assemble on the tarmac at Fort Bragg, the colonel is pleased to see the journalist take him up on his offer. While they are unloading at Da Nang, airplanes and helicopters constantly fly overhead and remind the viewer of America's much-vaunted air superiority. The base's signs are all posthumously dedicated to heroes who have died in this dangerous and very real conflict.

Touches of home abound from the officers' mobile home to the cold American beer in ready supply. Some of the men go to sample the very censored presentation of the pleasures of the city. Wayne is briefed on his mission to respond to a heavy buildup of enemy troops in the highlands. He is to reinforce a camp in "the heart of VC country." Aiding his company will be a full complement of Montagnards, the tribal minority that acted as crack mercenaries on behalf of the U.S. government.

For the journey to the perimeter camps, large Bell UH-1d ("Huey") helicopters ferry the men. The men orient their civilian guest to the contours of the Cambodian and Laotian borders below. The arrival at the outpost provides the filmmaker with an opportunity to familiarize the audience with this type of encampment. Off the landing zone (LZ) and above the entrance is a sign that reads, "Dodge City." Every night is "Charlie's" (the VC's) time to lob in mortars. The camp has a perimeter of cleared-out jungle, here 150 feet of "killing area." Wayne quickly orders that it be cut back 300 more feet. In a matter of hours, the Americans' bulldozers will clear out a thick jungle that has stood for thousands of years.

To reinforce the perimeter defenses, claymores are laid, concertina wire is placed, and pungi sticks are implanted. The first defense is a type of Army-issued land mine. The second is a sharper and deadlier cousin to barbed wire dressed with metal cans to reveal potential infiltrators. The pungi sticks are a "trick learned from Charlie" and become an obsession in the movie. Their use recurs many times and symbolizes the primitive nature of the guerrilla war. Despite all the superior U.S. weaponry, these sharpened stakes buried in the ground will exact many casualties. When the designated all–American kidder Jim Hutton proceeds to his hooch (quarters), he is tripped by a mischievous Vietnamese orphan boy. Ironically, a trip wire is one more economical VC-inspired implement of destruction in the jungle warfare. However, here it is just an adorable innocent's prank to make the big American man fall down. The adorable little boy lost his parents in the war, and the missionary fathers at his orphanage were assassinated by the VC. He lives among the troops as a kind of mascot. Hutton has been chosen as the new surrogate father. Little Hamchunk's Spam-inspired nickname is more often pronounced "Ham Chuck." The *New York Times* thought a more appropriate name for the character would have been "Up Chuck."

At night the quietude of card games and letters home is punctuated by mortar fire. While scurrying about, the new arrivals discover that a direct hit has been scored on the captain's quarters and the dispensary. Tragically the CO who is "short," meaning his tour of duty is almost complete, is killed. The men remark on the attack's accuracy. A South Vietnamese ranger sets them straight. It was not luck; the VC have "eyes" in the camp. The next day Sergeant Muldoon observes one of the South Vietnamese soldiers pacing off the compound. He must be preparing the coordinates for another devastating artillery attack. The burly sergeant punches the spy out. In the next scene, ARVN ranger Nim vigorously interrogates him. Janssen is appalled by the lack of "due process." His naive assessment of field procedure is belittled by Wayne, who sets the record straight when he intones, "Out here due process is a bullet!"

The troubled journalist wanders from the "inquisition" to the medical tent. Here the kindly Doc tends to the poor villagers. One little girl has lost part of her leg to a land mine. The village elder explains in Vietnamese how afraid they are every night. Their rice and livestock are often stolen by the VC. The colonel decides that these neighbors need to be brought into the camp for their own protection.

The next morning a group of Green Berets, Montagnards, and ARVN go out to the village. On the path a plethora of booby traps encourages the patrol to take another route. The allied forces wonder if the old chief was "wearing more than one face." But that is not the case. Upon arriving at the hamlet, the men are sickened by what they see. The chief has been hung with a note staked to his body. All the huts are destroyed, and there are many dead. Janssen, now in fatigues, inquires about the little girl he met the day before. The grieving women report that she was taken off into the jungle, thus implying rape. The soldiers find her mangled corpse in the bush.

Back at the camp, the recon team reports that Charlie is building caskets and ladders only a few clicks (measure of distance) away. The fort/base prepares for battle as Wayne is summoned to Da Nang to meet with the brass. In a nightclub they discuss a scheme to kidnap a North Vietnamese general. Using a beautiful South Vietnamese model, they can ensnare the enemy. The meeting is interrupted as Wayne is called back to his command for the impending attack.

From an action point of view, the human-wave assault is the film's most exciting sequence. The Green Berets dig in as incoming mortars and outgoing artillery are exchanged. The journalist escapes injury as the soldier standing next to him is blown to bits. Given the intensity of the battle and the outnumbered defenses, he decides to lend a hand by loading ammunition for the besieged combatants. Colonel Kirby's returning helicopter is forced to back off from the

LZ. He crash-lands and regroups with a platoon trapped out in the bush. Via radio he learns of the dire situation in the camp. One by one the inner positions are breached, with heavy casualties. The Americans pull back to their secondary lines of defense as the determined VC continue their costly surge. In the midst of the carnage, Hamchunk's puppy runs out of the foxhole and is killed by a rocket blast. The tearful little boy gives it a proper "Christian" burial. As he puts a stick cross on the grave, his protector Hutton scoops him to safety in one hand as his guns blaze in the other. The faceless hordes force the soldiers and villagers into their final bunkered position. Wayne makes it in from the rear, having missed most of the climactic battle in his own movie. Only U.S. air cavalry is able to save them. Two "birds," or jets, bomb the inner-base positions, thereby clearing the marauders out in the nick of time. The tide of battle is turned, and despite heavy losses, the American and South Vietnamese comrades repel the remaining attackers.

The next morning the many enemy bodies are piled up. American dead are "tagged and bagged," placed in green plastic body bags for shipment back to the States. A shaken Janssen now carries a rifle. The colonel is touched but remains stoic, comforting the wounded and directing the camp's rebuilding effort.

The film has reached its climax but detours to a subplot concerning the mission behind enemy lines to kidnap the general from his palatial villa. On the way back from a successful operation, Hutton steps into a sloop knot, which pulls him into a pungi stick–filled wall. He is impaled upside down and wide-eyed in a shocking death. So close to the end, this tragic casualty touches them all. At a field burial Wayne makes a few appropriate remarks. Eventually the men are evacuated to their base by helicopter.

The heroes exit the choppers as Hamchunk pitifully searches for his beloved "Peter-San." Wayne breaks the news to the little boy. A crying Hamchunk asks, "What will happen to me now?" John Wayne hands Peterson's beret to the boy and responds in his deep yet lilting voice, "You let me worry about that Green Beret. . . . You're what *this* is all about." Together they walk off hand in hand into the sunset as the theme song begins anew.

It is only fair to say that Wayne deserves credit for having the "guts" to make a combat film set in Vietnam while the conflict raged. By the summer of 1968, opinion polls showed that the war was already very unpopular. Renata Adler wrote in her review in the *New York Times* on June 20, 1968, "*The Green Berets* is a film so unspeakable, so stupid, so rotten and false in every detail that it passes through being fun, through being funny, through being camp, through everything and becomes an invitation to grieve, not for our soldiers or for Vietnam (the film could not be more false or do a greater disservice to either of them) but for what has happened to the fantasy-making apparatus in this country. Simplicities of the right, simplicities of the left, but this one is beyond the possible. It is vile and insane. On top of that, it is dull."[7] In an accompanying article on the next page of the entertainment section, Charles Mohr slayed the perceived inaccuracies in detail in the movie. He summed up the technical gaffes that fueled politically subjective criticism. The *New York Times* writer caught the following continuity problem when the American hero walks off into the sunset with his innocent little charge: "Unless they have moved the South China Sea, the sun disappears magically into the east."[8]

The firestorm of protest was not limited to the media, which took an understandable dislike to the unsympathetic portrait of them in Janssen's Beckwith. The politicians also got involved. Representative Benjamin Rosenthal of New York accused Wayne of ripping off the Pentagon. Wayne responded by calling Rosenthal "an irresponsible, publicity seeking idiot. . . . I wish this were the 1800's. I'd horsewhip him."[9]

The hullabaloo surrounding the film generated interest in seeing it. In some quarters the public was incensed by the film. In fact, instances were reported of members of the audience cheering every time an American soldier was killed.[10] Although such reactions were in very poor taste, many viewed the film and the war as obscene and deserving of such a response. Adler, reflecting on the current polarized climate, finished her *New York Times* review in the following manner: "This is not exactly the stuff of which heroic fantasies are made. This is crazy. If the left wing extremist's nightmare of what we already are has become the right wing extremist's ideal of what we ought to be, we are in deeper trouble than anyone could have imagined."[11]

As with traditional action-driven pictures, war movies are better off avoiding politics; *The Green Berets* chose not to do so. As Michael Herr, future collaborator on *Apocalypse Now* and *Full Metal Jacket,* comments in his powerful book *Dispatches,* the movie reflected the same "mythic tracks" that had led us into the war itself. The film became a favorite booking of the armed forces entertainment officers in the years to come. Some of the less initiated "cherries" at first bought into the formula. But often after a few months in-country, even the most thickheaded recruits began to enjoy the movie as unintentional high camp. Like anyone close to the real action that is recreated in a movie, they knew too much. Or perhaps it was not that they were so close to the subject, but rather that they were so far. After all, as Herr says, *"The Green Berets* doesn't count. That wasn't really about Vietnam, it was about Santa Monica." Just previous to that bit of cynicism, Herr observes the filmmaker's dilemma and the industry's present wartime situation by stating, "Vietnam is awkward, everybody knows how awkward, and if people don't even want to hear about it, you know they're not going to pay money to sit there in the dark and have it brought up."[12]

Despite the critical lambasting, the domestic box office gross of *The Green Berets* was close to $20 million. Given ticket prices in 1968, that was a brisk tally. Additional revenue was provided by licensing to television and a small foreign market. With Defense Department help, the film cost only $6.1 million to make. In light of the commercial reception, did *The Green Berets* legitimate other combat portrayals of the war? No, not at all. Hollywood executives attributed some of the business to the free publicity generated by the controversy. Corporate suspicions that this type of Vietnam combat movie should remain off limits were confirmed by countervailing public relations costs. To use a term much in vogue at the time, such a film was not worth the "hassle."

In contrast to *The Green Berets* were the irreverent sensibilities of *Greetings*, released in December 1968. It was an early low-budget effort written and directed by Brian DePalma and starring Robert DeNiro. The movie is a wacky, improvised feature that offers an amusing glimpse of the lifestyles of three New York City bachelors. DeNiro as a would-be filmmaker provides yet another through-the-camera's-eye refracted image of the war. Jonathan Warden and Gerritt Graham costarred.

The film opens in black and white with a shot of President Lyndon Johnson delivering a speech. As the camera pulls back, we realize we are watching the address on a television screen. Together with the yet-to-be-introduced characters, we are an audience for the beleaguered chief executive. This subject camera angle is a favorite of DePalma's, one he will utilize constantly throughout his career in a technique designed to heighten empathy. It tends to break down the separation between the visual perspective of the actor and of the viewer. In this way we are witness to the same things as the characters.

LBJ attempts to exhort the youth of America to support the Vietnam War effort as a way to protect their way of life and make a contribution to society. "I'm not saying you never had it so good. . . . But that is true, isn't it?" The president's question is still hanging in the air as the credits roll and the film switches to color. A hand-held camera awkwardly bounces to a mod 1960s ditty as it follows a bell-bottomed, long-haired Jonathan Warden into a seedy looking New York City bar.

The outside facade of the rough establishment is shown, but not the interior. A number of black patrons follow Warden in, as the camera frames the front entrance. Then we hear but do not see him ask, "Which one of you niggers is man enough to take me on?" After the sounds of a few grunts, a pummeled Warden is dumped out the front door onto 125th Street. This peculiar scene is clarified when it turns out that Warden had received his call for his preinduction physical. He was hoping he could beat the draft by having someone break his leg.

Desperate to find a way to avoid Vietnam, the three friends decide they must come up with a better tactic for Warden. In a series of long takes or awkwardly edited jump cuts from precisely the same camera angle, they discuss their desperate options. In loony, improvised conversation the three actors brainstorm. The camera then follows them around New York as they fine-tune their schemes. In a clothing store they decide that Warden must pose as a "fag" to avoid induction. We also learn that Graham is obsessed with the John F. Kennedy assassination and conspiracy theories. DeNiro is a peeping tom and would-be pornographic filmmaker.

The young men go to the Bronx Zoo, where they coach Warden on "how to walk like a homosexual." In case this ruse does not work, they also prepare Warden for the role of a wild right-wing reactionary member of a secret organization. In a hilarious final preparation for the call back, they deprive Warden of sleep to make him a complete wreck for the physical.

Outside of the army office, DeNiro and Graham see their friend off with a mock Nazi salute. At the physical, Paul and a bunch of other frightened, pimply faced boys are welcomed by an enlistment officer with the words "Greetings." The exam results remain indeterminate as the movie jumps around with other zany episodes.

In a self-conscious way, television reports intrude and convey information about the war, such as that 500,000 troops are now in South Vietnam. We also witness DeNiro trying to convince a woman to take her clothes off in his film. On television the "living room war" continues as a captain in the First Cavalry in Vietnam talks about the war. At a Greenwich Village party, a returning vet talks about the rampant drug use, thriving black market, and "Wyatt Earp" mentality of the U.S. presence.

The efforts on behalf of Warden may have paid off, but DeNiro must appear for his army physical. He decides to use the previously rehearsed right-wing fanatic ruse with the army psychiatrist. The officer seems totally oblivious to the lunacy.

In the next scene, DeNiro is in fatigues in the jungle of Vietnam. With a subjective mock documentary framing, an audio voiceover asks the private for a man-in-the-field interview. As DeNiro explains the meaning of this "search-and-destroy" mission, they are interrupted by Viet Cong sniper fire. Crawling through the elephant grass, DeNiro and the documentarian come across a Vietnamese girl. Interrupting the interview, DeNiro tries to convince her to take her clothes off for the camera just as he used to do in New York. The film ends by returning to the opening black-and-white footage of Lyndon Johnson on television. "The End" is printed over an American flag. *Greetings'* antiestablishment attitude and frequent use of nudity earned the film an X rating. Its youthful appeal resulted in a gross in excess of one million dollars on a $50,000 investment! DePalma's success assured funding for 1970's quasisequel entitled *Hi Mom!* Robert DeNiro starred now as a Vietnam veteran, who as he disembarks in the United States is greeted by a film crew and utters the title greeting. No longer shooting with a gun, a societally acceptable role for a soldier in Vietnam, DeNiro is soon shooting with a camera. The veteran becomes a full-time pornographic filmmaker and, as a hobby, an antiwar bomber. Vet DeNiro's new career in *Hi Mom!* is troubled by his technical gaffes. It seems a scene or two or his dirty movie is ruined when the observing stationary camera, mounted on a tripod, droops downward. The reference to an erect and then flaccid penis is obvious.[13]

In *Greetings* and *Hi Mom!* DeNiro's wacko persona predated Travis Bickle, the Viet vet antihero of Martin Scorsese's 1976 film *Taxi Driver*. That lead was the serious A film apotheosis of ten years of maladjusted veterans' portraits. The idiosyncracies of that performance are hinted at here when DeNiro talks to himself in mock reactive dialogue, dances about with lethal martial training techniques, or smiles with insane malevolence.

Greetings and *Hi Mom!*'s obsession with sex ranged from the mainstream horniness of three young men to the perverse voyeurism of DeNiro. The obsession with violence was a current running through the film, with the Kennedy assassination, the Vietnam War reports, and the finale in the poorly evoked Asian jungle. The relationship of violence and sexuality was a theme that would continue to fascinate Brian DePalma throughout his career. He returned to them and this book in 1989 in *Casualties of War*, an extremely harrowing, fact-based tale of the rape and murder of a Vietnamese girl by American soldiers.

As the decade came to a close, world attention focused on the Paris peace talks, which commenced on January 25, 1969. The public awaited Nixon's plan to end the war as U.S. involvement seemed first to escalate and then to diminish, only to escalate again. In early June, American planes bombed North Vietnam for the first time since November 1968. The following month, a 25,000-troop withdrawal was completed. A program of "Vietnamization" was implemented, involving the turning over of the war effort to the South Vietnamese. In the fall of 1969, the Laotian government requested additional support in its battle against communist forces.

On November 15, there were massive antiwar demonstrations throughout the country, with more than 250,000 marchers in Washington, D.C. The very next day it was first reported that hundreds of civilians had been massacred at My Lai the previous year. By the end of this turbulent year and decade, U.S. troop strength was at 474,000, down from 536,000 the previous New Year's Day. The United States' extrication from the war was going slowly, and increased involvement in Laos and Cambodia threatened to scuttle the peace process.

In February 1969, Columbia Pictures released *The Model Shop*. It was produced, directed, and written by France's Jacques Demy. The new film was typical of the internationalization of cinema in its day. A multinational crew and cast joined in a traditional romance infused with Vietnam War references.

The two romantic leads were current darlings of the art audience, Anouk Aimee and Gary Lockwood. He portrayed a young Los Angeles architect awaiting his draft notice. She was a lovely French woman in a "model shop" for amateur photographers. This is basically a place where attractive women take their clothes off for money. Eventually he receives his induction notice and discusses his fears with the model. After they sleep together, he returns to his wife. Before he can go off to the army and, as implied, to Vietnam, his wife leaves him for a television producer.

The lazy writing that had pervaded the exploitation genre vis-à-vis the vets was now invading urbane films in similarly tangential Vietnam references. As a dramatic impetus, the specter of the war or being drafted was less likely for an older upper-middle-class professional. However, the anxiety reflected a preoccupation with the continued conscription and high troop deployments. To further appeal to young adults, the soundtrack from Lou Adler was a blending of classic compositions with modern rock.

The music echoed the character of the film. A traditional tale of love and infidelity was updated in a hip setting. Modernity was enhanced by paying lip-service to the conflict.

In *The Model Shop*, voyeurism, photography/filmmaking, and Vietnam seemed to find a way of integrating into a self-conscious, late-1960s, McLuhan-induced obsession with media and the reality of secondhand imagery. The sexual revolution went hand in hand with the new society. By definition, this allowed for a greater permissiveness and a degree of alternative behavior. In films in the future when the veterans return home, their combat experiences would often render them sexually impotent. It is as if their combat-generated visceral feelings of fear and self-preservation had overwhelmed them, rendering them unable to partake of the sexual revolution and permissiveness back in "the world."

In a sign of the times, movies showed life being observed through a lens. Gary Lockwood in *The Model Shop*, Robert DeNiro in *Greetings*, Paolo in *The Wild Eye*, Yves Montand in *Live for Life* (and, definitively, David Hemmings in Antonioni's *Blow Up*) all viewed life through this artificial barrier. It was a way to avoid responsibility and feeling. This distancing was the way in which most Americans observed the Vietnam War: directly through television and indirectly through such films. Those in the military or in active opposition to the war remained in the minority. For the majority of Americans, the film industry was more than ready to oblige in failing to address the conflict in a head-on manner.

Warner Bros.' March 1969 release, *The Big Bounce*, concerned the melodramatic life of a veteran upon his return to the United States. The movie was directed by Alex March and written by Robert Dozier. It featured Ryan O'Neal in his first starring role; he played opposite his future wife, Leigh Taylor-Young.

The film opens as the vet is working in a dead-end job as a migrant worker on a California farm. He gets into a fight and is thrown out of town. O'Neal then drifts to another locale, where he has an affair with a wealthy landowner's mistress. She goads him into criminal behavior. They have a falling out, and the aimless young man moves on down the road.

Based on an Elmore Leonard story, *The Big Bounce* manages to subtly convey a number of classic depictions of returning veterans. Here is a man whose readjustment into society and the workplace is marginal at best. He is employed in some of the least-respected occupations that exist. He is violence prone, which causes problems with employers and the police. He is misunderstood and is a loner without a support system, either institutional or private. In other films, support is limited to other similarly situated veterans, fellow bikers perhaps. One of the few talents possessed is the combat-tuned ability in martial arts and survival training.

Any one such characterization in isolation may not be heinous or implausible. But it is precisely the aggregate effect that this book outlines that is most unfortunate. From what can be discerned, few real-life veterans bothered to watch most of these films. Damage was inflicted when nonveterans, lacking other models, were presented with these negative character traits.

Adding to the making of a cliché was the June 1969 release of producer-director Al Adamson's *Satan's Sadists*. Here motorcyclers have an assortment of colorful names, including Acid and Anchor, the latter played by Russ Tamblyn. However, the returning veteran has the traditional name: Johnny. Set, as usual, in southern California, Anchor's gang wreaks havoc at a roadside cafe. Surviving the carnage is the drifter Johnny. After taking a beating, he regains consciousness and uses his combat skills against the punks. Included is a brutal scene where he drowns a man in a toilet bowl. Johnny and a waitress escape to the wilderness. The mayhem continues as innocents are raped and murdered in a number of sordid scenes. The hero veteran puts an end to the nonsense by hurling a knife into Anchor's throat while driving at him at full throttle.

(Lest one worry that such "classic" films are lost forever, *Satan's Sadists* was just one of several motorcycle films that recently graduated into the ranks of rarified camp art. A print traveled throughout the country as part of a film retrospective entitled "Chrome and Celluloid." It was curated by the UCLA Film and TV Archives and played art museums and film society venues.)

Not all the Vietnam-related films released in the hot summer of 1969 were mindless, violent, lowbrow references. *Medium Cool* represented a thinking man's perspective on the war, the media, and our turbulent society. The title referred to Marshall McLuhan's definitions of "hot" and "cold" media. The movie was produced, directed, written, and photographed by Haskell Wexler. The film was loosely based on Jack Couffer's 1967 novel, *The Concrete Wilderness*.

In 1968, when Jane Fonda made her famous trip to North Vietnam, her group included her friend and cinematographer Haskell Wexler. He recorded the events for a later documentary. Fonda, Wexler, and the others believed their dialogue would hasten the peace process. The most controversial moment was their encounter with American prisoners of war held captive in Hanoi. Despite Wexler's "radical" credentials, he was able a year later to find a major film studio to distribute his new drama. As a sign of the times, even while X rated, *Medium Cool* was not considered off limits by Paramount.

The movie concerned a television news cameraperson played by Robert Forster and his sound engineer, portrayed by Peter Bonerz. They travel around the United States covering a panoply of late–1960s events for a Chicago station. The film had at times a "mock-dock" (pseudodocumentary) style. This feeling was underscored by the use of a hand-held camera covering well-known current events. The cinema vérité stylization coupled with a filmmaker protagonist was thus typical of the time.

The increasing politicization of the media employees suggested a journey to knowledge reminiscent of the actual filmmaker's. Initially in *Medium Cool* the dispassionate filmmaker is like the amoral documentarian in *The Wild Eye*. He films an auto accident, and only later does he call an ambulance. Later in Appalachia, they interview a woman whose husband is off in Vietnam fighting to preserve the "American way." This is an angry presentation of the paradox of the "have-nots" fighting on behalf of the "haves" in American society.

A romantic subplot and an FBI subplot develop. Finally in Chicago tension mounts as opposing forces assemble during the 1968 Democratic National Convention. The preceding year's real-life protests in the Windy City's streets had come to represent a domestic climax in violent clashes over the continuation of the war. The hippies' confrontation with the overzealous Chicago police and the National Guard was a sickening example of the serious civil strife produced by disagreement over the war.

Set to the music of Frank Zappa and the Mothers of Invention, the images of this domestic confrontation were well known. Into this fictionally recreated maelstrom are plunged the film's characters. The filmmaker/reporter now covers the events with much more sympathetic involvement. Among a full-blown riot and exploding tear gas, he and his girlfriend flee the scene. He loses control of their automobile, and she is killed. In a gruesome finale, a passing motorist stops to photograph – but not aid – them. The film's first scene involving the ambulance is echoed. *Medium Cool* ends with this last bit of life-through-a-lens commentary on the need to take a stand.

The movie's portrayal of a numbed populace turned off and tuned out by televised overexposure to the war was one of the last Vietnam-related films to use a filmmaker/photographer's perspective as a source of irony or intellectual sojourn. The anonymous viewer who turned off the television in the end of *The Ugly American* had become the nightly news watcher of battles and body counts served with dinner. The quagmire was tough to tune out. As the 1960s came to a close, the "message" was clear, and the "medium" as a self-aware costar became trite in its own right. It would be 1987 before the mock documentary style would return in *84 Charlie MoPic*. That film used a subjective camera as a character. In 1987, this was an attempt to bring freshness to a subject that had expanded to include many powerful direct-combat portrayals of the war.

As if to punctuate the end of the filmmakers-as-protagonist strain of Vietnam-related movies, 1969 featured one more incarnation of the returning veteran story. Originally entitled *The Soldier's Wife,* the movie changed its name to the bad pun *I Feel It Coming.* The pervasiveness of the war resulted in its inclusion in this movie by Sidney Knight, which was little more than a skin flick.

I Feel It Coming's aptly named protagonist, Peter, is a Viet vet. Excited to be reunited with his lovely wife, he is unable to perform. Impotency could accompany a combat-scarred psyche. However, it will become a recurring attribute in many returning vet portrayals. The coupling of the Vietnam combat experience with impotence seems to echo a perceived lack of potency of the U.S. military in the conflict. How fitting that the literal notion has one of its first overt manifestations in a sex film.

To add to the list of misunderstandings on the part of noncombatants, Peter's wife badly mishandles the episode. The distressed vet attempts to regain his sense of manhood with a prostitute but again fails to perform. Finally Peter and Rita reconcile and seek help. In a laughable consultation, a doctor tells him to try forgetting his wartime experiences. With renewed creativity the wife attempts to find appropriate means of sexual stimulation. Here the true voyeuristic nature of the film is able to go wild. They/we watch a striptease, lesbianism, and several imaginative couplings.[14]

None of these "therapies" sufficiently "relaxes" the troubled veteran. Finally, it is agreed that marijuana might have the desired effect. The drug's courier is an attractive woman who reminds Peter of an arousing situation back in Saigon. The uncooperative delivery woman refuses a ménage à trois. The film turns particularly ugly as an aroused Peter rapes the woman. Finally, Peter and Rita let the delivery girl go, and they reconsummate their marriage. The movie unfortunately integrates a number of loser vet currents while exploiting both violence and sex.

In October 1969, the now defunct National General released *Hail, Hero!* It was based on John Weston's book, published the previous year. Michael Douglas was "introduced" in the starring role as a college dropout who, despite his antiwar protests, enlists in the army. Arthur Kennedy protrayed his father, a conservative World War II combat veteran and patriarch of a wealthy Arizona ranching family. Peter Strauss was the older brother, and Teresa Wright played the mother. Gordon Lightfoot wrote and sang a number of original songs for *Hail, Hero!* The score itself is a kind of expansive Coplanesque celebration of the hero's exuberance and the American West setting.

Prior to induction, the spirited Douglas returns to his family homestead. What ensues is an exploration of the war, responsibility, manhood, and the ability to kill. It is as if *East of Eden* has met the draft anxiety movies. His older brother is crippled by an accident for which the father and Douglas hold themselves responsible. The long-haired flower child is torn by a need for parental love, absolution, and participation in a proud family tradition of military service. As his older brother is incapable of this duty, Douglas feels doubly compelled. The father venerates the military as a maker of men and defender of our country. He reminisces about fighting the Japs and "having" native women. The different circumstances of the two conflicts, World War II and Vietnam, seem lost on the older man.

At a party Douglas confronts a representative and a senator over the war. They listen but dismiss his idealism as youthful naïveté. Finally, the representative insults the young man, who responds by taking a swing at the politician. The reflexivity of this Douglas response intrigues Douglas as he has wondered about this ability to pull the trigger in combat. He concludes that ideals become nothing more than reflexes when young men are faced with the threat of death.

Douglas's brother still loves him and recognizes the pain and fear of confronting his sibling. The brother's attempt to reconcile the family on behalf of Douglas are lost on the oblivious parents. In the finale Douglas alone paints a red, white, and blue peace mural on the side of the barn. He then goes off destined for Vietnam. *Hail, Hero!*'s ambiguities were reflective of its desire to be topical, yet not too radical. In a prerelease version, the family joined the departing

He's afraid to die.
He doesn't want to kill.
And the Army
takes him tomorrow.

"HAIL, HERO!"

starring
Michael Douglas · Teresa Wright and Arthur Kennedy
Screenplay by David Manber. From the novel by John Weston. Produced by Harold D. Cohen.
Directed by David Miller. Music by Jerome Moross. Technicolor*
"Hail, Hero!" and "Wherefor and Why" composed and performed by Gordon Lightfoot.

Hail, Hero! (National General Pictures, 1969). In his first major role, Michael Douglas confronts the draft and manhood.

son in painting the peace symbol. If the film had been made today, the sunnier ending would have been utilized. But in the late–1960s films with antihero protagonists, the use of ambiguous or unpleasant finales was not looked upon as box office poison.

The angst experienced by the characters reflected domestic anxiety and despair produced as a consequence of the war. Aside from returning from Vietnam veterans and their problems, a number of movies concerned those awaiting military service or trying to avoid the draft. Their legal responsibilities, sense of duty, moral dilemmas, and disruptions in civilian lifestyles were sources of genuine concern. Although only marines were assured of a one-year tour of duty in Vietnam, a significant number of other draftees in all armed services were assigned to the fully mobilized conflict. One could be fortunate to be stationed at Fort Dix or Wiesbaden, but it was not something to count on. Aside from the moral questions the war presented, it was quite life threatening.

Hail, Hero!, The Model Shop, and other dramas concerning selective service were joined by the comedic send-up of *Greetings.* Another humorous treatment was *The Gay Deceivers*, the story of two draft-age heterosexuals who pose as homosexuals to avoid the army. Kevin Coughlin and Lawrence Casey starred in this Bruce Kessler film from American International that received its premiere in San Francisco. The mod West Coast comedy also featured Jack Starrett as the army recruiting officer.

The two young men move into a one-bedroom apartment in a very gay area. In a campy way, all sorts of "madcap hijinks" result. Danny's father is appalled, and their girlfriends believe they are actually gay. The girl-crazy young men are desperate to regain their old lifestyle and undo the damage that their successful ruse has created. Finally they decide to admit their deception to the army and proceed with the Vietnam-destined tour of duty. However, the recruiting colonel is unconvinced of their recant and upholds army policy (which remains in effect to this day) by refusing their enlistment. In a final scene, the colonel is revealed to have his own homosexual lover, a sergeant in the induction center. Aside from the comedic twist, the hypocrisy of the establishment figure is revealed.

If Hollywood found it impossible to deal with the war itself, the independents were at least more successful in dealing with the antiwar movement and counter-culture. Out-of-the-mainstream filmmakers were often, if not part of the milieu, then at least closer to it. These niche pictures' lower budgets also allowed for less corporate constraints as the risk of return on investment was diminished.

One example of niche marketing, which earlier East Coast filmmaker Robert Kramer had occupied, was the December 1969 Jana Enterprises release, *The Activist*. This X-rated production was written and directed by Art Napoleon. Because of severe budget limitations, *The Activist* was shot in 16 millimeter. By the time the film stock was blown up to the common 35-millimeter theatrical exhibition format, the resultant graininess lent a degree of cinéma vérité to the production. Enhancing this out-of-the-mainstream pedigree was the actual location shooting done in Berkeley, California.

Michael Smith starred in *The Activist* as an antiwar student radical. He flees a teargassed demonstration and seeks refuge in his girlfriend's apartment. She is absent, but her roommate, Lee, played by Leslie Gilbrun, is there. She and Mike begin a love affair, and she becomes involved in the antiwar struggle. Later on, at a demonstration at the Berkeley draft induction center, a riot breaks out. Mike is beaten up by the police, and Lee is arrested. She is frightened by these events and the fact that Mike has been expelled from school and has lost his deferment. She convinces him to seek guidance from one of his professors. Mike is put off by their compromised notions of protest and breaks off his relationships in order to continue more radical activism.

Alice's Restaurant was a United Artists release directed by Arthur Penn and starring Arlo Guthrie. The movie was an expansion of his hit song, "Alice's Restaurant Massacree." It had a pacifist attitude toward the war presented in a flippant but commercial format.

Arlo loses his draft deferment when he is thrown out of college. He and his hippie friends hang out at Alice's place. Eventually our wisecracking hero is jailed for littering and is then rejected from military service as an undesirable criminal! The "flower power" generation comedy features several poignant scenes where Arlo visits the deathbed of his real-life father, Woody Guthrie. In an inside joke, the real police and judge associated with the antiwar protest that inspired the "massacree" portray themselves.

Easy Rider **(Columbia Pictures, 1969). Peter Fonda as Captain America surveys the American landscape.**

Continuing in 1969's sign-of-the-times vehicles was another star-director, Italy's Michelangelo Antonioni. In a transition that is sometimes frightening for filmmakers, he was now in an English-language milieu with funding by America's MGM for *Zabriskie Point*. The film was produced by Carlo Ponti, and the screenplay was written by Antonioni, Fred Garner, Tonio Guerra, Clare Peploe, and Sam Shepard. The soundtrack featured terrific music by Pink Floyd, the Grateful Dead, the Rolling Stones, and so on.

Antonioni picked two unknowns for his youthful protagonists. Mark Frechette and Daria Helpern were cast mainly because of their perfect physical beauty. In an analogous way, their politicization and subsequent victimization at the hands of the overzealous police, the as it were "domestic military," are somehow akin to the bespoiling of America's natural and spiritual beauty. Cryptically, the European director presents an environmental message in his references to exploitation by capitalist polluters. This ruination is juxtaposed with the tarnishing of our innocence in an immoral war. The actions of the "unspoiled" youthful lovers are tainted by a muddled lack of motivation. Is their antiwar activism merely a popular show of solidarity with their generation, or is it truly heartfelt? The critics panned *Zabriskie Point* as unintelligible. Many dismissed any antiwar themes as secondary to a jumbled treatise on alienation and materialism.

Continuing a decade-ending descent into tangentiality was *Easy Rider*. The box office hit cost only $400,000 to make, so Columbia Pictures made a mint distributing this monument to a bygone era. Costars Dennis Hopper and Peter Fonda directed and produced the film, respectively. The movie is fondly remembered for the star-making performance of Jack Nicholson and the pulsating rock score by such late 1960s groups as the Byrds, the Electric Prunes, and Jimi Hendrix. Steppenwolf's "Born to Be Wild" became an anthem for a generation turned off by the war and turned on by sex, drugs, and rock and roll.

Despite a lack of overt references to the Vietnam War, *Easy Rider* was borne of the period and now helps define it. The movie had a uniquely Americanized picaresque theme presented against a psychedelic, heliotropic, rock-and-roll background. The characters sell marijuana in California and then begin an odyssey across country on their motorcycles. Along the way they encounter an ugly strain of hostility. The longhairs with jeans patched with the American flag and peace signs cannot escape violent overreactions. The intolerance that befalls the heroes is indicative of the spirit that gave rise to the war.

American society was so polarized by the war that soldiers returning from Vietnam were sometimes spat upon by antiwar demonstrators. This division was typified by the popular campus chant "Ho Ho Ho, Ho Chi Minh, the NLF [National Liberation Front] is gonna win!" No wonder then that combat portrayals remained strictly off limits. Some of the related treatments of the Vietnam War went further "underground" in their presentations. This different place, different time mentality can cause an overextension of subjective attribution to the conflict. This leads to instances of incorrect observation that a film is about the Vietnam conflict. An example is the following from David A. Cook's otherwise very fine 1981 book, *A History of Narrative Film*. He begins with similar conclusions by stating, "The years 1968 and 1969 witnessed some of the most original American films since the late forties. Like *Bonnie and Clyde*, many of them were aimed at the new youthful audience and were either covertly or overtly concerned with the political hysteria that had gripped the nation over the war in Vietnam."[15]

However, then he goes too far in his particulars by stating, "If *Bonnie and Clyde* were about the type of romantic rebel who would fight the military-industrial complex to end the war and usher in the greening of America, Sam Peckinpah's *The Wild Bunch* (1969) was about America's mercenary presence in Vietnam itself."[16] No, *The Wild Bunch* was about American gunfighters in turn-of-the-century Mexico and Texas.

Nevertheless, the violence (and, to a lesser extent, sex) graphically portrayed by filmmakers reflected a shocking challenge to the previous standards of depiction. As Cook and others have stated, the choreographed bloodletting in the finale of *Bonnie and Clyde* ushered in an age somehow more befitting the carnage in Vietnam and the revelations yet to come, such as My Lai. In an artistic and an industrial sense, this violence also paved the way for graphic portrayals in some of the best (read: least romanticized) Vietnam war films yet to come in a return to in-country combat depictions.

At this same time in 1969, a new medium was introduced in the industry that would rely on topical and inexpensively produced feature films as a source of programming: the made-for-television movie. This birth of the "long form" would become an important secondary source of Vietnam-themed motion pictures. At roughly feature length, these movies provided original treatments of controversial subjects. (A successful television presentation is seen by more people on one night than a moderately successful theatrical film is in the course of its entire run.)

With the current expansion of ancillary markets, these films have taken on added importance. The more successful television productions had been repackaged and released theatrically in the international marketplace. In the 1990s with the need for home video titles to stock the shelves of 10,000-plus cassette stores, these same movies are placed side by side with theatrical releases. Their more modest origins are lost on the general public, particularly younger viewers. So in 1969, the electronic purveyor of the conflict in a nonfictional sense joined the regular movies as a source of images relevant to the Vietnam War.

The Ballad of Andy Crocker, the first television movie to deal with the war, was aired on November 18, 1969, on ABC. The film was produced by two successful television heavyweights, Aaron Spelling and Danny Thomas. Actor Stuart Margolin wrote and associate-produced the film, which was directed by George McGowan. Lee Majors portrayed Crocker, and Joey Heatherton was his girlfriend. Supporting work was done by Agnes Moorhead, Pat Hingle, Jill Haworth, Peter Haskell, and actor-singers Jimmy Dean and Marvin Gaye.

Underscoring the budgetary constraints of the new medium, the film opens to a firefight in Vietnam that is shot on a soundstage and then poorly integrated with real-life footage. Crocker is wounded and sent home to encounter numerous postservice problems. In what will become prototypical traumatic domestic fashion, his sweetheart has married another man, his business has been run into the ground, he cannot relate to his father, and the flower power generation denigrates his decorated service. One fistfight and an extended motorcycle chase scene pay homage to contemporaneous theatrical releases. However, he does not solve his problems by using his military training to exact vengeance on a cruel world. Rather, as the film ends, he waits alone in the morning cold for the army recruiting station to open up. *The Ballad of Andy Crocker* was by no means a dramatic tour de force. However, it was refreshing that in this maiden Vietnam-themed foray, the new medium chose a more benign characterization in portraying the veteran.

As the new decade begins, so, too, does the next chapter. It is entitled "Hot Chrome and Hippie Cool" and reflects the continuation of many of the same refracted portraits of the war featured in this chapter.

References

1. Gilbert Adair, *Vietnam on Film* (London: Proteus, 1981), p. 73.
2. *Ibid.*, p. 74.
3. Robin Moore, *The Green Berets* (New York: Crown, 1965).
4. Ron Kovic, *Born on the Fourth of July* (New York: McGraw-Hill, 1976), p. 55.
5. Lawrence Suid, *Guts and Glory: Great American War Movies* (Reading, Mass.: Addison-Wesley, 1978).
6. *Ibid.*, p. 224.
7. Renata Adler, "Film Reviews," *New York Times*, June 20, 1968, p. 48.
8. Charles Mohr, "The Green Berets," *New York Times*, June 20, 1968, p. 49.
9. *The Hollywood Reporter* interview with John Wayne, June 26, 1969, as quoted in Suid, *Guts and Glory*, p. 226.
10. Ivan Butler, *The War Film* (London: Tantivy Press, 1974).
11. Adler, "Film Reviews," p. 49.
12. Michael Herr, *Dispatches* (New York: Knopf, 1972), p. 202.
13. Michael Bliss, *Brian DePalma* (Metuchen, N.J.: Scarecrow Press, 1983).
14. Richard P. Krafsur, ed., *The American Film Institute Catalogue of Motion Pictures* (New York: Bowker, 1976), p. 515.
15. David A. Cook, *A History of Narrative Film* (New York: Norton, 1981), p. 633.
16. *Ibid.*, p. 631.

Chapter 3

Hot Chrome and Hippie Cool, 1970–1973

As the first half of the 1970s began, the subgenres of indirectly related Vietnam War films continued, while the norms of presentation and the environment of reception were dynamically changing. *Easy Rider* had offered a decade's-end expression of America. Television helped challenge the means of production and exhibition norms. In response to industry and societal change, theatrical films by 1970 contained unprecedented explicitness in sex and violence. The 1960s end of the studio system had softened Hollywood's traditional role as defender of both morality and patriotism. The upheaval created by the Vietnam War offered a new moral challenge, which the film industry and society in general had great difficulty in addressing. In real life one unfortunate area of continuity in the midst of this dynamism was that the war itself continued.

In March of 1970 South Vietnamese forces attacked communist bases across the Cambodian border. On April 4 a rally was held in Washington, D.C., in support of President Nixon's conduct of the war. By the end of June Nixon had withdrawn U.S. infantry from Cambodia, but air strikes continued. On the last day of the year Congress repealed the Gulf of Tonkin Resolution. Following October troop withdrawals, the U.S. troop strength at year's end was 335,800.[1]

In January 1970 independent Manson Distributing Company released *The Ravager*, directed by Charles Nizet. No longer was the military background merely mentioned. This film actually began in Vietnam. The main character is a demolition expert who has become separated from his platoon. In a frightening sequence he witnesses the rape and murder of a young Vietnamese woman by two Viet Cong soldiers. Eventually he returns to the United States, where he undergoes six weeks of psychological therapy in a Veterans Administration hospital. The system fails miserably, and upon his relese this pre–"Son of Sam" psychopath begins to kill anyone he sees engaging in sex. Using his military expertise, he blows up cars of parked lovers.

This pre–"slasher" genre film exploits the soon-to-be-familiar equation of pubescent sex-violence-horror fantasies. Here the social maladjustment is thematically propelled onto the veteran character. The only thing missing is the exploitation of impotency, as the veteran does finally begin to rape his murder victims himself! By more clearly identifying the Vietnam background of the main character, the film intensifies the negative associations in the minds of the public. This type of graphic film would appear to be without entertainment or redeeming value.

Another release, *The Losers,* was an appropriately named Vietnam veteran exploitation feature. It, too, notched up the relevant profile by specifying in detail the combat experience of the main characters and by placing the on-screen action in Southeast Asia. Jack Starrett, an actor in *The Gay Deceivers,* directed muscular William Smith as the gang leader Link. Adam Roarke was his veteran comrade in arms and in axle grease.

The Losers represents the ultimate synthesis of biker flicks and Vietnam exploitation films. Link recruits a team of veterans and biker buddies to aid in a raid into Cambodia. The story is preposterous, but the setting is noteworthy, as the conflict has now overflowed into that neighboring country. Five now-civilian Hell's Angels go on the CIA payroll to infiltrate behind enemy lines and rescue a presidential adviser held captive in a prison camp. To accomplish this task, the men retrofit their motorcycles into armored war machines! Vic Diaz, the Viet Cong professor in *Operation CIA,* returned as a mechanic whose garage the bikers use to modify their choppers.

In one scene Adam Roarke escapes from the official army convoy and rides his cycle to his girlfriend's rural home. They run toward each other amid the elephant grass, arms open wide in a laughable reunion cliché. In another scene out of *The Wild One,* the bikers ride through a small town parade jumbling up the traditional Chinese dragon dancers and confounding the peasants. Beer drinking and whoring provide for several fight scenes, leading up to the no-nonsense preparation for the mission. Finally the men ride into the camp and liberate the nerdy CIA operative despite his peculiar reluctance to escape with them. Several of the protagonists die in the assault, as do countless enemy soldiers who never seem to take cover from the marauding machine-gunning bikers.

In a confusing final double cross, the object of the rescue mission seems to be a double agent. The one regular army officer who protected the interests of the bikers is killed by friendly fire. Another soldier kills the last surviving hero, William Smith, as he attempts to shoot the CIA ingrate. The sole identifiable survivor is the government spy. The internecine violence and unhappy ending connote a grim view of the war.

The film was originally titled *Nam Angels,* an amusing integration of the conflict with the genre. Movie mentor Roger Corman later utilized that name and similar story elements in a direct-to-video release in 1986. Back in 1970, however, American International preferred the more generic title *The Losers* for its summer drive-in release. It seemed to cynically convey the anticipated result of the conflict and the fate of its veterans.

The next Vietnam veteran portrayal was on a much more peaceful note. *Norwood* was a musical comedy that starred Glen Campbell as the title character and

Norwood (**Paramount Pictures, 1970**). **Glen Campbell readjusts to civilian life as a country singer.**

Kim Darby as his supportive girlfriend. Joe Namath, launching an acting career, costarred as Campbell's buddy and fellow vet. Jack Haley, Jr., directed this adaptation of Charles Portis's tale of a returning veteran's rise to stardom in the world of country music. It is a refreshing departure from the violent exploitation portraits. Albeit a small aspect of the story, the good-natured young man's military service did not seem to warp him for life. It just interrupted his inevitable cross-country odyssey and success in his chosen profession.

The new made-for-television movie medium provided a return to a generic conflict and enemy in a pacifist-oriented movie tale. *The Challenge* was broadcast on ABC on February 10, 1970, and starred Darren McGavin, Broderick Crawford, Mako, James Whitmore, and Sam Elliott. In a bit of Vietnam-era wishful thinking, the teleplay by Marc Norman posited a unique solution to war's human costs. Representatives of the United States and an "Asian" country with which the United States is at war agree to settle their differences by each sending one soldier to fight to the death on a deserted island.

Although a pleasant utopian means of resolution for a Vietnam-mired nation's viewers, the film's execution was as slight as its premise. In fact the real director had his name removed from the project in favor of the traditional Hollywood pseudonym, "Alan Smithee." That recurring moniker attached to a project's main credit ensures the inferior status of the end result. In essence no one wanted to take the credit.

American International's prolific exploitation factory churned out a March release simply titled *Explosion*. This Canadian-American coproduction was filmed in Vancouver under the name *The Blast*. It starred Don Stroud, Richard Conte, Gordon Thomson (later of "Dynasty" fame), and Harold Saunders. Jules Bricken wrote and directed the film.

The melodramatic story begins with a family trauma caused by the Vietnam War. The Evans family's eldest son decides to flee over the border into Canada to avoid the draft. His father persuades him to stay in the United States. He is inducted into the army, sent to Vietnam, and killed in action. The grieving younger brother, who is nearing draft age, rebels and runs away from home. He meets a hippie drifter played by Stroud, and they head for Canada in a stolen sports car.

In one bizarre scene Thomson tells his new friend about his younger days in military school. He is very strange as he marches about in recollection of the rigid regimen. Later we learn that the young rich kid was actually exempt from the draft, having been designated 1Y for mental instability. Finally the "psycho" blows his cool and guns down two police officers who catch Stroud stealing gas from a closed station. This exact same transgression of the law will be the impetus to the veterans' crime spree in the 1972 film *Welcome Home Soldier Boys*.

In racing to the tragic climax, the film is taken over by its exploitative thrust. Like all the downbeat endings indicative of the time, a final nihilistic shootout results in the death of the young men. Somewhere between the A movie freeze-frame stylized ending of the outlaws' saga in *Butch Cassidy and the Sundance Kid* (1969) and the graphic slow-motion end of the crime spree in *Bonnie and Clyde* (1967) is the journeymen-directed demise of these B movie hero-villains of the time.

Brief mention should be made of the March 1970 release of the Warner Bros. documentary *Woodstock*. The event represented the countercultural apotheosis of the era. The three-hour film, directed by Michael Wadleigh, was basically a concert movie. As such it chronicled the importance of folk and rock music to the younger generation and its integral unifying role in an antiwar movement. Between the songs was the intercutting of footage of the crowd and interviews with some of the 400,000-plus people assembled in the field in Woodstock, New York.

The politicization of the younger generation and its favorite musicians was apparent throughout. Jimi Hendrix's improvised electric guitar rendition of "The Star-Spangled Banner" was enough to send chills up the spine of any American Legionnaire. Country Joe and the Fish memorably led the huge crowd in the antiwar "I Feel Like I'm Fixin' to Die Rag."

Woodstock is now tritely referred to as more than just a place or three-day event. When the late radical activist Abbie Hoffman was asked, "Where do you live?" he replied, "Woodstock nation." When queried as to where that was, he said, "It is a nation of alienated young people. We carry it around with us as a state of mind, in the same way the Sioux Indians carry the Sioux nation with them."[2]

Hoffman's words also revealed the empathy that many young people felt for what they considered to be oppressed people – namely, the Vietnamese of the time and the American Indians exploited in our nation's bloody past. This notion changed Native American portrayals in the westerns of the period. Even though these Hollywood productions might not have been about Vietnam, they reflected a guilt-ridden sensibility about our conquest of the West. The savages of countless westerns were now portrayed as noble victims of a violent society.

There were several examples of Westerns released in the early 1970s with Vietnam-reactive sensitivity for Native Americans. An entire coda of American manifest destiny and pioneering spirit was called into question. Arthur Penn's *Little Big Man*, starring Dustin Hoffman, was a tragicomic retelling of Custer's Last Stand from the Indians' point of view. *Tell Them Willie Boy Is Here* featured Robert Redford and Katharine Ross in a serious tale of a modern Indian victimized by society. (Ironically the film's writer and director was Abe Polonsky, working for the first time since he had been blacklisted in the 1950s anticommunist hysteria.)

Ralph Nelson directed a 1970 release entitled *Soldier Blue*, which starred Candice Bergen and Peter Strauss. Its climax was the brutal slaughter of an entire Indian village by the once-heroic U.S. Cavalry. In light of the recent revelations about My Lai, this was a painful sequence. It would be years before any such atrocity could be directly attributed to our fighting troops in the modern context.

The last example of this recontextualized setting was the 1971 production *Ulzana's Raid*, directed by Robert Aldrich. The film starred Burt Lancaster. In the film an inexperienced cavalry officer attempts to kill Apache leader Ulzana. The U.S. officer is an academy-produced leader by virtue of his institutional rank only. Real leadership has to be earned. This cynical portrayal of a foolish lieutenant would eventually become a popular antimilitary character in many Vietnam-set films. The traitorous loyalties of the white-employed scouts were embraced by some as analogous to the South Vietnamese position at the time. Some critics mistakenly contended that these films were about Vietnam but that Hollywood felt compelled to change the setting for commercial reasons. These films were not secretly about Vietnam; they were just informed by it.

On May 4, 1970, four students were killed at Kent State University in Ohio during an antiwar demonstration. That same month four black students were killed at Jackson State University in Mississippi. The police and National Guard were establishment institutions directing violence against the college youth of America. Occurring domestically to noncombatants, these incidents had a traumatizing effect. They exemplified the sickness of the nation and horrified it in a way that the continuing combat carnage and statistics flowing out of Vietnam could no longer muster. Eleven years later in a well-made evocation of the times, the Ohio tragedy was recreated in the made-for-television movie *Kent State*.

Unfortunately at the time of these events and the real-life combat incursions into Laos and Cambodia, Hollywood could respond only lamely. Filmmakers did not have the benefit of perspective or the luxury of instantaneous production. The next three A budget productions reflected the bloated approach of the studio institutions to the perceived youth market and to current events.

Getting Straight was a Columbia Pictures release based on Ken Kolb's 1967 novel of the same name. This sign-of-the-times comedy-drama opened in May, the same month as the real-life campus bloodletting. Richard Rush was the producer and director of Robert Kaufman's screenplay. The film starred Elliott Gould and Candice Bergen. He played a civil rights activist who had served in Vietnam and has now returned to college to pursue a master's degree. As a teaching assistant to undergraduates, he is implored to join in the campus protests. Gould's tired character is more intent on finishing his education and bedding down pretty coeds. Eventually he is forced to take sides and joins in a student riot.

Not to be outdone by Columbia, MGM released a similar campus-based film in June entitled *The Strawberry Statement.* It was produced by Robert Chartoff and Irwin Winkler and directed by Stuart Hagmann from a screenplay by Israel Horovitz. It was based on the James Simian Kunen novel *The Strawberry Statement: Notes of a College Revolutionary.*

The drama elicited by the antiwar movement and draft-related anxiety was mollified by comedy from West Coast gag writers. Added to the mix was a youth-oriented musical score featuring Buffy Sainte-Marie; Crosby, Stills, Nash, and Young; and the notable anthem "Give Peace a Chance" by John Lennon. The cast included Bruce Davison, Kim Darby, But Cort, and Jeannie Berlin. The film was self-consciously full of superfluous camera angles, editing techniques, and slow motion.

The plot of *The Strawberry Statement* involved university student Davison's joining in campus demonstrations as a way to meet coeds. The once-noble purpose of civil disobedience and its anti–Vietnam War catalyst are largely a jumbled mass of background noise. Davison is coopted into activism by an implied enhancement of the possibility of his having sex. Sexual revolution is accepted as fact, but passé at that. Protests on any real social issue are now merely pop pontifications. Davison's cynical motivation reflects the entire production's duality of purpose in an equally dishonest characterization. In a massively staged climax, student demonstrators gather at the gymnasium, where they sing "Give Peace a Chance." As television crews record the events, gas-masked National Guard troops attack the students.

Columbia returned to its pursuit of a hit based on hipness when it released *R.P.M.* That abbreviation was a cutesy pun that stood for revolutions per minute. The film was a collaboration between producer-director Stanley Kramer and Yale professor, media celebrity, and author Erich Segal (*Love Story*). The movie starred Anthony Quinn as a university professor, Ann-Margret, Gary Lockwood, and Paul Winfield.

The film attempts to tell the campus unrest story from the point of view of a sympathetic faculty member torn between his own activism and his position's

R.P.M. (Columbia Pictures, 1970). The police drag off Gary Lockwood amid campus unrest.

inherent institutional responsibilities. Quinn is beloved by his radical students and is rewarded by enjoying a sexual relationship with graduate student Ann-Margret.

Radicals Paul Winfield and Gary Lockwood lead a student revolt that succeeds in ousting the university president. Quinn is drafted as successor because of his relationship with the student body. On behalf of the administration he begins a negotiating process with the radical leaders. They are absolutely rigid in their demands and thoroughly unsympathetic as they threaten to destroy university property. Unable to exact a compromise, Quinn is forced to call in the police and restore order. In so doing, he loses his constituency and becomes a victim of circumstances beyond his control.

Independent Cannon Films' July release, *Joe,* was an unexpected low-budget hit. Cinematographer John G. Avildsen added directing chores to his topical rendition of Norman Wexler's story about a blue-collar steelworker's and a white-collar advertising executive's reactionary response to the hippie subculture. Peter Boyle was praised for his portrayal of the lead character, Joe; Susan Sarandon and Dennis Patrick costarred.

This film reduces the counterculture to a bunch of hedonistic sex maniacs and drug addicts whose antiwar activism is no longer discernible. The ad exec and the steelworker unite as the "Silent Majority" to rail against the "free love"

Joe **(Cannon Releasing, 1970). Peter Boyle as Joe introduces Dennis Patrick to his buddies at the bowling alley.**

and substance abuse they equate with the flower power generation. But then the two men hypocritically get stoned and join in a sex orgy. In the final scene at a commune, the older men slaughter everyone in sight.

Joe was a consummate sign-of-the-times film. Like other well-grossing films, it appealed to diametrically opposed market segments. It had a way of fulfilling the viewer's perspective as opposed to challenging it. For the right-wing reactionary, it contained the requisite action and vengeance against a permissive society run amok. It felt good in its extremism. To a more liberal audience, it confirmed the intolerance of hawks and the hypocrisy of the older generation. In its depiction of the backlash against youthful radicalism and disrespect for societal institutions, the film's original title was more apropos: *The Gap.*

Most protest was limited to an acceptable social consciousness on behalf of the antiwar movement. However, a small violent fringe existed on the extreme Left of the counterculture. The Weathermen were such an underground organization. In July 1970 United Artists released an Edward Pressman–produced film dealing with a more hard-core antiwar activist. Jon Voight starred as simply "A" in *The Revolutionary.* The dramatic screenplay was written by Hans Koningsberger in an adaptation of his book. Paul Williams directed the film, which also featured Robert Duvall.

Filmed in London, the movie was set in an unnamed country. The code-named radical "A" was disenchanted with the compromised policies of his student

The Revolutionary (United Artists, 1970). Jon Voight finds himself in uniform for a cause he does not believe in.

group, similar to the character in the preceding year's film *The Activist*. Voight joins Duvall's violent working-class organization. However, "A" is drafted and called upon to suppress a labor strike. He deserts and teams with another fanatic to plan a political assassination. "A" and his accomplice fail to blow up a judge and are caught by the authorities.

The minimalism of time, place, and even the main character's name suggested a frightening neo–Orwellian extension of societal institutions. The succinct designation of "A" added a secret-"cell" dimension and was complementary to a popularly held notion that behind every campus radical was an anarchist or communist agent. In light of the recent bombing at the University of Wisconsin's mathematics buildings and the East Coast armed robberies on behalf of the Weathermen, a violent fringe element was a source of real fear among the populace.

The same month as *The Revolutionary*'s release was the debut of independent Jaylo Films' *Cowards* in New York. It, too, concerned the war, the draft, and the violence associated with the war. Simon Nuchtern produced, directed, and wrote the film, which starred John Ross. The lead is no longer a student, so this popular source of deferment is gone. However, his parents seek to find him another alternative source of deferral, a special type of job. He and his Greenwich Village girlfriend decide a better solution is to flee to Canada. His father objects to this illegal means of avoiding the draft, although he had no qualms about searching for a conventional dodging mechanism. Father and son become estranged as the former accuses the latter of being a "coward."

Contributing to the Vietnam-related tragedies are the death of the girlfriend's brother in combat and the wounding of a friend, who is left permanently disabled. The protagonist decides he must stay in the United States and fight against the draft and the war. In the finale he joins an antiwar group led by a priest as they destroy a draft board office. The last scene shows him in jail, arrested for his heartfelt convictions. Just as the Weathermen lent a degree of reality to *The Revolutionary*, the actions of Fathers Daniel and Phillip Berrigan lent authenticity to the fictional drama in the *Cowards* finale. Their exploits would be chronicled in 1972 in *The Trial of the Catonsville Nine*.

The heartland was not to be outdone by the East and West coasts' mad rush to portray in film the war's effect on noncombatants. National General Pictures' *Homer* was filmed in Canada, set in small-town Wisconsin, and premiered in Louisville. It told the tale of an 18-year-old facing the draft and coming of age. It was produced by Edgar J. Scherick, directed by John Trent, and written by Claude Hanz. Don Scardino and Tisa Farrow costarred. The September release featured songs by the movie's young star as well as by Led Zeppelin and the Byrds. The story also involved the long-haired youth's search for parental respect, his loss of virginity, and his dealing with the grief caused by a peer's death in Vietnam. Each of these important events led him to a mature stance against the war on moral, not expedient, grounds.

New York–based filmmaker Robert Kramer returned from *The Edge* to write, direct, and star in a new film, *Ice*. Released by art film distributor New Yorker in October 1970, the director now turned his attention to a futuristic look at U.S. aggression in Mexico. This indictment of U.S. foreign policy vis-à-vis a Third World country was meant as recontextualized anti–Vietnam War commentary. There was little interest at the box office for this view of a radical terrorist's opposition to the violent U.S. foreign policy. Coupled with radical vet Jon Rubin in *Hi Mom!* (see Chapter 2), the violent antiwar activists of *Ice, The Revolutionary, The Activist,* and other films began to assert themselves as common characters ready to join the wired loser vets in the pantheon of Vietnam-induced fictional clichés.

The last independent release in the fall of 1970 to be discussed here is the West Coast–produced Richmark presentation of *Captain Milkshake*. This film was made in Berkeley and San Diego and was produced, directed, and written by Richard Crawford. The film's musical score included contributions from Country Joe and the Fish, the Steve Miller Band, and Quicksilver. Unlike the tangential or recontextualized films, *Captain Milkshake* was firmly rooted in Vietnam.

Geoff Gage portrayed a United States marine on emergency leave from Vietnam to attend a family funeral. In San Diego he meets a cute hippie college student, played by Andrea Cagan. They smoke dope, visit a commune, make love, and smuggle drugs in from Mexico. It is all good, clean, sign-of-the-times fun and a welcome respite from the horrors of war. At an antiwar demonstration at the University of California, she breaks up with him. He does not flip out. Rather, as planned, he returns to Vietnam when his leave expires. Shortly after his return he is killed in action.

On television Universal Pictures offered up *Lost Flight*, a feature-length pilot for a proposed new series. Leonard Horn directed from a screenplay by Dean Riesner. The plot was an updating of the old story of a disparate group of people stranded on an island, this time because of a plane crash. They must decide how to run their microcosm of society. What is notable is the inclusion of Billy Dee Williams as a marine on his way home from active duty in Vietnam. Instead of being a weird antisocial powder keg, he is a calming influence on the others, with his keen survival skills. Despite his contribution to the group, racism makes him a victim and he is shot. His bigoted attacker flees from the group and is impaled on Billy Dee's food-gathering animal trap. Ironically, having survived his tour of duty, the vet dies. His attacker is killed by the Viet Cong–inspired pungi sticks. It is quick retribution for a lethal injustice. In the movie's final scene one of the women has a baby. The new arrival and the tragedy of the veteran's death unite the group in a communal forging ahead with its new society.

Tribes, broadcast on November 10, 1970, on national television, exemplified some of the inherent strengths of the new full-length "made-fors." It was frugally mounted, topical, and nongratuitous. The made-for-television movie was designed for one or two large exposures to a national audience. Because of the heterogeneity of that potential ratings source and sponsor concerns, overt politicism was compromised in deference to a more balanced counterpunctual presentation. Far from being reduced to pablum, this better-written film was able to speak to groups on differing sides of the issue. Perhaps it reconfirmed viewers' beliefs prior to tuning in, but to expect miraculous conversion was unrealistic. Rather, *Tribes* created an internal rhythm that echoed a societal dialogue at work.

Joseph Sargent helmed *Tribes*, and Tracy Keenan Wynn and Marvin Schwartz won an Emmy for their writing. Darren McGavin was the tough marine drill sergeant, and Jan Michael Vincent was a hippie draftee. The story follows the basic training of raw recruits into the once-hallowed U.S. Marine Corps in the middle of the Vietnam conflict. *Tribes* opens to a mournful folk song about "lonely soldiers." A busload of apprehensive, pimply faced young men bounce along the highway on their way to basic training. This is an eclectic bunch: blacks, whites, Hispanics; long and short hairs. One hippie type stands out as a handsome and internally peaceful presence. It is Jan Michael Vincent lost in a pleasurable daydream about his girlfriend. We abruptly rejoin reality as the bus pulls into the austere confines of the military base.

Gunnery Sergeant McGavin yells at the boys to get off the bus. His authoritative commands are more angry barks than coherent directives. The cadence and the gut-wrenching nature of the patter are familiar; only the language is compromised for television. When the sergeant sees the long-haired

Vincent, he cannot believe his eyes. He asks that young man what he is doing
here. The young man answers the NCO's query, "I was drafted. I didn't have
a choice."

The recruits fall out, the credits roll, and we then watch the new arrivals
receive their military haircuts. More accurately we see marine barbers shave the
young men's heads in slow motion. As the hair wafts to the floor, the first stage
of enforced uniformity and shared experience is accomplished. The same visual
composition was utilized later in Stanley Kubrick's introductory sequence in *Full
Metal Jacket.*

The drab uniforms are issued; the rules and regulations are ordered and
reordered. In jarring contrast to the noisy public persona, the film cuts away to
a quiet moment in the NCO's lounge. A soft-spoken McGavin shoots pool with
his friend and supervisor, played by Earl Holliman. The two career marines
discuss how they are going to get these boys fit for battle in Vietnam. Holliman
decries the use of marijuana among the troops in Nam.

Vincent is in the best physical shape and a natural leader. When he is able
to withstand a grueling exercise, it does not escape the notice of his DI and fellow
boot-campers. The anguished among them begin to take lessons in meditation
from their fellow trainee. Some of the more conservative members of the group
take issue with this breach of discipline and the alternative code of conduct they
believe it represents.

McGavin's fundamentals of pugil stick defense, marching, and so on begin
to shape the group into a presentable unit. However, he is troubled by the
perceived competition for the trainees' minds. Physical training is not enough;
they must think like marines. The hippie's outlook undermines this essential element of their education. In one funny scene the drill instructor turns on the light
at reveille and sees the entire platoon meditating in the lotus position on their
bunks! When Vincent refuses an order to shoot at the facsimile of a human
target, the situation has gone too far. Holliman is furious about the breakdown
in discipline and warns McGavin to take charge of these troops, or he will.
McGavin deliberates on a proper course of action. Holliman baits Vincent, asking him, "What kind of flower are you?"

In the middle of the night Vincent awakens and notices that the troubled and
now drug-addicted Quentin is missing from his bunk. When Vincent checks the
bathroom (a nocturnal scene more eerily used again in *Full Metal Jacket*), the
Zen master recruit finds that Quentin has slit his wrists. Vincent calmly applies
tourniquets and directs the other startled recruits to summon help. He has saved,
not taken, a life. McGavin realizes he is losing complete control over the situation. He gives Vincent a manual on how to most effectively kill an opponent.
After all that will ultimately be the most important business at hand.

Vincent is angry and can no longer reconcile his pacifism with the reality
of his situation. He begins to beat his pillow on the floor. The other recruits join
him in the therapeutic motions. The barrack erupts into a wild pillow fight
reminiscent of the social anarchism of the young boys in Jean Vigo's 1933 classic

Zero du Conduite. Their similar activity took place in the dormitory of their repressive institution, a boarding school.

By the next day, McGavin has reestablished his sense of mission. The passage of time makes the inevitable post-training assignment to Vietnam more imminent. As if to underscore the brutal reality, Vincent is forced to defend himself in a pugil stick competition. Each time he wins he must face another opponent. Finally, exhausted and bleeding, he collapses. That night McGavin calls Vincent in for a talk in his quarters. There are only two days left, and he must think like a marine. The sergeant sees this not as friendly advice but as genuine lifesaving natural law. The young man defiantly explains that no one can expect to change him and ignore his mind. McGavin tells him to shut up and understand the privilege of serving his country. We are at war, the sergeant declares.

The next morning we see Vincent out of uniform wandering around town. He heads past the recruiting office and into the bus station. With a calm resonance we hear an off-camera voice say, "You better leave the country. In thirty days you're a deserter. You're AWOL right now!" The sergeant has found his lonely soldier.

Vincent explains the movie's title in a scene of quiet intimacy. "We're from different tribes, Sergeant, two completely different worlds. You didn't understand mine, yet you force me to accept yours. Your whole world is four walls and some bunks. I think you've lost touch with life. . . . Your whole bag is death." McGavin, who has been patiently listening, responds, "My 'whole bag' is defending my country." Vincent responds, "I don't equate militarism with patriotism. I can't. . . . I'm never going to carry a gun, and I won't kill anybody, and that's where it's at, isn't it?" McGavin continues, "Not quite. I carry guns and I've killed men simply so that you and I can sit here and talk like this."

Tribes was entertaining and thought provoking. It successfully utilized humor amid its drama and was not afraid to tackle difficult issues in the intimacy of America's living rooms. After receiving good ratings and an Emmy, it was repackaged for a theatrical run overseas as *The Soldier Who Declared Peace.*

Of the three remaining 1970 films to be discussed, *Patton*, *Catch 22*, and *M*A*S*H*, each derived a portion of its power and entertainment value from the backdrop of the Vietnam conflict. Although not set anywhere near Vietnam, campus protests, or draft evasions, these films were consummate reflections of the intellectual currents operating at the time. Francis Ford Coppola wrote the screenplay for *Patton*, which opens with George C. Scott in front of a huge American flag rallying his troops on the eve of D day. Scott's speech is presented directly to the audience. "Men, all this stuff you've heard about America not wanting to fight, wanting to stay out of the war, is a lot of horsedung. Americans traditionally love to fight. All real Americans love the sting of battle. When you were kids, you all admired the champion marble shooter, the fastest runner, the big league ballplayers, the toughest boxers. Americans love a winner and will not tolerate a loser. Americans play to win all the time. I wouldn't give a hoot in hell for a man who lost and laughed. That's why Americans have never lost, and will never lose, a war because the very thought of losing is hateful to Americans."

This monologue was not a verbatim transcript of the real general's stirring message to his troops. Rather, it was poetic license that summed up the dichotomous nature of America's attitude toward war and spoke to the audience amid the ongoing Vietnam War. The general's charge did not just echo every American high school coach's halftime pep talk; it also summed up America's own fascination with war as a spectacle and tester of manhood. The words uttered in 1970 reflected a post–Tet realization that the current war was not going to be a sure winner by any means.

Patton was an Allied Artists film directed by the late Franklin J. Schaffner. The young Coppola's script was a powerful character study. Steven Jay Rubin in his book *Combat Films* sums up the appealing duality of the film for the American public: "*Patton* became a mirror through which warring doves and hawks viewed the confirmation of their own deeply emotional beliefs. To the former, General Patton was the anti–Christ, who symbolized the gutsy brand of militarism that had led to the Vietnam debacle. . . . To the hawks, Patton offered a nostalgic look at a simple time, a period when super heroes were also super patriots and when victory was made possible through military action. . . . Patton personified to them [hawks] a kind of man the absence of whom was a major factor in the Vietnam War."[3]

The two military comedies of 1970 understood the absurd and tragic dynamics of war and the appeal of dealing with current issues in an indirect manner. Paramount Pictures' *Catch 22* was directed by Mike Nichols from a Buck Henry screenplay based on Joseph Heller's book of the same title. Set in World War II at an air base on a Mediterranean island, the film starred Alan Arkin as Captain Yossarian. The comedy's basic dilemma and the source of the title is Yossarian's desire to be certified as insane. With such a designation he will be unfit to fly dangerous missions. However, these self-preservation instincts are judged to be rational, so the military psychologist cannot designate Yossarian as unfit despite his peculiar behavior.

The wonderful cast tweaks the military mentality at every turn. Heller's book, written in 1961, became a best-seller at the end of the decade because it appealed to an antimilitary irreverence born of Vietnam-inspired cynicism. The film ends as an injured Yossarian attempts to desert to Sweden. The fact that he is paddling a boat from the Mediterranean Sea does not daunt him in his effort. At the time in real life many Vietnam War draft evaders and military deserters were seeking refuge in that country as an alternative to the most utilized nearby destination, Canada.

The military comedy *M*A*S*H* (an acronym for Mobile Army Surgical Hospital) opened in January and played for the entire year. The ad campaign typified the current Vietnam-related character of the film despite its Korean war setting. The memorable logo featured a hand in a *V* for victory/peace sign offering of the upturned index and forefinger. A green army helmet was mounted on one of the digits. The hand was then grafted onto an attractive pair of female legs, which all together conveyed a degree of sexual provocativeness. The peace sign as a symbol of the Vietnam era supplanted the older but still recognizable *V* for victory interpretation of the same sign language.

Robert Altman directed *M*A*S*H* from a screenplay by Ring Lardner, Jr., in an adaptation of Richard Hooker's novel. Ingo Preminger produced the film, which was distributed by Twentieth Century–Fox. The black military comedy starred Donald Sutherland as Hawkeye Pierce, Elliott Gould as Trapper John, Tom Skerrit as Duke, Sally Kellerman as Hot Lips Houlihan, Robert Duvall as Major Burns, and Gary Berghoff as Radar O'Reilly (the only actor to reprise his role in the television series).

The hijinks of the 4077 are familiar, as the surgeons try to laugh in the face of unspeakable carnage and horror. As they operate on their young battlefield casualties, they joke about every-

M*A*S*H (20th Century–Fox, 1970). In this ad slick the *V* for victory meets the peace sign in a grand film logo.

thing. The flippant but skilled heroes are obsessed with women, golf, poker, and martinis. They debunk all "military logic" as oxymoronic and disdain all army protocol while attempting to survive and keep their wits amid the grueling pace of frontline medicine. They try to normalize their existence by transporting conventional aspects of Americana to their encampment. Hence when they play golf on the helicopter landing pad or rig the women's shower for voyeuristic pleasures, they relieve the tension and forget the horror of war. The by-the-book militarism and hypocritical religiosity of adulterous Major Burns and his lover, head nurse Houlihan, become representative of traditional establishment and military concepts worthy of derision. As in any merging of the mercy of the medical mission and the misery of war, the ultimate irony is the juxtaposition of saving life in the midst of a conflict inherently designed to take it.

M*A*S*H employed a realistic style and graphicness that were innovative at the time. Robert Altman preferred overlapping dialogue and sounds that reflected the chaotic ambience of an operating room rather than simple, straightforward dialogue filtered and uninterrupted by the noise that would in actuality be present. The battlefield casualties are not just off-camera litters that grunt and groan. They are sources of spurting arterial blood and eruptions of anguished cries. War becomes absurd and in essence the one really bad joke operating herein.

The 4077 Mobile Army Surgical Hospital unit is located just three miles from the Korean War front. The tragic loss of life it deals with daily is common to any war. However, the cynical, antimilitary, black comedy in the film is a modern phenomenon. Screenwriter Lardner admitted the true focus of this film and echoed a perspective found elsewhere when he stated that *M*A*S*H* was about "a special kind of war, an American one on the Asian mainland, and our habit of taking our culture along with us and ignoring the local variety."[4]

On Oscar night in 1971 the winner of the Best Documentary Short Subject award went to 1970's *Interviews with My Lai Veterans*. The Best Feature Length Documentary award went to *Woodstock*. *Patton* was the Best Picture winner, beating out *M*A*S*H*. George C. Scott won the Best Actor award, which he refused in a charged Hollywood atmosphere of controversy. Sally Kellerman was nominated for Best Actress as Hot Lips in *M*A*S*H*, but she and director Robert Altman did not win their respective categories. Ring Lardner, Jr., did triumph for Best Screenplay Adaptation for *M*A*S*H*.

In total *Patton* ended up winning the awards for best picture, director, screenplay, art direction, sound, and editing. When Francis Ford Coppola took home the statue for original screenplay, this helped assure his place in the creative community. His success led in part to *The Godfather*, which led to United Artists' entrusting Coppola with a huge project in *Apocalypse Now*. Therefore his work on *Patton* was integral in the construction of his "cineage" (cinema lineage). This concept is important in understanding how films are made, particularly about controversial subjects such as the Vietnam War. The expansion of the relevant movies is heavily dependent on this idea. Even famous directors such as Coppola and Oliver Stone had to start somewhere. No producer or studio entrusts them with millions for films before they have completed apprenticeships and achieved career-building triumphs.

As time passes and résumé items increase, then, like any business, responsibility grows. It is essential to understand this reality for two additional reasons. One reason is the personal and professional relationships forged by filmmakers in the early stages of their careers. These relationships become sources of collaborative effort in later works. The people with whom a future director rose through the ranks become a filmmaking "platoon." They provide the technical nucleus for future projects and help explain recurring names whose fascination with Vietnam-themed films became a line of development rather than the result of haphazard production assignments based on disinterested storytelling and disparate employment opportunities.

The second reason for the importance of the cineage is its part in explaining the paucity of combat portrayals of Vietnam until the late 1970s. The controversial nature of the war aside, the veterans as sources of firsthand recollection simply had not yet had a chance to rejoin civilian life. Even with a few years of readjustment to a noncombat existence, much less the distillation of painful memories, it would be several years before veterans such as Oliver Stone or Patrick Duncan (*84 Charlie MoPic*, 1989) or Jim Carabatsos (*Hamburger Hill*, 1987) would find jobs and mentors who would enable them to bring to the screen their own firsthand accounts of this war. In 1970 or thereabouts no one was going to welcome a vet home from his tour of duty and hand him a major motion picture. Even though Hollywood may have been fearful of the reception of direct Vietnam-themed films, practical script and professional considerations also entered into the process. Like World War I veteran Lewis Milestone or World War II vet Sam Fuller, Vietnam vet filmmakers would create some of the most honest and enduring portraits in this examination.

On February 8, 1971, U.S. air and artillery forces, along with South Vietnamese units, began a 45-day incursion into Laos. On March 29 Lieutenant William Calley, Jr., was convicted of murder in connection wtih the My Lai massacre on March 16, 1968. On April 7 President Nixon announced the withdrawal of another 100,000 troops by year's end. Later that same month 500,000 antiwar demonstrators gathered in Washington, D.C., with many other protests taking place throughout the country. On June 13 the *New York Times* began running the *Pentagon Papers*, which detailed the government's secret involvement in Southeast Asia. In the late summer allied forces from Australia, New Zealand, and South Korea began to withdraw from South Vietnam. In November 1971 Nixon announced a further troop reduction of 45,000 to be in effect by the end of January. In neighboring Laos the U.S.-supported regime was on the verge of defeat by communist forces. In response, in late December U.S. bombers massively attacked North Vietnamese targets for five days. This unwelcome Christmas-time escalation was reminiscent of 1969's broadening of the conflict into nearby Cambodia. By New Year's Day, the American troop strength was down to 140,000.

Summertree was typical of 1971's topical interest in the Vietnam conflict as expressed in a major studio release. It was adapted from Ron Cowen's acclaimed off–Broadway play. The property was bought by Kirk Douglas to produce as a vehicle for his son Michael. Brenda Vaccaro, Jack Warden, and Barbara Bel Geddes costarred. In a supporting role Rob Reiner played a friend, and exploitation star William Smith was featured in a straighter role as a lawyer specializing in draft cases. The Columbia Pictures release featured a dramatic story about intergenerational mistrust and wartime anxiety. Pop singer Anthony Newley directed the film.

Michael Douglas's character is a young man with a dilemma. How will he respond to his draft notice? With a minimum of understanding, his parents try to give him direction. Douglas, seen in a similar debuting role in 1969's *Hail*

Hero!, really just wants to hone his musical skills and aid a troubled black youngster he has befriended. His father vehemently opposes his son's plans to flee to Canada. Nevertheless, the "old man" and his wife are terrified of what might befall their son if he goes to Vietnam. The nature of self-sacrifice, responsibility, and guilt is given a muddled dramatic treatment. In one scene the parents are watching television news reports of the war in the comfort of their home. Their son's face is surrealistically flashed across the screen.

Michael Douglas's cinematic father in his earlier film *Hail Hero!* was played by Arthur Kennedy. The talented older actor returned as a similarly conservative World War II vet in Cinerama's 1971 release *Glory Boy*. Edwin Sherin directed this updated version of John Sanford's novel about World War I veterans. In regional tests the movie was distributed by its source material title, *My Old Man's Place.*

Michael Moriarity made his film debut as a Vietnam veteran. William Devane was his New York City streetwise fellow soldier, and Mitchell Ryan portrayed Sergeant Flood. Moriarity is guilt-ridden because he killed a Vietenamese woman during combat. Upon his return to the United States, he stops off in San Francisco, where he meets the psychopathic sergeant. The two vets return to Moriarity's pastoral northern California farm to visit his father. The "old man" has no patience for the problems of this new breed of veterans.

Meanwhile Devane has returned home to find that his wife has been unfaithful (a problem he confronted again in 1977's *Rolling Thunder*). He rejoins his army comrades at the California farm. The veterans seek solace together as no one can understand their painful recollections and the injustices they are encountering back in society. Along the way west Devane picked up a young woman hitchhiker and brought her to the farm. She is a committed peace activist from Canada. The crazed sergeant attempts to rape her but is stopped when Devane shoots him. While the sergeant convalesces, he reconsiders his way and promises acceptable civilian behavior. Moriarity makes healthy strides by reaching a better relationship with his father and by falling in love with the hitchhiker. The now-recovered sergeant decides to reenlist as a way to find a place in a world he understands. Just as the peaceful accommodations are being made, the film climaxes in violence. On the eve of his departure the sergeant rapes the young woman. When the old man comes to her rescue, he is shot. Returning fire, he kills the crazed sergeant despite being himself mortally wounded. With a last breath Kennedy and Moriarity make peace.

Moving in a descending order of production value is the returning veteran portrayal in Duque/Maron Film's *Jud*. The movie was directed and written by Gunther Collins and featured Joseph Kaufmann and Robert Deman. Perhaps the best-known player was Playboy Playmate of the Year Claudia Jennings. *Jud* concerned the adjustment to civilian life of another returning vet. He, too, has been dumped by his girlfriend. He, too, is haunted by painful wartime flashbacks. To add levity, the boarding house where he lives a seemingly pointless existence is populated by a host of bizarre loser types. A similarly motley crew populates the goings on in *Prism*, another independent release concerning draft issues. It starred Paul Greier and Dale Soules. The movie was written and directed by Anitra Pivnick.

The summer release *Clay Pigeon* from MGM featured Tom Stern as a vet who helps narc Telly Savalas fight drug kingpin Robert Vaughn. The cast, which also included Peter Lawford, John Marley, Ivan Dixon, Jeff Corey, and Burgess Meredith, reflected the higher budget qualities of the film. The returning vet character and star Stern also directed and produced the film along with Lane Slate.

In the film the veteran's righteousness is unquestioned. A former police officer, he served with distinction in the military. The film opens to a dramatic Vietnam-set scene where he hurls his body onto a grenade to save his buddies. Fortunately his altruism is rewarded as the grenade does not explode. Now back in his native Los Angeles, the charmed vet, who had himself flirted with drug abuse, becomes a crusader against the pushers.

The gritty urban setting and conventional style of the film are surprisingly altered in a last-minute surrealistic sequence. This becomes the film's most interesting and powerful image. After Stern violently dispatches a group of bad guys, we cut back to the film's first scene in Vietnam. The grenade does indeed go off and the hero dies. It is an abrupt and imaginative departure from the literal and linear. *Clay Pigeon*'s surprising bit of last-minute warrior cognition before death is either a flash forward, a final fantasy, or a divine mission. It is an upscale literary echo trapped in a downscale context. Ambrose Bierce's classic returning Civil War veteran's short story, "The Occurrence at Owl Creek Bridge," taps this same poignant and truncated life fantasy of a doomed soldier. Bierce, too, begins a tale with imminent death, diverts to a panoply of life experiences, and then abruptly hurls his reader back to the continued moment of death alluded to and supposedly eluded in the beginning. The preceding narrative is just an instant of internal cognition and the source of personification of a soldier's life and death. (The exact same device was used in the 1990 film *Jacob's Ladder,* which again concerned a Vietnam vet, who was shown in a frightening opening sequence as being bayoneted in a fierce ambush.)

Clay Pigeon's title conveyed the sacrificial sitting-duck aspect of the soldier-victim. The 1971 incarnation was known overseas as *Trip to Kill.* That moniker allowed for quick action-exploitation flick identification. *Clay Pigeon*'s urban setting began to connote a change in marketing strategy and in location shooting. The inclusion of Ivan Dixon and other black cast members heralded the beginning of Blaxploitation. Many films in the next few years were made with primarily black casts and designed for the African-American city-centered audience. Black stars such as Fred Williamson and Jim Brown became huge box office draws in these films. Often they played returned Vietnam veterans combating drugs and crimes in the streets of America with the skills they had learned in the military in Nam.

The returning veteran, motorcyclers, and race relations are all integrated in the Burt Topper–written and directed release *The Hard Ride*, from American

International Pictures. Robert Fuller escorts the body of his comrade Lenny back to the United States. In flashback his interracial friendship with Lenny, played by Alfonso Williams, reveals a color-blind, in-country camaraderie. Survivor Fuller is entrusted with his buddy's prized possession, "Baby," a gorgeous, low-slung chopper. He sets out to find his slain comrade's girlfriend and Indian friend "Big Red" and bring them to the funeral. Along the way he learns about his friend's pre–Nam life and has a love affair with the girlfriend, played by Sherry Bain, a white woman.

The movie begins as the casket, covered in the Stars and Stripes, is loaded off the transport plane into the hearse. Bill Medley, half of the Righteous Brothers, sings "Swing Low, Sweet Chariot." Following a basic formula, the picture extols the freedom of the open road, displays an almost fetishistic love of hot chrome and glistening steel, and features a number of rumble sequences. The alternative lifestyle of the bikers, the implied but unseen interracial love affair, and the idiotic ranting of a drunk reactionary fulminating about the war seem to advocate tolerance. This message, along with the smoking of grass and mild sex scenes, appealed to a youthful drive-in audience and managed to integrate sign-of-the-times, exploitation, and returning vet elements into the story.

Three times the film reverts to Vietnam to show the soldiers' friendships, the former's death, and the latter's grief. Back in the United States Fuller is well adjusted sexually and socially and fights only when provoked. The viewer cares about this vet character more than is usual for such a movie. *The Hard Ride* ends in typical biker flick tragedy as the veteran, having survived the war, is killed in a gang battle here at home. He and his comrades are buried with full military honors side by side, the way they fought in Vietnam. On the soundtrack we hear the scene again where the black soldier is dying and pleads to his friend, "Don't leave me." His white buddy and hero of the story replies, "I'm right here" as the camera pulls back to reveal the flag-draped coffins. The priest, the bikers, the grieving woman who loved them both, and a full military honor guard make for a strange assembly paying their last respects.

The returning veteran biker tale as cliché was acknowledged in the self-mocking title *Chrome and Hot Leather*, released by AIP. It took the star of *The Losers* and other such flicks, William Smith, and made him the nemesis of four ex–Green Berets. Lee Frost directed the vets, played by Tony Young, Michael Stearns, Peter Brown, and singer Marvin Gaye. Together they exact revenge on the "Devils" cycle club that contributed to the auto accident death of Young's fiancée. The veterans are experts who are forced to exert their brand of justice rather than crazed, unprovoked sociopaths who initiate mayhem. Their well-disciplined teamwork is enhanced by the use of a veritable arsenal of military equipment they have squirreled away, including mortars, grenades, guns, and field radios. The battlefield has shifted from Nam to America. The combat effectiveness of the Special Forces members brings victory. In this vein the film allows a sense of triumph and a vanquishing of the enemy not permitted by the actual events of the war.

Chrome and Hot Leather (American International, 1971). The Green Berets take on the bikers in a cycle gang war.

The biggest hit of 1971 involving a veteran was the independent production *Billy Jack*. Director and writer T. C. Frank was actually star Tom Laughlin. His wife was the writer Teresa Christina, the nom de plume of his costar, Delores Taylor. The character of the half-breed American Indian Vietnam vet Billy Jack had been introduced in the 1967 cycle film *Born Losers*. Independent filmmaker Laughlin played up his underdog status and Hollywood outsider image. Against all odds he saw to it that his very personalized project got made. Despite opposition, he was able to star in this hit, which spoke to the youth of America and achieved repeat business and cult status to boot. He had triumphed over a studio-controlled production apparatus. Along with the fictional protagonist, Laughlin himself was part of the phenomenon. Despite the eventual studio distribution deal that was struck, this "hook" made great copy for the film.

Upon his discharge Jack returns to a domestic terror set in the prototypical American minimalist landscape of the Southwest. He is denied his portion of the American dream because of overt racism and is forced to rebalance the odds and exact justice. Herein the revisionist westerns of the time with their sympathy for Native Americans commingled with current indictments of a reactionary America. The film thereby spoke to an in-vogue interpretation of the white man's inherently racist treatment of the yellow-skinned peoples in Southeast Asia and the victimization of the soldier. Despite these undercurrents, the movie operated only a few notches above the title character's motorcycle movie origins. When the inevitable justifiable revenge occurred, it was a cathartic but gruesome exhibition that left audiences cheering for more.

When one innocent is murdered and a teacher is raped, the veteran cannot contain his rage. He uses hand-to-hand combat and other U.S.-government-sponsored training against the bigoted townspeople and crooked agents to law enforcement who protect them. This ultimate triumph appealed to a public subliminally attuned to the trauma of losing the war in Vietnam. In the film's climax the pacifist victim schoolteacher convinces Billy Jack to give himself up to the authorities. The children cheer their hero as he is led off to jail and an uncertain future in the American criminal justice system.

Fortunately for fans of the film, the Vietnam veteran's return was assured by the huge box office appeal of the hero. In 1974 the first sequel (or second if one counts the resurrected-from-the-dead Billy Jack of *Born Losers*) appeared with an appropriate sense of continuity, *The Trial of Billy Jack*. The next sequel, released in 1977, was called *Billy Jack Goes to Washington*. Frank Capra and Jimmy Stewart did not have to worry about anyone forgetting their similarly titled work. Actually Capra's son, Frank, Jr., produced the film for Tom Laughlin, who now starred as Senator Billy Jack. His election to public office in that film was an interesting precursor to Laughlin's recent activities. He announced that he was seeking the Democratic nomination for president of the United States in 1992. Unlike another actor-turned-politician, Laughlin's populist campaign was not taken very seriously.

Not to be outdone by the returning veteran flicks, the sign-of-the-times counterculture films continued. One rendering was the irreverent Universal release *Taking Off.* It featured the English-language debut of Czechoslovakia's talented director Milos Forman. The expatriate refugee from the communist repression of the Prague Spring brought a fresh outsider's perspective to observations of the current American scene. The comedy featured Lynn Carlin, Buck Henry, Ike and Tina Turner, and, in one brief scene, Carly Simon. The film's title reflected the story of a runaway girl and her parents and, in a pun, the entire tone of the film itself and the new mores. Drugs, sex, the East Village, and verbal references to the war combined in an evocation of the times.

The one made-for-television "long-form" contribution of the year to this book was broadcast on ABC in September. *The Forgotten Man* was a returning veteran who had been a prisoner of war. Dennis Weaver starred as the lieutenant, Anne Francis played his wife, and Andrew Duggan and Lois Nettleton costarred. *The Forgotten Man* was directed and produced by Walter Grauman and written by Mark Rodgers. Dave Grusin provided the musical score.

The film begins as Chinook helicopters land on a beach. Vietnamese civilians look on as a bedraggled American soldier in POW garb is evacuated. The scene shifts to a military hospital in Hawaii, where the recovering lieutenant is being debriefed. He had been held captive for five years, finally managing to escape with one other POW, who died in the process. When the lieutenant's chopper went down on an intelligence mission in 1966, he anticipated capture and exchanged his dog tags with that of a dead enlisted man not privy to strategic information. This ruse did not save him from repeated interrogations and beatings, which are shown in flashback. However, they did result in his designation as killed in action by the army. Believing him to be dead, the soldier's wife remarried. Adding to his readjustment woes, Weaver's father died, and the family business was sold. Despite efforts to help on the part of his doctor, ex-wife, enthusiastic young daughter, family friends, and even his wife's new husband, the strain is too much. Lieutenant Hardy begins to experience post-traumatic stress disorder, the label given to this war's particular version of shell shock.

Emotional stress elicits flashbacks and disorientation. Several times he regresses to periods in prison camp and the interrogations by his nemesis, Major Thon, played by James Hong. A clerk behind a fence becomes a guard of a bamboo tiger cage. Orderlies in the hospital become North Vietnamese sentries and so on. Each episode, recreated in color and containing strange, cacophonous Asian music, reroots him in the terror of the past. Eventually in a less graphic manner than the theatrical treatments of such trauma, the lieutenant does flip out. However, in the end, through the intervention of loved ones and professionals at the Veterans Administration, he is able to get back on his way to a normal life.

The Forgotten Man was the first film to introduce by name the recently labeled malady affecting a substantial minority of vets. Made during the war, the film was thus very topical, a characteristic of the less expensive television movie. In crosscutting between the protagonist's stateside situational reality and the in-country events in his mind, the film establishes a pattern of depiction to be duplicated many times.

The public greeted 1972 with optimism that this would be the final year of the United States' involvement in the Vietnam War. On January 13 President Nixon announced further withdrawals of U.S. forces. However, every time the war seemed to de-escalate, events reversed the positive momentum. On March 30 North Vietnamese troops launched their biggest attacks in four years across the DMZ. In response, the aircraft carrier USS *Kitty Hawk* and other ships joined those already stationed off the coast of Vietnam. U.S. bombers were also reinforced in Thailand and at Da Nang. On April 15 there was renewed bombing of Hanoi and Haiphong. Almost at the same time Nixon announced a further cut of 20,000 troops. A tactical air presence was being strengthened, while the ground troops were being phased out. As always, our much-vaunted air superiority was hampered by triple-canopied jungle cover and a dug-in enemy force.

On May 1 North Vietnamese forces captured the town of Quang Tri. A week later the president announced the mining of North Vietnam's harbors. On June 12 the South Vietnamese army broke the two-month siege of An Loc. Two months later on August 12 the last American ground combat troops left South Vietnam.

The celebration of this historic event was muted by the presence of 43,500 air force and support personnel and the continued fierce fighting of our allies in the ongoing conflict. In September the ARVN recaptured Quang Tri city, but the outer province remained under communist control. In December after a two-month hiatus the United States resumed bombing of the North for a two-week period. By the end of 1972 the total U.S. troop level in the South was at 27,000.[5]

A made-for-television movie was the first contribution of the new year to the list of Vietnam films. In January 1972 CBS broadcast the Cinema Center production of *Welcome Home, Johnny Bristol*. The film had several similarities to *The Forgotten Man* broadcast just four months earlier. *Johnny Bristol* was directed by George McGowan from a screenplay by Stanley A. Greenberg. Martin Landau starred as Captain Bristol, an ex–POW. Jane Alexander was his nurse and eventual girlfriend. Martin Sheen and Forrest Tucker appeared as friends recuperating in a VA hospital. Pat O'Brien appeared as a guilt-ridden recruiting officer who had sent countless boys off to war. The key medical role was occupied by a black actor, a recurring bit of Hollywood overcompensation and positive television imagery. Brock Peters played the caring army psychiatrist who attempts to help Bristol. This role is similar to the selfless and pivotal aid of African-American actor Percy Rodrigues's character in *The Forgotten Man*.

Initially "welcome home" is an ironic salutation for America's troubled "Johnnies," the war vets. This psychological drama underscores the importance of a strong support network for overcoming wartime trauma. The movie is another early treatment of post-traumatic stress disorder. The film takes to a literal extreme the old maxim "You can't go home again." It opens in-country as

Captain Bristol is imprisoned in a tiger cage with another POW. They cling to life by discussing happier times. Bristol recites the comforting details of his childhood hometown, an idyllic Vermont hamlet. However, each time these recollections elicit on-screen imagery, the transition is accomplished in a kind of jarring use of reverse negative. The scene appears in black and white and then takes on Peter Max's 1970s psychedelic colors before settling into normal exposures of the pastoral scenes. It indicates that something is askew in his recollections of this happier period.

Bristol and his comrade suffer from poor rations and taunts from the villagers, who spit upon them in their publicly exhibited cell. Eventually during a bombing strike, shown with budget-saving but badly matched real news footage, the prisoners are able to escape into the bush. By the time the U.S. patrol finds them, Bristol's companion is dead and he is not far from it. As a sergeant tries to comfort Bristol, he passes out and envisions a July 4 celebration back in his hometown. When the captain reawakens, he is in a VA hospital in Boston. He vigorously embraces the physical therapy necessary to regain use of an injured leg. Mentally he provides a type of therapy for himself and his friends by spinning tales of his hometown.

Eventually a romance develops between patient and nurse. Upon release Bristol takes his fiancée on a trip home. Mysteriously the town is simply not there. This frightens both of them and leads to the captain's near-psychotic breakdown. As the reality of the situation begins to belie his recollections, he becomes desperate. Finally he is returned to the hospital psychiatric ward. Fiancée Alexander and the psychiatrist are persistent in their care. The captain accuses the army of covering up some type of nuclear or biological accident that eliminated the existence of his home. This is not altogether portrayed as the ravings of a lunatic. Rather, after years of the military managing and fabricating news from the Vietnam War front, this notion actually had a plausibility that intrigued the viewer. The U.S. government was at an all-time low level of esteem, and revelations about drug experimentation on American soldiers as well as careless safety associated with 1950s nuclear tests were current news items. Therefore, although odd, the captain's rantings were not impossible and led to suspense.

With the help of his wardmates, Bristol escapes from the hospital and begins a fact-finding tour based on clues in his own mind. None of them leads to a Charles, Vermont, but each does point to a painful realization that such a town never did exist. It was merely a creation of the mind in a desperate attempt to pass the time and muster the spirit. Only the psychiatrist and his girlfriend are able to supply him with the last pieces of the psychological puzzle, which reveal a terrible childhood trauma. Once these in-country and childhood demons are confronted, Johnny Bristol can finally be welcomed home to America.

As America's level of combat troops in Vietnam de-escalated, many more soldiers were returning home in large numbers. Because of the controversial nature of the war and the revelations of misconduct such as My Lai, most veterans were not afforded a very warm response. Only later when the POWs were released did America seem to realize the short shrift it had given the veterans and correct this with traditional hoopla. It would be nearly 20 years before ticker tape style recognition would be afforded the Vietnam vets in conjunction with the Operation Desert Storm victors.

If returning vet and POW Johnny Bristol literally cannot find his home, the four veterans in *Welcome Home, Soldier Boys* also have great difficulty finding their place back in "the world." Their odyssey of attempted reintegration takes the form of a road trip across America. To underscore a sense of isolation, it is set against the bleak desert of the Southwest on the way to the promised land, California. The only people the veterans can relate to are one another. This exploitation film from a major distributor, Twentieth Century–Fox, was also released regionally as *Five Days Home*. Richard Compton directed the screenplay by Gordon Trueblood. The four vets were played by Joe Don Baker as the leader, Danny; Alan Vint as the Kid; Paul Koslo as Shooter; and Elliott Street as Fatback. As usual the nicknames exemplify the strong bonding of the male characters forged in wartime. In fact the only female character of any consequence in the film is referred to simply as "the broad."

The film begins and ends in militarily contextualized scenes. A drab army green bus pulls out of Fort Liggett and delivers the four dishonorably discharged Green Berets to town. Pooling their resources, they buy a used Cadillac and begin their journey to the Kid's inherited land in California, where they hope to raise cattle. Theirs is a rather delusionary, shared vision of the future. Its pitiful naïveté is similar to that in the upcoming film *Heroes,* with its destined-for-failure dream of the vet characters to start a more irreverently conceived "worm farm."

Along the way they pick up "the broad," played by Jennifer Billingsley, who willingly has sex with all four men in the backseat. During an argument about money, she accidentally falls out of the moving auto. The vets move on, now with the woman's dog as a memento of the encounter. Danny takes his wartime friends to his home, where his boyhood room and total inability to relate to anyone bring an overwhelming sense of loneliness. He is not even willing to admit his military service in Vietnam to casual acquaintances who ask where he has been. Given that the men often walk around in their combat boots and pants, their military service is a difficult thing to conceal. Danny's father, like most members of his generation in this type of film, is a callous jerk who belittles the vets' dreams. Moving on, the men have a wild party at a motel run by Geoff Lewis, a Bible-quoting hypocrite who pimps for them. The men enjoy their sexual encounters, and each has a revealing chat with his companion for the night. Joe Don Baker says the only thing he ever really accomplished was that he killed a lot of the enemy.

The men's service in Vietnam earns them no respect and in fact is a subject of disdain. In Texas a scene that will become familiar in many of the returning vet pictures is injected. That is the impatient response of the veterans of America's other wars. A veteran of the Korean War and a farmer who served in World War II remark in tandem baiting, "No wonder that damn war's gone on for ten years. . . . You guys come home and it's still going on. . . . Oughta get the old army back there. . . . Clean it up in three months. . . . All they do is kill the damn civilians."

Moving onward to New Mexico, the four vets do all they can to corroborate such negative accusations. In the rather obviously named town of Hope, the exploitative nature of the road drama comes to a full degenerative climax. Like the pivotal scene in the 1970 flick *Explosion*, the men impatiently help themselves to gas at a station. The owner takes a shot at them, and it is as if they are back in a firefight in Vietnam. They unload their trunk to reveal an arsenal of weapons, including rifles, grenades, and a bazooka. Now in full Green Beret uniforms, they proceed to slaughter all the inhabitants of Hope. As the National Guard and state police prepare to respond, the men are resigned to die together in combat. Baker even articulates his brotherly love for the Kid in a quiet moment interrupted by a staccato radio transmission from a National Guard reconnaissance helicopter. The vets blow it out of the sky and continue the firefight until overwhelmed by tear gas.

In the final scene National Guard troops in gas masks advance in formation in a visual pattern that recollects Kent State or the Chicago streets of 1968 more than an in-country battle. The four doomed vets stand in the street amid the burned-out wreckage of Hope. Each throws a grenade and with outstretched arms, the movie goes to freeze-frame. We hear on the soundtrack overwhelming lethal return fire. As the film has certainly not been averse to showing violence, the end is merely a ripoff of the stylized conclusion of the popular *Butch Cassidy and the Sundance Kid*. As the movie concludes, Joe Don Baker in voiceover is heard to recite his army induction oath.

Just as motorcycle films had taken a tired recipe and updated it with soldiers, so, too, black films found this approach an easy source of topicality and rationale for all types of mayhem. For some films the African-American's tour of duty was incidental. In other films it was an integral part of the story. Either way themes of readjustment, anomie, and societal ingratitude were similar to those of white vet pictures. However, the irony of making a sacrifice for one's country and then being unappreciated for it seemed even more meaningful for some members of the black audience. The inability to obtain college deferments and other upper-middle-class-oriented exemptions was well known. The have-nots, whether poor whites or blacks, defending the haves' way of life reflected a skewed societal sacrifice in the conflict. The high percentage of blacks in service and among the casualties was a factor that contributed to an overall sense of injustice in the returning vet films.

By 1972 when box office star and football great Jim Brown starred in *Slaughter*, the prevailing characterization of the vet was not the old lunatic proactive type in *Targets*. Rather, it was of a rational but victimized and thus reactive man. Ex–Green Beret *Slaughter* was the first of the many black veterans who populated the Blaxploitation films. As if to punctuate the marriage of the various subgenres, Jack Starrett of *The Losers* was the director of this American International film.

The story was a simple one of revenge. Captain Slaughter's parents are killed by mafiosi. He declares war on the mob, and using expertise learned courtesy of the U.S. government, he wreaks havoc on the bad guys. The formula worked well, and the following year the same star and character reappeared in a sequel, *Slaughter's Big Rip Off.* This time Gordon Douglas directed, with costars Brock Peters and Dick Anthony Williams joined by Don Stroud and Art Metrano. Again the story line involved the mob, and the veteran was the means of street enforced justice.

In 1972 Jim Brown was the lead in a similar vehicle, *Black Gunn.* In the vet's exacting justice upon corrupt racketeers, his tangentially realized background comes in handy. He and his brother are small-time nightclub owners victimized by the "Man." When his sibling is murdered, Brown enlists the help of fellow black vets. Paul Winfield and his "Bro's" were to venture into remarkably similar territory in the 1973 film *Gordon's War,* to be discussed in that year's relevant productions.

The Vietnam War–related films of 1972 continued with alienated soldiers in *Parades.* The title of this independent Cinerama release was meant to be an ironic reminder of the lack of fanfare afforded the combatants. It was one of three titles under which the film was released. The alternatives were *The Line* and *Break Loose.* Robert J. Siegel produced and directed the film from a screenplay by George Tabori. It starred Russ Thacker, David Doyle, and, in an early role, Erik Estrada as simply "Chicano." The film begins in Ohio in 1969 as a bearded young man returns home from Vietnam. He is reticent about communicating his unpleasant experiences to his parents. He fights with his father and finds solace with his high school sweetheart. Eventually, army CID officers arrive and arrest the youth, who is a deserter.

He is sentenced to the Presidio stockade, which holds many other malcontents and troubled youth. There he is brutalized by a sadistic drill instructor, "Sergeant Hook," played by Brad Sullivan. He accuses the inmates of being "malingerers" and cowards. Protagonist "Rusty" begins a decline into suicidal behavior. He sometimes flashes back to an instant when he inadvertently shot a baby. Eventually he is able to fulfill his death wish as he is gunned down trying to escape. Press reports of the incident grab the nation's attention and galvanize the antiwar movement.

Some of the inmates join a crowd gathering at the fences in civil disobedience. A sit-in leads to a tense moment when the guards train their arms on the demonstrators. Several hippie types insert flowers into the barrels of the rifles. However, there is a discharge of weapons, and one of the protestors is killed. No one is tried for this tragedy. Rather, seven of the inmates are court-martialed for mutiny, a treasonous act. A public outcry leads to a reduction in the harsh sentences imposed.

Filmmaker Siegel had been a documentarian and herein was making an antiwar statement in a re-creation based on actual accounts given by inmates at Fort Dix and other base prisons and brigs. The movie's title song of pitiful yearning was called "I Am Your Child." It was written and sung by none other than Barry Manilow.

Actor Russ Thacker returned in a similar tale that very same year entitled *AWOL* (Absent Without Leave). This American-Swedish coproduction was directed by Herb Freed and costarred Isabella Kaliff. Other tangentially rendered veteran characters populated the 1972 releases *Georgia, Georgia,* from the now-defunct Cinerama, and *To Kill a Clown,* from Twentieth Century–Fox.

Youthful alienation among noninductees continued in *Outside In,* starring Darrel Larson, Heather Menzies, and Logan Ramsey. Allen Baron directed this film about a draft dodger who returns from Canada to attend his father's funeral. While home he visits two boyhood friends. One had gone off to Vietnam and returned in great emotional pain. The other is a draft dodger who, despite the protagonist's concern, commits suicide. Federal agents close in on the hippie hero, and the movie's original and more evocative title, *Red, White, and Busted,* reveals the fate of the young American forced to be an outsider in his own country. *Outside In* was a depressing drama. (This low-budget effort was the first production from author Harold Robbins's short-lived independent film company.)

One of the first major directors to address the war, albeit still in a noncombat manner, was a man well beyond his career prime, Elia Kazan. *The Visitors* was written by his son Chris. This nonunion movie was made for a mere $160,000 entirely on location at the director's home in Newton, Connecticut. Despite being terrible, it did reconfirm Kazan's ability to access talent. The movie casts James Woods in his first starring role as a Vietnam veteran and Steven Railsback as a fellow soldier.

Veteran Woods is enjoying his quiet rural lifestyle with his girlfriend, played by Patricia Joyce, and their baby boy. The young man has returned from the conflict as a committed pacifist. Living down the road is the woman's father, played by Patrick McVey. This alcoholic writer and World War II vet does not like Woods's politics or out-of-wedlock fathering of his grandchild. Entering the picture are two fellow platoon members who show up at the farm. The wired white sergeant is played by Railsback and the laid-back black enlisted man by Chris Martinez. They have just been released from the maximum security federal prison at Leavenworth, where they served time for raping and murdering a Vietnamese woman. It was Woods who testified against them.

At first their presence is not quite as hostile as logic would dictate. In fact they settle into an implausibly friendly period of simple visitation. But tension begins to mount as a neighborhood dog is found slain. Then the father hears the story about the crimes committed in Vietnam. Instead of condemning them, he accuses Woods of being a "queer" for not having participated in the rape. The acceptability of the group act and the concept that boys far from home "will be boys" seem perfectly normal to the grizzled old man. He sees Woods's wartime testimony as a betrayal of a moral duty to his comrades to remain silent.

Inevitably things get out of hand, and the crazed vets who committed rape on a defenseless Asian woman during the war now have the temerity to try a similar action on an American Caucasian woman in her own home. When Woods intervenes, he is beaten senseless. However, the film attempts to differentiate itself from the normal exploitation fare. Those films would end in mass bloodletting. Here the perpetrators are allowed to just wander off. Eschewing the conventional low-road ending is supposed to elevate the trite theme common to several returning vet sagas: the difficulty of readjusting in society and the ability to modify trained killer and aggressive instincts into decent behavior.

Kazen's foray into topical Vietnam-related themes was a dismal failure. The father and son filmmakers were accused of using union-busting tactics in their employment practices. The Screen Actors Guild condemned the film. The movie was derivative of the previous year's *Glory Boy*, which concerned the killing of a Vietnamese civilian woman. In *Glory Boy*, Mitchell Ryan was the psycho sergeant. In *The Visitors* Steven Railsback was the sergeant rapist and murderer. The preceding film featured Arthur Kennedy as a narrow-minded reactionary World War II veteran. In Kazan's film Patrick McVey was a similar but even more despicable character.

Like many films of the era, the conventionally unflattering portraits of the war and its combatants were fueled by real-life revelations concerning wartime misconduct. My Lai was the salient example of U.S. forces behavior that would have seen impossible and propagandistic only a few years before. The Viet Cong might do this, but not our own boys. Unfortunately instances like this did occur in this dirty war in which the enemy was often indistinguishable from the friendly members of the indigenous populace.

In May 1969 the *New Yorker* had published an article that became the source of Daniel Lang's book *The Casualties of War*. The title referred not only to the real-life young Vietnamese victim of rape and murder by several U.S. soldiers but also to the American perpetrators' loss of humanity and decency as an additional consequence of the war. In 1989 Brian DePalma returned to the Vietnam War context he had flirted with in *Greetings* and its sequel in a hard-hitting Vietnam-set film version of this same incident. Playwright David Rabe adapted the Lang book for this still-to-be-discussed graphic film.

What is interesting to note now is the probable shared nature of the source material as inspiration for Kazan's film made back in 1972 shortly after the initial article's appearance. *The Visitors* dealt with the wartime crime in a domestic context. Years later with a larger budget and no contraints to direct and explicit portraits, DePalma showed the actual crime in-country and its domestic aftermath. The filmmaking conventions of 1972 set the majority of the story out of Nam, and the conventions of 1989 put it firmly back in.

Even though it is not an English-language film a relevant 1972 international coproduction is worth noting. *Summer Soldiers* was produced by Japan's Yukio Tomizawa and directed by Hiroshi Teshigahara. The film was written by American John Nathan. It dealt with American soldiers AWOL in Japan and featured a mixed cast with English and Japanese dialogue sequences.

The fact-based story involved the relationships between Japanese families and American soldiers whom they welcomed into their homes when these soldiers deserted while on liberty from Vietnam. Some Japanese actually formed a group known as the Deserters Aid Committee. The movie explored the concepts and attitudes inherent in this controversial phenomenon. There was no action and very little resolution of the dilemmas and thought-provoking questions raised. The deserters reflected a gamut of motivations from philosophiocal or political opposition to the war to more personal factors such as fear and exhaustion.

In a move from the sublime to the ridiculous, the next Vietnam-related film of 1972 was also not American in origin. The Canadian-produced *Deathdream* was a horror film originally known as *The Veteran.* The main character is a vet, and the first scene is a re-creation of combat in Vietnam. It begins as Richard Backus and his friend are killed in action. The film switches to America as his parents, played by John Marley and Lynn Carlin, are informed of the news. The father grieves, but the mother refuses to accept the tragedy.

Several nights later, as if to confirm her feelings, Backus appears back home in uniform. His parents throw a party to celebrate the unexpected homecoming. Only the neighborhood children are willing to ask the young man anything about the war. He is noncommunicative and peculiar, but everyone attributes this to his rough experiences. The family dog is not so sure, however. It is very agitated by Backus and growls at its old master. Just like the foreboding animal cruelty in *The Visitors,* the vet's first domestic casualty is the dog. Backus shocks the guests by strangling it in front of everyone.

The father cannot believe this behavior and rushes his son to a doctor. The veteran has no pulse! The doc's shock is short-lived as he is murdered by the soldier.

The young man draws his victim's blood and injects it into himself. In an updating of the vampire myths, this revitalizes him. His crime undetected, the vet returns home in time to go to the drive-in on a double date with his sister. Understandably his date is terrified when she observes the vet decaying before her very eyes. In well-done but gruesome makeup effects, the zombie begins to degenerate both physically and behaviorally. Backus murders his date and his sister's boyfriend and then escapes to his house. His horrified father commits suicide in response to the shocking events. Despite all that has happened, a mother's love is too strong, and she leads him to a graveyard, where the near-skeleton is able to lie down and finally rest in peace.

Alternative titles that reflected the subject of the film included *Deathdream, Dead of Night, Death of Night,* and *Nightwalk.* These names were more reflective of the debt the film owed to George Romero's independent cult hit *Night of the Living Dead* (1968) than to any war-related story line. Despite the primary appeal to horror fans, some reviewers at the time did find the movie a clever variation on a now-overexposed subject. After all combat fatalities, a veteran's "readjustment" problems, violent proclivities, and treatment as a societal pariah were all integral parts of the story. Also, some of the positive response was due to the film's stylish technical achievements despite a low budget. This primarily involved the makeup and effects work of Tom Savini and Canadian Bob Clark's direction. Whatever one's reaction to *Deathdream* (aka *The Veteran*), the Vietnam returnee film had been pushed to a limit. The characterization was no longer of an alienated young man or a crazed sociopath. Now the veteran was a walking zombie!

Although borne of the talent of a genius, *The Trial of the Catonsville Nine* featured acting that the *New York Times* found so dreadful as to ensure the film a place on its list of the ten worst movies of 1972. The drama was based on the celebrated play written about the real-life protests of one of the film's participants, the Rev. Daniel Berrigan. The antiwar activist priest and his brother, Phillip, also a priest, were extreme examples of the committed clergy leading opposition to U.S. conduct in Vietnam. The brothers had served time in jail as result of their activities, which included demonstrations, draft card burnings, and herein the destruction of selective service records at the Catonsville, Maryland, center in May 1968. This film was the story of their controversial trial.

Daniel Berrigan and Saul Levitt adapted the former's play for the screen version. Gregory Peck produced the independent film. Gordon Davidson directed, and Haskell Wexler donated his services as cinematographer. Some fine actors were attracted to this important antiwar project, often deferring their usual compensations. Ed Flanders played Father Daniel; Douglas Watson was his brother, Phillip. William Schallert portrayed the judge, and Peter Strauss and Richard Jordan also appeared.

The film dealt with moral necessities of conscience in an antiwar context and whether they supersede human-made laws. Despite the deeply felt beliefs, the government won, and the nine were convicted at the trial. The importance and topicality of the drama were well known. However, its earnestness got in the way of its emotional impact. Hollywood was accused of ignoring the conflict at hand. This independent production was so current to the actual subject events and so intimately created by its direct participants that this very proximity compromised the film's effectiveness. Acting became speechmaking, and the film suffered from artistic and dramatic myopia. *The Trial of the Catonsville Nine* flirted with the demarcation between fiction and nonfiction, drama and documentary styles of filmmaking. Unlike the media-self-conscious quasidocumentaries with the fictional filmmaker protagonists of the late 1960s, this film was so literal in execution as to blur the delineation. The viewer almost expected Daniel Berrigan to portray himself rather than to bother to have the physically similar Ed Flanders do so.

In a similarly earnest left-wing vein, the Free Theater Associates got together in 1972 to produce an independent film named after their troupe, *FTA*. Francine Parker directed the movie, which Jane Fonda and Donald Sutherland produced. It was basically a filmed performance, an antiwar version of the old Andy Hardy staple, "Let's put on a show." Here the program was not so much to entertain the troops but to amuse the antiwar types assembled in the on-stage audience and viewing in the movie theater or college lecture hall. The screenplay was written by Fonda, Sutherland, and, among others, Holly Near and Dalton Trumbo. To the initiated the real meaning of *FTA* was more than just Free Theater Associates; it was the well-known initialism, "Fuck the Army." Either way it reminded us that the war was still raging and that films were continuing to address it in unconventional ways.

The last 1972 film to be discussed here is *Limbo*. This Universal film was a low-budget portrayal of the war's effect on noncombatants back home. *Limbo*'s balanced perspective was in stark contrast to shrill and dogmatic treatments on the war. The only in-country scenes are provided via newsreel footage. In a fashion typical of the era, the credit sequence is on a split screen. The left side features jet fighter planes taking off and attacking. The right side box shows surface-to-air missile batteries (SAMs) firing and some of the targets on the ground. The integration of the two sides of the raids is indicative of some of the strengths of the picture. In small but nevertheless atypical ways, the film introduces both prowar and antiwar sentiments via its characters. Using female protagonists, the movie dwells on feelings such as loneliness, fidelity, and sisterhood as opposed to more common male-dominated treatments concerned with rescue missions, confrontation, and frontline camaraderie. *Limbo* also has one of the first instances of a scene providing the enemy's perspective on the conflict in a domestic feature.

Mark Robson (*Lost Command,* 1966) directed *Limbo,* which was written by Joan Micklin Silver and James Bridges based on her original story. The movie altered the male perspective on war and its tragic consequences by dealing with three patriotic pilots' wives whose husbands are listed as either MIAs or POWs. Hence the women are in "limbo" as to how to run their lives. In one powerful scene the women watch newsreel footage of American POWs being harangued, beaten, and spat upon in the streets of Hanoi. This was famous real footage that angered and saddened the American public. Already, several films, such as *Welcome Home, Johnny Bristol* and *The Forgotten Man,* had recreated such heinous treatment. They showed the hatred but also the face of the enemy and yet another horror of war. Here in *Limbo* the question is dramatized, what must the prisoners' families watching these films be going through? The women are to shout if they recognize their loved one, perhaps resulting in a positive identification and a change of status from MIA to POW. One nebulous profile elicits several excited responses from the audience. An officer tells the women that 14 others in screenings across the country at air force bases have claimed the same man as their own!

The three women were played by three Kates: Kate Jackson, Kathleen Nolan in a particularly powerful performance, and Katherine Justice. Stuart Margolin, who wrote television's first Vietnam vet feature, *The Ballad of Andy Crocker,* costarred as a potential suitor to Nolan who becomes a friend when she insists on remaining faithful. As the wives of pilots as opposed to grunts (foot soldiers), the women reside in relatively comfortable surroundings near an air force base in Florida. Ever since their husbands were shot down, they have been existing in an anxious state of fear as they await word on the status of their spouses. Each women is different in age, economic situation, political view, and religious outlook. Nevertheless, their shared plight binds them in spirit and purpose. In their heterogeneity they create dramatic empathy across a wide spectrum.

The wealthy Katherine Justice character is hopeful but very unrealistic. Despite strong but inconclusive evidence to the contrary, she insists her husband is alive. Nolan is older with four children. Her husband has been a POW for five years. Jackson is the beautiful young woman married for only a short time when her spouse went off to war. She is torn by duty and her vows as she has met another man. Despite this dilemma, she joins her new friends in pursuit of information from the government. She moves in with Kathleen Nolan and her family, and this arrangement as well as the entire wife support network becomes a source of information, collective action, and solace.

Despite some caring liaison officers, the women experience no satisfaction from the air force. Therefore they lead a group of MIA wives to Paris, the site of the real-life ongoing peace talks. There they hope to meet directly with the representatives of North Vietnam and gain information. The opposition government is not forthcoming and instead dwells on its own painful and propaganda-rich perspective that the American fliers are perpetrators of atrocities on an innocent civilian populace. The women are forced to watch newsreel footage of the casualties in the North that result from American bombing raids. The three women weep as the human tragedy knows no nationality.

In another scene several of the women testify before a congressional committee. Unlike the other demure witnesses, Nolan's character expresses anger and frustration at the lack of substantive progress in the disposition of their husbands' cases. Later at a group assembly Nolan questions the very purpose of the war. She advocates withdrawal, while other wives angrily advocate a victory with honor. Amid the air force spouses, Nolan's articulating the idea that perhaps their husbands' sacrifices are in vain is very controversial. *Limbo* concludes as one of the women's husbands returns home and is greeted at the airport by his wife and then besieged by an eager press corps. As they hug in reunion the last frame freezes, and the image lingers on through the closing credits.

Despite requests from the major studio producer, *Limbo* did not receive any assistance from the U.S. Air Force. The war was still on, the MIAs' status was still indeterminate (as it remains for some even to this day), and the POWs were for the most part not yet on their way home. Therefore the government felt the one instance of marital infidelity of the Jackson character was unacceptable for morale reasons. Rather than make any story compromise in this area, the filmmakers did without the logistical help.[6]

The alternative title to Universal's film was *Women in Limbo* or the more melodramatic *Chained to Yesterday*. Interestingly the movie's feminine perspective was more than just a plot device. It reflected an uncommonly strong technical contribution by women. The aforementioned Silver's original idea and adaptation were only the most fundamental source of such input. In addition the producer was Linda Gottlieb, the editor was Dorothy Spencer, and the musical score was by Anita Kerr. The film's direct dealings with the war and its current events were a timely exception. Its interest in the difficult MIA status predated many gung-ho, male-oriented, and wholly unrealistic avenging action films, such as *Missing in Action, Rambo,* and their sequels.

The year 1973 was to mark the end of direct American involvement in the war in Vietnam. Unfortunately for the people of Southeast Asia, the carnage continued. On January 15 President Nixon agreed to suspend all U.S. military operations against North Vietnam as a result of the progress made at the Paris peace talks. On January 23 negotiators Henry Kissinger and Le Duc Tho initialed a peace agreement ending the hostilities and providing for release of all prisoners of war. On March 29 the last American troops left South Vietnam. On April 1, 1973, the last-known American prisoners of war returned to freedom at Clark Air Base in the Philippines. The American public emotionally watched television coverage of the repatriations and family reunions. Joy, relief, anger, and other deeply felt emotions greeted the cessation of hostilities and the return of the POWs. It was not until August 14 that all U.S. bombing raids stopped in Cambodia per formally mandated congressional action. As the year came to a close the Nixon presidency was embroiled in the Watergate scandal. In response to the perceived abuses of the executive branch, Congress overrode Nixon's veto of the War Powers Act. Thus in November that historic legislation became law.

Back on the domestic home front and neighborhood movie screens, Universal teamed Peter Fonda with a beautiful young actress making her feature film debut, Lindsay Wagner. Together these *Two People* were featured in a conventional romantic tale set against a turbulent war-related background. Robert Wise produced and directed the film. Fonda portrayed an army deserter from Vietnam who makes his way to Africa. There he meets all-American fashion model Wagner. They travel to Paris and discuss life and his current dilemma. They fall in love and have a child. Not wanting to remain a fugitive and eager to get on with his new life, Fonda returns to the United States and turns himself in.

The picture could at times be nauseatingly upbeat. However, the likable and attractive performers, the baby as a symbol of rebirth, and Fonda's decision to seek a resolution with the authorities all reflected the beginnings of a positive outlook that had been vacant from movies on Vietnam-related subjects. Thematically romanticism and upbeat endings were reappearing as opposed to the usual antihero cynicism, promiscuous sex, and climactic final death scenes.

Five years before the important film depiction of a maimed veterans' problems in *Coming Home* (1978), and concomitant with the POWs' return, a small independent picture merged the two issues in a sympathetic way. A low-budget work, *The P.O.W.* was created as a family effort. Jane Dossick produced the film; Phillip Dossick directed, wrote, and edited it; and Joanna Lee Dossick costarred.

Howard Jahre played a crippled Vietnam veteran attempting to adjust to life back in the United States and out of a VA hospital. The film was a simple nonexploitative portrait that had a cinéma vérité style enhanced by the use of nonprofessional actors.

Here the POW designation referred not only to Jahre's wartime status but also to his permanent disability. Everyday tasks, such as finding a job, negotiating the streets, and getting about his apartment, are recorded in agonizing detail. The audience was poignantly reminded of how it takes these activities for granted.

Lest the refreshing but facile Hollywood optimism of *Two People* or the cautious seriousness of the independent *The P.O.W.* seemed to establish too positive a trend, the next two films of 1973 returned to the old mold. *The Stone Killer* and *Trained to Kill* were exploitation flicks that superficially concerned veterans. *The Stone Killer* was a Columbia Pictures release in the late summer that teamed international action star Charles Bronson with director Michael Winner. Subsequent to *The Stone Killer*, the duo hit box office paydirt with the equally violent and reactionary actioner *Death Wish*.

With the success of *The Godfather*, films about the Mafia were much in vogue. Like the vigilante convention and very other commercial subgenre, it was only a matter of time before Vietnam veterans were integrated into these popular gangster stories. In *The Stone Killer* a Mafia kingpin, played by Martin Balsam, recruits a team of highly trained Viet vet killers. They are to act as gangland assassins in retribution for a crime committed years ago.

Charles Bronson was the no-nonsense title character, a cop known as the stone killer. Normal Fell and Ralph Waite costarred. The movie was indicative of the higher class of exploitation films. The story was enhanced by talented direction, acting, and a bigger budget. The increasing acceptability of "R"-rated screen violence was demonstrated by the mostly positive reviews the film received despite its stereotyping and mayhem. Roger Greenspan in his review praised director Winner and identified the sources of this admiration as "a strange combination of vulgarity and technical elegance . . . as close to inspired primitivism as we are likely to get in the movies these days."[7]

Style seems to have triumphed over substance. When these action pictures involving Vietnam veterans were the sole purview of independents such as American International, the releases were somewhat limited in their exposure and influence. However, here a major studio was using a bankable star in a vehicle that promulgated in an almost subliminal manner yet another negative and amoral caricature of the vet.

To carry out the contract killings in *The Stone Killer*, the Viet vet mercenaries are given additional training in a special desert outpost. In the next film, *Trained to Kill* (aka *The No Mercy Man*), the title character requires no such additional expertise. He has learned plenty of killing techniques from the usual U.S. government sources during his military service. Steven Sandor starred in this low-budget feature directed by Daniel J. Vance. The protagonist confronts a sadistic gang of teenage hoodlums who try to take over his hometown. The veteran is like a booby trap in Vietnam whose trip wire is activated. Once the sequence is in motion, it carries forward to its violent climax. Sandor is almost like a machine rather than a human being. After all, he is "trained to kill."

Not to be outdone by the expertise of the white veterans, the black vets returned in 1973 in Twentieth Century–Fox's *Gordon's War*. Here the veterans are at least on the side of the good and rational in nature. Nevertheless, they are called upon to use their military training in the service of the domestic war on crime. Blaxploitation, veterans, and gangsters all merge in this tale of a Green Beret's return to his Harlem neighborhood. Ossie Davis directed the picture, which starred Paul Winfield. Although vigilantes, the highly trained Green Berets are portrayed as well-disciplined, intelligent protectors of family and community values. Winfield's three veteran cohorts were played by Carl Lee, David Downing, and Tony King.

Gordon's War opens to a heavily decorated veteran Winfield in full dress Special Forces uniform standing at his wife's grave saying, "It would take an army to get dope out of Harlem." The credits roll, and images go to a split screen as the soul-pop score begins. We surmise that the spouse he had yearned for while away has succumbed to the urban plague of drug abuse. In his cozy Harlem apartment his deceased wife's picture and her drug paraphernalia confirm the tragedy. Outside the war hero encounters a big black drug dealer and pimp. In a flurry of rapid actions the veteran disarms and beats the much larger criminal. Combat training and experience combined with anger and sadness lend a degree of ferocity to the attack.

After this violent but just outburst, Gordon proceeds about the business of readjusting to civilian life. He flirts with a neighbor woman, goes to the library, researches potential jobs, and visits an aging black poet friend and history buff. Each of these sequences is naturally presented and designed to convey the vibrant and intellectual pursuits of life in what is often perceived as only a black ghetto wasteland. Winfield is pained by the debilitating drug subculture engulfing his neighborhood. He decides to put together a mission and goes to visit each of his Viet vet comrades who live in the area. Each man is handsome, well adjusted, family oriented, and gainfully employed. Again, despite the street crime milieu, these dramatic sequences are subtly positive in how they portray the black vets.

The four men plan out their course of attack against the pushers, pimps, and thieves. They proceed in an organized military fashion in setting up a command post in an abandoned tenement and securing weapons and communication equipment. Using military parlance, they infiltrate the enemy area, gather intelligence, and fight the "hostiles." They capture and interrogate a dope peddler, who is then so terrorized that he leaves town. Using sophisticated electronic surveillance techniques, they identify drug hotels and dealing areas. Then by a series of undercover exploits and nonlethal means of physical "persuasion," they clear out these gathering places. Having interrupted some means of distribution, they now go after the sources. In one scene the ex–Green Berets stop a courier on her way to deliver raw heroin to a processing lab. The woman is singer-actress Grace Jones in a bit role.

The vets have been so successful in adapting war skills to their domestic battlefront that the drug lords are forced to retaliate. One of the heroes is gunned down execution style. The other three escape the offensive on their command post. An exciting extended chase scene through New York City ends with the death of a major drug mobster. However, Winfield knows that this black hoodlum's death does not represent the end of the chain of command. Posing as garbage collectors, the three remaining good guys confront the white "suits" who run the Harlem drug operations from their corporate boardroom. The ultimate kingpin is killed, and the rest of the criminals, now exposed to the press and police, are left to the conventional justice system.

Gordon's War was full of both black anger and black pride. The veteran protagonists are determined not to be victimized nor to allow their people to be harmed by a corrupt power structure. Gordon's war both in Southeast Asia and in the ghetto back home is now over. The film ends as he peacefully strolls through Central Park.

Another proud vet was the lead character in the cult classic *Electra Glide in Blue*. The Vietnam background is merely verbally rendered character development. Robert Blake starred as a motorcycle highway patrol officer in the Southwest. James William Guercio directed Robert Boris's screenplay. Blake is a scrappy and incorruptible law officer who must contend with drug-addled hippies and other lowlifes. He must also confront condescension borne of his diminutive stature, class, and wartime service. His no-nonsense approach dictates that neither he nor his fellow vets get a reprieve from responsibility and honest behavior. Service in Vietnam is not an excuse for speeding or other law infractions. The stereotypical sociopathy of other movie veterans would drive him mad; he quietly does his duty without recrimination.

As 1973 came to a close the country rejoiced in the cessation of hostilities in Vietnam and the return of the POWs. Nevertheless, the losses and wounds caused by the war were deep. Also, the country was buffeted by revelations involving the Watergate scandal. Pop-cultural escapism has always acted as a balm for the individual and collective psyche. The 1950s became the decade of choice as America nostalgically embraced that period as one of perceived innocence. George Lucas's blockbuster *American Graffiti* typified the fond memories. The film took place at the end of that era, the summer of 1962 after high school. It featured a young cast that included Richard Dreyfuss and Ron Howard.

The specter of Vietnam subtly hangs over the film. America's preeminence and innocence have been shaken by the turbulent events of the 1960s. These young people stand on the threshold of adulthood, a time perfectly typified by the summer after graduation. America in 1962 is on that same brink, about to be engulfed in a conflagration in Indochina, political assassinations, and urban strife. Each of the characters in the film has to make fundamental choices that fateful summer as they all enter manhood. For one it is a job, for another it is college, and for the hapless nerd, "Toad," played by Charles Martin Smith, it is the military. *American Graffiti* was a feel-good movie seen by millions of young people, many of them upper-middle-class younger teens. For them Vietnam was a faraway place of sad but inchoate meaning. Therefore in the now-often-imitated epilogue title card sequence, when it was revealed that Toad had been killed in Vietnam, shock and grief were registered with an unexpected emotional impact.

Most of the films in this chapter catered to the baby-boomers who dominated the marketplace and were by now overwhelmingly opposed to the war in Vietnam. Unlike national film industries, Hollywood did not rely on government financing. Therefore the necessity of acting as a propaganda mechanism in support of American foreign policy did not exist. By the same token as for-profit corporations the "establishment" nature of the industry made criticism of controversial issues and the ensuing fiscal risks dangerous. Therefore the indirect and ambiguous strands of film related to the Vietnam War were all that could be mustered in the 1970–1973 period.[8] But in the era beyond the celluloid realm, one overriding fact was the relief the country felt at the end of 1973. For America the long, bloody Vietnam War, but not its consequences, was blessedly over!

References

1. Ray Bonds, ed., *The Vietnam War* (New York: Crown, 1983).

2. Roger Ebert, *The Movie Home Companion* (Kansas City: Andrews, McMeel and Parker, 1987), p. 656.

3. Steven Jay Rubin, *Combat Films: American Realism, 1945–1970* (Jefferson, N.C.: McFarland, 1981), p. 201.

4. Brock Garland, *War Movies* (New York: Facts on File, 1987), p. 136.

5. *World Almanac* (New York: World Almanac, 1990). For more historical background, see Bonds, *The Vietnam War*; Thomas C. Paterson, J. Garry Clifford, and Kenneth J. Hagan, *American Foreign Policy* (Lexington, Mass.: D. C. Heath, 1977); Jeff Stein, *The Vietnam Fact Book* (New York: Dell, 1987); Harry G. Summers, *Vietnam War Almanac* (New York: Facts on File, 1985); George Esper, *The Eyewitness History of the Vietnam War* (New York: Ballantine Books, 1983); David Halberstam, *Vietnam: The Making of a Quagmire* (New York: Random House, 1965); Stanley Karnow, *Vietnam: A History* (New York: Viking Press, 1983); and Edward Doyle, *Vietnam: A Collision of Cultures* (Boston: Boston Publishing, 1984).

6. Jay Hyams, *War Movies* (New York: Gallery Books, 1984), p. 194.

7. Roger Greenspan, "The Stone Killer Review," *New York Times*, August 30, 1973, sec. 3, p. 26.

8. Additional sources of synopses and cast not cited via direct quotation thus far include Patricia King Hanson and Stephen L. Hanson, *Film Review Index, Volumes 1 and 2, 1950–1985* (Phoenix: Oryx Press, 1987); Leslie Halliwell, *The Filmgoer's Companion* (New York: Avon, 1989); *HBO's Guide to Movies on Videocassette and Cable T.V.* (New York: Harper and Row, 1990); Leonard J. Leff, *Film Plots, Volumes I and II* (Ann Arbor, Mich.: Pierian Press, 1988); James L. Limbacher, *Feature Films on 8 mm, 16 mm and Videotape* (New York: Bowker, 1982); Leonard Maltin, *T.V. Moviees and Video Guide* (New York: New American Library, 1990); Gerald Mast, *A Short History of the Movies* (Indianapolis: Pegasus, 1971); and Steven H. Scheuer, *The Complete Guide to Videocassette Movies* (New York: Holt, 1987).

Chapter 4

Transition to Peacetime, 1974–1977

The Paris peace agreements were signed in January 1973, ending the United States' involvement as a combatant in Vietnam. In 1975 the South Vietnamese government fell to the communists. The war and its domestic consequences were a product of the 1960s. America could not move into the future without a physical, if not spiritual, resolution of the conflict.

From August 5, 1964, until May 7, 1975, more than nine million Americans saw active duty in the armed forces. The average age of the soldiers in Vietnam was 19. (In World War II the average was a more mature 26.) A full 97 percent of all veterans of this period received an honorable discharge.[1] American forces suffered nearly 58,000 dead and 153,300 wounded as well as some 2,000 MIA cases, which remain unresolved to this day. Countless Vietnamese and other Southeast Asians lost their lives in the conflict. Numbers cannot convey the anguish; they only provide information. Movies are also unable to fully convey the meaning of what Marlon Brando as Kurtz in *Apocalypse Now* referred to as "the horror" (in quotation of Joseph Conrad's *Heart of Darkness*). The movies show little safe pieces of the story for the majority of Americans who were fortunate enough not to have been there. When the war came to an end, the world of film would begin to address the conflict in more direct ways. This was a commercial decision and a function of production delay, lack of source material, the arrival and ascendance of firsthand accounts, and the healing processes of time and distance.

From 1974 to 1977 the old conventions continued, but the groundwork was being assembled in society and within the industry for the reappearance in 1978 of combat films set in-country. But in 1974 there was an unusual lack of films or characters related to the war. This production void represented a collective sigh of relief that was not to be compromised by rushed representations of the horrific events.

Unlike fictional films, the printed medium was in a production spurt that would continue unabated for the next several years. By 1975 there were more than 100 Vietnam-related first-person accounts and novels in print, several of which would become the source for feature films. Feature documentaries also had a production surge that was the inverse of the commercial feature's decline. The most notable documentaries of late 1974 and 1975 were *Introduction to the Enemy* and *Hearts and Minds.*

The television industry joined the theatrical domain in a hiatus on Vietnam-related coverage. Writing in *The American Experience in Vietnam,* the authors summarized the broadcast medium's initial response to the U.S. extrication from the conflict: "It seemed appropriate that America's first 'television war' be reexamined not just in print, but by the medium that had daily brought it into millions of living rooms throughout the country. Television's coverage of the war in Vietnam had been a source of much political contention. Presidents, policymakers, congressmen, and generals had accused it of bias, distortion, oversimplification, and sensationalism. Stung by such assaults on its integrity and competence, television quietly acquiesced in the country's postwar desire to forget Vietnam."[2]

As early as the tail end of television's so called golden age in 1964, "CBS Playhouse" had presented a powerful four-act play entitled *The Final War of Olly Winter.* It featured Ossie Davis as an American adviser in Vietnam in 1963. The teleplay opens to the rhythmic sounds of a whirring helicopter. An intimate portrait unfolds of a compassionate black American trapped in the jungles of Vietnam. In a poignant manner Ronald Ribman's play covered new dramatic ground concerning the widening U.S. role in the conflict.

Olly flashes back on his childhood as the helicopter makes its way over the Mekong Delta. He advises the South Vietnamese commander, but his words go unheeded. After a disastrous advance into an ambush in a rice paddy, Olly escapes into the jungle. There he meets a young Vietnamese girl, and gradually they gain a mutual trust. The lieutenant is forced to kill a Viet Cong guerrilla in hand-to-hand combat. To escape the emotional pain this engenders, he daydreams of his childhood in the big city. Gradually the trust of the big black American soldier and the delicate Vietnamese woman becomes a beautiful, unconsummated love. Tragically, like many real-life American soldiers, Olly Winter does not make it out of the jungle. This powerful drama went the way of all of television's earlier dramatic theater presentations. It would be years before renewed investigations of the complicated feelings about the conflict in Southeast Asia would be presented.[3]

During the conflict the nightly news coverage brought the war into the home and created a conscious immediacy for noncombatants. The war was easy to tune in or out. In *The Ugly American* the viewer at the film's conclusion chose to turn off his set before Brando as Ambassador MacWhite could impart his knowledge to the discussion. In the film version of *Born on the Fourth of July,* Ron Kovic's mother turns the channel from the nightly news' depressing battle accounts to the comedic escapism of one of the 1960s top-rated shows, Rowan and Martin's "Laugh In."

In 1968 coverage of the Tet Offensive became ubiquitous as the war spilled into major urban centers where reporters and camera people barely had to leave their hotels to provide graphic accounts of the war. The reporter in the bush or on patrol could not take along a full camera crew, so reports necessitated only a pad, pencil, and courage. Despite the intimacy that written coverage provided, it could not compete with visual reports. Film and then television diminished the audio and written word's power in favor of the literal, graphic, and visual. This is precisely why moving pictures had become the most powerful tools of propaganda and mass entertainment. The world of film had to share its power with the upstart medium of television. The sharing of the controversial imagery from Vietenam affected the style and means of commentary of each medium.

The foremost commentator of the media phenomenon of the 1960s was Marshall McLuhan. Although now viewed as passé, his observations are important in the analysis of the transition years that were concurrent with the movement from war to peace and from indirect to direct portrayal as well as changes in film editing and style that remain to this day. The language of the cinema was changing to reflect the youth-oriented and youth-understood images of the time. That same transition is asserted today as films take on the character of rock videos for the MTV generation. McLuhan with collaborator Quentin Fiore described in *The Medium Is the Message* the ascendancy of the mass medium and how it changed our culture. That change helped explain the massive unpopularity of the war and how film and television would choose to deal or not deal with it in the years to come.

Regarding film, McLuhan observed the "grammatical" changes of the late 1960s: "Critics of television have failed to realize that the motion pictures they are lionizing . . . would prove unacceptable as mass audience films if the audience had not been preconditioned by television commercials to abrupt zooms, elliptical editing, no story lines, flash cuts."[4] He alluded to the distinct susceptibility of the younger audience to these changes. "Youth instinctively understand the present environment—the electric drama. It lives mythically and in depth. This is the reason for the great alienation between generations. Wars, revolutions, civil uprisings are interfaces within the new environments created by electric informational media."[5]

Lest we dismiss McLuhan's observations as having died out with the hippies, all we need to do is sit with a ten-year-old and compare computer and video game skills to corroborate a belief in the instinctive electronic literacy of the young. The change in film language, the Vietnam films yet to come, the eventual plethora of made-for-television movies about the war, and years later the made-for-video treatments all are rooted in the transition of the country and its media. Taken to an extreme, the healing of time and the geometric progressions in the electronic medium coalesced the Vietnam conflict into nothing more than a video game for some of today's youth. The popular Nintendo brand of computer games now offers games entitled "Platoon" and "Rambo" for the children of America.

Much of the discussion of the new "global village" and the dissolution of the Iron Curtain has been attributed to the leveling internationalism of broadcast images showing how the other half lives. These transmissions know no borders.

Back in 1967 McLuhan quoted one of the principals affected by the anticolonial fallout in Southeast Asia when he said that "Hollywood is often a fomenter of anti-colonialist revolutions."[6] These were the words of Indonesia's Sukarno, who continued, "The motion picture industry has provided a window on the world, and the colonized nations have looked through that window and have seen the things of which they have been deprived. It is perhaps not generally realized that a refrigerator can be a . . . symbol of revolt to a people deprived of even the necessities of life. . . . [Hollywood] helped to build up the sense of deprivation of man's birthright, and that sense of deprivation has played a large part in the national revolutions of postwar Asia."[7]

These sentiments, despite being cloaked in the consciousness of the late 1960s, not only contextualize the changes and importance of the medium, film included, but also propel us to the present world and the dissolution of world communism. In the video age and a contemporary compendium on Vietnam War films, a self-conscious analysis now in a transitional stage agrees with the assessment on McLuhan: "Whatever his relation to an unfashionable '60s rhetoric of excess, McLuhan stands at the beginning of a shift in cultural criticism that we are only beginning to undertand."[8]

Although film and television, in the period 1974 to 1977, offered few Vietnam War treatments, the groundwork was being laid for further integration of the two mass media in Hollywood. The depressing and apparently noncommercial gamble of head-on portrayals of the war was softened by the lower production costs associated with the movies of the week. Therefore in the years to come many feature-length films about the war would come out of this programming area. "Television . . . favors the abstractions of language over the density of the image. . . . It's the lightness of TV movies that makes them favor 'heavy' subjects."[9] These would include post-traumatic stress disorder and, soon to come, war orphans and Agent Orange.

The television executives responsible for the made-for-television movie would go on to run the Hollywood studios in the 1980s and then the evolved multinational media conglomerates of the 1990s, which now dominate the global communications and entertainment industries. Michael Eisner and Barry Diller left ABC's television division to run Paramount and then split to head Disney and Twentieth Century–Fox, respectively. The worldwide ascendancy of American culture through the ubiquity of its entertainment products reflects a triumph never imagined in the postwar malaise of Vietnam and Watergate.

In 1974 in the theatrical realm, the filmography entries were feeble. An incidental veteran portrayal was provided via Disney family entertainment in *The Bears and I*. The Duke's eldest son, Patrick Wayne, starred with Chief Dan George in this nature tale. The kindly vet adopts three motherless bear cubs and fights on behalf of a Native American tribe's land rights. The weak *Mixed Company* alluded to a different type of orphan, Vietnamese children. The film starred Barbara Harris and Joseph Bologna as a couple that adopts a number of minority kids. Madcap interracial and cross-cultural hijinks are the order of the day.

The Crazy World of Julius Vrooder was also a comedy. This Twentieth Century–Fox presentation of a Playboy Enterprises film was originally entitled *Vrooder's Hooch*. However, few people knew that this in-country slang meant "hut" or "domicile." Arthur Hiller directed Timothy Bottoms and Barbara Seagull (now back to Hershey) in the starring roles.

As a portrait of a mentally unstable veteran, the film was an irreverent look at the tragic-comic characters in a VA hospital psycho ward. The "crazies" who populate the hospital are not limited to the current conflict but also include vets from both world wars. Vrooder is unable to relate to the real world. Using skills he learned in Vietnam, he constructs a booby-trapped shelter under an expressway overpass. Hershey, a sympathetic nurse, tries to help him. Of course he falls in love and dreams of running away with her to the peaceful confines of Canada. However, the veteran gets into trouble with another establishment institution, the phone company. It seems that he has been tapping into Ma Bell's lines inside his hooch and making illegal long distance phone calls.

No one was really interested in a comedy about Vietnam. In fact to this day there have been only a few comedies about the Vietnam War. One was the wildly successful *Good Morning, Vietnam* (1987). However, the box office was attributable to Robin Williams's stand-alone comedic jags. The big-budget *Air America* (1990), which was a supposedly humorous look at CIA operations in Laos, had a low gross despite matinee idol Mel Gibson. If Hollywood could not find anything funny about the conflict some 16 years later, then it certainly would not have back in 1974.

War still raged on in Southeast Asia. In January 1974 Phnom Penh, the beautiful capitol of Cambodia, came under communist siege. The South Vietnamese government reported 13,778 soldiers killed since the so-called January 1973 truce.

Despite the less intimate status of Americans in the conflict, controversy surrounding the war continued. Part of it was generated by *Hearts and Minds*. Despite being a documentary, this 1974 release is afforded an extended examination here because it achieved a breadth of distribution and exhibition rarely given to that particular type of movie. After being a cause célèbre at the Cannes Film Festival, this important antiwar documentary found a showcase in conventional venues such as upscale urban theaters. The title refers to the efforts of the United States to win the loyalty, affection, and cooperation of the indigenous populace to its cause and that of the South Vietnamese government. Peter Davis, known for his controversial television documentary *The Selling of the Pentagon*, directed *Hearts and Minds* for producer Bert Schneider (*Head*, 1968).

The movie summarizes and indicts long-term involvement of the United States in Vietnam. It features newsreel footage as well as original interviews with participants on all sides of the political issues. The main technical method by which it achieves its perspective is the editing process. The juxtaposition of powerful images with the preceding or ongoing testimony of various persons either supports or refutes their words. For instance, in one of the most controversial scenes in the film, the U.S. forces supreme commander in Vietnam, General William Westmoreland, is interviewed. At one point he states that "the Oriental doesn't put the same high price on life as does a Westerner." Belying his assertion is the crosscutting with a distraught father as he prostrates himself at the grave of his child killed in a B-52 bomber raid. This is a deliberate discrediting of the hawkish perspective, which was contrary to that of the filmmakers.

Former Johnson administration secretary of defense Clark Clifford outlines the post–world war and the cold war sensibilities that led us into the conflict. Footage from a Hollywood musical of the 1940s features gaily singing soldiers on their way off to a romanticized conflict. Clifford is utilized repeatedly as a spokesperson and former firsthand policymaker whose personal transformation from hawk to dove reflected the perspective of many people in America. He outlines the Truman Doctrine, the French presence, and so on. Archival footage is interspersed with images that include the surrender at Dien Bien Phu, President Eisenhower on the domino theory, JFK, LBJ, Nixon, the return of the POWs, the Gulf of Tonkin Resolution, veteran interviews, May Day demonstrations, Fourth of July parades, J. Edgar Hoover, Joseph McCarthy, the streets of Saigon, Daniel Ellsberg, folk singers, bombing sorties, grunt recollections, and battle footage. The end result is a discrediting of the hawks and a painful realization that our involvement in Vietnam was a huge and bloody mistake. The controversy engendered echoed the disagreement in the hearts and minds of Americans that still raged, but no longer in wartime itself.

Two other images from *Hearts and Minds* merit mention. First is the moving-picture footage that accompanied the famous *Life* magazine still photograph of a young naked Vietenamese girl running in agony after a napalm raid. American soldiers pour water on the burning skin of the civilians in an attempt to alleviate the suffering caused moments earlier by U.S. forces' misplaced discharge of the controversial antipersonnel weapon. A mother holds a baby whose skin is literally hanging off. It is a horrible sequence and seems to summarize the brutal contradictions of the war: the compassionate behavior of the young men on the ground versus the indecent behavior that would allow such a thing to happen. The United States was using chemical weaponry, something considered beyond the notion of the rules of war. The accidental nature of this particular famous discharge typified the missteps associated with the much-vaunted U.S. technology applied in the war. A tearful fighter pilot, Randy Floyd, who often dropped bombs but never saw their closeup effects, is in hindsight consumed by guilt. He states, "You try to escape what you learned and to not come to logical conclusions."

The other scene out of many worth mentioning is the brothel sequence. Here in incredibly candid and shameless footage, two callow soldiers engage in foreplay with young South Vietnamese prostitutes, or "gook" girls. It is too graphic and their jabber to the camera is too ugly to keep the scene from being obscene. In many ways it summarizes the corruption of a culture brought on by the displacements and the emplacement of a huge and overpowering American presence.

The two scenes evoke the filmmakers' desired effect: a nauseating antiwar conclusion. Between the destruction of the people and the countryside and the corruption and exploitation of the youth, a popular adage at the time—that in an effort to save Vietnam we helped destroy it—is supported. Those with a differing viewpoint were outraged by the one-sided presentation. However, for many people the film gave voice to a feeling of guilt and the loss of everything that America supposedly stood for and fought against in the war. The debate over our role in Vietnam continued. It would be many years before the opposing viewpoints in films would blur into a coalesced acknowledgment that, despite differing perspectives, the war was wrong, but not for political or humanitarian reasons (the original context). Rather, more safely and united we could all say that our soldiers suffered and died and that the military effort was compromised. The one transcendent lesson of Vietnam, regardless of politics, is the following: if we are going to fight, then we fight to win. This now-universalized conclusion skirts some of the real issues and nuances of the war debate of years past. Nevertheless, in the context of the recent Persian Gulf War, it is the constantly mentioned societal conclusion that seems to have been learned from the Vietnam War.

For many Americans, particularly Hollywood, which had primarily sat out the war, feeling guilty felt right. Therefore at Academy Award time, *Hearts and Minds* provided a national showcase for self-flagellation of the creative community. Warner Bros. had taken a chance in distributing the film, and it was no surprise when the controversial nominee won the Best Feature Length Documentary Oscar for 1974. (This was the third nonfiction Vietnam-themed film to be nominated for a similar accolade. In 1969 Emile de Antonio had garnered a nomination for the same prize for his feature *In the Year of the Pig*. In 1970 the Documentary Short Oscar went to the powerful *Interviews with My Lai Veterans*.)[10] It would be four years before the Oscar ceremonies would be dominated by the first crop of direct fictionalized accounts of the Vietnam War.

The Hollywood response to the announcement reflected the still deep divisions in the country. In the acceptance speech, *Hearts and Minds* director Peter Davis reminded the audience that the suffering and war still continued in Vietnam. Then producer Bert Schneider said, "It is ironic that we're here at a time just before Vietnam is about to be liberated. I will now read a short wire that I have been asked to read by the Vietnamese people from the delegation for the Vietcong at the Paris peace talks: 'Please transmit to all our friends in America our recognition of all that they have done on behalf of peace and for the application of the Paris accords in Vietnam. These actions serve the legitimate interests of the American people and the Vietnamese people. Greetings of friendship to all American people.'"[11]

The producer then strode off the stage amid boos and cheers. Backstage all hell broke loose. Conservative Hollywood institution Bob Hope "pinned" the show's producer, Howard W. Koch, against the wall and demanded that a disclaimer be read. Shirley MacLaine yelled back, "Don't you dare!"[12] Normal presentations went on, including John Wayne's award of an honorary Oscar to director Howard Hawks. Bob Hope and others hastily drafted a rebuttal. Hope handed it to the next presenter, Frank Sinatra, and threatened, "If you don't read it, I will."[13] The singer-actor went to make his Best Writer presentation. Before he gave out the award he said, "Ladies and gentlemen, do deviate a second . . . I've been asked by the Academy to make the following statement regarding a statement made by a winner. The Academy is saying, 'We are not responsible for any political references made on the program and we are sorry they had to take place this evening.'"[14] The audience's response was once again mixed.

The black tie star bickering continued backstage. Bob Hope called Schneider's speech "a cheap, cheap shot." John Wayne did not mince words when he called the producer "a pain in the ass and outta line and against the rules of the Academy.[15] Before the ceremony was over the pool reporters had dragged Frank Sinatra, Brenda Vaccaro, Marlon Brando, and Jane Fonda into a discussion of the merits of the forum for such a controversy.

It was then reported that the night's big winner for *Godfather II*, Francis Ford Coppola, put in a last word in Schneider's defense: "It's [*Hearts and Minds*] not a musical comedy, so the Academy in voting for that picture was sanctioning the message of that picture, which was in the spirit of Mr. Schneider's remarks."[16] In conclusion the triumphant director then answered queries and promised to venture into other avenues. Perhaps one of them was to be the jungles of the Philippines . . .

The press and pundits had a field day with the Oscar night controversy. All these glamorous people arguing about the remarks and in a one-step-removed process about the war made great copy. Hollywood felt very self-righteous, very involved and political, and "it hurt so good."

At the halfway point of the decade, the war finally ended in Vietnam. In March the North Vietnamese launched an offensive in the Central Highlands. In April Khmer Rouge insurgents forced Lon Nol from power in Cambodia. War raged in neighboring Laos. In South Vietnam communist troops from the North captured the town of Xuan Loc, only 38 miles east of Saigon. On April 30 they entered the environs of the city (American personnel and some South Vietnamese allies had chaotically carried out evacuations up to the last moment), and President Duong Van Minh of South Vietnam announced the country's unconditional surrender.

Bloodshed and conflict did not end there. In May U.S. marines died while freeing the captured American freighter *Mayaguez* from Cambodian communists. The situation in Laos degenerated, and by December that country had also fallen under communist rule. In Cambodia the ruthless Khmer Rouge under the leadership of Pol Pot formalized its victory by renaming the country Kampuchea. Three countries in the region had now fallen to communism, and the bloody streets and rice paddies of Vietnam were joined by these additional "killing fields."

In 1975 *Milestones* marked independent filmmaker Robert Kramer's return to the subject of the Vietnam War. The director of *The Edge* (1968) and *Ice* (1970) had one iconoclastic left-wing treatment remaining to complete his trilogy. The 195-minute movie is an American odyssey that follows several characters' discovery of the United States through a cinéma vérité interview process with the different people they encounter. With little binding exposition the film becomes a peculiar tapestry of 1960s images in transition.

Among the people we meet are a group of radicalized antiwar veterans, a student activist, a father estranged from his son, an intellectual who served time in prison for aiding deserters, assorted hippies and commune members, and a militant fugitive. The film is dedicated to Ho Chi Minh and the "heroic Vietnamese people." As such it reflects the same sentiments about our former enemy that the campus radicals used to honor in their peppy chant "Ho Ho Ho with Ho Chi Minh, the NLF is gonna win." Such was the division in society that this film chronicles. *Milestones* was interesting but already dated.

In the highly acclaimed hit *Dog Day Afternoon*, also from 1975, Al Pacino played a mentally disturbed but sympathetic loser. During a botched bank robbery, he and his partner take hostages and, in an attempt to convey their ruthlessness to the police waiting outside, state, "We are Vietnam veterans so killing doesn't mean anything to us."

The 1975 fall television season presented two made-fors. *Returning Home* was directed by Daniel Petrie and starred the still relatively unknown actors Dabney Coleman and Tom Selleck. It was an updated remake of the 1946 William Wyler classic *The Best Years of Our Lives*. It, too, dealt with vets and their readjustment to civilian life. Like the original film, it also profiled the struggles of a combat amputee. It would still be three years until *Coming Home* integrated William Wyler's film and Fred Zinneman's *The Men* (1950) into the Vietnam era in the theaters.

Another veteran's physical challenge and courage were profiled in a true story adapted for television, *The Desperate Miles*. Tony Musante and Joanna Pettit starred for director Daniel Haller in the tale of his 130-mile odyssey across America in a wheelchair.

In the realm of quasi-exploitation flicks was independent Colmar's drama *Two* (aka *Captive*). Sarah Venable and Doug Travis starred for director-writer Charles Trieschmann. Wired vet Travis escapes from an army hospital and kidnaps Venable. They develop a curious rapport during their two days together in a secluded mountain cabin. He returns to town to rob a bank and is killed, leaving his captive with mixed emotions about Travis's tragic fate.

In late 1975 George Armitage wrote and made his directorial debut with the film *Vigilante Force*. The adventure featured Kris Kristofferson as a returned vet. Costarring were Jan-Michael Vincent and Victoria Principal. The story involved the hiring of Kristofferson to aid the police in a small town in California that is overwhelmed by ruffian oil field workers. He assembles a crack team of mercenaries seasoned in combat to restore order. Unfortunately their success leads to excess, and they begin to take control of the town. The staging of the action sequences is better than the trite plot.

The lack of veteran portrayals and the fact that the two exploitation movies were not biker flicks reflected the realization that the convention was finally running its course. Aside from the staleness of the imagery, the drop-off was attributable to one more factor. By the mid–1970s the drive-ins in America were closing by the hundreds. The land on which they sat was infinitely more valuable as the site of suburban shopping malls than as a seasonal business based on box office receipts. Therefore the demand for the films that had indiscriminately provided the B movie programming was diminishing. It would be several years before the advent of the B movie would return in the form of made-for-video programming. When this took place in the 1980s, the old formulas were trotted out, and among them were the Vietnam-related action films.

America celebrated its bicentennial in 1976, and the trappings of patriotism were allowed to resurface from a moribund post–Vietnam state. In Southeast Asia bloodshed continued in Cambodia as the vicious zealots of the Khmer Rouge forcibly resettled the population and murdered thousands. Vietnam was officially united as one country, and Saigon was renamed Ho Chi Minh City. Despite the use of controversial reeducation camps, the wholesale bloodbath predicted in South Vietnam did not transpire. In November 1976 the United States vetoed Vietnam's application for membership in the United Nations.

The returning Vietnam veteran character reappeared at the tail end of the Blaxploitation production boon in the 1976 release *Mean Johnny Barrows*. The film was an aptly titled exploitative actioner. Fred "the Hammer" Williamson directed himself, along with costars Elliott Gould and Roddy McDowall. The generic "Johnny" moniker is once again placed on a tightly wired veteran. This soldier fights a white-dominated organized crime syndicate that preys on his inner-city neighborhood.

The film opens in Vietnam with a ground-level shot of combat boots in a training exercise. By the time the credits are finished, the strapping black soldier is being harangued by a racist superior. The deadly nature of the in-country terrain (unconvincingly staged in a California field) is apparent when the asinine officer steps on a land mine and is blown to bits. The hard-core action audience has already received its first bit of gratifying mayhem.

The ingratitude of the establishment toward the black soldier continues as he returns home. Despite being decorated with the Silver Star and being a popular ex–football player (as was the star in real life), the veteran cannot get a break. He is down and out when Elliott Gould comes to his rescue. Gould shows Williamson how to make money by getting involved in some shady undertakings. Like most of these films, there is a complete absence of any Veterans Administration or social service outreach to aid the readjustment to civilian life. Eventually the veteran runs afoul of the Mafia and is forced to use his killing skills to exact a modicum of ghetto justice.

Not all the portraits of returning black soldiers were so angry. Paul Winfield, who had starred in the 1973 release *Gordon's War*, returned as a vet in the made-for-television drama *Green Eyes*. The movie was directed by John Erman and costarred Rita Tushingham and Jonathan Lippe. Powerful recent real-life images are integrated into the film via newsreel footage. Not only does this quickly orient the viewer to notable events, it also saves considerable money in lieu of recreating crowd scenes. The film opens to such stock footage as a modest welcome greets soldiers deplaning from Vietnam.

However, it is "one year later" when Paul Winfield finally returns to the United States. In uniform he limps to the modest rural home of his buddy Noel. The young white man, played by Jonathan Lippe, has not returned from the war. He is missing in action and presumed dead. Winfield has come to pay his respects. Unlike the shrill and jingoistic response of the older generation in many earlier films, Noel's uncle is a World War II vet with an aching heart. Not only does he mourn the loss of the nephew he raised as his own son, he is also pained by why his country went to this war. It is he, not the returning veteran, who voices the cynical notion that the war was worthless.

Winfield attempts to overcome the older man's disillusionment and in the process convince himself that the sacrifice that took his friend's life and his own health was justified. Winfield says that Noel contributed something on behalf of his country. But the uncle will have none of this and dismisses the patent words of consolation. In doing so, he also orients the viewer to the events of the past year. He says, "You've been in the hospital in Guam too long; it's not that way with this one [war]."

Winfield returns home to Chicago. As he makes his way through the ghetto, we are reminded that so many have yet to share in the American dream. The point is driven home as the veteran greets his grateful mother. The family was evicted from its apartment because of financial reverses. Several days later the veteran sees his old friends but is struck by how little he now has in common with them. At night he cannot sleep and often looks at the picture of a young Vietnamese woman. Winfield goes to get his old job back, but it and other positions are unavailable. A job counselor tells him not to wear the uniform because having anything to do with Vietnam "puts people off." Physical labor is impossible because of his injured leg. Desk jobs are hard to come by as he has little formal education. The VA social worker tells him about the GI bill and its educational benefits. However, this is too long-term a solution for a man who needs a job now.

Winfield grows despondent and cannot tolerate his mother's support of him and the idleness of his existence. He misses the Vietnamese woman and their Amerasian child. Finally he explains that he must return to Vietnam. His mother is stung by the thought of once again losing her son. Vietnam is far away and dangerous, as the war there still rages. She screams, "No one is the father of a hooker's child. . . . You can't fix the whole war. . . . Go back to school. . . . No half-breed baby of a Chinese slut is going to throw out what I spent my life scrubbing toilets for." Her son allows her this outburst and then says he needs her forgiveness and support. They hug, and it is this type of support that allows him to go and make something of his life.

In the next scene Winfield in civilian clothes disembarks at Saigon's Tan Son Nhut Airport. It is a noisy metropolis bursting with refugees from the fighting in the countryside. The viewer is horrified by the shots of the injured, of beggars, and of the rampant poverty. His cabby lost a son at Pleiku and reports that every day the casualties mount. The veteran is dropped off at a Saigon neighborhood known as Soul Alley. Here black American GIs lived in a segregated community with their Vietnamese wives and girlfriends. Most were abandoned to this squalor when their men returned to their native country. Many of the sickly inhabitants gaze longingly, hoping he has returned to take them away.

Finally he finds his girlfriend's mother, who is angry that he abandoned her daughter. She tells him that their baby, known as Green Eyes, died. Winfield is devastated but disbelieving. He wanders aimlessly through the streets of Saigon. This is not a beautiful Asian and French colonial gem of Southeast Asia. It is a desperate, ugly, and demoralized city waiting to fall to the communists. The exhausted veteran sits down on a bench at a soldier's memorial. A young girl comes over and offers to sell her body. A few hours later a street urchin sits beside him. They talk and Winfield learns how the orphan boy lives by his wits on the streets of the city. In an ingenious diversion, the boy makes off with the tired vet's jacket and money.

The veteran is at an all-time low when he goes to an orphan resettlement center for information. Just when the bleakness seems overwhelming, an English social worker changes things. She convinces him that, although his girlfriend and child are gone, there is much work he could do right here at her orphanage. He is reluctant until he is besieged by the Amerasian children there. Winfield decides to help out at the orphanage.

That night he flashes back to several ugly episodes during the war. First is the memory of an innocent-looking little girl who was a human booby trap. Second is his sergeant asserting that "these people have no regard for life." Third is the memory of himself and fellow soldiers talking about grabbing the first girl they see and getting "some R&R." Fourth is seeing his friend Noel in the back of a truck right before it took a direct hit from a mortar. These sad thoughts are joined by the memory of the little children's faces he witnessed. Returning to the present, he looks across the street as kids swarm over the refuse fighting for scraps of food. Winfield whispers to himself, "How did this happen?" and the movie fades to black.

Winfield looks in vain for his child. Then he begins his volunteering and provides care to the *bui die*, literally "the dust." He is happy and life begins to have new meaning. He writes to his mother that finally "I have done something!" (This assessment is in marked contrast to the depressed veteran character Joe Don Baker had played in the exploitative 1972 flick *Welcome Home Soldier Boys*. His sense of worth was self-defined by his ability to "kill gooks, lots of them!")

Two coincidences dramatically propel the plot. First, Winfield happens to see the boy who stole his jacket. He catches him and befriends him. The boy, Trung, becomes Winfield's guide to the city and finds a home at the orphanage. Second, Noel surfaces alive and well and running a nightclub. Winfield is dumbstruck by the appearance of the man he thought he saw die. Apparently Noel escaped with only slight injury and faked his own disappearance. Now he is a wealthy black-marketeer and living off the exploitation of others. Noel says this has been easy because they "love Americans. . . . They love John Wayne." Winfield is disgusted.

Looking for additional information on his loved ones, Winfield makes his way through a portion of the city's outskirts that has nearly fallen into enemy hands. Amid the fires Winfield thinks back to an incident in the war when he and his platoon torched a village suspected of harboring Viet Cong. This recreation of a "zippo party" shames him.

Despite Noel's ugly lifestyle, he does make an effort to use his extensive connections to help Winfield. The veteran is concerned about his orphanage; his young friend, Trung, is about to be inducted into a desperate South Vietnamese army; and he still wants to find out more about Green Eyes, whom he refuses to believe is dead. The social worker, Margaret, finally explains the reality of the situation. Saigon is going to fall, and the children who are already discriminated against will be complete outcasts and possibly even killed by the new authorities. He must give up his search and prepare to leave. She intends to stay with her children.

Trung comes up with one more lead, which takes the veteran to another squalid area of the city. There Winfield sees the mother of his child. Their eyes fill with tears as in flashback the film recalls the day his unit shipped out and he waved goodbye to the forlorn woman. He feels horrible guilt, but she has no time for anger. He is relieved to hear that she has married a fine man, a pilot in "Region One." Finally, however, he must ask, "What became of our baby?" She confirms that he died of a fever. He weeps in her lap and asks for forgiveness. She forgives him and says to "no more cry."

Winfield walks the streets of Saigon and then returns to say goodbye to Margaret and promises to champion her cause in the United States. He then searches the streets for Trung, fearful that he might not find the boy in time. When he sees Trung, the big black American runs and hugs the little Vietnamese teen. We understand that he is going to adopt him as Green Eyes. The movie closes with the following postscript: "In the spring of 1975 the gates of Saigon closed, sealing in hundreds of thousands of orphans, many of them half–American."

This melodramatic film provided major national exposure to the plight of Amerasian children. As a fictional work based on true life events, it predated other films on the subject, such as *The Children of An Lac* and *Last Flight Out.* In addition the panicky and dangerous atmosphere that preceded the fall of Saigon was also recreated for the first time and predated the exciting finale of

The Deerhunter (1978) and a film entirely devoted to that period, *Saigon: Year of the Cat,* made in 1983.

American International presented Bo Svenson as a Vietnam veteran in a relatively benign romantic comedy entitled *Special Delivery.* He leads a group of down-and-out vets in a bank heist. Everything goes awry, and he hides the loot in a mailbox that belongs to Cybill Shepherd. Drug dealers and other characters intervene, but eventually the two fall in love and escape on an ocean liner. Perhaps most significant is the conventional leading man nature of the protagonist as a man fully capable of physical and emotional love.

International Rainbow Pictures was a New York based independent production house that had been responsible for *Hearts and Minds.* Shortly after that documentary was made, one of its producers, Henry Jaglom, directed the film *Tracks.* That film did not receive its theatrical release until 1976. The executive producer of Jaglom's returning vet drama was Bert Schneider. Most of *Tracks* takes place on a train going across the United States, hence the name. Dennis Hopper appeared as the main character, Vietnam veteran Jack Falen. Dean Stockwell costarred, and the film marked the introduction of Taryn Power.

In a plot line similar to that of the 1971 feature *The Hard Ride,* Hopper, just back from Vietnam, is escorting for burial the body of a fallen comrade. Like the other film, the white veteran is performing this honor on behalf of a slain black buddy. The shaky hand-held camera techniques at first nicely mimic the movement of a train. However, like the film itself, they soon become tiresome.

The movie begins as Hopper in uniform checks on the loading of the flag-draped coffin into the baggage car. As the credits roll we see President Nixon's television address in which he announces the peace agreements in January 1973. Then it is all aboard for the cross-country journey. A hodgepodge of bizarre characters are introduced, including a real estate agent, two college coeds, a chess aficionado, and Stockwell as a skinny antiwar activist in a hideous psychedelic polyester shirt. Hopper confides to Stockwell that he liked to get high on Thai sticks and watch the tracer bullets flicker in the night. The sergeant makes out with a cute college girl, and when she stops him from proceeding any further, he respects her wishes but begins a decline into weirdness.

Most of the passengers either ignore his Vietnam-themed rambling or seem to vaguely worry about his mental health. He begins to flash back to Nam and hallucinates that some of the passengers are raping the girl. Fortunately he does not use the gun he pulls out. A startled conductor, played by character actor Frank McCrae, discovers the vet wandering about the train nude. The vet's paranoid fantasies seem absurd. However, soon it turns out that Stockwell is a fugitive from the FBI from his underground radical activism days. The overzealous real estate agent turns out to be a government agent. Some of the hallucinogenic paranoia does not seem as whacked out given the nighttime activities of the Feds in their capture of the young man.

At a little town Hopper and his precious cargo are unloaded. Before the funeral he meets up with one coed from the train. They have sex on a hill, but then he scares her by his weird recollections of toy soldiers and West Point. The moment of orgasm seems to elicit some of his mental demons. He is alone at the funeral and disgusted and confused. He speaks to his buddy and then jumps into the grave and opens the coffin. There is no body but rather an arsenal. The sergeant puts on a helmet and battle fatigues and loads himself down with weapons and bullets. Then in a rage he yells, "You want to go to Nam?" He jumps out of the grave as if it is a foxhole and proclaims to the unsuspecting little village, "I'll take you to Nam!" There is a freeze-frame, and we hear an explosion. As this is the film's last shot, the mayhem he wreaks is left to our imagination.

Many of the songs that accompany this strange tale have a military theme. Gay renditions of nostalgic tunes remind us of old images of war and fighting soldiers. These tunes include interspersed audio of "Praise the Lord and Pass the Ammo," by Kay Kyser and his orchestra; "He Wears a Pair of Silver Wings," by Dinah Shore; and "We're Going to Have to Slap That Dirty Little Jap," by Carson Robinson.

The supposedly comedic elements are not funny. The irreverence is purposeless, and the portrayal of the veteran eventually degenerates into stereotypic sociopathy. As a result the film is quite annoying as its pretensions are beyond the exploitative, but its technical and thematic elements are actually worse than most low-budget movies with a similar character.

One of the most famous Vietnam movie characters is Travis Bickle in the 1976 release *Taxi Driver*. The film, directed by Martin Scorsese, is a stylish and disturbing tale of alienation set against the New York nocturnal netherworld. Contributing to the fascinating power of the film is Robert DeNiro's memorable performance in the lead role. Bernard Herrmann provided the evocative musical score shortly before his death.

In the beginning of *Taxi Driver* DeNiro is suffering from acute insomnia. He tells the taxi company interviewer that "I just want to work long hours." He will work anywhere and anytime. His odd work schedule and sparsely furnished, dingy little apartment seem to convey that he has no life and no friends. In voiceover narration matched with Michael Chapman's wonderful nighttime cinematography, Bickle introduces us to the "animals . . . filth . . . and scum" of the mean streets. Everyone and everything appear ugly in this nighttime hell on earth. Only the daylight seems able to wash away the bodily waste and fluids that seep out at night. The steamy wetness of the streets evaporates along with the messy blood and semen that are on the backseat of his cab every morning.

Bickle rages against the pimps, prostitutes, criminals, and hypocrites. Despite his moralizing, he, too, attends the peep shows, and pops pills. His insomnia aggravates his psychosis. He keeps this illness of the mind in check by a physical exercise regimen he learned in the marines. As he mulls over his mission in life, he fine tunes his body despite a nagging suspicion that he may have stomach cancer (an early allusion to recently emergent Agent Orange concerns). The physical and psychosomatic manifestations of his anomie precede the eventually recognized medical diagnosis of post-traumatic stress syndrome. This

This updating of shell shock is merely the idiosyncratic tick of a richly rendered sick character.

Bickle fixates on an upscale WASP beauty, played by Cybill Shepherd. She works for a New York politician running for president in 1976. Her fellow campaign worker is a protective and platonic friend, played by Albert Brooks. Also introduced is the abused teenage runaway Iris, played by Jodie Foster, and her pimp, Harvey Keitel. Peter Boyle played the "Wizard," a gregarious and opinionated fellow cabby whose bigoted pontifications echo reactionary musings similar to those of the lead character in *Joe* (1970).

The voiceover narration joins Bickle's diary in revealing his tortured outlook on life. Cleaned up in an ugly, drab sportcoat, he manages to charm Shepherd into accepting a date. However, he frightens her and she rejects him. In a confrontation at her workplace, Bickle is thrown out. He strikes a martial arts, hand-to-hand combat pose but decides to retreat to his cab. That night he condemns his beloved to "burn in hell" like the rest of the scum.

Bickle on an aspirin, sugar, and booze binge buys a .44 Magnum from an amoral gun merchant. In fact the taxi driver buys several weapons for his personal arsenal, all of which he is familiar with from his military training. He attends a Palantine for President rally where the candidate is surrounded by Secret Service agents and the facile slogan of his campaign, "We Are the People." The vaguely populist sounding message is sound bite pablum.

In a famous scene, Bickle straps guns and knives on himself in preparation for his mission as a political assassin. Perhaps this will get Shepherd's attention. In a prelude to violence he looks in a mirror and practices drawing his weapons. He eerily asks himself and the viewer, "You talkin' to me?" In so doing, this scene bridges the book. The warped idiosyncracies of Bickle are reminiscent of the same mannerisms and movements experimented with by the actor back in DePalma's early Vietnam-related flicks, *Greetings* and *Hi Mom!* The same twitchy and disturbed persona was being created by this inexhaustibly talented actor. Also, the herky-jerky martial-inspired movements performed in isolation predated a similarly quasiballetic dancing scene performed by Martin Sheen as the government-sponsored hit man in the yet-to-come *Apocalypse Now.*

In the dingy little apartment Bickle proceeds with preparation for his dangerous self-imposed mission. Like a soldier on the eve of battle, he gets his affairs in order. He writes to his parents and tells them he is working for the government in a sensitive area that he cannot reveal. In attempting to "recon" his battle zone, he goes to see Iris. The 12-year-old talks the disgusting lingo of a whore enticing a john. However, Bickle is not interested in sex and by implication is probably not capable of it. Rather, he explains he is there to liberate the downtrodden little girl. (In other films to come, Vietnam vets confound women by refusing their sexual advances.) Bickle is able to gain a modicum of bemused trust from the girl.

After some last-minute expert target shooting, Bickle confidentially proclaims that his "whole life is now pointed in one direction." He proceeds in his

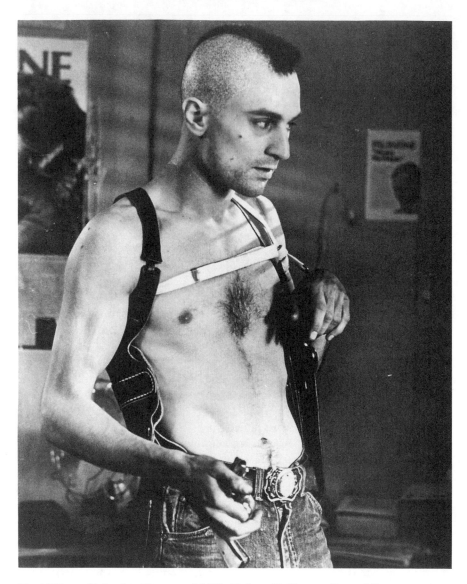

Taxi Driver (Columbia Pictures, 1976). Robert DeNiro as Special Forces veteran Bickle prepares for a stateside mission.

army jacket and a new Mohawk warrior hairdo to his appointed mission. His attempt to kill Palantine is thwarted, but Bickle escapes undetected. He then goes on a second mission. After swilling down a handful of pills and a beer, Bickle goes to where Iris works. He shoots the pimp at point-blank range. Proceeding into the building, Bickle shoots the manager as well. Then bursting into Iris's apartment, he chases her john away. As Iris huddles in fear, the wounded manager stumbles in proclaiming he is going to kill Bickle. The taxi driver blows the man's brains out against the wall. Our protagonist antihero then appears to want to commit suicide, but he is out of bullets. The police arrive as he mockingly places his blood-soaked finger to his head and pulls the trigger. An overhead camera shot lingers on the bloody scene. The movie fades out to an ironic explanatory epilogue. Tattered newspaper clippings from the New York tabloids hang from Bickle's apartment wall proclaiming, "Taxi Driver Battles Gangsters." Travis reads a letter of gratitude from Iris's parents, with whom she is now reunited. Bickle, now with a normal hairdo, returns to the cabbies at the coffee shop. Shepherd comes to see him now that he is a media hero. Bickle ignores her interest. As saxophone music rises on the soundtrack, the last nighttime shots of a misty neon-lit Times Square are reflected in the windshield of his taxi.

In the context of the Vietnam veteran portrayal, the final rejection of the object of desire once she has implied her acceptance of intimacy is notable. Throughout the film the sexuality of the Bickle character has been more firmly rooted in phallic expression through his guns, particuarly the slender magnums, than in any normative sexual pattern. In the final explosion of violence an individual and societal catharsis is unleashed. Retribution for sin is exacted on those that trade in the selling of sex. As the red bodily fluids gush forth in graphic arterial spurts, the viewer is subconsciously reminded of a long-suppressed orgasm. It is in some ways akin to what one critic of Brian DePalma's film *Casualties of War* referred to in the context of that Vietnam's tale's release as a "wargasm." Perhaps the ultimate irony of the film is the most inadvertent. In yet another instance of life imitating art, when John Wayne Hinckley tried to assassinate President Reagan, it became one more instance of the type of political killing that *Taxi Driver* alluded to. However, the irony was that the disturbed young man had attempted this desperate action as a way to gain the attention of actress Jodie Foster. It seems that he had seen *Taxi Driver* many times and became sexually infatuated with the young actress. He fixated on her and attempted this desperate act in an effort to reach her.

The military background of the sociopathic cabby is an integral but subtle part of his disturbed persona. As an ex-marine, his Vietnam background provides an A movie shorthand for his loner status, psychological problems, proclivity to violence, and strangely moralistic vigilantism. These traits could be part of the characterization of the nonvet. However, they might then necessitate longer initial exposition. Weaker films would be unconcerned with such factors, but Paul Schrader's script strives for a richer, multidimensional characterization. So the Vietnam vet status provides a shortcut to explain some of the sociopathy as inculcated by other more incidentally drawn characters.

In addition the taxi driver's veteran status provides an irony that the film's finale confirms. If *Taxi Driver* is primarily an indictment of America's corrupt and violent urban landscape and the way it alienates people, the fact that much of the lead character's problems stem from establishment or institutionally inspired sources helps broaden the problem into a macro-cultural commentary.

In other words the killer instincts of the Bickle character were, if not instilled, then honed during his marine service, and their warping is a commonly offered cultural response to the unconventional and unpopular nature of the conflict. His moralistic desire to rid the land of evil and corruption gets out of hand. In this way it mirrors the genuine hopes of the nation in getting involved in Vietnam and the subsequent degeneration of the positive national character of Americans once they were there.

After a failed political assassination attempt and premeditated murder, the outlaw veteran is commended by a vengeful society. The ultimate heroic lionization of this lowlife is a strange reward from a warped society. For Travis Bickle violence becomes a cleansing catharsis from a nearly toxic anomie. In America's bicentennial year Schrader and Scorsese managed to convey this same illness on a cultural and societal scale in a post–Vietnam-informed context. *Taxi Driver* represents the apotheosis of the tangential Vietnam veteran character. The combat films are yet to follow, and to this point most of the returned soldier portrayals had been formulaic renderings of exploitation films. Here, although not the main subject, the veteran status becomes upgraded in a talented A movie production. A major studio, Columbia, released the controversial and violent film as each of the people involved in its making were reaching a crescendo in their careers. Martin Scorsese had worked at American International, the king of the B movie studios. He was well aware of the motorcycle movie iconography and how it related to the Vietnam vets. In many ways Travis Bickle had traded in his metaphorical motorcycle for his taxi cab. In going from the slim B movies to a finely crafted A production, the veteran character was experiencing a transition that in the future would lead to a full-fledged examination of his status and indeed of the war itself in more direct and healthy portraits.

For the United States, the bicentennial year was to be one in which the trauma of Vietnam was put behind in a hopeful look forward. When this began to happen, then filmmakers could begin to examine the conflict in more depth, without such acutely negative emotional baggage as to render the complete commercial rejection of their work. The healing process was beginning and with it the healthfulness of dealing with the conflict and the problems it brought to its veterans and to American society.

Hollywood's reticence about combat films did not preclude it from making one notable action war drama in 1976, *Midway*. To the studios' relief, it became the sixth highest grossing film of the year. Although set in the more acceptable World War II conflict against an Asian enemy, the box office response to this conventional military picture provided some positive reinforcement for the speculation that the public might be ready for this genre's return. One question remained, however: did that include the most recent conflagration?

In January 1977 Cambodian Khmer Rouge troops raided border villages in Thailand. Civil war gripped neighboring Laos. In March anticommunists in the vanquished South blew up the Long Binh ammunition dump near the newly renamed Ho Chi Minh City. On March 17 the bodies of 12 missing American pilots were repatriated after much negotiation. By the end of June approximately 700,000 people had been moved from Saigon to rural agricultural resettlement camps. Fortunately such a forced relocation did not connote mass slaughter, as it had in nearby Cambodia. Throughout the year Thailand was able to successfully negotiate its way through the domestic upheaval and tensions created by massive influxes of refugees. In September Vietnam became a member of the United Nations. The lack of a U.S. veto exemplified a small turn toward still-unachieved normalization of relations. On the last day of 1977 the short-lived peace of the Vietnamese people ended when Vietnamese forces invaded nearby genocide-racked Kampuchea. In American minds the barely understood conflict put our ex-foes in a position of relative favor vis-à-vis the murderous government of Cambodia's Pol Pot. In response to economic and political dislocation in Vietnam, renewed conscription, and harsh communist rule, a steady stream of refugees poured out of the country. Many of them became the pitiful "boat people" tossed about the South China Sea in an effort to escape their dire living conditions. After much controversy and opposition, they began to be accepted in various countries, including the United States.

The writer of *Taxi Driver*, Paul Schrader, also fashioned, in collaboration with Heywood Gould, the screenplay for the 1977 release *Rolling Thunder*. This film was about a Vietnam veteran who becomes a vigilante crusader. Directed by John Flynn, it lacked the substantive characterization of Schrader's earlier film. Rather, it was ensconced in the exploitation elements of *Death Wish* and the crazed vet pictures from its studio, American International. *Rolling Thunder*, a Lawrence Gordon production, starred William Devane as pilot Major Charles Rane, a POW for eight years. Costarring were Tommy Lee Jones as Devane's wartime buddy, Dabney Coleman, and Linda Haynes as the love interest.

The film opens to Devane's hero's welcome. A local car dealer expresses the populace's gratitude by bestowing on him a brand new Cadillac and a silver dollar for every day he was held captive in "Hanoi's hellhole." Such a generous greeting was most often reserved for the POWs as opposed to the run-of-the-mill returning veterans. He graciously accepts his hometown's best wishes.

Perhaps the dust cover from the Blockbuster Video store best summarizes the plot: "After returning home to San Antonio, a former Vietnam P.O.W. loses his hand, and his family to a gang of repulsive thugs. Outfitted with a razorsharp hook, and aided by a fellow vet and a hitchhiker (blonde Haynes), he trails the killers to Juarez." Bear in mind that this blurb was meant to entice, not dissuade, teenage boys to rent this particular video.

Prior to the violence perpetrated on the vet's family, he had already figuratively lost his family. His wife had a new lover, and his child did not even know him. After the thugs rob and kill his family, they necessitate the claw hand by putting the veteran's arm down a kitchen disposal! It is a disgusting scene and is used as the justifying impetus to a veteran's tale of revenge. *Rolling Thunder* lacks pretension about violence in our society. It is a simple tale that allows the veterans, as victims of all manner of injustice, to entertain the audience by utilizing their combat experience and ordnance expertise in domestic service. Obviously such a heinous crime could elicit a violent response from any husband and father. Therefore prior to this scene the filmmakers have just hinted at a certain postincarnation oddness. In a bit of masochism Devane has challenged his wife's new suitor to torture him in a fashion that the North Vietnamese had employed. The boyfriend declines this peculiar request.

Like many veterans in preceding films, including *Taxi Driver*, the two vets carefully plan their mission of revenge. Devane and Jones relate much better than the lead character and his new girlfriend. Stereotypically, he is initially unresponsive to her carnal advances despite the fact that everybody else wants the comely blonde. In one particularly vicious integration of violence and sexuality, Major Rane hooks a bad guy in the crotch with his grafted weaponry.

Two major firefights are staged in the movie. One takes place in a stockyard. The other is set in a Mexican whorehouse, which subliminally seems to synthesize an uneasiness with sexuality and a Third World kind of setting in which to attack non–Caucasian lowlifes. Fellow vet Jones, lying in wait for the coordinated offensive, confounds the prostitute, in whom he shows no interest. In the climactic scene the evildoers are graphically but rather unrealistically slaughtered by the two veterans. Wounded in the process, the comrades help each other up and walk arm in arm out the door of the brothel. The asexual physical contact of the end provides the strongest example of touching in the movie.

In the course of the film several instances of stress trigger recollections of being in-country or in captivity. They are rendered in black and white so as to differentiate them from the present. The pilot is taunted as being a "fly boy." The title of the film ws the name given to the March 1965 air offensive against North Vietnam. Operation Rolling Thunder involved sustained and controversial bombing sorties.

In full exploitation of the film's bad taste, most of its publicity prominently featured the hook hand. Gilbert Adair summarizes the Hollywood mentality typified in *Rolling Thunder* when he says, "Vietnam was inextricably yoked to crime, with war-weary veterans attempting valiantly to 'go straight' but unable to shake off the lingering odor of carnage that attracted criminality to them and often brought about the violent death they had escaped on the battlefield."[17]

Black Sunday, a big-budget hit from Paramount, featured Bruce Dern as a former POW. The film integrated current global concerns about terrorism with the aftermath of the failed war effort. An international band of Black September terrorists assemble in Beirut to watch footage of then–Lieutenant Commander Dern being forced to confess war crimes in a crude North Vietnamese propaganda film. This same disgruntled vet has now approached the terrorists about making a grand and violent anti–American gesture. As he is now the pilot of the Goodyear blimp, a plot is hatched to rein terror down on the Super Bowl, hence the title.

Dern twitches and glares as an embittered psycho tortured by his wartime captors, cuckolded by his wife, demeaned at the VA, and now forgotten by his country. His grand traitorous gesture is "something to remember me by!" It is notable that most of the American forces brought to bear against the terrorists are ineffective. It is up to a savvy Israeli intelligence agent, played by Robert Shaw, to foil the heinous plot. The characterization of U.S. officialdom's impotency is a reflection of an intense American postwar self-doubt in this period.

By the late 1970s Chuck Norris had emerged as an international action star. He made his first foray into the realm of Vietnam veteran portrayals in *Good Guys Wear Black*. The title referred to the surreptitious nature of his character's in-country commando service during the war. Despite being set primarily in southern California, the film begins in 1973 in Paris as the peace talks are in the final stages of negotiation. To gain a last bargaining chip and prove the existence of additional POWs, the U.S. negotiator and the CIA decide to send Norris and his elite Black Tigers on a raid of a North Vietnamese stronghold to liberate captured Americans. In a much-used plot device (post–*The Losers*, pre–*Missing in Action*), this type of mission provides the opportunity for a lot of action with cheap sets and a lot of ambiguous political commentary.

As the commando team prepares for the operation, its members express concern that they not be the last U.S. casualties in the long war. Cheesy voiceover narration emanating from the peace talks tells us the war's end is imminent. Setting out from a desert terrain via helicopter, the men arrive about two seconds later in Vietnam. The raid takes place under cover of darkness, and the good guys wear black and camouflage face paint. Therefore it is often only the soldiers' teeth that reveal that any action at all is taking place in the chronically underexposed introductory sequence. A hasty retreat from the prison camp allows for spectacular explosions, which finally provide enough light for the raiders and the viewers to see the enemies as they line up smack dab in the line of fire. Every little grass hut seems to contain enough flammables to provide for spectacular secondary explosions. Norris, utilizing his real-life karate champion skills, dispatches communists in hand-to-hand combat. The commandos retreat to the appointed LZ (landing zone), but the helicopter never shows up. In the bush the heroic group sustains terrible losses, and only a few, including Norris's character, John T. Booker, are able to escape into the jungle.

The film then flashes forward five years to the present and finds the squad leader a teacher of political science. As if to confirm his manly nature, he is also a race car driver and has Anne Archer as a lover. In one of his lectures he explains that the Vietnam War was "beyond any kind of logic." The film then proceeds to tell the tale of how Norris and his men were betrayed by the suits and politicians who ran the government. A muddled plot surrounds the wartime double cross. Obviously by extension it is meant to exemplify the betrayal of all U.S. soldiers by the country's policymakers.

Among the villains are the secretary of state, played by James Franciscus, the amusingly named career bureaucrat and lush Edgar J. Harolds, played by Dana Andrews. Although not a psycho-type veteran character, Norris is wired enough to jump straight through an automobile windshield in order to kill the assassin of one of his surviving team members. Another team member, a mysterious Asian character Minh (as in Viet?), is sufficiently out of it to offer the following inadvertently comical query to his spook (CIA agent) contact: "Are you certain of your intelligence?"

It is hard to believe that Ted Post, the director of *Good Guys Wear Black*, is the same man who will helm the following year's very fine Vietnam war film, *Go Tell the Spartans*. The ad copy that accompanied the Norris film proclaimed, "In Vietnam, they were betrayed for peace. In America, they were marked for murder." The conspiracy and compromised military effort portrayed in Bruce Cohn and Mark Medoff's script struck a responsive chord in the American public. The movie led to another chopsocky (karate movie) sequel, with the same veteran character portrayed by Norris fighting drug pushers in 1979 in *A Force of One*. In another followup, the action star was similarly cast in *Forced Vengeance* in 1982.

Several years later Norris rode the revisionist avenge-and-win flick bandwagon with the back-to-Nam-to-liberate-our-boys tales in *Missing in Action* (1984), *Missing in Action II: The Beginning* (1985), and the final installment, *Braddock: Missing in Action III* (1988). Each of these films was remarkably unoriginal and similar to *Good Guys Wear Black*. They spent increasing amounts of time in-country as opposed to back in the United States. Each featured a mistrust of authority, the betrayal of the fighting soldiers, and an obsession with the peace talks as a symbol of compromise.

Another less familiar name making his first of several contributions to the genre was Filipino director Cirio Santiago. In collaboration with his mentor, American producer Roger Corman, he lensed *Fighting Mad* in his native land. It starred black action star Leon Isaac Kennedy; his wife, Jayne Kennedy; and James Inglehart. The intriguing premise was that an American GI is wounded and abandoned in the jungles of Southeast Asia. Instead of being captured by the current enemy, he falls into the hands of some old Japanese soldiers still fighting that war. This plot line underscored the ability to present a generic type of Asian enemy and thereby harkened metaphorically to the early films but was not as literally rooted in the previous conflict.

Boxing great Muhammad Ali portrayed himself in the screen biography *The Greatest*. Quite a bit of the film follows the controversy surrounding his draft refusal on religious and moral grounds. The world champion was stripped of his heavyweight title as a result. Ali states, "No Vietcong ever called me nigger," a refrain which was the title of a well known documentary made in 1968. Both reflected a militant Black perspective which rejected the opposition of one minority (Afro-American) against another (Oriental) in a "white man's war."

In the fall of 1977 Universal released *Heroes*. It starred Henry Winkler as a Vietnam veteran. His costar and catalyst to normalcy was Sally Field. The still-unknown actor Harrison Ford portrayed Winkler's buddy and fellow veteran. The film integrates comedic elements with drama and a love story via an on-the-road odyssey of discovery.

Jeremy Paul Kagan directed the film, and Lawrence Turman and David Foster produced it. Jack Nitzsche provided the musical score, while the pop-rock group Kansas provided a hit single in the form of the appropriately titled "Carry On My Wayward Son." The troubled veteran character does carry on, survive, and triumph. Real-life veteran Jim Carabatsos wrote the screenplay. His work represented the first production of a fictional film based entirely on the words of an actual veteran of the conflict. (Ten years later Carabatsos's second screenplay, the combat film *Hamburger Hill,* was produced.)

Heroes deals with the mental scars left on the veterans of the Vietnam War in the form of post-traumatic stress disorder. This disorder is characterized by depression, insomnia, and, in films, either a charming craziness or a flashback-induced violent psychosis. For the veteran in *Heroes* the illness initially manifests itself in the nutty, supposedly funny form to which Julius Vrooder succumbed in the 1974 film.

Heroes opens as Winkler enters an army recruiting office in Times Square. He interrupts the officer's gung-ho lecture to a group of pimply-faced prospectives and tells them it is all lies and that he should know. Police officers are called, and Winkler ends up back in the Veterans Administration hospital from which he had escaped. He is a favorite of his wardmates, some of whom date their stay back to Korea or World War II. Winkler dreams of starting a business, a worm farm. The other men entrust their savings to him to bankroll the scheme. It is a big responsibility for the troubled young vet.

In the first step in pursuit of his plan, Winkler needs to escape the confines of the hospital. He does so by masquerading as a doctor. In this scene John Cassavetes makes a cameo appearance as a VA physician. Using military lingo and training, Winkler organizes his party in a diversionary tactic that leads to a harmless search-and-destroy mission. After making his getaway, Winkler proceeds to the Port Authority. Here he meets another bus passenger, Sally Field, and the curmudgeonly driver, played by Val Avery. Most of the ensuing cross-country odyssey involves Winkler annoying the young woman, eluding the authorities, and eventually falling in love.

Winkler seeks out one of his partners, a good ole boy, played by Harrison Ford. The Camaro-driving "Ace" is currently mired in a sort of timid idiocy that tempts the local redneck population into derisive taunts of "Hey, soldier boy" at every opportunity. The genuine affection and understanding between the two vets are strongly demonstrated and bring out the best in Winkler. The two men share beers and reminisce, creating a sanitized nostalgia about their platoon and the conflict they experienced together. When Ford invites Winkler to fire his purloined M-16, the grunt buddy refuses. Ace urges him on saying, "The government spent all that time teaching you a skill." Since this is a different kind of veteran portrayal, the only firing done is directed toward the sky.

Much of the jargon the vets employ is government issue. In addition Ford is unable to take his dog tags off. Despite his friend's positive effect, Ford remains in the safety of his isolated rural home. When it comes time for the odyssey

Heroes (Universal Pictures, 1977). Sally Field comforts her beloved, flashback-tormented veteran, Henry Winkler.

to continue, he bestows his prized Camaro on Winkler. On the way to California Winkler and Field share their thoughts and a motel room. The inevitable question of sexual intimacy arises. Winkler nervously confides that "he hasn't been with a lady in a long time." Field tenderly touches his battle scar. This action is too frightening; and he runs out the door. He conveys fear of intimacy more than any explicit notion of impotence.

Having beat a hasty retreat, Winkler wanders about the little town. Two rednecks who earlier had taunted him for being a veteran beat and rob our hero. In his army pants he seeks out his attackers and in an effort to reclaim his belongings is beaten up. Only Field's quick action in Ace's Camaro saves our hero. She drives through the window of a bar, and the bloody vet climbs in as they peel out for California. Although the film continually touches on the trite conventions of violence, dysfunction, societal ingratitude, and bigotry, the screenplay manages to avoid stereotypical conclusions.

Field and Winkler continue their trek, and their love grows in an unconsummated way. Finally the travelers reach their ultimate destination: Eureka, California. The last partner from the old days is to be visited on behalf of the worm farm idea. Field accompanies Winkler as he goes to the home of his comrade, Larry. The soldier's mother answers the door and is delighted to welcome any friend of her son. As they go into the sitting room, we see a picture of Larry. His father proudly mentions his son's Distinguished Service Cross.

After these pleasantries Winkler politely inquires as to where Larry is now living. The mother goes ashen and breaks down in tears. Field and Winkler anxiously await an explanation for this sad reaction. Larry's father states what he knows should be obvious to Winkler: "Larry was killed over four years ago in Vietnam!" Winkler becomes hysterical and runs out into the street. There he begins a frightening flashback to a firefight in Vietnam. The movie protrays his psychotic dementia by crosscutting between the reality of cars and people and his superimposed images of these everyday objects as tanks and Viet Cong soldiers.

The flashback continues as the source of Winkler's mental problem is finally revealed. The film temporarily relinquishes the present to a scene set entirely during the war. Mortar fire envelops the platoon, and the soldiers try to evacuate onto helicopters caught in a hot LZ. Winkler is hit by small arms fire. Harrison Ford and the boy in the picture watch from the chopper. Seeing his friend go down, Larry jumps out and helps Winkler into the arms of their comrades. At the last second Larry is shot and killed. The helicopter lifts off.

The film rejoins a sobbing Winkler as he kneels in a vacant lot. He rails to Larry and the heavens, "You show off.... Why couldn't you stay in the helicopter?" He rages, he spits, he convulses in guilt and grief. The comforting hands of Field envelop him as she says, "You're alive." He rocks in her arms, and she tearfully intones, "Please don't be crazy.... I can't have you if you're crazy." He meekly smiles back, and the audience knows that together they are on their way to a new beginning.

Despite many flaws, the movie is ultimately a touching look at the Vietnam veteran's reentry into society. The cross-country odyssey is not only a journey of discovery for the film's title character but also part of a transition for all American society in the nature of its pop-cultural portraits of the war's veterans. As a serious attempt to deal with the effects of the war on the psyche of its veterans, *Heroes* represented a number of firsts. The theatrical feature was produced by a major studio and featured two up-and-coming stars. It was also a nonexploitative attempt to deal with a soldier's emotional trauma as a main element of the plot. It continued in-country footage and was actually seen by a large number of filmgoers.

The overall serious condition that *Heroes* dealt with was portrayed in the aforementioned 1974 release, *The Crazy World of Julius Vrooder*, and in the 1972 television movies *Welcome Home Johnny Bristol* and *The Forgotten Man*. In an exploitative and graphic vein, this condition was also portrayed in numerous movies, including *The Ravager* (1970), *Tracks* (1976), and *Rolling Thunder* (1976).

As far as real-life instances of emotional illness, it was estimated that 15 percent of combat veterans suffered from what the American Psychiatric Association officially recognized in 1980 as post-traumatic stress disorder.[18] To quote Michael Paris's historical and film-informed commentary: "In the case of Vietnam, adjustment problems were exaggerated by the divisive mood of the nation while the war was in progress. The [research] report claimed that over 60 percent of veterans studied either opposed the war at the time or did not understand why they were fighting. Returning home, the veteran was often castigated for going, called a 'murderer' and, in some perverse way, held responsible for America's defeat. In cinematic terms, the veteran who cleans up the streets, rescues the child prostitute, or executes a vicious killer when the police are unable to act is regaining the respect of the community and proving that he can be a 'winner' after all."[19]

As films began to seriously address the mental problems of the returning veterans, they also began to focus on the physically disabled. Each war had after a time featured these dramas that in their depiction of suffering and maiming were inherently antiwar. In October 1977 NBC broadcast a tale about a Vietnam paraplegic vet titled *Just a Little Inconvenience.* This story gained a great deal of poignancy because of its casting. Handsome actor James Stacy played the crippled Captain Kenny Briggs. Just a few years before this film was made, he had lost an arm and a leg in a motorcycle accident. Here in his return to acting, he brought a great deal of physical and emotional authenticity to the part.

Lee Majors, who as Andy Crocker had been television's first vet, played Briggs's friend, Captain Frank Logan. He produced the film with his actress wife at the time, Farrah Fawcett, for Universal Pictures. Theodore J. Flicker directed from the teleplay he wrote with Allan Balter. Barbara Hershey costarred as the female lead. The movie was based on a true story.

Just a Little Inconvenience begins in the beautiful snow-capped High Sierra Mountains in 1965. Two avid skiers traverse the slopes. Lee Majors and James Stacy are academy-trained officers who discuss their imminent departure to Vietnam. The next scene takes us forward four years. In a bit of costcutting, the southern California terrain inadequately serves as the setting for this in-country sequence. Stacy is ordered to lead his men into battle in an effort to save an ambushed platoon. Providing radio contact coordination of the effort is his old friend and fellow officer, Majors. A heavy firefight ensues, with American forces pinned down. At a critical moment the would-be reinforcements led by Stacy are themselves pinned down. Majors is forced to make a tactical calculation as to which group of men to rescue first. He objectively decides the other group is the preferred military option. Stacy does not believe that headquarters' decision accurately assesses his force's dire situation. In an effort to reach a command radio, he steps on a land mine. As it explodes the film shifts forward to San Francisco in 1971.

Majors in civilian garb enters a tavern with two tipsy fellow aerospace engineers. They flirt with some young ladies until Majors glimpses a solitary figure in the corner. He runs over and sees his old friend Stacy. Majors proclaims, "I spent a year trying to find you." A greasy, unshaven, drunk Stacy bitterly replies, "Take a good look at what you did to me." He then pushes his table aside and reveals himself in a wheelchair with stumps where his left arm and leg had been. Majors winces as he sees his old friend and ex–star athlete. Stacy continues to berate Majors, who finally leaves in embarrassment, disgust, and guilt.

In the next scene a Veterans Administration physician gives a weekly checkup to the withdrawn paraplegic. A few minutes later Majors has a consultation with the doctor, who chews him out for only now showing up to help his friend. Majors claims he lost touch when Stacy was evac'd out and then refused to respond to his inquiries from the field. Finally Majors asks what he must do to help. The doctor counsels him on how his friend is consumed by rage and self-pity. In an attempt to make others suffer with him, Stacy will not even wear his new prosthetics. He prefers to shock people by revealing his stumps.

The doctor sees Majors as a last resort to reach the embittered man. Majors hesitantly goes to Stacy's ward. He is revolted and frightened by the amputees he sees everywhere. Stacy once again berates Majors and tells him that his deployment of the reserve forces cost Stacy his limbs. This is a guilt trip and Majors storms out, but first he informs the doctor that he is still "in."

On the express medical and military orders of the doctor, Stacy is sent to meet Majors at a ski resort. Majors appeals to Stacy's fighting athletic spirit by telling him about a post–World War II German program that rehabilitated amputees through skiing. Stacy is skeptical, but as a onetime champion, he accepts the challenge. Majors tosses Stacy a specially constructed ski that when tucked under a stump and strapped to the shoulder approximates a leg and a ski pole. In a quiet, continuous take, Stacy attempts to strap the contraption on and stand up. He constantly falls down, and the only sound is his grunting as he tries to make the thing work. Majors deliberately shoos away a bystander who attempts to help. This is a frustrating and tragic sequence that ultimately ends in failure as Stacy lays on the snow exhausted.

After hurling some more emotional bile at Majors, Stacy returns the next day to attempt mastering the task. The next few scenes feature the men renewing their friendship as the anger subsides. Stacy begins to remaster the ability to ski, becomes more outgoing, and pays more attention to his appearance. Now showing a real interest in his rehabilitation, Stacy successfully modifies the ski. He also begins to wear his prosthetics whenever he is not skiing.

After some final confrontations and making up, Majors and Stacy sit together in the chalet bar having a drink. Barbara Hershey walks in, and she and Stacy are immediately attracted to each other. The two of them flirt as the lovely schoolteacher remains unaware of Stacy's condition. The next day Stacy traverses the slopes as Hershey dismounts from the lift and is taken aback by the sight of his stumps. He reacts by saying, "Disgusting, isn't it?" and skis away. Majors thought Stacy had told her. She is hurt and frightened as Majors explains the facts about his West Point, ski champion friend.

That night Hershey goes to Stacy's room and lays into him for shocking her that way. Together Majors and Hershey as "normies" attempt to understand the "amp." With great patience they are able to penetrate Stacy's defenses. Hershey falls in love with Stacy, whom she has to convince time and again of her feelings.

We also learn more about the reality of the situation that confronted Majors and necessitated his difficult wartime decision. Eventually the healthy emotional and physical love that Stacy shares with Hershey and the vigor he derives from his beloved skiing renew him. They also make him finally realize the inner pain and turmoil that have gripped his supposedly healthy friend, Majors, all these years. Now it is Stacy who forces Majors to confront his emotional demons. The amputee in his forgiveness and understanding is able to share the gift of internal peace.

In the end the three ski off into the sunset as Stacy remarks that his lack of an arm and a leg are "just a little inconvenience." Some criticized this true story as being as facile as its name implies. However, at this juncture in this book, the movie was a welcome effort on behalf of physically damaged Vietnam war veterans.

The last entry in this chapter is fitting as a transitional movie. Robert Aldrich's *Twilight's Last Gleaming* is an example of a film that some observers felt had little or nothing to do with Vietnam. As such it represented the end of the movies that necessitated cryptic recontextualizations or metaphorical analyses of the conflict. By the next year such works would be rendered obsolete with the surge in direct portrayals of the war.

Twilight's Last Gleaming was a multinational coproduction financed by both Allied Artists and West Germany's Bavaria Studios. It told the story of a former air force major, played by Burt Lancaster, who is relieved of his command because of an unsubstantiated murder charge. He has been framed because of his opposition to the Vietnam War. Along with three other inmates, he escapes from prison and takes over a Montana nuclear missile silo. Then threatening to start World War III, he attempts to blackmail the president, played by Charles Durning, into making public the notes of a cabinet meeting that took place early in the Vietnam War. In essence, "the document reveals that the president and his advisers were fully aware that the war could never be won and that they decided to continue it to prove to the Soviet Union that the United States was capable of irrational and inhuman acts. All the years of slaughter were nothing but a warning . . . to America's Cold War enemies."[20]

Twilight's Last Gleaming, as in the lyrics of "The Star Spangled Banner," represented one of the last films from mini-major studio Allied Artists before its corporate demise. (It was bought out by Lorimar, which was in turn purchased by Warner Bros. in a typical pattern of industry consolidation.) Further typifying the end-of-an-era aspects of the production, the director overused the once avant-garde technique of the split-screen image. Somehow the picture managed to integrate all the worst antimilitary left-wing paranoia in a kind of *Seven Days in May* warning about right-wing extremism and American nuclear capacity. It is an extremely long and peculiar movie with confusing and ambiguous antiwar sentiments.

On the subject of film politics, but specifically on *Hearts and Minds*, film critic Andrew Sarris writes, "It is . . . simplistic, tendentious, disorganized, and repetitious. Its onesidedness verges on vulgarity. . . . Ultimately, the images . . . vulgarize the enormous complexities of the subject."[21] Then in a generally apropos observation, Sarris declares, "Indeed it can be argued that all films are ultimately political either as statements or as evasions. When one looks back on the cinema one is startled by the infrequency with which Vietnam was mentioned. Yet this infrequency is in itself significant in that it reflects a society emotionally detached from that particular war. I suppose that there is an active and passive way to interpret this information. The active way is to scold (as a critic) the film industry for not making more movies about Vietnam. The passive way is to report the reluctance of the studios as a symptom of the public's lack of interest in the war."[22]

One more analysis of the medium pertinent to the transition in this book to well-known head-on entries about to come is contained in the article "The Filmmaker as Historian." In it Robert Brent Toplin states, "Attention to the filmmaker's craft is particularly important, because film producers, directors, writers, and editors are today assuming the role of the historian for larger and larger audiences."[23] The most important concept that the present work attempts to demonstrate is that for the young people of America, perceptions of the Vietnam War are more controlled by the imagery contained in *Platoon* and *Apocalypse Now* and the other films discussed than by any school text or adult dialogue on the conflict.

As a multifaceted controversy the Vietnam War does not lend itself to easy and abbreviated analysis. However, as academician Toplin points out, "Producers argue [that] a film quickly loses its audience to confusion and boredom if it attempts to present a detailed and highly complicated perspective on a topic. Because filmmakers must remain sensitive to an audience's reception in an industry in which production expenses are high and commercial marketability is essential, [they] must reduce their message to a principal idea and repeat the thesis over and over again in a variety of ways. Such a strategy may strengthen viewer ratings and clarify the audience's understanding, but it cannot satisfy . . . [those who search] for a sophisticated analysis that recognizes ambiguity and complexity."[24]

The director of *Hearts and Minds*, Peter Davis, observes that films work best when they excite feeling and emotion. Producer Bert Schneider "pointed out that he would not want to get his history from historical films any more than he would want to get his science from science fiction."[25] This concept of emotive stimulus will be particularly relevant in the analysis of the combat films about to be released. As bloody action-oriented features, they are most powerful in their inherent visceral nature, regardless of any intended political perspective. This is precisely why such scenes as the final firefight in *Platoon*, the morning helicopter charge in *Apocalypse Now*, the Russian roulette game in *The Deerhunter*, and the exploding arteries in *Born on the Fourth of July* will remain with the viewer much longer than the implied or quasi-encrypted politics of a John Wayne, an Oliver Stone, a John Milius, or a Burt Schneider.

In discussing the monumental reentry of television into the fray of Vietnam analysis in 1978 in the 13-part PBS documentary *Vietnam: A Television History,* Toplin notes that "no film on a controversial subject . . . can assume complete non-partisanship."[26] But in a countervailing argument concerning ambiguity, television drama producer Peter B. Cook reiterates that "ambiguity is the key to effective drama."[27]

Characterizing the controversial analysis of the use of the Russian roulette metaphor for brutality in the upcoming *The Deerhunter,* many were stymied by the lack of credible evidence that this cruel form of torture was ever truly perpetrated by the enemy against American prisoners of war. Perhaps that controversy, which embroiled the film community in both political and film critiques, is somewhat irrelevant. As Daniel J. Walkowitz states in another scholarly historical perspective on this debate, "Visual History: The Craft of the Historian-Filmmaker," "Particular details may be negotiated in a historical drama, so long as the overriding conceptual framework remains inviolate."[28] Toplin frames the question this way: "How should appropriate questions about accuracy and responsible representation apply to the loose treatment of fact evident in historical dramas?"[29]

In conclusion to this chapter's analysis and in preparation for the fecund objects of exploration about to come, let us consider Toplin's somewhat paradoxical remarks:

> A greater problem is the separation of the storytellers in two different worlds. Very few historians are significantly involved in the making of historical films, and very few filmmakers are themselves impressively literate in the scholarship of subjects they address in film. The division of territories, with one group assuming charge of written activity and the other of visual representation, has disturbing implications in the age of the electronic media. Filmmakers, assuming the role of historians, are interpreting the past for even larger audiences in the late twentieth century. Academicians often bemoan this state of affairs, troubled by a sense that flashy salesmen are intruding on their turf and marketing colorful packages to gullible clients. They fear for a future in which the public's historical "literacy" will be drawn from superficial products of the media. But expressions of anger and contempt will not make filmed history go away: the public's enthusiasm for it is likely to grow in the decades ahead.[30]

Toplin's analysis harkens back to this chapter's introduction and its discussion of the evolution of the imagery's means of transmission. Many conventional analyses of Vietnam War films begin where the next chapter does, in 1978. All that has preceded was deemed irrelevant to the group of films. To be comprehensive and acknowledge the concept of omission as well as commission, the preceding chapters were essential. Other books' conventionally abbreviated treatments are also often strident in their film criticism or political analysis. In the mid–1990s, given the tragic and controversial nature of the conflict, this methodology clouds, rather than clarifies, the investigation of Vietnam War movies. A familiarity with a comprehensive list of movies, aided by the reader's personal analysis through history and the screening of available films, is most worthwhile.

The paradox of Vietnam film output now comes into unmistakable focus with the production boom typified by the four horsemen and the apocalypse.

References

1. *World Almanac and Book of Facts* (New York: Pharos Books, 1990).

2. Clark Douglas and Stephen Weiss, *The American Experience in Vietnam* (Boston: Boston Publishing, 1988), p. 161.

3. Ronald Ribman, "The Final War of Olly Winter," in *Great Television Plays*, ed. William J. Kaufman (New York: Dell, 1969), pp. 259–301.

4. Marshall McLuhan and Quentin Fiore, *The Medium Is the Message* (New York: Bantam Books, 1967), p. 128.

5. *Ibid.*, p. ii.

6. *Ibid.*, p. 131.

7. *Ibid.*

8. Michael Paris, "The American Film Industry in Vietnam," *History Today*, July 18, 1988, p. 35.

9. Dave Kehr, "The Reel Difference," *Chicago Tribune*, February 22, 1991, sec. 3, p. 1.

10. *Variety's Directory of Major U.S. Show Business Awards* (New York: Reed Publishing, 1989).

11. Mason Wiley and Damien Bona, *Inside Oscar: The Unofficial History of the Academy Awards* (New York: Ballantine Books, 1986), p. 504.

12. *Ibid.*, p. 504.

13. *Ibid.*, p. 506.

14. *Ibid.*

15. *Ibid.*, p. 507.

16. *Ibid.*

17. Gilbert Adair, *Vietnam on Film* (London: Proteus, 1981), p. 101.

18. "Post Traumatic Stress Disorder," *Chicago Tribune*, March 2, 1990, p. 6.

19. Paris, "The American Film Industry in Vietnam," p. 36.

20. Jay Hyams, *War Movies* (New York: Gallery Books, 1984), p. 197.

21. Andrew Sarris, *Politics and Cinema* (New York: Columbia University Press, 1978), p. 103.

22. *Ibid.*, p. 6.

23. Robert Brent Toplin, "The Filmmaker as Historian," *American Historical Review* 93, 7 (December 1988), p. 1212.

24. *Ibid.*, p. 1213.

25. *Ibid.*

26. *Ibid.*, p. 1226.

27. *Ibid.*, p. 1227.

28. Daniel J. Walkowitz, "Visual History: The Craft of the Historian-Filmmaker," *Public Historian* 7 (Winter 1985), p. 60.

29. Toplin, "The Filmmaker as Historian," p. 1224.

30. *Ibid.*, p. 1226.

Chapter 5

The Four Horsemen, 1978

The title of this chapter refers to the four notable Vietnam War films that appeared in 1978. They were *The Boys in Company C, Go Tell the Spartans, Coming Home,* and *The Deerhunter.* They were important because they represented a renewed effort to deal with the traumatic conflict in a direct manner. Each of the films suggested the healthy healing process that allowed for examination of their subject matter without physical or metaphorical recontextualization and that, by extension, permitted the allocation of financial resources to the production. Other films that appeared this year will also be examined.

The Boys in Company C began in boot camp in the United States and then followed the recruits to Vietnam. It featured several combat sequences and was infused with instances of black comedy and cynicism about the military command structure. It was the first major studio release featuring extensive in-country combat since the gung-ho *The Green Berets* some ten years before. *Go Tell the Spartans* dealt with the early years of U.S. involvement in Vietnam and offered a glimpse as to how the country became bogged down in that quagmire. The film took place entirely in-country.

Coming Home was a serious A film examination of a crippled veteran and his rehabilitation and reintegration back in the United States and the changes the war wrought in the lives of those touched by it. *The Deerhunter* was a very controversial film that examined the war in a richly textured tale of life cycle events and male bonding interrupted and irreversibly altered by the conflict that engulfed its characters and, by extension, the entire nation.

The reemergence of the combat film did not by any means preclude the existence of other types of portraits. Serious examinations of the returning veterans and their problems still coexisted with exploitation films. Films evolved away from the campus unrest movies endemic to the 1960s and early 1970s and joined with coming-of-age dramas that indirectly concerned the war.

For the gamble of producing a full-budget and serious A movie production on the Vietnam War, American producers remained "gun shy." As stories and screenplays began to surface, domestic financing sources remained very frightened about the commercial potential of such film portraits. Therefore money for strong dramas was more forthcoming from foreign sources less traumatized by the conflict.

As production commenced on the new crop of direct portrayals of the Vietnam War, the traditional domestic Hollywood studios, such as Columbia, Warner Bros., and Paramount, began the preparation for selling and distributing these titles. Hong Kong producer Raymond Chow bankrolled *The Boys in Company C,* and the English firm EMI financed *The Deerhunter.* In the years to come English producers from Hemdale would ensure that *Platoon* and *The Killing Fields* got off the ground. Additional French, Taiwanese, Israeli, Italian, and other foreign money contributed to the flow of relevant product.

At the tail end of the transition-to-peacetime years, films such as *Rolling Thunder* and *Good Guys Wear Black* continued to feature veteran characters in ways similar to the preceding motorcycle and sign-of-the-times films. But each began to offer a certain postwar political ambiguity as an undercurrent. Acquiescing to the conventional wisdom and predominant opinion, the war was condemned. However, the individual soldier was often lionized as a superhero. The elite special forces of *The Green Berets* became the commandos of *Good Guys Wear Black.* The crack shooting in *Targets* became the handy gunplay in *Rolling Thunder.* Eventually superhuman comic book status would be bestowed on the vet in vehicles such as *Rambo* and its sequels.

"Implicit in all these features is the notion that the American fighting man (especially the Green Berets) is equal to any situation, hence if America lost the war it must be attributable to other more sinister reasons."[1] The mistreatment of the vet upon his return home in such films as *Mean Johnny Barrows, Green Eyes,* and *Gordon's War* is repeated in the in-country features. The stab in the back and double-cross from the powers that be leave the individual soldier in a position of weakness. *Good Guys Wear Black* posited such a theory in a cynical and vaguely hawkish way.

Eventually, despite widespread disagreement about the war, its motivations, its conduct, and so on, the American public would at least coalesce in a united assumption that the overriding lesson of the war was that if Americans are going to fight, Americans should fight to win. Anyone who doubts this eventual conclusion need only examine the Persian Gulf War debate of twenty years later, so informed with the trauma, imagery, and legacy of the Vietnam conflict.

William J. Palmer, writing in *The Films of the Seventies—A Social History,* somewhat gruesomely sums up the process that began in the transition-to-peacetime years and reached fruition in the period associated with the release of the four horsemen. "Since 1976, the movies have been picking persistently at the scab of memory." He then chides Hollywood for producing portrayals of the Vietnam War that were for the most part "misguided, insensitive, exploitative, cliched, unauthentic and just plain stupid."[2] Other Vietnam films he rejects as largely irrelevant to the war itself. But they were all that Americans had and they did reflect unpopular aspects of the war in film.

As part of what I identify herein as an evolving process, Palmer points out the similarities of the films covered in the previous chapter, *Taxi Driver, Rolling Thunder,* and *Heroes,* with the first film to be examined in this chapter, the 1978 release

Who'll Stop the Rain. Each contains "a climactic firefight scene meant to conjure images of Vietnam."[3] In both *Taxi Driver* and *Rolling Thunder* the vet unleashes his weaponry and fury in a brothel. In *Heroes* it is the emotional breakdown at the dead vet's parents' home that triggers the finale's flashback to conflict in Nam. All of these film characters thus exhibit behavior that in the years ahead would be associated with post-traumatic stress disorder. For a few years this condition was referred to more specifically as PVS, or post–Vietnam syndrome.

Who'll Stop the Rain and its source novel may have been popular precisely because they managed to incorporate elements of every identified strand of orientation in the Vietnam film series in an overriding tone of war-generated cynicism, betrayal, and disgust. The movie offered instances of exploitation and action mayhem along with the drama associated with the veterans' problems of mental health and reintegration. Also, there are in-country combat footage and domestic sign-of-the-times attention to drug usage, the old hippie commune lifestyle, antiwar sentiment and so on. Finally the film includes the popular late-1960s throwback to refracted imagery: a war correspondent as narrator.

This United Artists release was an adaptation of Robert Stone's novel *The Dog Soldiers.* In fact for a presumably more literarily attuned European audience, the film was released via that title overseas. Britain's Karel Reisz directed the Judith Rascoe screenplay, which the original work's author had attempted to help fashion but refused to be associated with in its final form. The film starred Nick Nolte as Vietnam vet Ray, Tuesday Weld as female lead Marge, and Michael Moriarity as the amoral member of the media. Each character was an inchoately rendered representative of greater societal problems and Vietnam-induced trauma. The film's extended in-country beginning shifts its locus to the United States for the balance of the feature. As such it managed to mirror the process that had actually taken place in the real world once the war was over.

Even before the credits roll, war correspondent and narrator Moriarity hits the dirt amid huge explosions. Friendly fire casualties result from the ubiquitous helicopters. Moriarity obscurely observes, "In a world where elephants are pursued by flying men, people naturally want to get high." Apparently this line is meant to summarize the assumption that the war was an absurd waste. An industrial power used its technology to bomb the jungle of this Asian country, metaphorically the home of elephants. The troops got high, the youth of America got stoned, and all this ridiculous reality is somehow a justification for the actions of the correspondent in the film's next scene.

He decides to smuggle heroin out of Southeast Asia and enlists the help of his friend Nick Nolte. Immorality joins with quintessential Ugly Americanism when the two characters try to make sense of the crazed environment. Facing death in combat or covering a war had at least at one time provided moments of epiphanous self-awareness. Now all the characters can come up with is the following exchange: "Don't they say that this is the place where everybody finds out who they are?" Moriarity asks. Nolte's only reply is, "What a bummer for the gooks."

This is an inglorious war, and morality seems to have broken down for all concerned. Moriarity's wife is a drug addict. The cops back in Oakland are corrupt, the politicians are crooks, the allies are black-marketeers, and the soldiers are dopers. Nolte makes stateside contact with Moriarity's wife Weld, while two disgusting Vietnam vets, played by Richard Masur and Ray Sharkey, pursue the heroin.

Romantically involved Weld and Nolte make a getaway to a deserted commune complete with a megasound-wired amphitheater. This setting, along with the title, harks back to the song of the same name by Creedence Clearwater Revival, which nostalgically recalls flower power. In the finale there is a firefight in the amphitheater amid rock and roll and strobing lights. Nolte, armed to the teeth, brings machine-gun-toting defiance to his last stand. Wounded, he bleeds to death alone in the vast isolation of the desert. Moriarity and Weld bury him, and the only words of eulogy are the familiar "Semper Fi." The much-sought-after heroin blows away like dust in the New Mexico winds.

For the combatants and the other victims of the war, cynicism and self-awareness were some of the nonlethal results of the conflict. As demonstrated in the previous chapters, confronting the draft and doing military service were profound and sobering influences that led to growing up. In the in-country and direct-combat films about to come out, the forging under literal fire was an extreme example of "a rite of passage" into adulthood.

As a transition from indirect to direct, two films from the summer of 1978 featured high schoolers and young adults on the cusp of adulthood whose crucible was to be the war in Vietnam. In *Our Winning Season*, directed by Joseph Ruben, the specter of the war hangs over the life of high school track star Scott Jacoby. Similarly but more overtly, the war forces an end to a last summer of innocence in the 1978 release *Big Wednesday*. The movie was primarily about surfing and afforded an opportunity for tanned hunks such as Jan Michael Vincent and William Katt to display their pecs. Eventually the beach music and lifestyle are forced to give way to the reality of war. However, the closest the film physically gets to Vietnam is the induction center and halfhearted attempts at feigned homosexuality and other possible deferments and exemptions. (The ruses are nowhere near as funny or elaborate as in *Greetings* or *The Gay Deceivers*). In a prewar setting the film is obsessed with male bonding and the ego-oriented challenge of catching the big wave. Aside from the photography of Bruce Surtees and the surfing scenes, the musical soundtrack featured now nostalgic 1960s (not 1950s) pop by Carole King, the Four Seasons, and Trini Lopez, among others. Most notable about the production of *Big Wednesday* is the credit for the machismo-hound John Milius as writer and director and Buzz Feitshans as producer. Together in one of those capacities these men would be associated with such Vietnam-related films as *Rambo, Uncommon Valor, Apocalypse Now,* and *Flight of the Intruder*.

In a progression to 1978's four watershed films, other entries bear mentioning. One is the fascinating portrait of moviemaking afforded via the troubled Viet veteran title character in *The Stuntman*. Richard Rush directed Steven Railsback, Peter O'Toole, and Barbara Hershey. The black comedy blurred the distinction between reality and make-believe. Fugitive drifter Railsback saves the leading lady from drowning, only to learn that he has interrupted filming. O'Toole as the intrigued director hires him on the spot. The mysterious young man's daring includes daredevil techniques he learned from the "gooks." He occasionally offers glimpses into his wartime past to his new lover, Hershey. He compares the war to a plague or a disease. His cryptic anecdotes employ pithy summations such as that stepping on a "Betty Booby" trap was not the problem: stepping off was. He lost many friends and admits he shot at anything that moved. When he returned home people looked at him "like I was going to start killing babies or something." This comment in conjunction with the growing suspicion/ paranoia tht the director (general) is callously risking Railsback's life in ever-more-dangerous stunts synthesizes the analogy between the filmmaking and war-making worlds. It coincidentally resonates with the concomitantly checkered production reports coming from the set of *Apocalypse Now* over in the Philippines. That film's release, delayed until 1979, really underscored cinema and war analogies. Unable to get a handle on how to sell *The Stuntman*, the studio did not distribute it for an additional two years after its completion.

American International Pictures released *Youngblood*, starring Lawrence-Hilton Jacobs as a vet returning to the Los Angeles ghetto. He recruits fellow vets to combat the urban scourge of drugs. This allows for action sequences against the pushers. However, the Neal Nosseck–directed film does take a serious dramatic look at the problems as well. This slice of street life is enhanced by a score by the group War.

In the realm of the newly created medium of the made-for-television movie was *My Husband Is Missing*. Richard Michaels directed the film, broadcast on NBC on December 5, 1978. It starred Sally Struthers as a young wife who goes to North Vietnam in an effort to obtain information on his MIA pilot husband, a plot line similar to that of *Limbo* back in 1972. On her journey she is joined by Tony Musante as a Canadian journalist who hopes to find a human interest story. He does, but it is not professional. He falls in love with Struthers, who does not even know if her husband is alive. James Hong appeared as a Vietnamese official. This role offered a slight variation on the characters he had or would portray in a number of films, including *Go Tell the Spartans*, *Missing in Action*, and *The Forgotten Man*. Rather melodramatically, *My Husband Is Missing* was originally entitled *The Reach of Love*.

As real-life attempts to determine the fate of MIAs proved inconclusive, frustration laid the groundwork for escapist and cathartic rescue movies on behalf of the POWs and MIAs. Such fictions would allow for triumphs not experienced on the battlefield and would corroborate the allegedly dishonorable nature of the enemy.

Before America could attempt to triumph fictionally in the war, it had to first more truthfully lose the war. *The Boys in Company C* was a Columbia Pictures

The Boys in Company C (Columbia Pictures, 1978). **A studio struggles with the marketing of Vietnam.**

release of a Golden Harvest film produced in 1977 and distributed in 1978. Producer Raymond Chow was a Hong Kong–based international film mogul. Director Sidney J. Furie wrote the screenplay along with Rick Natkin.

This initial foray back into the long-abandoned combat genre vis-à-vis Vietnam was quite dualistic in nature. On the one hand, its tone was one of antiwar cynicism and disgust. Coproducer Max Youngstein felt that by 1978 "America was ready to look back at what happened in Vietnam, warts and all."[4] The war effort is shown to be purposeless, led by idiotic officers who risk their mens' lives for personal and "corporate" gain based on inflated body counts and other false indices of battlefield success. The South Vietnamese allies are dismissed as cowardly, corrupt, and incompetent. The civilian populace is either VC, tragically and fatally suspected as being such, or noble and most often beautiful innocents awaiting slaughter at the hands of misguided combatants. Chaos, waste, compromise, and purposelessness lead to an inevitable sense of an obscenely flawed U.S. presence in the conflict.

On the other hand, *The Boys in Company C* narratively wrapped itself in the clichéd formulaics of many preceding war films. The modern indictment of the U.S. role in the recently concluded and immensely unpopular conflict is somewhat tempered and dated by the familiarity of the stock characters. The viewers follow their lives from induction through basic training and on to Nam. The attempted black and antimilitary comedy is more reminiscent of the recontextualized forms in films such as *M*A*S*H*.

Reflecting some of the uncertainty about the film's identity, at least from a marketing point of view, was the print ad campaign copy. It read, "The Real Vietnam," with an underline for emphasis. Then in staccato bursts of hyperbole the copy continued, "They lived it . . . died for it . . . wished to God they could forget it."

In case the public was not ready for this indictment of the United States presence, the narrative style at least bred familiarity and noncontroversy. The movie proceeded from *Tribes*-like basic training to action sequences of ultimately unavoidable excitement. Paradoxically any such return to combat sequences elicits an exhilarating reaction no matter how strong its preceding negativism. Aside from the tragedy of death, especially for the young, perhaps the film's most effective and original means of conveying its cynical perspective is the totally unseen nature of the enemy. The nervous young men are attacked immediately by VC upon their arrival in-country and continually ambushed either in the field or in supposedly safe havens. The futility of such a response is joined by the nagging uncertainty of combatant/noncombatant identification and the question of whether the real enemy is the North Vietnamese and VC or the Americans' own muddled war effort.

The film begins in August 1967 as five young conscripts report for duty at the U.S. Marine Corps depot in San Diego. To the strains of "From the Halls of Montezuma," the young men take leave of civilian life. Stan Shaw was Tyrone Washington, a big black kid from Chicago. Andrew Stevens was Billy Ray Pike, an athletic good ole boy from Galveston. Michael Lembeck was Vinnie Fazio, a gregarious Italian-American from Brooklyn. Craig Wasson was Dave Bisbee, a long-haired draft evader from Seattle who is delivered courtesy of the FBI. The last character is the narrator, who has provided these introductions. James Canning played Alvin Foster, the diarist from Kansas who provides the running audio commentary, a reflection of his note taking as a would-be journalist about to embark on the adventure of his life. In providing the narrator's voice and the viewer's perspective, Alvin joins the much more cynical Moriarity journalist-spokesperson in *Who'll Stop the Rain* and Fowler in *The Quiet American*. All of them have been our eyes and ears on this bloody conflict. A voiceover perspective will also be used in *Apocalypse Now* and *Platoon*.

The foul-mouthed drill instructure, Sergeant Loyce, attempts to form this motley crew of undisciplined raw recruits into a marine fighting unit, the men in Company C. This role marked the acting debut of real-life drill instructor and Vietnam veteran R. Lee Ermey. (The same type of role earned the tough guy rave reviews ten years later in *Full Metal Jacket*.) The steps in boot camp are familiar, with the training rigorous and dehumanizing. The "pukes" are destined for a tour of duty in Vietnam at the height of the raging conflict. Ermey clarifies the deadly nature of their future. To learn to kill is the order of the day; the alternative is to be killed.

Despite a growing professional competency, the men remain a disparate lot. A product of the ghetto, Shaw initially schemes to smuggle drugs back in the relative security of plastic body bags,. Unlike the weak Moriarity in *Who'll Stop the Rain*, the immorality of these activities ultimately dissuades the young black man (as it does the pilots in *Saigon* and *Air America*, who had similar opportunities to profit from contraband).

The waspy Kansas farm boy and the New York ethnic form a friendship, with the former's sensitive writer's perspective in stark contrast to the womanizing obsession of the latter. In preparation for a similar draftee's role in the upcoming *Go Tell the Spartans*, Craig Wasson as the ex-hippie espouses pacifism and plays folk songs on his guitar.

By October the unit can, in the words of Canning, "do no wrong." It is no surprise when each of the five characters is assigned to Vietnam. On the boat over Scott Hylands is introduced as Captain Collins. He is an idiot who espouses a theory that playing the "gooks'" sport of soccer will help the new marines learn to think like the enemy. After three months of advanced training and 40 movie minutes, the boat docks at Cam Ranh Bay. It is January 1968, and the Tet Offensive is under way. No sooner have the men reached shore than they come under heavy rocket bombardment on the dock. Now that the men are in-country, the enemy will remain faceless, quietude will constantly be disrupted by instances of death and danger, and any sense of overall military purpose will remain nebulous.

The men's first assignment is to accompany Captain Collins as they transport vital items to a forward position via convoy. In contrast to the stupid captain, a much more caring guidance is offered by Lieutenant Archer, played by James Whitmore, Jr. As helicopters continually fly overhead, the new arrivals try to absorb the sights and sounds of this beautiful but dangerous country. They must remain vigilant, maintain their "intervals," be on guard for booby traps, unseen VC snipers, and so on. For an audience in 1978, these realities of war in Vietnam in 1968 juxtaposed with the almost surrealistic presence of snippets of Americana in a far-off Third World land (e.g., bowling alleys and Budweisers) provided a detail-rich environment.

After the convoy is ambushed, the "essential" nature of the cargo is revealed: cartons of Jim Beam and cigarettes. This renders the loss of two men in the process of its delivery an obscene reminder of a wasteful and misguided war effort. The sensitive Wasson harangues the captain, who swears ignorance. Now deeper in-country, the men set off on their own agendas for a 24-hour liberty. Aside from an Esther Williams pool, a snack bar, and movies, the additional in-country pleasures of dope and hookers are readily available. Wasson goes off with his guitar and a claymore to blow up a cushy trailer destined for a general up the road. Such luxury in the midst of squalor and death is repugnant to him.

Observers sometimes criticized the movie's reliance on stereotypes, even though tempered by the newly represented negative imagery of sloppy discipline, whoring, drug use, and dealing. These manifestations of purposelessness and fear were appropriate, but they were perhaps more reflective of 1970s in-country morale problems than of anything at this 1960s juncture.

As a unit under Shaw's corporal and natural leadership, the young men function together as they attempt to save the life of the overdosing Stevens. The northern black man saves the southern cracker in a typical bit of in-country color-blind heroism. The men then proceed to a series of adventures in now-familiar locations such as Da Nang and Con Thien. On patrol the troops "hump" through the paddies, encounter booby traps and mines, and fight the heat and dysentery. All these travails are no longer noble adventures but rather the unromantic reality of survival.

While in a rice paddy, Washington steps on a pressure mine. Andrew Stevens returns the lifesaving favor when he disarms the activated explosive. The patrol, now back on the road, comes to an elevated bridge. The dimwitted captain tries to assess the "risk factor" in crossing. As an academy (read, political/institutional) product of the system, he of course miscalculates the danger. The career officer lieutenant counsels that to cross could lead to an ambush. Concerned about the timetable and lack of body count, the captain ignores the advice and the patrol proceeds. It indeed comes under heavy fire and lacking proper interval spacing, sustains heavy casualties.

In a vengeful mood the captain orders an air strike on the nearby village suspected of harboring the VC responsible for the attack. Lacking proper intelligence and firsthand observation, Wasson challenges the captain in another bit of unreal insubordination. In scenes that integrate incompetence with atrocious morality, the American soldiers proceed into the hamlet. The finding of a tunnel system seems to vindicate the captain's contention as to the presence of the enemy.

Old-fashioned innocence and Americana ironically blend with viciousness. The young men play baseball with a teenager suspected of being VC. From headquarters a helicopter arrives with a South Vietnamese interrogator. It turns out to be a corrupt and corpulent ARVN officer, Trang, played by Vic Diaz. Accompanying him is a humorless Aryan automaton special forces officer. They take the young man off for questioning as Stevens and Wasson protest.

As the men continue on they hear a shot and surmise that the questioning had turned into a bush execution. With a soulful countenance enhanced by closeups of massive features and big eyes, Shaw and his evolved consciousness in the midst of the carnage is joined by the others' growing awareness. Stevens refuses to play soccer for the captain, whom he holds responsible for the murder of the young Vietnamese. Wasson reconfirms his pacifism and sings sad folk songs. Canning writes everything down. Worsening the already poor morale are the interceptions of Hanoi Hannah's broadcasts, which remind the troops of just how lovely the weather is this time of year in Sweden.

The caring lieutenant manages to catch Shaw before he can "frag" the captain during a firefight. The lieutenant convinces the corporal to console himself by spending a million dollars, by which he means playing the game and calling in an air strike to destroy enemy positions on the hill. They radio in coordinates on an abandoned position and fabricate a body count to satiate the hierarchy. What follows is an awesome display of firepower.

Returning from the bush, the men are offered a way out of combat duty. Their soccer team is to begin a tour against the South Vietnamese army team. In a filled-to-capacity stadium the heroes proceed to a three to one halftime lead score. The arrival of the corrupt interrogator Colonel Trang and his special forces shadow portends sinister developments. After unheard consultations with the ranking American officers enjoying the game, the captain receives new orders in the midst of his locker room pep talk. The men are instructed to throw the game. Like the football game in the finale of *M*A*S*H* or the antiauthoritarian gridiron shenanigans of the convicts in the popular 1974 Robert Aldrich film *The Longest Yard*, sports are metaphorically transformed into a commentary on the conflict itself. Perhaps it is notable that "their sport," soccer, not the Americans', football or baseball, becomes the somewhat heavy-handed means by which to summarize the compromise of American effort and the corruption of U.S. allies. With, as Stevens puts it, one hand tied behind our back, America in essence threw the war. This is the implied message. The captain explains, "We're not supposed to win. The Vietnamese go for winners and right now they happen to think that's the Viet Cong. Now it's our responsibility to build up their confidence in their government and their army and their sports teams."

The men remain unconvinced and defiant. To solidify the instruction, they are told if they lose, then they go on to Bangkok, but if they insist on winning, then they go on to Khe Sanh. They vaguely know what the viewer knows: that the camp's siege was a meat grinder. The film annoyingly degenerates in this last sequence. The men spitefully and obviously begin to throw the game. The "enemy," here the allies of the United States, are unworthy of such largesse. Following Stevens's lead, the Americans instead proceed to victory. Their joy and the evil colonel's outrage are short-lived.

Viet Cong commandos attack the stadium. The cowardly colonel and his U.S. sycophant grab civilians as human shields. Observing this despicable act, the pacifist Wasson behaves in a manner he had intellectually disdained. He shoots the ARVN bastard and is in turn gunned down by his bodyguards. The company's captain abandons his men and is killed as he seeks shelter in the stadium's reinforced bunker. The other men fight valiantly against the VC suicide squads.

When the smoke clears, Shaw and the lieutenant insist that a slightly wounded Stevens allow himself to be medevac'd. After all it turns out that he is a now a father! Canning attempts to write everything down as his friend Lembeck stands around with a group of Vietnamese kids. Two ARVN soldiers are escorting out a captured VC attacker. All of a sudden the prisoner throws down a grenade. Everyone ducks except the sensitive and now heroic writer, who, seeing the children in harm's way, throw himself on the explosive and absorbs its full impact. Even though a grand war movie cliché of the highest order, it is nevertheless sad, especially as his surviving comrades' eyes well up in tears. The good CO gently coaxes the corporal to help a grieving Private Fazio rejoin the departing company. As they march away, the deceased chronicler's carefully kept notes blow away in the wind. In one final voiceover the martyred young man says, "We'll just keep on walking into one bloody mess after another until somebody figures out that living has got to be more important than winning."

The film did not shy away from instances of corruption, incompetence, racism, and so on. The "gooks" as "yellow niggers," the use of troops as "live bait" for airpower, and other ugly manifestations of the war not mentioned explicitly in the preceding description of the plot were also re-created. Most of all the picture was about lying, and the boot camp prelude was merely a conventional bridge to the unconventional but now acknowledgeable conclusions about the war. The punctuation of quiet moments with the sudden finality of death's intrusions would become the means by which combat films established a pattern of perpetual in-country danger.

The Boys in Company C fight for no cause other than their comrades in arms and personal survival. That is because there seems to be nothing else to fight for. From a real-life perspective this lack of clear goals and purpose led the troops in Vietnam to many of the morale and moral compromises depicted in the film. Given its relatively modest production and dramatic scope, the "first horseman" remains an important movie in this book as it represents the return of the direct-combat portrait set in Vietnam. Like the war itself, the film met with critical controversy and public apathy.

Another important movie in 1978 was the late mini-major studio Avco Embassy release *Go Tell the Spartans*. That film, set in 1964 when there were only 12,000 U.S. "advisers" in South Vietnam, was historically placed in a far different, dramatically pregnant moment in history. As the precredit footage stated, "In 1964, the war in Vietnam was still a little war—confused and far away."

Go Tell the Spartans managed to convey the blundering military and political milieu that contributed to the escalation of the U.S. commitment. However, the source of Wendell Mayes's screenplay was not a posttrauma treatise informed with the bile of hindsight. Rather, it was based on a novel by Daniel Ford entitled *Incident at Muc Wa*, published during the war in 1967.[5] The prophetic nature of the material was therefore quite startling. The film adaptation managed to incorporate the important and prescient thematic components while wisely eliminating extraneous subplots and characters. Nevertheless, it took seven years for the screenwriter to gt a green light for the production. Then almost four additional years passed before the production was completed and distributed. What resulted was a powerful and ironic film of minimal budget and staging that received tepid commercial returns but great critical acclaim.

Burt Lancaster starred as Major Asa Barker, a career soldier who had served in both World War II and the Korean War. He is the type of gruff but caring officer that soldiers love. His career has been stymied by his ultimate inability to kowtow to his superiors at the expense of the men in his command. The limp of an old wound and his cigar chomping add to a wonderful characterization by the beloved actor.

As the film opens Lancaster is seen saving the life of a Viet Cong prisoner who is being drowned in a rain barrel by an overzealous South Vietnamese interrogator, nicknamed with a bit of transplanted Americana, "Cowboy." Lancaster, retiring to his office in Penang, receives a directive to reconnoiter a small hamlet known as Muc Wa. As his troops' present position is totally understaffed and he is not anxious to establish yet another tactically dubious static position in the bush, the major fakes a position paper for his superiors. Lancaster then proceeds to interview several new arrivals, and in so doing, he and the audience are introduced to the film's characters.

In a manner similar to that which generated criticism for *The Boys in Company C*, the young recruits are a somewhat tired amalgam of cross-sectional platoon characters. Nevertheless, each was updated in a Vietnam-specific contextualization. Craig Wasson, almost reprising his role from the preceding film, was Corporal Courcey, a college-educated draftee who actually volunteered for service in Vietnam. His sensitive, vaguely pacifist tendencies puzzle the experienced commanding officer, Lancaster.

Joining Wasson at the new outpost is gung-ho Lieutenant Hamilton, played by Joe Unger. As a product of the formal military training system, this young officer lacks any semblance of either common sense or military expertise. He is quite anxious to get out and kill communists. In his overzealous naïveté, complicated by the responsibilities of rank, this character is one of many who will appear in future in-country portrayals of the war. Most often, as in *Platoon* later on, it is the seasoned sergeants who have to keep their men alive as the inexperienced but hierarchically superior fools from HQ jeopardize soldiers' lives. Perhaps Unger's character is beyond compare in his intense idiocy, and his presence allows for some blackly humorous moments.

The battle-seasoned and weary sergeant character is played by Jonathan

Go Tell the Spartans (Avco Embassy, 1978). An ad slick for this combat tale set entirely in-country.

Goldsmith as Oleonowski. The actor, who had appeared in the recent *Green Eyes* as the soldier who faked his own death, portrays a broken man who served under Lancaster in Korea and is now seeing one too many tours of duty in Vietnam. Rounding out the characters are Dennis Howard as the drug-addicted medic rather heavy-handedly named Abraham Lincoln; the aforementioned sadistic but very battle-competent South Vietnamese soldier-interpreter, Cowboy, played by Evan Kim; and Lancaster's superior officer, General Harnitz, played by Dolph Sweet.

Allan F. Bodoh and Mitchell Cannold produced the film, and according to them, the choice of a group of relatively unknown actors to surround the familiar star was an overt attempt to "coincide with the American consciousness of those early years in Vietnam, when we knew little more than what the president or the generals told us and the battle lines were being manned by the anonymous volunteers of our special combat forces."[6] perhaps unstated were the additional budget-saving aspects of such casting. In fact the film was rather sparely filmed in the hilly outskirts of Los Angeles. Newly arrived South Vietnamese refugees were employed as extras. It is precisely the modest character of the film that allows it to best convey the isolated and still small-scale nature of the conflict for U.S. forces back in 1964.

General Harnitz, whose name begs for the obvious nickname of "Hard Nuts," arrives at Lancaster's outpost by helicopter. He knows that the major has faked his report on Muc Wa as it contains several factual errors, not the least of which is its estimated population of 200. In fact Muc Wa turns out to be an uninhabited outpost abandoned by the French in defeat back in 1954. A reluctant Lancaster orders Montagnard mercenaries, South Vietnamese irregulars, and some of the newly arrived American advisers out to the area to establish the mandated forward position in the very heart of VC, or "Indian," territory.

Not only does Lancaster feel the mission is dangerous and purposeless, but the seasoned Sergeant Oleonowski is also very worried, especially given the newly arrived Lieutenant Hamilton's official leadership of the party. Barker apologizes to his old subordinate and informs the entire group that, despite the lieutenant's rank, it should rely heavily on the sergeant's experience. In a pep talk to these ragtag troops, the nominally in control young officer speaks with pride about their important mission in defense of liberty. When Cowboy translates this speech, it is met with derisive and convulsive laughter from the Vietnamese.

In the reconnaissance of the area, Wasson finds a cemetery that contains the bodies of French soldiers from the immediately preceding Vietnam War. Above the cemetery entrance is the inscription that gives the film its title. The college kid translates from the French, "When you find us lying here, go tell the Spartans we obeyed our orders." The quote is from Greek historian Herodotus' story about the battle of Thermopylae in 480 B.C. in which 300 Spartans died defending their ground. Aside from the obviously foreboding nature of this scene, the almost ghostly presence of a one-eyed, grizzled old Vietnamese man on the outer edge of the cemetery startles the young corporal. Is this a mysterious VC warrior or an apparition? Tad Horino's one-eyed man conveys the unseen or at least fleeting aspect of the enemy so prevalent in *The Boys in Company C.* It also serves as a dramatic device, as if he is a historical witness to the proceedings. In addition the cemetery and the reference to the French are meant to convey the historical continuity of the conflict. The U.S. presence just now tragically escalating is merely a fleeting moment in the history of the country. And it is precisely the victory of the Vietnamese over their previous opponents that bodes poorly for the ill-conceived effort at hand. As a student of other conflicts, Lancaster knows the futility of staffing this isolated post, but he is forced to obey orders.

A number of local Vietnamese civilians are encountered near the newly established outpost. The men react differently to the civilians' presence. The young Wasson befriends them and, like a good GI in France, offers them chocolates. Cowboy is convinced they are VC. The cynical and alcoholic Oleonowski is wary of the "dinks" and disdainful of the corporal's attempts to win what the young lieutenant refers to as "their hearts and minds." Soon thereafter when Lancaster arrives to survey the scene, he inquires as to whether the friendly Wasson is screwing one of the young girls. The corporal replies, "No," to which the incredulous old major replies, "Well somebody ought to!" He then pragmatically suggests to the medic that "you better pump that little cunt full of penicillin before the whole barracks comes down with the clap." Continuing with the odd and unromantic realities of the field operation, the commanding lieutenant has developed the dreaded "quick step," or dysentery, and is temporarily sidelined.

Back at headquarters Lancaster and his aide are forced to listen to a psychological warfare intelligence officer explain the newly conceived "incident flow priority indicator." The two officers can hardly contain their skepticism about this Pentagon-inspired nonsense. Back in the field the medic Lincoln, stoned on drugs, climbs to the garrison watchtower and begins to deliver the Gettysburg Address during a mortar attack. Shortly therafter Cowboy catches some of the civilians stealing weapons and ammunition. This would seem to confirm his suspicion as to the true identity of the villagers.

Near Muc Wa a patrol is ambushed by the river. Sergeant Oleo and others escape, leaving a wounded man on the other bank. He is hopelessly pinned down. The young lieutenant heroically but foolishly insists on attempting to save this South Vietnamese farmer-soldier. With Wasson laying down cover fire, the lieutenant makes it to the other side, only to find the man has died. In a retreat the lieutenant, too, is killed. Everyone is shocked, and Oleo feels quasi-guilty and disgusted that this wasteful sacrifice was attempted on behalf of a "dink." He is so burned out that for him there seems to be no difference between enemies and allies. He sees this conflict as "their war." When the young corporal goes to see the Korean War vet, he receives an earload of dispirited bile from the alcoholic Oleo. Shortly thereafter the sergeant commits suicide.

Back at command Lancaster is deeply troubled by the deaths as well as the apparent upsurge in enemy activity near the isolated post. Knowing his remaining men are severely outnumbered, he goes to see a corrupt South Vietnamese colonel, played by Clyde Kasatsu. Lancaster is seeking troops and artillery support for the garrison. Only through bribery is he able to prevail upon the official at their meeting in his opulently appointed home. Stereotypically the set reflects post–French-colonial excesses in taste and lifestyle that stand in marked contrast to the reality of the existence of the Vietnamese and the soldiers in the bush.

Upon Lancaster's return to Penang, Olivetti and the nerdy intelligence officer inform the major that Muc Wa is under attack. At this point it is the inexperienced Wasson, Cowboy, and other troops who are left in defense. The situation is desperate, but Lancaster's request to Harnitz for air support is denied. It seems that political considerations will compromise the military situation. A rumored coup in Saigon has grounded all air support in deference to the needs of the unstable government. Lancaster is able to prevail on Harnitz as only an old comrade who does not care about his political future in the military organization can do. Much to the staff's disbelief, Lancaster tells the general that if he does not send help, then Lancaster will "shoot his [the general's] balls off." This indelicacy convinces the general to accept the dire reality of the situation and commit the planes to Muc Wa. Air superiority, not shown but only reported, is able to temporarily end the assault on the camp. Nevertheless, sensing the untenable position of the isolated and outnumbered garrison, the brass decides to abandon the outpost, which Lancaster never wanted to staff anyway.

Lancaster is ordered to "extricate" all American personnel. He himself arrives via helicopter to get the remaining U.S. soldiers out. In a dramatic scene the still-idealistic young corporal is appalled when he learns that the South Vietnamese with whom he has fought side by side will not be allowed on the chopper. Therefore he refuses to leave and instead elects to take his chances with them in a ground retreat back through the jungle. The crusty major attempts to convince him to get on the helicopter amid the swirling elephant grass and whir of the blades. As the chopper takes off the camera pulls back, and we see that a reluctant major has heroically elected to stay with the stubborn, principled young corporal and the others.

The two Americans converse about fairness, duty, and war. Lancaster says that the young man is merely a tourist in this war. "It's too bad we couldn't have shown you a better war – like hitting the beach at Anzio . . . . That was a real tour. This one's a sucker tour, going nowhere, just around and around in circles." As the retreat begins the group is ambushed. Jumping out of a camouflaged position, one of the young Viet Cong girls who had been in the compound as a civilian kills Cowboy, who is out on point. Everyone is wounded, and the young corporal passes out. Heroically a mortally injured farmer-soldier ally hides the unconscious American in the bushes. The next morning when the corporal awakens, he finds the dead, stripped, and looted bodies of the major and all the others. As the "tourist" hobbles past the cemetery, he spots the mysterious one-eyed man. For a moment it appears he might kill the surviving American. However, the old man lowers his gun and a relieved and bedraggled young corporal says, "I'm going home, Charlie" as the film comes to an end.

As if to echo the recurring theme of continuum, the conclusion title card merely states, "1964," as if this is more a beginning than an end. The film is loaded with a sense of irony, moral ambiguity, imperfection, and absurdity. Aside from the unknown nature of the enemy, nothing is as it appears. The idealist Courcey is simply wrong about who is or is not VC. The bloodthirsty Cowboy, who at one point actually beheads a man, is the most competent fighter, speaks four languages fluently, and ultimately is correct in most of his assumptions. Barker is a hero but compromised by the system and forced to issue orders of a dubious nature. Ultimately his dinosaurian sense of duty leads to his death in godforsaken isolation.

Even at this early juncture the existence of substance abuse is shown. Bridging the generations, the means to getting stoned differ, but the necessity of escaping from the tortured and bewildering reality is the same. Oleo drinks Jack Daniels, and Lincoln smokes dope. As for the overall military and hierarchical establishment, its lack of understanding of the prevailing dynamics of the Vietnamese culture and the nature of the war is legendary. Their (the American) understanding is that of a tourist on a brief trip. Whether in *The Boys in Company C* or in *Go Tell the Spartans*, the institutional military command becomes a treacherous hindrance to the troops in the field. Ironically the absurd "indicator chart" was actually correct! Also, like most head-on portraits of the war, the South Vietnamese are shown in the most unflattering terms. Perhaps one point of divergence between quality and exploitative treatments to come is the depiction of the enemy. A respect for their tough fighting ability, as opposed to a cartoonish and heinous portrait of incompetent barbarians, helps differentiate the level of veracity of many subsequent works.

Go Tell the Spartans nicely brackets the conflict and the series of films. Set in 1964, the American involvement is just beginning. Like *The Boys in Company C*, some of the characters are trite and mired in earlier conflict depictions. However, the negative and updated specifics transcend the hackneyed and propel the films forward in an overt, now postwar-informed indictment of a hated chapter in American history.

The director of *Go Tell the Spartans*, Ted Post, had recently contributed to the group with the Chuck Norris star vehicle *Good Guys Wear Black*. It also cynically treated the powers that be who exploited and victimized the individual fighting soldier. Post was quoted as saying as production began that now the American people "are open to disillusion." It's safe to cope with the issues the war raised."[7] And Post, like other observers at the time, attributed part of this new openness to the trauma of Watergate as well as the Vietnam War.

By 1978 it was easy to have 20/20 hindsight about the war, but consensus remained illusive. Nevertheless, the recognition of much of the irony of the doomed circumstances and actions was unavoidable. When the ignorant Lieutenant

Hamilton says that we can't lose, "We're Americans," the audiences cringes. This sentiment will be repeated in many of the upcoming films.

In *Go Tell the Spartans* the title, the references to the French defeat, the use of words such as *esprit,* which Harnitz objects to as "French," the harkening back to other "better" or more defined wars, and more, all contribute to a sense of doom from the outset. The mysteries of Asia were cultural, racial, religious, historic, and geographic. The triple-canopied jungles of Nam seemed to physically symbolize the multilayered and obscured dimensions of the entire setting for America.

In *Go Tell the Spartans* the metaphysical continuity of time and history and the more temporal but equally challenging lack of clear enemy identification all coalesce in the one-eyed character. This is what William J. Palmer in *The Films of the Seventies* refers to when he states, "That mythic image of the one eyed soldier captures that vague sense of a 'secret sharer' which many American combat soldiers in Vietnam experienced. One combat veteran described it in these terms: 'I always sensed he was out there, used to think about him all the time, like he was my twin or something. Some VC, like me, wondering what the hell was going on . . . but not understanding.'"[8]

In this film the overriding feeling, one apparently shared by the public, seems to be expressed by the tragic Oleonowski when he says, "It's their war." As the head-on portraits continue, each thematic chord that strikes a response in the postconflict audience will be reinforced by actual wartime events. In *The Boys in Company C* the unsafe-anywhere aspects of the watershed Tet Offensive trigger a sense of identification and verisimilitude. In *Go Tell the Spartans* and several other films, the costly defense of an isolated outpost that is subsequently abandoned harkens to numerous real-life campaigns, notably the siege of Khe Sanh. In the upcoming *The Deerhunter,* the fall of Saigon offers such identifiable re-creations of nonfictional milestones.

The totally recontextualized and noncombat portraits of the preceding chapter are being updated in realistic ways in *The Boys in Company C* and in hybrid and surrealistic scenes in *Go Tell the Spartans.* The dynamic tension between the differing states of reality endemic to the conflict will become a fascinating source of filmmaker exposition. The metaphorical renderings in *The Deerhunter* in the context of graphic and harrowing sequences such as the game of Russian roulette were criticized as untruthful.

Apocalypse Now and *Platoon* operated in both realms because the realistic battle scenes only confirmed the chaos and mind-bending aspects of the war. The drug abuse depicted in both contributed to mind-altering perceptions of reality. The dichotomous nature of the very real and very unreal aspects of war, especially this one, also reflected the rhythmic nature of peace and war. This conflict in the history of the United States reflected the historic reality that every twenty years or so Americans seem to need or find a war. The ebb and flow of conflict and nonconflict also reflected the gut-wrenching intrusion of danger and destruction into times of peacefulness and quietude.

Although *Go Tell the Spartans* was embraced by the critics, the public remained uninterested in the two lower-budget, lesser-profile entries already discussed. While they were in release, the general press continually referred to the plethora of head-on portraits of the war about to come to a neighborhood theater. Beating *Apocalypse Now* into distribution in 1978 were the remaining two "horsemen" of this chapter's title, *Coming Home* and *The Deerhunter*. Both were big-budget pictures with high-profile casts and marketing campaigns as well as grand production values. Unlike the preceding films, the public found these two impossible to ignore, as did the Academy Awards and other sources of accolades at the end of the year. Like many Vietnam War films yet to come, much of their success and notoriety were borne of the continuing inherent controversy surrounding any work dealing with this particular conflict.

Contributing to the controversy surrounding the upcoming United Artists release *Coming Home* was the intimate association with the project of its female star and original production impetus, Jane Fonda. Much of the American public had never forgiven the actress for her visit to North Vietnam while the war raged on. Especially controversial was her meeting with American POWs held in Hanoi. Thus the fine actress and second-generation Hollywood star became for some a treasonous political pariah worthy of the moniker Hanoi Jane.

Nevertheless by 1978 Fonda was firmly ensconced as a star, and she and her partner, Bruce Gilbert, had already spent several years working on an appropriate Vietnam-themed theatrical vehicle. In fact some five years had passed since screenwriter Nancy Dowd had started on the then-titled *Buffalo Ghost*. Sensing the commercial apprehension surrounding a movie about the just-completed war, Fonda decided to hedge her bets by fleshing out the concept with a love story. Talented screenwriter Waldo Salt began rewrites.[9]

As preparation for the film proceeded, Fonda hired Englishman John Schlesinger to direct. However, the uniquely American flavor of the story put off the Brit, and he was replaced by Hal Ashby, recently triumphant with *Shampoo*, which, like this project, was set in the year that epitomized the turmoil of the previous decade, 1968. Attempts to cast the male lead began with Jack Nicholson, who was already booked. Al Pacino and Sylvester Stallone were discussed. Finally Fonda's producer Jerome Hellman suggested Jon Voight. It was to become his career's most important role, along with that in *Midnight Cowboy*.

With Voight set as the paraplegic Vietnam veteran, Bruce Dern was hired to portray the husband, Captain Bob Hyde. The officer's wife, perky ex-cheerleader, center of the story, and the focus of change was Fonda as Sally Hyde. Penelope Milford played her friend Vi Milford, the girlfriend of Sergeant Dink Mobley, played by Robert Ginty. Vi's troubled brother, psychologically scarred for life after only two weeks in Vietnam, was played by Robert Carradine.

Robert C. Jones shared the screenplay credit with Salt, and original writer Nancy Dowd received a story credit. Fonda's companion in North Vietnam and documentarian on that trip, Haskell Wexler (*Medium Cool*), served in his primary profession as cinematographer.

One significant costar remained on the production. That was the conspicuous and integral 1960s rock music on the soundtrack. The constant use of songs not only evoked the times but also commented on the screen action and served as a bridge between differing but related scenes. Although some felt this technique was intrusive, the prominence of this filmmaking component was unprecedented for such a drama.

Coming Home is about the effect of war, in this case the Vietnam War, on its participants as well as those at home. It deals with physical as well as spiritual or emotional debilitation and the resultant rehabilitation and healing or lack thereof. Additionally it deals with change and growth. All these elements are conveyed in the context of the lead characters. However, each of their journeys reflects portions of American society's dynamic altering during the course and aftermath of the recently concluded war.

The male lead, played by Voight, is veteran Luke Martin. The onetime captain of the high school football team went off to war with romantic notions of glory. He came back crippled and embittered. The film attempts to grapple frankly with his readjustment and rehabilitation, including his notions of sexuality, virility, and wholeness in the wake of his terrible injury, trauma, and paralysis. His apostle's name is no coincidence.

For the female lead, Fonda as Sally Hyde, the film takes a stock character, the repressed and dutiful military wife and ex-cheerleader, and chronicles her transformation as she evolves into a freethinking liberated person. For the physically whole career soldier and husband, Captain Bob Hyde, Bruce Dern represents the traditional and conventional military establishment. In the context of this war his character must contend with a mind-numbing transformation from gung-ho patriotism and notions of glory to awareness, pain, bewilderment, shame, and a lack of belonging as a result of his in-country service. His eventual, implied sexual impotence, and cuckolding are meant to comment on the general fate of the soldier and the military establishment during the war.

The precredit opening features several veterans in wheelchairs playing pool in a VA hospital. Amid the actors, including a listening but silent and bearded Jon Voight on a gurney, are actual veterans. The scene is shot in a quasi-documentary style that recalls the same technique of using nonprofessionals that Fred Zinnemann employed in the 1950 drama about a crippled World War II vet, *The Men.* That film, starring Marlon Brando, dealt with the physical and mental rehabilitation of a paraplegic veteran. With the exception of the television movie *Just a Little Inconvenience, Coming Home* represented the first theatrical film about a crippled Vietnam veteran.

Using very realistic dialogue, the men discuss Vietnam. One asks the others if they would go back or go to Sweden or Canada. These men are attempting to make sense out of their experience and their great sacrifice, to find a degree of purpose or meaning. When one of the crippled young men says he would return, the others cannot believe it.

The strains of the Rolling Stones' "Out of Time" intrudes over the intimate opening scene as the film cuts to a pair of running legs. These juxtaposed physically healthy limbs belong to a jogging captain, Bruce Dern, doing some last-minute road conditioning in anticipation of going off to Vietnam. Intercutting between the men in wheelchairs and on stretchers and the virile marine traversing the base sets the ironic contrast.

Dern and Ginty continue preparations for their new assignment with target practice as the base's helicopters roar overhead in a bit of implicit audio foreboding. Afterwards Dern meets Fonda at the officers club. As he enters, the assembled guests are watching television coverage of the Tet Offensive. Any apprehension is masked by the macho bravado of the officer. "A Time of Innocence" plays on the soundtrack as only the woman is allowed to show her fear and concern, both tempered by the need of a loyal officer's wife for stoicism and bravery.

That last night together Dern (with his dog tags on) and Fonda make love. She is preoccupied and nonorgasmic; he seems oblivious, as the familiar strains of "Hey Jude" well up. At breakfast she admits she is afraid but proud. He feels that as a marine, Vietnam is where he belongs. In a manly gesture as head of the household, he mundanely fixes the toaster. At their good-bye she lovingly but also insecurely gives him a wedding band, something he has never worn but promises to never take off. Such traditional sexual roles are consistent with the innocence that these characters have about the fate about to befall them.

In seeing her husband off, Fonda meets Vi, played by Penelope Milford, as she says good-bye to her boyfriend, Dink, Dern's friend. Despite Vi's free-spirited attitude, a contrast to Fonda's straitlaced and repressed nature, the two women become good friends. Vi's brother is in the psycho ward at the Veterans Administration hospital. Fonda decides it would be helpful and worthwhile to volunteer there.

The film cuts to the hospital as a massive machine rotates an imprisoned and crippled veteran in some type of unpleasant therapy. This is a crowded, noisy, sad, and desperate place. Jon Voight, not yet ready for a wheelchair, ambulates about the ward on a gurney by using two canes as a means to push off the floor. He is in a rage, totally unreconciled with his horrible fate.

As a determined, yet nervous Fonda enters the facility, Voight accidentally rolls into her. In the collision his full urine bag is spilled. Fonda tries to maintain her composure as the identity of the liquid dawns on her in an instance of nonverbal recognition. This moment of subtle acting, like so many others in the film, immensely contributes to its strength. Overcome with embarrassment, humiliation, and anger, Voight launches into a tirade directed more at the overworked staff and the world in general than at the pretty young women who hurries off to the volunteer orientation. Voight's fit of anger results in an involuntary dosage of Thorazine and the use of restraints. He objects and pleads, "Just take care of me." Years later this unimaginably horrible stage in the recognition of one's permanent fate as an early part in the rehabilitation process will also be memorably recounted by Ron Kovic in *Born on the Fourth of July* and re-created by Tom Cruise in the film version of that veteran's memoir.

It turns out that Fonda recognized the troubled veteran. In fact they went to a nearby high school together. That night as she and Vi prepare to move into an apartment together, they discuss the past. As if to signify lost youth and innocence, out in the yard some children are playing war games. Vi, entrusted with the care of her troubled brother, says cynically, "They tore down my past and built a shopping center." Continuing the scene's sense of passage, they look at the yearbook and see a handsome, young, clean-shaven Voight as he appeared years ago, the head of the football team. As the ex-cheerleader reads her insipid adolescent wish for the future, "a husband," the rite-of-passage dimension of her living off base with this free-spirited young woman is apparent.

Determined to persevere in her duties, Fonda returns to the hospital as she passes out doughnuts and self-consciously learns to feed a vet who has lost his ability to speak without being plugged into a machine. In the meantime a restrained Voight refuses to be fed, proclaiming that he is not a child. The ravages of war are varied, humiliating, and horrible. When Fonda goes to see Voight and remind him of their previous acquaintance, he is abusive. His self-pity makes him feel she is being patronizing. Gradually the biting quality of the abuse becomes more jocular as Voight begins to accept Fonda's attention and persistent friendship. In fact he constantly refers to her as "Bender," as in her maiden name and as in the boyhood fantasy of "Bend 'er over," a revelation that shocks the prissy Sally.

Feeling very independent and productive now, Fonda buys a new car, a sporty Porsche, and changes her severe hairdo to a curly and natural style. She and Vi move into an apartment right on the beach. Even Vi kids her about these changes and her newfound liberation now that Dern is overseas. Despite his absence, Fonda remains dutiful in writing and loving her husband. Vi shares with her the romantic "present" that Dink sent her from Vietnam: an ear! This casual reference to in-country mayhem forebodingly refers to the misconduct and horrors of this war.

Voight, who was a sergeant, continually challenges his new friend, Bender. "Why aren't you teeing up balls at the officers club?" When he says something awful about her husband coming home in a body bag, he has gone too far. She calls him on this, and her completely appropriate anger is a response that is in no way tempered by his incapacitation. This movement beyond his condition is an important step in their growing friendship.

Now enjoying new levels of self-awareness and purpose, Fonda attempts to get the ladies club newsletter to write about some of the awful problems at the VA hospital right there on the base. Like much of America, the women view this as much too depressing and insist that the rag be limited to Little League scores and gossip.

Back at the hospital, one of the vets has a flashback to Vietnam while everyone is watching the Smothers Brothers. At home Fonda is fixing her hair in the mirror and listening to Robert Kennedy talk about the just-assassinated Martin Luther King. Like most of the film, in 1978 these scenes carried a poignancy and omniscience unknowable to the characters in 1968.

The next day at the hospital Fonda is excited to see that Voight has finally gotten his wheelchair. This added mobility happily affords the veteran a new confidence. She invites him over to her house for dinner. It is the Fourth of July, and like any other Americans, the vets gather at the hospital for a picnic. Games of wheelchair frisbee and basketball convey a sense that life will go on. As a legionnaire drones on reading an essay on how proud he is to be an American, the camera pans the crowd of young men who have given so much for their country. They are oblivious to the speech as they converse, smoke dope, and so on. Vi's troubled brother joins her, and Fonda, and Voight at a picnic table. After some coaxing, he begins to sing but breaks down in tears. Only his fellow vet can comfort him, extending a hug and, more important, a shared sense of knowing the truth and the source of the pain. Fonda admires Voight's caring and tells him so as they go to their dinner.

They are both very nervous at this private social engagement, and Voight's jocular self-mockery not only breaks the ice but also reveals his continuing strides toward emotional health. When she apologizes for her music, he retorts, "You probably won't like the way I dance either." They began to share intimate details and feelings. Voight explains that when he dreams, he still pictures himself as whole with legs that work. He then confides to Fonda that he spends 95 percent of his time at the hospital thinking about making love to her. She is a bit taken aback, but not at all repulsed by the sentiment. Finally she merely says that she has never been unfaithful to her husband.

Soon thereafter on the hospital patio, Fonda is given a telegram. She holds her breath, fearing the worst. Instead it is merely her husband requesting her presence in Hong Kong, where he will be on leave. Feeling it her duty to join him on R&R, she goes to tell Voight. As the Rolling Stones sing the now descriptively ambiguous "My Girl," she disembarks in Hong Kong, once again sporting her old hairdo. Dern is generally agitated and distant and chauvinistically opposed to his wife's working, especially in the hospital. Dink is angry that Vi could not join them. Dern seems as much concerned about his comrade as about his wife. They have difficulty talking, and she must convince him of the necessity of spending some time together alone.

In the privacy of their hotel room, the extent of Vietnam-induced emotional trauma becomes apparent. Cryptically railing against the preeminent medium of the time, Dern responds to Fonda's inquiries by saying, "TV shows what [Nam] is like; it sure don't show what it is." The essence of that she cannot understand. Voight and Vi's brother can. Interspersed with this scene and Rolling Stones music are scenes of Voight back home beginning to enjoy his life again and regaining his emotional equilibrium. He takes great joy in driving his specially outfitted Mustang, with the license plate "VET 210," and other tasks that one takes for granted, such as moving into his own apartment and grocery shopping.

Returning to the hotel room in Hong Kong, Dern twirls his dog tags, while Fonda sits there in an absurd-looking coolie's hat, a tourist's memento of that day's sightseeing. She listens intently as her husband tells of a second lieutenant, "a Camp Lejeune whiz kid," who asked if it was okay to put the heads of the enemies they had killed up on poles. After all "it scares the shit out of the VC." Almost in tears, the career soldier is deeply troubled that his men were chopping heads off. This is a painful moment from a dirty war. In the far background of the room, sitting on the bed, Fonda seems a world apart from her husband as he disintegrates. Subliminally that stupid little hat she still has on is reminiscent of the look of the Viet Cong.

Their physical contact is limited to her brief back massage of her husband. He insults her with a jealous and insecure jab, and all other intimacy ceases. In essence the strapping captain has been rendered impotent by the horrors of war. Reiterating the ironically contrasting message is the crosscutting with a scene in which the physically crippled Voight meets with a hooker.

Back at the hospital Vi's brother, played by Carradine, is in a crazy manic mood. Alarmed by this jag, the vet who spoke in the film's beginning and seems to be a ward leader calls Voight to come and help their mutual friend. By the time Voight arrives, the young man has committed suicide by injecting air into his vein. The other hospital-bound vets witnessed it all through a wire mesh door, unable to get in and aid the troubled casualty of war.

Returning from Hong Kong, Fonda tries to comfort a grieving Vi. Also troubled is Voight, who is moved to a desperate act of antiwar activism. He proceeds to the marine corps recruiting depot, where he chains himself to the entrance gates. He is berated by the young sentries and arrested.

Fonda bails Voight out of jail, and as they return to her beach home, we see the FBI conducting surveillance on the now-suspect radical veteran. Here the film manages to integrate another component of the domestic fallout from the conflict. Antiwar activism and internal dissent in America are construed as threats to the government.

In a very difficult, yet effective and poignant scene, Voight and Fonda make love for the first time. Their intimacy and caring lead Fonda to ecstasy. Again implicit is the reverse potency of Fonda's two lovers in the film. Once again a song is used to bridge to the action into the next scene. The Beatles' "Strawberry Fields Forever" follows the lovers as they go about their activities in a postcoital bliss. The newly bonded lovers make a handicapped access ramp for the house, fly a kite via a bike and wheelchair hookup, and watch a slide show of Voight's happier moments in Vietnam. This is the closest the film gets to the modern no-dialogue montage style of inserted rock video.

Abruptly ending this mood are two events. One is the viewer's, not the characters', growing awareness that all this is being recorded by the FBI on film. Two is the announcement that Dern is scheduled to return home because of an injury. The two lovers talk and Voight is resigned to the reality that Fonda will rejoin her husband upon his return. Although sad, Voight cherishes the time they had together and reveals an inner peace unthinkable only a few months before.

As the strains of "For What It's Worth" play, Dern disembarks on the tarmac. As the wounded in stretchers and the dead are off-loaded, Dern limps toward Fonda, who awaits him on the other side of the airport fence. When he sees her, he wonders, "What the hell did you do to your hair?" She has no longer bothered to straighten it for him. She is a changed person, and this is merely an outward manifestation of it. This is a less than stellar opening line, but Dern is quite pleased, announcing, "Outstanding" at the new little sports car. As they speed off through the entrance gate to the base, Dern flips the "bird" (middle finger) to an antiwar protestor. Once again in a recurring physical motif, fences, gates, and wire meshes have served as physical barriers that typify the separation of people and lack of emotional connectedness depicted in the film.

Dern is overwhelmed in his return to the United States and bewildered and challenged by the lifestyle changes he witnesses in Sally. When Vi and Sally query him on the circumstances of his leg wound, Dern reluctantly admits it was a self-inflicted M-16 wound suffered when he slipped on the way to the showers. This is all very humiliating, and he flees their welcome home party, taking solace in getting drunk with a group of soldiers he hardly knows. He passes out asleep with his revolver in his hand.

Compounding Dern's embarrassment, guilt, disappointment, and disorientation is the revelation of his wife's infidelity. He calmly goes to see Voight and resignedly says that a resolution is up to Sally. Voight feels very guilty about what he has helped inflict on this fellow vet. When Dern returns home to Fonda, he appears crazed. Herein the travails of the returning vet in the exploitation movies are given a brief, more controlled reprise. With an M-16 the uniformed, broken man confronts his wife. Fonda proclaims her love and says that she would have told him but that he has seemed too distant since his return. He dismisses this as nonsense and expresses a raging commonality with other vets when he proclaims, "I do not belong in this house . . . and they're saying I do not belong there [in Vietnam]." Set to receive a Purple Heart, the irony does not escape Dern. He rages, "I don't deserve that fucking medal either. How can they give you a medal for a war they don't even want you to fight!?"

Dern's dreams of heroism have proven elusive. When Voight arrives to help diffuse the tense moment, he behaves bravely and, ironically, heroically. Dern is on the edge, and some of the film's only false dialogue occurs when in homage to ten years of crazed vet films, the agitated captain threatens his wife with defensive, ugly words in a duress-induced flashback: "Get back slope cunt!" The slang is off, and so is his reality. She is not a "slope"; she is a Caucasian, and she is his wife. A calm Voight explains from his wheelchair to the menacing returnee, "I'm not the enemy. The enemy is the fucking war. You don't want to kill anybody here. You have enough ghosts to carry around." His ability to convince Dern to come to his senses is borne of the shared wartime pain that allowed Voight to empathize with and relate to the late Carradine as well.

Coming Home (United Artists, 1978). Bruce Dern returns from Vietnam and confronts his wife's lover.

With this brave speech Voight manages to set the direction of most Vietnam films yet to come. The nuances of the particular wartime debates have become irrelevant. They are now subordinated to the tragedy of the individual soldier's experience and the collective suffering that resulted from it.

The heavily decorated soldier, shaking but restored to his senses, apologizes and collapses in anguish. As his wife confronts him, Voight quietly disarms Dern's M-16 and leaves the house. The next day Dern is forced to endure the tales of heroism that accompany his fellow medal recipients' awards at a formal ceremony. A sense of hypocrisy, worthlessness, irrelevance, and betrayal consume the once-proud soldier.

The film concludes by crosscutting between the two men in Fonda's life. At a high school assembly a smartly dressed marine addresses the young boys and potential recruits. His spit-and-polish assurance that the Marine Corps builds body, mind, and spirit rings out menacingly. Years later the gung-hoism of such speechmaking was repeated by the handsome Tom Berenger at a similar gathering in *Born on the Fourth of July.* Unlike the impressionable youth in that film, here the boys are afforded another perspective.

Voight begins a powerful speech, deriving meaning as much in how he says and acts the words as what he says. Ultimately as the hero of the film and the real survivor, his insight and assuredness stand in marked contrast to the man he was at the beginning of the film or to the suffering and nearly destroyed Dern.

As Voight starts to address the high school boys, Fonda is seen conversing with her husband at her beach house. He is unresponsive when she offers to have a nice barbecue and attempts to comfort him with some favorite food. He is now lost in his own far-off land. She asks, "It's been a long time since you've lit a BBQ, isn't it?" It seems a throwaway line based on some notion of lost domestic bliss. However, Dern's subtle and inscrutable hint of a smile at this inquiry implies another meaning. The smile is one of pained insider information. Undoubtedly, horrid memories of the intentional torching of a suspected VC hamlet is called to mind. Dern's response is lost on Fonda as she and Vi go off to get the groceries for dinner. Her return to simple domesticity will not work any more than his return to civilian life will, but his dilemma is now the one in focus and the more acute one.

As the mournful song "Once I Was a Soldier" plays on the soundtrack, the film intercuts between Voight's speech and Dern's gradual undressing on the beach. The wheelchair-bound vet explains to the boys, "You know you want to be a part of it . . . and patriotism and go out and get your licks in for the U.S. of A. and . . . when you get over there it's a totally different situation. . . . You grow up real quick. . . . All you're seeing is a lot of death."

Now half-naked, Dern leans on the lifeguard stand as he removes the ring he promised his wife he would never take off. Voight continues, his voice increasingly choked with emotion, "And I know some of you guys are going to look at the uniform and you're going to remember all the films and you're going to think about the glory of other wars and think about some vague patriotic feeling and go off and fight this turkey, too . . . and I'm telling you it ain't like it is in the movies. That's all I wanna tell you because I didn't have a choice when I was your age. All I got was some guy standing up like that man, giving me a lot of bullshit, man, which I caught. . . . I wanted to be a war hero. I wanted to go out and kill for my country . . . and now I'm here to tell you that I have killed for my country or whatever, and I don't feel good about it because there's not enough reason, man." Then in tears in front of a hushed assemblage, he concludes, "to feel a person die in your hand, to see your best buddy get blown away, I'm here to tell you it's a lousy thing, man. I don't see any reason for it, and there's a lot of shit I did over there that I find fuckin' hard to live with, and I don't want to see people like you, man, comin' back and having to face the rest of your lives with that kind of shit. It's as simple as that. I don't feel sorry for myself, I'm a lot smarter now than when I went, and I'm just telling ya that there's a choice to be made here."

Back to the beach a now nude Dern runs into the pounding surf of the Pacific Ocean, choosing to end his life and thus his pain. Somewhat ruining the powerful moment is Ashby's misstep of showing an unknowing Vi and Fonda entering the grocery store with the name of the chain as a pun declaring, "Lucky Out."

The cursive script credits begin, and the extensive and wonderful soundtrack contributions are given. Among the musical contributors not already noted here were Buffalo Springfield, Jefferson Airplane, Jimi Hendrix, Simon and

Garfunkle, and Steppenwolf. Although many of the sign-of-the-times films featured original or acquired music, *Coming Home*'s soundtrack was the most extensive, and undoubtedly expensive, usage of the actual artists' recordings from the era yet to be featured in this book.

Coming Home mostly received great praise. The leads were extremely well acted. Some criticism surrounded the lack of dimension of the pivotal Bruce Dern character as written. Others felt the film deified the Voight character too much. Still other observers objected to the prominence of the soundtrack as obtrusive.

Some observers merely detested Fonda and felt compelled to condemn the film. Producer Jerome Hellman had anticipated this when he told her, "You get up on a soapbox and we'll sink like a rock. They're going to be looking for that from you."[10] This led to the tempering of various antiwar messages. Some accused the producers of offering up pablum. Commenting on the feminist aspects of the story line, one would expect *Ms.* magazine to have been kind. However, it dismissed the film by saying, "Its message seemed to be that doves are better than hawks in bed, and it was pious as well as sentimental."[11] Stanley Kauffmann disliked the film, calling it "a shaky sentimental triangle drama that could essentially have been about the war of 1812."[12]

Still other critics objected to the ultimately unchallengeable tragedy certified with 20/20 hindsight by the intervening decade. But herein lies one of the strengths of the film and its place in the book. It accurately reflected the growing consensus about the war circa 1978 and did so with the integral participation and contribution of a radical celebrity. The apolitical factors that prevented Hollywood from tackling these films during the conflict had now dissipated, and this film and others in 1978 contributed to the process of national healing and reconciliation. No one wanted to see a political diatribe like *Hearts and Minds* anymore. A time of postwar healing was beginning, and the political compromises that softened the edges of *Coming Home* and opened it up to some haranguing were far more humanistic and purposeful at this point than some fictionalized account that did not convey with half the power the human tragedy of the war. Root political causes and analysis have their place, but rarely in a fictional film contextualization.

The film manages to integrate several related subgenres. It deals indirectly with the effect of combat. It chronicles veterans' problems, ranging from physical to emotional maladies. Rehabilitation and reintegration become subjects of graphic depiction. *Coming Home* touches upon domestic opposition to the war. It evokes aspects of the era ranging from unquestioning naïveté to embittered awareness and knowledge. Pop-cultural and sign-of-the-times aspects are summarized via the soundtrack and other references. Most of all *Coming Home* is a drama that contains universal themes and tragedy but is informed and given meaning and context by the Vietnam War.

Ultimately, as Roger Ebert puts it in his glowing review, "*Coming Home* considers a great many subjects, but its heart lies with the fundamental change within

Sally Hyde."[13] Each of the film's characters managed to personify some of the collective consciousness that surrounded either the wartime era or its aftermath. Because the characters' evolution exemplifies the change and growing awareness among the American people of the tragic human costs of the Vietnam War, the film succeeds and takes its place as one of the more important movies in this book that does not feature in-country sequences.

Like the other films of 1978, *Coming Home* is antiwar in nature because of its depiction of the effects of war on its central characters. The similarity of tragedy with previous wars does not homogenize the effect. It echoes previous antiwar film perspectives but without a doubt roots them in the specifics of the Vietnam conflict. Any additional tragic consequences of that war's unpopularity, losing result, compromised conduct, and immoral or dubious catalysts, purposes, and pursuit serve to specify the documentation and fictionalization.

Any controversy surrounding *Coming Home* was relatively muted compared to the firestorm of virulent protest surrounding the release of another 1978 film, *The Deerhunter*. The amount of political controversy this film engendered and the powerful visceral emotional effect it had on its viewers are testament to the strength of the filmmaker's vision and execution as well as the raw nerve that Vietnam still represented in the American psyche.

During three hours *The Deerhunter* presents a rich tapestry of characterization, tracing the effects of war on both the combatants and those left at home. Like a fine and classic play it is divided into three acts or as others put it, movements (as in a symphony). The beginning shows the rituals of life and friendship in a small and gritty steel mill town as three young men prepare to go to war. The middle features in harrowing closeup the in-country experiences of those same men. The final portion reveals how the war has changed their lives forever.

The Deerhunter was a Universal Pictures release that was largely funded by the British entertainment conglomerate EMI. It was directed by Michael Cimino, whose only previous theatrical credit was the Clint Eastwood film *Thunderbolt and Lightfoot*. Cimino worked from a script he had penned along with Deric Washburn, Louis Garfinkle, and Quinn K. Redeker. The talented Vilmos Zsigmond contributed greatly as the cinematographer. The best known of the film's performers and the main character was Michael, played by Robert DeNiro. He prepared for his role by visiting Steubenville, Ohio, to pick up local color in the steel mills. Joining him were a number of relatively unknown young actors, including Christopher Walken as Nick, John Savage as Stephen, the late John Cazale as their buddy Stan, Chuck Aspegren as Axel, George Dzundza as John, and Meryl Streep as Linda.

When *The Deerhunter* was completed, Universal knew it had an important but difficult-to-watch three-hour potential masterpiece. Perceiving the film as a "downer," the studio wisely chose to release it on a limited-platform basis. With that distribution pattern, word of mouth would slowly generate box office and allow the film, with its ambiguous title and challenging themes, to survive the plethora of upbeat Christmas competition. To qualify for the Oscars, *The Deerhunter* opened for only one week in New York and Los Angeles. As planned, acclaim, interest, and indeed, controversy gradually mounted, and so did the breadth of release and box office return. The distribution became a classic rollout pattern that generated previously unprecedented returns for a Vietnam-related film.

In synopsis here is a description of what the public saw in this epic film. Stanley Myers's sadly evocative music and John Williams's integral score accompany the credits, which when completed lead to the dawn of a new day. It is morning, but inside the dingy and dirty steel mills of a small Pennsylvania town the night shift is just ending. The movie introduces one of its recurring images as the camera focuses on the powerful brightness of a blast furnace's fire. Paradoxically dangerous and helpful but always powerful, this element will recur with regularity and meaning. As the shift's whistle sounds, big and inarticulate Axel (Aspegren), little and weasely Stan (Cazale), Michael (DeNiro), Nick (Walken), and Steven (Savage) head to the showers. This is an exciting day for the latter three Ukrainian-Americans; it is their last day on the job as they prepare to go off to a tour of duty in Vietnam. (Details of their enlistment, training, why they already know their assignment, and so on are largely irrelevant. Similar small problems or questions appear but deserve to remain ignored in the context of the overall execution.)

It is also an auspicious day as it is Steven's wedding day. In celebration the five back-slapping, beer-drinking, working-class buddies go off to the neighborhood bar to have a good time. The film is packed with rich physical and thematic detail. On the way from the parking lot to the tavern owned by their friend John (Dzundza), two more recurrent elements are introduced amid the scenes establishing the camaraderie and boyish joking that help constitute male bonding. Michael, looking at the clear sky, remarks on the good omen it foretells for their imminent deer hunting trip. And on the way to the watering hole, as the men pile in Michael's old Cadillac, Nick bets him that the car can outrun a big truck sharing the tight road. This dangerous bit of adolescent high-speed hijinks is the first depiction of Nicky's penchant for gambling and risk.

In contrast to the men's world, the film cuts to the lesser-defined female characters, led by Linda (Streep), sloshing through the muddy streets of the dingy town they call home. Dressed as bridesmaids, they prepare for the "opening act's" main life cycle event, the wedding. This occasion allows the filmmaker to linger on the rich ethnic traditions and homey nature of this small slice of Americana and the events that give purpose and texture to everyone's lives. The town, its architecture, the fat old ladies in babushkas, the pretty young girls, Linda's abusive alcoholic father, and the small-town grocer who doubles as the wedding crooner all richly render texture to the initial portion of the film.

Back in the male milieu of the bar, the men get drunk together and shoot pool. Nicky bets on billiard shots and the beloved Pittsburgh Steelers, while the quiet Michael reveals his role as the leader and the characters' other attributes

begin to be defined. Axel is just a big dumb gentle bear, Stan a womanizing con-
niver, Steven a sensitive and soft young man preparing to marry his bride (pregnant by someone else) and ship off to war in a few days. In a memorable scene
the men revel in their companionship and slight intoxication as they sing along
with Frankie Valli's rendition of "You're Just Too Good to Be True" on the
jukebox. The outside world intrudes as Steven's mother drags him out in
preparation for his big day.

Best friends Michael and Nicky return to their modest trailer home on a hill
overlooking the town and its belching mills. Standing in sharp contrast are people's ugly, yet familiar edifices and the grandeur and beauty of the nearby
natural environment of God's making. As the men put on their tuxedos, they
discuss their anxiously awaited deer hunt, and Michael explains his almost
spiritual code. The prey, the deer, must be killed with one shot! Anything else
is "pussy." This very language separates the sexes and connotes the manly
nature of the event. By using sexual slang, the men further exclude the women,
a fact that the experience of war also accomplishes for the group.

Not only does the hunt foreshadow the war; it also codifies a sense of fair
play and dignity that others do not adhere to in the context of the hunt or of the
war to come. Unbeknown to these young men, notions of honor, mercy, and,
ultimately, control over events will become obsolete. To the prey, which they
themselves will become, the ultimate truth is survival, not the means by which
it is achieved. Michael's noble code will be severely challenged. But for now it
is the calming regularity of life, exaggerated and exemplified by the rigid ritual
of this ethnic wedding and of the hunt that will define existence, knowledge, and
a sense of place in the community and cosmos.

The worlds of men and women, peace and war, and other spheres of existence and consciousness are continually contrasted within the frame and
through crosscut editing. The beauty of the day, the proud opulence of the Russian Orthodox church, the pomp and circumstance of the ceremony, and the
togetherness of the friends all stand in the foreground, while in the background
the despair of a drunk on the corner, the black eye of the lovely but abused
Linda, and the pregnancy of the white-clad bride all echo the contrasting,
underlying fabric of real life. When the film goes to Vietnam, the beauty and
ugliness will switch place in the respective foreground and background of the
film and the lives depicted.

At the wedding reception the shy Michael stares inarticulately at Nicky's girl,
Linda. The spry little Steven energetically dances to a folk tune. And in a traditional ceremony he and his bride drink out of a double cup together. Legend
holds that if not a drop is spilled, then they will have good luck and happiness.
In extreme closeup, beyond the vision and awareness of the characters, like so
much of reality, a small drop of wine does trickle onto the bride's white dress.
In a contrasting redness, the wine resembles blood.

For the first-time viewer the foreboding of this scene is obvious. However,
only later or on repeated viewing do other aspects of the film's careful construction

The Deerhunter (Universal Pictures, 1978). Meryl Streep and Robert DeNiro at Stevie's wedding.

become apparent. The talented and quick step of the groom will be replaced by the despair of a legless amputee.[14] The concentrated intent of the bride will be lost in a daze of catatonic mourning. The off-limit desire of an innocent young man for his best friend's girl will become the shared comfort of lovemaking borne of grief and loneliness.

The wedding reception is in the American Legion hall, a modest and typical setting for such an event, and its military nature is underscored by the proud poster-sized pictures of the three young men set to go off to war. They share the glory of the day's event as they are prominently displayed on the walls. A banner declares, "Serving God and country proudly." As the lascivious master of ceremonies sings the familiar "You're Just Too Good to Be True," some of the men retire into the public bar area of the hall. There a solitary Green Beret sits drinking. The naive men about to go to war are intrigued and quiz the soldier on what life is like over there. He rather rudely ignores them, off in his own pained world. The men bluster about their eagerness to go off to where the bullets are flying and to the implied glory of war. Unresponsive to their queries, the Green Beret is again questioned about the reality of in-country and can only say, "Fuck it."

As the reception breaks up the buddies chase the bride and groom as they drive off to their honeymoon. An intoxicated Michael runs after them through the town streets, uncharacteristically losing his inhibitions and shedding all his clothes along the way. When Nicky catches up to Michael, they together emotionally and vocally strip away to the inner layers of their souls. Nicky gives words to the fear that they might not come home alive from the war. He declares that he "loves this fuckin' place." Then he makes Michael promise that whatever happens in Vietnam, "don't leave me over there." Michael nude, supported by Nicky, promises.

The film cuts from the darkness of the night to the blinding outdoor brilliance of a sunny day up in the beautiful mountains. The deer hunt is on. Michael is disgusted with the immature conduct of his cohorts, who refuse to take the hunt as seriously as he does. Nicky acts as a peacemaker and bridge to the rest of the group. The hunting scene is handled like another religious ceremony. It is a rite that Michael pursues in a state of isolated concentration. As he stalks a beautiful buck, the grandeur of nature is featured in stellar wide-screen composition. A choir of chanting voices echoes the assemblage that performed at the wedding in the church, and brings meaning to the hallowed and holy nature of God's cathedral, here the mountaintops, canyons, and cataract. Michael achieves his goal, cleanly, honorably, and gloriously bagging the animal with one shot. The telescopic lens he uses cuts to an extreme closeup of the terror in the eye of the deer as death comes to it. Clearly Michael is "the Deerhunter" of the film's title.

The men load their trophy, gear, and beer into the car and head back to town. In tired repose they enter John's bar and now pensively listen to the big man as he softly plays the piano. There is no dialogue, merely sweaty and greasy men uncharacteristically quiet as the reality of this hunt's conclusion becomes apparent. It is the end of an era and of innocence, and their unknown fate renders them speechless and nearly tearful. As the camera explores each of their faces, the soundtrack gradually replaces John's peaceful and melodic tones with the powerful mechanized whir of helicopter blades.

The audio transition gives way to a dramatic visual change as the next act is introduced by fire. We are now in-country, and mortars explode everywhere with great force and noise. As fire rains down an enemy soldier brutally shoots an injured civilian girl. In quick response this brutality is met by a filthy Michael, who appears to us now as a crazed-looking soldier in the midst of combat. He sprays the North Vietnamese soldier with a flamethrower, utilizing fire to torch the man.

As pigs gruesomely eat the singed flesh of the soldier, the sounds of helicopters overhead connote relief to the besieged Michael and what is left of his group. Jumping into the hastily arranged LZ are Steven and Nicky, reunited with Michael, apparently after a long absence in-country from their friend. Michael is so preoccupied, intent, and adrenalized that he barely acknowledges or recognizes his lifelong buddies. Any reunion (however implausible this might be here in the bush) is cut short as the smoke clears and the camera pulls back to show an NVA or VC onslaught closing in on the Americans as the hamlet battle scene.

The film abruptly cuts to its most harrowing and controvesial sequence as the protagonists must endure captivity as prisoners. The details of their capture are not shown, nor are they important. The young men are now trapped in tiger cages in a river, with water up to their necks. There underneath a little hut they wallow cold, beaten and ill-fed. The brutality of their captors is not fully revealed until the sound of gunfire is heard. The prisoners are being used in a deadly game of Russian roulette, while their captors bet on the outcome. With a portrait of Ho Chi Minh on the wall, the guards brutaly run this ultimate gambling game, which results in graphically depicted point-blank deaths. As blood realistically spurts from the heads of unlucky American and South Vietnam soldiers, our protagonists await their fate within close earshot of the sick undertakings. Stevie is almost hysterical with trauma and fear. Only Michael is able to give him a semblance of comfort, holding him and speaking to him in an effort to keep him alive and sane.

When it is our heroes' turn to play the deadly game, the extreme closeups heighten the tension to an unbelievable level. The short, brutal, and foreign clicks of the enemies' language as they bark out a demand for each man to pull the trigger are designed to make the viewer hate them. (This one-dimensional portrait of not just an enemy but an Asian one led to charges of racism and xenophobia.) As Stevie faces his anonymous fellow victim, the suspense mounts, and the very movement of the gun, the near inability to pull the trigger, and the almost slow-motion rolling of the cylinder to its next potentially deadly bullet chamber are all detailed.

Forced to endure and ever the leader, Michael must convince a hysterical Stevie to take his chances and pull the trigger or be shot and killed outright. Michael rallies him with the exhortation "You can do it!" Understandably quivering, Stevie pulls the trigger, releasing a bullet but only grazing his head as the projectile flies into the ceiling. Everyone laughs because his shaking has saved his life. This bit of luck allows him to return to the pit as Nicky is ushered in to play against his best friend.

With great bravado Michael convinces the evil captors to increase the number of bullets in the gun. He and Nicky then each take their chances, hoping to advance the cylinder to a bullet — Michael then abruptly turns the gun from his own temple to the enemy leader. Scoring a direct hit in the forehead, he quickly unleashes all his shots as Nicky springs to action and dispatches the others. The hysterical and embittered Nicky repeatedly beats the skull of a now-dead captor, and Michael has to pull him off to effect their hasty retreat. They release Stevie from his cage and under Michael's leadership wade onto a log to float away from this horrid place. The carefully staged Russian roulette scenes remain one of the most harrowing and memorable sequences in the history of recorded film. Some observers declared this to be easy and cheap theatrics based on no factual accounts or historic records of any such incidents in Vietnam. This fictional technique became the source of cries of racism, moral and historic inequity, and dramatic opportunism.

Whether such a brutal game ever really took place, and no evidence since the film supports that it did, is irrelevant to the power of the imagery based on realistically staged violence. The use of Russian roulette, like other imagery in the film, will recur. At this juncture it is a continuation of the already alluded to gambling aspects of life. However, the invention of this fictional device is very effective and justified. It creates in an unprecedented film manner a sequence of brutality that goes a long, even if not entire, way in demonstrating the ugly brutality of war. The wounds are not clean but horrid, resulting in instantaneous spurts of blood. The triumph over the captors is hollow as the men are brutalized and become in turn brutal. Russian roulette is able to convey the random aspects of combat death associated with war, the questions of luck and fate that hound combatants and confound survivors.

Gut-wrenching skill continues in the escape of the three heroes. Nicky is barely holding on to the log in attempting to survive the ordeal. Stevie is kept alive and above water only by the strength of Michael. Eventually they float under a rudimentary hanging bridge. Hearing rapids around the bend, Michael orders them to grab hold of the span and leave their log as it tumbles onward toward the deadly falls. The bedraggled and wounded men flag down a U.S. helicopter crew, which attempts a difficult midair evacuation.

The camera shoots in a downward angle from the helicopter as we see Nicky pulled up into the copter. As the others struggle to make it, a weakened Stevie loses his grip and tumbles downward into the churning river. Michael, undoubtedly strong enough to hold on, heroically lets go in an effort to save his friend from certain drowning. Michael is able to rescue Stevie, and together they make it to the banks of the river. Stevie's legs are broken, and he is in great pain. "The deerhunter" carries his comrade for miles, finally encountering a ragtag convoy retreating from the front. As planes scream overhead and fires burn in the hellish background, soldiers and civilians clog the road in a desperate attempt to escape the area. Michael stops an ARVN jeep and after some initial miscommunication is able to convince the young officer to take the badly wounded Stevie to a hospital. Michael precariously rests his friend on the only space available, the hood of the jeep, and, bewildered and exhausted, continues on foot alone amid the crowded column of desperate humanity.

The film abruptly cuts to the clear, bright, clinical confines of a U.S. Army hospital in Saigon. It, too, is a noisy and crowded place but for now is far away from the war front. A confused, sad, trancelike Nicky sits alone on the hospital patio ledge consumed with inner pain. He cannot think or properly answer the simplest personal questions posed by hospital staff, as if his previous life had never happened. Later a slightly improved Nicky runs through the hospitall, tragically populated by amputees and other casualties of the war. Anxiously he reaches a phone bank set up for GIs in Saigon to call home. When the operator puts through his call to Clairton, and Linda, he is unable to speak.

The extent of Nicky's pain and trauma is extreme. He wanders the streets of Saigon, dramatically re-created in great detail as a rough-and-tumble place full of whorehouses and tacky touches of Americana that cater to soldiers. Young Vietnamese girls bump and grind to country and western music as drunk GIs ogle. Nicky goes with a prostitute to her room. Her crying infant is in the same room where they are to have sex. Nicky is sickened by the tawdry nature of everything. The whore tells him he can call her "Linda" if he likes. He says to forget it and escapes the room in a desperate attempt to gain a symbolic breath of air and relief from the oppressive place. Judging by similar scenes in other films, Nicky's lack of interest is understandable but inherently implies a probable sexual dysfunction as well.

Wandering past a dark alley, Nicky hears gunshots and cheers and sees dead bodies being unceremoniously dumped near the garbage. He is frightened and intrigued. As he approaches, an older Frenchman welcomes him (an immoral man who profits in the black-market underbelly of this teeming city and a living throwback to the days of the previously defeated Western power).

Ushered into the all-male, smoke-filled confines of a big Russian roulette game, Nicky winces as he watches the "performers." A one-eyed, chain-smoking Vietnamese barks instructions to the doomed players in a manner similar to their captor on the river. Something snaps in Nicky. He rushes toward the game and deliberately grabs a gun, puts it to his head and pulls the trigger without hesitation. As he runs out, amid surprised and delighted shouts, a member of the audience runs after him. It is Michael, now bearded and in civilian clothes. He is not able to catch his friend, and is driven off by the Frenchman. The latter does not want to lose this crazed Caucasian so willing to participate in such a deadly game of chance.

Nicky's mental instability and especially the way this evil game elicited such a flashback exhibit the type of behavior associated with post–Vietnam syndrome. His mental illness is a continuation in a long line of such film characterizations. The fact that we have seen and not merely heard about some of the causes solidifies the reality of his sick response.

The final sequence of the film begins as Michael returns home to Pennsylvania. In this third act he will attempt to confront his experiences and make some sense of them and in so doing will be able to reintegrate into a civilian life. Complicating this process will be the guilt he feels at having left Nicky in Vietnam and at having survived the inferno.

In full special forces uniform and on the outskirts of town, he instructs his cab driver to drive past the sign that proclaims, "Welcome Home, Michael." In fact he goes beyond his trialer and assembled friends, escaping detection as he seeks solitude in a nearby hotel room. He is a changed man, no longer the Michael who left. As evocative string music wells up on the soundtrack, the green bereted soldier crouches on the floor in solitude, clenching his pounding head. His inner turmoil, what he has seen, his perceived failure to help his beloved friends, all pain him. The headache is a physical manifestation of the psychological damage, a symptom also associated with post-traumatic stress disorder. Like Walken back in Saigon, DeNiro is able to convey his anguish through subtle grimaces and sad eyes without the necessity of overblown theatrics or expository dialogue.

That night Michael looks longingly at a tattered old picture of Linda, which he, too, has carried throughout his tour in Vietnam. As dawn breaks over the town, old buddies and partygoers leave Nicky and Michael's trailer home, where Linda now lives. Michael waits until everyone else departs before he goes "home." The scene of reunion is dramatically understated, an elegant moment that encapsulates the reasons DeNiro and Streep are perhaps the preeminent performers of their generation. They do not know what to say; time and events have separated them. Pain, worry, and ugliness have intervened. They are old friends, potential lovers, happy and awkward at the same time. Like countless homecomings for men returning from war, they are choked with the emotion that conveys relief and joy in having survived.

Finally Linda says, "I was hoping Nick was with you." He remains AWOL. As an American flag hangs prominently from the wall, Linda sayas, "I'm glad you're alive" and hugs Michael. He walks her down to work at the local grocery and receives the attention and adulation of many townspeople. Then for a moment we believe the film has returned to Vietnam as a violent orange inferno engulfs the screen. As the whole scene is illuminated, we find it is once again only the blast furnace at the mill. Michael is ready to see his friends again. They tell him nothing has changed, and we believe them. But for Michael and the others who went to Vietnam, everything has changed. The buddies innocently ask him, "How does it feel to be shot?" Stan has taken to carrying a silly small-caliber gun to protect himself from jealous husbands. It stands in absurd contrast to the weaponry that we have seen and that Michael intimately knows.

Michael goes to pay a call on Angela, Stevie's bride. When he arrives at her mother's home, he finds the young woman in a nearly catatonic state of despair. He wants to know what befell Stevie. Angela is unable to speak but writes out a response. As Michael leaves this tragic scene, a little boy, the one Angela was pregnant with back at the wedding, points a toy gun at Michael.

Michael calls the nearby Veterans Administration hospital where Stevie is staying. We see the subdued young man in a wheelchair, missing two legs and an arm. When he takes the phone call from Michael, Stevie is overcome with emotion and terminates the call.

Meanwhile Linda makes dinner for Michael and suggests that they go to bed together in an effort to "comfort each other." Michael cannot bring himself to do so and leaves, saying, like many a returned and bewildered vet, "I feel far away." Later the old gang goofs off at the bowling alley, but for Michael all the fun has gone out of these activities. He has great difficulty relating to his old crew, their inane hijinks, and civilian life. Only the lovely and sad Linda seems to offer any hope of reaching Michael.

The remaining male members of the group go on the film's second deer hunt, only it is not, as one of them say, "like old times." Michael again stalks a buck alone, while the others cavort. Finally he has it face to face squarely in his gunsight. He chooses to spare the magnificent animal, instead shooting into the air. Then in an affirmation of hiw own health and of the future, he shouts to the heavens, "OK!" He no longer wants to shed blood. Empathizing with the hunted, he knows what he must do. The remainder of this deer hunt is a sad disaster. Michael is fed up with Stan's asinine whining and abruptly pulls the trigger of Stan's little revolver, its cylinder rotated randomly, pressed to its owner's forehead. The others are shocked into silence by this potentially fatal and crazy overreaction. With this last bit of antisocial behavior, and the cathartic effect of being in the mountains, Michael begins to take steps to return to normalcy. He and Linda make love. Overhead in the side of the frame is the old stuffed buck's head from the first hunt now so long ago.

Michael goes to see Stevie at the local VA hospital. Michael tells Stevie he must return home to his wife and baby. Frightened, the crippled veteran says, "I don't fit." Then he shows Michael all the cash that keeps coming from Vietnam. Together they realize this provides a new clue to Nicky's whereabouts.

The transition to the next scene begins with the familiar whir of a helicopter. Michael is back in Vietnam, where he promised to never leave Nicky. It is 1975 and the country is in chaos, about to fall to the communists. This only recently completed time in history is excitingly re-created in crowded street scenes that convey the panic of a city out of control. The chaos of the hinterlands convoy of the second act has in essence now reached the outskirts of this urban capital. The familiar and destructive force of fire is seen everywhere as buildings smolder from rocket attacks. Artillery and sabotage have rendereed the river and canals, despite their watery nature, floating infernos. People riot at the gates of Tan Son Nhut Airport and the U.S. Embassy. Interspersed in these harrowing scenes is recent newsreel footage, which adds to the sense of authenticity.

Dressed as a civilian Michael makes his way to the old gambling house. There he meets the familiar French proprietor preparing to evacuate the beleaguered city. Despite the danger in remaining, the greedy man is convinced to take Michael to Nicky. The two men make their way through the crowded streets and canals in a scene that resembles hell on earth.

As everything comes down around them, with artillery bombardments heard on the outskirts of town, a game of Russian roulette goes on. The same one-eyed man runs the contest, and as a contestant shoots himself, Michael catches a glimpse of Nicky. Preparing to go "on stage," Nicky sports the red band around the forehead and tacky muslin white shirt that constitute the uniform, such as it is, for these desperate "players." Nicky is glassy eyed. He does not recognize Michael, who attempts to get through to him. Nicky is pale, with rotten teeth and the bewildered demeanor of a heroin addict. Michael declares, "I came 12,000 miles to get you. . . . I love you. . . . You are my friend." This does not seem to awaken Nicky from his trance, nor does slapping him.

In a last desperate attempt to reach his friend, Michael attempts to buy his own way into the roulette game opposite Nicky. Even the cynical Frenchman is touched, contributing the money Michael gave him as a bribe. Now face to face in closeup amid the howling and yapping mass of lowlife South Vietnamese and equally despicable Caucasian American spectators in business suits, the two friends are once again reunited as they were in the little hut above the river.

Michael beseeches Nicky to come to his senses and come home with him. Using the repetitive tic of a rhetorical question, DeNiro, in a fashion similar to that which we saw him use in *Taxi Driver* and in the early film entry in this book, *Hi Mom!*, pleads over and over, "Is this what you want? Is this what you want?" as he threatens his own head with the gun. A desperate Michael tells Nicky again that he loves him and pulls the trigger. There is no bullet, and the spectators scream with excitement at this seemingly crazed new player. Michael is exhausted with relief. He is glad to be alive, having found that life is still worth living. Perhaps this sacrifice made point blank to his friend will reach Nicky as nothing else can.

Nicky reaches for the gun, having evinced with some degree of recognition at Michael's actions. As Michael looks at poor Nicky's needle-tracked arms, he screams, "Talk to me. . . . Remember the mountains. . . ? Remember." He is too late. Nicky cocks the gun to his head, pulls the trigger, and blows his brains out! Michael tries to grab him and cries out in agony, but he cannot save Nicky.

Cimino grounds Michael's sad return to the United States from his unsuccessful "mission" in an historical context. The final retreating U.S. forces are seen scuttling their helicopters off the deck of the USS *Hancock*. ABC television Hillary Brown presents the coverage of this real-life rout and defeat as the steeple of the Clairton church appears. The scene of the wedding is now the occasion of the final life cycle event, Nicky's funeral. Michael, Axel, Stan, and John are reunited again as pallbearers. Linda, Angela, Stevie in his wheelchair, and their families mourn together this tragic casualty of war. All have now come home in one form or another.

Hardly anyone is really able to speak as what remains of the old gang gathers afterward at John's bar. Everyone tries to busy their hands and minds, but the sadness hangs heavily. As the sweet and musically inclined bachelor John prepares the food, he seeks comfort in half-consciously humming a melody. The others hear the familiar tune and pick up on it. Sadly but once again collectively, they sing the words to "God Bless America." The film ends.

Like much of the rest of the movie, *The Deerhunter*'s ending was ambiguous and controversial. Some people thought it absurd that after all that has occurred, these poor people have learned nothing. Others thought that in the midst of so much antiwar and anti–American sentiment, this must be a statement of patriotism. Rather, it is simply a comforting reaffirmation that, despite all, life will continue.

These folks are simple working-class Americans touched and changed by the war, and their song is in no way political. It is comforting, it is familiar, it is a harking back to ritualized moments in elementary school or church, to less troubled times, to values that although altered, survive. The less than clear meaning of the final scene was a filmmaking strength, not a weakness. Why not send people out of the theaters from this powerful tour de force discussing its meaning, intent, and pathos? The discussion, the controversy, the creative vision, and even the business milieu that allowed this film to be made were a measure of the beginning of the collective healing process.

Because the film is ultimately about the hugely controversial and unpopular war, observers chose to criticize or react to it in ways that reflected their own political bias. Some bestowed upon the film right-wing, gung-ho, and racist attitudes and then in a manner similar to that reserved for the much inferior film *The Green Berets* panned the film despite its breadth, power, and crafts. In this way *The Deerhunter* and other direct movies of the period revealed the continuing controversy and pain the war generated.

If the film was ambiguous in its politics, this provided others with another source of criticism: that the film was gray or purposely confusing. Given the nature of the conflict and the world's lack of pat black-and-white reality, this became one more ridiculous contention. The film was condemned on the one hand for being too political and on the other for not being political enough. Fortunately the handwringing and haranguing generated enough controversy to urge others to view the film themselves and draw their own conclusions. Both the box office return and the year-end accolades revealed, at least if nothing else, an understanding of the film's artistic beauty as a rich and powerful piece of filmmaking, not a history lesson.

Cimino was quoted as saying his protagonists are simply "trying to support each other. They are not endorsing anything except their common humanity."[15] Like most men going off to war, and like the United States itself, the heroes had no idea what they were getting themselves into. For most people pain and suffering, although often endured in isolation, are healed only through collective comforting. The film's sense of tradition and community echoes the rehabilitative powers of our country and culture itself.

Also, in this way the film joins other works, such as William Wyler's tale of three World War II vets returning to America in the classic *Best Years of Our Lives*. Gilbert Adair observes "that Cimino's intentions are basically the same as Wyler's: to restore his audience's confidence in their country's regenerative powers, which took a bad mauling in the 60's."[16] When *The Deerhunter* was entered in the Berlin Film Festival in 1979, the Soviet delegates withdrew from the event in protest. They categorized the film as "racist" and a "criminal violation of the truth."[17]

In the context of a fairly negative review, Stanley Kauffman defends the film's use of symbolism. On the Russian roulette, he writes, "First, the Viet Cong were quite capable of barbarism. . . . Second, the sequence fits the film, thematically and metaphorically." Then he goes on to say, "*The Deerhunter* is not about Vietnam: it's about three steelworkers, bonded in maleness, who work and drink and hunt together, who enlist together . . . who are captured and tortured together, escape together, and who then . . . move on to . . . differing resolutions of that experience."[18] Philip French in the *London Observer* parallels some of these opinions when he writes, "The picture is about the perennial American preoccupation . . . with male friendship . . . and is constructed deliberately to eliminate discussion of war-aims and the larger issues involved in the Vietnam conflict."[19]

Roger Ebert, in his refreshingly unstrident manner, writes as follows: "It can be said that the film . . . is the most impressive blending of 'boxoffice' and 'art' in American movies since *Bonnie and Clyde*. . . . *The Deerhunter* is said to be about many subjects: about male bonding, about mindless patriotism, about the dehumanizing effects of the war, about Nixon's 'silent majority.' It is about any of those things that you choose, but more than anything else it is a heart-breakingly effective fictional machine that evokes the agony of the Vietnam time. . . . If it is not overtly 'anti-war,' why should it be? What *The Deerhunter* insists is that we not forget the war."[20]

The Deerhunter powerfully integrated a number of subgenres within the group of films. In an unusually brutal manner, it features instances of combat and in-country sequences befitting a ruthless war. It examines the effects of the war on both those left at home and those returning home. Ultimately antiwar in its harrowing depiction of the tragic effects, *The Deerhunter* is not overtly so. By reaffirming basic American values, the film is the opposite of most sign-of--the-times films' desecration and rejection of institution and "establishment" values.

In chronicling the experiences of three young soldiers, the film also deals in a powerful manner with the problems of returning veterans, physical and emotional reintegration, and rehabilitation. The film's action sequences are so bloody and well staged that the film was able to appeal to the least discriminating male audiences as well. Therefore *The Deerhunter* managed to integrate all the subgenres identified in Chapter 2. In 1978 the American film industry finally responded to the seminal event of the preceding decade.

As major A movie productions involving a controversial subject, both *Coming Home* and *The Deerhunter* generated a huge amount of interest. As mentioned, both were critcally acclaimed but had vocal detractors. For the former, criticism centered around artistic elements or its more conventional soap opera undertones. The latter film engendered virulent journalistic, industry, and general public reactions. A whirlwind of controversy and accusations of racism surrounded the portrayal of the enemy.

As noted previously in the context of *The Green Berets*, this firestorm merely heightened curiosity, afforded free publicity, and ultimately contributed to the films' box office performance. *Coming Home*, perceived as a dovish, left-wing treatment, grossed nearly $30 million in its domestic first-run release. *The Deerhunter*, most often seem as a more hawkish or at least politically ambiguous portrait, went on to gross nearly $60 million.

The year 1978 stood as a watershed in the collection of films, and as such that year's productions, along with the eagerly awaited but still delayed *Apocalypse Now*, typified the industry perception that the American public was finally able to examine the bloody conflict. Already a majority consensus had developed that the war was wrong and wasteful. However, the factors that contributed to that conclusion and the overall assessment of American motivations and conduct in the war were, and are still, subjects of great contention.

Each film was a fine exercise in screenwriting, directing, acting, and all the elements that make for great movies and translate into deserved public interest. The two came to dominate the year-end critical accolades and ceremonies, which increased their box office performance. Ultimately this bottom-line factor contributed most directly to the conclusion that films about the war should continue to be made.

The Deerhunter won the Academy Award for Best Picture, beating out *Coming Home* and others. It won the top award of the New York Film Critics as well. For the Oscar for best actor, Jon Voight won over Robert DeNiro. Jane Fonda took home the Best Actress award for her project. Competing for Best Supporting Actor were Bruce Dern and Christopher Walken. Here *The Deerhunter* role won. The Supporting Actress category was represented by Penelope Milford in *Coming Home* and the relatively unknown Meryl Streep in *The Deerhunter*. Neither of the two wonderful performances won.

Michael Cimino won for directing *The Deerhunter* over Hal Ashby for *Coming Home*. Continuing the numerous nominations for each film, their screenwriters faced off in the written directly for the screen category. *Coming Home*'s Waldo Salt and Robert C. Jones won over *The Deerhunter*'s four-writer team. In the other screenwriting category, for adapation, a little-known, real-life Vietnam vet named Oliver Stone won for his thrilling work on life in a Turkish prison, *Midnight Express*. In the film editing awards *The Deerhunter*'s Peter Zinner triumphed over *Coming Home* and others. *The Deerhunter* was also nominted but did not win for sound nor for Vilmos Zsigmond's wonderful cinematography.

The night belonged to Best Picture winner *The Deerhunter*, but *Coming Home* also captured two major awards. For the viewing public and for industry insiders, this showing by Vietnam films seemed to exonerate those who had persevered in their making. Jane Fonda, who remained much disliked for her conduct during the war, showed great insensitivity when she condemned the racism she said was inherent in *The Deerhunter*. She actively campaigned against *The Deerhunter* in the prevoting Hollywood jockeying that preceded the ceremony. However, she admitted to the *Los Angeles Herald Examiner* that "I haven't seen it."[21]

At the end of the night the totals were three Oscars for *Coming Home* and five for *The Deerhunter*, including the big one and the one that translates into most box office reward. The evening exemplified the renewed interest in important portraits on a decidedly unglamorous subject. The medium of film was reclaiming its role as a means of fictionalized historical recreation and dramatic analysis of the lives touched by the Vietnam War. The "four horsemen" were decidedly different films that represented a vigorous return to direct exposition for the year 1978.

References

1. Michael Paris, "The American Film Industry and Vietnam," *History Today* (London, July 18, 1988), p. 23.

2. William J. Palmer, *The Films of the Seventies—A Social History* (Metuchen, N.J.: Scarecrow Press, 1987), p. 181.

3. *Ibid.*, p. 182.

4. Max Youngstein, "The Boys in Company C," cited in Lawrence Suid, *Guts and Glory* (Reading, Mass.: Addison-Wesley, 1978), p. 319.

5. Daniel Ford, *Incident at Muc Wa* (New York: Doubleday, 1967).

6. Mar Vista Productions, *Production Notes*, cited in *Guts and Glory*, p. 321.

7. *Ibid.*, p. 411.

8. Palmer, *The Films of the Seventies*, p. 209.

9. Mason Wiley and Damien Bona, *Inside Oscar: The Unofficial History of the Academy Awards* (New York: Ballantine Books, 1986), p. 554.

10. Brock Garland, *War Movies* (New York: Facts on File, 1987), p. 61.

11. Wiley and Bona, *Inside Oscar*, p. 554.

12. Stanley Kauffman, *Before My Eyes* (New York: Harper and Row, 1980), p. 118.

13. Roger Ebert, *Movie Home Companion* (Kansas City: Andrews McMeel and Parker, 1987), p. 118.

14. Palmer, *The Films of the Seventies*, p. 196.

15. Frank N. Magill, ed., *Magill's American Film Guide* (Pasadena: Salem Press, 1987), p. 866.

16. Gilbert Adair, *Vietnam on Film* (London: Proteus, 1981), p. 133.

17. Kauffmann, *Before My Eyes*, p. 326.

18. *Ibid.*, p. 328.

19. Philip French, *London Observer*, cited *ibid.*, p. 329.

20. Ebert, *Movie Home Companion*, p. 150.

21. Wiley and Bona, *Inside Oscar*, p. 538.

Chapter 6

And the Apocalypse, 1979

Meanwhile in the Philippines, hurricanes, heart attacks, and other natural disasters were plaguing the production of Francis Ford Coppola's eagerly awaited epic, *Apocalypse Now*. It was to have been the first major film about the war in release. However, the unexpected events rendered it the last completed. Having relinquished its lead-off position, and having become a rather notorious undertaking, the film's ability to live up to the hype was a huge problem for Coppola, his Zoetrope Studios, and United Artists. The world would have to wait for the Cannes Film Festival (where it would win the coveted Palm d'Or grand prize) and the fall, for the domestic audience to see the finished product.

Back in the United States television continued to contribute "made-fors." On April 22, 1979, ABC broadcast a lengthy (180 minutes) film based on true-life events in Vietnam and their effect on a family back home. *Friendly Fire* was based on C. D. B. Bryan's controversial book, which, as the title suggests, involved the tragic loss of life of Iowa farm boy Michael Mullen as a result of actions by his own side in wartime. The transition of young Mullen's family from patriotic, unquestioning, heartland supporters of the war to pained and cynical antiwar activists mirrored the general populace's change during the course of the conflict.

David Greene directed Fay Kanin's screenplay. Carol Burnett and Ned Beatty starred as the parents, Peg and Gene Mullen. Sam Waterston portrayed the author Bryan. Dennis Erdman was Michael, and his little brother was played by a very young Timothy Hutton. Among the in-country footage's platoon members were Hilly Hicks, the radio engineer in *Go Tell the Spartans*; Kevin Hooks, and David Keith.

As the film begins it is 1969 and Michael is preparing to leave for the war. An idolizing younger brother asks, How can you kill someone when you can't even watch a hog being slaughtered? Michael replies, "They teach you." As his anxious family says good-bye, his father gives the medal he won during World War II to his son.

Initially the young man's experiences in Vietnam are conveyed via voiceover readings of letters home. In a relatively brief time Michael rises to sergeant. Nevertheless, he begins to reveal disillusionment and confusion, particularly concerning the inability to identify the enemy. Soon thereafter a drab army car rumbles down the rural road. When the local priest gets out of the vehicle with the officer, the truth is apparent. Before the messengers can speak, the father asks, "Is my boy dead?" The officer reads the statement declaring that Sergeant Mullen "died while at a night defense position when artillery fire from friendly forces landed in the area."

Expressions of grief overtake everyone in the family, except Mrs. Mullen, who suppresses it in an angry effort to find out more particulars. The phrase "friendly fire" seems particularly absurd to her. Thus begins an odyssey of discovery and change, a personalization of what has been nebulously referred to as the "national tragedy" of Vietnam. Many of officialdom's responses are either unsatisfactory or incomplete. The Mullens write letters to other platoon members and interview a just-returned comrade in neighboring Waterloo. He bitterly tells them of his own homecoming experience and of how people are preoccupied with knowing whether he killed anybody. Truths beyond that seem of little interest.

The parents become increasingly embittered and mistrustful. Once-sympathetic friends are alienated by the antiwar activism that consumes the grieving parents. Using the paltry payment the army made them to help defray funeral costs, the Mullens run an ad in the *Des Moines Register* depicting 714 crosses for each of the Iowa sons who have died in the war. Peg Mullen joins her daughter, the local pastor, and others in a journey to Washington, D.C., to protest against the war. There Peg meets with wounded vets, politicians, and other activists. She questions the government's reporting policies vis-à-vis friendly fire because its lack of inclusion masks the true casualty rate. The visit of the Mullens to the rural Kentucky home of another grieving couple whose son died in the same friendly fire incident, leads to Peg's first tears. Also emitted is a shared sense of guilt that they taught their sons to obey and allowed them to march off to war without sufficiently questioning what cause it was they might die for.

One day author C. D. B. Bryan arrives in his VW microbus replete with painted peace sign. He has arranged to tell their saga. Bryan is able to form a bond of friendship while still maintaining a reporter's professional sense of objectivity. Returning to Washington, D.C., Bryan begins to interview officers who were either present or responsible for the First Battalion. Belying his preconceived notions, the military's culpability is almost nonexistent. Professional and deeply regretful officers attempt to shed light on the human error that led to the deaths. As officers and enlisted soldiers reveal details of the fateful evening, the action is recreated on screen on an hour-by-hour basis. The tragedy was ultimately caused by human error, a mistake in calculating the height of nearby trees, which hindered the trajectory of the shells and caused them to land too close. The stereotypic postwar imagery of a horrible government in conspiracy with a callous military is revealed to not be the case. However, the authorities are less than forthcoming on details, and civilian policymakers are less than sympathetic. By the same token the sympathetic characterization of the grieving parents, particularly the mother, is compromised by her almost irrational, near-obsessive, paranoid vision.

Bryan had tried to make the Mullens' pain his own. He sought the truth concerning their son's death as the only means by which to allow them to finally be able to let Michael go. The liberal antiwar author was predisposed to find a military-political conspiracy. Instead he merely found human error and with it a poignancy and dramatic tragedy beyond the grief of this one family's loss and representative of the entire nation's search for meaning.

The characters' ambiguity revealed a fine depth of characterization and struck a responsive chord that ultimately earned *Friendly Fire* an Emmy for Outstanding Drama, Best Director, Best Music (by Leonard Rosenmann), and Best Sound Editing. The film was nominated but did not win for Best Screenplay, Actor (Beatty), and Actress (Burnett).

As far as the tragedy and inevitability of friendly fire were concerned in Vietnam, a 1968 study revealed a contributory rate as high as 20 percent![1] Despite the mercifully and remarkably light casualty rate in Operation Desert Storm, incidences of friendly fire did take their toll. In October 1971 after seeing the Mullens, C. D. B. Bryan went to a Virginia apartment to interview the commanding officer of Sergeant Michael Mullen's battalion in Vietnam. The grieving family was, as it turned out, unfairly incensed at the lieutenant colonel. That man was none other than H. Norman Schwarzkopf! As has been reported, he was no stranger to friendly fire, having been bombed once himself by U.S. B-52s in Vietnam.[2]

As revealed to America in his Persian Gulf War briefings, the thoughtful general was also depicted as such in Bryan's book. In the film actor William Jordan portrayed the now-famous interviewee. In connection with the film project, Schwarzkopf recently revealed in his humorous manner tht he wrote actor Jordan at the time. The general said, "When I heard *Friendly Fire* was going to be made into a movie, I wondered where they would find someone handsome enough to do me justice."[3] (No doubt Scharzkopf himself will someday be the central figure in a telefilm or theatrical biography.)

To quote from an article that bridges twenty years from this episode in Vietnam, Steve Daley writes in the *Chicago Tribune*:

> Alternately dispassionate and angry, Schwarzkopf talked to Bryan about his Vietnam experience with candor and some insight.... As he discussed the accusations made against him by the Mullen family, Schwarzkopf told Bryan, "I hate what Vietnam has done to our country, I hate what Vietnam has done to our army." And still later he spoke about the doubts churned up by his tours in Vietnam.
>
> "When they get ready to send me again," Schwarzkopf said, "I'm going to have to stop and ask myself, 'Is it worth it?'"...
>
> Obviously, the general found a satisfactory answer to his question . . . [and] some measure of relief from the anger he felt over Vietnam....
>
> The Mullens were angry about the small lies the government told them about his [their son's] death. But they also came to be angry about the big lies. And there were big lies about U.S. military involvement in Cambodia, about the bombing of Laos, about the "secret plan" and the body counts and the unblinking light at the end of the tunnel.[4]

Daley goes on to report that Peg Mullen, now a widow, had recently gone from her home in Texas to the nation's capitol to protest Operation Desert Storm.

The reporter finishes his article, entitled "Not Only Generals Had to Exorcise Vietnam Demons," by writing, "National moods ebb and flow, and the way we feel about our institutions . . . is altered by time and circumstance. And sometimes history is subject to review, depending on who is doing the writing."[5] As the post–Vietnam War group of movies continues, that history continues to be shaped by precisely who is doing the filmmaking as well.

At this juncture in the book it is appropriate by way of introduction to the next movie to note again that during the Persian Gulf War one of the sources of the allies' stunning success was the genuine cohesion of the international force arrayed against Iraq. Going beyond diplomatic condemnation and opposition in a post–cold war environment, the military effort, although led and staffed primarily by the United States, still featured significant participation on the part of allied nations. Many countries participated in the campaign, including the United States, Britain, France, Saudi Arabia, and Egypt.

This international cooperation had been attempted in the Southeast Asian conflict as well. In the beginning of U.S. involvement in South Vietnam in 1961, the "more flags" policy was adopted. To varying degrees this policy's deployments were unsuccessful because of a lack of commitment, direction, and purpose. Nevertheless, at the height of the deployment of the Free World Military Forces, as they came to be known in 1969, there were some 68,889 troops. Thirty-nine countries had permitted their names to be listed as having sent aid to the allied effort, and several had deployed peacekeeping and noncombat forces.

Five countries contributed combat troops. They were the SEATO member nations of the Philippines, South Korea, Thailand, New Zealand, and Australia. As one veteran of both the Vietnam and Iraq tours recalled, the South Koreans were most famous for their raids on the well-stocked American PXs. All these allied nations faced internal opposition to their participation. It was the Australian contingent that peaked at a deployment of 7,672 and saw the most direct-combat action.

In 1979 as the government-sponsored Australian film industry continued its meteoric rise, that country's role in the Vietnam War was finally addressed in a head-on manner after a painful hiatus similar to that in the United States. Tom Jeffrey wrote and directed a film appropriately titled *The Odd Angry Shot*. This production's negative appraisals of the war effort were similar to those being produced in the United States. Receiving fourth billing after several fine Aussie actors was the now-well-known international star Bryan Brown. Appearing as the young man coming of age in the war was John Jarrett as Bill.

The film opens as the pimply faced young man is cheered on his imminent departure to Vietnam. To the strains of Peter, Paul, and Mary's "Leaving on a Jet Plane," Australia's Special Air Services wing over on Qantas. The young men quiz some veterans of the Southeast Asia tour. "How do we know the difference between Charlie and the villager?" They hang on the sergeant major's every word, understanding little of what he says. We also learn that, unlike the rotation of American soldiers as their tour of duty comes to an end, Aussies choose to rotate units all together so that there was continuity for each group.

In-country the film takes pains to recreate the mundane minutiae of daily existence. The torrential "fuckin' rain" becomes a leitmotif. It typifies the periods of enforced isolation and boredom, the inhospitality of the native environment, and the utter lack of control over events, and acts as a segue to moments of utter destruction. Clearing weather means renewed patrols in the bush.

A strength of the film is the moments of bonding that take place via male rituals such as playing cards, wisecracking, and drinking in the tent environment.

Films from *The Green Berets* to *Platoon* contained similar scenes that helped establish characters, relationships, and hierarchies, and, most important, provided a contrast to the sudden, heightened, and sometimes deadly level of reality of combat. One night the poker game is interrupted by incoming mortars. The first casualty is taken, and absolute confusion reigns among the men. The film then carefully nurtures the yin and yang rhythm of quiet and noise, boredom and adrenalized hyperawareness, life and death. Then the men wile away the hours with scatological and sexual banter. The rains abruptly stop, and the men go into battle.

Unlike their conscripted American counterparts, the Aussie soldiers are professionals. Their level of discipline and training is high. Nevertheless, they have a nagging suspicion that the people back home question, oppose, or do not care about their sacrifice. A seasoned vet declares, "The great majority of the people back home couldn't give two stuffs whether you lived or died." Each patrol leads to a wounding or a quick death of largely unseen origin. Then moments of quiet or harmless hijinks appear. It is the latter that infuse the film with a humorous and, in this setting, black comedic flair.

Recreational drinking, as opposed to debilitating drug abuse, seems the extent of these troops' addiction. One hilarious scene involves the Aussies pitting their spider against the American GIs' scorpion. Betting on the outcome and beer drinking lead to a massive brawl in the mud. These scenes are genuinely funnier than similar attempts at humor in *The Boys in Company C.* They are reminiscent of some of *M*A*S*H*'s inspired moments.

The discipline of the troops maintains order despire cynicism about corrupt politicians and the troops' awareness of their own societal status. They are merely working-class blokes who function as, in American slang, grunts. Again the negative-positive tonality recurs as Bryan Brown is wounded while on patrol. The men go to visit him a field hospital, and he greets them with "G'day." Then they inquire as to whether he still has his balls. When the sheet is pulled back and their continued existence is confirmed, a rousing cheer goes out among the men.

One last major battle scene takes place, excitingly staged on a nondescript bridge. The helicopter evac takes the troops away from their last battlefield encounter. On the way home we hear the lyrics of a mournful folk song. The young men come home to an anonymous lack of welcome. They sit ignored in a bar and toast their fallen comrades and their own good fortune in having survived.

As the nascent Australian national film industry expanded and met with critical acclaim, direct head-on examinations of that country's role in the Vietnam conflict gave way to other war-related and antiwar recontextualizations. In this way the Australian film group was opposite to the American experience of building up to such a direct point. The year after *The Odd Angry Shot*'s release came the powerful *Breaker Morant* (1980). That riveting drama starred Edward Woodward, Bryan Brown, and John Waters.

The film, directed by Bruce Beresford, concerned the Australian presence on behalf of the British colonial authority in South Africa during the Boer War. Soldiers in the field are on trial for alleged atrocities committed in a brutal conflict involving the mixed-up status of combatant and noncombatants among the Afrikaners. Parallels to the cryptic identity of VC and to friendlies and the excesses of My Lai are readily apparent. The governmental hierarchy in league with politicians betrays the soldier in the field and makes them examples in an unpopular war and a muddled cause. A sense of betrayal, waste, and lack of honor and purpose pervades this antiwar, antiauthoritarian film infused with post–Vietnam sensibilities and parallels.

The 1981 release *Gallipoli* was set during the infamous and bloody anti–Turk campaign in the Dardanelles in World War I. Directed by Peter Weir, it starred Mark Lee and a relatively unknown, handsome young actor named Mel Gibson. Herein the Australian soldier is once again exploited in behalf of the colonial power, Britain. Commanders offer up innocents as human waves of cannon fodder in politically dubious and militarily absurd maneuvers on far-off foreign soils. Like young American men naively anxious to "kill communists," Aussie soldiers become representative of their country's pressing need to prove its self-worth among the family of nations.[6]

Concomitant with the growing international coopting of the native Australian film industry, Peter Weir and Mel Gibson teamed with American star Sigourney Weaver and United Artists for the 1983 release of *The Year of Living Dangerously*. This wonderful adventure/love story served as a final example of the post–Vietnam, partially recontextualized Aussie examination of conflict in Indochina. It involved journalists caught up in the intrigue of the Indonesian rebellion in 1965. Such a romance set against the greater Southeast Asian political backdrop has never been made successfully in America.

Back in the United States the return of the head-on Vietnam film and the specific and frank discussion of veteran issues did not preclude the ongoing existence of other familiar thematic strands. As noted, the sign-of-the-times films by definition had to switch to a depiction of protest or draft evasion. Most often they evolved into the coming-of-age flicks harking back to the just-completed era. In *American Graffiti* the epilogue alluded to the tragic fate of Toad in Vietnam. In the summer of 1979 that film's sequel, *More American Graffiti*, was released.

This far inferior film used the war as a tangential and topical contributor to the plot's basic analysis of growing up in the 1960s.

Two of the original's female characters have now joined the Haight Ashbury rock-and-roll scene. In contrast to the crazy domestic scene, Charles Martin Smith and Bo Hopkins are off fighting in Vietnam. Using differing techniques, the film juxtaposes the two circumstances in an effort to reflect the turbulence of the times. A sense of realism and medium-self-conscious newsreel authenticity is given to the in-country sequences as they were filmed in 16 millimeter and blown up to the 35-millimeter standard. Despite these technical efforts, the film is most notable for the minute early roles afforded Harrison Ford and Rosanna Arquette.

The filmed version of the ultimate 1960s play, *Hair*, also appeared in 1979. Immigrant Milos Forman, who had so successfully skewered the crazy era in *Taking Off*, now returned to film this quintessential topical stage production. The Age of Aquarius, like the war itself, was a thing of the past, subject to postevent analysis only. The film adaptation seemed almost an obligatory exploitation of what must have been viewed at one time as a very hot property upon which to option the film rights. This musical examination of the hippie lifestyle, with its flower power imbued with antiwar sentiment and reaction, was fun but already qualified the film as what one observer called the source of "the first signs of Vietnam nostalgia."[7] With the war having been only barely examined in a meaningful way, this tangentially related rendition was notable only in terms of its stellar young cast, which included Broadway veterans such as *The Deerhunter*'s Stevie, John Savage, and Treat Williams and Beverly DeAngelo.

Saint Jack was the story of a Korean War vet played by Ben Gazzara who runs a brothel in Singapore in the early 1970s. Much of his trade is GI's on R & R from Vietnam. The film's director, Peter Bogdanovich, also appeared as a shadowy gangster with possible ties to the CIA. Old AIP mentor Roger Corman teamed with Hugh Hefner to produce this fascinating character study based on Paul Theroux's novel.

The local hoods try to control the pimping trade but the enterprising American receives powerful assistance because, "The Army is still in the cathouse business." Busloads of GI's arrive for pleasure and morale boosting." Observing his clients as they cavort with comely Asian women, Gazzara remarks with paternal regret, "we're in the slaughterhouse business, we're the ones who fatten them up." The war's end brings the extended, often nightmarish, but lucrative R & R business to a close.

Utter depravity was the order of the day when the Vietnam veteran portrayed by Marjoe Gortner in *When You Comin' Back Red Ryder?* terrorizes the patrons of a small-town Texas diner. Milton Katselas directed Mark Medoff's adaptation of his own play. Supposedly serious drama, the film is yet another characterization of the maladjusted returnee. Adding a bit of sign-of-the-times balance is his stateside hippie sweetheart, played by Candy Clark, When Gortner rants and raves, he reminds us of his real-life roots as a child preacher.

More American Graffiti (Universal Pictures, 1979). Charles Martin Smith as "Toad," now a helicopter pilot in Vietnam.

Without pretension was the Chuck Norris martial arts action feature *A Force of One.* Here the hero police officer's status as a special forces veteran is revealed verbally. This film and *Octagon* (1980), *An Eye for an Eye* (1981), *Lone Wolf McQuade* (1983), and the previously mentioned MIA films *Forced Vengeance* and *Good Guys Wear Black* all to varying degrees cast the karate champion as a vet. His numerous contributions to the films in this book were no coincidence. Working-class hero Norris had a strong interest in the subject because he had

Hair (United Artists, 1979). Milos Forman directed this sign-of-the-times hit play for the big screen.

lost a brother in the war.[8] A self-styled "archconservative," the athlete-turned-actor notes, "When Wieland was killed, I realized finally that it was a war that we should not ever have been in."[9] Another personal fact only recently revealed and bearing on the film vehicles to come was that Norris's father had briefly been declared MIA in Germany during World War II.

Norris's characters are always good guys, generally a law officer victimized by a bureaucratic hierarchy. As a lone warrior he must triumph over this additional adversity to exact justice and triumph. In these stateside renderings, the B action star was laying the groundwork for later films of revisionist Vietnam triumph.

In the fall of 1979 NBC television contributed a made-for to the list of films. *When Hell Was in Session* was a true story based on navy commander Jeremiah Denton's experiences during the seven and a half years of captivity in North Vietnam. His harrowing tale of torture and stubborn and inspiring resolve was quite powerful. Hal Holbrook starred, with Eva Marie Saint as Mrs. Denton, Ronny Cox, and the ubiquitous James Hong and Mako. Paul Krasny directed, and the real war hero served as technical adviser.

Shot down during a bombing mission in 1965, the officer endures mistreatment by steadfastly organizing a resistance movement whose only real means of communication is through rudimentary Morse code. Nevertheless, such actions in conjunction with heartfelt faith and determination become a means to survival. Integrated into this narrative are the events at home surrounding the POW families. A year after the film's release Denton was elected U.S. senator from Alabama.

Most notable about this film are its unapologetically patriotic message and embrace of traditional values that a film like *The Deerhunter* hinted at only in ambiguous terms. This much slighter made-for-television entry contains none of the knee-jerk antiestablishmentism of most of the earlier films or the gray ambiguity and the strength represented in *Friendly Fire*. Rather, this film praises the bravery and determination of the individual soldier, previously portrayed as victimized by the system as much as by the enemy. It should then be no surprise that *When Hell Was in Session* was the first Vietnam film since *The Green Berets* to receive the cooperation of the Department of Defense.[10]

The 1970s had begun with the United States still mired in the deadly conflict in Vietnam. In 1973 our combat troops were finally extricated, but it was not until the hasty retreat from Saigon in 1975 that the war actually ended. With the 1980s prepared to dawn, the eagerly awaited and already controversial Vietnam-themed *Apocalypse Now* was finally released on September 26, 1979.

Set entirely in-country, the mammoth production featured recreated combat unprecedented in scope in the Vietnam films. Like *The Deerhunter*, it went beyond mere condemnation or depiction of the war. More than just a literal journey into the depths of the Southeast Asian jungle, the film was also a figurative exploration of the characters' descent into a hellish "heart of darkness," into the depths of their capacity for primitivism and evil. By extension that underlying metaphorical odyssey could be applied to the United States' long, corrupt, and ultimately ill-fated role in the war.

If a number of films of the late 1960s featured an on-camera, self-conscious, media-oriented attempt to view the war through refracted imagery, *Apocalypse Now* presented the opportunity for a real-life parallelism among the war, the movies, and the process of producing that depiction. Before examining the plot and themes of the epic, it is interesting to follow the checkered production of the film. An oft-heard, only partially serious refrain was the analogy that the indeterminate nature of the project, the delayed process of its conduct and completion, and the cost overruns and logistical nightmare it became all echoed the course of the U.S. role in the war itself.

As discussed in Chapter 3, Francis Ford Coppola had written the Academy Award–winning and career-enhancing script for *Patton* in 1970. Somehow even then as America remained in the throes of the actual Vietnam War, he had been able to carefully craft a script about a man who unabashedly acknowledged that he loved war, and to make it powerful and at the same time ambiguous enough to be embraced by both the hawks and doves of the polarized period. The following year with the original *Godfather*, Coppola was able to establish himself as one of the preeminent auteur directors of the second half of the century. These successes allowed for the massive financing of *Apocalypse Now*, much of which came out of his own pocket.

The concept of a Vietnam War film first came to Coppola in 1969. University of Southern California alums George Lucas and John Milius (*Big Wednesday*) approached their friend with a rudimentary idea for such a film, with the former actually set to direct. At this time Coppola conceived of using Joseph Conrad's novel *Heart of Darkness* as a basis for the metaphysical descent as well as employing that work's literal story of a journey by boat as a means to show anecdotally various aspects of the U.S. role in the conflict. In typical Coppola style the project kept evolving and escalating in scope. At one point it was an inexpensive, gritty, quasi-documentary to be shot in 16 millimeter in Vietnam while the war still raged.

Milius and Lucas completed the script, which Warner Bros. bought for $15,000.[11] The studio that had released *The Green Berets* subsequently backed off, and Coppola was forced to buy the script back for $400,000! He intended to use his own studio, Zoetrope, to make and even perhaps distribute his Vietnam treatment.

Consistent with the now-grander vision was Coppola's casting. He was able to convince Marlon Brando to return from self-imposed career exile to portray Colonel Kurtz. However, the casting of that role and of Captain Willard, the star and narrator, had proved very problematic. It was reported tht the following stars had for various reasons all declined to take one or the other role in Milius's script: Robert Redford, Jack Nicholson, Gene Hackman, Al Pacino, and James Caan. Steve McQueen had agreed but dropped out for perhaps the most compelling, negative reason that all had expressed: the difficulty of an up-to-six-month location shoot in the Philippines.

Throughout the casting process the gambler Coppola utilized the prestigious names of varius potential actors to obtain financing on the project. Like most of the Vietnam films of the period, this money came from foreign sources that were less reticent about the conflict and its box office potential. It was the Japanese who provided Coppola's Zoetrope with a much-needed infusion of $8 million in preproduction funds. Brando was finally signed for $2 million for five weeks of work. This unprecedented salary was just the beginning of the runaway budgeting. With a major star and director attached to the project, the U.S. distribution rights went to United Artists, which promptly kicked in several million more dollars.

Coppola sought the cooperation of the Department of Defense for logistical aide. The U.S. government had little interest in supporting a project that did not conform to its public relations needs. Given the number of extras and necessity of equipment, especially helicopters, Coppola persisted in attempting to interest the Pentagon in cooperating. He and his longtime producer, Fred Roos, had several meetings with military officials.

After some initial interest and script negotiation, the army rejected any role in the production. As the preeminent chronicler of the stormy relationship between the military and the film community, Lawrence Suid in *Guts and Glory* reports on the continuing flirtation between the institution and the artist. Quoting government officials and documents, he writes:

> [The Army] informed the Public Affairs Office that there was little basis for cooperating "in view of the sick humor or satirical philosophy of the film." Several "particularly objectionable episodes" presented its military actions "in an unrealistic and unacceptable bad light." These scenes included U.S. soldiers scalping the enemy,

a surfing display in the midst of combat, and an officer obtaining sexual favors for his men and later smoking marijuana with them. . . . The Army and the Defense Department probably would have been able to live with at least some of these negative incidents. . . . But [they] . . . strongly objected to the main plot line . . . in which Colonel Kurtz (Brando) sets up his independent operation in Cambodia and Captain Willard (Sheen) is sent to "terminate" him. In its initial response to Milius' script, the Army said Kurtz's actions "can only be viewed as a parody on the sickness and brutality of war." . . . While the Army washed its hands of the project, Defense Department Public Affairs officials attempted to keep communications open with Coppola, as he had hoped they would."[12]

Apparently the government was anxious to have a film made about the war, restoring a sense of action and adventure to a moribund genre that in previous incarnations had led to interest in the armed services. Even John Wayne had had trouble fashioning an acceptable script. Now in a postwar treatment of the unpopular war, an acceptable basis of cooperation indeed appeared to be a real long shot. Nevertheless, in 1975 co-producer Gary Fredericksen visited Fort Bragg, North Carolina, to observe a training facility that was a mock Vietnamese village. Coppola finally concluded that time was being wasted and sought cooperation from the Australian armed forces. They lacked the extras and types of planes and helicopters he needed but rejected the director first, saying their army was "not a film extra agency."[13]

In an appropriate instance of an American invasion an Asian Third World country, the cast and crew descended on the Philippines. Production designer Dean Tavoularis oversaw the construction of huge sets. The laborers were paid a dollar a day, so it was easy to employ hundreds at a time. Coppola continued an unfruitful dialogue with the American army in nearby Clark and Subic bases. Finally following a meeting with Ferdinand Marcos, Coppola made a deal with the Filipino armed forces. Sometimes in the middle of a shot, the defense forces were called away to fight communist insurgents in the nearby jungles. This not only delayed production; it also added to the aura of analogy with the subject being depicted.

By March 1976 when Coppola and his family arrived in the Philippines, the script was already more than six years old. Casting still remained a problem. Steve McQueen had dropped out as Willard, to be replaced by Harvey Keitel. After watching a few days of rushes, Coppola fired Keitel and replaced him with Martin Sheen. At the same time Coppola continued to tinker with the script, intent on presenting a masterful "personal vision."[14] In fact his unique "make-it-as-you-go" approach would continue throughout the production.[15] Eventually the lack of an ending would nearly drive him mad with frustration.

Cost overruns continued as the unprecedented battle re-creations mounted. For instance, in the scene where Robert Duvall's air cavalry squad drops napalm, 5,000 liters of gasoline were burned for what became 90 seconds of on-screen footage. Eventually Martin Sheen suffered a heart attack during the grueling production. This crisis and a hurricane that soaked the crew and destroyed an entire set forced shutdowns and delays in the project. Coppola used these respites from the "hellish" process to return to "civilization" and seek additional stopgap funding.

After a whopping shoot of 200-plus days, the film wrapped on Mary 21, 1977. Like preproduction and principal photography, the postproduction process remained a huge obstacle before completion of the film. Finally almost a year later in April 1978, a recruited audience saw a sneak preview of the film. Notable was the addition of voiceover narration provided by Martin Sheen and written by the author of the evocative Vietnam book *Dispatches, Esquire* correspondent Michael Herr. Francis Ford Coppola, John Milius, and Michael Herr were strange collaborative partners. Their respective contributions added dimension but also ambiguous perspective to the product nearing completion.

Coppola furiously continued to oversee the film's editing, which was being done by Walter Murch and his crew. The distributor and creditors were eager to open the film but the lucrative Christmas 1978 season came and went. Beginning with a $12 million budget, what emerged more than three years later was a $30.5 million production. *Apocalypse Now* was finally presented at the Cannes Film Festival, where it tied in winning the coveted grand prize. After some additional editing and tinkering, a 153-minute version went into release in the United States in the fall of 1979.

Some four years before Julian Smith had written in his early examination of the relationship of the Vietnam War to movies, *Looking Away: Hollywood and Vietnam,* "Vietnam was like a movie that had gotten out of hand: gigantic cost overruns, a shooting schedule run amok, squabbles on the set, and back in the studio the first auteur dying with most of the script in his head, the second quitting in disgust, and the last swearing it was finally in the can, but sneaking back to shoot some extra scenes."[16] This analogy managed to integrate the two worlds – factual and fictional, Vietnam and movies – and exemplified *Apocalypse Now*'s notorious production history. Coppola loved the comparison of the technology of war and cinema and the director as general. He emerged from the jungles to Cannes, encouraging the analogy. At a press conference he proclaimed, "My film is is not a movie about Vietnam. It is Vietnam. It is what it was really like. It was crazy. And the way we made it was very much like the Americans were in Vietnam. We were in the jungle, there were too many of us. We had access to too much money and too much equipment and little by little, we went insane." That particular process was to be richly chronicled in a fascinating documentary (to be discussed later), *Hearts of Darkness: A Filmmaker's Apocalypse,* released in 1991. Its narrator was the filmmaker's wife, Eleanor Coppola, who had written a diary in the Philippines (*Notes*) and had shot some 60 hours of footage at the time for Zoetrope. Both became a primary source for the later study and contributed greatly to the story behind the scenes.

The attempt to make Conrad's *Heart of Darkness* into a film was an even greater challenge to Coppola because another audacious auteur, Orson Welles, had tried to do so back in the 1940s and had abandoned the project. Coppola, reveling in the gloss of literary antecedents, also brought in elements of Homer's

Odyssey. Later Coppola compared Duvall's Kilgore to the Cyclops and the Playmates to the Sirens. At one point in the depth of self-doubt, Coppola referred to the movie as his "Idi-odyssey" (idiocy-odyssey). Other literary echoes abound. Conrad's Mr. Kurtz of the Congo jungle, now Colonel Kurtz of the Cambodian wilds, quotes T. S. Eliot.

Apocalypse Now opens to the hypnotic, drug-enhanced strains of the consummate 1960s burned-out visionary hero, Jim Morrison, singing with the Doors, "This Is the End." The soundtrack enhances the striking on-screen visuals. Sometimes, however, the added voiceover monologue contributes to a nagging suspicion that it is necessary as much for explanatory exposition as for surrealistic imagery. Voiceover about the prey and the war is joined by comments such as "I watched a snail crawling along the edge of a straight razor . . . and surviving. That is my dream."

The pop music of the Doors, Jimi Hendrix, and other psychedelic rockers contributes to the perception of the mind-altering aspects of combat and also the chaotic influences of mixed messages, unseen enemies, and uncontrolled forces particular to the Vietnam War. *Coming Home* very effectively evoked the era through music, but many of its artists were more mainstream. William J. Palmer succinctly introduces this film, contextualizing it in the filmography, when he remarks, "If *The Deerhunter* is a symphony, then *Apocalypse Now* is a rock and roll light show. It captures the audience visual with action, spectacle, and dramatic shock."[17] The first on-screen image is the lush, green, triple-canopied jungles of Vietnam. Using mind-bending techniques of double exposure and slow motion, helicopters, the preeminent visual and audio leitmotif of the book, are shown dropping napalm on the forest. The fiery conflagration is both beautiful and horrifying. Immediately it suggests the mundane factuality of American air superiority, the brutal and destructive forces arrayed in the war and against the environment, and the all-consuming power that eventually was to prove futile and impotent.

As the credits recede, the blades of the helicopters evolve into the whirring blades of a ceiling fan. The jungle longshot shares and then relinquishes the screen to the sepia-dominated tones of a Saigon hotel room. Bourbon, cigarettes, a woman's picture, and a gun under the pillow accompany the introduction of a stupefied and bored Captain Willard, played by Martin Sheen. He is a man who when he was last in Nam wanted to be home and when he finally got home could not wait to get back in-country. The on-the-edge sickness that would lead a man back to Nam, especially as it is revealed that he is a CIA assassin, is underscored by the drunken, spastic, half-nude karataka dance of the captain in the isolation of the dank hotel room. In balletic and martial repast he cavorts to mind-altering Doors music in a scene reminiscent of the out-of-kilter preparation of Robert DeNiro as Travis Bickle for his self-appointed mission in the *Taxi Driver.* Finally Sheen breaks the mirror, cutting his hand and wiping the primordial red fluid all over his nude and sweaty body. It was later revealed that much of the scene was improvised and that Sheen was on the verge of a nervous breakdown when he made it.

This fascinating and bizarre opening gives way to a scene of straighter and soberer reality. Detached and emotionless, Willard the narrator says, "I was goin' to the worst place in the world and I didn't even know it yet, weeks away and hundreds of miles up a river that snaked through the war like a main circuit cable plugged straight into Kurtz," the rogue commander, played by Marlon Brando, whom Willard is to kill. Kurtz, a career officer on a fast track, has apparently flipped out and has begun to operate a ruthless independent organization prosecuting the war from the isolated ruins of ancient Angkor, deep in the Cambodian jungle, beyond the rules of command or notions of decency.

Willard continues, "This mission is more like a penance. . . . It was no accident that I got to be the caretaker of Colonel Walter E. Kurtz's memory. . . . There is no way to tell his story without telling mine, and if his story is really a confession, then so is mine." Coppola chose an assassin as our eyes and ears on the conflict. In the context of a ruthless war, fine lines dividing human from beast, sane from insane, good from evil, were infinitely grayer.

The lethal nature of Willard's penance is explained with greater detail at the meeting with his superiors at the base in Nha Trang. It is a strange, nondescript place, where tight closeups enhance the nervous claustrophobia of the scene. G. D. Spradlin is brilliant as a southern general who offers his hospitality and in-country touches of imported Americana, Texas beef, and Budweiser at their working lunch. A silent and androgynous man in civilian garb (Jerry Ziesner) joins the proceedings. He is undoubtedly some type of spook, a CIA operative. The mechanics of the briefing, including tape recordings, and dossiers, are presented by a bespectacled junior officer, a small role played by Harrison Ford. Using the military's penchant for obfuscating terminology, Willard is told to "terminate" Kurtz's command with "extreme prejudice." The inherent surrealism is summarized when the intelligence officers remind Willard that this meeting, this conversation, and this assignment never took place.

As the odyssey begins we are introduced to the crew members of the small patrol boat (PB) that will escort Willard to his appointed destination. They are mostly kids, draftees unhappy to be there. In the grand tradition of war films they are a cross-section, but specific to this war they are mainly unfortunate have-nots forced to participate in this conflict: the Louisiana saucier "Chef," played by Frederic Forrest; the blond, muscled, and tanned California surfer Lance, who could be out of Milius's *Big Wednesday,* portrayed by Sam Bottoms; and the young black from the Bronx, "Clean," played by Larry Fishburne, who really was only 14 years old at the time. Skippering the boat and boss of his domain is the older black man "Chief," played by Albert Hall.

The men wile away the hours listening to the rock and roll of the Rolling Stones and Armed Forces Radio. Oblivious to the war nearby, the three young men dance about and get stoned, and Lance even water-skis behind the boat as long as they stay in "friendly" territory. Like the cracked mirror in the opening scene and the businesslike lunch in the air-conditioned trailer, this is a strange reflection of a particularly American attempt at creating a sense of normalcy.

Surfing, giant and wasteful PXs, mass entertainment, and sexual vulgarism are as inscrutable to the indigenous populace as its simple lifestyle will be to the Americans. The institutionalized Ugly Americanism and racism of the intruding presence are typified by the speeding boats' disruptive, rippling wake, which uncaringly swamps a few peasants in their simple little boats that share the winding river.

As the PB proceeds farther down the river, Sheen explains more about his mission and his prey, Kurtz. The outlaw special forces officer was being "groomed for a top spot in the corporation." The antiseptic, all-business metaphor is still operational. When the boat arrives at a rendezvous point for a brief escort, the arc lights of a B-52 bomber raid illuminate the sky in a beautiful and frightening fashion. Huey helicopters join the fray as the men disembark from the boat and look for their contact. As they run by the carnage and smoky remains littering a fresh battlefield on the beachfront, they encounter a news crew shooting the proceedings. In a cameo appearance Francis Ford Coppola directs the mock documentary camera crew.

Sheen and his group seek the captain in charge of the attack, Robert Duvall as Kilgore. As the commanding officer of the air cavalry, he is an idiosyncratic, fascinating, and uniquely American throwback to the days of the Old West's Indian wars. In a hat befitting Custer and with a touch of panache provided by a yellow kerchief and cavalry sword emblems, Duvall leaves ace of spades playing cards as a signature on the bodies of dead VC.

This is an absurd and memorable scene as everyone except the seemingly oblivious or immune Kilgore, ducks remaining incoming fire. He is excited to find Lance, a surfer he knows and admires by reputation. That night in one more bit of imported homeyness, the men join the air cavalry unit in a China Sea beach party complete with guitars and T-bones. As they discuss surfing, the commander invites the men on the air cav's mission the next day. The scene that results is the famous air assault on a North Vietnamese village as Wagner's "Ride of the Valkyries" blares from helicopter-mounted speakers.

The boat crew does not know what to make of this air assault as the scene begins. The men imitate their hosts by removing their helmets and sitting on them so as not to have their balls blown off. It pays to be in the know. As Duvall's copter takes off, he remains in contact with the other lead chopper under the command of real-life Vietnam vet–turned–actor R. Lee Ermey (effective as the DI in *The Boys in Company C* and destined for an Academy Award nomination in *Full Metal Jacket*). Meanwhile down on the ground, the villagers, including women and children going about their schooling, are forced to run for cover, while others go to their battle stations as the assaulting forces approach. The squadron of helicopters set against the beautiful Southeast Asian sky almost appears as a benign flock of birds. Then as it approaches, perhaps the formation is more like locusts about to wreak havoc with their noisy air assault. Beauty and danger once again coalesce as the music blares and the attack begins. The camera subjectively looks down on the proceedings, as the "slopes" scurry about.

Wagner's rousing music, explosions, and speed combine to give an exhilarating, near-hallucinatory impression to the attack. The viewer's excitement is intense, visceral, and palpable. My God, can one begin to imagine the reality of the real thing? Sequences such as this one, or those in combat veteran Oliver Stone's films later, will hint at but never be able to convey the fear and reality of war. A U.S. helicopter goes down, belying the seeming invincibility of the air cavalry forces. A young girl in peasant civilian garb throws a grenade into a medical evacuation helicopter, killing all aboard. The copters in the air follow her with a vengeance, strafing and killing her as she attempts to flee.

As the mop-up of the operation continues, the gung-ho nut case Kilgore insists that Lance and others strip down and surf in the excellent conditions that surround this seaside village. The LZ is still hot as the surfers are coaxed into the water by the zealous commander. Maddeningly some snipers still persist in hindering the recreation. Kilgore calls in a massive tree line air strike to clear out these last vestiges of opposition. As the jets drop their payload and light up the ancient jungle, Duvall delivers his now famous line: "I love the smell of napalm in the morning. . . . It smells like victory." The men in Kilgore's command love him, but Willard and the boat crew are anxious to get on with their voyage as soon as possible. Willard remarks in voiceover, "If that's how Kilgore fought the war, I began to wonder what they really had against Kurtz. It wasn't just insanity and murder. There was enough of that for everyone."

The first adventure of the renewed boat voyage is the encounter with a tiger. Chef convinces Chief to stop on the bank long enough for Chef to procure some mangoes. In an eerie, dark jungle he and Willard, on guard for VC, instead encounter a beautiful and ferocious Asian tiger, which chases them back to the relative safety of the boat. "Do not get off the boat unless necessary" becomes the operable sentiment.

The renewed odyssey takes another bizarre twist as the men arrive at an isolated U.S. river base. Two tall phallic towers anchor the ends of a stage. Here in the middle of nowhere, a helicopter arrives carrying a USO morale-boosting troupe of gorgeous Playboy Playmates. As the real life "Bunnies" bump and grind suggestively for the lonely and horny throngs, the scene degenerates into chaos. Out-of-control soldiers storm the stage; MPs fight them off as the scantily clad beauties clamber back onto the copter and pull off amid a full-scale riot. Willard remarks, "Charlie didn't get much USO, dug in too deep or moving too fast."

As the boat proceeds upriver, Willard continues to peruse his top-secret files on Kurtz. We learn about the colonel's family and career and his behavior since arriving in-country. From star officer to embarrassment, from professional soldier to self-appointed leader of killers, Kurtz's career fascinates Willard. He wonders just how similar they may be. The difference is that "Kurtz got off the boat. He split from the whole fucking program."

The actors had approached a responsive director about their desire to shoot a "My Lai–type" scene. Bottoms later sheepishly admitted that he was on speed at the time to give him the right edginess. What results is horrifying because it makes the unthinkable seem perfectly possible. Coursing down the river, the boat encounters a sampan. Chief decides to take a look, despite Willard's protests. Is there VC contraband aboard, or are some innocent South Vietnamese merely trying to ply their meager trade? Chef boards the vessel while shouting unintelligible English instructions to the frightened family. Clean looks on from behind his stationary high-caliber forward gun. Paranoia engulfs him as uncertainty and marijuana combine their effects. Suddenly the young girl makes a quick movement toward a wicker basket that Chef is about to inspect. Clean opens fire, his bullets ripping at the flesh of the entire family. As Chef investigates the basket, he finds a little puppy. An innocent family lies dead, except for the young girl, who is wounded and moaning. The men scream, cry, and yell obscenities in shock and guilt. They have just killed her whole family, but now they want to save her life and keep the darling little puppy. But the delay is too much, and the mission cannot tolerate a wounded civilian. Willard the professional assassin now resignedly and without discussion shoots and kills the girl at close range. The men, who just wasted the entire family, thinks this is really horrible. They wince as Willard declares to Chief, "I told you not to stop." The men are now cold toward the outsider Willard. He feels an additional empathy with the object of his mission, his prey.

As the boat approaches the last army outpost on the river, rocket and mortar fire light up the nighttime sky. An LSD-tripping Lance watches the fireworks in a bemused daze. The place is in a shambles under heavy artillery assault, the "asshole of the world." The enemy soldiers are so close that the frontline dug-in troops can hear them talking. A terrified black huddles in the night, almost invisible. The confused troops almost shoot their own men. This is an image of Khe Sanh on LSD, an indictment of a strategically dubious presence. Two men are blown to bits off a bridge as Willard searches in vain for the commanding officer. "Aren't you the CO?" the terrified men ask Willard.

We feel as if the boat is descending into increasingly hellish situations. As Willard reads a newspaper clipping from home about Charles Manson, Clean plays a cassette tape sent from his mama. The daytime recreation is punctuated by sniper rounds from the shoreline. The loving black mother's voice continues to play as we discover that Clean has taken a hit. He dies as she is heard in the background saying how much she looks forward to seeing him soon.

The men are grief stricken and want to turn back. Willard insists they go on, sensing their proximity to his prey: "He was close. . . . I couldn't see him yet, but I could feel him." Fog drifts in and out, obscuring their full vision of the flotsam of war. The wreckage of an airplane represents the last metallic vestige of "civilization." The boat once again comes under fire, this time from spears and arrows, the weapons of a primitive culture. As the boat pulls away, Chief is impaled from behind. The means of attack, like the river journey, is right out of Conrad's novel. With his last bit of strength, Chief tries to pull Willard onto the same spear protruding from his own body.

Apocalypse Now (United Artists, 1979). **Dennis Hopper welcomes Martin Sheen and Frederic Forrest to Kurtz's camp deep in the Cambodian jungle.**

Finally the boat and its remaining crew, Willard, Chef, and Lance, arrive at their destination. Primitive tribespeople, Montagnard guerrillas, ragtag American deserters, and mercenaries line the shores by an ancient Cambodian temple, the ruins of Angkor. The men have no choice but to enter Kurtz's strange lair. Greeting them is a gonzo, babbling, burned-out American combat photographer, a hanger-on in this netherworld. This sycophantic court jester, this tour guide in hell, is played by the 1960s druggie, counterculture icon Dennis Hopper. He tells Willard that Kurtz is a genius, a poet-warrior in the grand tradition.

As the film enters its third and final hour, Willard is ushered into the inner sanctum where Kurtz decays. Kurtz proceeds with polite small talk, but he knows the purpose of his visitor's presence. "Are you an assassin?" he asks Willard. He replies, "I'm a soldier." Then Kurtz says disdainfully, "You're neither. You're an errand boy sent by grocery clerks."

Next morning Willard is imprisoned standing upright in a bamboo cage. Will Willard be executed? He does not know. Chef, who was left on the boat to remain in radio contact and, if necessary, call in an air strike, is killed. His decapitated head is presented to a terrorized and hungry Willard.

In pursuit of some purpose known only to Kurtz, Willard is spared and once again ushered in to listen to the leader's pronouncements. Brando as Kurtz, in a slow, intelligent, but ultimately deranged manner, explains what he has seen in this bloody conflict and why he is doing what he feels he must do in response to such madness. "I've seen the horror," Kurtz declares. He tells Willard, "You have the right to kill me but not the right to judge me." Kurtz then relates a story. "Horror and moral terror are your friends." Years ago when he was still in the special forces, the Americans had inoculated South Vietnamese children. That evening fanatical Viet Cong had hacked off the left arm of every inoculated child. Kurtz admits that he "cried like some grandmother." He remembers the revelation he had at that moment, "like being shot with a diamond bullet." My God, he exclaimed, "the genius, the will to do that . . . it's perfect and pure." These enemy cadres had the "strength to do that!" He judged them to be "moral" and at the same time able to utilize primordial instincts to kill. Kurtz hates the "stench of lies" and the weakening "judgment that defeats us." This realization and a response to it became Kurtz's self-appointed destiny.

The strange confession/speech speaks to the brutalizing realities of war. However, it also specifically recognizes that conventional notions of force cannot and will not triumph over this committed and determined opposition. Kurtz knows what the audience knows in 1979: that the Americans will be defeated just as the French were defeated. The people of the iron age, the civilized in self-appointed name only with their boats, airpower, refrigerators, and canned beer, are no match for the weapons of the natives. Herein dramatically the natives are just that, stand-ins for a primitive, misunderstood society. Coppola is commenting more on the American culture than drawing an analogy to the enemy. Kurtz and his primordial, indigenous force, which appears savage, are perhaps metaphorically really only the nakedness of visceral commitment. The tale of evil and the scent of death are indicative of the horrors of war, a phrase we hear but are unable to comprehend.

This revelatory sequence bridges the group of films in an important way. Up to now this has been a war film cloaked in style and made to echo the mind-altering and -bending rhythms of war. It is a dream, a nightmare, and, as Coppola admitted, a "journey." The last such specific tale of Viet Cong heinousness, which Kurtz's story echoes, is the traumatized hamlet back in *The Green Berets*. The rape and murder of the little girl and the villagers were horrible and helped explain why Americans were involved in this conflict on the side of justice. Accompanying the cynical appraisal of the U.S. role in the war common to the films of 1978, *Apocalypse Now* in 1979 contains Kurtz's tale, which echoes such horrors but frightening assigns a morally ambiguous nature to such conduct. Furthermore, the assassin Kurtz is now the prey of an officially sanctioned assassin, the film's narrator.

What is unmistakable is the bridging effect of the ambiguity. *The Green Berets* outlines enemy atrocities; *Apocalypse Now* reiterates them and then questions U.S. behavior as well. By 1986, in films from *Platoon* to *Casualties of War*, American film will be offering up on-screen atrocities committed not by the enemy but by our own troops.

Coppola seeks a transcendent explanation for the evil people do but in the process confuses a film whose strength emanates from its very evocation of the confusion, chaos, and cross-purposes of this country's wartime role. The boys who slaughtered the family on the sampan were not evil, but they acted badly. Everyone, given the circumstances, is capable of such behavior. That is the moral ambiguity. The narrator admits, "On the river I thought that the minute I'd look at him I'd know what to do, but it didn't happen." Back in Kurtz's private domain, Willard is not even guarded. But as the captain admits, "I was free, but I wasn't going anywhere. He knew more about what I was going to do than I did."

In a final, masterfully intercut scene Willard stalks his prey, rising up filthy from the depths of the water to stealthily slaughter the big bull of a man, Kurtz. At the same time in a primitive ritual the tribespeople slaughter an ox in a sacrifice to their gods. The lights strobe and the elemental fire glistens in the night as the Doors scream, "Come on Baby Take a Chance." Quickly the editing pace increases, crosscutting and accentuating the parallels in the knife-wielding death scene. As Kurtz lies dying, his last words are "the horror, the horror." The assassin has been assassinated, but also the chief, the king, has been replaced. Emerging from his abode with the weapon of death, Willard is hailed and lionized as the subservient masses bow to this new king.

Willard and the proverbially stoned Lance return to the boat and flee this place. Static, electronic radio transmissions follow their departure. As the end credits begin to roll, an air strike begins. Bombs and napalm engulf the enclave, destroying the ruins and presumably all those who remain in them. The film runs out, never stating the end, merely fading from fiery reds into darkness and black.

Francis Ford Coppola explained tht the film ended with "a moral choice." However, Coppola was much more intrigued by "Will Willard become another Kurtz? Or will he learn from his experience and choose another direction? I wanted to leave the end open."[18]

Apocalypse Now remains one of the most visually striking films ever made. "Coppola . . . is intentionally making war so beautiful, so fascinating, presenting it with such visual virtuosity, that the audience is seduced into a suspension of all civilized restraint, all moral judgment, all abhorrence for that which is innately evil. The audience is captured by the awesome beauty to the point that it forgets the lethal reality."[19]

Aside from the distracting beauty, the film is rich in detail meant to convey the extent of transplanted Americana gone wild. Placed in an alien culture, Ugly American attempts at imposed cultural hegemony become opiates to our soldiers. The committed bands of Kurtz or the unseen VC are not bogged down and bloated with drugs and beer. Playmates cavort and corrupt only a flawed and distracted effort. In an all-too-common in-country manner, substance abuse provides a delusion of fuller and heightened knowledge while really delivering an impaired and flawed analysis. Double exposures are used throughout the film, echoing this theme of American distraction and ill-defined purpose. Other films yet to come illuminate the corruption of a generation of young farm girls into Saigon prostitutes and thus symbolize the elements of American weakness.

Most conventional attributions of parallelism were to Joseph Conrad's *Heart of Darkness*. That novel's river journey through the Congo into Africa and interior became a literary framework overlaying the construction of the film. However, this attribution is limited in its ultimate applicability. Strange partners are collaborating here. Screenwriter John Milius would later contribute Vietnam action pictures void of handwringing self-deprecation in *Uncommon Valor* and *Flight of the Intruder*. (And in the muddled 1990 film *Farewell to the King*, he was able to examine the subservience of native peoples to another Caucasian visionary.) Here he wrote, "I love the smell of napalm in the morning."

Michael Herr, who wrote the stream-of-consciousness-filled *Dispatches* from Vietnam, was called in to pen voiceover narration and dialogue. Fascinated with movies' place in creating a reality borne of celluloid images, he described in his book "coming out of some heavy heart of darkness trip, overloaded on the information, the input."[20] Herr's ear for idiom combined with Conradian reference led to dialogue such as that uttered by the photojournalist character Hopper when he babbled about being "overloaded on the input." Later referencing the Nha Trang briefers and the type of operation that Kurtz ran, Herr spoke of the "spook war . . . irregulars working in remote places under little direct authority, acting out their fantasies with more direct freedom than most men ever know."[21] The intoxicating and corrupting power is unmistakable and unavoidable.

Herr informed his dispatches with the importance of rock-and-roll music to the grunts. "Hendrix had once been in the 101st Airborne."[22] Herr helped bridge the films and added to Coppola's appeal to a generation of filmgoers with observations that typified the sign of the times meeting the newly informed and resurgent combat film. "Out on the streets I couldn't tell the Vietnam veterans from the rock and roll veterans. The Sixties had so many casualties." Then in a remark to be used later in Willard's narration, he continued, "Its war and its music had run off the same circuit for so long they didn't even have to fuse."[23]

The talented writer, observer of the surrealism of the war, knew he would have to someday "make movies." *Apocalypse Now* provided this uniquely qualified author with his first important contribution to this group of films. Another auteur, Stanley Kubrick, would once again turn to Herr for the screenplay of *Full Metal Jacket*.

The critics all agreed that *Apocalypse Now* was visually and physically brilliant. Stanley Kauffmann called it a "jungle discotheque. . . . Despite its simplistic relation to Conrad's *Heart of Darkness*, it is at its best in delivering the texture of the first freaked out, pill popping, rock accompanied war."[24] To paraphrase Roger Ebert, *Apocalypse Now* did not necessarily explain why things happened, but it showed how they could have happened. For the post–Vietnam television generation, this rendering of the "television war" was sufficiently grand to eclipse the small fictional scope of the tube. As with the controversy surrounding the four horsemen, some veterans' groups were put off by the depiction of the war, the military, and the conduct shown, fearing the film reduced all soldiers to drug addicts or assassins. Ironically this was the type of portrait featured in the exploitation, indirect treatments of the preceding years. Other observers simply saw *Apocalypse Now* as a validation of the notion that war is hell. Many could not escape the production costs and notorious stories from the Philippines. *New West* offered its opinion in another reflection on art imitating life: "Coppola has come up with a movie that unwittingly mirrors the spirit of the Vietnam war: a heartless exercise in logistics, a monumentally oversized catastrophe."[25]

Apocalypse Now grossed very well ($71,646,000 in first-run billings) but because of its $30 million-plus budget, it had initial difficulty recouping its investment. Coppola finally stated, "The most important thing I wanted to do in the making of the film was to create a movie experience that would give its audience a sense of the horror, the madness, the sensuousness and the moral dilemma of the Vietnam War."[26] To President Carter, the filmmaker later said, "I'm cauterizing old wounds, trying to let people put the war behind them. You can never do that by forgetting it."[27]

The call for clear-cut political delineations and the lack thereof were indicative of this period of revitalized postwar movies. Polarized elements of the populace demanded recognition for their position or were prepared to vilify the film. Nevertheless, issue-raising motion pictures were once again being produced. These films, like life, lacked pat answers. In totality, *Apocalypse Now* is antiwar, but, like the war itself, *Apocalypse Now* is unconventional and at times undeclared.

Apocalypse Now was nominated for the 1979 Best Picture Oscar but lost out to *Kramer vs. Kramer.* Other nominations went to Robert Duvall for supporting actor, Coppola for director, Milius and Coppola for best screenplay based on material from another medium, art and set direction, and film editing. The film did not win in those categories but did capture the sound award, and Vittorio Storaro won for cinematography. Having publicly flaunted and exorcised some Vietnam War demons the previous year, Hollywood halfheartedly honored *Apocalypse Now.* The previous year's releases, *Coming Home* and Best Picture winner *The Deerhunter,* robbed Coppola's entry of historic significance, but its artistic contribution to the films of the dawning decade and to the collective body of Nam movies was unmistakable.

The out-and-out negativism toward the war or the military of *The Boys in Company C, Go Tell the Spartans* and *Coming Home* gave way to the ambiguous but still antiwar decrying of *The Deerhunter, Apocalypse Now,* and the made-for-television entries of 1978 and 1979. The full frontal examination of the war was the major legacy of this fecund two-year period, politics being a secondary issue. Nevertheless, as historian Stanley Karnow (soon to be documentarian of the famous PBS examination of the war, "Vietnam: A Television History") summarized, whether from the Left or from the Right, the coalescence of opinion was that Vietnam was wrong. For the Left that perspective centered on negative notions of our involvement's inherent immorality, racism, stupidity, duplicity, and overzealous world police role. From the Right the fight against communism was wrong because it was flawed by the inability of the soldier in the field to be allowed to win the war. Films in the newly direct environment were going to run the gamut. The source of agreement was the necessity of nonglorifying negativism.[28]

In the years to come romanticism would begin to creep back into the military film. However, in the immediate future the return of head-on Vietnam War depictions would begin to evolve from the antiwar and provocative well-constructed films of 1978 and 1979 to the cartoonish revisionism and gung-ho exploitation of the early 1980s. Even these films would remain antiwar in the framework of what befell the fighting soldier.

Perhaps if the nuances of film politics and the evolution of perspectives are difficult to discern, what is most clear is the indisputably traumatizing aspect of the war depicted in both the aforementioned and forthcoming films. They dealt with loss and defeat. As an unprecedented fact in American history, this acknowledgment of loss, both in individual and collective terms, typified and informed the films of the 1970s once they got around to addressing the war in their differing manners.

In the next chapter, as the chronology proceeds into the 1980s, with the election of Ronald Reagan and a fatigue with the events of the 1960s and 1970s — civil strife, assassinations, Vietnam, and Watergate — the lineup will begin to change. The films that acknowledge individual and collective loss will be joined by those that fictionally attempt to do what the country and its fighting troops were not able (or allowed) to do in the actual war: win it. The next chapter examines that trend, culminating in the cultural ascendance of the superhero mythology surrounding Rambo(ism).

References

1. "Casualty Reports That Win No Friends for Today's Army," *Chicago Tribune*, June 21, 1990, op-ed page.

2. *Time* (February 18, 1991, p. 24.

3. Army Archerd, "Just for Variety," *Daily Variety*, May 6, 1991, p. 2.

4. Steve Daley, "Not Only Generals Had to Exorcise Vietnam Demons," *Chicago Tribune*, March 3, 1991, p. 4.

5. *Ibid.*

6. William J. Palmer, *The Films of the Seventies — A Social History* (Metuchen, N.J.: Scarecrow Press, 1987), pp. 230–250.

7. Gilbert Adair, *Vietnam on Film* (London: Proteus, 1981), p. 11.

8. Tony Williams, "Missing in Action: The Vietnam Construction of a Movie Star," in *From Hanoi to Hollywood*, ed. Linda Dittmar and Gene Michael (New Brunswick, N.J.: Rutgers University Press, 1990), pp. 129–141.

9. Rod Lurie, "Chuck Norris Interview," *Penthouse* (March 1992), p. 50.

10. Alvin H. Marill, *Movies Made for Television: The Telefeature and the Mini Series, 1964–1984* (New York: Zoetrope, 1984).

11. Numerous preproduction details are from Jean-Paul Chaillet and Elizabeth Vincent, *Francis Ford Coppola* (New York: St. Martin's Press, 1984).

12. Lawrence Suid, *Guts and Glory* (Reading, Mass.: Addison-Wesley, 1978), p. 310.

13. *Ibid.*, p. 311.

14. Chaillet and Vincent, *Francis Ford Coppola*, p. 60.

15. See production notes for similar quandaries encountered in the making of *The Godfather III* as chronicled in Peter J. Boyle, "Under the Gun," *Vanity Fair* (June 1990), p. 133.

16. Julian Smith, *Looking Away: Hollywood and Vietnam* (New York: Scribner's, 1975).

17. Palmer, *The Films of the Seventies*, p. 196.

18. Chaillet and Vincent, *Francis Ford Coppola*, p. 68.

19. Palmer, *The Films of the Seventies*, p. 228.

20. Michael Herr, *Dispatches* (New York: Knopf, 1968), p. 6.

21. *Ibid.*, p. 20.

22. *Ibid.*, p. 194.

23. *Ibid.*, p. 278.

24. Stanley Kauffmann, *Before My Eyes* (New York: Harper and Row, 1980), p. 107.

25. Mason Wiley and Damien Bona, *Inside Oscar: The Unofficial History of the Academy Awards* (New York: Ballantine Books, 1986), p. 573.

26. Brock Garland, *War Movies* (New York: Facts on File, 1987), p. 28.

27. *Wisconsin State Journal*, June 27, 1976, p. 1, cited in Suid, *Guts and Glory*, p. 316.

28. Stanley Karnow, *Vietnam: A History* (New York: Viking Press, 1983).

Chapter 7

Winning the War, 1980–1985

This chapter covers the films released from 1980 to 1985. Following the damning indictments of American involvement in Vietnam represented in the tragedy of the four horsemen and the apocalypse, there was a lack of head-on films (i.e., those that addressed the war directly and not metaphorically or analogously). This lag in 1980, 1981, and 1982 approximated the dearth of depiction in the transition-to-peacetime years. The film zenith of 1978 and 1979 was achieved by recreating an emotional nadir vis-à-vis the conflict. The production pendulum had swung from no films about the conflict to too many.

Despite grossing well and receiving many accolades, the 1978-1979 entries had ruffled some feathers, just as the direct portrait in *The Green Berets* had done some ten years earlier. Among the perturbed were the veterans themselves, who already had been afforded a raw deal in the loser vet flicks. Some vets took exception to the conduct depicted in *Apocalypse Now, The Deerhunter*, and so on. In fact later marketing campaigns found a more traditional way to exploit commercial appeal. United Artists sold *Apocalypse Now* as a "high epic adventure" and *Coming Home* as "one of the most beautiful love stories you'll ever see."[1]

In 1983 when combat films reappeared from the new hiatus, they were very different movies. The new film heroes provided opportunities to triumph in ways never achieved on the battlefield. These delusionary escapist adventures reflected a renewed American optimism evolving from the country's malaise. Once again pop entertainment not only reflected the collective mood but also helped create it.

Real-world political events corresponded to the film industry's evidence of a new spirit. At about the time *Apocalypse Now* was playing in theaters, American hostages were being taken in Iran. Washington outsider Jimmy Carter, elected president in the post–Watergate cynicism, seemed powerless in his attempts to free the Americans and restore a sense of pride still damaged by the Vietnam War, Watergate, and this newest humiliation. As if to underscore the impotence of the American military, the rescue effort mounted in April 1980 to free the hostages was a dismal failure.

Carter had pardoned the Vietnam draft evaders back in January 1977 as one of his first acts as president. He saw that controversial action as an important step in the healing process of the nation. Now at the end of his term he was wholly ineffective in freeing the innocents held captive by the ruthless Islamic fundamentalists in Tehran. On November 4, 1980, Ronald Reagan defeated Carter for the presidency. He blended an ebullient, can-do pioneering persona with political conservatism and gung-ho patriotism.

In January 1981 immediately after Reagan's inauguration, the Iranian fundamentalists released the hostages after 444 days in captivity. Joy and relief swept over America in a manner similar to that reserved for the return of the Vietnam War POWs. After this latest humiliation Americans did not want to be depressed or self-flagellating in their examination of the Vietnam debacle.

The new Vietnam War films depicted the individual fighting soldier as a victim of misguided and compromised government policy. In this way the cynicism about politicians borne of Vietnam and Watergate could remain, but the soldier and, by extension, individual Americans could be absolved of guilt. In addition the newly revisionist films of triumph could integrate recent frustration involving the incarceration of the Iranian hostages with concerns about the MIAs and the popular notion that POWs were still being held in Southeast Asia. What evolved to accommodate the desire to win, the need to be entertained, and the cathartic notion of liberating American captives were films that featured heroic rescue missions back in-country.

Uncommon Valor, Missing in Action, and *Rambo* showed that the communists could be beaten and that patriotism could be restored. The revenge that Rambo exacted against the communists was also directed at our own government policymakers. In this way the on-screen depictions reflected an evolution to the explicit from the implied double cross of the soldier in the field in earlier films such as *The Losers* way back in 1970 or the 1977 actioner *Good Guys Wear Black.*

The two issues that now seemed to preoccupy the postwar films were the resolution of the POW-MIA questions and a continued awareness of the veterans' problems now associated with post-traumatic stress disorder. The subgenre concerning the veterans was thus able to evolve in both A and B manifestations around this much-talked-about health issue. Serious films such as *Birdy* in 1984 dealt with attempts to understand and confront this illness. Exploitation flicks such as *The Exterminator* in 1980 used the illness as an excuse for violence. A film such as *Cease Fire* in 1985 seemed to toe the line between a dramatic attempt to explore the malady and a commercial desire to exploit the quirkier aspects of the illness.

If the combat films in this period fundamentally evolved from losing to winning the war, and the veteran subgenre managed to adapt to more topical concerns, then the sign-of-the-times films desperately needed updating now that the war was over. Thus for the most part the depictions of the late-1960s domestic, war-concomitant scene continued the trend toward coming-of-age nostalgia. *A Small Circle of Friends* in 1980, Arthur Penn's *Four Friends* in 1981, and the epoch-defining megahit *The Big Chill* in 1984 all managed to make the war a backdrop to the baby-boomers' march to nothing else but inevitable adulthood and responsibility. The hippies, antiwar protestors, and draft evaders were becoming parents and stockbrokers. This trend reflected the 1980s growing conservative embrace of Reagan and the restoration of good feelings.

War and military-related depictions, which at one time derived meaning from commenting on the war in a differing place or time context, found that masking was no longer necessary. After all the war was over, and head-on depictions had already returned with a vengeance. Therefore the films of relevancy in recontextualized forms were disparate reflections on the new positive attitudes of the public and its willingness to move on from the Vietnam War. Military comedies and the romantic depiction of handsome men in uniform returned from fifteen years of exile. Each of the subgenres evolved in a way that mirrored the evolution of American society from pessimism to optimism. The period from 1980 to 1985 thus restored currents that would continue to coexist with the negative and more realistic depictions of the war that would reemerge in the late 1980s. (These films will be covered in the next chapter.)

As the new decade of peace and renewal began, changing attitudes were joined by evolving technologies. Video was altering the entire entertainment industry. Film entries were no longer limited to the theatrical and made-for-television features. The thirst for product for the burgeoning home video stores led to a new source of programming, the direct-to-video movie. Like the early-1950s cheapie B movies for double bills, or the 1960s drive-in fodder, the new source of exhibition tended toward exploitation depictions. Therefore the action-oriented mayhem associated with the cyclers and loser vets was updated along with the avenge-and-win-the-war mentality into newly emergent video-only vehicles. Until the end of the decade they would be popular rental titles and thus sources of cognition about the war for young viewers. (Not until the 1990s did the public begin to tire of these made-for-video B titles. The novelty of the new medium had worn off, and much of the public felt "burned" by these lamely mounted productions. Proven A picture commodities would reattain their preeminence in both rental and the newly expanding "sell-through" video purchase market.) As the individual examination of the films of the 1980s begins, this introductory look at history, the entertainment industry milieu, and the evolution of the Vietnam War movie subgenres will come into focus.

The title *The Exterminator* quickly orients the audience to the simpleminded exploitation nature of this release from the now defunct Avco-Embassy Pictures. Robert Ginty starred as yet another crazed Vietnam veteran. In a ripoff of the popular *Death Wish* series, Ginty kills street punks who terrorize his neighborhood. Christopher George played the police detective who hunts the overzealous vet. A subplot involves some devious interference from the CIA.

In an effort to outdo the hook-hand from *Rolling Thunder* and other gruesome weaponry employed by crazed vet characters, Ginty at one point employs a blow torch to carry out his vigilante justice. Samantha Eggar costarred in this gory piece of junk written and directed by James Glickenhaus.

The traditional B action movie audience, young males, found this Vietnam veteran character to be enough to their liking to generate a sequel, *Exterminator II*, in 1984. Mark Buntzman directed Ginty in that installment. Mario Van Peebles costarred in an effort to expand the audience to the old black exploitation crowd as well. In this trashy sequel seasoned combat vet Ginty operates out of an armored garbage truck. *The Exterminator*(s)' muddled view of the CIA and the police appeals to a general mistrust of authority and speak to the notion of official hampering of the effort of the fighting soldier to get the job done.

A much more pretentious but ultimately dreary portrait of the veterans was presented in the 1980 release *The Ninth Configuration.* This adaptation of William Peter Blatty's (*The Exorcist*) novel *Twinkle Twinkle Killer Kane* was written and directed by the best-selling author. The theatrical release of the film was negligible and occurred under both titles in a futile effort to find an audience. Stacy Keach appeared as the title character, Kane. Costarring in this release from yet another moribund independent company, New World, were Scott Wilson, Jason Miller, Neville Brand, Ed Flanders, Moses Gunn, and Robert Loggia.

The muddled story line involved a secret army asylum for officers. This mental institution is located in a fog-shrouded castle in the Pacific Northwest (actually filmed in Hungary). The movie attempts to attach humor to mental illness, a rarely funny matter. In this case the psychosis is Vietnam-induced trauma, thus fitting into a topical interest in the diagnosis of post-traumatic stress disorder. In its quasi-humorous treatment of Vietnam vets' mental illness, the film is a descendant of the line represented by *Julius Vrooder* and *Heroes.* The more malignant portraits belong to the *Exterminator* school of depiction.

Aside from the "loony" goings-on, such as men who walk around in boxer shorts, sing songs, and speak in nonsequiturs, there is a mystery/conspiracy component. The men are treated as captives, and the army experiments on them. A cryptic half-baked story implies that their condition was caused by government drug experimentation in-country. This treachery tapped into current postwar accusations of CIA-sponsored use of LSD on troops in Vietnam as revealed in numerous sources, including CBS's "Sixty Minutes." These alleged immoral actions fit with recent information on the debilitating effects of Agent Orange on the ground troops. This powerful defoliant was used on the thick jungle but ended up being carcinogenic. *The Ninth Configuration* lamely speaks to the nature of insanity, the Pentagon's imperturbability, and popular conceptions of the victimization of American soldiers in uniform. The film was released in versions running from 99 to a whopping 140 minutes.

The year 1980 had one tangentially relevant contribution to the now nostalgic sign-of-the-times domestic Woodstock generation. United Artists released *A Small Circle of Friends.* A fine young ensemble cast including Brad Davis and Karen Allen starred in director Rob Cohen's adaptation of Ezra Sacks' screenplay about late-1960s college students. The film attempts to address the sexual revolution, women's liberation, and concerns about the big background event, the war in Vietnam. During the war the major studios' renditions of campus events were instantly stale contributions such as *The Strawberry Statement* or *RPM*. *A Small Circle of Friends* joined *Hair* in a nostalgic look at the flower power generation and failed to capture the feeling any more successfully than its bloated predecessors.

One notable and realistic draft-related scene in *A Small Circle of Friends* does strike a chord of amazed recollection. The young friends sit around watching television and having a lottery party. They watch as selective service officials draw birth dates out of a tumbler and assign call-up rankings to them. All across America young men and their families watched this frightening attempt to bring an equal dose of luck to the draft-age populace via this nonjudgmental means of assigning priority to the wartime draft pool.

Finally in September of 1980 there was a head-on combat portrait of the war presented. On two nights CBS broadcast an adaptation of veteran Phil Caputo's controversial autobiography, *A Rumor of War*. This Charles Fries production was directed by Richard T. Heffron and written by John Sacret Young, the man who would later be responsible for the weekly television series set in Vietnam, "China Beach." The late Brad Davis portrayed Caputo, who has gone on to be a noted combat journalist and author. The cast included Keith Carradine as Lieutenant Murph McCoy and Michael O'Keefe as Walter Cohen. Also appearing were Brian Dennehy, Stacy Keach, Lane Smith, Richard Bradford, Chris Mitchum, and Jeff Daniels as the chaplain.

Because of the book's strong indictment of the war and admission of misconduct among American troops, it took over five years for this first-person memoir to reach the screen. Originally intended as a theatrical feature, the lengthy teleplay was partially funded by the British firm Hemdale, the same foreign source that would pony up the money for *Platoon*. *A Rumor of War* featured omniscient voiceover narration by the main character, the author-lieutenant. In accessing the war, this first-person rendition was a harrowing breakthrough that had won the Pulitzer Prize. No longer was a stranger to combat, such as a journalist or filmmaker, interpreting events.

The film follows the book in tracing Caputo's evolution from naive college student to marine officer to embittered veteran. It opens as First Lieutenant Philip Caputo is accused of the premeditated murder of a citizen of Vietnam. A military tribunal stands in judgment of this capital offense. The movie then flashes back three years to Chicago as the young man cavorts with his girlfriend, oblivious to a background foreign policy speech by President Kennedy.

The college student eventually feels confronted by his need to make certain life decisions as he approaches graduation. In a bar a World War II vet proudly talks about his contribution at Tarawa. The assassination of John F. Kennedy becomes the impetus for the young man, along with many others, to enlist in the marines. His parents wonder what he is trying to prove. Like countless young men who preceded him, Caputo wants to test his mettle and notions of manhood and courage.

In boot camp the boys are exhorted to "survive! survive! kill! kill!" Italian-American Caputo and a young Jewish soldier, O'Keefe as Cohen, become friends. Soon they are deplaning together from their C-130 transport at Da Nang. The war and the VC seem nowhere to be found in this beautiful and very hot foreign land. The men are like most newcomers here in the early part of the war, anxious to see action, or, as they put it in their generational lingo, to "rock and roll!"

As an intelligent college graduate Caputo has completed officers candidate school and arrives in-country a very green second lieutenant. As seen in *The Boys in Company C* and *Go Tell the Spartans*, despite his official rank, the men's lives will be in the hands of the combat-seasoned career sergeants. Caputo is ready to fight communists and defend a free way of life. The mundane realities of dysentery, headquarters reports, and so on prove frustrating.

Soon combat comes, and aside from those killed, innocence is also a casualty. The specifics of in-country life, such as the process of securing camp perimeters, and the landing zones, are all now more familiar to a fictional film audience. Via the ubiquitous helicopters, Caputo and his squad take part in a classic "hammer-and-anvil" maneuver. In response to rounds from an unseen enemy, the men wildly fire. In a village an ARVN interpreter viciously interrogates an old man suspected of being VC. Like Cowboy in *Spartans* or Vic Diaz in *Company C*, the allied officer's brutal treatment of his countryman shocks but also serves as an eventual example for the young officer.

Caputo and his comrades are confounded by their inability to sort the enemy from the indigenous friendlies. In addition they suspect that their maneuvers lack a coherent overall objective despite the plethora of body bags resulting from their actions. This is not the war Caputo expected. It is on a helicopter-transported "commuter shuttle" with no victories, only strange incursions and firefights. The people that the Americans were there to defend seem either unworthy or unappreciative of attempts to win their hearts and minds. As casualties mount the Americans begin to relieve their pain and frustration "by inflicting it on others." "We learned just how brutal a 19-year-old American boy can be." This revelation was a shock and recalled Americans' collective trauma at realizing what conduct their soldiers were capable of at My Lai. *A Rumor of War* speaks in the first person in a fact-based recollection of what Kurtz described in *Apocalypse Now* as "the horror."

In an attempt to find respite from the carnage, the men go to DaNang for R&R. Already in 1965, it is a huge bustling city full of whorehouses and other support for the burgeoning U.S. presence. Back in the bush Caputo's friend dies in his arms. The next day he snaps in an interrogation and brutalizes a villager. Caputo's friend Cohen slaps him to bring him back to civility. Caputo is transferred to paper-shuffling duty. One night the relatively safe compound comes under heavy fire, and Cohen is killed.

Caputo is consumed by hate, and upon his transfer back into the field, he becomes a brutal leader. One night, following an informer's lead, he and two of his men ambush a group of suspected Viet Cong booby trap experts. It is an independent action that results in the wrong people being killed. The film cuts from the ambush to the present and a lawyer in the courtroom interrogating the young officer. Caputo does not deny the killings but takes exception to the charge of murder. He objects to such judgment when the demarcation between legitimate and illegitimate conduct is so muddled.

The military defense lawyer convinces Caputo to cop a plea and be reprimanded rather than subject himself to a trial and harsher punishment. Unlike some fictional rendering that would result in an indictment of the system and absolution for the individual soldier, the film is more nearly realistic. Caputo does what he must to survive, just as he had learned to do in Vietnam.

As the film ends a wise and weary Caputo gazes at fresh-faced recruits arriving in huge numbers on the tarmac. At the same time C-130s are loaded with coffins destined for the United States. In voiceover, he states, "For me the war was over. Yet it was not to let go; it would ride with me. I had survived, but that was my only victory." As the credits roll a stylized, vaguely Asian instrumental rendition of the "Halls of Montezuma" is heard.

As a sad assessment of the American involvement in a losing conflict, *A Rumor of War* fit into the cynicism that pervaded the four horsemen and the apocalypse. The necessity of English money was also met by a reluctance to allow this first-person account to be filmed in the United States. Rather, the film was made in Mexico, thereby saving production funds and avoiding controversy. Real-life Lieutenant Colonel Harry McCloy, played by Keith Carradine in the movie, was the technical adviser. The source material and the contribution of the real-life Nam veterans as tech advisers lent a veracity to the on-screen re-creations.

A Rumor of War managed to incorporate a number of personally based first-hand perspectives on the war. Some accounts needed "to document what fighting the war was actually like for the American soldiers. Others emphasized the chaotic nature of the war and the impossibility of recounting the soldiers' experiences. A third theme, common to most . . . personal accounts, was the soldiers' disillusionment at having been asked to risk their lives for a cause that neither the government nor the American people would allow them to win."[2] A confessional Caputo sums up his thoughts in his award-winning book this way:

> At times the comradeship that was the war's only redeeming quality caused some of its worst crimes — acts of retribution for friends who had been killed. Some men could not withstand the stress of guerilla fighting. . . . Others were made pitiless by an overpowering greed for survival. Self-preservation, the most basic and tyrannical of all instincts, can turn a man into a coward or, as was more often the case in Vietnam, into a creature who destroys without hesitation or remorse whatever poses even a potential threat to his life. A sergeant in my platoon, ordinarily a pleasant-going man, told me once, "Lieutenant, I've got a wife and two kids at home and I'm going to see 'em again and don't care who I've got to kill or how many of 'em to do it."[3]

In an effort to expiate guilt, the misconduct of Caputo in his confessional memoir *A Rumor of War* served as a bridge in this group of films. At the time of

The Green Berets American soldiers' participation in the killing of civilians seemed impossible. In 1971 the My Lai convictions took place and seemed to symbolize everything that had gone wrong with American presence in Vietnam. Gradually in the returning vet pictures, such as *Glory Boy* in 1971, or *The Visitors* in 1972, atrocities were alluded to as aberrations. By 1978's in-country depictions, in a still-once-removed circumstance, the South Vietnamese allies were shown executing suspected Viet Cong sympathizers. Here in Caputo's 1980 film American soldiers themselves killed the wrong civilians. What eventually would evolve from here in this continuum of misconduct was the accidental killing of children in 1983's *Memorial Day*, the overt crimes in DePalma's *Casualties of War*, the bloody misconduct in *Platoon*, and the inadvertent shedding of children's blood in *Born on the Fourth of July*. Serious nonexploitative films would eventually offer up such a wealth of ugly incidents or, at the very least, professional incompetency that veterans' groups would object to the evolving portrait of the troops as "baby killers."

Theatrical treatments of the war remained elusive in 1980 as television contributed film entries. Charles Fries, the same production house responsible for *A Rumor of War*, provided *The Children of An Lac* in October. Once again a firsthand account provided the source material. This feature was inspired by the work of the late actress Ina Balin on behalf of the orphans of South Vietnam. Balin served as story consultant and associate producer and appeared as herself in the telefilm. Shirley Jones costarred along with two Asian actors seen throughout: Vic Diaz and Kieu Chinh. John Llewellyn Moxey directed the screenplay penned by Blanche Hanalis.

Actress Balin had become interested in war orphans in Saigon during a USO tour in 1970. An Lac was the name of the orphanage she championed. It meant "Happy Place." The movie told of her unceasing efforts to effectuate the evacuation of 219 orphans from South Vietnam amid the panic and politics of the April 1975 communist triumph.

The Children of An Lac brought national attention to heroic efforts on behalf of orphans in war-torn Vietnam. In this way the film followed up on the more particular problems of the Amerasian children depicted in *Green Eyes* and predated other similarly social, not military or political, depictions of the effects of the war. In chronicling the chaos in a desperate Saigon, it predated features such as *Saigon: Year of the Cat* and a television film *Last Flight Out*. All managed to convey the panic that engulfed the South Vietnamese as the United States withdrew in the inevitable prelude to defeat.

Balin, American Betty Tisdale (Jones), and Madam Ngai, played by Beulah Quo, all combine compassion with determination to save their beloved orphans. They cajole a besieged U.S. diplomatic contingency into providing a C-130 transport for the mission. Negotiating the clogged streets of Saigon becomes yet another adventure. The embassy, Tan Son Nhut Airport, and elsewhere are all scenes of chaos. Underlying much of the desperation is the widely held belief that the approaching communists have a death list. Presumed to be on this VC register are many loyal allies who had anything to do with the long American presence in South Vietnam. Personal and collective responsibility for their safety becomes an undercurrent in this and other evacuation tales.

The story of *The Children of An Lac* is heartening. Fortunately the planeload of children did make it out and arrive safely in the United States. In fact Balin went on to adopt three girls as her own. Many such planeloads of orphans, some full Vietnamese and some Amerasian, flew out in the final days of the war. Unfortunately in one last-minute wartime tragedy a full C-130 did crash with the entire crew and precious cargo of children killed. It became a shocking symbol of waste and death to a jaded American public anxious to be out of Vietnam, a place Americans thought they had left in 1973, only to be still retreating from in 1975. (Tragically, the compassionate Ina Balin died in June 1990 of a chronic lung disease at the young age of 52.)

Only a month after its previous television movie about Vietnam, CBS broadcast the made-for melodrama *The Promise of Love*. This Pierre Cosette production starred Valerie Bertinelli, Jameson Parker, and Craig T. Nelson as Major Landau. Directed by Don Taylor, this is a simple tale of tragedy and renewal that follows a teenage bride from war-induced widowhood to recovery and a new romance. In its harking back to the recent sad past the film is a personalized account of a collective trauma. In its hopefulness and rebirth it is an optimistic look at an individual and, by extension, national future. The romantic drama was originally called *Personal Effects*. This dually meaningful title referred to the sending home of a dead man's possessions and to the results of the war on the loved ones back home.

Less than one month passed before ABC had its own made-for-television Vietnam-themed presentation. On December 7 the MTM Enterprises presentation of *Fighting Back* was broadcast. Once again a fact-based first-hand account was the source of the melodrama. Directed by Robert Lieberman and written by Jerry McNeely, this film told the tale of Pittsburgh Steelers star Rocky Bleier's inspiring comeback from wartime injuries. Based upon Bleier and Terry O'Neil's book, the recovery of the soldier was a miraculous tale of perseverance and inspired optimism.

Robert Urich portrayed Bleier, and Bonnie Bedelia costarred. Art Carney played Steelers owner Art Rooney, and Bubba Smith and several real-life teammates appeared in the film. Howard Cosell overacted even as himself. The television film, like its predecessors, was at times heavy-handed but worked quite well in the low-budget broadcast milieu for which it was intended. Most of the 1980s made-fors offered optimism and recovery as opposed to the recent guilt-ridden pessimism that had pervaded the national consciousness after the war.

(In conjunction with the plethora of made-for-television movies about the Vietnam War or its aftermath, weekly shows began to introduce veteran characters for the first time. Appearing at this time was the live action but cartoonish adventures of the "A Team." These crime-fighting professionals gained much of their expertise as soldiers in-country. Also in a slightly more reality based cop program, Don Johnson as Sonny showed a detective seasoned under fire as a veteran of the recent conflict in the hit series "Miami Vice.")

The year 1981 began with great elation following the release of the hostages in Iran. Nevertheless, the first film released that featured Vietnam War veterans was a throwback to earlier days. *Search and Destroy* had been filmed some three years before. Only now, attempting to exploit the burgeoning demand for undiscriminating action titles for home video, did the film find distribution. The movie starred Perry King and Don Stroud. William Fruet directed the picture, which opened to an in-country sequence set in 1968.

U.S. Special Forces troops are escorting a high-level South Vietnamese government official. A Viet Cong ambush results in one of the American's being wounded. In an effort to escape, the callous ally refuses the man medical aid. This so infuriates the remaining Americans that they abandon their charge. The film then jumps forward ten years to the United States. There the same South Vietnamese official attempts to extract revenge for the mutual wartime double crosses. Several ex-soldiers are killed before there is a climactic firefight at Niagara Falls.

Although a facile exploitation flick, *Search and Destroy* did reflect the undercurrent of mistrust between the United States and its South Vietnamese ally. In fact the film seemingly makes no distinction between the North and the South, merely referring to the "Vietnamese." This went beyond the common depictions of the South Vietnamese as corrupt, brutal, ungrateful, or cowardly allies. Like most negative stereotypes involving the hated war, this characterization was a great disservice to the many brave South Vietnamese soldiers who served their country and the allied combined war effort with distinction. The generic Asian bad guy was a throwback to the earliest Vietenam movies.

Other veteran depictions in 1981 were tangential renderings that served as background color for movie characters. *I, the Jury* featured Armand Assante, and *Nighthawks* starred Sylvester Stallone, as detectives who happened to be vets. Both were savvy practitioners of gunplay partially learned while soldiers in Vietnam. Although both were pretty violent and wired guys, neither was a loser in a movie hero sense. They were not destined for disaster, but rather operated professionally (and sexually) in exciting ways associated with leading men over the years.

A fuller depiction of a veteran was in the peculiar, low-key film *Americana*. This Crown International release was produced and directed by David Carradine, who also wrote the musical score. Richard Carr's screenplay was based on Henry Morton Robinson's novel *The Perfect Round*. Carradine's real-life love, Barbara Hershey, appeared as the romantic interest.

Americana was another film that had sat in a vault for years because no one quite knew how to sell it to the public. It was slow and meandering, like a merry-go-round on a hot summer day. That analogy may seem odd, but it is appropriate because that is what the film is about on the surface. Carradine is a vet in uniform who wanders into a small Kansas town. He is intrigued by a broken-down carousel sitting in an abandoned field.

The townspeople are suspicious of the transient but give him odd jobs to perform for cash. He uses this money to purchase paint and wood to restore the merry-go-round to its former grandeur. As he works he watches the lovely Barbara Hershey. He does not rape her, an ugly act to which other films have resorted. Rather, they form a tentative liaison. The local sheriff, although watchful, does not victimize or beat the wandering vet. Local rednecks at one point do taunt the drifter with the nickname "Airborne" and later rough him up. What is operating here is a man on a benign mission. He takes great pride in his peaceful work. It is a task rendered not for money but for an aesthetic sense of beauty, and the story extols the cleansing nature of good hard physical labor. If this task is a penance for some unknown misdeed, it is never revealed. The only behavior explicitly inspired by in-country experiences is the vet's formation of an enforced security perimeter around his project. This is necessitated by local vandals who resent his presence. At one other point flashback recollections are conveyed by the nighttime whir of helicopters on the soundtrack. This audio symbol of war never escalates into visual depictions. They would be outside the minimal thrust of the film's budget and of its intent.

After completing this task, the veteran moves on, having left the town and its children a legacy of fun in the beautiful carousel, the "perfect round." This peculiar little film is a refreshing change in the depiction of the vets.

Another challenging and fascinating depiction was featured in *Cutter's Way* (aka *Cutter and Bone*). This United Artists release directed by Czech expatriate Ivan Passer was criticaly acclaimed and swept the Houston Film Festival. Jeff Bridges starred as Cutter, a handsome man with no convictions. His best friend, Rich Bone, is the vet, memorably played by John Heard. Bone lost an arm and an eye and has a bum leg as a result of wartime injuries. His patch and scruffy demeanor make him appear as a modern-day pirate. He decries hypocrisy and evil societal manipulations by the rich and powerful. However, he sometimes aspires to their pleasures and subconsciously manipulates his friends, lovers, and strangers with his physical infirmities.

When Bone uncovers a murder plot involving a wealthy town leader, he has found his cause. Cutter is a reluctant participant in his friend's quest for the truth. Lisa Eichorn, as the vet's long-suffering wife, provides the film's third compelling performance. The vet is a gray, multilayered, and cross-motivated character. Like the murder mystery plot line, the film inconspicuously unfolds in its depiction of the vet as well as the other emotionally troubled characters. At one point vet Bone rails at his buddy that "while you were getting laid in the Ivy League, I was gettin' shot at!" Bone is irate at the injustices inherent in the Vietnam sacrifice, usually skewed along class lines. Bone finds the powerful businessperson, hypocrite, and murderer a fitting personification of those who "never put their ass on the line" but kept soldiers in the rice paddies for profit and patriotism.

Bone eventually dies trying to kill the powerbroker. Cutter takes a stand and finishes the job on behalf of his martyred buddy. The downer ending went against the renewed vogue of happy endings and, along with the cryptic nature of the film, eventually consigned it to commercial oblivion.[4]

By 1981 a military comedy could once again become a hit. This was notable because for years that subgenre had been avoided amid the carnage in Vietnam and the discrediting of the institution of the armed forces. *Stripes* starred Bill Murray in a farce set among U.S. forces assigned to NATO in Europe. At one point while attempting to rally his ragtag troops, the comedian says in his whiny voice, "C'mon, we're Americans." Then in reference to our collective history and recently tarnished record, he declares that as far as wars were concerned, "We're ten and one." Like a sports team, the ten represent wins, and the one is conspicuous as a loss. Obviously that loss was Vietnam. By 1981 that line could get a laugh.

Commemorating events of some 11 years before was the poignant telefilm *Kent State*. It began with the following scrawl: "On May 4, 1970, four students were killed at Kent State University. Their deaths ended a decade that began in innocence and ended in despair." The long form's power was in its quiet and deliberate rendition of facts on a day-by-day basis leading up to the fateful Monday. By following characters representing the students, the National Guard, and the faculty, the movie was able to personalize the tragedy and begin to address the question "How could this happen here?"

James Goldstone directed Gerald Green and Richard Kramer's script. Will Patton, Ellen Barkin in a NLF shirt, Keith Gordon, John Getz, and Sheppard Strudwick costarred. On Thursday April 30 President Nixon addresses the nation on the necessity of an offensive against "enemy sanctuaries along the Cambodian border." The next morning a poorly attended campus protest distracts some students from their class schedule. Each of the four doomed students is introduced, and their activities are chronicled. By Friday night overzealous college hijinks combined with the rowdiness of a local cycle gang lead to a riot in downtown Kent, Ohio. Police in riot gear are taunted as they break up the disturbance.

During the weekend rumors that the ROTC building will be torched lead to great anxiety among the police and faculty. In light of the recent destruction of these facilities at other colleges, the possibility is not at all farfetched. By Saturday a contingent of Ohio National Guard exhausted from a violent Teamsters strike arrive on campus. The Guard's presence inflames the student body. The soldiers are a cross-section ranging from reactionary rednecks to young men merely trying to serve duty here in lieu of an in-country tour. So, too, the student body ranges from radicals to concerned peace advocates to those just going about their studies.

Despite the fact that the audience already knows the tragic results, the film is able to convey a mounting sense of tension and reveal the miscalculations that led to four deaths and nine woundings. Saturday and Sunday bring no respite, and by Monday the campus is a powderkeg. Crosby, Stills, Nash, and Young's anthem "Four Dead in Ohio" rings out as the film dramatizes the fateful day and

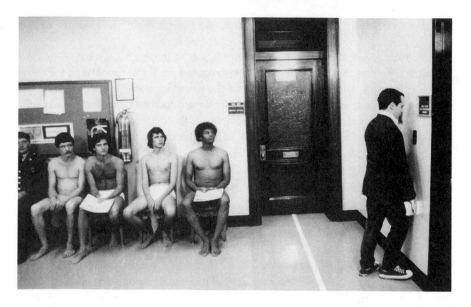

Purple Haze (Columbia Pictures, 1983). **A young man acts like an idiot to get out of the draft.**

incorporates images burned into the American conscience. Most notable is the anguished supplication of a coed as she kneels over the body of Allison Krause, another visual image from the era frozen in our minds by a Pulitzer Prize–winning photo. The tragic climactic "battle," as it were, leaves the viewer dripping in sweat and nauseated in a manner that the best in-country firefight re-creations of the films in this book also elicit.

The pleading speech of a faculty member to avoid further tragedy is powerful. He tells the shocked, grieving, and angry mob to "sit down. . . . We've had bloodshed. . . . There are too many of you that are too damned good to die in this stinking field." His words are so true, and the same went for thousands in some far-off rice paddy. The Vietnam War had set American against American, and *Kent State* became a monument to the nation's loss.

In September ABC telecast An Lac Production's *Fly Away Home.* The film starred Bruce Boxleitner, Brian Dennehy, and Kieu Chinh. Paul Krasny directed the film, which was written and produced by Sterling Silliphant. The movie was actually a pilot for an unbought series following the exploits of a combat cinematographer in Vietnam.

The film, firmly set in-country, begins in Saigon around the time of the Tet Offensive. The historical events are seen from several perspectives, including those of the cinematographer, his cynical bureau chief, a young draftee, a navy pilot, and a South Vietnamese family. With subplots concerning local corruption, the film recalls early black-market tales. The naive idealism of some Americans, as opposed to any forthright miscalculation and poor motives, echoes the characterization elicited in the compromised film version of *The Quiet American.*

The first entry in 1982 also took place in the dramatic year of Tet, 1968. *Purple Haze* was a coming-of-age tale that utilized the title from Jimi Hendrix's hit song. That musician, who died before his time of a drug overdose, had become a pop-cultural symbol of the late–1960s era. His expert guitar playing and ahead-of-its-time use of electronic feedback were most often appreciated in an altered state of consciousness. The two protagonists in *Purple Haze,* portrayed by Peter Nelson and Chuck McQuary, both abused drugs as part of their experimental years. As a result they dropped out of college and lost their deferments. This tale of their quest for maturity, meaning, and safety in the summer of 1968 is played for both drama and laughs. Director David Morris did a good job balancing the two elements.

Director Peter Werner's *Don't Cry It's Only Thunder* was set in Saigon in 1967 and based on a true story. Dennis Christopher starred as a cynical drug-dealing medic who is blackmailed by an idealistic army physician, played by Susan Saint James, into assisting a desperate group of orphans. The GI uses his black market connections to provide supplies.

Paramount Pictures' 1982 release *Some Kind of Hero* was a serio-comic look at a returning veteran's adjustment problems. Directed by Michael Pressman, the film starred Richard Pryor, whose ability to play tragedy as well as comedy was proven.

Like most previous attempts at using Vietnam-related humor to soften a serious story, the necessary balance was hard to maintain.

The film opens in a swamp in Vietnam when Pryor is captured with his pants down while attempting to relieve himself. The image of him with arms raised in surrender and in boxer shorts became the print ad for the film. He is sent to a Viet Cong prison, where he is beaten and coerced into signing an antiwar statement.

Real-life POWs were subjected to this disgusting treatment until they relented and provided these worthless shreds of propaganda. He only agrees in order to save a beloved cellmate, played by Ray Sharkey. His friend dies, but the film again pulls its punches by sublimating grief into comedy with a new cellmate, a pet rat.

Finally repatriated, the brave soldier is haunted by the document as his loyalty is called into question. Ronny Cox played a kindly colonel who tries to guide him through the labyrinth of army nonsense. Now-familiar tragedies befall him at every step. His mother has a stroke, his wife loves another man, his business is ruined, and his back pay is held up pending an investigation of his confession. Margot Kidder as a kindly hooker gives the troubled vet some moments of pleasure, although the interracial love scene probably gave some exhibitors fits. Out of desperation the vet engineers a swindle of some gangsters. Unlike the films some ten years earlier, he does not blow the bad guys away with a bazooka. Rather, he merrily goes on his way in a contrived happy ending.

Some Kind of Hero (**Paramount Pictures, 1982**). **Richard Pryor and Ray Sharkey as prisoners of war.**

In contrast to the preceding widely distributed studio tale was the typical oblivion to which independent Mypheduh Films' *Ashes and Embers* succumbed. Haile Gerima wrote and directed this tale of a black veteran's confrontation with racism and poverty back home. John Anderson and Evelyn Blackwell starred in an American film that finally voiced what the enemy in previous movies had been trying to exploit, but without success. That was the inherent injustice/irony of fighting on behalf of the "oppressor." Some of the angrier Blaxploitation flicks had hinted at it, but only this film made it a central theme. The veteran's psychological trauma is exacerbated by this factor. When he has a tearful breakdown with his girlfriend, her son is basically unmoved. "My father was killed in Vietnam!" he remarks. By extension his alienation is grounded in the overall context of the suffering of the entire underclass. When the vet understands the remark, then he can begin to reintegrate into his subculture.[5]

Tangentially relevant to this book were two successful items from 1982. One was the debut of handsome Tom Selleck as a Viet vet character on the long-running weekly television show "Magnum PI." He and his private investigation team's expertise were garnered in-country. He is a ladies' man and a professional success and as such joins the more positive portrayals of the vets emerging in the 1980s. Aside from being likable, he is not the least pitiable. He is a far cry from the dysfunctional vet and sociopath characters of the 1970s. In the third season, the show would briefly return to Southeast Asia to show the initial bonding of its familiar characters.

The second item was the release of *An Officer and a Gentleman.* It became the third-highest-grossing film of the year and one of the finest romances in a long time. It is mentioned here not because of Vietnam imagery but because of the dashing romantic portrait it provides of a man in uniform. Now in peacetime, training camp is no longer a prelude to Vietnam. People can argue whether a restoration of a positive image of the military tarnished by Vietnam is a good thing. However, in terms of film images Richard Gere's lusty pilot kicked off a dress white sex appeal that within ten years would be attached directly to Vietnam warriors in films such as *Flight of the Intruder.*

In a surprise hit from Orion, Sylvester Stallone starred as special forces veteran and one-person army Rambo in *First Blood.* Ted Kotcheff directed the film, which featured Richard Crenna as Colonel Trautman, Brian Dennehy as town sheriff, and Jack Starrett as Galt. Buzz Feitshans was the producer of this Carolco-funded feature. As such he and the principals of that production company were to make numerous contributions to the list of films in the years to come.

The films opens as muscular loner John Rambo walks down a beautiful Pacific Northwest road in combat pants and boots. He arrives at the town of Hope, an obviously ironic moniker already used in *Welcome Home Soldier Boys* from 1972. There he seeks out an old comrade from Vietnam. The Medal of Honor winner is distressed to find out that his pal died of cancer caused by Agent Orange.

Although Rambo is minding his own business, the town sheriff tells the transient to move on out of town. The vet defies the order, resulting in his arrest. As Rambo is booked, we see not only his dog tags and big knife but a warrior's scarred body. As the redneck cops throw the monosyllabic vet in jail, he flashes back to his incarceration and torture by the Viet Cong. Rambo goes berserk, and using his hand-to-hand combat expertise, is able to escape despite overwhelming opposition. A chase ensues, and he reaches the lush woods with the police in hot pursuit.

In well-crafted action sequences, the war hero's survival skills make him more than a match for an eventual 500-officer onslaught and modern law enforce-

First Blood (Orion Pictures, 1982). This ad slick shows a veteran who tries to read-just. A pop-culture legend is born, Sylvester Stallone as Rambo.

ment technology. He employs in-country tricks and other decidedly primitive weaponry such as pungi sticks and bow and arrows. As a hunted animal or killing machine of primordial efficiency, the vet had learned his military lessons well. In an attempt to effect his surrender, the police and National Guard bring in a loved one to try talking him down. The loved one is not his mother but Crenna, his special forces commander from Vietnam, who declares, "God didn't make Rambo. I made him." The surrogate father tells the authorities to get plenty of body bags ready if they charge. Meanwhile the media swirl about like a bunch of vultures.

The film has functioned as an entertaining action showcase for the physical acting of Stallone and the cold and wet beauty of the American rain forest (actually British Columbia). Managing to escape back into town, Rambo meets up with the colonel. In this scene Rambo uses more dialogue than in the entire film so far to articulate the victimization of the veteran. Crenna tells him to give up; these are "friendly civilians." Rambo replies that there are no friendly civilians and that the war still is not over. "Somebody would not let us win," and back in "the world" vets were spat upon and called baby killers. He cries for his fallen comrades and for himself so lost in this world.

Eventually he mercifully spares the evil sheriff's life and surrenders. Very few films overtly articulated a belief that the Vietnam War was wrong per se for the United States to be involved in. Rather, *First Blood* espoused the less overtly political belief that the war was wrong because the soldier was not allowed to win. He was victimized and the war effort compromised by cynical political considerations, liberal manipulation, or a lack of will. In broad strokes the antiwar protestors became irresponsible fools who taunted innocent soldiers trying to do their duty. By the same token it seemed as if every U.S. combatant eventually became a baby killer or was accused of such behavior.

The mistreatment becomes so universally accepted that it cuts across the spectrum. Stallone's character describes what Bruce Dern alluded to in a much-different vehicle, *Coming Home*. Rambo articulates what *Taxi Driver* Bickle kept to himself. As the credits roll Rambo's private war begins a truce that will last until 1985 and the megahit sequel, *Rambo: First Blood II*. That film will become the conservative post–Vietnam film epoch of the 1980s.

Finishing up 1982 was the CBS television movie *Deadly Encounter*, starring Larry Hagman and Susan Anspach. William A. Graham directed this tale of a Vietnam helicopter pilot now in Mexico. The adventure contributed to the high profile of the chopper in the post–Vietnam group of films as the preeminent inanimate object associated with the conflict.

The big-budget spring 1983 release *Blue Thunder* actualy starred a helicopter. Although set far from Vietnam, the John Badham film strongly echoes unresolved personal and social conflict from the war. It features a superchopper that right-wing reactionary police elements attempt to use for surveillance and suppression of the crime-ridden underclass in America's slums. Roy Scheider, Daniel Stern, Warren Oates, and Malcolm McDowell starred.

Chief pilot Scheider is a Vietnam veteran who under pressure flashes back to a moment when, during an intense interrogation, his cohorts dropped a Viet Cong soldier to his death. Scheider is determined to not be used again in the service of uncontrolled technological abuse of an indigenous populace. As noted in *Commonweal*, "The helicopter is the technological icon of the eighties: beautiful, mobile, graceful, and deeply threatening. The fighter plane, the icon of World War II and Korea, was unidirectional, fast, and sure of purpose. The helicopter—no, the chopper—the icon of Nam, is omnidirectional, ambiguous, and capricious. It is the technology of the shrug."[6]

Each week on television Tom Selleck as Magnum PI played the ex–Vietnam chopper pilot. Since Marshall Thompson's flicks in the 1960s, the chopper had typified Vietnam military technology. The association was strengthened in the memorable air cavalry raid in *Apocalypse Now*. By the 1980s just providing the audio whir of the blades instantly conveyed Nam to the conditioned audience.

Blue Thunder was the name given to the sleek, metallic weapon. Its chrome beauty updated the male fetishism bestowed on the other "chopper," the motorcycle of earlier flicks. Both appealed to a male gear fantasy. In some ways this proactive imagery attached to the Los Angeles police was prescient of the war on drugs carried out against the gangs as copters with search lights noisily scanned the ghetto in the early 1990s. Incidentally director Badham that same year made *War Games*, a big hit that also warned of the danger of uncontrolled military technology.

Television's most memorable contribution to the Vietnam War films in 1983 was the controversial 13-part PBS special "Vietnam: A Television History." The documentary aroused great debate and passion. Historian Stanley Karnow in his companion book sums up this fascinating work's central theme that "America's leaders . . . carried the U.S. into Southeast Asia with little regard for the realities of the region."[7]

Most appropriate to this primary analysis of fiction films is the coalescence of opinion occurring from *Apocalypse Now* to *Rambo* that Vietnam was wrong. Again Karnow identifies the perspectives. For the Left the war was immoral, racist, stupid, and none of our business. For the right we were correct in fighting communism but wrong in not pursuing victory. The documentary, funded by France's Antenne and Britain's Central Television, was accused of no such evenhanded portrayal but rather of a dovish revisionism. By the way the credits for each installment featured the sound of a helicopter.

Britain's Thames television was the production source for 1983's *Saigon: Year of the Cat*. Now internationally renowned Stephen Frears directed Judi Dench and Frederic Forrest in this look at the final days of South Vietnam's capital before the 1975 communist takeover. The film begins with the American withdrawal and ends with the panicked last flight out of Westerners and the frightened longtime allies left behind in the final moments.

One of the strengths of this adventure/love story is its depiction of the vestiges of colonialism in the South. The French presence has receded into the background. However, the United States had replaced that power as a huge employer, cultural influence, and political and military benefactor. The British are employed in mercantilism and represent complementary capitalist interests. The characters sip drinks at Saigon hotels with the CIA spooks and other corporate warriors and reminisce about the good life mercilessly crashing down.

By Christmas the party chatter is about who will be the last to evacuate, what will happen to native employees and friends, and whether there will be a wholesale bloodbath. The American ambassador, played by E. G. Marshall, is beset by bad intelligence, a problem that plagued MacWhite way back in *The Ugly American*. The English, far more experienced in these matters of colonial dissolution, with stereotypical calmness present a stiff upper lip, a detachment worthy of the more benign side of Fowler way back in *The Quiet American*.

By operating from an English perspective and by integrating current events with a well-worn soap opera set in a foreign land, the film has the style of an old black-and-white feature. However, thematically it harks back to the most prescient early Vietnam War films and confirms their prewar fears. Chaos, then dishonor, and eventually defeat are the tragic final steps. In the finale civilians employed by the departing Westerners await an evacuation truck that never arrives. ARVN soldiers hurriedly change into civilian garb, trying to blend into the populace in a manner in which the Viet Cong were masters. And once again using real-life footage, the film shows once-proud marines scampering for helicopters and the last flight out.

Continuing 1983's rhythm from direct to indirect portraits of the conflict was the tangential contribution *Streamers*. Robert Altman directed David Rabe's adaptation of his own play. The film starred a talented young emsemble including Matthew Modine, Mitchell Lichtenstein, and George Dzundza. It took place entirely in a stateside army barracks during the Vietnam War. The conflict becomes a specter hanging over a parable about themes of manhood, race relations, sexual preference, and death.

The title refers to a song that involves a man streaming to his death because his parachute will not open. Apparently that is what awaits these young men as they prepare for the war and adulthood. This pretentious, dramatic nonsense works in the intimacy of live theater but becomes claustrophobic in its static film rendition. Once again Vietnam has been reduced to a kind of tragic generic irony for a troubled generation coming of age.

In November Charles Fries productions provided CBS with the made-for *Memorial Day*. Once again Joseph Sargent directed a series entry, this one starring Mike Farrell as a Vietnam veteran, Shelley Fabares as his supportive but confused wife, and Edward Herrmann as a concerned colleague. The film begins with positive imagery as Farrell, a successful lawyer and family man, goes to a reunion of war buddies. Reminiscing leads to a drunken depression on the part of one of the veterans, played by Robert Walden. Other platoon members— Danny Glover in a wheelchair from wartime injuries and Jonathan Goldsmith (Oleo in *Go Tell the Spartans*)—seem well acclimated to their postwar fate.

When the troubled vet commits suicide, the others are forced to reexamine long-suppressed emotions, such as grief and guilt. Farrell probes his past but is unable to share his thoughts with those who care. Once again the horrible nature of the in-country experiences makes only peers capable of understanding. The vets feel victimized by a military policy that had no overall strategic plan for victory. They also hated the integration of combatant and noncombatant death. In an effort to add zest to this uniquely Vietnam quandary, the film hints that the men have something to hide. By now in the film, it is readily apparent that some type of wartime atrocity took place. Unlike the wired psychos of the early films, the power is in the fact that this mysterious conduct was on the part of regular, good men put in horrible circumstances. Finally after turning to drink and beating a client, Farrell reaches a breaking point and purposely chooses an inappropriate social setting for his tearful confession. At a Memorial Day picnic he reveals the truth that haunts him. The whir of helicopter blades ushers in the revelation that at Bin Moi, Farrell shot and killed a number of children. Even though he was only following orders, the tragedy took place, and the pain is still there. Like many vets, Farrell admits, "I lost part of me over there, and I'm never going to get it back." The veteran who is physically maimed shows his sacrifice every day. But less obvious is this invisible mental component, which is also an important casualty of war. Farrell was afraid that if he started crying, he would never be able to stop.

In Vietnam the soldiers' loss of innocence echoed that of the entire country. Once again, even with serious nonexploitative films, the combatant as baby killer becomes such an oft-used means of conveying the mangled nature of the war that it seems as if every soldier must have such an atrocity story. (Like the earlier negative stereotypes, this was quite perturbing to veterans' groups.) The reaction of Farrell's guests reflects a range that mimics the film world's treatment of the entire conflict. One couple refuses to listen and leaves, ignoring the entire episode. Another couple lasts a little longer but tries to soften the information by misinterpreting and recontextualizing it. Only the best friend and wife take it head-on and in this manner come to help in the recovery process. So, too, despite the panoply of issues that populate the filmography and the value of metaphor, the most important contributions remain the direct portraits of combat and its effects.

One of the biggest hits of 1983 was the fall release of Lawrence Kasdan's emsemble drama *The Big Chill.* The story involves a group of former 1960s college kids who reunite for a weekend. In an updating of the sign-of-the-times campus dramas, the former students are now responsible yuppies who attempt to examine their lives while reminiscing about a past age of innocence. A wonderful 1960s musical soundtrack accompanies this tale of the inevitable process of becoming part of the "establishment." Interestingly the least functional character is the drug-addicted William Hurt, the sole military veteran of the Vietnam War. The film was basically a slicker remake of John Sayles independent film *The Return of the Secaucus Seven,* which featured the reunion of a group that had never quite made it to an antiwar rally. That 1980 release had a similar air of noncombatant nostalgia for the war era.

At Christmas 1983 Warner Bros. released *Twilight Zone—The Movie*, directed by John Landis and produced by Steven Spielberg. One of the three anthology parts featured a Vietnam sequence. Vic Morrow is running with two children through a rice paddy in a firefight. Overhead screams a helicopter churning the waters amid exploding artillery. The re-creation of the conflict was all too dangerous. Because of faulty special effects and an overzealous pursuit of realism, a charge went off near the hovering helicopter and blew its rotor off. In the ensuing crash actor Morrow and the two Vietnamese children were decapitated. The film did little business, and the scene is a monument to bad taste. The irony of the two child actors escaping the carnage of real-life Vietnam via the boatlift only to be killed on the set of a movie about the war was immense.

By 1983 America had become obsessed with the notion that unaccounted-for MIAs were still being held in Southeast Asia. Various live spottings, rumor, and wishful thinking combined to make this a widely held belief. Many people accused the Pentagon of not pursuing these leads vigorously enough. Out of frustration various patriotic entrepreneurs, veterans, and mercenaries began plans for rescue efforts. The most celebrated was Texas oil billionaire Ross Perot's bankrolling of retired Colonel Bo Gritz's unsuccessful mission to Southeast Asia to search for MIAs and POWs. Once again fortuitous timing was to catapult a fictional film to prominence as it told a remarkably similar tale.

Paramount Pictures released *Uncommon Valor* at Christmas, and it became a surprise hit. The film kicked off the on-screen cathartic rendering of victory in Vietnam and the liberation of American soldiers still there. The timing may have been coincidental, but the cinematic lineage of the film was anything but. The movie was directed by Ted Kotcheff straight from his success with the angry vet tale *First Blood.* John Milius, who had written *Apocalypse Now* and directed *Big Wednesday,* produced the film. His partner Buzz Feitshans had produced Rambo's introductory tale, and together they went on to do that entire series. Director of photography Steve Burum was second unit head on *Apocalypse Now.* Associate producer Burton Elias as a first lieutenant had commanded a platoon near the DMZ. Technical adviser Chuck Taylor was also a veteran and weapons expert. Finally actual veterans of the conflict were making their way to Hollywood to lend their knowledge to Joe Gayton's screenplay. They combined with filmmaking insiders who had already demonstrated their interest in the subject matter.

The cast was headed by Gene Hackman, himself a marine veteran. He proclaimed for the press, "It's not just an adventure story. This has something to say about the war, and about the unresponsiveness of the U.S. government towards people who have been affected by the Vietnam war ten years down the line."[8]

The inscription on the marine monument in Washington, D.C., reads, "Where Uncommon Valor was a Common Virtue." This film began to restore the honor of the individual fighting soldier in the context of a mostly in-country return to combat. The movie opens in a rice paddy in Vietnam in 1972. Under heavy fire a platoon attempts to evacuate onto a helicopter gunship. Because the series is shot from the vantage of the chopper with little depth of field to convey distance, it is difficult to tell whether the men will escape the pursuing North Vietnamese. In near slow motion they labor through the swirling elephant grass and swampy terrain. As each get aboard, they lend a hand to the others. One who has made it to relative safety jumps out to help a fallen comrade. Time is up and the craft has to take off. The men cry out as they watch the hero and his wounded friend fall into enemy hands. The credits begin against the backdrop of television coverage of the joyful return of POWs.

The film then jumps ahead to peacetime as Gene Hackman, a Korean War vet and the father of the heroic young man, begins to put together a rescue mission. He talks to Pentagon officials, who ignore reports of more than 400 live sightings. He ventures to Bangkok for more information and photo evidence and finally to Texas to secure mission funding. His benefactor, played by Robert Stack, is the father of the wounded young man who was left in the harrowing first scene. Hackman sets out to convince the survivors to risk their lives once again in Vietnam.

The rest of the cast exemplify the war film paradox of an extremely topical story packaged in a clichéd fashion. The cross-section of rerecruited platoon members features the nicknamed "Blaster," a California surfer played by Reb Brown. Also, Fred Ward was Wilkes, an artist who suffers from claustrophobia because of his in-country service as a tunnel rat in the Viet Cong labyrinths. Tim Thomerson was Charts, a burned-out chopper pilot. Harold Sylvester played the only well-adjusted one in civilian life, and he reluctantly returns out of group loyalty. Tex Cobb as Sailor is a throwback to the wired psycho stereotype as he wears a grenade around his neck and is in and out of stateside jails. Rounding out the group was then-unknown Patrick Swayze as a young marine who must fight for acceptance among the tightly knit unit. It turns out in one more Vietnam-induced generational tragedy that his father is MIA.

Nearly ten years have passed since the opening sequence by the time the soldiers reassemble for intense training at a Texas desert mockup of a Laotian POW camp. The men's expertise and fierce esprit de corp are in stark contrast to the frightened cherries or drug addicts or trigger-happy killers who populated previous films. On the eve of the departure for Asia, Hackman gives a rousing speech to his troops. "You're thought of as criminals because you lost." Then in slap at the corporate greed that has come to typify the 1980s, Hackman concludes with disgust, "You cost too much and didn't turn a profit." Now the situation is different, and no one can dispute the rightness of this mission of mercy and revenge.

No sooner has the team arrived in Bangkok than its equipment is confiscated. CIA interference is implied in this attempt to scuttle the mission. However, the savvy vet turns to a greasy French black-marketeer to resupply

Uncommon Valor **(Paramount Pictures, 1983). A rescue mission takes soldiers through a tough Laotian jungle.**

them. They make their way through the jungle with the aid of a Hmong guide and his two pretty daughters. Several excitingly staged firefights ensue on the way to the camp. Finally reaching their destination, the men commence a raid in a big-budget and more realistic fashion than similar missions in *The Losers* or *Good Guys Wear Black*. Unlike the real-life raid in 1970 on Son Tay Prison in North Vietnam to liberate POWs, the men do find American captives. Great bravery and heroism result in several bedraggled prisoners' being liberated. However, there has been a great price as several of the rescuers have paid the ultimate sacrifice in the quest. The pain of the years consumes Stack's grateful son as he confides to Hackman that his son is dead. As the film ends the proud but mournful major leads a press conference confirming the existence of American captives.

Shot on location in Hawaii and Thailand, the film represented a major studio effort that confirmed the box office appeal of adventure-combat flicks. More important, it spoke to a post–Vietnam hankering to triumph on film in a manner not attained in the real debacle. The dust jacket of the videotape release teases the would-be viewer with the line, "The final battle of the Vietnam conflict is about to begin."

In 1984 karate champion and action star Chuck Norris continued the rescue mission theme in *Missing in Action*. The film costarred M. Emmet Walsh and James Hong as a North Vietnamese official. Israeli moguls Menahem Golan and Yoram Globus produced the film, which was directed by Joseph Zito. As the Cannon Films logo appears on the screen, we hear the familiar whir of a helicopter.

Amid the Philippine location stand-in for Nam, Norris and his platoon fight their way through mortar fire to reach a very hot LZ. Several copters are blown to bits as pursuing soldiers bayonet wounded Americans left in the desperate evacuation. The superhero fantasy tone of the film is set immediately as the enemy seems incapable of taking cover from Norris's machine gun bullets or his karate kicks. Basically the old chopsocky adventure vehicle from Taiwan or Hong Kong has been westernized, and a Vietnam component has been laid over one more existing genre formula.

The film flashes forward to Norris in a hotel room listening to reports of MIA talks between the old combatants. The wartime prologue to a postwar present echoes the initial structure of Norris's previous Vietnam foray, *Good Guys Wear Black*. Both films will posit the double cross of the soldier in the field and the necessity for real men to take action against the enemy, whether it be barbarous Asians or corrupt domestic politicians. In flashbacks we see Norris as a POW tortured by his heinous Asian captors. The veteran is now a delegate to the POW/MIA talks. He refuses to shake the hand of the former enemy negotiating team and in fact recognizes one aide as a sadistic prison guard. His snub embarrasses the naive diplomats who make up the rest of the American contingent.

The American delegation goes on a fact-finding tour to Ho Chi Minh City, formerly Saigon. This gives Norris a chance to sneak away, gather evidence, and kill a few bad guys. Eventually Norris returns to the bush to rescue POWs who, despite official pronouncements, are still held by the North Vietnamese. Unlike Rambo, this hero uses the finest military technology to elicit the biggest explosions. At the first prisoner camp he finds that the Americans have already been moved. This disappointment again echoed the real-life Son Tay operation and in its frustrating result was also recreated years later in the CBS weekly television series based in Vietnam, "Tour of Duty."

Tracking down the convoy of emaciated POWs, Norris and some fierce locals overcome a great force to liberate the men. Via helicopter the men proceed directly to the government office, where a press conference is taking place. In the background hang portraits of Lenin and Mao as an unctuous party official denies that any Americans are still held in the Republic of Vietnam. Norris and his living proof burst into the room as a ravenous press corps goes berserk with this dramatic story. *Missing in Action* grossed so well that it spawned two sequels.

After a long hiatus romance also returned to Vietnam in *Purple Hearts*. The film was directed by Sidney J. Furie, who had helmed *The Boys in Company C*. Handsome Ken Wahl starred as a dashing navy doctor, and lovely Cheryl Ladd was a nurse. The film tries to integrate standard soap opera with the war and action sequences. Like the uneasy alliance of comedy with Vietnam, the blend is very difficult.

The film begins with a dedication to the 347,309 Americans who received the Purple Heart in the Vietnam conflict. As the credits roll the sound of choppers blends with the increasingly familiar voice of vet-turned-actor Lee Ermey barking commands. A well-staged firefight ensues, and Doctor Wahl is introduced during the rigors of frontline "meatball" surgery. Later at a hospital in Da Nang the attractive leads meet. A romance ensues, and Wahl uses every manner of excuse to get back to his beloved. The doctor's frontline duty allows the film to continually show the startling contrast of the wartime carnage.

Like the characters in Furie's previous Vietnam foray, most superior officers are complete idiots. The too damn smart, handsome, and lucky doctor is thus transferred out of sheer spite to Con Thien. The real-life siege of that camp in October 1967 was horrific as marines were attacked by the wave after wave of Viet Cong that followed almost nightly sapper probes. The doctor performs his duty admirably, as well-staged battle scenes enliven the proceedings. Finally in complete desperation the doctor is forced to abandon surgery and take up arms; as Sergeant Ermey points out, "Forget about the Hippocratic Oath and take a few of the bastards with you." At the last moment the camp is saved when an air strike is called in on the overrun position itself. The desperate final act by outnumbered but dug-in U.S. forces was used in many Vietnam films from *The Green Berets* to *Platoon*. It epitomized our stopgap countervailing tactical air superiority in the face of committed Asian fighters.

Reassigned to the hospital ship *Repose*, Wahl is reunited with Ladd. They proclaim their love for each other, something she had been reluctant to do, as her last beloved was killed in action. Almost every woman in a war film seems to have such a tragic history. In return for a blissful R&R in Manila, the doctor agrees to accompany a secret mission behind enemy lines to free American POWs. At a mission training center a bizarre CIA type instructs the team, using a mockup of the camp.

When the infiltrators reach their appointed destination, the POWs are nowhere to be found. The film thus manages to incorporate the cathartic POW rescue rage with the emotional frustration and ineffectiveness of the would-be liberators. This emotion typified the war itself and duplicated the first unsuccessful raid in *Missing in Action*. The Viet Cong attack the retreating team, and at a hot LZ one helicopter is blown to bits as another takes off back to command. The doctor is reported as killed in action. A distraught Ladd grieves for him back in Da Nang.

Actually the doctor and a small band are in the bush. After encountering enemy patrols, they reach friendly lines. Meanwhile underscoring the lack of safety anywhere in the country, the nurses' barracks are hit by enemy rockets. Having survived his ordeal, the doctor now learns of his beloved's death. The grieving lieutenant receives the Navy Cross and returns to a safer assignment on the *Repose*.

Upon his tour of duty's expiration the man destined to be a "million-dollar-a-year" surgeon chucks that career in favor of doing some good by helping the war's wounded back at a Veterans Administration hospital in the United States. While touring his new facility, the doctor encounters none other than his beloved nurse. She was not killed after all; it was her roommate, who had had Ladd's dog tags on at the time. A tearful reunion brings yet another happy ending to a film set in a place that had no such happy endings.

Once again a hackneyed plot has been updated within the context of a Vietnam War film. The return of romanticism and optimism is reflective of the overall societal healing process that most of this chapter's films reflected vis-à-vis the war. So, too, the films in some of their action and drama components hark back in a full circle to the early predebacle Vietnam War films discussed in Chapter 1.

Far from romantic was the tragedy that befell Nicolas Cage and title character Matthew Modine in *Birdy*. The curious film from Britain's Alan Parker was a unique look at the physical and mental damage wrought on two boyhood friends as a result of their duty in Vietnam. Based on William Wharton's novel and Sandy Knopf and Jack Behr's screenplay, the film flashes back and forth among the present at a Veterans Administration mental ward, the streets of Philadelphia, and, for brief moments, the jungles of Asia.

Post-traumatic stress disorder is given a whole new rendition via the powerfully quirky and physical acting of Modine. *Birdy* opens in the VA hospital as Modine squats birdlike and catatonic in his room. His visitor is his best friend, Cage, in uniform with his head wrapped in a bandage from in-country physical injuries. Cage's outward manifestation of hurt is clearly of a less life threatening nature than his friend's, who seems to have lost all sense of reality. Cage is also brilliant in conveying frustration and filial love. He tries to coax his friend out of his trance by reminiscing about their days together in high school. The mean streets of working-class Philly are given a gritty beauty in this evocation of a simpler time that nevertheless reveals Modine's early peculiarities and his obsession with flight and ornithology.

Cage laughs as he says that on the way here on the train he felt like the "invisible man." In his bandages not only does he look like Claude Rains, but as a troubled vet of an unpopular war he also feels the description is apt. Modine's frustrated doctors have called in Cage to try communicating with the unresponsive mute. Bruno Kirby played a kindly conscientious objector orderly who was lucky to escape such Vietnam-induced scarring. The film jumps from interesting adolescent adventures that create a strong sense of bonding to the present and Cage's attempts to ascertain if his buddy is just acting to get the hell out of Vietnam. The internal rhythm created by such cutting is vaguely reminiscent of the contrast created in the better in-country features between peacefulness and destruction. The Philadelphia of the nostalgic past is the relatively safer base camp. The forever altered present is like the bush patrol, fraught with anxiety.

Again eschewing the conventional, the film never shows the source of Modine's in-country trauma. He was a strange "bird," and certainly any number of tragic circumstances could have sent him over the edge. The VA hospital has other victims whose mental illness, unlike the uneasy theatrics of other films, is not used for cheap laughs. One soldier spits all the time in an effort to "get a bad taste out of his mouth." Other vets are maimed and crippled in more conventionally recognizable physical ways.

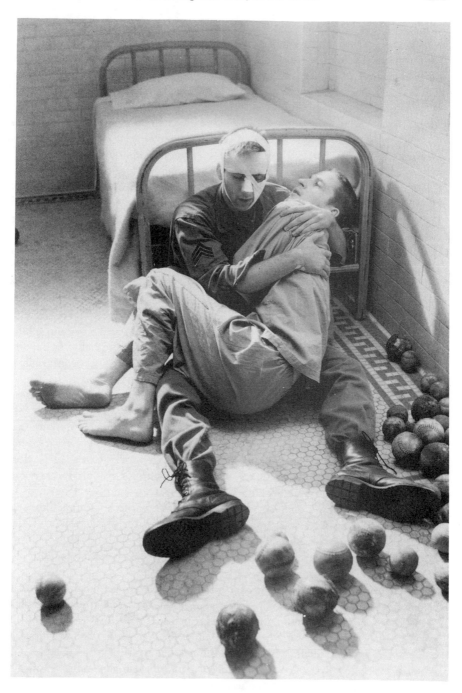

Birdy **(Tri-Star Pictures, 1984). A physically wounded Nicolas Cage comforts a mentally ill Matthew Modine, both victims of the horrors of war.**

After a scene of playing baseball as kids, the story returns to Cage, who must return to Fort Dix. The audience immediately tenses, not fully realizing how pleasantly it, too, was lost in this evocation of childhood. Later Cage muses to his pecking and strutting friend, "Oh, man, we didn't know what we were getting into with this John Wayne shit, did we? Boy we were dumb."

Soon it becomes apparent that Cage's monologuic visits are as therapeutic for him as for the still-catatonic Modine. One day the bandaged young man tries to feed his friend, but he refuses to eat. A frustrated Cage thinks back to a firefight in Vietnam as the whir of a copter elicits the time and place. Then on screen we see mines exploding, death, and frantic evacuation from the bush. Cage screams in terror and beseeches his friend to join him back in this world: "I need you." In another scene of in-country terror hundreds of beautiful tropical birds flit about the thick jungle. Suddenly napalm ignites their home, and we realize that they are being incinerated along with any hapless enemy soldiers who may have been present. Like other films' similar scenes, this destruction of nature speaks to a subliminal environmental concern but also typifies the overkill of the wastrel U.S. war effort. Here it stands nicely as a symbol of Birdy's destruction in the jungles of Southeast Asia. In fact as the film cuts back to the present, Modine freaks out and cowers like a wounded sparrow. His friend also cries out in emotional pain, "They got the best of us there. We're both totally screwed." *Birdy* is a peculiar and challenging character study that goes beyond Vietnam concerns to deal with themes of male bonding, nonconformism, nostalgia, and lost youth.

Receiving token theatrical runs in 1984 prior to their video releases were two forgettable Vietnam-related action features that went through numerous title changes in an effort to attract customers. *Final Mission* was a cheap film directed by Cerio Santiago and starring Kaz Garas. This clichéd tale involved a Green Beret veteran who uses his combat skills to battle the new urban scourge, Los Angeles street gangs. *Angkor: Cambodia Express* featured Robert Walker and Christopher George in a lamely staged actioner that also allowed Americans to triumph over Asians in a fantastic manner. What is notable about this film is its main character, an American journalist who escaped from the ruthless Cambodian communists, the Khmer Rouge. He returns to try finding the woman he loved. Directed by Alex King, this exploitation drivel was the B flip side of our next important A feature.

The Killing Fields was a powerful drama that showed the horrors of war in Cambodia in the 1970s. Sam Waterston starred as *New York Times* correspondent Sydney Schanberg, the author of this true story. An actual survivor of the killing fields was the Cambodian doctor Haing S. Ngor making his film debut as Schanberg's local assistant, Dith Pran. John Malkovich and Craig T. Nelson costarred in David Puttnam's production of a film directed by Roland Joffe. It is a harrowing tale that evokes the tragedy of war in a manner equal to any of the entries in this book.

In telling a story from a civilian point of view, this film alters the usual perspective on the war by demonstrating that most casualties were actually non-combatants. In sharing the westernized Causasian perspective of Schanberg with the Asian hero Pran, the film is also unconventional. In chronicling the guilt felt by Schanberg at having abandoned his friend to the heinousness of the Pol Pot regime, the film speaks to American complicity in the destruction of this ancient culture. By extension this antiwar humanist perspective subtly condemns the escalation of the Vietnamese conflict into Cambodia as a partial result of U.S. policy. Also in depicting the fall of Phnom Penh and the chaotic evacuation of foreigners, it echoes the last-flight-out sagas from Saigon. However, the film then traces the tragedy that befalls those left behind.

The Killing Fields opens to Chris Menges's photography of the gorgeous countryside. The quietude of a peasant boy and his water buffalo is shattered when two jets screech overhead. The journalist-as-narrator returns as Waterston tells of his love and pity for Cambodia. The time is 1983, and foreign journalists and photographers hang out in the hotel bars of Phnom Penh waiting to cover the inevitable fall to the communist forces. Urban terrorist bombings reminiscent of the Place Garnier interrupt the once-placid lifestyle. Correspondent Schanberg and his translator-aide Pran attempt to cover the war out in the countryside. American information officer Nelson tries to manage the flow of news, but the savvy journalism team manages to ferret out the stories.

At a swanky pool party an embassy official, played by Spaulding Gray, tips Schanberg and Pran on a tragic B-52 bomber raid that delivered its payload on a civilian target. (In 1987 raconteur Gray talked of his days in Cambodia and the filming of this movie in his one-person show *Swimming to Cambodia.*) Pran, Schanberg, and colleagues negotiate treacherous rural roadblocks and other dangers to find the site. They relish the excitement of the hunt and are appalled when they encounter the devastation; but they still manage to interview and photograph the victims with professional detachment. As time passes the once-distant artillery fire becomes more audible from the patio of the Hotel Phnom Penh. At the embassy officials shred documents and arrange for evacuations. Just like in the last days of Saigon, Cambodians are desperate to escape as they anticipate a bloodbath.

As most foreigners leave Schanberg arranges passage for his aide and family. Surely such an employee of an American company is in grave danger. Pran refuses to leave his beloved homeland. Severe tension mounts in a number of powerfully evoked scenes. When the journalist teams are captured by a nervous and trigger-happy Khmer Rouge cadre, only Pran's fast talking saves them all from summary execution. Later the prototypical gonzo druggie photographer, played by Malkovich, rises to the occasion when he forges a passport for Pran. However, the ruse does not work, and Pran is taken away as the foreigners are finally forced to leave the foreign capital. Unlike the end in Saigon, wholesale brutality and murder do follow at the hands of the ruthless new communist rulers.

A guilt-ridden Schanberg is haunted by his last memory of the frail Pran being led away in April 1975. When the writer accepts a "journalist of the year" award, his glory is short-lived as Malkovich confronts him on why he did not make Pran leave while he still could. Was it Schanberg's ego and the thrill of the big story that clouded his assessment of the inevitable danger to his colleague? Schanberg continues a letter-writing campaign in an attempt to locate his lost friend. Meanwhile the film shifts to depicting the horror that has befallan Pran.

In a concentration-type camp muddy and starving slave laborers succumb to disease or execution at the hands of zealots. Each night the indoctrinated instruct the prisoners on their reeducation. The new Cambodia, now Kampuchea, has turned into a killing field. Millions of civilians will die in the madness that accompanies the Khmer triumph. With nothing left to lose Pran daringly finds an opportunity to escape into the jungle. He encounters a mountain of human bones, which stand as a monument to the evil of which humans are capable.

Once recaptured, Pran feigns no knowledge of French or English or any education and is thus spared; he becomes a cadre leader's cook and babysitter. Anticipating his own execution, the Khmer officer entrusts his baby son to Pran and arranges their escape. The competing factions continue the bloodletting among the victors and the vanquished. Pran and companions hurriedly pass by the ruins of ancient Angkor and a once-thriving Buddhist civilization based on humane and religious teachings. One by one his companions die in the desperate journey. In one harrowing scene the baby is killed by a land mine. Pran is overcome by grief and the senselessness of such death. Amid the horror, moments of compassion do occur. A young red-kerchiefed boy saves Pran's life by showing him where a booby trap lies.

The tragedy in Cambodia is interrupted as the film cuts to an excited Schanberg running through the press room. Pran has been located! He has made it to a refugee camp in Thailand. Schanberg flies over, and John Lennon's homage to peace, "Imagine," wells up a bit obtrusively on the soundtrack as the two old friends are reunited. As they hug it is nearly impossible for the viewer not to cry. Schanberg asks, "Do you forgive me?" Pran replies that there is "nothing to forgive for." The reunion on October 9, 1974, ends four years of terror in the killing fields of Southeast Asia. Unfortunately the carnage in Cambodia continued, and Vietnamese forces finally intervened in their neighboring country. The ruthless Khmer Rouge continue to fight for power, although the international community has effectuated a frail truce in the bloody civil war that has left millions dead.

The real Dith Pran came to America and became a photographer for the *New York Times*. Schanberg continued as a correspondent and wrote the powerful, award-winning book on which the film was based. Doctor-turned-actor Haing S. Ngor won an Academy Award for Best Supporting Actor. He went on to other acting roles, including several films in this book. *The Killing Fields* was nominated but did not win for best picture, for actor (Waterston), and for best adapted screenplay. Menges and the film editors did win in their respective categories. The Goldcrest film was an English-funded production that enhanced producer

Puttnam's already respected image as a maker of quality humanist films. In a move reflective of the globalization of the film community, he went to Hollywood to head Columbia in a brief and tempestuous reign. One again Roger Ebert nicely sums up the movie and its place in this work: "As a human story, this is a compelling one. As a Hollywood story, it obviously will not do because the last half . . . is told from his [Pran's] point of view. Hollywood convention has it that the American should fight his way back into the occupied country (accompanied by renegade Green Berets and Hell's Angels) . . . blast his way into a prison camp and save his buddy. . . . Sitting in New York writing letters is not quite heroism on the same scale." But in a bow to the unfortunate realism of this war, what else could Schanberg and Dith Pran do? Ebert concludes that by telling Pran's true story and respecting it, *The Killing Fields* "becomes a film of an altogether higher order than the Hollywood revenge thrillers."[9]

The suffering of the innocents so eloquently conveyed in the last entry was updated in the serious but flawed 1985 release *Alamo Bay*. Between the final evacuations from Saigon and the desperate refugees among the boat people throughout the decade, several hundred thousand Southeast Asians had resettled in the United States. Their postwar adjustment and problems were the subject of this film from Frenchman Louis Malle. This fact-based story involves Vietnamese fishing families who settle on the Texas Gulf coast. There the immigrants attempt to ply their trade in an already depressed economy. Prejudice, including Klan harassment, greets them. Ed Harris played a vet torn by a sense of decency and pity for the desperate immigrants and a "good ole boy's" kinship with the indigenous fishermen's needs and problems. What weakens this look at one more consequence of the Vietnam War is its onesided characterization of the evil white person and the saintly Asian. It is the reverse of the reactionary or early depictions and thus suffers from the same dramatic pitfalls as did their clichéd characterizations of the brave American and the heinous Asian.

In 1980 the American Psychiatric Association recognized post-traumatic stress disorder as an illness typified by symptoms including nervousness, depression, insomnia, nightmares, emotional numbness, and survivor guilt. Experts felt that a disproportionate number of Vietnam vets suffered from this ailment as a consequence of the failure of society to absolve them of their part in a losing cause and the nature of the guerrilla opposition interspersed with civilian casualties.[10] Recent studies of this similar but distinct version of World War I's shell shock or World War II's combat fatigue found that almost 15 percent of Vietnam vets suffered from the disorder. That means approximately 450,000 vets were afflicted to some degree with the syndrome.[11]

This topical concern was the central theme in a 1985 film entitled *Cease Fire*. David Nutter directed Don Johnson and Robert F. Lyons as vets and Lisa Blount as the former's supportive but confused wife. George Fernandez adapted his one-act play for the screen. Each time Vietnam flashbacks occur to the troubled protagonist, they are elicited by helicopter noise and are presented in drab army green and mud brown that are evocative of sepia tones. Johnson awakens in a cold sweat from a nightmare about a hamlet raid. He proceeds to the unemployment office, where he recognizes another vet from his army jacket. They go to a bar and revel in the use of in-country lingo as they "reminisce." Vietnam is omnipresent in their minds, intruding both day and night. The scars on Johnson's body are nothing compared to the emotions he has bottled up. One night he does share with Blount the striking contrast in Vietnam between the beautiful and the dangerous. "How could something with so much life hold so much death?"

In only one scene does the film degenerate into exploitation. Johnson flips out and crawls around his apartment with a knife in his mouth ready to kill VC infiltrators. Other scenes are more grounded and include the vets' reluctant visit to therapists and Johnson's observation with his buddy that "some asshole changed the rules in the middle of the play." One night Johnson receives a call from Lyons, who is distraught over a fight with his wife. He believes that "Charlie is at the wire." Before Johnson can help, his friend commits suicide. The tragic death becomes the impetus for Johnson to enroll in a veteran counseling support group. There he is able to confront the in-country demons that still torment him fifteen years later. In an important step toward renewal, Johnson and Blount go to Washington, D.C. There the film utilizes the dramatic new monument to the Vietnam veterans as a reminder of the past and a symbol of rebirth. Johnson touches a friend's name engraved on the black granite wall and welcomes himself home.

In contrast to *Cease Fire*'s earnest but uneven attempts at dealing with the war, two more nearly direct-to-video releases were throwbacks. Lawrence Hilton Jacobs, Gerritt Graham, Paul Koslo, and Andy Woods starred in Charles E. Sellier's *The Annihilators*. In Atlanta a wheelchair-bound vet and his neighbors are terrorized by vicious street punks. The ex–GI is murdered, and at his funeral his old squad members resolve to use their expertise to combat the thugs. Several in-country flashbacks of decimation stand in contrast to their righteous and ultimately successful stateside mission. *Heated Vengeance* featured Richard Hatch as a soldier who, like the one in the previous year's *Angkor*, returns to Asia to free a woman trapped there. The lovers join the MIAs in conveying the feeling that we left something in our retreat from Southeast Asia. Hatch encounters a ragtag group of American deserters who choose to live in Vietnam as an outlaw gang. Michael J. Pollard costarred in this video descendant of drive-in fare.

Still more maladjusted veterans made their appearances in 1985. *White Ghost* featured Reb Brown and William Katt. The titular hero/misfit was an army intelligence officer who disappeared into the jungles. He still roams about displaying the cunning of a Native American warrior. Also showing great skill but dubious purpose was Tommy Lee Jones in the dreadful made-for *The Park Is Mine*. The usual troubles (wife, job, no respect, etc.) beset the ex-soldier. He decides to singlehandedly take over Central Park to publicize the plight of the veterans. Overzealous politicians are no match for the populist hero. Search-and-destroy missions, men "on point," and booby traps are meant to conjure up images of the war. However, the lamely staged action on location in Toronto did little to elicit any sense of either the Big Apple or Southeast Asia.

Barely six months after the first installment, Chuck Norris returned as Braddock in *Missing in Action II: The Beginning.* Lance Hool directed the action star in another avenge-and-win flick that was barely a cut above the direct-to-video releases. The only differentiation was the recognizable star and the use of better ordnance. Filmed in the Philippines, this mindless actioner had an international crew and appeal. This film is actually a prequel as it takes Norris back in country ten years to his original tour of duty. The first half takes place in a POW camp, where a sadistic colonel tortures his captives in a stereotype worthy of the worst Japan-bashing flicks of the 1940s. However, utilizing more permissive conventions of depiction, there are graphic renderings of the mistreatment. When the men finally escape their tormentors, the vengeance is justified and ruthless.

When Sylvester Stallone returned in the big-budget summer release *Rambo: First Blood Part II,* the apotheosis of the revisionist winning films was reached. Not only did the actioner become the highest-grossing entry in this entire group of films (domestic $150,415,432), it also provided a culture-defining character. Ramboism was to replace John Wayneism as a noun connoting the cowboylike justice dispensed by American men of action. Rambo helped define a new sense of patriotism and an unwillingness to be bogged down in the losing and depressing malaise associated with Vietnam. Rambo entered the international lexicon in the process of becoming a worldwide hit. During the Gulf War the title was often used to refer to a renewed American vigor and can-do militarism.

International film moguls Kassar and Vajna of Carolco financed *Rambo,* with action director George Pan Cosmatos at the helm. James Cameron and Stallone wrote the screenplay, and cold warrior Buzz Feitshans (*Uncommon Valor,* etc.) produced. Richard Crenna returned as Colonel Trautman from *First Blood,* and Charles Napier and Martin Kove costarred.

The film opens to a huge explosion. As the camera pulls back we see convicts working in a quarry. A sweaty and muscular Rambo is serving time for his offenses in the first movie installment. Trautman arrives to recruit the skilled vet for a secret mission to recon for POWs still held in Vietnam. Before Rambo will accept the government's assignment, he asks with disdain, "Do we get to win this time?"

On the politicians' turf in Washington, D.C., a CIA operative briefs the special forces vet on his mission. He is to provide photographic proof of POWs, not to engage the former enemy. In the technocratic military jargon, "extraction" will be someone else's job. This is a solo assignment requiring no help for the killing machine except some high-tech weaponry. When the timid politicos observe Rambo's expertise and appetite for action, they are informed by Trautman that "what you choose to call hell, he calls home." In a bit of homoeroticism the camera lingers on Stallone's rippling muscles as he sharpens a huge knife and assembles his bow and arrows. His aura of primitivism reveals a nonthinking animalism that was conspicuously absent from the handwringing war effort.

Rambo First Blood Part II (Tri-Star Pictures, 1985). **Rambo proves that Americans are still being held captive in Southeast Asia.**

Analogies to Native American spiritually based competency in the hunt are also made.

Stallone parachutes back in-country, and his local contact is a comely Asian woman played by Julia Nickson. Like many a cowboy in the old oaters, Stallone remains chaste in a no-nonsense pursuit of the mission. He explains, "To survive a war you have to become war." Upon arriving at the POW camp, Stallone disobeys orders and takes out the sentries with his crossbow. Like a cat, he infiltrates the perimeter and locates Americans. He escapes with one POW and the enemy in hot pursuit. Exciting and expensively staged action sequences accompany the retreat. He finally reaches a predetermined LZ where the copters hover, but they are ordered by the suits in radio contact to abort the pickup. Trautman, listening at the command center, demands to know what gives. As the copters pull away leaving Rambo stranded, the government's man, Charles Napier, explains that Rambo was not supposed to find anyone!

The again-victimized man of action is chained and interrogated not only by his Asian captor but also by a visiting communist sadist from the USSR. Rambo is tortured and made to watch as other American POWs are abused. He seizes the moment to break free and with the help of the beautiful Asian ally on the outside he is able to escape the compound. In a brief respite the bare-breasted Stallone shares a moment of intimacy with his skilled cohort. She asks that he take her to America with him. They kiss and the "Ponderosa Effect" is evoked as she is shot and killed immediately thereafter. Back at command Trautman is under arrest. Rambo is again truly alone in his predicament. Amid monsoon rains the warrior emerges for battle with stone-age weaponry, not high-powered guns. Subliminal is the realization that pungi stick primitivism in conjunction with high motivation triumphed over high-tech American ordnance in a compromised effort.

In a cartoonish superhero finale this one-person army destroys a hugely superior force of international communists. Eventually Rambo is able to commandeer the Soviet helicopter and fly it to a secret CIA base in Thailand. There he pursues his last enemy, American government official Murdoch. Amid the high-tech electronic gadgetry of the command center, Rambo lets out a primordial yell and sprays the room with bullets from a huge machine gun. When the smoke clears our hero has spared the life of his American nemesis. He tells Murdoch, "There are more Americans out there. Find them or I will!"

Surrogate father Trautman reunites with Rambo, and they discuss what went awry. The Crenna character says that the war might have been wrong but not to hate America for it. Rambo replies, "Hate? . . . I'd die for it." "Then what is it you want?" Trautman queries. Like the end of the preceding Rambo installment, the warrior makes a speech that probably equals all his previous dialogue in the film. Medal of Honor winner and felon John Rambo says, "I want what . . . every other guy who came over here and spilled his guts and gave everything wants . . . for our country to love us as much as we love it." He then marches off into the Thai sunset.

It should be stated unequivocally that *Rambo* is an excitingly staged action film that can be very entertaining. But it is also very political. President Reagan loved the film and joked in the context of the American hostage crisis in Beirut that perhaps Rambo could get the hostages out. Given the actor-turned-politician's love of filmic mythology, he was able to overlook the indictment of government conspiracy in the suppression of MIA information. The ink spilled about *Rambo* in the editorial pages of America's papers was similar to the controversy surrounding other key entries in this book, such as *The Green Berets* and the soon-to-be-released *Platoon*. *Time* made the film a cover story and said the country was gripped by "Rambomania."

Rounding out the year were two more highly contrasting tales of minority veterans' Vietnam-induced trauma. The studio release was Columbia's successful drama and dance feature *White Nights*. It made the Vietnam background merely part of the overall character development. Gregory Hines played an unemployed black tap dancer from Harlem who ended up a frightened and angry boy in Vietnam. He became disillusioned by the corrupt and ruthless war effort. Then he succumbed to the propaganda that the white race was the oppressor and that the black and yellow races were allies. He caused quite a stir when he defected to the other side. This tearful tale is related in the present to Mikhail Baryshnikov, who plays an acclaimed ballet dancer and defector to the United States from the USSR. Now more mature, Hines realizes that he was used by the communists for their publicity purposes and then consigned to oblivion in Siberia. What evolves is an adventure tale as he helps the Soviet expatriate get back to his adopted country and in the process allows himself to finally return home. As Hines states, the whole Vietnam scene "was a long time ago." The film nicely underscores the cynical cold war politics of both the KGB and CIA, and it shows the inherent, systemic rottenness of the now-failed system in the former Soviet Union.

The other minority vet feature was the minuscule-budgeted *Latino,* directed by left-wing filmmaker Haskell Wexler. It starred Robert Beltran as Captain Eddie Guerrero of the Green Berets. The Hispanic career officer who served in Vietnam now finds himself fighting communists as an adviser in Central America. Here he cannot escape the racial solidarity he feels for the indigenous people. Like the slick renditon of Gregory Hines's dilemma or the modestly staged plight of the protagonist in *Ashes and Embers,* Guerrero fears he may be fighting for "the man." His problem remains largely unresolved in this new front line against the perceived enemies of America. The movie was actually filmed in Nicaragua and represented the director's first return to a nondocumentary since the film entry *Medium Cool.*

Coincidental to *Rambo*'s release was a proposal from Hanoi to conduct the first high-level talks concerning the MIA cases. The unresolved MIA issue that the films in this chapter tried to address followed the end of the trauma of the hostage ordeal in Iran. In times of great individual and collective emotion the still-traumatic wounds of Vietnam surface. In 1991 it was no coincidence that the exhilaration of the triumph in the Gulf War contributed to renewed frustration, guilt, and interest in the remaining POW/MIA cases. The notion that the government is less than vigorous in pursuing reported live sightings and photos continues. With the dissolution of the Soviet empire, a KGB agent has come forward to report the transfer of POWs to his country during the war for interrogation purposes. American representatives sent to investigate such claims include Vietnam veteran and U.S. senator John Kerry of Massachusetts. He has received unprecedented aid in Phnom Penh, Hanoi, and Saigon. Additional word from Moscow is still being awaited. Perhaps Kerry and others' investigations will reveal some outlaw mountain tribes or bands of Khmer Rouge insurgents as captors of unfortunate Americans. However, the former enemy in Vietnam has no interest in keeping such soldiers as the Vietnamese government is intent on integrating its centrally planned economy with much-needed foreign investment.

The superhuman stature and muscular physique of Norris, Stallone, and others were in stark contrast to the remnants of our Vietnam debacle represented by the emasculated victims of an evil enemy and an uncaring government. The liberated POWs in these films were simply incapable of fighting. They were a tragic living legacy of the impotence that had defeated us in Vietnam. These fantasy films played on a collective desire to triumph in a manner that "depict Vietnam as dehumanizing and morally insupportable."[12] They were not as much fun to watch and fetured "the vulnerable, smaller, and often wounded bodies" of

Christopher Walken (*The Deerhunter*), Jon Voight (*Coming Home*), Martin Sheen (*Apocalypse Now*), and, later, Willem Dafoe (*Platoon*) and Michael J. Fox (*Casualties of War*).[13] The revisionist fantasy casting required action heroes, not skilled actors. The stereotype of the inarticulate insular veteran was perfect for these less verbally skilled movie stars.

The action films were very popular internationally because they required little translation. As Norris and Stallone were appearing in the exploitation Vietnam flicks, the entire film industry continued its march to globalization. Many national film industries were in decline, with American films beginning to achieve cultural hegemony. Taking up the exploitation slack and B Vietnam portrayals were the new independent and globalized players. A notable example were Israeli cousins Menahem Golan and Yoram Globus, who bought the American independent studio Cannon. Also poised to emerge as important global players in the financing of Vietnam-related action was the influential independent production company Carolco. Its original principals, Mario Kassar and Andre Vajna, would produce numerous contributions to the list of Vietnam films, including *First Blood, Rambo, Bat 21, Air America,* and *Jacob's Ladder.* Longtime international players in conjunction with successful American film producers began to pool their resources in an effort to finance, produce, distribute, and even exhibit film product throughout the world. (This march to globalization via core American film industry companies reached a crescendo in the mid–1990s. Companies such as MGM/UA, Twentieth Century–Fox, Columbia, and MCA-Universal had been so successful that they were all purchased by foreign companies.)

Action movies were the genre of first choice for theatrical export and a source of programming for the nascent video industry. They went from filling the programming vacuum that had been relinquished with the decline of the drive-in industry to filling that associated with the decline of indigenous filmmaking communities. As previously demonstrated, the Vietnam War veteran was a very suitable character to lay over a formulaic, action-oriented coda. This imagery was now offered up throughout the world.

In *Film Quarterly,* Gaylyn Studlar and David Desser use principles of psychoanalysis to explain the appeal of Rambo. In so doing, they also set the stage for the wave of Vietnam War films in the next chapter. "The pain of history, its delimiting effect on action is seen as a political, a cultural, a national liability. Therefore, an ideological battle . . . seeks to rewrite, to rehabilitate, controversial events."[15] But the film industry prefers to hedge its bets. First, very few people go to a movie to see a political harangue, and second, the lessons of Vietnam have been repressed anyway. Therefore political and emotional ambiguity remains a key to success, just as in the four horsemen era.

Nevertheless, general labels can be applied. This chapter featured the right-wing perspective where the question of whether we should have been in Vietnam at all was replaced by the questions "What is our obligation to the veterans?" and "Why were they victimized by an incoherent and compromised policy?" The next wave, typified by *Platoon*, is less cartoonish and more dovish or left wing. But despite the differences in imagined or real politics and the level of realism in battle depictions, they, too, present a universally indisputable and therefore less controversial thesis on the victimization of the fighting soldier. Both *Rambo* and *Platoon* evoke sympathy for the grunt. Refracted images give way to refracted guilt, and the lessons of history will eventually be sublimated to the belief that if we fight, then we fight to win. Regardless, the continued production of multiple head-on film entries in the second half of the 1980s reflected a psychic recovery process from the trauma of Vietnam.

References

1. Edward Doyle and Terence Maitland, *The Vietnam Experience: The Aftermath, 1975–1985* (Boston: Boston Publishing, 1988), p. 169.

2. *Ibid.*, p. 166.

3. Phil Caputo, *A Rumor of War*, cited *ibid.*, p. 166.

4. For an extremely full and interesting treatment of the disabled veteran here and in other films, see Martin Norden, "Portrait of a Disabled Vietnam Veteran," in *From Hanoi to Hollywood*, ed. Linda Dittmar and Gene Michaud (New Brunswick, N.J.: Rutgers University Press, 1990), pp. 217–225.

5. Rick Berg, "Losing Vietnam," *ibid.*, p. 65.

6. Frank McConnell, "A Name for Loss—Memorials of Vietnam," *Commonweal*, August 9, 1985, p. 442.

7. Stanley Karnow, *Vietnam: A History* (New York: Viking Press, 1983), Introduction.

8. Paramount Pictures, "Handbook of Production Notes," *Uncommon Valor* (Los Angeles: Paramount Pictures, 1983), p. 10.

9. Roger Ebert, *The Movie Home Companion* (Kansas City: Andrews McMeel and Parker, 1988), p. 307.

10. Myra MacPherson, *Long Time Passing: Vietnam, the Haunted Generation* (New York: Doubleday, 1984).

11. "Study of Twins Bolsters Evidence of Vietnam Stress," *Chicago Tribune*, March 2, 1990, p. 6.

12. Linda Boose, "Theaters of War," *Dartmouth Alumni Magazine* (May 1991), p. 14.

13. *Ibid.*, p. 15.

14. Gaylyn Studlar and David Desser, "Never Having to Say You're Sorry: Rambo's Rewriting of the Vietnam War," *Film Quarterly* 42, 1 (Fall 1988).

Chapter 8

The Grunts, 1986–1987

The Vietnam veterans memorial in Washington, D.C., was dedicated on November 13, 1982. Anyone who has visited it cannot help but be touched by its black granite beauty etched with the names of the 58,000 Americans who gave their lives. This is not a heroic action monument recalling combat, like the dramatic Iwo Jima statue; it is a quiet testament to the fallen soldier.

So, too, the important films in this chapter from 1986 and 1987 are celebrations of the sacrifice of the foot soldier, the grunt. What makes some of these films more powerful is that their creators are veterans of the conflict. *Platoon's* Oliver Stone is the best known ex-grunt filmmaker. However, *Full Metal Jacket, Hamburger Hill,* and *Dear America: Letters Home from Vietnam* all featured the participation of first hand witnesses. The development of the cinema of war had reached fruition. These men attempted to show how it really was in Vietnam. Whether or not they succeeded became one more source of controversy.

In the core genre of combat films, the first portrait of Vietnam in *The Green Berets* was criticized as being mired in the anticommunist sensibilities of the 1950s and dramatically structured like the war films of the 1940s. The important wave of the late 1970s featured films either set stateside, were limited in their evocation of combat by budget constraints, or were more concerned with an overall rock-and-roll chaotic ambience or literary metaphor. The film entries of the early 1980s wanted to refight the war and this time win it. All were important reflections and creators of concurrent Vietnam War feelings.

The grunts present the war from the trench or bush. They primarily retreat from macrosocietal and political commentary and let the intimate and graphically depicted experience of the individual GI convey greater antiwar or anti-Vietnam themes. The films feature ensemble casts without stars. Far from superman fantasies, they are realistic in showing individual death and destruction of innocence. In focusing on combat and "war as hell," the films eventually arrive at conclusions similar to those of such disparate films as *Rambo* and *Coming Home*: that the soldier was a victim. The war effort is compromised and lacks strategic military significance. The individual soldier suffers in such a context and his heroism becomes that of merely surviving or perhaps saving a comrade, but certainly not any higher attainment such as a triumph over communism or totalitarianism. The inevitability of such fictional conclusions is necessitated by the factual antecedent: America's loss of consensus, innocence, and the war. Could have and should have do not change Ho Chi Minh City back to Saigon (although the momentum of the current destruction from within of the failed ideology of communism may eventually bring this desired result).

Although 1986 and 1987 offered up some of the finest direct portraits of the war in this collection, as usual the other conventions and lesser contributions continued. In a ripoff of incidental vet characters, *Billy Jack* met "Miami Vice" in the 1986 movie *Band of the Hand*. Television actor Paul Michael Glaser directed James Remar and Stephen Lang in this theatrical release. It told of a Native American Vietnam vet who trains five punks in the "jungles" of the Everglades to fight crime on the streets of Miami.

Riders of the Storm was an English film that took its title from the Doors' song. Dennis Hopper and Michael J. Pollard starred as embittered vets who broadcast their messages from a B-29 bomber. They are a motley crew of maladjusted druggies who oppose a right wing political candidate.

Real-life motorcycle buff Gary Busey got to play a veteran for director Richard Sarafian in *Eye of the Tiger*. Using combat skills, Busey defends his town against drug dealers. One of the originators of the old drive-in cycle flicks, Roger Corman, now owned his own independent studio, New World. In 1986 he returned to directing with Brad Johnson in the made-for-video *Nam Angels*. That was to have been the original title of 1970's prototypical meeting of the subgenres, *The Losers*. Obviously originality was not the made-for-videos' strong suit. In fact the B movie label is too charitable. Other such fodder with tangential Vietnam interest included *American Commandoes*, *American Ninja*, and *Hitman*. These films were referred to in the video distribution industry as C and D titles.

Really slumming was *Combat Shock*, a release from Troma designed for inner-city action houses and undiscriminating video renters. Buddy Giovinazzo produced, directed, and wrote this story of a vet again forced to use in-country skills against a domestic enemy. This time it was New York City street punks.

Displaying a nearly nonexistent budget was the direct-to-video release of *No Sweat Blues* from a company appropriately titled Video Treasures. This film is mentioned here as it typifies a number of videos that blend cheap documentary footage with stories or narration and appeal to war film buffs who will shell out a mere six to ten dollars to buy these films. This "feature" had grunts singing songs that were popular in-country, including "Firefight," "Laid Around Vietnam Too Long," and "Who Cares About a Marine." Media Home Entertainment's company name connotes its direct-to-video orientation. *War Bus Commandoes* was its Philippine-lensed release whose hero was Green Beret "Johnny Hondo." Here he battles Soviet and Afghan communists in what was described as the "Soviet Union's Vietnam." This cheesy actioner follows the usual story of a vet's near-superhuman triumph in combat against a cartoonish enemy. (In 1990 the poorly titled *The Beast* featured a more serious look at the Afghanistan war. The film, which starred Steven Bauer and George Dzundza, drew the analogy between America's Third World debacle and that of the Soviets.)

The ripoffs of *Rambo* and *MIA*'s popularity continued in longtime B movie purveyor Manson International's release *No Dead Heroes*. Here a Green Beret goes on yet another jungle rescue mission on behalf of POWs whose very existence is denied by all governments. He becomes a prisoner of a ruthless KGB adviser to the Asian enemy. The captured captain is implanted with a microchip that makes him a killing machine. He is programmed to assassinate the pope and the president! Only another Viet vet is able to save the day. When he confronts the killer in the new front line against communism, Central America, he also discovers a whole brigade of American POWs programmed in this horrible manner. J. C. Miller produced and directed this low-budgeter.

In attempting to entice renters for *Killzone*, the video distributor paid homage to the more famous Vietnam War film contributions. The dust jacket reads, "The savagery of *The Deerhunter*, the brutality of *First Blood*, and the unbridled power of *Rambo* come together to create the most intense film yet about the effects of the Vietnam War." This drivel involved a military training school where the course is so realistic that it elicits psychotic flashbacks for one vet.

Cannon offered up another avenge-and-win flick with the straightforward title of *P.O.W.: The Escape*. Gideon Amir directed David Carradine in this retread of *MIA*. The film opens to the 1973 Paris peace talks. The cease-fire is to take effect in five days, and Carradine is ordered on a mission to prove the existence of remaining prisoners. An Israeli crew joins an American cast in a Philippine shoot that typifies the internationalization of such fodder.

Once again the commandos arrive too late and find the prison camp deserted. In trying to evacuate under heavy fire, Carradine goes back for a wounded comrade. Of course the would-be rescuer is himself captured. The dirty Viet Cong commandant was played by Mako. After torturing his American captives, Mako decides to make a deal with Carradine. He proposes to release Carradine if he will take this torturer to live in America. This is a throwback to the ethnocentric notion that behind every Asian is an American trying to get out. Carradine agrees as long as "everybody goes back home." The other escapees are the usual band of "dirty dozen" types. They hijack a truck, sing "Proud Mary," fight the enemy, and eventually, after several instances of heroic self-sacrifice, escape to America minus the deceased would-be restaurateur, Mako.

This plethora of B movie releases updates the exploitation genre that began with the second half of the double features, continued with the drive-in flicks, and now provided programming for a still-undiscriminating video audience. These films are often barely feature length, and the commonality of low production values joins with a lazy aura of anticommunism and jingoism. Soviets, North Vietnamese, Viet Cong, and Chinese are all evil caricatures. Even the late 1980s entries feature either overtly racist stereotyping or undelineated Asian characters. In a post–Vietnam context these films all seem to ignore reality in a desire to allow Americans to triumph on film. Here the worst aspect of the American experience in Vietnam was its legacy in producing psychopathic killing machines or victims of government conspiracy.

Two 1986 non–Vietnam, but military-themed films are worthy of note at this juncture. Both Clint Eastwood in *Heartbreak Ridge* and Tom Cruise in *Top Gun* helped restore luster to a recently discredited uniform. Eastwood was a leathery old gunnery sergeant and veteran of both Korea and Vietnam. The cigar-chewing character is quite memorable as the actor manages to breathe life into the cliché of a proud marine who must whip a bunch of green recruits into fighting soldiers and thereby save their lives. This film, written by Viet vet Jim Carabatsos, was directed by the star. Uniquely it depicts the triumphant invasion of Grenada. That incursion and the invasion of Panama were combat preludes to the Gulf War, which all served to restore the U.S. combat record to the "win" column and thereby overcome post–Vietnam trauma and a lack of confidence in our armed forces. Grenada, a small operation, served as the perfect television war, where the Pentagon could carefully manage the flow of information out from the quick campaign.

If Eastwood's film typified the real-life television war, then the megahit *Top Gun* was a thrilling video arcade game blown up to the big screen. Sexy young actors cavorted around the thrill-seeking elite fliers for the Navy. Cruise played "Maverick," whose father was a jet pilot in Vietnam and remains MIA and presumed dead. His son wishes to prove his manhood, but the young colt must first learn to be a team player. This Paramount release featured absolute state-of-the-art aerial flying sequences. It took a rather safe and ambiguous tack toward the enemies by putting them in Soviet-made MiGs but not really identifying the nationality of the pilots.

These sequences, along with the firefights in *Platoon*, provide viscerally exciting re-creations of combat in very different manners. The muddy, ground-level intimacy of the Vietnam picture is in marked contrast to the sterile, long-distance destruction in the entertaining *Top Gun*. The number-one-grossing picture of 1986, *Top Gun* (at $176,781,728), and the number three, *Platoon*, both owed a great deal of their appeal to making war exciting again to an apolitical younger male audience.

Top Gun and Paramount's earlier 1982 release, *An Officer and a Gentleman*, both demonstrably aided recruiting for the military and confirmed the desire of that institution to cooperate again with Hollywood. The latter featured a hit song fittingly hopeful in its title, "Come Lift Us Up Where We Belong." The film created and reflected the post–Vietnam healing process that began with the Reagan presidency and reached a real-life military apotheosis in the Persian Gulf War "victory" of 1991. (Back in 1986 the lame series of *Iron Eagle* films also debuted. They featured heroic combat against a new, stereotypically drawn foe, the Arab. Illustrating the post–Vietnam shift in emphasis away from communists, here the heinous bad guy was modeled after Libya's Khaddafy. This film and its sequels starred Lou Gosset, Jr., and were helmed by Sidney J. Furie, who had directed *The Boys in Company C.*)

While beckoning to the future, Hollywood also continued to look back at the tragic Vietnam debacle. The veterans remained witnesses to the Vietnam experience. Just like the 241 marines killed in the barracks in Beirut in 1983, they were victims in campaigns that seemed to lack a coherent objective and strong public support. Nothing typified this tragic mistreatment by the powers that be more than the Agent Orange issue. In November CBS broadcast a television movie on the subject entitled *Unnatural Causes.* John Ritter was powerful as a doomed vet, and Alfre Woodard was heartrending as the devoted veterans' benefits counselor. Her character, Maude DeVictor, was the real-life heroine responsible for much of the recognition of the link between the defoliant spray and the myriad illnesses it caused.

The film was written by John Sayles and directed by Lamont Johnson. It opens in-country as Ritter leads a squad through the swamps. They look up to see an army C-130 plane spraying the countryside. The defoliant rains down on the men in the bush. The jungle clears as they enter "Death Valley," an area denuded of shrubbery from the spray. The liquid is meant to deprive "Charlie" of a place to hide and sources of food. The Americans are ambushed and take heavy causalties. As Ritter calls for a medevac, one of his men dies in his arms. Shortly thereafter Ritter's tour of duty is over, and as he climbs aboard a helicopter, he takes his last look as soldiers unload barrels on the tarmac. They contain a bright orange stripe down the middle.

The film now flashes forward nine years to Chicago in 1977. The veteran is a divorced high school teacher but seems quite happy and is a fine father to his young son. The film then begins to intercut with DeVictor at the Veterans Administration. In an acknowledgment of years of unfortunate stereotyping, Native American actor Graham Greene approaches the counselor and says menacingly, "I'm a walking time bomb." Nonplussed the woman says, "I work *for* the veterans at the VA, *not for* the VA. If you can stop being crazy for a few minutes, then maybe I can help you get some benefits."

The film cuts back to Ritter, who collapses in class and is rushed to the VA hospital. His ward has a number of friendly men from several wars. Mocking the clichéss, the World War II soldier talks about John Wayne, and the Nam vets decry the acidhead, baby killer labels. This socializing is interrupted when a doctor somewhat callously informs Ritter that he has terminal stomach cancer. It is labeled a nonservice-related illness, and he becomes an outpatient. A shocked Ritter returns home and uncrates his wartime memorabilia. He sadly peers at the platoon group shot, his medals, and so on.

Meanwhile DeVictor goes to see a Vietnam veteran whose wife informs her that he has died of cancer. Meanwhile Ritter, with a nagging suspicion about his illness, looks up a number of his comrades. Some are okay; one even says, "You can't blame everything on the war." However, another has also died of cancer before his time. His buddy, a fellow vet played by John Sayles in a cameo role, tells his story.

DeVictor back at the VA has started to see a pattern of various illnesses in Vietnam vets, including cancer, rashes, insomnia, and impotence. The more she digs for information, the more the government bureaucracy shuts her out. Slowly she cuts through the Pentagon labyrinth and learns about the use of more than 18 million gallons of the defoliant in Vietnam. It turns out that the active ingredient of Agent Orange is dioxin, known to be one of the substances most toxic to humans.

Eventually through the veteran grapevine, Ritter and DeVictor become allies in the search for answers about Agent Orange. The doomed vet sees it as his legacy, and the devoted ex-navy nurse sees it as her duty. The vets do not much like the VA, but they love DeVictor, who must continually overcome the harassment of her superiors. Research into illness patterns and interviews with vets show one more injustice perpetrated on these soldiers. Once again the irony of having survived combat only to die stateside is underscored. DeVictor receives calls from vets all over the country telling her of their illnesses. The army was ignorant of its abuse but exceedingly careless in spraying more than 6 million acres in-country. Compounding the mistake is the army's insistence that no causal link has been medically proven. Therefore it has no obligation to the thousands of men exposed to the agent. Some research has been conducted by the University of Hanoi Medical School, but that is largely ignored.

The scene in which a very ill Ritter says good-bye to his beloved son is truly heartrending. It is extremely well acted, as is the entire film. DeVictor goes to say good-bye to her friend, and they agree tht she will fight on because "if the American people really knew, they wouldn't let this happen." They decide that she should go public with the story. Ritter and his wardmates watch Bill Kurtis's in-depth television report that breaks the story. In response, thousands of vets besiege DeVictor with calls. As she helps the survivors, she chokes back her tears, having just learned that Ritter has died.

This humanist tale plays like a tragic detective story. It was made by ITC in Toronto and almost featured Diana Ross as DeVictor until director Johnson threatened to quit over that miscasting. In a credit postscript the filmmakers acknowledge the inspiration of Paul Reutershan, the founder of the Vietnam Veterans Agent Orange Victims group who died in 1978. DeVictor was eventually forced to leave the VA in a "labor dispute." On May 7, 1984, veterans groups reached an out-of-court settlement to their class-action suit against seven chemical companies. The $180 million judgment was the subject of several appeals.

A made-for-television movie of a benign nature was Disney's tangential foray into the genre via *The Girl Who Spelled Freedom*. Australian Simon Wincer directed this true story about a Cambodian teenage refugee who arrives in the United States in 1979 speaking no English. Four years later the bright little girl wins the national spelling bee. Wayne Rogers and Mary Kay Place starred, and Vietnamese expatriate actress Kieu Chinh made yet another appearance in the list of films.

Several other theatrical releases had veteran characters. The horror film *House* began as William Katt sits down to begin a novel. He sees this as therapy to purge himself of Vietnam-induced flashbacks and fears. His graphically depicted thoughts of wartime terror deteriorate into wild, demonic fantasies. Played much more for laughs but reinforcing the stereotype of maladjustment was the cameo appearance of Sam Kinison in Rodney Dangerfield's star vehicle *Back to School*. In one scene university professor Kinison asks a young coed about the causes of the Vietnam War. She gives a reasonbly astute answer that infuriates the vet, who launches into a tirade. As he practically froths at the mouth, the students recoil. (In another incidental moment Dangerfield poked fun at the military mentality in his 1992 release, *Ladybugs*. There he torments a gung-ho coach by yelling "incoming" and watching as the wired jerk vet hits the ground.) Back to 1986's tidbits, independent Aquarius films released the largely unseen *Whatever It Takes*. It featured Tom Mason as a Vietnam veteran.

In Chapter 2 the quest of living legend John Wayne to make a combat film about the Vietnam War during the conflict was described in the background to *The Green Berets*. Roughly a decade later another important entry, *Apocalypse Now*, had a compelling production history as well. Observers likened the filmmaker's odyssey to the plot line itself and to the real-life debacle encountered in Vietnam. That checkered production became the basis of a fascinating documentary released in 1991 entitled *Hearts of Darkness: A Filmmaker's Apocalypse*. However, the analogies between filmmaking and war were ultimately publicists' hooks or critics' musings. Wayne's and Coppola's adventures were of moviemakers visiting a war zone. Oliver Stone, however, was a soldier first, a grunt, and only later did he become a filmmaker. To briefly tell his story and career path is to set the stage for arguably the most important single entry in the entire book, *Platoon*. His life and that of the film project suggest an evolution common to America and to Hollywood.

Stone was a rebellious youth from a privileged family who dropped out of Yale in 1965. At 19 he went to Vietnam as a civilian to teach Chinese students at a Catholic school. The day he arrived in-country the VC blew up a well-known restaurant in Saigon just like the Viet Minh had done in the 1950s film *The Quiet American*. This naif was there to find himself and in his own way to fight for the American way. After six months he went on a brief tour in the merchant marine, traveled some more, and wrote.

He then volunteered for the infantry. "It was a way of announcing to my father that I was a man. . . . Also I had a serious dose of patriotism. I believed in our country, believed in the ideals, believed that the Communists were undermining us everywhere."[1] Later Stone put it this way: "I believed in the John Wayne image of America."[2] In a speech he stated, "We were the good guys; we were going to win. It was the war of my generation. It was glorious."[3]

In the fall of 1967 the 21-year-old found himself in Vietnam as a member of the 25th Infantry Division stationed near the Cambodian border. After only two weeks in-country he froze up and was wounded when the NVA attacked. Gradually he became a more competent soldier, even receiving the Bronze Star for combat gallantry to go with his Purple Heart. After surviving the Tet Offensive, he was at one point disciplined for insubordination. His one-year tour of duty expired in November 1968, and he returned to the United States as a decorated veteran.

He admitted that he smoked a lot of dope in Vietnam. It was because "I didn't want to know what was going on anymore. All notions of romanticism had vanished."[4] Reflecting back years later, he mused, "We brought a corporate Miami Beach/ Las Vegas mentality to Vietnam. . . . When Johnson pulled out in March 1968, it was metaphorically over. The grunts sensed it right away, we were never going to win, but we had to withdraw with a semblance of dignity. That semblance of dignity took four more years of deceit and death, and in the moral vacuum, there was never any clear reason to us why we should die."[5] Shortly after his return he ventured to Mexico, where he was arrested for marijuana possession. His father bailed him out, and he wound up in New York, where he enrolled in the New York University film school on the GI bill. He was an angry loner who managed to find inspiration from one of his professors, Martin Scorsese. Finally the alienated would-be filmmaker produced a fine short entitled *Last Year in Vietnam*. (Incidentally in his student days Scorsese had made an experimental short film entirely about a man shaving and repeatedly cutting himself. Later he explained the bloody mess was supposed to be an analogy for America's involvement in Vietnam.) Stone was emboldened by the response to his student project. As he put it, "It's a good thing Scorsese gave me film as a way to use my energies, because after the war . . . I could have turned out . . . something like [*Taxi Driver*'s] Travis Bickle."[6]

Later Stone again used the previous film is self-analysis when he confessed, "If I went over to Vietnam right wing, I came back an anarchist. Very much like Travis Bickle . . . a walking time bomb."[7] Stone was close to living the stereotypic, B film, returned-vet life minus the exploitation violence. His marriage was breaking up, his career was stalled, and he often thought of his days in-country. This immediate post–Vietnam experience was a huge culture shock. "Nobody was fighting the war. That was the problem. It wasn't the hippies or the protestors. They were a very small group. It was the mass indifference. Nobody cared. That was what hurt. Nobody realized their sons were dying over there. People were going about the business of making money."[8] This domestic reaction would be recreated in Stone's second Vietnam-themed film, *Born on the Fourth of July*, released in 1990.

Upon graduation from film school Stone drove a cab because he was able to sell only one B horror movie screenplay. Finally, around the July 4, 1976, bicentennial celebration, Stone turned to a story that had been in development in his mind for eight years. He quickly completed *Platoon*, and several producers expressed an interest. However, it would be nearly ten years before it was made. His cinematic development needed further résumé building before his intimate and controversial version of Vietnam would reach the screen. In the ensuing decade the original draft would change very little. "*Platoon* isn't about politics or the government's fault: it's about boys in the jungle. . . . Let's peel the onion, let's get to the truth of Vietnam."[9]

Based on the strength of the unproduced *Platoon* screenplay, Stone was assigned to write the adaptation of *Midnight Express*. That tale of an American imprisoned in Turkey on drug charges became a hit, and Stone won an Oscar for the screenplay. Suddenly he had made it, and he moved to Los Angeles. There he became known as a hard-partying wild man. He directed a flop entitled *The Hand* but followed it up with the screenplay to *Scarface*, directed by Brian DePalma. Stone worked with John Milius on the screenplay to *Conan* and then wrote *Year of the Dragon* mostly because he wanted to work with its director, Michael Cimino (of *The Deerhunter* fame). The film was a controversial depiction of Chinese-American gangsters and starred Mickey Rourke as a tough, disturbed New York City cop and Vietnam veteran. Cimino and *Dragon*'s producer, Dino DeLaurentiis, had both indicated an interest in getting *Platoon* made. Those deals fell through, so Stone went on to write the screenplay for *Salvador*. All these films had in common the drug subculture, foreign characters of varying ethnicity, and exotic locales.

Salvador, set in Latin America, featured a combat photographer, played by James Woods, who follows the dirty war against communism in that country. Many felt that this film was Stone's way of commenting on the "Vietnam of the 1980s" in another context. The filmmaker noted that when he arrived in Latin America to research the project, "I had a flashback . . . [to] Vietnam, 1965. . . . It was hot, wet, and the American kids were 19 again in green uniforms. . . . I talked to the young GIs . . . and they were gung ho. . . . They were fighting communism again."[10] In fact in *Salvador* many of the characters are media vets of Vietnam who keep alluding to it. The producers of this controversial film were Englishmen John Daly and Derek Gibson of Hemdale Pictures. Stone's association with these producers led to their funding of *Platoon*. Stone's vision of Vietnam not only had to survive his own demons and fester for eight years before being written; it also had to overcome Hollywood's commercial angst and insider's club for another ten years to be produced.

Stone and his cast and crew gathered in the Philippines to begin shooting, with the writer now able to direct his creation. The highly autobiographical version of a grunt's tour of duty had a mere $6 million budget. Charlie Sheen was the 19-year-old son of actor Martin Sheen, who had starred in *Apocalypse Now* and nearly died in the Philippine jungle making that epic. Young Charlie was to play Chris, Stone's alterego. Like his father's lead role and many other protagonists, Sheen was to provide voiceover narration. The key roles of Sergeant Barnes and Sergeant Elias went to two talented but still relatively unknown actors, Tom Berenger and Willem Dafoe, respectively. The rest of the ensemble included Forest Whitaker, Kevin Dillon, Francesco Quinn, John G. McGinley, Keith David, and Johnny Depp.

Retired marine captain Dale Dye served as the technical adviser and appeared as Captain Harris. This veteran of Vietnam, Lebanon, and Nicaragua had formed a company called Warriors, Inc., and in the next few years would find quite a bit of business as a guide to directors depicting Vietnam combat. Dye put the actors through two weeks of training in the jungle. This was to give them a sense of the hellish conditions, gain authenticity in their military portrayals, and build a sense of camaraderie. Dye put it this way: "I nailed their ass. I wanted animals. Because that's what we were when we were nineteen in that jungle."[11] Stone allowed Dye to conduct midnight raids and forced marches. Stone wanted that dog-tired, enraged attitude to shine through. The young actors were not stars and they understood the ultimate aim, so they persevered and their performances were terrific.

If Sheen was Stone, then the other characteres were based on real people or composites. Berenger's Barnes was the malevolent sergeant whose scarred face reflected a survivor, a consummate soldier, but a broken spirit. He was a killing machine who, despite being shot in the face, reenlisted to get back to Vietnam. He was a hero to the poor white, redneck troops whose preference in "poison" ran to Jack Daniels and huge quantities of Budweiser. Dafoe's Elias was based on a 23-year-old, dashing, half–Apache soldier-warrior. His charisma reminded Stone of rock star Jim Morrison of The Doors (whose film biography Stone made in 1991). Elias's minions were the dopers, stoned whites, ex-hippie draftees, and blacks. The allegiance of the troops to these respective leaders came to typify the division among the grunts in a less than united and motivated American fighting force. So, too, in dramatic fashion the two sergeants became metaphors for the good and evil, the animal and the human that exist within everyone.

Platoon's soundtrack had its share of 1960s music, from the country strains of Merle Haggard to the rock of Jefferson Airplane to the Motown of Smokey Robinson. The eclectic mix is meant to reflect the crackers, dopers, soul brothers, and others who were disparate in their roots but integrated in their role as the underclass sent to fight the war. However, what stays with the listener is Georges Delerue's original music and his conducting of Samuel Barber's haunting "Adagio for Strings." This classical work evokes melancholy in a completely different manner from the chaotic tragedy of the rock-and-roll war in *Apocalypse Now* or the often clumsy evocation of a bygone era via the soundtrack in *Coming Home.* Arnold Kopelson produced the film along with execs Daly and Gibson and A. Kutman Ho. Orion Pictures released it domestically. The director of photography was Robert Richardson, Claire Simpson was the editor, and Simon Kaye was in charge of sound. All three made tremendous contributions. What follows is a brief synopsis of a film that is worthy of several viewings.

A quote from Ecclesiastes, "Rejoice, o young man, in thy youth," introduces a story that has many themes, of which the loss of innocence is one. It serves as a microcosm of America's dilemma in Vietnam. The apprehensive young recruits deplane from their C-130 in oppressive heat. Passing the "new meat" are grizzled veterans who cannot be much more than a year older than these new arrivals. In the background are cartloads of body bags. The film cuts to the thick jungle as a title reads, "December 1967 – Bravo Company, 25th Infantry Division – Somewhere near the Cambodian Border." Sheen's Chris is sweating profusely trying to hump his pack, carry his M-16, and whack at the jungle with a machete. The members of the platoon are introduced visually as they struggle. They pass a decomposing "gook," but only the cherries react to the horror of seeing flies and worms eat a dead man. Random radio transmissions punctuate the sounds of grunting as a frightened-looking lieutenant speaks to command. Barnes tells Chris to pick up the pace, "you sorry ass motherfucker." Elias tells him he is packing too much gear and lightens his load. Another cherry, a rotund Georgia kid, is ready to pass out. A redneck nicknamed "Bunny" urinates in the mouth of the dead body.

Back at the dingy little camp the company reinforces a perimeter with claymore mines and sandbags. The usual banter and minutiae of daily existence are recreated, and in the process other characters are introduced. Rhah is a gravelly voiced warrior; King is a kindly black guy missing a few teeth; Big Harold is a gentle giant; Francis is a handsome, baby-faced black man; O'Neill is a redneck syncophant to Barnes; and so on. There are a lot of minorities and poor white trash. As Chris observes his fellow soldiers, he realizes that they are America's underclass. The poor draftees cannot believe he was so stupid as to enlist in this war. It is Stone's commentary on his own naïveté but also on the less than egalitarian manner in which America fought this war. Unlike World War II, when everybody served, Vietnam is a "sucker's tour." Chris puts the matter this way later in voiceover: "They come from the end of the line. . . . They're the bottom of the barrel—and they know it. Maybe that's why they call themselves 'grunts'."

Chris is overwhelmed by everything he must learn. He is always exhausted and scared. The other men keep their distance because the new guys are dangerous in their inexperience. Sheen is assigned to nighttime guard duty. He is sleepy, tormented by mosquitoes, and terrified. Sure enough during his watch the Viet Cong appear. At first he is not sure that the solitary silent figure in the jungle is really there. Does he awaken all the others? Does he press the claymore trigger? The film evokes his horror, his racing heartbeat, his indecision. All of a sudden all hell breaks loose, chaotic and lethal. Explosions go off, the men are under attack, and cries of pain ring out as tracers light up the night. The other cherry panicked, stood up, and is now dead. Chris thinks he is dying, having taken a glancing bullet by his ear. The men yell at one another and glower at Chris.

Despite the stellar re-creation of action, Stone is not above platitude and clichés. Some of the voiceover becomes intrusive, overly analytical, and omniscient. But when he employs hackneyed scenes, this choice seems more a homage to the convention and a self-conscious bow to preceding mythic tracks or filmic ancestors. For instance, the death of the new guy is preordained because in an earlier scene he shows Chris a picture of his girl back home.

Chris is medevac'd out along with the body bag. He returns a week later, and the men are decidedly cool to him for his mistake. King, the kindly black man, befriends Chris as they empty latrines. They smoke dope while silhouetted against a beautiful Southeast Asia dusk. At night the men break off into their cliques. Chris is initiated into the rituals of the "heads," or dopers. Rhah offers him a three-foot-long Montagnard bong. Elias shows him how to use an M-16 barrel as a marijuana pipe. While they escape reality in their underground bunker, the other group, led by Barnes, gets drunk and plays cards. The lieutenant attempts to fit in with the poker players but quickly exits as he has no place among the enlisted men. Their respect for authority stops at the level of the skilled sergeants.

The next day on patrol they encounter a tunnel system, and Elias bravely enters it and kills a VC. Meanwhile the others hang out in the eerie atmosphere; everybody chain-smokes and peers about for the enemy. One young blond kid finds some documents in a box among the enemy gear. When he lifts the box, a booby trap explodes and he is killed. As they prepare to push on, they realize Manny is missing. After a search they encounter his body, throat slit, eyes protruding in terror. A quiet chill descends over the men. As they approach a hamlet, they see back in the distance a young man in civilian garb running away. Barnes nails him with one shot. When they arrive in the village, they are enraged. They are looking for VC or evidence of them. The local chieftain chatters in unintelligible excitement as the soldiers tear things up and Bunny shoots a pig just to do so. Several villagers are found cowering in hiding, and there is a stockpile of grain. Some of the Americans take this as confirmation that there are VC or that they are being harbored. The men begin a roundup, and the chieftain tries to explain through an interpreter that the villagers are innocent but that the VC terrorizes them.

Barnes is impatient when the frightened villagers are slow in coming out of their hiding places. He tosses a grenade into a hole. The discovery of a weapons cache infuriates the men, and they are abusive. Something comes over Chris when he enters a hut. An old woman and her retarded son recoil in fear of the big American men, all angry and armed. Bunny calls the woman and child "Ma and Pa Kettle" and eggs Chris on to shoot the "greasy gooks." Chris demonically makes the confused young man dance by spraying bullets at his feet. O'Neill lamely tries to intervene. A tearful Chris finally stops, terrified at his own sadism. But Bunny is not satisfied; he cold-bloodedly smashes in the boy's head. As blood splatters on Bunny's face, he grooves on the boy's brains spilling out. The old lady wails as she huddles over her dead son. Even veteran O'Neill is ready to vomit.

The horribly mutated war effort and the cliché of the baby killer have now been offered up in a harrowing on-screen rendition of graphic horror. American boys are committing atrocities, and their motivation or lack thereof has been dramatized on camera. How it could happen has been shown. Absolute fear, grief, and frustration have led to the heinousness. Outside the slaughter is about to take on My Lai proportions. Some angry GIs shout at Barnes to waste the entire village. Others just stand around dazed. The babbling and clicking of the agitated wife of the village chieftain lead Barnes to execute her in front of her

Platoon (Orion Pictures, 1986). The men separate the two sergeant warriors.

entire family. The chief is overcome with grief and resigns to die. Returning from the other end of the village, Elias interrupts the impending atrocity with the shout, "Barnes . . . what the fuck you doing! You ain't a firing squad, you piece of shit." He jumps on top of the other sergeant, and they beat each other. The lieutenant breaks the fight up as the platoon mentally takes sides. In a scorched-earth policy known as a "zippo" raid, the men torch the suspected enemy haven. The string music wells up as the Americans and the Vietnamese evacuate. Some of the GIs carry children on their shoulders, an irony that for a moment reminds one of a kindly soldier in World War II.

Back at command Elias breaks some muddled notion of a code of silence and reports the incident to the brass, who seem more embarrassed than outraged. Barnes remains defiant, and there is great distrust between the dopers and rednecks. Chris is frightened by the realization that evil lurks in him. He has seen his primordial self. However conscience, rationality, and tribal loyalty dictate that he embrace the saintly Elias. The splitting asunder of the platoon can be analogized to hawks and doves, good and evil, and so on.

A tentative investigation begins as the company digs in. One night Chris and Elias get stoned together. The veteran remarks on how much has changed since 1965. Then he believed in what we were doing. Now, however, "we're gonna lose this war." Chris is incredulous. Elias continues, "We been kicking people's asses so long I guess it's time we got our own kicked." His speech continued, but the balance was left on the cutting room floor. In Stone's original version Elias alludes to the importance of Chris surviving and going back to the United States as a witness to the lack of glory. This urging foreshadows a self-realization that he will not make it out of the jungle.

Monsoon rains drench the platoon as it patrols among Buddhist ruins and the men discuss what they are going to do back in the "world." A few days later the men are caught in an ambush. Chaos and casualties reign as Chris now acquits himself like a seasoned warrior. He makes his first up-close kill of an NVA. All his other shots up to now have been panicked firings in the direction of an elusive enemy. The men are under heavy fire but bravely fight and aid their comrades. The hapless lieutenant radios in faulty coordinates, so the air support results in friendly fire casualties. The sergeants run about directing the defense. In the thick jungle Elias encounters Barnes and smiles, relieved that he is not the enemy. However, the malevolent look of the scarred killer wipes the toothy grin off Elias's face. Barnes takes advantage of their isolation to shoot his fellow sergeant and would-be accuser. The other men fight their way out to a hot LZ, where they clamber onto helicopters. As they lift off several realize the one sergeant is missing. They look down to see a badly wounded Elias trying to escape pursuing enemy forces. The helicopters attempt to train their guns in support, but it is futile. The men watch silently as the brave sergeant is riddled with bullets. In slow motion he falls to his knees, arteries exploding, his arms outstretched to the heavens in a heavy-handed evocation of the suffering of Jesus. As the helicopters pull away, Chris flashes Barnes a suspicious glance.

Back at camp Elias's grieving minions accuse Barnes of murder. Rhah hates the man but voices in-country superstition when he remarks that Barnes has been wounded repeatedly and is not going to die. When Chris implies he might exact revenge, the glowering sergeant catches him in the tirade. Barnes enters the den and menacingly intones, "Y'all know about killing? . . . Y'all love Elias, want to kick ass. I'se here—all by my lonesome. Nobody gonna know. . . . Kill me." Waiting a moment, Chris lets out a yell and attacks him. Barnes quickly gets the upper hand and presses a knife to the protagonist's throat. Rhah appeals to the sergeant's reason, pointing out that killing Chris will lead to prison. As Barnes withdraws he contemptuously cuts Chris's face.

The next day the platoon acts as bait for a maneuver near the border. The men return to base amid rumors that an entire NVA regiment is massing nearby. The men are assigned to two-person foxholes in anticipation of a horrendous offensive. They are severely outnumbered, and the veterans' sixth sense tells them they may all die. Some men are in a panic, some are fiercely defiant, others are cowardly. What ensues is as excitingly staged a ground combat sequence as has ever been recreated. The grunt-turned-filmmaker infuses the action with the realism of the confusion and ferocity that accompany such a horrible battle. One by one the perimeter positions are overrun in a battle with fluid lines. Near the bush Chris and the others fight for survival. The night is lit up with flares, bullets, and mortars.

Back at command a major, played in a cameo by Stone, and his officers are killed when a suicide sapper with explosives infiltrates the bunker and blows it to bits. Nearly face to face with enemies murmuring in their native language, Chris blazes away with his M-16 yelling, "Die you motherfuckers!!! YAAAAAAA!!!"

Junior yells, "I ain't dying in no white man's war," abandons his hole, and is promptly bayoneted. O'Neill survives a probe by hiding under a corpse.

Dale Dye as the captain and the lieutenant call for an air strike on their own position. This desperate act is the only way to clear out the overwhelming enemy forces. They pass the word for the troops to take cover. As Chris runs about, he encounters a wounded Barnes, who looks like the devil incarnate. The sergeant is pure adrenalized obsession as he smashes Chris with a rifle butt. Barnes is about to deliver a skull-crunching blow when the phantom jet roars overhead and delivers its payload. The movie fades to black and then gradually in a manner subjective to Chris's consciousness reawakens in the vaguely lit sunlight of a new day.

Chris is dazed and in pain as he sees hundreds of ashen marauders' bodies strewn about. Nearby he hears American soldiers shouting and the sounds of armored personnel carriers. He picks up a dead NVA's AK-47 and staggers onward. Then he encounters a badly wounded Barnes, who calls for a medic. Chris merely stares at him, and the wounded sergeant understands, just as Elias had earlier. Barnes shouts defiantly, "Do it!" as Chris kills him.

The mop-up crew arrives as the numbed Chris is littered out to the LZ and takes his last look at the horror. Soldiers collect souvenirs from dead bodies, bulldozers pile up the enemy corpses, and Rhah lets out a yell, a primordial farewell to his fellow grunt. As tears stream down Chris's grimy face, he remarks, "I think now, looking back, we did not fight the enemy, we fought ourselves, and the enemy was in us. . . . The war is over for me now, but it will always be there the rest of my days—as I am sure Elias will be fighting with Barnes for . . . possession of my soul." The mournful score wells up as a dedication to those who fought and died in Vietnam is offered.

Had Chris become what he disdained—a killer? Was the murder of Barnes the ultimate corruption of Chris's soul, and did it mean that evil had triumphed? These dramatic points were more important as questions than as answers. Some observers took exception to the profundity attempted in the Elias/Barnes dichotomy. Elitist critic John Simon said that Stone wants to be a philosopher-poet and that he thinks in clichés and "tie-dyed prose."[12] Stone fueled the intellectualization by alluding to Homer's *Iliad* as a source for the symbolic journey.

The controversy the film engendered also concerned the accusation that once again the soldiers were portrayed as undisciplined, racist, substance-abusing fraggers and baby killers. In other words they were the losers who had coopted the pop-cultural portrait and here were shown in a graphic manner. The debate was very animated. Some veterans proclaimed that finally someone had shown what it was really like to be in Vietnam. Others condemned the portrait and said that they had never seen anyone kill civilians and that morale had not been nearly this bad, especially in 1967 and 1968. An early request for Pentagon logistical assistance in the production was turned down.[13]

Ultimately *Platoon* was about Stone's personal experiences in Vietnam and how a witness recreated them in a firsthand manner. Nobody shoots combat better, period. As in all the important film entries, the debate and resulting press attention enhanced the box office "wanna see."

On January 26, 1987, *Time* featured the film on its cover with the header "*Platoon*: Viet Nam As It Really Was." Inside the magazine welcomed the renewed debate about the war that the film had sparked. "*Platoon* the picture is now Platoon the phenomenon."[14] The article correctly noted that this entry, along with *Apocalypse Now, The Deerhunter, The Boys in Company C*, and *The Killing Fields*, had been largely financed by non–American sources. The article summarized the disagreement among veterans and the general public. *Time* noted the critical momentum that was leading to the spring Oscar ceremony.

An upscale audience embraced the film as carefully constructed and well acted. Others merely ignored or missed political cues and were enthralled by the film's visceral evocation of action. In this manner ambiguity or misunderstanding once again contributed to the gross. An unlikely source, *Mademoiselle*, praised the film, noting, "It's not about whether this war was right or wrong. . . . It's about the texture of the experience. What it is like to be there."[15] The controversy exemplified a furthering of the healing process vis-à-vis Vietnam. That cathartic renewal was mirrored in the life of Stone himself. *Platoon* won the Best Picture Oscar, and the grunt-turned-filmmaker was the toast of Hollywood. He not only won Best Director accolades but was also nominated for *Platoon*'s original screenplay and for *Salvador*'s adaptation! The filmmaker was happily remarried, had a baby son, and was off drugs. Friends said he was much mellower and, like many vets, had come to grips with his experience.

Other *Platoon* Oscar nominations went to Willem Dafoe and Tom Berenger for supporting actor and Robert Richardson for cinematography. The film editor and sound editors won their categories. The relatively inexpensive production garnered an additional 25 percent box office boost after winning the Oscar. When the picture finished its domestic theatrical run, it had grossed $138 million!

Following the immense critical and commercial success of Stone's Best Picture, there was a veritable "platoon" of direct portraits set in-country. The year 1987 featured *Hamburger Hill, Full Metal Jacket, Hanoi Hilton, Good Morning, Vietnam*, and others. These medium- to full-budget films were depictors or celebrators of the grunts. They had begun production at the same time as the making of *Platoon*, so their go-ahead was not primarily dependent on that film's notable success. Rather, like the fecund period exemplified by the four horsemen and the apocalypse, a commercial and psychological coincidence was taking place. The first wave of combat films had occurred roughly ten years after *The Green Berets*. This second wave happened approximately a decade after those films. The four horsemen were perceived as dovish or ambiguous. The revisionism of *Rambo* and the romanticism of *Top Gun* were perceived as hawkish. Now the list of films was steeped in bloody and muddy realism, and politically it seemed as if the old ideological conflict was being resynthesized.

As America continued to sort out its feelings about the war, the new crop of films offered up realism again wrapped in ambiguous politics. In reference to Francis Ford Coppola's *Gardens of Stone* then in production, the paradox was described by coproducer Michael Levy as "a pro-military, anti-war film."[16] What was also important in the new movies was the participation of other veterans as filmmakers or technical consultants. At about this same juncture many educators were wrestling with how to incorporate the Vietnam War into the curriculum in a meaningful and apolitical manner. They realized that in the twelve or so years since Saigon's fall, the war had not been taught and that most of its images for the young had been provided by motion pictures.

Made-for-television films were in short supply as they could not compete in scope with the theatricals. Sign-of-the-times films and recontextualizations were also unnecessary given the plethora of head-on depictions. However, the B movie exploitation films continued unabated in a copycat style designed to fill the video market. They were less than innovative, and in their appeal to an unsophisticated audience they generally were one cycle late in their adventures. In other words the actioners of 1986 and 1987 were primarily ripoffs of the success of *Rambo* and *MIA*. Only later did slightly higher-quality B flicks begin the emulation of the new A title hits. The late 1987 release *The Siege of Firebase Gloria* and the spring 1988 release *Platoon Leader* owed more to *Full Metal Jacket* and *Platoon* than to the last cycle of Vietnam films of the *Rambo* mold.

The sole made-for contribution in 1987 is important only in that it illustrates one more evolution of the industry. *Proud Men* was a made-for-cable feature designed to fill the programming needs of this new type of television. A pioneer in this area, Turner Broadcasting, produced the film, which starred Charlton Heston and Peter Strauss. If these films met with success, they were either released theatrically overseas or sold to cable stations in Europe as original programming. William A. Graham directed this cliché-ridden tale of an embittered rancher estranged from his only son, who deserted the army during his tour in Vietnam and has lived for the past 15 years in Paris. The mother seeks to reconcile the two "proud men" because father Heston is suffering from terminal cancer.

The World War II vet's lack of understanding, the ranch setting, and Strauss all contribute to an echo of 1969's *Hail Hero*. Many defenses are up when father and son greet each other. The farmhands are split between those who welcome the prodigal son home and those who condemn his treason. In a bar a vet berates the now-38-year-old photographer. He seeks to earn respect by reembracing such manly pursuits as rodeo riding and cattle roping. Occasionally the film lapses into conversation about Vietnam in which it gives lip service to such notions as World War II as the last "good war," and the fact that our country "bailed out" on its own soldiers. Each time, the film cuts to another scene in order not to have to confront difficult issues or provide the dialogue they would necessitate. After all Vietnam is actually just the background for a tale about father-son love.

Eventually the reason that combat-decorated Strauss went AWOL comes out. He saw his buddy get shot by a Viet Cong woman. When he killed her, he inadvertently killed her baby as well. To add to the irony the very same village in which this battle took place reverted to "Charlie" the next week. The absurdity was too much and he made the difficult decision to turn his back on his country. In the process he lost his family for 15 years. Just as his father begins to understand the extent of his son's sacrifice and pain, the police arrest Strauss on an outstanding warrant for his desertion. After all this time the army administrator is interested only in having the soldier sign an affidavit declaring that the case is finished and that he agrees to a less than honorable discharge. This riles some rednecks, who see it as a "slap on the wrist." When one begins to beat Strauss, his father comes to the rescue. Exemplifying the trite story is the final scene in which father, son, and grandson ride off together into the sunset.

Major theatrical releases in 1987 provided veteran characters whose incidentally drawn in-country service was steeped in the shorthand of years of stereotyping. The megahit police buddy picture *Lethal Weapon* starred Mel Gibson and Danny Glover. These two L.A. cops are both veterans of the war. However, the former is a maladjusted nut case who lives on the edge with a death wish. His domestic problems elicit reckless behavior that is serio-comic and is partially derived from old in-country experiences. His partner, family man Glover, seems unscarred by his wartime service. The duo returned in two sequels, also directed by Richard Donner. All were huge successes.

Suspect starred Cher as an attorney investigating a murder case. The first person suspected of the heinous crime is a pitiful street person played by Liam Neeson. He is a deaf mute and, as it turns out, a Vietnam veteran. He is mistrusted by society and victimized by the criminal justice system. Of course the heroine intervenes on behalf of the innocent secondary character.

The cheap, avenge-and-win, made-for-video ripoffs of *Rambo* continued, with most being shot in the Philippine jungles. Schlockmeister Roger Corman's newest company, Concorde, released *Eye of the Eagle*, directed by Cirio Santiago. Brett Clark starred as the leader of the elite guerrilla unit Eagle Team. The team infiltrates the jungle stronghold of the "Lost Command," a rogue band of MIAs and deserters. They are the B movie incarnation of Kurtz's renegades in *Apocalypse Now*. Romance with a female reporter joins in with the usual action sequences. A sequel appropriately titled *Eye of the Eagle II* was released in 1989.

Proving that the profitability of such fodder was assured for its video distributors, the next similar film also spawned a sequel. Media Home Entertainment released *Behind Enemy Lines*, also directed by Filipino Cirio Santiago. In this barely feature-length adventure, Green Beret "John Ransom" is captured shortly before the American pullout from Vietnam. He is tortured by the NVA and its sadistic ally, a Soviet adviser. Star Robert Patrick manages to escape and encounters love in the jungle. The romance aspects are a throwback to the early Vietnam actioners but have been updated to allow the video dust jacket to show some comely woman. *Behind Enemy Lines II* featured the same characters in a 1989 release.

Soldier's Revenge, directed by David Worth, showed how far John Savage's career had fallen since his performance as Stevie in *The Deerhunter*. This picture lacked a rating, having never received a theatrical release before going to video.

Savage is an embittered Vietnam vet who returns home to no welcome at all. Rather, he is branded a traitor for misunderstood in-country infractions. He returns to Southeast Asia to save the woman he left behind.

In *Steele Justice* Robert Boris directed Martin Kove and Sela Ward. Veteran Kove is forced to use his combat training in southern California against the drug-running Vietnamese mafia. Since the fall of Saigon the immigration of Southeast Asians had brought not only law abiding citizens but also a criminal fringe. This element, versed in the martial arts, was the enemy in several chopsockies. When a friend and comrade is killed, the veteran is forced to take revenge.

Backfire was directed by Gilbert Cates and starred Karen Allen, Keith Carradine, and Jeff Fahey. It opens to a firefight in Vietnam amid torrential rain and multiple explosions. As a body floats to the top of the water, a terrified Fahey awakens from his nightmare. The vet is agitated, aloof, and alcoholic. He has not recovered from Vietnam despite nearly 15 years of trying. Each time the sufferer thinks of Nam, the film reverts to drab green and brown hues instead of the usual technicolor. At a party he hears helicopters and makes a fool of himself. When Carradine shows up and starts sharing the troubled vet's wife, Fahey's suicide looks suspiciously like murder. The mystery thriller treats the revelation of Fahey having saved Carradine in combat as ironic given the postwar double cross. The police chief, played by Bernie Casey, is also a Vietnam veteran.

David Carradine portrayed a street gang–fighting, flashback-plagued vet in *Armed Response*. Crime fighters/vigilantes employed their in-country skills in the "world" in *Savage Dawn*. In *Fear*, the vet is a murderer who also suffers from flashbacks. *Bell Diamond* featured an unknown cast in the tale of an unemployed vet who suffers from Agent Orange exposure. *In Dangerous Company* at least featured an interesting look at Los Angeles' "Little Saigon" community. *The Forgotten Warrior* began as a tale about escaped POW's and then became a standard unintelligible chopsocky. The disservice to those that served continued in the new video releases of theatrically unplayable junk that had been gathering dust in film vaults. Examples include: *The GI Executioner, Outlaw Force, Hardcase and Fist, Nightforce, Night Wars, Street Trash, Zebra Force, Operation War Zone* and *Moon in Scorpio*. All featured violence prone, poorly adjusted vets. Despite larger budgets, *Extreme Prejudice*'s band of mercenaries, *Let's Get Harry*'s soldiers of fortune, the ex–CIA hitman in *Malone*, the assassin in *The Package*, the pilots in *Opposing Force*, the deserter in *Wolf Lake* or the drug addicts in *O.C. & Stiggs* and *Tough Guys Don't Dance* did little to elevate the image of the Vietnam veteran.

Usually a purveyor of action flicks, Cannon released the next important entry, *Hanoi Hilton*. This true story of American POWs held at Hanoi's notorious Hoa Lo Prison was directed by England's Lionel Chetwynd. It was originally intended as a four-hour television miniseries. The harrowing tale starred Michael Moriarity, Jeffrey Jones, Paul Lemat, and Lawrence Pressman as incarcerated navy pilots. It was the fullest re-creation of the American POW experience, taking place entirely in North Vietnam. In its depiction of the enemy captors, it was to be very controversial.

The film opens to a television crew interviewing flier Moriarity on the occasion of the Gulf of Tonkin incident in 1964. As he prepares for his mission at this early juncture in the war, the proud pilot says he is here to serve his government. By the end of the credits he has been shot down, and he and his copilot lie wounded on the ground in North Vietnam. The peasant warriors who capture them execute his comrade, who has suffered a broken leg. Moriarity is taken to the concrete prison in downtown Hanoi. Here he is interrogated as portraits of Mao and Ho Chi Minh look on approvingly. In the background are the noises of the busy city. He refuses to give any information except name, rank, and serial number. He is accused of being a criminal and is told he is not protected by the Geneva Convention because there is no declaration of war. Aki Aleong, who was sadistic as Chuck Norris's tormentor in the *MIA* films, reprises his evil ways in this feature. His performance typifies the paradox of the film. It aspires to be a serious A movie about the POWs but is often mired in the subpar elements of Cannon productions.

In solitary confinement Moriarity reads inscriptions etched by French prisoners from their Indochina War. Despite loneliness, rats, and poor rations, Moriarity survives his interrogations. Finally in the autumn of 1965 he is placed with other prisoners. He rejoices in the human contact, and the men discuss everything. The ranking American officer insists that the prisoners maintain a fine line of not cooperating with but not antagonizing the enemy. The Americans maintain discipline and morale by following a chain of command and aiding one another whenever possible. By 1966 the North Vietnamese authorities are incensed at their inability to break the spirit of the POWs. The beatings in the notorious Room 18 become more brutal, and one by one the men are broken. To do otherwise is impossible. In the spring of 1966 the days pass slowly as the men are subjected to Radio Hanoi propaganda. They are told they have been deserted by their country, and their forced confessions of war crimes are aired. How each man chooses to survive is shown in agonizing detail.

In a re-creation of the notorious incident already portrayed in *Limbo* and *The Forgotten Man*, the prisoners are led through the streets of Hanoi. They are spat upon and pummeled by the angry mob. The men try to maintain their dignity and are grateful when they receive mail at Christmas 1969. The film shows how brutally and how long some of these men were held captive. A visiting Cuban communist sadist joins in the interrogation and, on a variation of the theme of the downtrodden black soldier, tries to appeal to his shared ethnicity with a Hispanic-American flier, who will have none of this manipulation. The men discuss the children they have missed growing up, listen to Hanoi Hannah, and watch as some of their comrades succumb to disease and despair. Adding insult to injury is the appearance of an American actress-peacenik modeled after Jane Fonda. The men detest her as a traitorous apologist who is useful only in that she is able to win the release of three men.

Finally several men make a desperate escape attempt in which one dies. His last words are "I die not so much for love of country as for love of my countrymen." In this speech the film shows the evolution from the naive idealism of 1964 to the cold reality of winter 1970. All purpose is gone except standing by comrades. In this way this tale of highly trained, mostly older officers joins the infantry grunt portrayals in their sympathy for the victims of a wrong or compromised policy.

By the summer of 1971 conditions have eased. In 1972 the prisoners survive heavy American bombing of Hanoi. In 1973 dramatic music accompanies the announcement that the men are going home. Their tearful jubilation gives way to the credit postscript, which reads, "From 1963 until the fall of Saigon in 1975, 3.4 million American men and women served in Southeast Asia. Of these 58,135 never returned. Of the prisoners of war 725 were repatriated, leaving 2,421 still unaccounted for." The filmmakers then thank 17 ex–POWs for their technical assistance on the film. Included are John McCain, who is now a U.S. senator. The Department of Defense provided cooperation to the production.

Hanoi Hilton was perceived as a hawkish film. The director denied this saying, "It does not glorify the people who fought the war–there is a genuine sense of despair . . . and it has a very sobering effect. But neither does it show the Vietnamese as a childlike people brutalized by Western technology. From their captives, I learned that they were smart, sophisticated, worldly wise people with a whole inventory of torture–learned from their colonial masters, the French, who tortured the Arabs in Algeria. We take a dim view of the North Vietnamese Army–so in that sense you could say the film is right wing."[17] In a way the director's quote harks back to *The Lost Command* and defines the parameters of the films' depiction of the Vietnamese. It shows the wide spectrum between the cartoonish depictions of a heinous Asian enemy in the B films and the innocent, victimized peasants who took on near saintly status while suffering at the hands of baby killers like the overzealous Bunny in *Platoon*. Somewhere in between was the spartan VC warrior or the disciplined NVA regular.

In July 1987 Warner Bros. offered the eagerly awaited contribution of Stanley Kubrick to the lineup. *Full Metal Jacket*'s wide release was representative of its distributor's belief in its commercial appeal. Most observers expected a fall debut for the more adult and critic-oriented filmgoers. However, following *Platoon*'s box office success, Vietnam had a shot at big grosses. The gamble paid off in a modest hit that is fascinating not for the auteur's expectedly iconoclastic contribution but for the film's purposely derivative and self-conscious core. In terms of the group of films, the movie reflects the earlier Vietnam-based entries in a manner in which the first Vietnam films were descendants of the World War II films. The Vietnam combat genre had now produced enough entries so that this one wrapped in unique surroundings and visuals was actually in its conventions and references an homage to the imagery that had gone before.

Stanley Kubrick had directed many memorable films, including antiwar classics. Therefore when he began production some two years prior to release, the public and press eagerly awaited his version of the Vietnam War. Like the much-anticipated *Apocalypse Now* from Coppola, delays heightened the anticipation and hype. Both films relied on Michael Herr for collaborative screenplay contributions. And like lead Martin Sheen's heart attack on the set of the 1979 film, *Full Metal Jacket*'s production was delayed nearly three months by the near-fatal auto accident of technical adviser and actor R. Lee Ermey.

The ex-marine drill instructor and Vietnam vet who had appeared in *The Boys in Company C* in a similar role trained the ensemble of baby-boomer actors for their portrait of grunts. Like Dale Dye for *Platoon*, Ermey put them through on- as well as off-screen drills. This was designed to elicit camaraderie and realism. Actor Dorian Harewood, who portrayed "Eightball," said, "It was as close to war as I ever want to get. . . . It was the army!"[18]

If Ermey was the sergeant, then the general was Kubrick. Michael Herr reported in his foreword to the publication of this film's screenplay that the auteur had for years wanted to make a movie about Nam but had lacked the proper story. The author of *Dispatches* had spent hours talking to the Englishman, but it was not until they came across Gustav Hasford's novel *The Short Timers* that they had the proper source material.[19] All three men eventually collaborated on the screenplay. Hasford skeptically alluded to what Herr had referred to as the "mythic tracks" that led us into Vietnam. This specifically took the form of references to John Wayne as a cultural icon, a notion previously quoted in Ron Kovic's hero worship in *Born on the Fourth of July*. Now enough time had passed so that the preoccupation with "pulling a John Wayne" was evocative not only of *The Sands of Iwo Jima* but also of *The Green Berets*. In one scene from the script, cut from the film, the grunts laugh derisively at a screening of the Duke's Vietnam foray.

The look of the film and its title had been preordained in Kubrick's mind. Years before he had seen the phrase "full metal jacket" in a gun catalogue and found it "beautiful and tough, and kind of poetic."[20] Although set in the historically pregnant and now commonly evoked moment of the 1968 Tet Offensive, this version of the Vietnam War is not in a thick, green jungle. Rather, the urban setting of an abandoned coke-smelting plant in Beckton and its depressed East London neighborhood became stand-ins for a bombed out Hue. The rock-and-roll extravagance of combat in *Apocalypse Now* and the gut-wrenching realism in *Platoon* were not to be competed against here. The scenes of vicious street-to-street fighting are reminiscent of the European theater in World War II films. The setting, the language, and the characters reflect a debt to the Hollywood imagery of the past and the mind-set that accompanied the new generation of soldiers into battle in Vietnam.

In an initial 45-minute sequence the raw recruits are molded into marines at Parris Island. The rituals of depersonalization are now familiar from *The Boys in Company C* and *Tribes*. This prelude to war introduces themes of manhood and sexuality that run throughout the film. Ermey's language is at once hilarious and frightening. "If you ladies . . . survive recruit training . . . you will be a

Full Metal Jacket (Warner Bros., 1987). Real-life drill instructor–turned–actor R. Lee Ermey berates Vincent D'Onofrio as Matthew Modine looks on.

weapon . . . praying for war. But until that day you are pukes!" So far this is familiar harassment, but the experienced ad-libbing of Ermey goes one step beyond. "You are nothing but unorganized grabasstic pieces of amphibian shit!"

Soon everyone is assigned nicknames by the DI. Matthew Modine, so memorable in *Birdy,* is the lead character and a voiceover narrator. His moniker "Joker" reflects his wisecracking comments. He does a feeble John Wayne imitation. Arliss Howard, who bears a great resemblance to Craig Wasson, is "Cowboy." However, it is Vincent D'Onofrio as "Gomer Pyle" who is most memorable in the opening sequence. His television character nickname is anything but funny, as he is mercilessly ridiculed by the DI. Pyle cannot keep up with the unit and is clearly doomed. Reflecting the enforced evolution from boys to men, the others begin to excel, but the hapless Pyle sucks his thumb and marches with his pants down as punishment for his incompetence. At first the others seek to help him, but he drags down the unit. One night the harmless nocturnal pillow fights of boys are replaced by the savage beating of Pyle by the entire unit wielding soap wrapped in towels as a weapon. The already traumatized loser now descends into insanity.

The sublimation of sexuality into the phallic worship of the rifle is explicit when the recruits are instructed to sleep with their M-16s. "You give your rifle a girl's name!" Later sublimations include "This is my rifle. . . . It is my life." After the obstacle course and other training, Pyle finally finds he excels at sharpshooting. Remarking on a proud tradition, albeit a perverse example, the sergeant asks who Lee Harvey Oswald is. Most of the men do not seem to know, but the intelligent Joker identifies him. Ermey extols the skill that allowed Oswald as well as Charles Whitman to pick people off at hundreds of yards. Ermey attributes this to their marine training. This blackly humorous exchange manages to subliminally echo twenty years of portraits of soldiers as crazed killing machines. The military-induced skills of the sharpshooter way back in *Targets* and, in the interim, in many other wired Vietnam vets, have been inculcated. The scene also propels us to the next horror.

A few weeks later at night in the barracks, Joker awakens to find Pyle in the latrine with a rifle. The scene is bathed in an eerie nocturnal green and gray. Pyle stares ominously and says, "I am in a world of shit!" The drill instructor confronts the armed man with the impatient query "What is this Mickey Mouse shit?" When Ermey demands that Pyle surrender the rifle, Pyle shoots the sergeant at point-blank range. Joker watches in horror as Pyle then splatters his own brains against the drab wall.

This domestic horror fades to black as the film shifts to Saigon. Nancy Sinatra's "These Boots Are Made for Walkin'" belts out as a hooker offers herself at a café. This moment instantly conveys that this is a bustling and corrupt city bursting with an overpowering U.S. presence. The women are all hookers and the South Vietnamese men are pimps and thieves. Joker is now a correspondent for an army newspaper full of propaganda and false body counts. The cynical Joker and others laugh at the attempts to show America winning the populace's hearts and minds. The phrase "diplomats in dungarees" is a source of derision. This is the language John Wayne used in describing what he wanted to show the public in *The Green Berets* in his letter to President Johnson.

Quick verbal orientation is offered to the frightening offensive via buzzwords such as the "U.S. Embassy" and "Khe Sanh." Joker finally gets into the field to cover a story. His helmet, like many others', has a slogan inscribed on the front. However, his is a paradoxical blend of the words "Born to Kill" and a peace sign. When a general asks what the hell that means, Joker flippantly replies that it reflects the duality of humans, the "Jungian thing." It somehow serves as an absurd reminder that boys are masquerading as men, that innocents can and do become killers, and that in a war zone surviving is a lot more important than peace.

Joker hooks up with his old friend Cowboy in a besieged area of Hue. A roving documentary crew interviews Joker and his new band, including Adam Baldwin as the machine-gun-toting, baby-faced warrior known as "Animal Mother." The young men have little to say to the filmmakers in a scene used in *Apocalypse Now* and soon to be recreated in *Hamburger Hill*, each in an effort to convey the viewer's voyeuristic participation in the "TV" war. The spectacle of war as entertainment is underscored when the young men pass the time by making up the plot to what they call "Vietnam . . . the Movie." They laugh as they choose roles alongside none other than John Wayne, Ann-Margret, and the "gooks" as the Indians.

Using colorful in-country jargon, the young men negotiate for a teenage prostitute's services. After this they continue their patrol through the urban wasteland. A child's doll yields a booby trap that kills one of the squad. That begins a descent that culminates in a shootout with a sniper. As the men try to advance, the crack shot picks them off. They return immense firepower to the general direction of the killer. Each time a man is shot, the others feel compelled to expose themselves to danger to retrieve the wounded or the corpse. This absurd sense of duty and heroics propels them in a manner inculcated in countless war films. Instead of just retreating, they so much want to kill the killer of their friends that they are willing to be killed. This sequence is excruciating as one by one they die. Cowboy is wounded and in the book is shot by Joker in a cynical realization that he cannot be helped and should not suffer. Kubrick chooses to divert here and continue the absurd heroics. Eventually the survivors reach the building and amid fires and garbage search for the sniper. When they encounter the black-pajama-clad Viet Cong zealot, it is not at first clear whether the diminutive crack shot is a little "gook" man or, as it turns out, a young girl. Photographer-soldier Rafterman shoots her, and as she lies wounded she begs to be put out of her misery. Joker accommodates her at point-blank range.

The film ends as the platoon evacuates from the city, only a silhouette in the night against the fires raging in the background. As this and other squads hump toward the Perfume River, they sing the Mickey Mouse Club theme song. It is absurd but believable for this generation of soldiers raised on the refracted images of war in film and the black-and-white comforts of the television. Joker's voiceover speaks for all the grunts when he says, "I'm in a world of shit . . . yes. But I am alive."

The killer babies as baby killers is underscored when the young hero shoots the even younger girl. The thumbsucking child Pyle did not even get in-country. But the young protagonist in voiceover is no longer so innocent. Like the lead in *Platoon,* part of his goodness and youth is an additional casualty of war. Another recurring theme is that of the combat-sex connection. It is underscored throughout the film, just as Herr had constantly alluded to it in his book. In trying to convey the visceral feeling of combat to a nonparticipant, he made it akin to the exhilaration of the first sexual experience. It is significant that the phallic rifle analogy joins with all women portrayed as sex objects and then gives way to the ultimate expression of misogyny: the killing of the female sniper. This undercurrent was criticized by feminists who missed its multiple purpose. One meaning was the jargon-accompanied, self-conscious evocation of the war film as an exclusively male milieu. Another purpose was the conveying of the warping sensibilities of war as a male-engendered but misguided effort at conflict resolution. And the skill and perseverance of the VC are meant to typify them as superior fighters who as highly motivated soldiers will eventually triumph. This message was echoed in many films that had the hindsight of the American defeat. The existence of female as well as male combatants underscores the depth of conviction ascribed to the enemy.

Full Metal Jacket received several Academy Award nominations but was greeted with mixed reviews. Some took exception to its dramatics; others reacted, albeit subconsciously, to perceived politics. Once again ambiguity did not connote filmmaking cowardice but managed to reflect a coalescence in the wrongness of this conflict. Root causes and historic fact were replaced by survival and reconciliation. Everyone can agree on the absurdity and waste, and this film, in its cinematic lineage and its reflection of the leitmotifs of films that preceded it, reaffirms the centrality of Vietnam films in the culture.

Actor Lee Ermey had another tour in the independent release *The Siege of Firebase Gloria.* This 1987 English-language release was bankrolled in Hong Kong and shot, like many of the actioners, in the Philippines. Wings Hauser costarred and Brian Smith directed. The plot was very basic. An army outpost is under siege by the Viet Cong during the salient fear-inducing event, the Tet Offensive. An old-fashioned on-screen scrawl sets the stage and underscores the familiar cavalry-and–Indians movie antecedent.

This time it is Ermey who provides the voiceover narration as the marines proceed in-country. In the wake of the VC, the stock characters encounter heaps of bodies and heads on stakes at a hamlet. The marines explore the "dinks'" tunnel system and liberate a traumatized American imprisoned in a cave. The American response is hampered by poor intelligence and bad morale. Although drug problems became endemic only later in the war, filmmakers continue to feature it prominently even at this early juncture as a way to exemplify the compromised American war effort. At the titular firebase the commander is a fool, and the men try to frag him. The tough sergeant and his longtime friend, a captain played by Hauser, must take de facto control. They secure the camp in anticipation of an assault.

Every cliché is trotted out from the doomed black man who is "short" to the stoned gonzo combat photographer trapped with the grunts. Sappers probe the base as word of the U.S. Embassy fiasco reaches the men in the field. With Ermey also acting as technical adviser, the combat is excitingly staged. The men are amazed as "Charlie" keeps charging despite heavy casualties. The air cavalry keeps the enemy in check, but finally the perimeter is breached, and even the doctors must kill or be killed. The heroic defense of the firebase is respectfully contextualized in relation to the enemy in an old Chinese proverb: "The courage of your enemies does you honor."

The early films' portrayal of the Asian as cowardly, lascivious, and disorganized has been firmly supplanted by a lionization of the Asian's bravery and tenacity. Perhaps now that the real war has been lost, it is essential to impart extreme credit to the skill and character of the opposition. By joining this film's first scene of the ruthless execution squad's heinous crimes with the later anonymous, determined waves, this B picture illustrates the utter commitment of the enemy that Kurtz in *Apocalypse Now* sought to emulate. The film notes in a postscript that the Tet Offensive resulted in more than 55,000 Viet Cong deaths and thus, despite its psychological effects, the offensive was in fact a military disaster. The South Vietnamese–based opposition never recovered, and it was the North Vietnamese regular army that took on the burden of the war effort.

The grunt in combat as recreated by a vet-turned-filmmaker continued in the early fall of 1987 when Paramount Pictures released *Hamburger Hill*. It featured an emsemble cast in a fact-based account of the assault on Dong Ap Bia. That ten-day battle began on May 1, 1969, in the Ashau Valley. The area had been used as a staging ground for the Viet Cong's Tet Offensive on Hue (the setting for *Full Metal Jacket*). As a result of the ferocity of the battle, Hill 937 became known as "Hamburger Hill." Back in the United States Senate, the army's tactics in the siege were called "senseless and irresponsible" and led to a series of investigations.[21]

Hamburger Hill begins with the sound of helicopters and then crosscuts between the credits and the Vietnam veterans memorial. As the camera tracks quickly to screen right, the individual names on the black granite are blurred, and we whisk back to 1969 and chaos. In a hot fire zone casualties are being evacuated. A black medic tends to a dying man as bombing sorties quiet the attacking ground fire. The brilliant "fireworks" typify the contrasting images of Vietnam, where destruction and beauty coexist. This now-familiar dichotomy is underscored in the image of a pretty little girl under a bright parasol on a muddy, convoy-convulsed road. Henceforth, *Hamburger Hill* will be visually rooted in this danker realism.

Amid random radio transmissions Sergeant Frantz, played by Dylan McDermott, is introduced. In tones of sepia brown and muted green the new recruits make sandbags and reveal that they have no clue as to what is to come. In typical fashion they jabber about girls and boast. They are a disparate group of cherries. Tim Quill introduces himself as Beletsky by showing a picture of his girlfriend to the other new arrivals. Languilli, played by Anthony Barrile, insults the reputation of the young lady in typical locker-room/foxhole banter. The two are restrained from fighting by the others, who know it "means nothing," a phrase and concept that will become profound later. Beletsky's name conveys his Polish background, and "Languilli" grounds us equally in the world of grunt middle-class Italian America. "Motown," McDaniel, Duffy, and others make their appearances and either by name or color convey the melting pot character of the platoon.

Cutting from the sandbagging detail to a bathhouse, sergeants Frantz and Worchester enjoy two beautiful, bare-breasted Vietnamese women. The only females in the film either are prostitutes or are requested to be such by the boys in passing trucks. Conversely the female back home is a vision of Caucasian virtue and source of heartache. The banter in the bathhouse is filled with the jargon of the war.

The steamy bath is replaced by the oppressive heat at the base camp. Beginning a one-year tour of duty, the new arrivals are briefed and instructed to fill out next-of-kin forms. The three blacks already hang out together. They are experienced and bespectacled "Doc," played by Courtney B. Vance; the fresh-faced

Anthony Michael Boatman (later to be a regular on television's "China Beach") as "Motown"; and Dan Jones as McDaniel. Their discussion runs to the black soldiers' lack of opportunity to escape grunt duty.

Orientation continues with a recitation of the various organisms and disease that prey on the American body. Doc snaps to the casual listeners, "Listen to people who know . . . [or] I'll be tagging you." Then Frantz, with the help of a camouflaged Vietnamese man, instructs them on the importance of respect for their enemy, known as "gook-slope-slat-dink-Han." The sergeant mentions that whether they are for or against the war is now irrelevant because here the aim is merely to survive.

In the calm before the storm the young men cavort in the water to the strains of Country Joe and the Fish's "I Feel Like I'm Fixin' to Die Rag." Back in camp a luxurious mobile home rolls by bound for a general up the road. In *The Boys in Company C* a similar mobile home was destined for a claymore mine; here it is just shown already riddled with potshots. Finally the recruits confer nicknames on one another. This is the in-country moment that has inspired so many colorful film monikers. The relaxation, even tedium, is interrupted by incoming artillery. Instantaneously death visits the camp, and nearly as quickly a fire mission quiets the enemy in the bush. The silence is heightened by the stillness of death. The first casualty had his head blown off and remains anonymous.

The first patrol begins as helicopters ferry the new soldiers over the lush mountains. The sweating and silent peer out as the Animals' "We Gotta Get Out of This Place" shares the soundtrack with the mechanized whir of the blades. They jump off and into the bush as the sergeant barks commands. Soon unfamiliar jungle bird noises are punctuated by fire from an unseen enemy. The "short" guy on point, black man McDaniel, is killed. A trail of blood leads to the enemy's abandoned belongings, which include his wife's picture. Later back at camp Doc is furious. Why was the "short guy" on point? Was it because of experience or because he was black? The other blacks calm Doc with the recitation of "It don't mean nothing." This steely chant is beat out hand to fist and man to man. This oft-heard grunt phrase did not deny grief or condemn the war. Rather, it allowed soldiers in combat to not "lose it," for to do so meant to not survive. Sergeant Frantz sits alone and contemplates that one of his men died today. No longer do these soldiers believe that they fight for their country or anticommunism. As Sergeant Frantz says, there are only "you and Third Squad." They are all there is, each man dies for nothing else.

Now the 11 bloody assaults begin, and the date of each of the ten days is imprinted on the screen. The soldiers are advancing up and retreating down the same hill. Torrential rain and the voice of Hanoi Hannah torment them. Her broadcast claims their country has abandoned them as we hear a scream of pain in the background. The enemy is very close, so Sergeant Frantz reminds the men of their safety precautions. Beletsky wonders how he can remember "No half-canteens" (too noisy), "Poncho on head if you smoke" (to help cover the red glow), "Take your pills!" (malaria).

Once again on May 15, 1969, the troops fight their way back up the hill, trying to get a foothold while bullets rain down from the enemy's superior position. Where is the air cover, and what is the purpose? The absurdity is mired in the mud with the exhaustion. The NVA is dug in, so every new foxhole means hand-to-hand combat. When the Americans finally secure a bunker, a helicopter accidentally strafes them. In one horrible instant friendly fire silences the momentarily triumphant. No dialogue accompanies this irony. Rather, a lone helmet topples down the hill from where they came. Torn from the head of a dead man, the helmet suffices as an exclamation point for the scene.

That night Beletsky listens to a tape from his girlfriend. Her voice touches them all. It also provides for the commentary that everyone back home is acting as if nothing is going on in Vietnam. The next day is another assault, and that night the delivery of foot powder and mail does not have the desired morale effect. Sergeant Worchester's girl has dumped him because her college friends have told her that writing to him in Vietnam is immoral. This adds to the sense of futility and the feeling that the troops are unappreciated.

The assault on May 17 is distinguished not by its ferocity but by the appearance of a documentary camera crew. The weary privates have no comment, but Sergeant Frantz tells the reporter that he has no right to be there. If Frantz sees him on top of the hill, he will personally blow the reporter's head off. The scene joins sequences from *Apocalypse Now* and *Full Metal Jacket* in conveying a sense of the press as a voyeur. That night the 101st Airborne Screaming Eagles receive two new replacements. The new men now confirm the status of the others as seasoned veterans.

On rainy May 18 Doc is wounded while tending to a casualty. Beletsky, who months ago seemed a racist, a concept from out there in "the world," treats him. Doc holds on, awaiting medevac as Sergeant Frantz uses his own body to guard Doc from the wind. Black and white they are united, as Doc puts it, "all dumb niggers on this hill." That night as grief and exhaustion engulf the group, there is more discussion of "home." Sergeant Worchester admits he reenlisted because he could not fit in. He tells a story of insensitive college kids calling a mother whose son had died in combat and saying they were glad! Worchester is back, but the ethos of country and anticommunism have been replaced by the camaraderie of the field. The understanding from another grunt cannot be duplicated. The filmmaker uses Senator Kennedy and college as buzzwords for the situation that led to the political betrayal of the soldier in the field. These elements are facile and thus intrusive in the context of the superior physical staging of the agonizing assault.

May 20 is accompanied by the relentless melancholy and onward beat of Phillip Glass's musical score. Will this day bring triumph? That concept is now obscene and irrelevant. More appropriately, gaining the top brings rest and survival, no more or less. On the way a mortar blows off one man's arm and kills another man. The music and imagery blend with the heavy breathing of an anonymous, terrified, blinded man who waits to be evacuated out. The men proceed upward, upward, up the hill. Sergeant Worchester is now a bloody walking corpse who waits to rest in Sergeant Frantz's arms before dying. Motown is killed on pungi sticks, and the number of the men surviving dwindles. Will anyone make it? It is up to Beletsky to get Sergeant Frantz to "buck up" and continue. A hideous assault ensues, and when the smoke clears, Frantz, Beletsky, and Washburn are sitting silently sharing a canteen.

As their hair brushes back in the breeze, we realize they have made it to the top of the hill. The moment is dramatic because it is quiet and unannounced either verbally or musically. One step was still up the hill, and the next was on top. The enemy is vanquished, but there is no triumph. The geography is nondescript, as nebulous as the objective. There are no beautiful vistas from the top and certainly no celebration. If not for the resting and the tears in the men's eyes, we might not even know that this battle is over.

The helicopters clear the smoke away as they join the weary troops at the top. Where they were before is not clarified. A sign reads, "Welcome to Hamburger Hill." The sergeant, the private who has grown up and shown leadership (the next sergeant perhaps?), and the black man take long looks downward from where they came. Tears clear the grime away from the still-boyish face of Beletsky. A postscript reads, "Hamburger Hill was secured on 20 May 1969, the war for hills and trails continued, the places and names forgotten, except by those who were there."

The radio announces one final audible transmission: "Fire mission over." Philip Glass's haunting score begins as a poem slowly scrawls across the screen and then the credits in the tradition of World War II combat films show a brief exposure of each actor's face. Of the 14 featured players, eight are dead, three are wounded, and three have survived and reached the top. The numbers reflect the costliness of the campaign.

Hamburger Hill was directed by John Irvin, and the screenplay was written by Jim Carabatsos. The film was produced by Marcia Nasatir, Larry De Waay, and Carabatsos. The filmmakers represent a group of craftspeople who to differing degrees have had recurring association with the Vietnam War. Carabatsos served in the First Air Cavalry Division. He wrote the screenplay for the 1977 Vietnam vet film *Heroes*. He also wrote the screenplay for *Heartbreak Ridge*, starring Clint Eastwood.

Marcia Nasatir's son served in Vietnam. When she met Carabatsos, he complained, "I want to write the real story about what it was like to be 19 years old and be in Vietnam . . . but nobody wants to listen."[22] Nasatir hired John Irvin as director. He had been in Vietnam in 1969 as a documentary filmmaker for the BBC making a film about other combat photographers. He was able to see firsthand the experiences of the young soldiers and was deeply touched. Irvin stated, "The difference between us was that I was ten years older, and I had a ticket home. The . . . kids were asked to do things beyond anyone's imagination. They bleakly knew they were fulfilling the expectations of their country. . . . I wanted to make a film that would honor the men who fought there."[23]

Hamburger Hill (RKO Pictures, 1987). Survival is the only triumph.

Executive producer David Korda had worked previously at Hemdale, the British company that financed *Platoon*. Like many Vietnam War films, most financing for *Hamburger Hill* was from foreign sources. Fourteen unknown young actors who were composites for characters Carabatsos had served with underwent actual military training at the Subic Bay Naval Base in the Philippines.

Command Sergeant Major Albert Neal, who served three tours of duty in Vietnam including the battle of Hamburger Hill, was the instructor. This type of training was similar to that administered to the cast of *Platoon* and *Full Metal Jacket*. It was becoming a standard way to build camaraderie and evoke the most technically and emotionally correct performances. The technical adviser for the film, retired colonel Joseph B. Convey, Jr., was actually the brigade commander of the 101st Airborne Division at Hamburger Hill.

Hamburger Hill's 11-week shooting schedule required a great deal of cooperation with the U.S. Department of Defense and the Philippine Defense Department. The former provided F-4 fighters and CH-46 helicopters, and the latter gave personnel support. The cooperation was not a major issue as it had been with many other productions. The script was an acceptable match of the filmmakers' logistical needs and the armed forces' image and budget considerations. Physical production problems were substantial. A huge pool was constructed to hold sanitized mud for the battle scenes, thus ensuring the actors' health. The 1,800-foot-high hill required more than 1,000 trees to be planted and a series of five off-camera stairways to be built for access.

The director of photography, Peter Macdonald, had been in charge of the helicopter units on *Rambo*. Special effects coordinator Joe Lombardi had been the first to use napalm in a motion picture as part of *Apocalypse Now*'s production team. He had also worked on *Uncommon Valor*. Additional authenticity and "Vietnam film" experience were provided by technical adviser and actress Kieu Chinh, who had been born in Hanoi. She was a top actress in South Vietnam and appeared in the United States in many film entries in this book. She advised on the authenticity of Vietnamese villages and costumes and interpreted for the extras.

What *Hamburger Hill* conveyed in a fashion often superior to the better-known films is that all that matters is the individual soldier's and his buddies' survival. This film makes greater commentary on the war almost irrelevant. The reduction of the tragedy down to the heroism of the soldiers in the field makes the Vietnam War film more universal to all wars. The tragedy is not the Left's insistence of immorality or lack of mandate or the Right's cry that the press, civilians, bureaucracy, and politicians kept America from winning the war.

As a movie that dramatically portrays the utter futility of a battle, *Hamburger Hill* is reminiscent of World War I vet–turned–filmmaker Lewis Milestone's *Pork Chop Hill* from 1959. In both films as peace talks continue, the soldiers are painfully aware of the imminent cessation of hostilities. They are determined not to be the last battlefield casualties, yet have no choice but to fight on. The battle is only symbolically, not strategically, important as a bargaining chip at the negotiating table.

Contributing to the film's relative obscurity were its lack of stars and the cannibalizing of the gross by other big box office entries. This is a relentless and depressing film and thus was difficult to sell to the public. One final note: shortly after Ap Bia Mountain was secured, it was abandoned as nonstrategic.

Also released in the fall of 1987 was Bill Couterie's *Dear America: Letters Home from Vietnam*. It was to documentaries what *Platoon* and *Hamburger Hill* were to fictional, fact-based films. It told the story of the grunts but this time in their own words using only real footage. The movie added a 1960s rock score to the images and had a who's who of stars read the actual letters of soldiers. Contributing dramatic voices were, among others, Tom Berenger, Willem Dafoe, Robert DeNiro, Matt and Kevin Dillon, Sean Penn, Michael J. Fox, Howard Rollins, Jr., and Martin Sheen.

The movie opens to David Brinkley reporting on the Gulf of Tonkin incident. Then in intimate 16-millimeter home-movie footage young Americans frolic in the surf in the South China Sea. Soon the boys are being joined by ever-increasing numbers of 18- and 19-year-olds. Like this book, *Dear America* juxtaposes concomitant historical events with expressions of fear, gallantry, friendship, confusion, and grief. Thus in 1965 the young men write of opposing communism here rather than letting it reach back home to Kansas. They remark on the beauty of the country and soon learn of its dangers as well. As the casualty rate mounts, television correspondents join with familiar faces, such as that of

William Westmoreland, in discussing the escalating conflict. However, the footage of antiwar protests and the journalists and generals recede in the face of the simple musings of the foot soldiers in dramatic testimony.

At one point a young man provides a glossary of in-country lingo for the uninitiated stateside. At the end of each year the ground force strength and the casualty rate are presented on the screen. But it is the faces and voiceovers that must be seen and heard. When Ellen Burstyn reads the last letter home from a slain young man to his mother, it is heartrending. Like many of the film's poignant moments, the tears of grief and longing are so much more cathartic than the false thrill of combat triumph in the movies. The film ends at the Vietnam veterans memorial in Washington, D.C., and is accompanied by Bruce Springsteen's "Born in the USA," the hit homage to the Vietnam soldier. His musical contribution, like that of all the other performers and actors, was donated to the project, which was coproduced by the Vietnam Veterans Ensemble Theater Company and HBO Productions. The film's proceeds were earmarked for the former group and the New York Vietnam Memorial Commission.

Although a documentary, the film is mentioned here because it received a theatrical run that also serves to illustrate the evolution of the entertainment milieu. The film was intended as one of Home Box Office's productions designed to raise the pay cable service's profile in original programming. *Dear America* was so good that there was pressure to release it to theaters, something filmmaker Couterie wanted. In October the film was released theatrically for one week, thereby qualifying it for the Academy Awards. By the time influential critics such as Roger Ebert and Gene Siskel sang its praises, the audience was hard-pressed to find the film in theaters. The audience then had to wait for the exposure afforded on cable. Several distributors offered a full release, but HBO preferred to keep the property for a small screen premiere. Subsequent to the HBO run, the film went back into an unsuccessful wider theatrical release. The indecision reflected the ongoing fear of the commerciality of such a Vietnam War film. It was difficult to know how to market such a picture, and unfortunately the organizations set to benefit from the film's profits suffered as a result.

Writing in *American Film*, J. Hoberman contextualizes *Dear America* as follows: "The war's casualties included our longstanding sense of national innocence and feeling of invulnerability—not to mention the broad national consensus that had defined American foreign policy since World War II—and the paradox is that Couterie's documentary is the most heavily mythologized grunt ensemble film yet. Historical context dissolves in subjectivity, the war emerging as a no-fault collision whose victims are entirely American. Despite everything, we are a 'dear' people after all. This defusing of blame is a key aspect of the new Vietnam films."[24]

The problem with this analysis is that the tone of most commentary is by definition critical. What the observations reflect is the inevitable relinquishing of polemics that occurred with the end of the war. Inevitably the causal roots are too difficult to dissect, so the healing process coalesces in the abandonment of

Gardens of Stone (Tri-Star Pictures, 1987). James Caan leads the ceremonial unit at Arlington National Cemetery.

all but the human tragedy. Perhaps this is why wars recur, but for generation after generation this is the component that remains relevant and contributes to the much-desired reluctance to commit men and women to arms. One other critical rallying cry is the lack of films from the Vietnam perspective. The following chapter, Chapter 9, includes films from Vietnam; their outlook on the war, because of the overriding human component of lost loved ones, is remarkably similar to Americans'.

When Francis Ford Coppola announced another contribution to the Vietnam films, it was anxiously anticipated. Perhaps it was too much so because *Gardens of Stone* was a quiet disappointment. On the one hand, it fit in with the latest production surge in paying homage to the individual soldier. On the other hand, it was set entirely stateside and out of combat, so it seemed relatively insulated and far removed. Ron Bass wrote the screenplay from Nicholas Proffitt's novel. The Tri-Star Pictures release featured James Caan, Anjelica Huston, James Earl Jones, Dean Stockwell, Mary Stuart Masterson, and D. B. Sweeney.

Like many of the new films, *Gardens of Stone* is set in 1968. As the year of Tet that time was a turning point from the early years' innocence but was still prior to the American deescalation via the 1970s "Vietnamization" program. In a fitting monument to the soldier and in a place that typifies the continuity of the sacrifices of the United States armed forces, the movie is set in the most famous garden of stone, Arlington National Cemetery. It tells the tale of the "Old Guard," which provides the ceremonial burials and pomp and circumstance for our fallen soldiers. It is a proud military tradition that seems far removed from the carnage in Asia that provides the newly arrived bodies.

James Caan is the decorated sergeant who runs the guard at this hallowed place. He wrestles with a sense that his time has passed and that the current war belongs to another, younger generation. However, as his beloved corpsmen fight in a seemingly dubious enterprise, he feels that perhaps his place is with them. "We're toy soldiers," one member of the detail remarks.

Gradually a naturally evoked romance develops between the thoughtful soldier and an antiwar *Washington Post* correspondent, played by Huston. Their long talks provide an opportunity for a window on the current conflict. Frequent television broadcasts in the background provide additional grounding in current events. At a cocktail party a drunken liberal insults the handsome, uniformed Caan, who is minding his own business.

Meanwhile a young man whose father served with Caan in Korea is assigned to the detail. He is a likable kid who desperately wants to see combat duty. Caan and officer James Earl Jones understand the youngster's hankering for the real thing; in fact they share it. However, as they suspect this is a compromised effort, they are torn by their paternal sense of protection. Ultimately they know they cannot stand in his way. When Sweeney ships out, he leaves his beautiful and thoughtful newlywed bride, Masterson, stateside. She, too, was an army brat, once considered off limits to the NCO's son as she is the daughter of a high-ranking officer. This is one more subtle aspect of the film's constant sense of military tradition and continuity.

With its quiet characterizations the film provides a small and interesting humanist snapshot of the greater conflict. The inevitability of the tragedy is never in doubt. The film is as understated as *Apocalypse Now* was blown out.

Quiet was not the operable word for the loud comedic tour de force unleashed by Robin Williams in the Christmas 1987 release *Good Morning, Vietnam*. The film, set in Saigon, is loosely based on the story of grunt-beloved Armed Forces Radio morning disc jockey Adrian Cronauer. Barry Levinson directed from Mitch Markowitz's script. Forrest Whitaker costarred as a private assigned as driver and escort for Cronauer. Bruno Kirby was hilarious as a tight, by-the-book lieutenant. *Time* magazine called the film the "best military comedy since *M*A*S*H*." *Newsweek* said this film was about "comedy and culture, not body counts and bloodshed." Director Levinson explained that "we've already seen the combat stuff in *Platoon* and *Full Metal Jacket* . . . so I wanted to give a sense of what it was like in 1965. This movie is on the train tracks heading for the wreck."

The movie begins with the sugary innocence of "Around the World in Eighty Days" instrumental music, which would eventually seem so out of place in the rock-and-roll chaos of Vietnam. Deejay Williams arrives with a burgeoning American contingency. As he deplanes he is blinded by the intense sun of Southeast Asia and captivated by the beautiful women and landscapes. The strains of Montevani and boring public service announcements clog the airwaves of Armed Forces Radio. The new arrival is full of quips and steals the show, reducing it to a stand-up act when he gets behind the microphone. He is

Good Morning, Vietnam **(Touchstone Pictures, 1988). Robin Williams as deejay Adrian Cronauer entertains the troops.**

hilarious and has a good beat. The grunts depicted in cutaways to the bush truly enjoy him. However, the officers and military censors are terrified of such irreverence. As in *M*A*S*H,* all those who extol army protocol are constipated jerks, and the hip, funny types unite with the lowly soldier in the field just trying to have a good time and survive.

The on-air performances of Williams are hilarious manic-comedic jags. One example reserved for an officer who berates him to tone his show down is this rapid-fire mockery of military jargon: "Excuse me, sir, seeing as the VP is such a VIP, shouldn't we keep the PC on the QT cause if it leaks to the VC he could end up an MIA, then we'd all be on KP?" Cronauer's choice of once-taboo rock and roll is also a welcome departure from Pat Boone and the "Polka Hour." However, when the film attempts to reground itself in the war, it suffers from a shifting tone that has been difficult for all comedies about this unfunny war.

Williams is attracted to a young Vietnamese girl from a fine family and thus off limits to the perpetually horny GIs. Her protective brother forms a friendship with Williams, and the deejay learns firsthand about the native culture. In a bar frequented by soldiers the young boy is insulted, and Williams and his fellow deejays must take on a contingency of neanderthal-type racist soldiers. In an instance of clashing cultures, Williams takes the girls and her entire entourage of chaperones to the theater to see *Beach Blanket Bingo* with Vietnamese subtitles. Everything about the American presence is bloated and absurd. Using the omniscience of fictional hindsight, the ultrahip Williams must fight a reality-inducing melancholy to maintain his manic effervescence. The soundtrack is extremely entertaining but becomes way too heavy-handed when Louis Armstrong's evocative "What a Wonderful World" is played over a montage of ugly Saigon carnage, including the roundup and summary execution of suspected VC and riots in the streets. Like the Place Garnier sabotage and other instances depicted way back in *The Quiet American,* when the American hangout is bombed and many innocent civilians die, the war has gotten very close. Covered with blood, the hero reads censored material on the air and is booted off the station. An understanding general tells the kowtowing subordinates to get the greeting "Gooooooooooood Morning Vietnam" back on the air because the soldiers in the field love it and that's good for morale.

The suspended deejay takes a ride out of town and observes the beauty of the countryside and the Buddhist shrines. Back in Saigon in a traffic jam the loyal private tells Cronauer that he must return to the station, but the frustrated deejay refuses. Much to his chagrin, Whitaker introduces the famous character to the boys in the transport trucks adjacent to their jeep. They egg him on, and he finally launches into an impromptu show. They love it, and their carefully studied, joyous young faces move the audience and the hero. He knows what his wartime duty is and returns to the station. A tragic subplot develops concerning the young friend who, despite his seemingly youthful innocence, is indeed Viet Cong. Finally like all the other American soldiers, Cronauer's tour of duty is up, and he returns to the United States with the final salute "Gooooooooooood-bye Vietnam!"

The film was shot in Thailand for a mere $13 million. The entire war prop inventory was six trucks, three helicopters, and one plane. The rest took place mostly in the radio station studio, and Williams poured out his hilarious patter in just seven days of filming. The director maintained the anarchistic exuberance of the star and echoed the chaotic ambience of a degenerating situation by using constantly moving multiple cameras. The film is thus visually and audibly exciting at all times. A great contributor to the latter strength was the 33 musical tracks credited at the end.

Ultimately Williams is so hip and hilarious that the film becomes a comedic crowd pleaser that happens to have a Vietnam background. This tangentiality probably allowed the film eventually to gross $124 million and to garner Williams a Best Actor nomination.

For years Hollywood had resisted making the movie because of uneasiness about its setting and delicate balancing act. Real-life deejay Cronauer said the film was best in depicting how Saigon went from a "sleepy little French colonial town . . . to a nightmare."[25] His continuing story is supposed to be chronicled in a sequel still in preproduction entitled *Good Morning Chicago.*

The production pendulum had swung to a lack of Vietnam films following the surge represented by the four horsemen and the apocalypse. However, as the next chapter, which covers the years 1988 through 1990, will demonstrate, no such downturn accompanied the plethora of films appearing in this chapter. *Good Morning, Vietnam* went into wide release along with several major productions, many B films, and several weekly television shows about the war. Vietnam was no longer necessarily a box office gamble. The passage of time had finally blunted some of the pain, and the grunt films had looked at the war as directly as they could, from the ground level. The soldier was a sentimental hero once again in films, and he, like the country itself, would somehow survive the trauma. The continuing number of films about the Vietnam War confirmed that it could not and would not be relegated to cultural limbo.

References

1. Peter Blauner, "Coming Home," *New York Magazine*, December 8, 1986, p. 64.
2. Marc Cooper, "Oliver Stone Interview," *Playboy* 35 (February 1988), p. 51.
3. Oliver Stone, Address to the National Press Club, Washington, D.C., April 7, 1987.
4. Blauner, "Coming Home," p. 64.
5. Oliver Stone and Richard Boyle, *Platoon and Salvador Screenplay* (New York: Vintage Books, 1987), p. 250.
6. Blauner, "Coming Home," p. 66.
7. Cooper, "Oliver Stone Interview," p. 61.
8. Pat McGilligan, "Stone's Throw," *Film Comment* 23, 1 (February 1987), p. 18.
9. *Ibid.*, p. 20
10. Stone and Boyle, *Platoon and Salvador Screenplay*, p. 251.
11. "Cameos," *Premiere* (January 1990), p. 44.
12. John Simon, "Film Reviews," *National Review* (March 13, 1987), p. 54.
13. See "War Ripens Military Pic Prospects," *Daily Variety*, March 5, 1991, p. 45.
14. "*Platoon*: Vietnam as It Really Was," *Time*, January 26, 1987, p. 56.
15. "Movie Reviews," *Mademoiselle* (April 1987), p. 96.
16. "Horizons," *U.S. News and World Report*, February 2, 1987, p. 59.
17. "Films," *World Press Review* (May 1987), p. 59.
18. "Behind the Scenes," *American Film* (June 1987), pp. 11–12.
19. Gustav Hasford, *The Short Timers* (New York: Harper and Row, 1979).
20. Michael Herr, "Foreword," *Full Metal Jacket Screenplay* (New York: Knopf, 1987).
21. For more information, see Samuel Zaffiri, *Hamburger Hill* (Novato, Calif.: Presidio Press, 1988).
22. Paramount Pictures, "Hamburger Hill," *Handbook of Production Information* (Los Angeles: Paramount Pictures, 1987), p. 2.
23. *Ibid.*, p. 3.
24. J. Hoberman, "America Dearest," *American Film* (May 1988), p. 45.
25. "Black Humor Goes to War," *Newsweek*, January 4, 1988, pp. 50–51.

Chapter 9

Born Again, 1988–1989

This chapter covers the films that were released in 1988 and 1989. The continuity of the subgenres was maintained, but there was a shift in the new movies from the ensemble casts discussed in the previous chapter to greater star power. Such casting was meant to continue vivifying the box office now that spectacle and action had been reintroduced.

To be born again, one must have died at least figuratively. Certainly the nation's collective psyche and institutions had nearly succumbed in the debacle of Vietnam and Watergate. The death of young people and innocence was seriously examined in Chapter 5 and then in Chapter 8. Recovery took on a vengeful catharsis, as demonstrated in Chapter 7. Now the rebirth had matured, rendered with more drama and less adventure. In addition television would begin the first weekly series set in-country rather than just featuring vet characters. These shows would help genericize the Vietnam experience into the realm of a bittersweet 1960s that were now long ago and far away.

Concomitant to these changes were the real-world events that underscored the death and rebirth theme. Of preeminent importance were the unraveling and eventual dissolution of European-based communism. America's post–World War II foreign policy had been based on a containment of this global threat. By the end of the 1980s that ideology was collapsing with great alacrity. The death of one enemy necessitated the birth of another. Asian enemies began to be replaced in films with Arab villains. The PLO terrorists of the 1970s, the Iranian hostage takers, Moammar El Khaddafy, and eventually Saddam Hussein all contributed to the American identification of Arab, not communist, villains as the number one threat to the United States' interests.

Several films discussed in this chapter, and the Vietnam Film Project, attempted to humanize our old Vietnam War foe. Some observers thought this exemplified the maturation of the imagery. The antecedent was addressed by former Agence France press correspondent Lawrence MacDonald when he wrote, "Hollywood has supplied the American imagination with two types of Vietnamese: enemies and victims. . . . Unlike the American stars, the Vietnamese extras have no names, no past, no future. . . . The cameras pan the devastation just long enough to prove the American protagonist's victory or motive his subsequent guilt."[1]

Oliver Stone answered this type of criticism by stating, "I did *Platoon* the way I lived it. I did a white infantry boy's view of the war."[2] Ultimately this chapter's designation is merely an echo of the title of Stone's preeminent *Born on the Fourth of July*. Ron Kovic collaborated with Stone on the screenplay, which was full of loss and death, recovery and rebirth.

It is the notion of the abandonment of our ethnocentric perspective that acts as a segue to a body of work that by virtue of its exhibition in the United States connotes the open-mindedness that leads to rebirth. This attempt to communicate with a former enemy is the first step to rapprochement and signals renewed emotional vigor and the healing that accompanies the passage of time. The Vietnam Film Project was a series that traveled throughout the United States featuring movies about the war made in Vietnam. Ultimately the films proved most fascinating not because of the differences they illustrated but because of the similarities shared with American movies. In an evocation of the human tragedy of the war, these films are universal.

In 1986 the Toronto Film Festival had featured a series about the emerging cinema of Southeast Asia, including one Vietnamese entry, *Karma*, directed by Quang Minh. It told from a South Vietnamese point of view about the loss of traditional cultural values in the war and the onslaught of a huge American presence. A young woman is forced to become a "B-girl" after her fiancé is killed. By the time the English-subtitled, Vietnamese-language films began their tour, all the entries were from the North or from the post-unification South studios.

Reflecting increased contacts between the former combatants, three members of the Hanoi filmmaking community were allowed to travel on visas from the U.S. State Department to the Hawaii International Film Festival in 1988. For five evenings at the fitting venue of the Pearl Harbor Memorial Theater, Vietnamese films were shown. Then there was a symposium with the director, the founder of the Vietnam Cinema Department, and the drama critic who had at one time headed a government censorship committee. This cultural dialogue is typical of the type of communication that begins a process that evolves into economic and political arenas. The audiences were struck by the lyricism and beauty of the black-and-white films, which, despite minuscule budgets, conveyed compelling stories. Nevertheless, distrust and controversy existed below the surface of this exchange. In covering the event, *Film Comment* likened it to "group therapy."[3] Americans were amused or insulted by the fact that they were portrayed as bumbling and obnoxious and, worst of all, were played by Asian actors. There were some fascinating moments in the dialogue, including the first night when a veteran proclaimed himself "reborn" and presented a written apology to the delegation signed by a number of vets.

In public discussions outside the venue, some veterans groups and members of the Southeast Asian immigrant population took exception to what they viewed as a platform for communist propaganda. When the festival went on the road, it was portions of the South Vietnamese expatriate community that showed the greatest hatred for the North Vietnamese representatives and their work.

Jeff Gilmore of the UCLA Film and Television Archives curated the 18-month tour originally set for 25 U.S. cities. Following Honolulu was the Los Angeles show, which brought out demonstrators who dubbed the festival "KGB approved."[4] The UCLA Archives received two bomb threats. The controversy associated with anything about Vietnam and the entire group of films, American or foreign, continued in New York, Boston, and Minneapolis. Nevertheless, it was the dialectic itself that was of importance.

About 70 films had come out of the government-sponsored Ho Chi Minh City Film Company since 1975, with even more produced for years out of Hanoi. These were government-sponsored projects that rarely exceeded a $500,000 budget. Local curators usually ran seven films plus a panel discussion for their exhibitions.

Predating the U.S. withdrawal from Vietnam was the Hanoi production of a documentary entitled *Victory at Dien Bien Phu*, originally made in 1964 and updated with new footage in 1974, the twentieth anniversary of the triumph over the French. The old newsreel stock is fascinating and easy to follow given the conventions of the medium, such as maps, footage of rallies, combat sequences, and rousing patriotic music. Closeups are used to show affection for the avuncular Ho Chi Minh and to personify the evil of the French generals. Historically the inclusion of the new anti–American footage makes for the type of continuity from the Vietnamese perspective that a film such as *Go Tell the Spartans* tried to allude to in a fictional American context.

Desert Field (aka *The Abandoned Field—Free Fire Zone*) was made in 1979 by Nguyen Hong Sen, one of the most successful Vietnamese directors. It had won the top prize at the Moscow Film Festival. A peasant, his wife, and their baby live on the Mekong River shortly before the Tet Offensive. They are indeed Viet Cong and are constantly fired upon by American helicopter gunships searching for guerrillas. The sophisticated weaponry stands in marked contrast to the simple lifestyle of the family. Like the vision of the communists in Sam Fuller's *China Gate*, the American pilots are shown here as drunken, undisciplined, and frustrated. The helicopters become characters themselves in the film, "endowed with an abstract and institutional evil."[5] However, the humanity of the Americans is underscored when we see a dead pilot's picture of his wife and son.

Surname Viet, Given Name Nam was produced in the United States by Vietnam-born Trinh T. Minh-ha. It weaves documentary, drama, and folk poetry into a study of Vietnamese women and American attitudes toward them. *Brothers and Relations* was directed by Tran Vu and Nhuyen Huu Luyen. It is an indictment of those who are prepared to forget the war and the sacrifice of the veterans, who, like their American counterparts, are unappreciated and cannot find employment. The similarity with the serious A film treatments of the vets such as *Coming Home* is joined by a parallel with such flicks as *Tracks* and *The Hard Ride* when a vet is asked to escort a fallen comrade's body for reinternment in the North. The same postwar period was covered in the 1986 release *A Quiet Little Town*, directed by Le Duc Tien. It is interesting that these films were allowed to be made, which reflects a liberalization of government policy as this satire is an indictment of the bureaucracy.

Like many an American coming-of-age film, *Fairy Tale for 17-Year-Olds*, directed by Nhuyen Xuan Son, is antiwar in its depiction of lost innocence and the gung-hoism that sends young people off to die. Two teens just out of high school flirt, while in the background railroad cars loaded with tanks churn toward the front. In the tradition of Asian cinema romance, the music is syrupy and the young lovers are very beautiful. One night the girl goes out to view her beloved's picture in the moonlight. In silhouette she pulls out a slingshot, and surrealistically a tree limb falls into the water, causing it to ripple and glisten. To use the familiar Judeo-Christian legend, is the primitive weapon of David meant to signify Vietnam at war with Goliath? Scenes at the front are interspersed with an allusion to the continuity of sacrifice and strife in this nation. The young girl's father is a proud veteran. Eventually the attractive young woman, unsure of her lover's fate, is tempted by another man. As he, too, departs for the war, a photographer gaily snaps pictures. Other scenes echo similar themes and moments in American films, such as the progress of the war being injected via radio reports. An image of a beautiful waterfall tainted by clothes or toilet paper floating by not only alludes to the dichotomy of the country so often identified but also foreshadows the bandages of the war's wounded returnees. The film ends with the triumph over the U.S. imperialists. However, the joy of the protagonists is tempered by their reverence for their ancestors.

A blend of the ancient traditions of the Vietnamese society with the present is featured in the poetic *When the Tenth Month Comes*, directed by Danh Nhat Minh in 1984. This black-and-white film opens to an image of the beauty of the countryside. Flute music introduces the beautiful actress Le Van as she is ferried across a river. She reads a letter informing her that her husband has been killed in action. The camera mimics her disorientation as she reels in grief. Barely able to disembark from the boat, she is immediately confronted by a little boy pointing a toy gun at her. The allusions to the tragic continuity of warfare are forward looking here and backward looking in later references to French, Chinese, and other invaders. She is unable to tell her in-laws of the tragedy and enlists the help of a kindly male schoolteacher to continue writing letters as if they were from her husband. His beloved parents hang on every word each time the mail arrives. The teacher is smitten by the beautiful widow and expresses his love through the words of the deceased husband he mimics.

The love of the extended family is conveyed in the native tongue in a manner that makes the American viewer take notice. We are conditioned by *The Deerhunter* and other films to think of the Vietnamese language as ugly, with quickly clicking phrases shouted in anger or commands or bastardized with pidgin English. Here the language is lyrical, soft, and comforting. The contradictions within the native film industry is underscored by the fact that the beautiful cinematography is compromised by the obtrusive use of zooms and other overt camera movements. This is the result of single camera usage as opposed to a battery of high-tech filmmaking equipment. Like the European cinema, the takes tend to be longer and linger without dialogue on the facial expressions.

The neighbors and parents continually ask when their son will receive liberty and return home. His wife suffers alone, trapped in her lie and unwilling to acknowledge the affection of her teacher accomplice. Other characters include a sister-in-law, who remarried a wounded vet after her husband was killed at Quang Tri. Adorable children and loving grandparents evoke the richness of the family experience in this small town. Shots of a hat floating on the water or of a woman flying a kite allow the movie to soar to its poetic destiny. The widow is granted her wish of being able to see her beloved one more time at a Buddhist festival that celebrates such moments in time between kindred souls. Implicit is the realization that being allowed to say good-bye will allow her to get on with her life. By the time the reunion takes place, the enraptured viewer has completely forgotten the race or nationality of the characters or of the film.

Not part of the Vietnam Film Project but also screened in the United States were several other films. Le Hoang Hoa directed a series that follows the exploits of a communist agent in South Vietnam in the 1960s. This is the flip side of *Operation CIA*. The 1988 release *Girl on the River* told the tale of a prostitute who saves a Communist Party official wounded in a firefight. After the war he refuses to acknowlege her bravery. This film by Tran Van Thuy was very controversial as it not only showed the villainy of the Communist Party member but also featured nudity. Its filmmaker has not been granted a work permit by the Hanoi government since that effort.[6]

Prodigious Nguyen Hong Sen made the very humanistic *Left Alone,* juxtaposing the struggle of a wounded American pilot with those of a Montagnard woman and child whose village was bombed. Here suffering is universalized. Sen's latest film is, with a sense of rebirth, entitled *The Refrain of Hope*.[7]

At the same time the Vietnamese films were making their controversial rounds, the American industry continued with its images of the war. In 1988 20th Century–Fox released *Off Limits*, starring Gregory Hines and Willem Dafoe as military police investigators in Saigon. Basically this was a police buddy tale directed by Christopher Crowe, the cowriter with Jack Thibeau. Fred Ward, Scott Glenn, and Amanda Pays costarred.

The sordid metropolis is, as Hines summarizes, "the cesspool of the world." Far from saving the indigenous populace, the Americans are killing allies and corrupting their culture. Others urge the investigators to forget about the murder of a prostitute because no one cares. The images of American cultural hegemony hinted at with the mobile homes and cavorting playmates in earlier film entries now has degenerated even further. As the partners go on their rounds, they encounter drug sales among the locals carried on in clipped pidgin English. Young women are destined for prostitution or stripteasing to the strains of American rock and roll. Using familiar but irrelevant buzzwords such as "Khe Sanh," the filmmakers try to ground this generic story in Vietnam, but it remains merely background locale.

Off Limits (20th Century–Fox, 1987). Gregory Hines and Willem Dafoe are MPs in Saigon, 1968.

A chaste love affair develops between Dafoe and a gorgeous nun, and somehow the doomed and asexual relationship echoes the entire war effort. The street scenes, including a huge urban riot, are well staged. That the serial killer is a high-level U.S. Army officer comes as no surprise. The South Vietnamese police, like many a filmic counterpart in the ARVN, are unmotivated or corrupt. The goodness of the hard-boiled detectives is underscored by their tenacity in continuing the investigation despite official pressure. Their competitive spirit and support of each other make them more, not less, determined. Their motivation is to do something that will have meaning and resolution in the midst of an overall effort that lacks such qualities or conditions.

Off Limits was a major studio attempt to repeat the success of the stateside vets–turned–buddy cops adventure *Lethal Weapon*. However, a tawdry nature, in-country setting, and lack of humor doomed *Off Limits* to mediocre box office. Without pretension but as always totally derivative were the made-for-video flicks released in 1988. Several had themes similar to *Off Limits*. Richard Young starred in *Saigon Commandos* as a military police officer who battles corrupt politicians and drug dealers in the lawless city. Clark Henderson directed, with P. J. Soles costarring.

Drug dealing and black-marketeers were the subject of Cirio Santiago's sequel *Eye of the Eagle II*. The corruption endemic to the South Vietnamese government officials and U.S. hierarchy was again confronted by the lowly soldier fighting a virtuous but losing battle. This Philippine-lensed feature made good use of the seamy side of Manila to recreate the bars and brothels of Saigon. It begins in the bush with pungi sticks, chaotic firefights, fraggings, heroin addiction, and convoluted justifications for the nudity of comely Asian women. It is as if a checklist of the ills of the U.S. war effort has now been prescribed for every B movie. Uncovering the drug ring, the hero becomes a fugitive. With his old unit's help, the decorated corporal and his local woman escape to Thailand. There he is pursued by an evil American major who, instead of a uniform, wears a white suit and carries a gold club. Asian thugs and French hanger-ons join the climactic chase, and the good guy triumphs because the film has reached the point where it qualifies as a full-length feature.

Ripping off the winning formula of Robert Aldrich's *The Dirty Dozen*, which had already been Vietnamized in *The Losers*, was *The Expendables*. Anthony Finetti starred in this tale of a commando team captain who leads a band of misfits on a mission to rescue nurses held by a Viet Cong colonel. The women in peril were the descendants of the victimized in *Five Gates to Hell* (see Chapter 1). Further exploiting the concept of nurses in peril was 1988's *Charlie Bravo*, a cheapie release from Star Classics Video. It is available for less than ten dollars, wherever bad videos are sold. A woman in peril was the motivator for mayhem in *No Retreat No Surrender II*, the sequel to the 1985 film. A martial arts master ventures to Cambodia to save his Vietnamese fiancée, who has been kidnapped by the Soviets and their Asian henchmen. Loren Avedon starred in this hodgepodge of clichés integrated into the chopsocky format. Corey Yuen directed this Hong Kong–financed film shot in Bangkok, where it begins. (Incidentally the mayhem connoted in the term joining "chop suey" and "sock" can be given a Japanese-based spelling in its alternative form, "chopsaki.")

Crossfire, directed by Anthony Maharaj, featured a six-person squad sent to save MIAs, not women. Their clandestine mission would be disavowed by the government if it were revealed. *Mercenary Fighters* took a ragtag band of veterans of the Vietnam War and transplanted them to Latin America, the new front line against communism. The cast was a cut above the usual fodder, featuring Ron O'Neal, Peter Fonda, and Reb Brown. In *Private War* Andy Warhol's leading man Joe Dallesandro starred as Sergeant Ryker (rather close to John Wayne's Sergeant Stryker of *The Sands of Iwo Jima* fame). He returned from his tour of duty a psycho and now wreaks havoc as a drill instructor.

Video Treasures released *Chopper Wars*, starring Richard Lynch, a film that blended documentary footage with re-creations and voiceover narration. Thus it was typical of the minuscule-budget features that appealed to a niche audience that loved war documentaries, aviation videos, military programs, and so forth. Distributors reported that it was a brisk seller and kept rackjobbers busy despite having no illusions to even a token theatrical release. The sequence on "Recon by Fire" is compelling as it shows the dangerous maneuver in which choppers fly in low and draw Viet Cong fire so that jets can then pulverize the enemy. With video as an important source of revenue to the film studios, the lines were blurred on the programming continuum. Some films received small theatrical releases before becoming video titles, and others were designed directly for the video sell-through market.

The made-for-television features had also become sources of tape cassettes. Broadcast for the previous calendar year, *In Love and War* was such a release. Despite a stellar cast including James Woods, Jane Alexander, and Haing S. Ngor, this Paul Aaron–directed feature was rather flat. It is the adaptation of navy commander James Stockdale's story of his eight years as a POW often subjected to brutal torture. His perseverance is juxtaposed with that of his brave wife back home, who acts an organizer for the POW wives. By adding the captive's firsthand account with that of his spouse, some of the conditions that could only be surmised back in the war-concomitant 1972 production *Limbo* are dramatized as well. (Stockdale was Ross Perot's running mate in their 1992 independent bid for the White House.)

"The television war" was about to provide fictionalized in-country images in prime time. The pilots for these series as well as expanded year-ending shows and the editing together of several episodes provided the requisite program length to justify release on video. The features that resulted are only of marginal importance in the collection; much more significant is the fact that television execs now viewed their far-reaching medium as ripe for tales set in Vietnam. The perception that Vietnam was too depressing or box office poison was ending. *Platoon* and *Full Metal Jacket*'s performance was the impetus for the networks to spring into action.

First out of the block was cable network HBO with *Vietnam War Story,* a trio of half-hour in-country tales. Because the cablers were not bound by the same rules of censorship as the broadcasters, they utilized rough language and graphic violence. For instance, a black grunt on the way to a Qui Nhon brothel exclaims to a reporter, "Gonna get laid!" and then is briefly shown doing so.[8] When the soldier stays too long, he is shocked to realize that at night the patrons of this same establishment are the Viet Cong. The second segment features a "Twilight Zone"–type dilemma in which a grunt steps on a pressure mind and cannot move for fear it will explode. He must endure for hours in the intense heat. The last segment concerns maimed vets who learn to survive with the help of their teacher, a fellow amputee. The executive producer of the show was Georg Stanford Brown, who noted that the anthology format provided great freedom. "Since we don't have to stick with the same characters, we can explore Vietnam's full scope. . . . Every veteran fought in a different war. There are as many Vietnam realities as there were warriors."[9] Initially broadcast in August of 1987, the episodes were packaged as a videotape anthology. A second and third trio followed the same pattern, and by 1989 there were cassettes titled *Vietnam War Story I, II,* and *III.*

Also premiering on television in 1987, followed by feature-length video versions, was the CBS series "Tour of Duty." This tale of a platoon of grunts starred Terence Knox and was produced by Zev Braun. The stock characters included a soul brother from Detroit, a cracker from the South, a Bronx Hispanic gang

Braddock: Missing in Action III (Media Home Entertainment, 1988). **Chuck Norris returns to Vietnam for his Amerasian son.**

member, and so on. Ratings and standards and practices precluded obscenity and also acted to soften the stories, thereby eliminating the theatrically in-vogue clichés of drug use, fragging, and so on. What evolved was a "Combat"-type weekly story that happened to be set in Vietnam. One episode was presented from the point of view of the Viet Cong. This humanizing of the enemy was indeed controversial.

The pilot for the series entitled *Hard Rain—The Tet 1968* found its way into the video stores. Director Bill Norton set the stage once again by utilizing this event as a line of demarcation. Set in Saigon, the film juxtaposes the South's preparation for a truce and New Year's celebration with the VC's preparation for the ruthless onslaught.

From the time of the pilot to the end of the show's two-year tour of duty, it had greatly improved. Cynicism, grit, and realism had joined with action tales to make for compelling drama. The last five shows featured Lee Majors as a hardened vet who joined in this tale of a mission to rescue POWs. It opens a helicopter assault enhanced with Rolling Stones music. Then it shifts to mission preparation accompanied by Creedence Clearwater Revival. Via the many in-country theatrical features, the jargon of the war and the peculiarities of pungi sticks and intervals between grunts on patrol are now readily accessible even to the youngest viewers. The plot recycles the failed Son Tay raid where the POWs have already been moved. Here the brass are no longer the conventional uncaring or corrupt officers. When the film flashes forward, each of the characters is visited. Their success in readjustment to civilian life varies. The same closing of the circle was to be utilized in the finale of the acclaimed Vietnam war series "China Beach," which also spawned a number of cassette releases yet to come.

Returning to theatrical movie releases was the 1988 sequel for Chuck Norris as the colonel in *Braddock: Missing in Action III*. His brother Aaron directed this Cannon medium-budget actioner, which costarred Aki Aleong. The film begins with a well-staged evocation of the fall of Saigon. Norris believes his wife has been killed in an artillery attack on their apartment. As he shepherds desperate souls into helicopters on the roof of the embassy, his Asian wife tries in vain to enter the compound. Flashing forward some dozen years to the present, a missionary priest visits the colonel and tells him of evidence that his wife is still alive. He largely dismisses this as absurd but does make a few inquiries. Only when the CIA vigorously denies the tale does he then start to believe it. This one-person army returns to North Vietnam to search for his wife and the Amerasian son he has never seen.

Eventually with the help of the priest, who runs an orphanage, Norris locates his family amid the squalor of Ho Chi Minh City. Their reunion is short-lived as a sadistic Vietnamese colonel executes the woman. He then subjects Norris and his son to torture. When Norris effectuates his inevitable escape, he wreaks havoc on the enemy. Then like the Pied Piper, he leads a ragtag band of Amerasian children to the border. The kindly priest and Norris's son aid this superhuman effort. With joy the man of God and the long-suffering innocent boy both idolize the man of action.

The continued use of POWs, wives, or kids trapped in Asia seemed to connote a longing or sense that Americans had left something over there. Being able to identify and find "it" was a comforting psychological balm for the intangibles that in reality could never be retrieved, such as youth, innocence, goodness, health, and, for some, life itself.

For Memorial Day weekend Tri-Star released the Carolco-funded feature *Rambo III*, directed by Peter MacDonald. Coscripter (with Sheldon Lettich) Sylvester Stallone returned as the Vietnam vet, and Richard Crenna reprised his role as Trautman, Rambo's former superior. Shot in Thailand and Israel, the latter was a magnificent stand-in for the stark mountainous topography of Afghanistan. The film is an important transitional document in the list of films. It begins as Rambo tries hard to put his Vietnam past behind him. Reflecting a newfound spirituality and desire for inner peace, he resides in a Buddhist monastery near Bangkok. Trautman comes to see him concerning a mission into Afghanistan against the Soviet communists. The colonel urges Rambo to come to terms with who he is not through denial but through acceptance and to realize that "his war" is now long over.

As usual the unctuous local American diplomat reminds Rambo that if he is captured, his very existence will be denied. The skeptical vet mutters, "I'm used to it" and declines the offer. Trautman respects his friend's wishes and goes on the mission with the brave mujahadeen guerrillas. He is promptly captured by the Soviets and subjected to torture. The communists are ruthless to the

Rambo III (Tri-Star Pictures, 1988). Stallone (right) as Rambo and his beloved colonel from the old Vietnam days, played by Richard Crenna.

indigenous populace as well. They terrorize with helicopter gunships, employ chemical weapons, and disguise explosives as toys. Their genocidal campaign merely emboldens the fierce resistance to this newest in a long line of unsuccessful invaders. The notion that Afghanistan is the Soviet Union's Vietnam is both implicitly and explicitly stated.

Rambo must abandon his peaceful existence and rescue his friend since officialdom is incapable. What ensues is a big-budget adventure filled with action and excitement. Once again the muscular Special Forces veteran finds aid from brave locals, but ultimately is the prototypical lone warrior. He combines the iconography of the frontier sheriff who fights injustice with attributes (long black hair, bow and arrow, stealth) associated with the other player in the classic western, the Native American. The filmmakers manage to top the scene in the last installment when Rambo sewed his own wound. This time he pushes an arrow through the other side of his body, pours gunpowder into the gaping hole, and lights it. Fire explodes through the wound, cauterizing it in one painful burst.

The comrades from Vietnam—the colonel and the warrior—bid farewell to the brave Afghan resistance fighters and drive off into the sunset. Here the Arabs are allies fighting the communists; in fact the film is dedicated to them. By the time the feature reached video release, ironically it contained a trailer for the theatrical debut of *Iron Eagle II*. That feature showed the United States and Soviet Union cooperating in a joint maneuver against an Arab foe.

Stallone attempted to summarize his character's development: "In *Rambo III*, he learns he has a cause to live for. He purposefully seeks out his . . .

challenge, not so much because he wants to fight but because he must do it for himself. Rambo realizes . . . he is what he is."[10] Like his character, the successful actor-filmmaker has difficulty articulating the notion that, like any country, people are the sum of their experiences. Despite grossing well, this third installment did not come close to the take of the previous entry and lacked the perfect timing of its predecessor. Nevertheless, Stallone confirms that he and the producers are working on a script for a new adventure, presumably *Rambo IV.*[11]

Reflecting a subtle concern that perhaps the Hollywood action heroes were getting a bit old was the introduction of new leading men in the next two features. Steven Seagal wrote and produced his starring vehicle *Above the Law.* Andrew Davis directed costars Pam Grier and Henry Silva. Real-life aikido black belt Seagal portrays a Chicago police officer who continues the shift for veteran characters from outlaws to law officers. Their in-country service and training now serve them under fire in the United States. During the credits, newsreel footage of the Chicago riots and Richard Nixon connote the late–1960s era. Then the film begins in 1973 at the Vietnam-Cambodia border, where Seagal, a young CIA recruit, awaits the arrival of his fellow operatives. Silva and some Special Forces types begin the interrogation of prisoners. Seagal is horrified at Silva's brutality and confused about his questions concerning opium. Finally the young man shouts, "Are you soldiers or barbarians?" He and Silva stab at each other, and only the intervention of Seagal's friend saves the naive soldier from the agents.

Real world reports persist that the CIA involved itself in the drug trade out of the Iron Triangle in order to fund some of its covert operations. As yet another example of an immoral exercise of government power in the context of this dirty war, the story has resurfaced many times and is depicted in several films. After this prologue *Above the Law* flashes to present-day Chicago, where the old nemesis resurfaces to ply his narcotics trade until Seagal can exact justice. An analogous air of "in-country" and "back in the world" hierarchical corruption to the detriment of the foot soldier/police officer pervades this and other such films.

Aaron Norris left the Philippines to direct fresh-faced Michael Dudikoff in Cannon's ripoff of *Platoon,* titled *Platoon Leader.* The feature was lensed in South Africa, an atypical stand-in for Vietnam. Four screenwriters adapted James R. McDonough's book for the screen.[12] Dudikoff played a green lieutenant who must earn the respect of his 103rd Airborne troops and their experienced sergeant, played by Robert F. Lyons.

The film begins as the lieutenant is helicoptered into an isolated base camp. He is determined to follow the book, and the enlisted men and NCOs find his attention to detail a real drag. The previous CO had spent the entire last two months of his tour in his heavily reinforced bunker not wanting to jeopardize his "short" status. Entrusted with the mission to keep a nearby hamlet secure and probe the enemy, the new officer insists on daily patrols. The unmotivated lot has its share of druggies and slackers. The enemy remains largely unseen, but trip wires and other booby traps take their toll. Lots of explosions accompany these forays, including one in which the young lieutenant is wounded. He is medevac'd out and while recuperating is visited by his earnest superior, played by William Smith. The possibility of troop reinforcements is ruled out, and Dudikoff returns to the camp with a more realistic outlok. Gradually he gains confidence and respect and motivates his troops to do their duty without his previous pretensions of glory instilled at West Point. Firefights bring casualties, and one Hispanic soldier dies as the result of an overdose. In one scene the men rescue a baby whose mother has been mowed down by the Viet Cong. Later they exact revenge against the heartless enemy unit. Sapper probes and intelligence tell them an offensive is imminent, and the perimeter is reinforced. In a climactic battle scene reminiscent of *The Green Berets,* the VC are turned back. However, their wrath is turned on the innocents in the nearby hamlet. Unable to adequately protect the noncombatants, the GIs survey the senseless civilian carnage. Both the sergeant and the lieutenant are wounded in this last maneuver, and everyone joins in saving their comrades' lives. As the platoon leaders recuperate together in Saigon, they show a mutual understanding and filial love that give them purpose as they return in the last scene to the outpost knkown as the "Country Club." The attempt at character development in this independent feature is notable.

The appearance of Seagal, and, to a lesser extent, Dudikoff, as heirs apparent to Chuck Norris's minions symbolized an attempt to find new B movie stars who could rise to prominence in A action features. Bronson and Eastwood had long ago been replaced by such box office forces as Stallone and Norris. But several factors now conspire to limit the appearance of Vietnam as a tangential character trait for the emerging action stars. One is the globalization of the industry resulting from international co-ownership, day and date release of films in both American and international markets, the proliferation of cable and satellite television in Europe, and the explosion of video. What happens is the emergence of international stars and heirs to the action throne such as Jean Claude Van Damme and Arnold Schwarzeneggar. Unlike their predecessors, these actors lack prototypical American characteristics. Coincidental to this, and exemplifying the passage of time, is the fact that these stars are too young to be believable as veterans of a conflict whose soldiers are now in their forties. The diminution of even incidental veteran references will increase as time passes.

One last summer release exemplified this aging process and the relegation of Vietnam to the pantheon of America's conflicts. Paramount's release *Presidio* was a murder mystery that takes place on the famed army base outside San Francisco. Mark Harmon is a former MP who coordinates his civilian investigation with that of head military law officer Sean Connery. The mature Scotsman is somehow a Vietnam veteran, as are a number of other characters both good and bad in the picture. Most notable for our purposes is the scene where Connery goes to see his friend Jack Warden, curator of the Presidio Army Museum. Conducting a tour for grade-schoolers, Warden is persuaded to shift from the World War II uniforms to his own story of winning the Medal of Honor. A photo shows the then-forty-something officer being congratulated by President Lyndon Johnson. Familiar actor Warden is, like his avuncular character, now a man in his midsixties. This is somewhat shocking given the attention to the grunts, cherries, naifs, and so on who come of age within the films. Underscoring the aura of ancient history and its implicit contrapuntal empowerment of filmic images for youth is a nine- or ten-year-old boy's honest questions. As Connery looks on the child asks Warden, "What's Vietnam?" Then amid the glory and pomp that surround the child in the military museum, he queries with the language of the inner city, "Did we kick ass?" Thus ends the school tour.

Two good true life stories were broadcast in the fall. *My Father, My Son* starred Karl Malden as Admiral Elmo Zumwalt and Keith Carradine as his son. The younger Zumwalt, a Vietnam veteran, battles cancer most likely caused by exposure to Agent Orange. The irony is that his father ordered its usage. It was a moving tale that centered on the father-son relationship without recriminations. The other "made-for" was *To Heal a Nation* starring Eric Roberts. It was the story of veteran Jan Scruggs and his championing of the cause to build a Vietnam Veterans Memorial in Washington, D.C. This powerful monument was, like most things related to the war, born of controversy. Scruggs is shown first conceiving of his idea while watching *The Deerhunter.*

Sidney Lumet's *Running on Empty* was an outstanding motion picture written by Naomi Foner and starring Judd Hirsch and Christine Lahti. They portrayed 1960s Weathermen-type radicals who have lived for years as fugitives. Each time the FBI is on their trail, they move and assume new identities with the help of a support network. This nomadic lifestyle may work for them, but it is increasingly unfair for their children.

River Phoenix is touching as the son coming of age and finding first love with Martha Plimpton. He longs for a place to call home and must decide whether he will stay when his beloved parents are forced to leave for crimes committed years ago in a very different time. The scene where a heartsick Lahti visits her own father, played by Stephen Hill, is absolutely riveting. She beseeches him to take in her son so that he can pursue his dreams. The onetime antiwar radical fears she will now lose her beloved son just as her father lost her. Only now does she fully understand the pain she caused him.

Briefly intruding into the family drama is L. M. Carson as a fellow member of the underground. Hirsch and Lahti cannot relate to him as he remains mired in a violence-prone reaction to a war now long over. Twenty years have mellowed these college lovers, who now must live the consequences of their actions. They do not want to be political anymore; they just want to be a father and a mother. Coming on the heels of the resurfacing of such antiwar leaders as Abbie Hoffman, the film was additionally fascinating.

Less successful was the melodramatic fall release *1969,* starring Robert Downey, Jr., Kiefer Sutherland, and Winona Ryder. Written and directed by Ernest Thompson, it told the story of two high school buddies who go to college together to avoid the draft. Gradually their coming-of-age exploits, such as the loss of virginity, first love, drug experimentation, and the development of a social conscience, react with the ugly realities of an intruding Vietnam War. Richard

Nixon is inaugurated president, and it is the "Age of Aquarius," as the music proclaims. Sutherland's father, Bruce Dern, is a proud World War II marine vet who has instilled a sense of duty in his eldest son. He departs for Vietnam, but his little brother, the immature Sutherland, does not know what the audience presumes to be inevitable. At State College Downey struggles not to flunk out, and antiwar rallies take place in the background. When the families arrive for a campus visit, they are caught in a riot at the administration building. Returning home at break, the young men pick up a pimply faced draftee on his way to Vietnam despite the intrusion of a radio message from Nixon saying the troops are coming home. As affection stirs in Sutherland, he listens to Downey's little sister deliver a blistering antiwar valedictory. Dern is decidedly uneasy at the politics. Downey nearly overdoses on LSD, and a road trip in a VW microbus allows for more sign-of-the-times visits to the counterculture of the hippies. This semiauto-biographical tale plays at this point like an anthropological study.

The once-far-removed specter of the war begins to intrude more mightily as the draft board hounds Downey and Sutherland's brother is declared MIA. A fearful and grief-stricken father and his pained and confused son have an ugly confrontation. Downey gets arrested after breaking into a draft records center. Sutherland, who was not caught in the escapade, takes off on the night of the Apollo moon landing for the Canadian border. His love Ryder convinces him to turn back and fight for the antiwar cause however he can. On their way back they pass a convoy of army trucks loaded with young men who either flip them the bird or share a peace sign salute with them. The next scene is the funeral of Sutherland's brother, his status now changed to killed in action. As the guns fire in military tradition, the mourners wince. His mother refuses the ceremonial flag, which the father solemnly accepts. Younger brother Sutherland is moved to issue a call to action. He declares to the mourners that he used to think it was not his war but that he was wrong: "It's everybody's war." Then he apologizes to his fallen brother and to his father, remarking that his was a "good war" but that this one is not. They march to the courthouse to demand Downey's release as various townspeople join the black-clad procession. The sympathetic sheriff releases the young man to his family, and as the friends hug, the film ends. In voiceover Sutherland recalls that 327 people from his county, including his dad, joined more than 700,000 others in a march in Washington later that year. That protest as well as this film is dedicated to "Peace."

Having a similar title and draft related subject was *'68*, an independent feature. Once again the young man coming of age tries to avoid the draft, this time by feigning homosexuality.

The aging of the Vietnam veterans also meant that their offspring were now coming of age. Paramount's *Distant Thunder* starred John Lithgow as an emotionally scarred U.S. Navy Seal officer who has never recovered from his tours of duty. Based on real-life "bush vets" who remain outside mainstream society, the post-traumatic stress sufferer lives with other vets in the rain forests of the Pacific Northwest. Ralph Macchio costarred as his son, who upon graduation

Distant Thunder **(Paramount Pictures, 1988). Bush vet John Lithgow's son, Ralph Macchio, is now approaching manhood.**

from high school hankers for a meeting with his long-lost father. Robert Schaffel, who served in the U.S. Army Special Forces in Vietnam, produced the film, which was directed by Rick Rosenthal.

Distant Thunder begins with the familiar orientation of helicopter noise at an LZ in North Vietnam in 1969. Soon Lithgow's team is caught in a firefight and sustains heavy casualties. In retreat he drags one of the wounded into a swamp and waits in terror as the enemy patrols only a few feet away. This is a desperate situation, and he must muffle the anguished cries of his comrade so as not to give away their hiding place. A closeup of Lithgow's terror-filled eyes serves as a transition to his pained and bearded countenance some twenty years later. Amid the beauty of the Olympic Peninsula, the veteran peers up through the thick canopy to a civilian helicopter flying overhead. He gathers ferns for

Seattle florists to earn his living. On this trip he has gone to visit a fellow bush vet who resides in a trailer. His sobbing wife tells Lithgow of the desperation that has gripped her husband. Lithgow goes to look for him and finds him on the railroad tracks about to commit suicide. The ragged-looking vets in their military jackets confront each other. Lithgow tries to tell his friend that "it don't mean nothin', man," but the man goes through with his desperate act.

The film cuts from Lithgow shaking in the drizzle to the warmth of Macchio's room in Illinois. As the valedictorian prepares his cap and gown, he gazes at a picture of a considerably younger and clean-cut version of his father. The film then cuts between footage of the young man on his paternal quest and of the pained veteran and his troupe in the woods. Eventually with the help of an understanding woman in a nearby logging camp, played by Janet Margolin, the reunion takes place. She had lost her brother in Nam and holds great affection for the troubled vets. When she aids Lithgow and defends him from the inevitable taunts of redneck jerks, it stirs in him long-suppressed emotions and desires. However, the only love expressed in the film is the caring of the vets for one another and that mixed with hate on the part of the abandoned son.

Lithgow is inarticulate, timid, and haunted by memories of his days in combat. Fellow recluse Reb Brown is a violence-prone, "trip wire" vet, and Dennis Arndt is a goofy alcoholic and junk food addict. When the son finally reaches their remote camp, whose perimeter is reinforced with pungi sticks and such, he is in fact captured like a VC infiltrator and threatened in Vietnamese. Reconciliation under such circumstances and after so many years is difficult. Finally the two embrace and share some intimacy as the father tries to explain to his son what he went through in Vietnam. However, the tone quickly shifts in a shrill climax by the campfire, accompanied with music by Credence Clearwater Revival. Despite brotherly love, a drunk Arndt taunts Lithgow to tell his son about a man named Watson. This angers the father, whose recollection is once again introduced by the soundtrack's thunder of distant helicopters. The audio clue gives way to a full-blown flashback in which it is revealed that the episode at the beginning led to the death of the wounded comrade. In a desperate attempt to silence him, the frightened team leader actually suffocated Wilson. Everyone sobs at this confession. Like the tearful admission at the end of *Memorial Day* or the powerful request for forgiveness to come in *Born on the Fourth of July*, these overt and powerful moments are cathartic. The eruption of long-suppressed truth and tears replaces the vengeful mayhem that further sublimated such emotions into additional violence in the revisionist action tales.

A confused and solemn son prepares to leave, but his departure is stymied by vet Brown, who has totally flipped and thinks the boy is a VC infiltrator. Lithgow is forced to save his son's life, and Arndt dies trying to aid them. The firefight in the forest leaves Macchio wounded and recovering in a nearby hospital. When he awakens he finds a note of apology from his father. Macchio senses his father's pain and leaps from bed. Racing against time, the son drives along the railway and, as suspected, finds his dad about to "walk the tracks." Macchio confronts Lithgow and bravely saves his father's life by standing next to him as the train approaches. The only way for Lithgow to save his son is to spare himself, and they tumble out of the way at the last moment.

The filmmakers expressed gratitude to the Vietnam Veteran Rap Group and the Port Angeles (Washington) Family Counseling Center. Despite the best dramatic intentions, the film suffers from an inability to trust its dramatic components. It feels compelled to expand its cinematic horizons to exciting firefights and flashbacks. A gentle portrait of pained vets who remain isolated and brutalized gives way to yet another clichéd and damaging view of these men as trigger-happy nut cases. The film received only halfhearted distribution.

In 1985 *Harpers* magazine offered the estimate that there were 2,700 combat veterans living on the remote Olympic Peninsula. A presidential commission had determined that veterans had a 23 percent higher suicide rate than others in their age category.[13] *Time* reported on the bush vet phenomenon in "Lost in America," in which it told the story of post-traumatic stress disorder sufferers living in the wilds of the Hawaiian jungle. The magazine estimated that 479,000 Vietnam vets suffer to some degree from this multisymptomatic malady.[14]

Joining the new generation of matinee idols Macchio, Sutherland, and Downey in roles of interest to this collection was Christian Slater in the tangential entry *Gleaming the Cube.* Herein the skateboard, not motorcycle, subculture encounters drug dealing and adventure amid the Southeast Asian immigrant community in Los Angeles. This is one of several films whose only reference to the war is its depiction of the refugees who have fled homelands still buffeted by war. (Following the fall of Saigon, a reunified Vietnam became embroiled in the civil war in Cambodia in 1978 and in a border war with the Chinese in 1979.)

Returning in-country was *Bat 21*, which featured older on-screen protagonists. Although set during the war, this more mature soldier story creates empathy with an aging vet populace and contrasts to the fresh-faced emsembles that had populated the grunt tales. Both *Distant Thunder* and *Bat 21* were apolitical, "refusing to offer a political or moral context for the veteran's memories, just like the war, by implication."[15] *Bat 21* was a Tri-Star release of a Carolco film featuring Gene Hackman as real-life air force lieutenant colonel Iceal B. Hambleton, who not only inspired the story but also acted as technical adviser.[16]

Hambleton is a Korean War vet who coordinates high-tech bombing missions from the relative safety of his desk at HQ. As a senior officer he takes advantage of the perks of power that accompany his long military service. For instance, as the film opens he is playing golf at one of the exclusive officers courses in Vietnam. A messenger arrives via helicopter, which hovers over the green as his presence is requested. Reconnaissance appears to show an offensive being mounted. Hambleton decides he should take a closer look and goes up on a relatively routine mission. As he flies over the countryside, its great beauty is once again revealed. However, his plane is shot down, and the older man is forced to parachute out. This senior officer of great intelligence value to the enemy finds himself stranded alone on the ground.

What ensues is an exciting tale of the effort to rescue the downed man. Tension is heightened by the fact that the area in which he is stranded is due to be carpet bombed. Valiantly trying to locate Hambleton is Captain Clark, played by Danny Glover. The thick Malaysian jungle provides an authentic-looking location for the story, which presents the very different realities of this country from an aircraft and from the ground. In essence the sterile long-distance power that Hambleton has often brought to bear is forced to give way to an up-close, grunt-level view of the war, including the devastation wrought by U.S. bombers.

Glover, nicknamed "Birddog," flies a tiny Cessna Skymaster, an unarmed surveillance plane that is often within potshot range of the enemy. Via walkie talkie Hambleton and his would-be rescuer do not just plot strategy and coordinates. Rather, the black flier acts as an emotional lifeline for the frightened and slightly injured white senior officer. The first night on the ground Hackman hides from an NVA patrol. Weather and security considerations lead to an inability to immediately extricate the officer. He acts as a scout on the movement of the NVA armored column preparing for the offensive. When he calls in the "birds" for a surgical air strike, he is horrified by the destruction he witnesses. Back at base Glover disobeys policy to continue his search, which has now become an obsession. Fearful that their radio contacts will be intercepted, they devise a code based on golf jargon. However, the black man has never played the country club game and must quickly learn from a borrowed handbook.

Several powerfully staged scenes ensue on the ground. Hambleton comes upon a peasant hut and ravenously eats the rice he finds. The family returns and confronts him. The large man tries to explain in sign language that he is hungry and means no harm. However, the farmer feels threatened and attacks the officer. Suddenly thrust into hand-to-hand combat, the American slays the civilian with his machete. Despite killing in self-defense, Hambleton is consumed by remorse as the wife and child have witnessed the tragedy. He escapes off into the bush. An attempted evacuation near a hamlet leads to the helicopter's being shot down. Hambleton watches helplessly as a brave young pilot (David Marshall Grant) sent to rescue him is forced into a mine field to his death. Hackman cries out, "People keep dying around me" and prepares to give himself up. His realization of what really transpires in a war zone is painful. An air strike clears the enemy before Hackman can come out of hiding.

The next day Hackman encounters a young boy on a rickety bridge. They pass because the American has no intention of harming the child, but Hackman does worry about what the boy will do. Suddenly the boy runs past him to the end of the bridge and reveals a booby trap that surely would have killed him. Grateful, Hackman gives chocolate to the boy and waves farewell. As the B-52s' deadline approaches, Glover flies in solo in a chopper for a last-minute rescue. He is rusty with the controls and crashes when the helicopter comes under fire. Finally the men meet face to face and are now united in their fate on the ground. Hambleton understands the sacrifice, but his gratitude must wait as they run to safety amid the flames that engulf the forest. They survive the ordeal and share

Bat 21 (Tri-Star Pictures, 1988). **Fear gives way to kindness as a young Vietnamese boy saves the colonel's life.**

a laugh as the rescuer remarks, "It's probably time to find another way of making a living." The remark is flippant and is meant to lighten the tone. However, implicit in it is the awareness that Hambleton has gained concerning the human cost of what he has directed from afar as a leader in the "corporation." Also contained is the notion that his effort cannot continue and that there are better ways for them and America to conduct them- selves.

The film is most important as it is clearly set in Vietnam but is a traditional Hollywood tale of heroism and adventure in a war zone. It is this straightforward storytelling largely unburdened by handwringing and metaphysics that has made it a favorite of cable television programmers.

There were other made for television and cable movies from this period. Many of these features were of a more benign nature, reflecting their inability to rely on lazy violence prone writing. Their melodrama is apparent in their titles. Wings Hauser starred in *Code of Honor,* Teri Garr portrayed a female POW in *Intimate Strangers,* David Birney was MIA and nearly declared dead in *The Long Journey Home,* Wayne Rogers has an Amerasian child in *The Lady from Yesterday,* Richard Dean Anderson is blind in *Ordinary Heroes* and Tommy Lee Jones nearly loses his ranch and livelihood in *Stranger on My Land. Shooter* was the story of combat photographers and contained a tribute to those journalists who lost their lives covering the war.

The year 1989 featured a number of quality small- and medium-budget entries. In January came *84 Charlie MoPic,* a fascinating grunt's view of the war.

***84 Charlie MoPic* (New Century Vista, 1989). Left to right: MoPic (Byron Thames), OD (Richard Brooks), and LT (Jonathan Emerson) in the Central Highlands.**

Vietnam veteran Patrick Duncan wrote and directed the ensemble cast. He had spent five years trying to get the film made, only succeeding after achieving acclaim as the writer and producer of HBO's *Vietnam War Story.* Then the Sundance Institute bankrolled this project, and accolades at several film festivals led to its general release. The film's novelty was the manner in which it was shot. The story is told almost entirely through the eye of a documentarian's camera as he/it accompanies a six-person patrol into the bush. The voice of the chronicler cinematographer is heard, but he is only seen once. Shot in super 16 millimeter, the film thus takes on a mock documentary feel.

Although seemingly a throwback to the old omniscient journalist-narrator or other such media character in the films, Duncan gained authenticity and maintained identification with the group itself. The viewer is thrust into the platoon rather than distanced from it. Indeed, the physical movement of the camera actually mimics the motions that would accompany jumping off into an LZ or humping in the jungle. "Taking the 'I am a camera' idea further, while admitting to the common view that Vietnam was the first war-as-media event, Duncan seizes the medium away from the authority of network journalism and claims it for the infantryman."[17] Dispelling comparisons to Oliver Stone, draftee Duncan noted that he was truly a product of America's underclass. Duncan insisted that *Platoon*'s combat scenes still made "war look like fun . . . [when] in reality a dead body's a very ugly thing, and it's hard to carry. Life isn't cheap and I wanted to rub that in the audience's face."[18]

The film begins with the clapboard being snapped for the commencement of filming. Then by using long takes and extreme closeups, as if the viewer is walking right behind the guy in front, Duncan creates intimacy. The heavy breathing of the pack-laden men and the military filmmaker with his camera on his back pervade the soundtrack. Duncan refused a 1960s soundtrack, preferring these natural noises and a few unobtrusive Donovan tunes.

"MoPic," short for motion picture, becomes the moniker bestowed on the visitor as he interviews and gets to know the other men. They are not an entirely unfamiliar lot. The lieutenant, or LT," tries hard, but his corporate designation as boss must acquiesce to the natural leadership and experience of the black man "OD," played by Richard Brooks. Another youngster is a gung-ho poor white, another a jokester, and so on. When the filmmaker asks "Carolina," an older family man, about the state of race relations, the normally calm fellow gets agitated at the ignorance of the reality on such a patrol. "That's a question from 'the world.'" The viewer shares the embarrassment of the interviewer. The jargon is thick and colorful, connoting a sense of in-the-know authenticity also furthered by the recitation of mundane concerns such as foot fungus. Using real time for marching and muted conversations leads to a sense of tedium interspersed with instances of hyperalertness on the recon mission.

Eventually booby traps and firefights take their toll at close range and in disoriented confusion as the camera is forced to hit the dirt along with its holder. Death is forever present, but, unlike other in-country features, the enemy is not always anonymous. The men finish off a wounded VC for lack of other alternatives. "When you're in the bush just watching to see how the enemy is spending his day, what he's eating, how often he takes a shit, you get a very human picture of that guy. So if you have to kill him . . . you're not killing a Vietnamese, not a gook, not the 'enemy,' but another human being whose face you've seen laughing, losing at cards, and just doing his job."[19] Indeed at the Hawaii Film Festival the delegation that accompanied the Vietnam Film Project congratulated and embraced Duncan for the method in which Vietnamese were portrayed.

Commenting directly on perspective and indirectly on film predecessors, Duncan remarked, "I didn't need Michael Herr. I respect him, but his is once more the point of view of an educated observer, someone who can put himself outside the conflict to understand it."[20] In a relative sense the author of *Dispatches* seemed quite knowledgeable and articulate compared to the refracted imagery in the early films. But here a grunt-turned-filmmaker lays explicit claim to an even more intimate relationship to the war. Echoing a phenomenon already identified in terms of the better-grossing combat portrayals, Duncan remarked that "Truffaut once said that you can't make an antiwar movie, because battle scenes have a visceral impact all their own. . . . I'm hoping to prove him wrong."[21]

Like the preceding film, the next movie found it necessary to alter perspective in some manner tht would bring originality and understanding to the increasingly self-derivative collection of films. Independent producer Scotti Brothers' feature *Iron Triangle* shared an American's view of the war with that of a Viet Cong character as well. Supposedly based on the diary of an unknown VC soldier, the movie starred Beau Bridges and Haing S. Ngor. Eric Weston directed the tale, set in the infamous area near the Ho Chi Minh Trail.

Voiceover by Bridges grounds the film in the realm of survivor recollection. Initially we see the Americans conducting maneuvers, dropping leaflets meant to win hearts and minds, and acquiescing to brutal interrogations conducted by South Vietnamese officials. Crosscutting with the spartan conditions of the guerrillas, the movie sets up a rhythm that provides for a type of equality. Further enhancing this balancing act is the fact that each side in the war effort has dual representatives, one of whom is good and one of whom is bad.

When the army captain is captured by the source of the story, a young VC warrior played by Liem Whately, it is the humanity of the pajama-clad lad and the moments he has shared with Bridges that compel him to protect the American from a stereotypically heinous commander. Turning the tables, the Asians refer to Bridges in racial terms as "round eyes." The appearance of a French legionnaire who survived Dien Bien Phu as well as references to the Chinese invaders connote the continuity of conflict, the transient nature of the American presence, and notions of nationalism more than communism as the enemy motivation.

Eventually intruding is American air superiority, which wreaks havoc down in the jungle. The devastating B-52s leave orphaned children in clichéd evocations of the tragedy immortalized in the newsreel footage of the bombing of Shanghai by the Japanese. *Iron Triangle* is a curious drama from a surprising source that does indeed embrace the concept expressed by Bridges: "On the other side of the gun was a man like me."

The inclusion of a crazed Vietnam vet characters in comedies that had nothing to do with the war underscored how well established the stereotype had become. The casting of Bruce Dern in *The 'Burbs* as the wired neighbor in combat boots was in fact designed to poke fun at the persona he had had in *Coming Home* and *Black Sunday*. Randy Quaid was another neighbor/vet/idiot in *Moving*. Weird Al Yankovic did a Rambo sendup in UHF. Like the vet professor in *Back to School*, the tangential parodies were unfunny and the characterizations perpetuated rather than refuted the negativism.

Firsthand accounts of the war continued to surface in theatrical features. Stephen Metcalfe adapted his off–Broadway play *Jackknife* for the screen. *Distant Thunder*'s real-life veteran, Robert Schaffel, produced the independent drama directed by David Jones. Its profile rose with the casting of leads Robert DeNiro, Ed Harris, and Kathy Baker. Once again reflecting current real-life status was the age of the actors portraying the vets, conveyed in paunch and receding hairline. The release began with a public service announcement by DeNiro on behalf of the Agent Orange hotline and outreach program.

The story unfolds as DeNiro tries to help his war buddy Harris recover his emotional health. Harris attempts to block out shared memories, but DeNiro will not let him. In the process the better-adjusted vet falls in love with Harris's plain–Jane sister. A few on-screen scenes recreate combat and trauma in Vietnam. Like many such tales survivor guilt blends with in-country behavioral guilt in paining the veterans. Temporary solace is sought in alcohol abuse. Climactic moments of breakthrough are achieved as helicopter noise foreshadows self-revelation. Eventually the trio makes a pilgrimage to a nearby Connecticut Vietnam memorial. Despite the sister's love, Harris' redemption and rebirth are ultimately achievable only through the intervention of a fellow vet who can truly understand. The film ends on an upbeat note as Harris joins a therapy group and DeNiro and Baker profess their love.

By May 1989 the lack of public interest in these Vietnam War dramas made the producers of Columbia's *Welcome Home* nervous. They were determined to sell the late director Franklin Schaffner's (*Patton*) last film as a romance. Thus the radio spot went like this: "He was shot down in Vietnam and declared dead . . . [the sound of helicopters]. Seventeen years later he's returned to the woman he loved . . . . Now . . . [music wells up] . . . nothing is the same . . . . I promised myself I'd never stop loving you."[22]

The renewed use of the ironic title employed in the early 1970s exemplified the hackneyed project. Kris Kristofferson portrayed a soldier trapped in the mountains of Cambodia who has an Asian family with a tribeswoman, played by Kieu Chinh. We have witnessed the still-very-beautiful Vietnamese native actress age from the earliest film entries. Jo-Beth Williams has remarried because her husband was proclaimed KIA, the error a result of misidentified remains. Brian Keith is the widowed father happy to have his son back. Sam Waterston played the same role Andrew Duggan had way back in the feature *The Forgotten Man*, the supportive husband unnerved by the appearance of his wife's first love. Additional family pathos is injected as Kristofferson must see his 17-year-old son, whom Waterston has raised as his own.

Trey Wilson creates some sympathy as a colonel who is merely the executor of a policy that insists in a clichéd conspiratorial sense that the returnee keep quiet about his situation. The overt justification is to not disrupt important negotiations on behalf of the MIAs. Implied is a series of coverups and incompetency in the process of investigation throughout the years. A threat to investigate totally unsubstantiated collaboration charges is dismissed, but Kristofferson does cooperate in a quid pro quo for assurances that the government will help locate his Cambodian loved ones last seen in a Thai border camp.

World War II vet Keith recalls that he believed the "movies and politicians and war stories at the Rotary." The parents loved having a boy who was a flier, but mom and apple pie did not mean a damn thing when they received that box with a flag on it. "Instead of being so proud of you in that John Wayne suit, I should have tied you up and driven you to Canada myself."

Eventually Kristofferson decides he must search for his Asian family, last seen shepherding him to the camp and evading the Khmer Rouge. A senator in charge of MIA-POW investigations runs interference with the ineffectual, paranoid navy brass and in fact accompanies Kristofferson to his reunion with his children, whose mother died in an artillery attack on the refugee camp. The new family returns to the United States, where grandpa, ex-wife, and son all live nearby and happily ever after. Kristofferson's buddy Willie Nelson sang the title song, which had as much schmaltz as the screenplay.

Also both thematically and titularly unoriginal was the made-for-cable television feature *The Forgotten.* In fact only the medium of programming itself was new. Like the preceding feature, this movie concerned longtime MIAs who suddenly surface and embarrass the Pentagon, which has been busy denying their existence. It seems the men have been kept by a rogue band, and now in an allusion to the very current events, the North Vietnamese, eager to normalize relations, have discovered and liberated the six.

The U.S. government is not quite as treacherous as in some of the earlier entries, but its attempts at damage control and public relations underscore the military as a cynical "corporation." Keith Carradine and Steven Railsback starred as the long-imprisoned special forces officers. James Keach directed the film, and his brother Stacy appeared as the villain. Like Kristofferson, the men are subject to suspicion in terms of collaboration with the enemy, which they vigorously deny. Eventually they must take matters into their own hands and escape from the West German castle where the U.S. government keeps them captive.

The vet father played by Brian Keith in *Welcome Home* voiced the notion that some fifteen years after the war, he did not care whether Vietnam was right or wrong. All he knew was that the government told him his son was dead and that was wrong. The image of an unsympathetic boor had retreated since Arthur Kennedy portrayed the old breed in *Hail Hero* and *Glory Boy.* Along with Keith, mellowing was hinted at by Charlton Heston in *The Proud Men.* Time had healed old wounds, and the arguments about the war were fading into oblivion. The very fact that the personally conservative Heston played such a role was indicative of the change. Nevertheless, controversy did (and does) still surround the Vietnam War, particularly the lessons learned or, more importantly, those not understood about the conflict and American involvement. So, too, controversy continues to surround certain Vietnam War movies. In 1971 Elia Kazan made *The Visitors.* It was probably based on recent My Lai revelations as well as Daniel Lang's true story about the rape and murder of a Vietnamese girl that first appeared in the *New Yorker* in May 1969. Now twenty years later in 1989, Brian DePalma made his return to this genre with *Casualties of War,* also based on Lang's article. This Columbia feature had considerable marquee value as it starred Michael J. Fox as Private Eriksson and Sean Penn as Sergeant Meserve. Viet vet David Rabe (*Streamers*) wrote the screenplay, Ennio Morricone composed the evocative score, and Art Linson produced the harrowing feature.

Instead of taking place entirely in-country, the story is bracketed by a prologue and epilogue set stateside. In this manner the film is rooted in the realm of recollection as if the unfolding flashback is a collective nightmare. Introduced as commuter Fox dozes on a subway car, the very insinuation of the imagery is meant to elicit subliminal notions of a collective consciousness. Playing off the universalizing process was the casting of Fox, who was mostly known as a comedic actor, in a purposeful attempt to inject his boy-next-door image into the quagmire as a source of audience empathy. Sean Penn exploited his bad boy persona, and the two young stars reflected the moral dichotomy of Barnes/Elias and the cross-purposes that corrupted the American war effort. Ultimately the rape and murder become an allegory for the United States' entire Vietnam sojourn and evokes discussion of sexual metaphors within the collection of films. DePalma's fascination with violence, sex, and voyeurism had been demonstrated not only in *Greetings* and *Hi Mom!* but also elsewhere in his filmmaking career. Inextricably joined in the film's title as casualties are the Vietnamese victim of the crime and the perpetrators' very humanity.

The San Francisco newspaper headline reads, "Nixon Resigns" as Fox notices an Asian woman across the aisle and then nods off to sleep. It is 1966 in the Central Highlands, and mortar fire has the platoon pinned down. Fox falls halfway into a VC tunnel, trapped as he flails about yelling for help. Below the surface DePalma uses a fluid subjective camera to build tension as a VC tunnel rat with a knife crawls toward the American. At the last moment battlefield leader Sergeant Meserve plucks his private to safety and sprays the tunnel with bullets.

It is no coincidence that the in-country designation of Fox as a cherry is also the slang used to connote virginity back in the world. The audience surrogate ingratiates himslf to the locals in the next scene by handing out Hershey chocolates as if he is a GI in the "good war." The more experienced platoon members are attuned to the dual identity of many a seeming innocent. Squad members include Don Harvey as Clark, who enjoys the excuse war gives him to kill. John C. Reilly is Hatcher, a dullard who follows the leader, and John Leguizamo is the frightened new Hispanic arrival who tries to fit in and survive.

It is readily apparent that Penn's Meserve, like Berenger's Barnes, is a consummate warrior. Staying close to this guy could very well mean the difference between life and death. Various familiar images are conveyed in fine style via Stephen Burum's Thai-based cinematography. For instance, soldiers smoke dope, wonder at the beauty of the landscape, and encounter death and destruction. At base camp the touches of Americana abound as Budweiser and whorehouses provide R&R. If all Asians are "gooks," then all women are "slits" and prostitutes. Fox hangs out with his buddy from another unit, thus separating himself from the others as they cavort. Meserve homoerotically reserves compassion solely for his troops. Sex is for women, but love is for his men. Perhaps a quasi paternal or filial context is more appropriate as he cradles one of his wounded troops as he bleeds to death.

As the men prepare to go back into the bush, they are in surly moods because of their casualties. Meserve, who is only 30 days "short," hatches a plan to provide for some "portable R&R" as a morale booster. They sneak into a hamlet, and Clark picks a pretty young woman sleeping in her home as the victim. In amazement Fox nominally stands guard as some of the others kidnap the girl, played by Thuy Thu Le. Despite the tearful protest of her mother and sister, the soldiers make off with the young woman into the darkness. All Fox can do is mutter a lame English phrase as the unit departs: "I'm sorry."

Mockingly Clark tells Fox, "We're going to win her heart and mind if she has one." The girl is gang-raped despite the protests of Fox. At first Diaz refuses

Casualties of War (Columbia Pictures, 1989). Left to right: Michael J. Fox, Don Harvey, and Sean Penn contemplate the grim reality.

to participate but gives into peer pressure. Meserve confronts Fox and baits him, calling into question his heterosexuality and esprit de corps. Later when the sergeant speaks of his penis as the most potent weapon of all, he links the sex and violence metaphors of other films, including *Full Metal Jacket*. In an ironic reversal of a bootcamp training chant, the war lover grabs his genitals and declares, "This is a weapon." Then raising his rifle, he says, "This is a gun." Back to his crotch, "This is for fighting" and then to his M-16, "This is for fun." The cultural hegemony that the Americans imposed on the Vietnamese led to Ho Chi Minh's charge that Americans had turned all local women into whores.[23] Certainly the imagery of native women in the films has done little to refute this charge.

The men have not only denied the humanity of the innocent Vietnamese girl; they have also broken the Uniform Code of Military Justice in kidnapping, raping, and beating her. It is an incredibly ugly and graphically depicted crime that the conventions of cinema had not allowed until the early 1980s. Fox is, if not passive, then ultimately impotent in his attempt to protect the victim. Thus he not only personifies the overall war effort and the relegation of goodness but also becomes a metaphor for the silent observers that allow such things to happen — namely, the American people vis-à-vis the war. As the men proceed further in-country, they continue their abuse of the girl, and Fox attempts to free her. He incurs the squad's wrath, and Meserve hints that the "VC sympathizer" could be killed "real easy." Diaz seems tormented by all this, while Hatcher is a pathetic idiot, Clark grooves on the sadism, and Meserve recites the familiar in-country variation on Psalm 23: "I fear no evil for I am the meanest motherfucker in the valley." Finally as the men approach their evac zone, it becomes apparent that the girl must be murdered in order to conceal the crime. During a last-minute firefight, she is riddled with bullets.

Back at the base camp Clark reminds Fox that "what happens in the field stays in the field." Obviously all notions of decency have disappeared, replaced by absurd codes of secrecy and duty to fellow soldiers. Throughout these films, particularly in regard to some of the outlaw biker characters, the malevolence that resides in some men was shown to have predated their tour of duty but to have found a real home in the absence of morality in Vietnam. However, it is the impressionable followers and the less than evil characters who are most frightening as they become the means by which we explore how such things could happen. Were the perpetrators of My Lai really that different from the audience? Relatively speaking, Rabe softened the premeditation of the murder here from the portrayal afforded in Lang's article and book.

Overcome by guilt, Fox goes to his superior to report the incident. The black career officer is uncomfortable and tells the young man not to "buck the system." "Relax and try to forget about it." Once again the hierarchy acts in such a way as to protect and cover up such misconduct. As Fox tells the story to his friend from another unit, a cherry just off the transport steps on a "toe popper," a land mine. The ever-present danger registers on Fox, who tells his buddy, "Just because each of us at any second might be blown away, everybody is acting like we can do anything. . . . Maybe [it's] just the opposite because we may be dead. . . . [We've] got to be extra careful. . . . Maybe it matters more."

Fox then goes to see another superior, this time played by veteran and technical adviser Dale Dye. He is already aware of the allegations and assures Fox that the matter is receiving "max attention." Dye admits that Meserve blew it but reminds Fox that the same sergeant saved his life. Shortly thereafter Fox survives Clark's attempt to frag him in the latrine. The private escapes the grenade blast at the last moment and marches into the tent where the perpetrators calmly play cards. Fox smashes Clark's face with a shovel.

As Fox sits in a bar with a gun in front of himself for protection, a chaplain notices the troubled young soldier. He coaxes the story out of him, and the film shifts to the interrogation process preceding a court-martial trial. Dye is disgusted that Fox could not let the matter lie, and the enlisted man tells the officer to go to hell. Hatcher and Diaz break under inquiry, but Clark and Meserve remain defiant. The men are sentenced to varying terms at Leavenworth, with the sergeant shown leniency for his stellar service record. As they are led out, the audience is not allowed to hear what Meserve whispers to Fox. However, just the recollection of the threat startles the veteran awake as he wipes the sweat from his face and peers about in the present.

The Asian woman who reminded Fox of the incident exits at her stop. Fox runs after her, and she says, "Do I remind you of someone? You had a bad

In Country (**Warner Bros., 1989**). **Emily Lloyd consoles her distraught veteran uncle, Bruce Willis.**

dream, didn't you? It's over now . . . I think." The sunny day connotes rebirth and renewal. The chaplain became the means of confession and a prototypical Asian representative of her entire race became the means of absolution.[24]

Following the late August release of Michael J. Fox in Vietnam was a September vehicle for another television actor–turned–movie star, Bruce Willis. *In Country* employed as its title the phrase whose meaning was now widely recognized. This Warner Bros. release was produced and directed by Norman Jewison from a Frank Pierson screenplay based on a novel by Bobbie Ann Mason. This drama gender-bent the coming-of-age tale, using English actress Emily Lloyd as a young woman whose father was killed in the war and whose uncle, veteran Willis, remains troubled. The story begins on the threshold to adulthood, the summer after high school graduation.

Willis and his buddies from high school, mostly fellow vets, still hang out together. They have trouble relating to their wives or girlfriends, drink and smoke too much, and blame the inevitable aches and pains of aging on Agent Orange. The young woman searches for her roots by asking Willis numerous questions and going through her father's and his collective memorabilia. She inquires as to how her father died, and this is very troubling for her uncle. When hardly anyone shows up at a dance honoring the Vietnam veterans, the men are depressed. They debate the war they could not win versus the war they were not allowed to win. Lloyd begins to clue in on the collective disservice and why most people prefer to leave the war in the past. Exemplifying the passage of time and the coming of age, the daughter of the fallen soldier, now a young woman, beds down with one of the vets. Not incidentally he is unable to perform.

Vietnam is invoked on screen through Willis's recollections, including that of her father's last patrol. However, the in-country recreations are distractions from the drama, the nature of memory, and the march toward reconciliation and the future. When Lloyd's mother attempts to explain how things were twenty years ago, the very place of the films in the creation of images of the war for the youth of today is underscored. As time passes the war becomes ancient history.

Eventually visiting her grandparents, Lloyd reads from her father's diary about his day-to-day existence in Nam. When she discusses it with Willis, he weeps and admits that he is half-dead himself. Lloyd asks her grandma, "If you could do it over, would you have sent Dwayne to Canada instead?" She replies, "People don't have choices like that. Besides, he did a good thing for his country. I take comfort in that." Lloyd continues, "What good did he do for his country? Fifty-eight thousand guys died for a stupid war. Emmett [Willis] says they all died for nothing." Grandma says, "Well, Emmett can talk. He didn't die." Lloyd disappears into the back woods, the bush as it were, and contemplates the lives that predated her own birth.

Sensing a need for redemption and renewal, the young lady coaxes her mother and uncle into a trip to Washington, D.C., to visit the Vietnam veterans memorial. This important new symbol of sacrifice reflects their faces as they seek out the husband, father, brother's name. Each brings tears and their own unique offering to the wall. For the widow it is a plant, for Lloyd it is a picture of herself in a cap and gown all grown up, and for Willis it is his medals and a pack of Camels. The film ends as they stroll arm in arm past the other veterans and their loved ones. Canadian director Norman Jewison remarked, "The Wailing Wall of America is what the Wall has become."[25]

Despite compelling stories and the presence of stars, none of the 1989 releases about the war grossed very well. The top box office performance was mustered by *Casualties of War* at a mere $19 million domestic gross. Attempting to jump-start interest in the increasingly important global market, the ad campaign for the Penn-Fox picture practically ignored Vietnam in favor of a psychodrama. In France it was retitled *Outrages* and in Sweden *The Final Settlement*. The new tack improved the take in Europe. *In Country* relied on Lloyd's star power in Britain for its marketing.[26]

The final entry in this chapter relied most heavily of all on star power to tell its dramatic story. Both Tom Cruise and Oliver Stone brought this component to *Born on the Fourth of July*. Universal sought word of mouth and Academy Award qualification by releasing the film on only four screens in North America on December 22, 1989. By January 1990 the film had broadened out to 1,300 screens, a whopping total for such a powerful drama about the Vietnam War and, as the publicity line said, "Innocence Lost and Courage Found."

The background of this extremely important entry is testament to the importance of timing in Hollywood and the empowerment of cinema. In 1976, to correspond with America's bicentennial, McGraw-Hill had published Ron Kovic's autobiography, *Born on the Fourth of July*. That day is not only the country's birthdate but Kovic's as well (1946). The book is a powerful account of a young man who felt he had to answer John F. Kennedy's stirring inaugural call of 1961: "Ask not what your country can do for you—ask what you can do for your country."[27] Kovic, who was quoted in Chapter 1 in regard to his hero worship of Audie Murphy, also wrote of John Wayne as his generation's source of imagery on the glory of war. The movie buff recalled that *The Green Berets* was the first movie he saw when he returned from Vietnam to the United States: "It made me sick to my stomach. . . . This is not the way it was."[28]

A Hollywood agent contacted Kovic about his book and set up a meeting. Movie producer Martin Bregman optioned the story, and Al Pacino was set to star for director Daniel Petrie. In 1978 four days before shooting was to commence, the deal fell through. Kovic recalled, "The whole culture seemed to be resistant to what I had to say about the war."[29] Instead Kovic was hired by Jane Fonda as a consultant on her production concerning a wheelchair-bound vet returning to "the world" in *Coming Home*.

Around this same time Oliver Stone still could not get *Platoon* made but nevertheless already had a sequel in mind entitled *Second Life*. It was to be based on his own experiences back in the United States after his tour of duty.[30] Stone admired how Kovic's tale told of his experiences before, during, and after the war. "Ron's story is a coherent vision of the whole Vietnam experience. . . . There was a second war when we came back. . . . It was a real booby trap. . . . We were out of step. People didn't care about Vietnam. Their attitude was, 'I'm sorry. That was a waste of time.' It wasn't hostility. It was indifference. And so with Ron's story, I felt I could fit pieces of my own story and others."[31]

Finally Stone met with Kovic, who was disillusioned by the tabling of his film adaptation. Recalling their first meeting, and reflecting what some critics now refer to as his great excess, Stone said, "It was as if we had been linked by destiny . . . chosen as God's instruments to get a message, a memory, out about the war."[32] Nevertheless, nearly a decade would pass before Stone could find the financing to get their joint project made. Following the success of the foreign-financed *Platoon*, he renewed his efforts on *Born on the Fourth of July*.

The producers and director all agreed on the pragmatic necessity for a star in the main role. Tom Cruise, anxious to shed his matinee idol image and hone his craft in serious vehicles, read the Stone-Kovic script. He recalled, "I could feel the script in my balls."[33] Meeting with Stone and Kovic, Cruise promised to work for deferred compensation and do whatever was necessary to see that the film was finally made. Given his part in the gung-ho hit *Top Gun*, Cruise was asked if this was penance for that glorification of the military. The thoughtful star dodged the criticism by placing that role in perspective in terms of the development of his own career. He admitted his peer group's ignorance about the Vietnam War and felt strongly that this story had to be told. In fact Stone had once remarked on *Rambo* and *MIA*-type flicks, "I'm sick of revisionists who want to refight the war. Why don't they just understand that we never could have won it."[34]

Then Stone went on to identify his films as the "antidote to *Top Gun* and *Rambo* . . . because fuckin' *Top Gun* man — it was essentially a fascist movie. It sold the idea the war is clean, war can be won . . . [to] a lot of people who learned nothing from Vietnam."[35] However, Stone and Kovic dispelled their preconceptions of Cruise because of the young actor's earnestness and their own pragmatism regarding what was required to get A films made about this controversial and depressing subject.

With star director and actor attached, Universal approved a measly $17 million budget. Cruise spent time with Kovic and, in between other movies, nearly a year and a half in wheelchair- and Vietnam-based research for his role. Willem Dafoe was set in a small but pivotal role as an embittered vet who hangs out with Kovic in Mexico. Also from *Platoon*, Tom Berenger made a cameo appearance as a handsome marine recruiting officer who impresses the young Kovic. Frank Whaley was powerful as a fellow returnee, and Kyra Sedgwick was the first love. Raymond Barry and Caroline Kava played Kovic's parents. The entire cast was superb. Cameos went to Oliver Stone as a news reporter, Kovic as a vet from another war, Dale Dye as a colonel, and Abbie Hoffman as a college antiwar protest organizer. Dye once again put the young actors through a boot camp training and acted as a technical adviser. The film was dedicated to the recently resurfaced, colorful, antiwar activist–turned–fugitive Hoffman, who died during production.

The talented crew included *Platoon* alumni Robert Richardson as cinematographer and Bruno Rubeo as production designer. John Williams provided the haunting semiclassical music score. Twenty-one songs were credited on the soundtrack in helping evoke the twenty years that the film covered in the life of the protagonist and of America. This longtime frame accompanied the use of diverse locations in helping convey an epic scope. In fact with the parades, political demonstrations, and conventions, nearly 12,000 extras appeared.[36] The Philippines once again stood in for in-country scenes. Technical advisers Dye and Hoffmann symbolized the opposite extremes of the political discussion that accompanied the Vietnam War. Their respective expertise in combat and in domestic protest scenes enhanced the epic scope of the film.

Casting a handsome golden boy like Cruise as a hero was not at all unique in the history of war films. However, here heroics derived from a different type of bravery. No longer was Cruise a handsome sex symbol. Rather, he was often unshaven and ugly, embittered and unruly. He was paralyzed and his sexuality, his very manhood, was compromised. If initially the audience could not believe that it was Cruise up on the screen, then so much the better. On a subtextual level his emasculation, trauma, and eventual regeneration struck a subliminal chord in the American audience. In a reflection of admiration and gratitude, at the completion of filming Kovic bestowed upon his screen alter ego the Bronze Star he had received for bravery in Vietnam.

Born on the Fourth of July is 143 minutes long, but only 17 are set in-country. Nevertheless, its effect on Kovic and, by extension, on all America is unmistakable. Vietnam adds poignancy to all that precedes and follows it.[37] The film opens to a voiceover recollection of a little boy's dreams of becoming a man. The time is 1956 in Massapequa, Long Island, as ten-year-old Ronnie plays war with his buddies in the woods. The camera roams about freely with the inquisitive energy of a youngster's mind and body, and the omniscience of an adult's painstaking recollection.

The credits roll over a Fourth of July parade as the Kovic family and townspeople wave flags and cheer the marching vets. Some of the soldiers in wheelchairs since World War II or Korea recoil as firecrackers explode near them. Ronnie's a bit scared when he makes eye contact with an amputee but is quickly distracted when his friend Donna gives him a Yankee's cap as a birthday present. His mother fits him with it and proudly proclaims, "You're my Yankee Doodle Dandy." That night during the fireworks display Ron shares his first kiss with Donna (Sedgwick). The inculcation of cherished American values and the innocence and exuberance of youth are recreated. Ronnie hits a home run in Little League. He listens to JFK's inaugural address on the old black-and-white television, and his doting mother cryptically says she had a dream that someday he, too, would make an important speech in front of a huge crowd. This is an idyllic childhood with his siblings in their devout Catholic home. Cut from the final film was one additional scene in which Ron and Donna watch an old John Wayne war movie.

Ideals of country and family are joined by competitive spiritedness and athletic prowess as the film shifts to Ron's adolescent years and Cruise takes over from child actor Bryan Larkin. A gym instructor shouts commands to the boys like a drill sergeant, thereby foreshadowing later events and weaving a rich texture into the film. Kovic wants to be the best and gives 110 percent to everything he does. His teachers and parents instill in him that victory requires sacrifice. He gives it his all but loses an important wrestling match before a packed crowd.

The film cuts to two marine recruiters addressing a male-only assembly. Flanked by the American flag, they proclaim that America has never lost a war because of the type of excellence the marines require and develop. In Ron's attentive mind military service is a proud shortcut to manhood. He is convinced to enlist and tells his many friends not to miss out on history, to defend America as their Dads did, and to stop communists. Many of the young, gawky boys are skeptical. As the seniors ponder their future at the malt shop, weighty issues such as college or military service give way to girls and the prom.

Ron loves Donna but is frightened by her and the feelings she stirs in him. Although he thinks she likes him, he hesitates and someone else asks her to the prom. The night of the big event, Ron packs for his imminent departure to marine boot camp. The film cuts between the pleasant dance and the serious soul-searching of the thoughtful boy on the threshold of manhood. Down the hall his little brother strums on a guitar and quietly sings Bob Dylan. Emerging from the bedroom replete with Yankees memorabilia and a crucifix, Ron sits with his loving father. His dad watches a television report featuring Oliver Stone as a reporter interviewing Dale Dye playing a colonel in Vietnam. We cringe as the officer says what we now know is naive nonsense about the enemy and the soon-to-be-victorious American effort. Ron's parents are anxious, but he reassures them by proclaiming his sense of duty in defense of what they taught him had to be protected: the American way. In one other instance of the television war's intrusion, his mother flips from a battlefield report to the mindless escapism of Rowan and Martin's "Laugh-In."

Returning to the privacy of the bedroom, Ron prays to Jesus that he has made the right decision. Then Ron runs out the door into the pouring rain to the prom. He enters soaking wet intent on finding his beloved. As the romantic "Moon River" plays, he shares a final slow dance and kiss with Donna. This is meant to be a magic, loving, almost dreamlike moment as the camera twirls them about deliriously.

A fade to blackness is followed by a bright, nearly blinding sunlight. At once it recalls the skyward shot that began the film as the boys played in the woods and conveys the heat of the exotic locale of Vietnam. It is October 1967 among the sand dunes near the Cua Viet River. Natural leader Kovic is now a sergeant on his second tour. He reassures a frightened cherry from Georgia. As dusk approaches they are about to go into a hamlet amid heavy fire. Chaos reigns as Kovic leads his squad in amid the deafening noise of combat. Once again the fluid confusion of such moments is memorably conveyed by Stone and his cinematographer. Some of the men, it is always difficult to tell exactly who, including the retreating NVA, fire into a hut. Inside Kovic discovers that they have slaughtered an entire family. He screams for a medic, crying as he attempts to tend to a baby. Then instantly the front shifts, and they must retreat to the sand dunes. Under heavy fire the confusion is exacerbated by the blinding light of the sunset. The men are merely silhouettes as they clamber toward safety. Even the experienced Kovic is terrified as his men and the enemy seem interspersed all about. Bullets whizzing by his head and his heavy breathing are magnificently engineered onto the stereo soundtrack.

Turning abruptly, Kovic fires at the outline of a soldier. As he falls it is apparent that the victim is Wilson, the young Georgia boy. Blood spurts from his arteries as Kovic and the others run to him. Kovic in a panic screams, "What happened?" but he knows. The young man is bleeding to death before our eyes. That night Kovic goes to see his commanding officer, played by John Getz. Choking back tears the still-youthful sergeant confesses, "I think I killed Wilson." His superior tells him it was convusing out there. Kovic persists in trying to accept blame and is finally ordered to shut up and is dismissed. Aside from portraying the familiar, self-interested hierarchy, the scene is nuanced with the superior's interest in dispelling this fine soldier's pain. After all why admit the deed? Who can be sure? And if so, it was a tragic accident. This not entirely unsympathetic aspect of the major's stonewalling is indicative of the film's strong writing and

Born on the Fourth of July (Universal Pictures, 1989). Tom Cruise as Ron Kovic is seriously injured while on patrol.

acting. Also nearly undetectable is the disapproving gaze of the young sentry (played by William Baldwin), which serves to reaffirm Kovic's assessment of the tragedy of his friendly fire.

Determined to move on from this event but riddled with Catholic guilt, the only thing the young sergeant can do in penance is to be an even better soldier. It is now January 1968 as several squads approach a village. Their eyes dart about trying to detect danger amid the huts and oxen. Suddenly the soldier operating the radio is struck by a bullet and blood explodes from his face. Shot in slow motion the impact is frozen and in great contrast to the quickness of action that ensues as the men get pinned down in the field. Like a machine, a movie warrior, Kovic fires round after round from his M-16. Suddenly his heel is ripped open by a bullet, and he falls down writhing in agony. Instead of staying down and waiting for a medic, he props himself back up and continues to fire. A bullet rips into his back, and the camera whirls about as he crumples to the ground. Suddenly his world is upside down as a brave black soldier scoops the now terribly wounded sarge to safety at great personal risk.

The chaos of the battlefield is replaced by the horror of the field hospital as countless casualties overwhelm the doctors. In a barely conscious state Kovic's life blood oozes out of him as he sees others suffering with gaping wounds, emergency amputations, and convulsions. A priest administers last rites to Kovic and he passes out. The fade to black ushers in the stateside story of his physical rehabilitation.

The terror of the MASH unit is replaced by the horrid squalor of the Bronx

VA hospital. The hallways are clogged with neglected and crippled veterans, flotsam of a far-off war who overwhelm even the most caring staffers. One man's catheter overflows with its unattended urine. Rats run about, and the evocation of filth is so powerful as to almost conjure up the amazing stench that must accompany such a terrible place.

Kovic is still bedridden; the sores on his buttocks protrude through the fitted stretcher, adding to the overall unkempt, sickly, and greasy look of the once-handsome man. The paralyzed vets are showered as if in a car wash, the system creaking with casualties as impersonality triumphs and adds insult to injury. Still determined to rise above all this, Kovic makes his bed like a good marine. He watches coverage of the riots at the Democratic National Convention and rails at the long-haired demonstrators as they burn his beloved American flag. He embraces physical therapy, determined that he will walk again. In an uncharacteristic anachronism, "American Pie" plays as he struggles on the parallel walking bars. He refuses to accept the truth when a doctor tells him he will be confined to a wheelchair for the rest of his life. Finally, he does ask if he will ever be able to have kids. The reply is a concise and deafening "No."

A black orderly reflects changing attitudes when he tells Kovic that Vietnam is a white man's war and a lot of nonsense. Kovic again rises to the establishment defense. He reflects on his situation, while next to him, with no privacy, a prostitute sits astride another wardmate. His determination and denial continue in the next scene as he drags his limbs about with the help of crutches and sheer upper body strength. This is really just a delusionary balancing act as he has no tone or feeling in his legs. Nevertheless, as concerned doctors look on he smiles in self-congratuation that he is "walking" again and yells, "Semper fi, motherfucker." He joy is short-lived as he collapses and in doing so breaks his leg, with the bone protruding sharply through the skin.

In a dream sequence, eerily evoked in the nocturnal corridors of the hospital, Kovic sees himself as he once was, a handsome young man running through the halls amid the sad amputees. Reaching full stride, he breaks into a toothy grin. Abruptly reality intrudes as he awakens suspended downward in a special rotating bed. He stares at his vomit-covered face reflected in a mirror placed upon the floor. Enraged he yells for help, which is a long time in coming. Despite the advice of doctors, he is trying to save his leg from amputation. The pumps that drain the poison from the infected limb keep breaking. A harried young doctor attempts to rig up a replacement, remarking that funding is not available for new equipment. After all the Vietnam War keeps draining the government budget. The victims of that war now suffer again with this inadequate care. Finally the orderly tells Kovic that if he would just let them take his leg, he could be out of here. Kovic cries out, "It's my leg, dammit" and bravely suffers to save his useless limb and thus a modicum of wholeness and dignity.

The film again fades to black, establishing each location as an important interior vignette. Each introductory shot serves as transition in an imaginative manner. Now it is 1969 and a car door opens to reveal Kovic with both legs about to return to his home. His father lovingly lifts his grown son into his wheelchair as if he were still a boy. Hesitantly his family greets him with hugs and kisses. His mother can barely bring herself to look upon his body. The neighbors gather about welcoming him home. They self-consciously do not know what to say, so they remark, "You look great" even though he still looks awful. His denial has been replaced by the denial of those around him. Only his father can reveal genuine emotion, kissing his son and tearfully saying he is glad Ron is home alive. Kovic gazes at his old room and his many athletic trophies.

In the next scene in Massapequa, Ron visits with an old high school buddy who went to business school while Ron was off at war. The comely waitresses in miniskirts show how fashions have changed as Ron shyly watches them sashaying around. The entrepreneur offers Ron a job in his burger joint, but he declines. After all the government pays him monthly compensation. Finally his old buddy admits that no one back here really cares about Vietnam, that America is getting badly beat up there, and that all this stuff about communism is ridiculous anyway. Ron continues to defend what led him to Vietnam. However, unlike what less astute critics proclaimed was a quick transformation, Cruise conveys in his eyes the pain that is evoked every time he hears such proclamations. He is listening to every word. After the orderly and then his buddy, his brother too challenges the war and the purpose of Ron's sacrifice. At the dinner table domestic peace has been replaced by politics and railing as Ron tells his brother off and yells, "America, love it or leave it!" His sisters weep at the family strife.

As "It's a Grand Old Flag" belts out, Ron's dad helps him prepare to be the honoree at a Fourth of July parade. His smart parade dress uniform contrasts with the mundane reality that his father must change his catheter before the legionnaires arrive. Ron waves from the convertible as the surrealism of such an event confronts him and the audience. Murky slow motion accompanies the scene as he, too, winces when firecrackers remind him of bullets in combat. The old storefronts have become head shops, and some of the hippies wave, while others flip him the middle finger. Awaiting his introduction, the decorated vet nervously surveys the crowd. His family and neighbors stare back at him as if he is a curiosity at a fair. The speaker proclaims the ultimate sacrifice of many a Massapequa son in this conflict and says America is going to win this war! Kovic momentarily misses his cue as his mind wanders off amid the whir of helicopters and the sound of a crying baby. He begins to speak but is unable to continue and is mercifully whisked from the stage. As his family carries him off, his old friend Timmy, played by Frank Whaley, rushes to hug him. He lingers in embrace with this long-haired fellow vet in an Army jacket. Their tear-filled eyes convey a truly mutual understanding of the pain.

That evening in the backyard, Ron and Timmy have a cathartic heart to heart. They laugh as they reminisce and cry over everyone and everything that died in Vietnam. Finally in relaying the story of his crippling wound, Ron admits he should have stayed down but thought he was "John fucking Wayne." Timmy, who suffered a head injury, tries to cheer Ron up: "It's your birthday; you're alive." But it is not just his injury and lost friends that trouble Ron; it is that he believes he failed. He says he made mistakes and killed some people. This is a muddled confession that Timmy tries to ease by remarking how crazy it was over there. All Ron knows is that he is paralyzed, castrated, and, now he admits, stupid.

Ron travels to Syracuse University to see Donna. The campus is enlivened with antiwar activity. They are excited to see each other. So much has happened and she strongly opposes the war. No longer is Ron a potential lover; he is now an object of pity. Donna invites him to lend his experience to the antiwar movement, but Ron prefers just to listen. As Donna goes off to a demonstration planning meeting with some guy, a boyfriend perhaps, Ron's impotence is underscored by the fact that he cannot maneuver his wheelchair over a high curb. The next day at a rally at the administration building Abbie Hoffman plays the spokesperson. An angry black vet throws his medals away in protest, as if in a moment of rebirth at a religious revival. The overzealous police fire tear gas and move in clubbing unarmed students. Ron is horrified at the domestic battle that swirls all around him.

Integrating the familiar scene of the reaction of vets from another war, Ron and Timmy shoot pool at a bar back in Long Island. Kovic is drunk and obnoxious as he whines and moans about the war. Finally a tough old marine says they oughta bomb the hell out of Hanoi and if Ron was not in that chair, the man would beat him up. The disillusioned hero is led to safety by his friends. He drowns his sorrow by drinking and wildly dancing in his wheelchair with a cute girl. She does not take him seriously, and eventually he tips over his chair and passes out.

He is an abusive and embittered drunk when his buddies finally drop him off in the wee hours at his quiet suburban home. His father tries to help him in; a portrait of Nixon hangs next to Jesus in the entryway. Ron's mother is angry and embarrassed by the late-night carousing. What ensues is one of the most powerful scenes of anger and angst in the book. It escalates out of control as Ron swears and spits, his mother rails at his debauchery, and his father attempts to maintain household order. The whole family, if not the neighborhood, is awakened as Ron shouts in self-realization about what a fool he has been. He sees his sacrifice as having been for nought and his parents as a party to the lies and propaganda that led him to his current state. He shouts about his broken body and his useless penis. The very use of the word infuriates his mother, so he yells it over and over to torment her. Finally she says to hell with him and storms off as his siblings break down and sob. His father carries him to bed, reattaches his catheter, and gently suggests that perhaps he should leave for a while.

This blackout leads to Villa Dulce in Mexico in 1970. Many paralyzed veterans have escaped here for the weather, the drugs, the tequila, and the prostitutes. Ron meets Charly from Chicago, played by Willem Dafoe. He shows Ron the ropes, including how a crippled man can be with a woman. Like the poignant scene in *Coming Home,* the sex is secondary to the desperately needed intimacy. Ron lapses in and out of drunken debauchery, which the others seem to easily revel in. His thoughts take him to Wilson, the young Georgia boy he shot. Ron writes and reads amid the episodes of carousing. Summarizing his descent, he is finally able to eat the worm that sits in the bottom of the tequila bottle. Thrown out of one whorehouse, Charly and Ron venture to another. When they start fighting, the cab driver abandons the two wheelchair-bound men in the desert. The stupidity of their drunken argument and the escalation of their anger are enhanced as the camera careens in a circle as they spit at and punch each other. Charly taunts Ron and asks him if he ever killed a baby. They flail at each other, finally collapsing in the sand sweaty, exhausted and stranded. Quietly Ron cries and wonders what happened to the men they once were, "before we got so lost." He has reached his nadir.

Trying to reclaim his way, Kovic ventures to Georgia. First he pays a visit to Wilson's grave and then proceeds to his house. The father ushers Ron into the ramshackle rural home, and mother, widow, and young son welcome any friend of their fallen loved one. Just seeing a comrade who knew him is painful for the family. The little boy plays with a toy gun as Ron looks about the room in this awkward social situation. Memorabilia from the father's service in World War II completes a three-generational reference to the continuity of war. Finally Ron gets around to the purpose of his visit. He chokes back emotion as he slowly tells how the young man died. Sensing his pain and their own fear, the mother politely says in her thick but friendly southern accent, "We don't have to hear this." However, Ron must continue. Finally he says it: he killed their loved one. The words fall out amid the tears; the confession pent up for years has now been shared. The young widow is the first to speak to the trembling Ron. "What's done is done. I can't ever forgive you, but maybe the Lord can." It is not said with malice; it is just how she feels and conveys a faith in God that evokes the religious "mythic track" that is only one of many operating here. With great compassion the mother merely says, "We understand Ron. . . . We understand the pain you've been going through." As this now-quiet pivotal scene set in Dixie fades out, the strains of "When Johnny Comes Marching Home" are faintly heard.

Having confessed his sin, Ron is now able to begin getting on with his life. He has reached an accommodation with his physical circumstances, but it is his mental transition that provides the analogy for much of America's evolution. Ron is now pushed along by a fellow vet as they march in protest at the 1972 Republican National Convention in Miami Beach. They wave the flag of the Vietnam Veterans Against the War. Inside, shot like a television image, is newsreel footage of Nixon accepting the nomination and accolades of the crowd. Now a leader of the antiwar veterans, Ron and others attempt to get on the convention floor. Security tries to prevent them as curious journalists converge on the fracas. They thrust microphones at Ron as he proclaims that he loves America but that the war is wrong. His poignant speech is cut short as delegates rail at the traitor, and one even spits upon him. In the parking lot a riot ensues as tear gas swirls about in a police helicopter's wake. It not only evokes an image of combat but also recalls the previous antiwar riot. One of the vet protestors turns out to be an FBI spy who roughs up Ron while attempting to arrest him. Protestors battle police as a big black vet takes advantage of the chaos to whisk the immobile Kovic off the ground to safety. The brave actions of years ago when Ron was wounded and his life changed forever are echoed as he is carried off over the shoulder of this protective comrade. In the rear the sergeant leader, the Yankee Doodle Dandy, rallies his troops. Ron proclaims, "Let's take the hall!"

There is fade to black and it is now four years later. America and Ron Kovic have come a long way. The Vietnam War is over, and the 1976 Democratic National Convention is under way. No longer is the representative of the veteran's group on the outside trying to get in. He is about to be introduced as a featured speaker. Ron looks happy and handsome again. As he is wheeled out to the awaiting throng, lightbulbs flash and Ron thinks back to the triumphant childhood moment when he hit the home run and when his mom predicted he would make an important speech. He has regained the exhilaration of the Little Leaguer and answers a reporter's query as to how he feels by proclaiming, "I feel like I'm home." America's son has returned and as the patriotic "It's a Grand Old Flag" belts out, he receives a huge ovation from the crowd in the hall bedecked in red, white, and blue. He flashes a grin and the peace sign, and this time the movie fades to white.

This tour de force received a panoply of positive coverage. In a glowing review *Time* pointed out the painful debate the film evoked. For Kovic the "regeneration" was only partial. Never did the film provide a pat reconciliation with his mother or a final kiss with Donna.[38] The hero has come a long way, but there is still more healing to go, and none of it can ever make his life all better. The theme of manhood that runs throughout the film allowed for only a partial sense of renewed virility and potency. For America films like this only hinted at an evolving process that may have reached a crescendo in the "triumph" of the Gulf War.

Vincent Canby in the *New York Times* conveyed the synthesis of the pertinent subgenres when he wrote, "Stunning. A film of enormous visceral power. [It] connects the war of arms abroad with the war of conscience at home." In a momentous march to acclaim, grunt-turned-filmmaker Oliver Stone won the Director's Guild of America award. Twenty years to the day after being shot in combat in Vietnam, Ron Kovic won the Golden Globe award for best adapted screenplay. Tom Cruise received numerous acting awards but was edged out at the Oscars in April 1990 by Daniel Day Lewis for *My Left Foot*. Stone and the film editor took home Academy Awards among eight nominations.

Perhaps hinting at America's continued reluctance to embrace such challenging and controversial Vietnam War films was the awarding of the Best Picture Oscar to the noncontroversial *Driving Miss Daisy*. Ultimately the gross of this major star vehicle but depressing drama also reflected the desire of the public for escapism and the residue of reluctance that continues to contribute to reticence in the production of serious Vietnam War films. The domestic first-run tally for *Born on the Fourth of July* was a respectable but disappointing $70 million. (To put this figure in context, Tom Cruise's exceptionally shallow 1988 movie *Cocktail* grossed some $10 million more.) Foreign box office and videotape rentals were outstanding.[39]

Shortly after *Born on the Fourth of July*'s award triumphs, Loretta Smith produced a documentary on the same subject entitled *A Good American: The Ron Kovic Story*. By the end of 1990, America would be marching to the drumbeats of a new war, to begin in early 1991 in the Persian Gulf. The final contributions to the Vietnam War films released in the new decade will be covered in the next chapter. To conclude this one it is fitting to mention the circumstances surrounding the positive reception that Kovic, Stone, and their film received at the Berlin Film Festival. Taking place in the capital of another onetime enemy, the drama of the films in competition was overshadowed by real-world events. As the festival prepared for its finale, so, too, did the decade. The leaders of the Iron Curtain communist foes of the West announced their intention to clear away the symbol of the cold war, the Berlin Wall. It fell on November 9, 1989, to the cheers of the crowd. Middle-aged director Oliver Stone and his peer, activist-writer Ron Kovic, gathered amid the throngs at the Brandenburg Gate. Years before they had answered their country's call to fight communism, and now how poignant it was that they could be there at the moment that symbolized the downfall of that ideology and the possibility of renewed cooperation among the people of the earth.

References

1. Lawrence MacDonald, "Vietnam Movies Distort Reality and Erase Identities," *Chicago Tribune*, April 6, 1990, p. 23.

2. Marc Coopper, "Oliver Stone Interview," *Playboy* 35 (February 1988), p. 58.

3. "Speak Your Peace," *Film Comment* (March-April 1989), p. 14.

4. "Brotherly Media," *The Nation* 248, 23, (June 12, 1989), p. 826.

5. Karen Jaehne, *Cineaste* (Fall 1989), cited in the University of Minnesota Film Society Program Notes, February 16 to March 11, 1990, pp. 1–4.

6. Uli Schmetzer, "Vietnam Idles Critical Filmmaker," *Chicago Tribune*, December 15, 1991, p. 18.

7. *World Press Review* (London), 35, 9 (September 1988), p. 63.

8. "Lifestyle," *Newsweek*, August 31, 1987, p. 68.

9. *Ibid.*, p. 69.

10. Tri-Star Pictures, *Rambo Production Notes* (Los Angeles: Tri-Star Pictures, 1988), p. 38.

11. Army Archerd, "Just for Variety," *Daily Variety*, October 29, 1991, p. 2.

12. James R. McDonough, *Platoon Leader* (Novato, Calif.: Presidio Press, 1985).

13. Paramount Pictures, *Distant Thunder Handbook of Production Information* (Los Angeles: Paramount Pictures, 1988), quoting *Harpers* and other sources.

14. "Lost in America," *Time*, February 11, 1991, pp. 76–77.

15. William Adams, "Still Shooting After All These Years," *Mother Jones* 13, 1 (January 1988), p. 48.

16. William C. Anderson, *Bat 21* (Englewood Cliffs, N.J.: Prentice-Hall, 1980).

17. Karen Jaehne, "Company Man," *Film Comment* 25, 2 (March-April 1989), p. 13.

18. "Cameos," *Premiere* (April 1989), p. 66.

19. Cited in Jaehne, "Company Man," p. 12.

20. *Ibid.*, p. 12.

21. *Premiere* (April 1989), p. 66.

22. Adam Rifkin, "The Secrets of Movie Advertising," *Premiere* (October 1990), p. 38.

23. Mac, "Casualties of War—Film Reviews," *Daily Variety Annual Review*, August 11, 1989, p. 234.

24. Gavin Smith, "Body Count: Rabe and DePalma's Wargasm," *Film Comment* 25, 4 (July-August 1989), pp. 49–52.

25. Jay Scott, "Back to the Wall," *Film Comment* 25, 5 (September-October 1989), p. 11.

26. Don Groves, "Casualties Campaigns Strong in Europe," *Daily Variety*, January 22, 1990, p. 50. Box office grosses throughout are from *Variety, Daily Variety*, miscellaneous general press, and Entertainment Data, Inc., of Los Angeles.

27. John F. Kennedy, "Inaugural Address," January 20, 1961, as cited in Ron Kovic, *Born on the Fourth of July* (New York: McGraw-Hill, 1976), preface.

28. Robert Scheer, "Born on the Third of July," *Premiere* (February 1990), p. 52.

29. *Ibid.*

30. Cooper, "Oliver Stone Interview," p. 112.

31. Alan Mirabella, "Mad About Filmmaking," *St. Paul Pioneer Press*, January 4, 1990, p. 10.

32. *Ibid.*

33. Robert Scheer, "Tom Cruise Interview," *Playboy* 37 (January 1990), p. 58.

34. Cooper, "Oliver Stone Interview," p. 59.

35. *Ibid.*, p. 58.

36. Universal Studios, "Born on the Fourth of July," *Universal News* (Los Angeles: Universal Studios, 1989).

37. Richard Corliss, "Cruise Control," *Time* (December 25, 1989), pp. 74–79.

38. *Ibid.*, p. 76.

39. Jack Putman, "U.S. Roster Strong Overseas, 'Born' Bows Hot," *Daily Variety*, March 5, 1990, p. 9.

Chapter 10

To the Gulf
and Beyond, 1990–1993

The 1990s began with great optimism as the cold war came to an end. However, by the end of 1990 the United States and an allied United Nations force were marching toward a "hot" war in the Persian Gulf. That conflict, more than any passage of time or diminution of communist threat, would have a great impact on the American view of the Vietnam War and its veterans. The initial historic debate over a response to Iraq's aggression against Kuwait would be filled not only with lessons learned or missed concerning Vietnam but also with the iconography of the films now thoroughly integrated into the domestic as well as international psyche. While the drums of war beat, both Saddam Hussein's foreign minister, Tariq Aziz, and President Bush referred to *Rambo*. It was now clear that character had supplanted John Wayne as a representative of the persevering American fighter unburdened by self-doubt.

By 1991, amid other great geopolitical events, the war of words would become Operation Desert Storm. The means of coverage, which contributed to the notion that Vietnam was the first television war, were completely antiquated relative to the instant purveyors of the images in the Gulf of the video and satellite age. As always these real-life events altered motion picture images, while at the same time more traditional entries continued into the list of films.

Around the time Oliver Stone was collecting his Oscar for *Born on the Fourth of July, Time* conducted a poll among Americans on the subject of Vietnam some 15 years after the fall of Saigon. In conjunction with CNN, *Time* asked, "Was the U.S. right or wrong to get involved in the Vietnam War?" Respondents were broken down into the general public and Vietnam vets. The public response was "Right—29%, Wrong—57%." The vets said, "Right—58%, Wrong—32%." "Should the U.S. re-establish diplomatic relations with Vietnam? . . . Public Yes 48%, Vets Yes 44%." "Do you believe that any American MIA's are still alive in Vietnam? The reply was yes from 62% of the public and a whopping 84% of the vets."[1] Despite joy and pride concerning the apparent victory of democratic values over totalitarianism in Eastern Europe, Americans remained pained, guilt-ridden, and embarrassed by our one military defeat and its huge human cost.

Discussion of a diplomatic rapprochement between the former enemies continued but were heavily dependent on joint cooperation with MIA-POW investigation teams. Several Vietnam veterans, some of whom had even been POWs, were now U.S. senators, and they took a leading role in this dialogue. In fact as the crumbling Soviet Union retracted its economic and political support, the Vietnamese hinted that perhaps the United States would like to lease its former bases at Cam Ranh Bay and Da Nang (especially in light of the anticipated loss by the Americans of similar facilities in the Philippines). Immediately prior to the outbreak of hostilities in the Persian Gulf, pop culture did its part to maintain the previous war at the forefront. *Born on the Fourth of July* played at the movies, ABC's "China Beach" aired weekly on television, and the hottest ticket on Broadway was for *Miss Saigon.*

Reflecting the globalized nature of cinema, Australia's Philip Noyce directed Holland's Rutger Hauer as a blind Vietnam veteran in Tri-Star's *Blind Fury*, which integrated martial arts with the samurai legend and in fact credited Japan's Ryozo Kasahara for its original idea. The star's loss of sight is a consequence of his wartime service, after which he benefited from mental conditioning by a Zen master. This holistic training connotes a postwar desire for inner peace and recovery. Thus Hauer's character joins Rambo and the entire country in striving to move on from the trauma. Nevertheless, the interdisciplinary expertise does come in handy when the hero is forced to take on the Mafia.

Completely incidental was the verbal admission that the hotshot pilot played by Kevin Costner in *Revenge* was a Vietnam naval aviator. This February 1990 release from Columbia was a misstep in the star's rise to box office prominence.

Reflecting sign-of-the-times nostalgia was Paramount's comedy *Flashback.* Like most films dealing with the domestic scene during the war, it had difficulty evoking the era. Franco Amurri directed Kiefer Sutherland as a rookie FBI agent who is an uptight yuppie entrusted with the task of escorting a federal prisoner back to justice. The longtime fugitive is played by Dennis Hopper doing an Abbie Hoffman imitation. The actor associated with *Easy Rider* and the drug subculture thus integrates his own persona with that of his character, Huey.

The self-parody begins as the graying "radical court jester" babbles about the politics and sex of twenty years ago. The uptight suit, Sutherland, finally asks what Huey did to become a fugitive. He did not blow up a building; he merely played a prank on Spiro Agnew. Eventually Hopper manages to slip LSD into Sutherland's drink, and the drugs lighten the kid up, allowing him to have sex but nearly costing him his job.

It turns out that Sutherland is the child of hippie commune dwellers but is ashamed of his past. Carol Kane shows up as an old friend who explains amid the peace signs, love beads, and Hendrix music what the 1960s were all about. Her grainy home movies merely confirm the feeling of a bygone era and bring tears to the eyes of Sutherland. Richard Masur and Michael McKean are amusing as solid citizens and parents who relish the opportunity to relive their college activist days by aiding Huey in his attempted escape.

Flashback (Paramount Pictures, 1990). The psychedelic 1960s collide with the Reagan 1980s. Kiefer Sutherland (left), Carol Kane, and Dennis Hopper star.

Producer-screenwriter David Loughery writes several lines that take a jab at the "Me" decade of the 1980s. For instance, Hopper tells Sutherland that during the Reagan administration, all the poor people were homeless and all the rich people were in the Betty Ford clinic.[2] Comedy and chase sequences are uncomfortably mingled with observations on the massive bombing of North Vietnam and other serious subjects. The film is most successful in showing how conservative and liberal ideals ebb and flow in America, the recently past 1980s in marked contrast to the unrest of the late 1960s. Inevitably the depictions of the 1960s take on a feeling of fuzzy nostalgia that is unable to evoke the powerful angst of that era.

Shortly after *Flashback*, New Line released another 1960s Rip Van Winkle tale entitled, with appropriate lingo, *Far Out Man*. Tommy Chong starred as a hippie who reawakens in the present. The Vietnam War was even less prominent, and this movie made *Flashback* seem like extremely astute cultural commentary.

In March, Robert Ginty, who played Dink in *Coming Home*, directed and starred in *Vietnam, Texas*. He portrayed Father Thomas McCain, a veteran-turned-priest who feels compelled to confront his past and search for the family he abandoned. His quest takes him to the Southeast Asian immigrant community in Houston. There he locates his old lover, once again played by the graceful Kieu Chinh. Their daughter, played by Tamlyn Tomita, is now nearly an adult and believes her GI father died back in Nam. The new husband and surrogate father is an Asian mobster played by Haing S. Ngor (*The Killing Fields* and *Iron*

Triangle). The coincidences with previous film entries continue as Ginty enlists the help of reluctant fellow vet Tim Thomerson (*Uncommon Valor*). Aiding them is their earnest Asian buddy, who yearns to be a stand-up comedian and imitates Robin Williams in the recently released *Good Morning, Vietnam*. In a subplot reminiscent of *Alamo Bay*, Ginty champions the cause of the immigrant fishing families who are discriminated against by the Americans who feel their livelihood is threatened.

The film is full of recriminations and confessions. Ginty begins his adventure by confessing to his monsignor. Later he must confess to his Amerasian daughter. Chinh in turn must confess the sin of taking up with a gangster, albeit one who offered security to a woman and her victimized child, shunned for their connection to an American. Eventually Ngor's goons attempt to crucify the priest using ice picks in a packing house. He escapes, but the film, like the war itself, does not have a happy ending. Perhaps this independent effort was meant to subtextually convey that like the well-meaning intervention of the United States into the conflict, this American's intrusion into the postwar scene and his attempt to remedy the past merely bring additional tragedy.

Reflecting the overall shift from enemies to friends was the cultural exchange of films and the employment of U.S. theater chains and studios to build modern multiplexes in various countries of the former Soviet Union. Premiering in Moscow was a Vietnam-related film from RKO/Pavilion Pictures entitled *False Identity*. James Keach directed Genevieve Bujold and his brother Stacy as a naval intelligence officer who was listed as dead. He now returns 17 years after the war has ended. It turns out he was the victim of an attempted murder on the part of some murkily drawn government operatives. Disc jockey Bujold becomes intrigued by the mystery when she finds an abandoned Purple Heart at a Veterans Day garage sale. Keach's circumstances and the steel plate in his head all conjure up memories of his other appearances in equally bad films such as *The Ninth Configuration* and *The Forgotten*.

In another cultural exchange known as the Peace Marathon, *Heart of the Warriors* was screened. This 1990 release equated the U.S. and Soviet experiences in Vietnam and Afghanistan and examined the traumas shared by the young veterans of each war. It was produced by Michael Franck and directed by Steve Peck.

An independent feature that quickly went the video route was the generically titled *Fatal Mission*, shot in the Philippines. Here sporting a bit of a paunch was Peter Fonda as a CIA operative in the 1960s. The in-country tale opens in Haiphong during the war as Fonda poses as a French journalist. He is covering a communist rally in which an NVA general whips the crowd into a frenzy beneath a huge picture of Mao Zedong (not Ho Chi Minh?). Using a camera equipped with a gun, Fonda assassinates the official and escapes amid the chaos, which includes the indiscriminate spraying of the crowd with bullets. Witnessing all this is lovely Tia Carrere, a Chinese agent who was sent to do the same job. As if she is "the Girl from U.N.C.L.E.," Carrere retreats to a little shop that leads to a huge underground intelligence complex. Fonda meets up with his contact in the bush, played by Mako. The password they use to make contact is "Purple Haze" followed by "Jimi Hendrix." The Asian guide cannot wait to get to the LZ as he has been promised passage to America, where he intends to open a restaurant. As with 1986's *P.O.W.: The Escape*, this is an elusive dream for Mako's character, who is killed by Carrere. The beautiful and mysterious agent remains hot on Fonda's trail.

Eventually a helicopter sent to rescue Fonda is shot down. In a twist representative of the now well-established CIA double-cross theme, the American pilot, Chris Mitchum, is actually there to terminate Fonda. Carrere saves Fonda's life at the last moment. She captures him and they are eventually forced to cooperate in order to elude the pursuing North Vietnamese. Who is holding whom captive changes several times but becomes irrelevant as a love-hate relationship develops and is eventually consummated on screen. Their banter reveals the chauvinist notion that most Americans view Asian women as "gook slits" and explains that, despite the fact that Americans think all Asians look alike, there is great rivalry between the Vietnamese and Chinese. The film occasionally flashes to Saigon as CIA types beneath a picture of LBJ attempt to track their wayward agent. Several firefights ensue in the jungle and along the river. At one point the two fugitives take cover in an abandoned French-era plantation. In another scene they enlist the help of Buddhist monks, who seem to rise above the earthly carnage that surrounds them. Eventually Fonda is able to steal an airplane and escape without Carrere, despite the fact that she fought off an approaching patrol so he could effectuate the takeoff. She escapes into the jungle to an unknown fate, and Fonda lands in Laos. In the last scene he approaches what should be the safety of the American Embassy. Near the gate he is assassinated.

After *Born on the Fourth of July*'s run ended, it was television, not the theatrical market, that was to provide the highest-profile imagery of Vietnam in the first half of 1990. "China Beach" met with great critical acclaim and was nominated for seven Emmy awards in its second full year. John Sacret Young, who had contributed to *A Rumor of War*, created and wrote most of the shows. In April and September the weekly one-hour series was expanded into two-hour telefilms, which eventually made their way into the video stores. Lead Dana Delaney brought intelligence and beauty to her role as a devoted nurse at a hospital and R&R center by the South China Sea. The ensemble cast allowed for a variety of stories. The drama evolved from evocations of the old nurse-in-peril episodes to crisp *M*A*S*H*–like writing in the inherently ironic field hospital setting. The series was bold in flashing some episodes forward to the present in order to examine the effects of the war. Music from the era helped evoke bittersweet memories. Although a very sad time, the participants eventually look back on the heightened awareness and vitality that their existence in a war zone provided versus their present existence. The series does not glorify the war, but it does convey the centrality of that experience in the characters' lives and self-awareness. By extension it evokes similar emotions in its core audience. Concomitantly real-world events were confirming Vietnam's place as a fundamental source of national development. When "China Beach" at last received its cancellation notice, the finale featured a tearful trek to the Vietnam veterans memorial in Washington, D.C.

Featured on NBC's Monday Night at the Movies was a sign-of-the-times portrait in *Flying Blind*. The title connotes the innocence that recedes with adulthood and sometimes leads young people into war. Two talented young actors, Frank Whaley and Richard Panebianco, who had both appeared in *Born on the Fourth of July,* starred. Vince DiPersio was the writer-director. The film opens in 1965 in Phila-

"China Beach" (ABC Television Network, 1990). Dana Delaney as an army nurse in the weekly television drama set in Vietnam.

delphia as several buddies graduate from high school and confront the draft and their future. College, Vietnam, drugs, and sex await the various characters.

The same network also offered up the made-for-television *The Girl Who Came Between Them,* starring Cheryl Ladd and Anthony John Denison. Mel Damsk directed this story of an Amerasian orphan, or *bui dui* (pronounced boo die), "a child of the dust." Once again coming to terms in a head-on fashion with a Vietnam legacy became an important prerequisite to rebirth. No longer could the war be suppressed in the back of its participants' psyches.

Denison is a vet who is a successful businessperson and has a lovely wife. We are way past the unemployed and impotent soldiers by now. Nevertheless, he does visit a VA counselor every week to sort out wartime experiences. Denison does not flashback in the sense of a psychotic episode; rather, he finds his mind turning back to memories of his pregnant in-country lover, whom he abandoned when the war ended. Like many a film vet he both torments and relieves himself by going through his Vietnam memorabilia. Inevitably the uniform barely fits, the black-and-white photo of the platoon reveals a bunch of mere kids, and the medals gather dust.

Denison's wife tries to understand but feels threatened by her husband's dwelling on the past. With the help of the counselor, played by Joe Spano, the loving wife becomes a party to the search and eventual reconciliation. They offer the only chance of "making up for the betrayal and ugliness of that war." This type of story is perfect for the television medium and is the melodramatic variation on the B action movies' attempt at reunion and renewal. In those films tension is mounted through gun play. Here it is the mystery of penetrating the bureaucratic labyrinths that both the United States and Vietnam maintain. Eventually the offspring of the long-past union is located using a lead from a *Life* magazine photo. Denison is skeptical that the mother is the same woman he once knew and with whom he fathered the girl. Nevertheless, they come to live in the United States. Despite the plethora of material comforts and the aid of Denison's entire American family, the adjustment is difficult. Finally it becomes clear the "mother" is actually not the old lover, who died years before. However, she, too, is allowed to stay and begin a new life in the United States. The film contains a postscript concerning the 40,000 Amerasian children from the war. It notes that they are victims of discrimination in their homeland and that only 9,700 have been successfully relocated to the United States.

Similar to the previous month's entry and blending predecessors such as *Green Eyes* and *The Children of An Lac* with the impending doom in *Saigon: Year of the Cat* and *The Killing Fields* was the telefilm *The Last Flight Out*. This true story filmed in Bangkok starred Richard Crenna as a Pan Am pilot, James Earl Jones as the airline head in Saigon, Haing S. Ngor as his loyal local assistant, Arliss Howard as chief mechanic, and James Hong as an immigration official. Larry Ellikan directed this docudrama from a Walter Halsey Davis script. In the background the BBC announces that Da Nang has fallen to the communists, a fate that soon awaits Saigon. Bravery, altruism, and even trickery combine in an effort to secure safe passage for orphans and Vietnamese employed by the United States. This is a desperate situation, and those associated with the longtime U.S. presence are believed to be on a death list. As each of the commercial airlines ceases operations and the diplomatic corps is evacuated, it becomes clear that soon time will run out. Nevertheless, Pan Am station manager Topping manages to get at least two packed planes out each week. This is the story of Pan Am 8732. It is compelling television drama that traces each day leading up to the takeoff of that last flight out on April 30, 1975, with 463 lucky passengers on a 375-seat jet. The crew was an all-volunteer force assembled in Manila and mindful of the grave dangers that accompanied their effort. Several of the real-life heroes contributed their expertise to the production.

Aside from being well acted, the film was interesting in its depiction of the lives of a number of South Vietnamese middle-class families. This was in marked contrast to the usual characters, who were black-marketeers, prostitutes, corrupt government officials, nondescript ARVN soldiers, peasants, or VC. Academy Award winner and real-life refugee from Pol Pot's killing fields Haing S. Ngor was asked if these films trivialized the true story. He replied that it was important to try because "if we don't get the story out, understanding is blocked—if you don't tell me your story, I don't know you as a human."[3]

Air America (Tri-Star Pictures, 1990). Mel Gibson adds glamor to the CIA's secret operations in Laos.

The summer of 1990 was conspicuously lacking in any Vietnam films. Instead there were attempts to glorify the military in matinee idol vehicles such as *Navy Seals,* starring Charlie Sheen, and *Fire Birds,* starring Nicolas Cage and actress Sean Young as Apache helicopter pilots. That aircraft was to have a prominent role shortly in the Gulf War. These films, like the post–cold war thriller *The Hunt for Red October,* all received military assistance in their productions as their scripts conformed to the positive imagery that the Pentagon was seeking.

Receiving assistance from the Royal Thai Armed Forces was the late-summer release *Air America,* with Mel Gibson and Robert Downey, Jr. Carolco Pictures was responsible for the film, using its usual distribution partner, Tri-Star Pictures. Essentially the film's "Terry and the Pirates"–type intrigue is no different from the 1948 entry *Saigon.* Exploiting handsome stars and exotic location, studio publicists did a tremendous job in placing stories in the general press prior to the film's release. In each of these features the Southeast Asian setting was secondary to the promised good humor and adventure. The film attempted to blend comedy into the Vietnam War context and, like its predecessors, was largely unsuccessful. (Perhaps Billy Wilder's *Stalag 17* and, in a differing manner, *M*A*S*H* have been most successful in integrating black comedy into films set in wartime and in so doing enhancing the overall dramatic effect.) *Air America*'s entire production history is testament to the depoliticization of the Vietnam conflict in an attempt to enhance box office appeal.

The print ads featured copy that was a takeoff on the army's ubiquitous new recruiting campaign. The copy read, "The Few. The Proud. The Totally Insane . . . *Air America* . . . Anything. Anywhere. Anytime." What inspired this tale was the real-life U.S. government–owned airline in Southeast Asia that grew out of the Flying Tigers of World War II. By 1947 it ferried supplies for Chiang Kai-shek's Nationalist Chinese. That same year the CIA was formed and took over the operation. It began support flights for the anticommunists in Southeast Asia and expanded the operation in the early 1960s on behalf of American allies in the Laotian civil war. The pilots were a rowdy group of hellraisers who thrived on danger and partied to legendary extremes in the nightspots of Vientiane, the Laotian capital. As the secret war effort expanded, so, too, did the fleet of C-123s and their payload. One of the items transported was the opium crop of friendly warlords who commanded the Laotian mercenary forces. Apparently the ends justified the means, and this cargo funded the rest of the clandestine operation on behalf of more conventional military and political objectives. In fact the CIA sold the airline in 1976 and turned over $20 million to the U.S. Treasury. British journalist Christopher Robbins had documented the colorful enterprise in his book entitled *Air America.*

Back in 1978 Lorimar Films had bought the rights to Robbins's book. The first script was unacceptable, so director Richard Rush (*Stuntman*) fashioned another. Sean Connery agreed to star, and by now Carolco had acquired the rights. Producer Dan Melnick fired the director and brought in a new screenwriter. The first three script versions had elements of black comedy and focused on the naïveté of the young American protagonist and the turmoil in the Asian culture amid the war. The new writer, John Eskow, was actually a contributor to "Saturday Night Live." He along with Melnick and newly assigned director Roger Spottiswoode altered the film's vision and in so doing removed most of its political controversy.[4] The new scriptwriter actually bragged in a high-profile *Premiere* magazine article that "it's a fun, zany thing for the whole family, with laughs aplenty and big things blowing up."[5] Despite the film's early–1970s setting along the Ho Chi Minh Trail, director Spottiswoode went so far as to say it was not a war film at all but rather a tale of "loyalties torn" and "morals under pressure."[6]

The other types of prerelease publicity found it rollicking good fun to focus on the travails of the cast and crew in their Third World locationing. Producer Melnick brought in "200 Western style toilets and 170 water heaters in these little Thai hotels." Star Downey joked, "I'm not a Southeast Asia kind of guy. . . . One walk through the meat market, and I'll never eat anything with a heartbeat again."[7] *Premiere* magazine had nearly become a shill for the studio publicists by the time it reprinted the Thai police's safety instructions to the crew, which included "Try not to walk in darkness place of trekking in jungle alone."[8]

An obtrusive rock-and-roll score was used throughout the film. It opens in Laos in 1969, intercutting between President Nixon lying about no U.S. military presence there and the dropping of various supplies to isolated villages. Finally a pig in a crate comes crashing into a grass hut, and as it runs off squealing, the film cuts back to Nixon's lips. Viewers are probably annoyed by the lack of subtlety, but in the very next scene the film momentarily wins them back. A lone peasant sniper fires one shot at the Air America plane. He then walks off, while over his shoulder in the background we see smoke trailing out as the plane goes down to an off-screen crash. The moment is funny, but we are not positive why. The film proceeds in this flawed manner, unable to reach an equilibrium in tone.

The pilots rush out of the airfield bar. David Marshall Grant (from *Bat 21*) restrains fellow pilot Mel Gibson from going into the flaming wreckage. An official notes, "We're not here right now. This didn't happen." Gibson remarks disgustedly, "Tell that to the dead man." Cutting to Los Angeles, the film shows traffic helicopter pilot Downey crash his rig and get fired. Arriving at his apartment, decorated with peace signs and Hendrix posters, some mysterious suits offer him a new job full of adventure. The naïve kid signs up and winds up in Laos.

Gibson takes the bewildered rookie under his wing and admits, "What's considered psychotic behavior anywhere else is company business here . . . [but] we're not here." The remark at once subliminally recalls Gibson's familiar character Martin Riggs, the wired vet from the *Lethal Weapon* series, and also the analogy between the government, especially the doublespeak expert CIA, and corporate America. Nevertheless, the very fact that in the next sequence the film tries to get a laugh out of the old oxymoron "military intelligence" shows the staleness of much of the script.

Lane Smith played a senator who arrives at Vientiane airport. He is on a fact-finding tour concerning allegations of covert actions. His overbite conveys a Jerry Lewis type of humor that is underscored when he commits a huge faux pas: he hands his official greeter, a general, his bag, mistaking the officer for a porter. Gibson takes Downey on a mission running guns to the mercenaries. The beauty of the lush jungle and the true nature of the operation are both revelations to the young man. At night the gonzo pilots drink and cavort into the wee hours. The hijinks continue as a hungover Downey is transported over the rooftops of Vientiane in his bathrobe. The bumbling visiting politician remains oblivious to the true nature of the airline. However, Downey's growing awareness of the endemic corruption troubles him. In a post–Vietnam informed way, Gibson's world-weary acceptance of the pragmatic realities is meant to summarize the moral compromises of the entire war effort. Whether he will regain his ethical bearings becomes the dramatic core of the film.

Various missions and brave rescues are expensively staged and entertaining. Along the way a few pilots are killed, and this elicits arguments and discussion among their bereaved comrades. Underscoring the local warlord's corruption and, by extension, that of the war effort and corporate ethos is the use of a Pepsi Cola bottling plant as a heroin processing center. The men relax with Putt Putt golf, and the local general yearns for a Holiday Inn in California. The film tries to have it both ways. It decries the bloated American infrastructure imposed on the locals but then utilizes the old ethnocentric canard that behind every Asian is an American trying to get out.

Downey cannot accept the fact that he works for the government but is party to the shipment of drugs that addict U.S. soldiers. His idealism inevitably wakes up the amoral Gibson. In the end Gibson gives in and risks his life not for some contraband cargo but for a group of desperate refugees. Gibson has done the right thing and his girlfriend, Nancy Travis; his protégé, Downey; and fellow pilot Tim Thomerson all beam with pride. The credits begin to the strains of Frank Sinatra's "Come Fly with Me." A postscript humorously ties in the film's 1970s villains to the Iran/Contra and Panama/Noriega drug scandals run by the zealots of the 1980s.

The reviews were damning, including the usually agreeable trade papers. One critic slammed it as "*Rambo* meets *M*A*S*H*."[9] With a production cost of $35 million, this was the most expensive "Vietnam" film to date. Arriving at a final domestic gross of approximately $31 million obviously did not please the producers. It did contribute to the still-very-much-alive notion that perhaps Vietnam was box office poison after all.

The fall of 1990 brought a number of medium-budget films that proved that incidental Vietnam veteran characters were still subjects of stereotyping. *The Deerhunter's* Michael Cimino directed a remake of William Wyler's 1955 film *The Desperate Hours.* Anthony Hopkins was the patriarch of a family victimized by a ruthless criminal played by Mickey Rourke. Although sporting an English accent, Hopkins's character has been updated to that of a decorated Vietnam veteran. As one reviewer pointed out, he is now looking for a "good" fight, one "he might be allowed to win."[10] Another commentator on this aspect of the film said that he went so far as to be a "suburban Rambo imitator."[11]

Two other characters' sociopathy and insanity were more quickly suggested by their associations with Vietnam. In *Graveyard Shift* Brad Dourif is a fruitcake cellar-dwelling vet who acknowledges that everybody thinks he is nuts because he was in Nam. In David Lynch's award-winning *Wild at Heart*, Willem Dafoe is veteran Bobby Peru, a rapist, murderer, and thief whose malevolence is physically manifested, like Dourif's, in his rotten teeth. The casting of Dafoe as the killer who loved the excuse war gave him to do what he enjoyed was somewhat of an inside joke. It is no wonder, then, that in a case of life imitating motion picture art, the following news item appeared: in a trial concerning the Los Angeles slaying of the producer of the film *Cotton Club*, the defense attorney actually utilized the argument that his client had been taught as a Vietnam veteran that "sometimes bad people had to be killed." Therefore in light of such government-sponsored training, he should be shown leniency.[12] Fortunately the jurors did not buy this argument.

When in November Carolco's moguls Mario Kassar and Andrew Vajna offered up yet another entry, *Jacob's Ladder,* they were straddled with a reported $40 million negative cost. Although the film's character was integrally a Vietnam

Jacob's Ladder (Tri-Star Pictures, 1990). Veteran Tim Robbins is haunted by memories of Vietnam and victimized by mysterious CIA types.

vet and several in-country scenes were prominent, the preview trailers stressed the horror aspects of the film. The big budget was attributable to the frightening evocation of purgatory on the screen.

Tim Robbins starred as Jacob, Elizabeth Pena was his girlfriend, and Danny Aiello was his chiropractor and confidant. Jeffrey Kimball's photography and Maurice Jarre's music added greatly to the production. As the credits begin the audience is thrust back to Vietnam with the familiar whir of helicopters, staccato radio transmissions, and behemoth insects. It is October 6, 1971, in the Mekong Delta. The tired platoon of grunts smoke dope and jabber about the gooks, dinks, and so on. Robbins' nickname is "Professor," reflecting his intelligence and bookishness. All of a sudden there is vague movement in the trees; bullets start flying, and then the men begin to vomit, pass out, or go into convulsions. Chaos reigns, a comrade is blown to bits, and Robbins manages to escape into the bush. Out of nowhere an enemy soldier appears and bayonets him in the stomach.

The graphic sight is supplanted by Robbins in another uniform awaking on a New York subway car. The postal worker has fallen asleep and either had a nightmare or a flashback to that traumatic in-country moment. When Michael J. Fox had a similar dream sequence while doing what we all do, commuting, in *Casualties of War*, it came to connote both the personal and collective nightmare of Vietnam. Here "Jacob" will begin a journey that places him on a ladder between heaven and hell, as in the biblical tale, and between sanity and insanity.

The reality of the subway gives way to the sight of a man with a tail. Or is it? Then Jacob is trapped in the station. Or is he? Trying to refresh himself, he showers but is suddenly back in Nam crawling through the grass with a gaping abdominal wound. Then he is back with his girlfriend. The film weaves in and out, abruptly blurring the lines between reality and fantasy. It becomes so fluid as to allow anything to be possible, and the audience begins to empathize with the character's inability to differentiate levels of consciousness. Gradually it is revealed that Jacob's child (played in flashbacks by Macauley Culkin) died and his marriage broke up. He received a doctoral degree but did not use it, preferring an unchallenging existence at the Postal Service.

Someone tries to run Jacob down, and he is beset by fever and hallucinations. His girlfriend and chiropractor try to help, but he is afraid to reveal fully the terror that grips him. The Veteran's Outreach Program has no file on him. His beloved VA counselor died in an accident! But Jacob should have known that. Or did he? At a party sexual fantasies give way to dripping orifices, attacking birds, and other recreations that underscore the true nature of the film as a horror flick.

Fearing for his sanity, Jacob contacts his fellow platoon members. Their shared cognitions lead them to believe that in that last firefight they were exposed to some type of drug testing. Like the brainwashed POWs in *The Manchurian Candidate,* only the corroboration of comrades offers the hope of rational explanation for these horrifying hallucinations. The film murkily posits some type of government coverup and the immoral victimization of the grunt in the field. When one comrade is blown up, it not only evokes a flashback to Nam but also reveals a modern plot as well. The old platoon gathers at the funeral and further corroborates all their symptoms. The men hire a lawyer to get to the bottom of the confusion. However, days later several back out from pursuing an investigation or lawsuit. Anonymous government agents beat and threaten Jacob and tell him, "Let it lie." He is dumped out of their car and winds up as a John Doe in the psycho ward. Horror upon horror grip him, but he gets better and returns home. He goes through his Vietnam memorabilia and watches grainy 8-millimeter films of his days in-country. Some mysterious sixties radical calls him and arranges a meeting. There the radical offers a long explanation about how he was arrested for antiwar activity and as a gifted young scientist was forced to manufacture LSD for the military. Then the military set up a lab in Saigon and experimented on monkeys. After the animals were tested, the drug was administered to Vietcong POWs. Both experiments elicited the same result: the victims tore one another limb from limb. Now the military hoped to temper the result and make ferocious warriors out of the moraleless U.S. troops. But the military rushed the tests, botched the dosage, and Jacob's battalion was the guinea pig.

Jacob runs to the brownstone where his wife and child live. No one ever died. He awakens from his nightmare. He imagined his girlfriend and his life as a postman. He gets out of bed, gazes at his wife, and peers toward a blinding light. Zap and he is back in Nam as two exhausted doctors cover Jacob, who has bled to death from the bayonet wound. "He put up a hell of a fight." They walk away as his corpse lies on the gurney.

The viewer wonders what he or she has just seen. Was there any level of reality in this film, or was it merely an exercise in piling one horrific image on another? A postscript reports on the Pentagon's denial of rumors that drug experiments were carried out on the troops in Vietnam, something that "60 Minutes" and other investigators had alleged for years.

One critic called the film "a cross between *Platoon* and the . . . *Twilight Zone*."[13] In fact in one scene in Vietnam the helicopter downdraft blows off tarpaulins and uncovers a line of corpses, a horrid sequence already recreated in Stone's film. The filmmakers went so far as to hire Gordon Smith, the prosthetics designer for *Platoon* and *Born on the Fourth of July*, for the demon scenes. Cannibalizing the corpus of Vietnam films further was the now-hackneyed production convention that Dale Dye had to be recruited to train young actors in the nuances of combat. In fact star Robbins wrote an article in which he talked about how they had to eat C-rations and stare at body bags.[14] Robbins turned in a fine performance and was earnest when he said in reference to the grunts, "Betrayed by greed and political posturing. Betrayed by lies of patriotism. Safe in my bed, I am hoping the job I've done shows respect for some of these men."[15]

The body of films reveals other antecedents. In 1971 *Clay Pigeons* began in Nam, told an entire stateside story, and then revealed it as illusion when the film returned to the instant when a grenade explodes, killing the protagonist. That plot twist was noted as derivative of Ambrose Bierce's classic Civil War tale, "Incident at Owl Creek Bridge." In 1961 when *The Manchurian Candidate* came out, the torturers were the Chinese. (This cautionary tale of the overreaction of domestic McCarthyite zealots was pulled from release because of its final scene, which involved political assassination. In the wake of the murder of President Kennedy, the film was too harrowing. Released years later for video, the movie struck a responsive, post–Vietnam chord in a public now conditioned to mistrust government authority and anticommunist zealotry.) Also using surrealism, *Jacob's Ladder* revealed just how tarnished was the public's view of American institutions post–Nam (and Watergate). Prior to the debacle this movie would have been lunatic ranting.

Despite being primarily a horror film, *Jacob's Ladder* implicitly synthesizes many real-life Vietnam and film elements that have evolved from collective myth into accepted reality. It uses subtle class bias to reveal a noted lack of postwar success: the troubled Jacob is a postman in a walk-up flat with a passionate but plain-looking Hispanic girlfriend. But the well-adjusted Jacob is a professor who is briefly shown living in an expensive townhome with a gorgeous WASP wife. The troubled vets remain mired in their in-country experiences. The film dresses the vets in green army jackets that would have worn out long ago. Possible drug testing abuses, like the Agent Orange controversy, meet with conspiratorial silence. The preeminent audio leitmotif of Vietnam — helicopter noise — intrudes often and nearly subliminally. The American government's betrayal of the quirky white grunts, black bros, and Hispanics in-country is repeated in the fratricide stateside. The hippie radical is stereotypically a New York Jewish intellectual resembling Jerry Rubin. The bland, spook-type agents are always shown as big, nonethnic automatons.

The reviews were mixed, and the film ended up grossing only $25 million. Some negative assessments contextualized it among the list of Vietnam films in this manner: "The movie uses America's conduct during the Vietnam War in a phony, pious way—as a moralistic hook for exploitation fantasies."[16] The conduct of the United States in Vietnam will remain forever tainted. However, events will soon change some of the perceptions of the military itself.

Jerry London directed 1990's last entry, a tale of government betrayal based on a true story. *Vestige of Honor* was a television movie starring Michael Gross and Gerald McRaney. Actor Gross was the sensitive dad from television's "Family Ties" series, and coproducer McRaney was the titular Vietnam vet marine from the weekly comedy "Major Dad." In this film the former was a civilian engineer who helped construct a hospital for Montagnard tribespeople in Vietnam. The latter was the Special Forces captain who trained the ferocious warriors as American mercenaries. Previewing the CBS Sunday Night Movie, one media critic wrote, "Just when you thought it was safe to think about Vietnam again, along comes another set of fingernails to rake across the still-festering national wound."[17]

The Montagnards were a distinct ethnic minority that suffered discrimination at the hands of the Vietnamese of both the North and South. They felt very isolated and were fiercely loyal to their American benefactors. The film begins in-country in 1969 as Gross puts the last nail in his field hospital. The celebration is short-lived as incoming mortars begin a firefight. McRaney organizes his troops to repel the North Vietnamese attackers, and Gross and the Montagnard civilians take cover.

The film then flashes forward to 1985, where Gross is a successful construction executive. He lives with his lovely wife, played by Season Hubley, and their children, including an adopted Asian boy. The lad is having trouble at school because of his first exposure to racial prejudice. Meanwhile an old war buddy calls Gross and informs him that the Montagnards are trapped in a squalid refugee camp on the Thai-Cambodian border. This sends Gross to his chest of war memorabilia. A bracelet takes him back to the ceremony when he received the gift. He and McRaney were proud to be made honorary brothers of the Montagnards.

This scene segues to the 1975 fall of South Vietnam. Chaos reigns and a bloodbath is anticipated. McRaney and his forces arrive to evacuate the Montagnards to safety. He leads a column through the bush to a prearranged LZ. Gross jokes to the captain that he is like John Wayne. Gross is ordered to board the sole helicopter, and as he bids a tearful goodbye, he and the captain promise the other copters will arrive shortly. Back at the embassy amid the destroying of documents and the rooftop evacuation, Gross and McRaney harangue a State Department employee, played by Cliff Gorman. The helicopters never arrived, and now they are told by this harried bureaucrat that there are none available to effectuate the promised evacuation. The man suggests that maybe the ARVN can do the job. McRaney slams him against a cabinet and explains that the South Vietnamese hate these people. Gross envisions in his mind the slaughter that ensues at the hands of the advancing North Vietnamese Army.

The Montagnards fled South Vietnam and made it to Cambodia, where they were persecuted by the ruthless Khmer Rouge. Finally the decimated band made it to the Thai refugee camps, where they remain trapped. Now some ten years later Gross ventures back to the American Embassy in Bangkok, where he encounters the usual bureaucratic stonewalling about the internal affairs of Thailand. Coincidentally stationed there is Gorman, the State Department official who could not help years before. He now tries to do what he can to facilitate Gross's mission.

Gross finds McRaney hanging out with some fellow Special Forces vets in the red light district of Bangkok. The former captain has sunk to a lifestyle of whoring, drinking, and black-marketeering. The knockabout adventurer has lost all sense of purpose and demands payment to effectuate bribes. The once-proud soldier is embittered, having been "riffed" (RIF=reduction in force) from the military before his time and, as he admits, left void of civilian skills.

Gross skirts the government hierarchy and with the captain's connections gets into the border camp. There he is overcome with emotion as he witnesses the suffering. Finally he locates his beloved Montagnard friend, played by Harsh Nayyar. Their tearful reunion is reminiscent of the climax in *The Killing Fields*. Here it is just a prologue to a tale of frustration and renewal. When Gross hears the tragedy that has befallen his friends, it makes him even more determined to get them out. They accept his explanation for what happened and bid him adieu with the chant "God Bless the United States." Back in Washington, the State Department denies any responsibility for these people. Gross is certain that there was a written agreement to support them from the U.S. Embassy in Saigon. Gross's constant lobbying and financial contributions nearly cost him his marriage and bankrupt the family. Nevertheless, his promise is now a crusade.

He returns to Thailand with his Asian son. A brief subplot develops concerning the adopted Asian boy as an American and a blond-haired Amerasian lad in the camp who is a Cambodian. Notions of racism, nationality, and the tragedy of war combine in these youthful characters. Gradually McRaney's mercenary attitude subsides, and he fashions a plot to aid Gross. If slowly developing diplomatic progress fails, then he and his band of aging Special Forces vets will break the "Nards" out. Eventually the Montagnards are granted exception status and allowed to emigrate to the United States. However, last-minute tension is evoked as McRaney's troops must escort the tribe through the frontier, which is beset with roving Khmer Rouge, minefields, and so on. Fulfilling the promise of a dozen years earlier, the Montagnards are brought to America. Their new chance has also become the source of reawakening for McRaney and redemption for Gross.

The tragic reality of the Montagnards' fate is summarized in a postscript that states that of the approximate 4,000 tribespeople in 1975, only 213 survived to see their new home in Greensboro, North Carolina, "where they've become proud, productive, and self-sufficient citizens of America." The composite characters in the film as well as the Camp Lejeune community that helped in the resettlement continue to work on behalf of Montagnard families and Amerasians still trapped throughout Southeast Asia. The real-life immigrants were extras in the movie, which was shot in Thailand and North Carolina.

By the fall of 1990 Iraq had invaded Kuwait, and the United Nations, led by strong American and allied resolve, was determined to impress a "new world order" through economic sanctions or force to remove the aggressors. In January 1991 Operation Desert Shield became Desert Storm as Iraq was bombarded by air and then defeated on the ground. The Persian Gulf War was everything the Vietnam War was not. Instead of 58,022 deaths and years of conflict, the international effort was brief and resulted in few casualties for the allies.

Despite the tragedy of renewed conflict, America viewed the war as a winning effort, and amid the hoopla welcoming the troops home was the realization of the short shrift the 2.7 million veterans of Vietnam had received. The Vietnam War had been prominently featured in the debate over the proper course of action in the Gulf and the commitment of U.S. troops to war in a far-off land. Concomitant with the discussion of lessons learned was a huge subliminal attention to the iconography of war as inculcated through the medium of motion pictures.

As Congress debated whether to sanction President Bush's possible use of force, more than 430,000 U.S. troops were already in Saudi Arabia. The feeling that history was in the making electrified the speeches and conveyed a moment that was paradoxically both very similar and very dissimilar to the days surrounding the Gulf of Tonkin Resolution. Representative and former Vietnam POW Pete Peterson (a Florida Democrat) opposed the authorization of force by saying, "When I sat in Hanoi, I made a vow never to allow any president to send troops into battle without the backing of the American people." Senator Bob Kerrey (Democrat from Nebraska), a congressional Medal of Honor winner in Vietnam and two years from being the first vet to run for President (in 1992), declared that "I am profoundly uneasy about the instant deployment of . . . troops, sold to the American people on false assertions that Saddam Hussein is Adolf Hitler, that our way of life is at clear and present danger."[18]

Another Vietnam veteran, Democratic Senator John Kerry (of Massachusetts) said everyone sought the same goal, but "one offers more patience (the use of sanctions); the other contemplates more devastating action soon."[19] Republican Senator Mark Hatfield (of Oregon) opined, "If we are divided now, think how we will be when our young people begin coming home in those human-remains pouches."[20] (Wanting to eschew the jargon of Vietnam, the Pentagon had renamed a number of items; this was the new phrase for "body bags.")

In general the military spokespeople were now much more astute in public relations. The Pentagon tried to distance itself from Vietnam but referred to that conflict openly in its role in the decision-making process. Many senior level officers were veterans, and they, along with civilians and tacticians, declared that if America fights, it fights to win. This became the indisputable conclusion derived from the Vietnam conflict.

Eventually after reasoned debate and many a bar and living room discussion, the use of force was sanctioned. Before and after the eruption of full-scale conflict, notions of war attributable to Hollywood were voiced. Senator David Pryor (Democrat from Arkansas) "found myself saying, 'I was against this a few days ago, but now I feel like Rambo all of a sudden.'"[21]

Henry Allen wrote an article in the *Washington Post* that some editor saddled with the title "Desert Shield Troops' Conception of Combat Is Based Largely on War Movies They've Seen." The quotes Allen derived from the troops stationed in Saudi Arabia are highly appropriate to the present study: "The last war is always the real war. When Vietnam was just starting, the real war was World War II. Now in the desert the real war is Vietnam"; "'We've seen all the movies, *Apocalypse Now, Platoon*,' said Lance Cpl. Benjamin Bradshaw. . . . 'Remember in *Platoon* . . . when they pour the fuel oil in the outhouse barrels. . . ? We do that here, just like in *Platoon*.'"[22]

Private First Class Joseph Queen of Washington, D.C., referred to *Full Metal Jacket*, saying, "At the end, they send that guy out here by himself looking for that sniper. They never should have done that man." Marine Captain Bret Shomaker observed, "When John Wayne got killed, that's it, he just fell down. . . . Now, in the Vietnam movies these guys see, there's body parts all over the place. . . . *Born on the Fourth of July* is scarier." "'Hollywood completely colors their way of seeing war,' said retired Col. David Hackworth, who was in Korea and is the most-decorated living veteran of Vietnam."[23]

Correspondent Allen continued his report: "The god of war, the psychic totem at least, is on display all over. At the press center in Dhahran, the reporters and public affairs officers sit around watching *The Killing Fields* on television."[24] And: "The god appears; the god vanishes. . . . Just think only last spring we were thinking he had gone for good [the end of the cold war]. Experience shows, though, that he will come again. . . . Old gods, new gods, and always room out here in the desert for one more."[25]

The television war had progressed to round-the-clock instant satellite transmission of images.[26] This had many strange consequences, as evidenced by these random examples. War coverage was interrupted to give NFL football scores. Saddam Hussein allowed CNN to continue broadcasting from Baghdad, and this won praise for the commentator on the spot, Peter Arnett. But others tried to impugn his editorial integrity. They accused him of being used as a propaganda tool on behalf of Iraqi victims of the air campaign. Somewhat reminiscent of the bombast associated with the suspicious senator back in *The Ugly American*, Wyoming Republican Senator Alan Simpson's method of discrediting the reporter was to tote out stale accusations that he was "married to a Vietnamese whose brother was active in the Viet Cong."[27] Instead of the audio cassettes sent to the troops in Vietnam, the new breed of soldiers received videotapes of family greetings made free of charge by stateside boosters. Several amateur videos became the source of news reports smuggled out of the war zone. Footage from cameras directly linked to the eye of the bombers was supplied to the press moments after their mission. Like a giant video game they showed the pinpoint bombing of targets from a midair vantage point. Perhaps most surrealistic was the blending of media and war via the outfitting of portable news cameras with infrared scopes that mimicked the peculiar green-hued night vision of the allied desert warriors.

The Persian Gulf War was quickly fought and won, if that word is appropriate to war. More than any film or additional years of healing, the conflict helped dispel the ghost of Vietnam and restore pride in the United States' armed forces. This is both a blessing and a curse. In terms of pride, honor to the veterans, and the possibility of a new world order, the conflict's results were good. But in the context of the danger of glorifying war, the compromising of heartfelt reluctance to commit American troops to combat, and future reaction to the options in conflict resolution, the conflict's results could be bad. Ironically bridging the two wars was the hero of the hour, General Norman Schwarzkopf. He was previously mentioned in conjunction with his role as ranking officer during the tragic incidents depicted in 1979's telefilm *Friendly Fire.* As far as veterans were concerned, the Desert Storm forces were welcomed home with open arms not only for their sacrifice but also in recognition of the disservice that had been done to the Vietnam vets when they came home. As one commentator put the past injustice, "After the defeat, the Vietnam veterans were inconvenient witnesses to an experience the nation wanted to deny—so the nation denied them too."[28] Arlo Guthrie of *Alice's Restaurant* fame summarized the new feelings when he admitted, "We had to learn a big lesson in Vietnam: that we need to support those people who are in the Middle East even if we disagree with the policy."[29]

Concomitant to a war in which some of our allies were Arabs was the release in January of no fewer than four films depicting Muslims as the enemy. *Not Without My Daughter* starred Sally Field as an American housewife imprisoned with her children in Iran by her Islamic fundamentalist husband. *Ministry of Vengeance* concerned Arabs who terrorize an American woman and child in Lebanon. The telefilm *Held Hostage: The Sis and Jerry Levin Story* chronicled the imprisonment of a television correspondent in Beirut. *Hangfire* was about Libyan "raghead" terrorist squads, and one of its heroes was a Vietnam combat veteran.

Coincidentally on January 15, 1991, the deadline President Bush had given Saddam Hussein to pull his troops out of Kuwait, Paramount released *Flight of the Intruder.* This adaptation of Stephen Coonts's popular novel about the A-6 Intruder bomber pilots in Vietnam had struck a responsive chord by examining this notion of fighting to win or not bothering to fight at all.[30] Several cynics thought the release date was an attempt to exploit the impending real-world hostilities. This was not the case as the date had been planned since the film's removal from the previous summer lineup so as not to compete with *Air America* and other big-budget movies. Nevertheless, distribution execs thought that perhaps the topical nature of the film would indeed boost the gross. As it turned out this was not the case because free and much more dramatic on-the-spot war footage was being provided to a nation glued to CNN and other coverage of events from the Gulf.

Mace Neufeld and Robert Rehme, who had worked closely with the navy on *The Hunt for Red October*, produced *The Flight of the Intruder*, directed by gung-ho John Milius. Paramount sent 110 people out to sea on the aircraft carrier the USS *Independence* for ten days. The unprecedented cooperation extended to the use of real A6 Intruders, A7, and VA-122 aircraft. What was notable about Defense Department cooperation was that this was finally a Vietnam-based story. Milius, who had been associated with *Apocalypse Now* and *Uncommon Valor*, had also dealt with the red menace in *Red Dawn*. He bragged, "Give me a liberal, and I'll bring him back a raving zealot."[31]

Despite the Vietnam setting, producer Neufeld admitted, "Action and adventure are the backdrop for a story about men keeping faith with each other."[32] John Milius echoed that with, "When everything else in combat may fall apart, the one thing that endures is the bond between the men themselves."[33] What emerges is an old-fashioned war movie that uses Vietnam as the ultimate illustration of a compromised effort, purposeless policy, and effrontery to the virtues extolled in the camaraderie of the fighting soldier. What Milius and other hawkish observers decried about Vietnam were not the root miscalculations but the lack of codes by which the troops lived, such as honor, duty, bravery, and sacrifice. Milius noted that America never should have been in Vietnam. "One, it was a lie between the President and the grunt. . . . And two, you can't walk away from a fight. If you get in a fight, for whatever reason, you fight to the end."[34] This was the area of greatest potential resonance between the film and concomitant world events.

The remainder of the crew and cast exemplified the importance of cinematic lineage and the cannibalizing of the Vietnam film corpus in casting decisions. Danny Glover (*Bat 21*) was Commander Camparelli. Brad Johnson, who got his break in Roger Corman's cheapie *Nam Angels*, was the dashing Lieutenant Grafton. Rosanna Arquette played the love interest, a pretty pilot's widow afraid to let herself or her daughter be hurt again by the war. *Platoon* and *Born on the Fourth of July*'s Willem Dafoe was Lieutenant Commander Cole. Pilot "Boxman" was portrayed by Tom Sizemore from "China Beach." J. Kenneth Campbell as "Cowboy" was a real-life vet with two Purple Hearts. Ving Rhames as the chief petty officer had appeared in *Casualties of War, Tour of Duty*, and *Jacob's Ladder*. The colorful flyboy monikers were more reminiscent of the surgically clean *Top Gun* than the many ensemble grunt films.

Flight of the Intruder **(Paramount Pictures, 1991). The ads read, "The only thing they can count on is each other." Pictured are Brad Johnson, with Danny Glover in the foreground.**

Two more incidental casting notes are of interest. Madison Mason, who played the air group officer, had appeared as Oliver North's Vietnam-based commander in the television movie *Guts and Glory: The Rise and Fall of Oliver North*. That reference to the Iran/contra government scandal brings the "mother of all political scandals" to mind, Watergate. Actor Fred Dalton Thompson, who appeared as the prosecutor in the court-martial scene, had been in his previous career the minority counsel to the Senate Select Committee on Watergate.

The crew of the *Enterprise* and the moviemakers watched *Platoon* together one evening. The next day Willem Dafoe was teased relentlessly. When it came time for the premiere of *Flight of the Intruder*, it was on the same ship, this time stationed in the Persian Gulf. Like *Air America* and *Jacob's Ladder*, the publicity campaign was geared to the elimination of the Vietnam aspect. Instead the film was set in "the South China Sea." The ad copy read, "The only thing they can count on is each other."

As the credits roll, LBJ and Nixon are shown in newsreel footage, each escalating U.S. involvement in Vietnam. By the time the film opens in 1972, much of the naïveté is gone, and the men are merely trying to survive a compromised war effort. The first excitingly staged aerial sequence typifies the politically constrained and militarily worthless nature of the missions. Brad Johnson and his best friend and copilot drop bombs on a suspected truck park, and even that turns out to be empty North Vietnamese countryside. On the way back a single lucky shot from a rifle kills the copilot. Johnson is barely able to land the plane safely on deck. As he climbs out of the blood-soaked cockpit, he is griefstricken.

The other pilots express their condolences, and all the men decry the lack of strategic targets on which they risk their lives. The A6 jockeys are particularly vulnerable as their bombers are virtually defenseless, sometimes even used as bait for the extensive North Vietnamese SAM batteries. Once these bombers draw flak, the fighters pulverize the air defense systems. The men assemble on the bridge in dress whites for a full military burial at sea.

Glover reminds the surly Johnson that targets are picked for "political considerations," not as military objectives, and that these decisions are none of the troops' business. The film is replete with pithy military axioms and jargon. The commander warns that half the time it is not the mission someone is flying, but the one before that kills him. The men gather daily in the briefing room, and the discussion turns to the peace talks in Paris as well as Jane Fonda and locker-room humor. Willem Dafoe arrives as the replacement copilot, and of course he must earn the others' respect, which he does in macho displays of flying skill.

Finally the men get a much-deserved liberty in Manila. They drink at the notorious Po City red light district, which is teeming with GIs on R&R. The enormous whorehouses and strip joints recreated in film make nearly every Asian female appear to be a fallen woman. The overindulgence leads to a good old-fashioned barroom brawl, with some rednecks, rock-and-roll cavorting, drinking until the drinker pukes, and other rituals of male bonding. Nursing hangovers, the pilots move upscale to the officer's club, where Johnson spots the comely Arquette. They dance to the strains of "This Magic Moment." He asks hopefully where her husband is, to which she replies, "Scattered all over North Vietnam." In deference to esprit de corps, they take a momentary pause and make inane conversation for a few days before they sleep together. Johnson is very loving with the frightened widow and her young daughter, and they agree to write one another.

Returning to the ship, Dafoe explains to his copilot and now buddy why he is on his third tour in Vietnam: he loves to kill SAMs. He's gung ho, so Johnson finally confides his thoughts to Dafoe. Enough of these worthless targets, let us bomb Hanoi! The death of yet another comrade persuades Dafoe to proceed with the plan. Watching a Swiss television crew doing a story from Hanoi, Dafoe spots the legendary "Sam City" in the background. This is the center of the capital near the government buildings where the missile batteries are stored. Apparently the enemy is quite secure that at this juncture in the peace talks, these targets are exempt from attack. According to the hierarchy's orders they are, but not for purposes of "payback."

It is as if *Thirty Seconds Over Tokyo* and *Twelve O'Clock High* meet Vietnam when the heroes make two passes over the center of town. Amid walls of flak, they release their payload and light up the Hanoi sky. The concussion of secondary explosions assures them that they have hit Sam City. In the use of miniatures and simulators in the re-creation of this bombing mission, the sequence was actually more reminiscent of the central aviation attack in George Lucas's 1977 megahit *Star Wars*.[35] There the final airborne assault of Luke Skywalker on the Death Star featured flak suppression raids against antiaircraft batteries in a linear cavernous approach as well.[36] (In fact at the time of that film's release, some observers applied the old Vietnam recontextualization commentary to the science fiction blockbuster.)

Dafoe and Johnson return triumphantly to the carrier, ready to accept their punishment. Glover rails at them about how they may have jeopardized the peace talks. And in fact one French news report says they hit a school, something the professional pilots know to be a propaganda fabrication. The defiant fliers await court-martial proceedings at Subic Bay. It is an open-and-shut case, and the men are given a chance to explain their rash actions. Dafoe is eloquent when he sadly notes that 50,000 Americans have died. He asks rhetorically, "For what?" "This war is confusing. . . . Nobody wants to fight. . . . Nobody wants to win . . . but people do die. . . . [We] know the difference between dying for something and dying for nothing." Despite the end of their careers and possible prison, the men are glad they performed this act together.

All of a sudden a relieved Glover announces to them that the charges have been dropped. It seems they cannot be court-martialed for doing something that President Nixon had just ordered them to do—namely, the resumption of sustained bombing of the capital. All the fliers are delighted to be allowed again to let loose against strategic targets. This is not only a way to hit the enemy; it is also revenge against what is going on back home. After all there are riots, and people are spitting on returning soldiers. The soldiers conclude that all they really have is each other. Rousing music ushers in the renewed American firepower.

Returning safely to the deck, Dafoe and Johnson must go out again to rescue the downed commander. As they approach Glover pinned down near an NVA patrol, the heroes also crash-land. Dafoe is injured as he ejects into the bush. Nevertheless, he draws the enemy fire on the ground as Johnson, with guns blazing in each hand, makes it to their comrade. The other jets provide air cover, but a tank approaches at close range. Via radio contact a smudged and bleeding Dafoe reports that his back is broken. He calls in coordinates and lights a final cigarette as the "birds" pulverize the enemy. Altruistically he dies a hero as the firepower engulfs him, too, and Johnson and Glover are able to escape to a helicopter evac.

At the hero's funeral on the flight deck, Glover reveals that he is getting command of his own ship. Glover and Johnson joke about the lack of black admirals, and then in a John Wayne imitation, Johnson says he would be proud to serve on that duty. The camera pulls back to reveal the massive ship streaming along in the South China Sea.

The title of the film provided a satiric field day for the bad reviews. Desmond Ryan in "Misguided Flight" wrote, "There is no escaping the status of the bomber as the chief symbol of the high tech, indiscriminate savagery of modern warfare. . . . Whenever the Intruder touches down on their home carrier, they land on a flight deck jammed with . . . war movie cliches."[37] No dovish apologist, the *Charlotte Observer* headlined, "Low Flying Intruder."[38] Other heartland reviews seized the opportunity; for example, the *St. Paul Pioneer* wrote, "Intruder Off Course," and the *Milwaukee Sentinel* proclaimed, "Intruder Grounded."[39] *Daily Variety* summarized the reaction by saying, "*Flight of the Intruder* enjoys the dubious distinction of being the most boring Vietnam War picture since *The Green Berets,* but lacks the benefit of the latter's political outrageousness to spark a little interest and humor."[40] The domestic box office tapped out at a paltry $15 million.

Milius admitted that he had always wanted to be a naval aviator but was rejected for service because of asthma. What he failed to realize was that in fulfilling his dreams on the aircraft carrier with a $30 million budget, he was creating new fantasies for the children of the present day. The nuances of political discussion would be lost in the imagery of flying and parade dress white uniforms.

The staging of some of the film's sequences visually appealed to the intense focus and peripheral parameters utilized in the new age of video games popular among the computer literate teens of America. In fact Software Toolworks Corporation had a joint licensing agreement with Paramount for a video game featuring the logo and characters from the film. This tie-in was by no means unique, as another company featured an arcade game known as "Missing in Action" in which the player attempted to free POWs from captivity. These adventures were joined by the previously mentioned interactive Nintendo cartridges for *Rambo* and *Platoon.*

The Vietnam film entries in 1991 were few and weak. However, those that do exist are replete with the hints of sentimentalization and nostalgia beginning to intrude even in an in-country context. Real-world events continued to conspire to make the issues surrounding the Vietnam War seem moot. By the fall of 1991 the reactionary coup in the Soviet Union had failed, and Mikhail Gorbachev and Boris Yeltsin were initiating the reforms that resulted in the dissolution of the Communist Party. In November a historic Mideast peace conference commenced. December marked the fiftieth anniversary of the Pearl Harbor bombing that provoked the U.S. entry into World War II. And by the end of the year Secretary of State James Baker was broadly hinting that the United States and Vietnam might normalize relations, especially in light of the recent peace accords in the Cambodian civil war and progress in the joint MIA investigations. Paradoxically these changes were progressive and positive but fraught with danger and the damning effect that would result if the past were forgotten or subjected to too much historical revision.

Two made-for-cable television features were broadcast in February. The USA Network presented *Tagget,* starring Daniel J. Travanti and directed by Richard T. Heffron. The ex–Green Beret seems very successful and well adjusted. He owns a high-tech electronics firm and has a striking career women, played by Roxanne Hart, as a lover. A limp is the only physical evidence of his wartime trauma. However, night sweats and scary memories do intrude from time to time. Utilizing these moments, the film flashes to sequences of torture at the hands of the North Vietnamese. Tagget (Travanti) becomes haunted by a single cryptic word, "Queensway," which keeps creeping into his consciousness.

What evolves is a tale of international intrigue and unrequited cold warriors who are now motivated by a desire to scuttle the transition of Hong Kong from a British back to a Chinese territory. Cynical CIA associates from the Vietnam days seek to silence Travanti as he begins to sort out the past. Eventually it is revealed that the electronics wizard was assigned the task of placing sensors along the Ho Chi Minh Trail in the mid–1960s. His own side brainwashed him with a false story about a nearby village's collaboration with the Americans. Outfitted with a false story at a secret location in Hong Kong on Queensway Road, the victimized soldier was released for inevitable capture. He was tortured and eventually broke, revealing what he was programmed to tell. The vicious enemy then murdered the entire North Vietnamese village accused of collaborating. This slaughtering by the North Vietnamese of their own people was designed by the policymakers to distract attention from the My Lai massacre. The incredible cynicism of the suits and the victimization of the soldier are now a rather stale image. However, the addition of Hong Kong 1997 and the existence of a friendly Soviet agent manage to update this unwieldy integration of the past conflict into the present tense.

Cabler TNT produced *Which Way Home* with an eye toward foreign theatrical distribution as well as domestic airing. Cybill Shepherd starred as an American nurse working at a refugee hospital in Cambodia in 1979. John Waters was an Australian boat captain in director Carl Schultz's production of Michael Laurence's teleplay. Filling in the checklist, the altruistic woman finds herself stranded on a rickety boat with a group of children who must evade pirates who rape and pillage. The ne'er-do-well smuggler captain must overcome his mercenary cynicism to aid the desperate refugees. Romance, adventure, and redemption are the eventual result.

Another made-for-television film, *Carolina Skeletons*, was an adaptation of David Stout's novel. Previous film contributors collaborated on a tale that integrated Vietnam War themes, the civil rights movement, and a murder mystery. *Green Eyes* director John Erman helmed this screenplay by Tracy Keenan Wynn, who had penned *Tribes*. Lou Gossett, Jr., portrayed a decorated Special Forces officer who returns from Vietnam to his childhood backwater South Carolina town. He is determined to prove the innocence of his brother, executed in the 1930s for a murder he did not commit.

The irony of a proud black man serving his country while his people are denied the "American Dream" back home is reiterated amid the squalid cabbage patch conditions, racism, and long-ago miscarriage of justice. Bruce Dern portrayed the white sheriff who sides with the truth, rather than pragmatic convention, and aids Gossett in his quest. Several redneck World War II vets taunt the lifer as "boy," which implies that the same mentality that gives rise to slurs like "nigger" also allows "gook" to compromise one's vision of other people's humanity.

Theatrically the slim pickings continued with a tangentially relevant entry from director Oliver Stone. This chronicler of the 1960s created a noisy and controversial screen biography of poet-rocker Jim Morrison in *The Doors*. This musical drama was replete with evocations of the hedonistic excesses of the era. It was impossible for Vietnam to be completely absent. In one scene a stoned Morrison watches television images of the war. At other times the war is merely mentioned. However, in this film and other Stone works, the integration of sex, drugs, rock and roll, and Vietnam all create a tapestry that in essence is meant to evoke the "formation of our generation—the values we shared. People were out there, experiencing things, changing things. There were no limits, no laws."[41]

Also in the spring, Martin Sheen appeared as a DI and made his directorial debut in the military brig melodrama *Cadence*, from New Line Cinema. He cast his son Charlie and fellow *Apocalypse Now* alumnus Larry Fishburne as young men coming of age. Despite the movie's setting in 1965 (in West Germany), Vietnam was virtually ignored. Also released in this period was the nearly direct-to-video, *Last Stand at Lang Mei* starring Steve Kanaly. Similar to *The Siege of Firebase Gloria*, it was inspired by the Battle of Khe Sanh.

In the important summer playtime not a single film entry appeared, except a two-hour episode of the television series "Quantum Leap" set in Vietnam in 1969. Caroline Kava, who played Ron Kovic's mom in *Born on the Fourth of July*, was Scott Bakula's in this special. Further exhibiting the cannibalizing of the imagery, a firefight in a rice paddy gave way to guys water-skiing with a helicopter and journalists hanging out at the Hotel Continental. The jargon was fast and furious. The VC operative was a beautiful female, as if no men or ugly women ever joined that cause. The climax featured a POW rescue.

In July "China Beach" rebroadcast its season finale in a two-hour telefilm version. The third-season premiere in the fall was also a long form, as was the show's final episode. Set in-country and back in the United States, the show was effective. Television's weekly images had evolved a great deal, mirroring the pioneering steps of theatrical films but obviously never able to approach the scope or graphicness of that medium. In the 1970s the action shows from "Mannix" to "Hawaii Five-O" had their share of crazed veterans. Adjustment, responsibility, and eventual respect were bestowed upon Thomas Magnum in "Magnum PI" and Sonny in "Miami Vice." Cartoonish folksiness accompanied the vet crew in the "A-Team." Set in-country, "Tour of Duty" and *Vietnam War Story* provided action and adventure, but it was the acclaimed, now-canceled "China Beach" that represented the dramatic apotheosis of weekly television on the subject.

Late August did bring one tangential verbal reference to Vietnam in the surf adventure *Point Break*. In order to convey just how young and green a new FBI recruit is, veteran Gary Busey remarks that the novice was pissing in his diapers while Busey was being bombarded at Khe Sanh. This throwaway cross-generational line was notable because many a movie had made the same point;

but the reference had always been to Guadalcanal or Anzio. It underscored the aging of the Vietnam veteran populace and the admission to the pantheon of that particular siege.

Premiering in October on first-run syndication television, yet another programming outlet, was "Street Justice." The first episode was a two-hour introductory telefilm, which, like similar projects, should receive limited shelf space in a video store as a feature rental. Carl Weathers starred as a Vietnam veteran crime fighter. The story begins as he attends a Vietnam veterans therapy session. His recollections of his tour are preceded by the familiar audiotrack of helicopters. One such flashback reminds him of a small boy who saved his life some twenty years ago. Eventually he reunites with the street hustler, and they team up back in the United States to fight the Mafia and other criminals. The subsequent episodes are as laughable as this initial premise.

The exploitation actioners provided three nearly direct-to-video entries. Miles O'Keefe, a bigger star overseas than in the United States, teamed in *So Cool* with bodybuilder Lou Ferrigno as Vietnam vet buddies who fight criminals in urban America. Myrl Schreibman directed this independent feature. In *Cartel* O'Keefe starred with the 1970s star Don Stroud in a tale about a Vietnam pilot framed by a drug cartel. When he escapes confinement, he wreaks havoc on the new international bad guys. John Stewart directed and William Smith also appeared. Asher Brauner wrote and starred in *American Eagle*. Robert F. Lyons, of *Cease Fire* and *Platoon Leader*, costarred for director Robert Smawley. This Triax release took three Vietnam buddies and set one against another some 20 years later.

Since American producers seemed once again uninterested in the old and losing conflict, it was up to foreign imports to provide imagery to the U.S. audience. American and British actors appeared in a Philippine-lensed adventure featuring a largely Italian crew entitled *Dog Tags*. This international collaboration starred Clive Wood and Baird Stafford in a Romano Scavolini writing and directing effort. The production values were relatively high, and the film became a staple of cable channels in a dubbed version. A platoon is ambushed in the jungle, and there are heavy casualties. The survivors become lost in the Cambodian countryside. One of them goes mad and is blown up by a booby trap. Another steps on pungi sticks and has to have a field amputation. However, their luck begins to change when they find gold bars in a crashed ARVN helicopter. Some type of corruption is afoot as the stash is bugged for tracking, and the American command is also in hot pursuit of the loot. When the men retrieve the treasure from its watery resting place and must trek it out on a rickety bridge, the movie reaches its apex. The set is excellent; it appears at any moment that the bridge will collapse into the thick jungle. After great hardship the men make it out and keep their booty as a reward for their trouble. A postscript quotes an unnamed U.S. Senate investigation committee hearing stating, "During the war . . . profits from theft, bribery, opium smuggling, extortion and black market dealings exceeded $100 million each month. Much of this sum was converted into gold for easy handling."

American interest in the dynamic cinema of Hong Kong brought the import of director John Woo's *A Bullet in the Head* to several film festivals. Corruption was the subject in this graphically violent tale of Asian drug dealers operating in the Vietnam War zone. This gangster movie quickly shifts from Hong Kong to Saigon. Three Americans are captured by a vicious band of VC, and one betrays the others out of greed and fear. Also making the rounds was a film from Hong Kong originally made in 1983 called *The Boat People.* Ann Lui directed this heartbreaking tale.

That the successful capitalist economy of Hong Kong was providing images of the Vietnam War to Americans was not so strange when compared to the emergence of a feature film from war-ravaged Cambodia. *White Page* was such a project. Vietnamese-born Ho Quang Minh, who directed *Karma,* wrote and directed this feature starring Phuong Dung. The story involved a Cambodian woman living comfortably in Paris with her two children. She is summoned back to her homeland by her husband, a Khmer Rouge official. Upon her arrival she is sent to a reeducation camp amid the killing fields of Kampuchea. It turns out that her husband has been "purged." A harrowing tale unfolds, all the more poignant as it was filmed on location. Her children die, she is raped, and death is all about. Finally the Vietnamese liberate Kampuchea and begin the process toward a Cambodian peace initiative and coalition government. Taken in conjunction with the English-language entry *The Killing Fields,* this Swiss-financed drama underscores the fact that the Khmer Rouge murderers have never been brought to justice.

In a related feature broadcast in the fall, American Playhouse presented the telefilm *Lethal Innocence.* Helen Whitney filmed the Cambodia-set tragedy in Thailand. Blair Brown, Teresa Wright, and Vanthy Roth starred. Loosely based on real-life events, the movie begins in a refugee camp on the Thai border. A 13-year-old boy is rescued by British aid workers and winds up adopted by an American couple in Vermont. The arrangement does not work out, and he goes to live with another family. Gradually his horrible wartime experiences come out, evoked in sepia tones. This film, like the angry Thai black-marketeer character in the previous year's *Vestige of Honor,* firmly notes the causal relationship between the U.S. conduct of almost two decades ago and the fallout that continues in the region to this day.

Undoubtedly the most fascinating entry from 1991 is the documentary *Hearts of Darkness: A Filmmaker's Apocalypse.* This feature-length look at the making of *Apocalypse Now* was written and directed by Fax Bahr with George Hickenlooper. Showtime cable network premiered the ZM/Zoetrope production on October 12, 1991. Atypically a limited theatrical release followed from Triton and then a renewed video push from Paramount Home Video for the antecedent and this companion study.

More than 60 hours of behind-the-scenes footage from the Philippines had been shot by Eleanor Coppola. The director's wife acts as nominal narrator, and her historic record from the vaults of Zoetrope Studios is often interspersed with footage from the feature film itself. Nothing is more critical to effectiveness in this genre than the editing, here performed by Michael Greer and Jay Miracle. Although documentary films remain primarily outside this book's focus, this highly original work is included as it is entirely about the making of a film that is discussed herein.

With the exception of Brando, all the principals involved in the crazy four-year process from the mid- to late-1970s are interviewed. Some details and confessions are new, but most were previously reported or contained in Eleanor Coppola's published diary from the set, *Notes*. Nevertheless, to hear the information directly from the artists and then to see the resultant scenes or unused takes make the film all the more interesting.

What emerges is a revealing look at the unique blend of art and business that defines the process of making a film of this magnitude. Additionally this film underscores the filmmaking and Vietnam analogies that were previously acknowledged in the discussion of *Apocalypse Now* in Chapter 6. In fact the film begins with Coppola's remark at Cannes about the huge infusion of American personnel and capital into the jungle and the resultant abuses and insanity that flowed from it. Surrealism, destruction, industrial versus Third World cultural hegemony, a lack of strategic planning and a finishing point, and an overall drug-infused, rock-and-roll ambience during the whopping 238-day shoot complete the analogous aspects.

Francis Ford Coppola's appearance changes throughout the film from heavy to trim, in a suit to half-nude in the jungle. So, too, his demeanor goes from commanding and brilliant to depressed, frightened, and blocked. He babbles about the metaphor of the journey into the self, not just in Conrad or here in the movie but also in the process of making the film. He fears that he has staked his entire personal fortune on a $40 million disaster. Worst yet, aside from being bad, he suspects it is pretentious and thus deserving of critical barbs. At one point he only half-jokingly admits, "I'm thinking of shooting myself." The film is full of such intimacies. However, from these moments emerges a sense that if nothing is ventured, then nothing can be gained. Others dismiss Coppola's worries as the usual "Francis works best under pressure." He insists that this is much worse, and what befalls the crew lends some credence to his fears.

After the credits the film begins with Orson Welles's 1938 radio adaptation of Conrad's *Heart of Darkness*. Then it tells of his aborted attempts to film the story. The documentary then cuts to interviews with George Lucas and John Milius and the early evolution of the film. Milius admits that under the original plan in the late 1960s the filmmakers would have run right into the actual Tet Offensive. Describing the immensely difficult undertaking for the camera in the present day are actors Martin Sheen, Albert Hall, Frederic Forrest, Larry Fishburne, Robert Duvall, Dennis Hopper, and Sam Bottoms. Cinematographer Vittorio Storaro, set designer Dean Tavoularis, and producers Fred Roos and Tom Sternberg also add their reminiscences. Eleanor and Francis Coppola continually infuse their recollections and insight.

The physical staging of several scenes is chronicled, such as the construction of the Angkor Temple ruins and the filming of the helicopter raid on the North Vietnamese village. The scope of such undertakings was enormous and unprecedented in this Third World setting. A typhoon in May 1976 brings destruction to some of the sets, but not before Coppola, misunderstanding its magnitude, tries to film during it. The parties that accompanied the dubious milestones of day 100 and 200 of shooting are briefly shown. All the while Coppola wrestles with economic and creative demons, especially the lack of an ending.

Some footage of the excised French plantation scene is revealed. This was to provide a kind of ghostly presence to the descent along the river. It was as if the PB boat and its crew had wandered back into the 1950s. It would convey the sense of continuity to the battle alluded to by other films, such as *Go Tell the Spartans*. The Americans are merely replacing the French, but the locals have and will outlast them.

Sam Bottoms somewhat embarrassingly admits that drug use was rampant on the set. He used speed to help himself convey the right edginess. Reformed druggie Dennis Hopper clearly was stoned in many of his scenes, which was fine since his weirdo photojournalist character was in another dimension. Scenes of Hopper improvising give way to similar moments with Sheen and Brando. This in addition to script meetings and motivational talks with the actors reveals what Albert Hall says was the huge respect and collaborative influence the director had on his screen personnel.

Several takes from the initial Saigon Hotel scene hint that Martin Sheen was on the verge of a nervous breakdown. He revealed his inner self on camera, pain and tension welling up until he punched the mirror and broke it. He then insisted that they keep filming as he wiped his bloodied hand, sweat, and tears all over his nude body. Shortly thereafter he suffered his heart attack, and the production slowed for five weeks until his return.

Eleanor's on-set footage introduces the tribespeople who acted as extras and were rumored to be cannibals. One night the cast and crew observed the tribe's animal sacrifice, and this was later integrated into the film's final scene. Anecdotes abound, such as the difficulty the actors who were playing severed heads had as they had to sit motionless below ground in the heat for take after take. Brando showed up very overweight for his three million dollar, three-week performance. Coppola tried to work with him to fashion an ending and flesh out Kurtz's motivations. The scenes between Brando and Sheen involved three weeks of improvisation. Coppola felt that turning the camera on them would give better results than forcing dialogue and a nonapparent ending. These scenes fluctuate between great power, spontaneity and energy, and boredom, pretentiousness and nonsense. At one point Coppola finds Brando brilliant, but later it occurs to Coppola that Brando has never even read Conrad's novella. In one daily rush the off-screen director keeps coaxing the actor for more improvised dialogue. Finally Brando walks out and declares, "Fuck it." However, in the words of Coppola what they were attempting to do was make a leap of faith, a transmutation, a rebirth, a purgation. This would allow them to see their inner selves and convey it on screen. At other points the director is merely a business-man trying to keep his investment from going up in smoke.

This film concludes with the final scene of Sheen emerging from the primor-dial ooze and carrying out the assassination. Then a postscript notes that the movie finally opened on August 9, 1979, grossed $150 million, and garnered many awards. Coppola's parting wish is that with all the video cameras now out there in America, "some fat little girl in Ohio" will become an artist with the lens. Ultimately he is wishing for the ascendancy of the form over the mechanical and business aspects of the process. And ultimately that is what this revealing documentary is about: the dialectic, the creative process. One is relieved that despite its flaws, *Apocalypse Now* remains fifteen years later a very worthy effort and one of the preeminent entries in the present study. (On the heels of Showtime's success with the Coppola documentary in 1991 was a recent, in-teresting, shorter-than-feature-length examination entitled *Oliver Stone: Inside Out.*)

When *Time* ran an article beginning with the phrase "Hello, Kuwait. Good-bye, Vietnam," it did not just refer to the "exorcising of an old demon."[42] It simultaneously evoked the aura of Vietnam films themselves as exemplified in the trademark dialogue from *Good Morning, Vietnam*. Now set to join the overall body of war films were the tales of the Persian Gulf triumph. Not surprisingly the first out of the box was a television movie that necessitated less production time. *The Heroes of Desert Storm* presented on the ABC Sunday Night Movie in October 1991 was current in both subject matter and execution. It typified the evolution from the television war to the video war. It combined docudrama re-creations with mock documentary footage designed to imitate amateur video-tape. Combat scenes in Kuwait City were meant to remind the viewer of smuggled-out footage shot at great danger and close proximity by the observers. The testimony of actors playing recent participants, the re-creation of the homefront, and the integration of real Defense Department footage all con-tributed to the new hybrid presentation of war in film.

Other theatrical films about the just completed Persian Gulf War included *Desert Storm—The Movie; Desert Shield, S.E.A.L.S., Shield of Honor*, and *The Heroes of the Desert*. *Daily Variety* had summarized the anticipated onslaught in a cleverly titled article, "Coming Soon: Iraqi Horror Picture Show."[43]

By the end of 1991 communism in the Soviet Union had ended, and the en-tire country itself had unraveled. Coinciding with the demise of America's primary cold war adversary were the commemorations of Pearl Harbor. Now twenty years after the fall of Saigon, these milestones in conjunction with the Gulf War all conspired to relegate Vietnam to ancient history. It was no longer America's last war, but it would forever be their inglorious one.

Four American films from the 1991 fall and Christmas season all illustrated the renewed background status of the Vietnam War. Each in their varying man-ners reduced the conflict to tangentiality once again. None of the releases featured it in the foreground or as the main story line. Rather, with the passage of time and intervening events Vietnam had become a part of the American tapestry, along with many other threads of history. This is not bad or good per se; it is the way of the world. But one can hope that it does not preclude further direct examinations of the conflict, its causes, and its effects.

Opening the same week in October were two small films destined for obscurity. Sean Penn made his directorial debut with the very fine character study *The Indian Runner*. It was a stylish and challenging tale of two brothers in the mid–1960s. One is a small-town law officer, played by David Morse, and the other is his rabble-rousing brother, portrayed by Viggo Mortensen. The film opens as the former guns down a fugitive in self-defense. He is deeply troubled by his use of lethal force despite societal acceptance of his role and actions. Shortly thereafter his brother returns from Vietnam. Before he left he was a wild man, and his irrational and violent tendencies remain despite his tour, in which his penchant for mayhem was also temporarily subject to societal approval. It is always clear that his antisocial tendencies are not a result of Nam but predate it. The misfit's inner pain and anger are unfathomable to his concerned brother and wife. What evolves is a challenging study of a tormented soul, who runs away after beating bartender Dennis Hopper to death for no particular reason.

The other fall film was director Nancy Savoca's *Dogfight*, distributed by Warner Bros. It takes place in November 1963 and eventually features a single in-country sequence. However, the specter of Vietnam hangs over this coming-of-age tale. River Phoenix and his buddies, including Richard Panebianco, portray marines on R&R in San Francisco before shipping out for Vietnam. They are a swaggering, cussing, and drinking band tapped into the traditions of their corps. They hatch a rather cruel plan to pool their money and throw a party. Then they are to find the ugliest date they can, and whoever is judged to have the homeliest companion wins the "dogfight" and the cash. Their prank is born of ignorance, naïveté, societally imbued sexism, and other factors that make them unenlightened victims themselves more than cruel human beings. Phoenix's date, Lili Taylor as Rose, finds out the true nature of the evening, and her pain and eventual tenderness raise Phoenix's character's awareness level. In contrast to the gung-ho, indoctrinated marine, Rose is a folk-singing peace activist and hippie-to-be.

Set early in the conflict, the female lead is able to get away with the following query underscoring the naïveté theme: "Vietnam? Aren't they fighting there or something?" The line is inconsistent with her social activism and intelligence but conveys this early juncture in the escalation of U.S. involvement. The dogfight becomes the metaphor for the nonsense and cruelty that pervade society, including the relations of the sexes and the lies that lead young men to their deaths. The characters lie to each other, and the government lies to them. The young men lie to themselves, covering their fears and insecurities with macho bravado.

Finally reaching a modicum of understanding and tenderness, the two young people make love. The next morning Phoenix and his crew ship off to Vietnam. That same day, adding to Lili's emotions, President Kennedy is assassinated. Apparently the departure of young marines to a far-off war was not a poignant enough moment in history, so this additional pathos had to be injected. The film then flashes forward three years to Chu Lai, and the same merry band of buddies are still rather implausibly all together playing cards. All of a sudden incoming mortars wreak havoc and blow Phoenix's friends to bits before his very eyes. In a confusingly staged action sequence, a wounded Phoenix is medevac'd out.

The film fades to black, and a limping Phoenix is back in San Francisco looking for the café where the girl he last saw three years and thousands of miles ago worked. It is now the heyday of the Haight Ashbury scene, and the hippies abound with a vengeance. They stare at the crewcut marine in uniform using a cane. One yells, "How many babies did you kill?" He wanders into a bar where some World War II marine vets at first ignore him and then finally offer the returnee a free drink and their condolences on what a "bummer" tour he had. In case the viewer has not noticed, even the new jargon is meant to connote that the times are changing. Phoenix pushes on to Lili's café, and despite the fact that he never once wrote, she senses his pain and they embrace as the film ends.

For no particular reason other than self-derivative homage to the other more central Vietnam War film entries, the young actors in *Dogfight* also went through a period of boot camp training. These five days were meant to create esprit de corps and heighten realism. Ironically the training did not take place at a marine base but rather on Vashon Island near Seattle, a rural haven for ex-hippies and naturists.[44]

In creating contrast between the peacenik and the misguided young warrior, the screenwriter Bob Comfort created a truly saintly young woman. As one reviewer observed, "She is also the most spiritual creature to come along on this earth since Mohandas K. Gandhi, emitting a steady stream of advanced pacifist philosophy, impeccably liberal political thought and unlimited sweet under-standing."[45] Another commentary stated, "The pitting together of a soldier headed for Vietnam and a future hippie on the last night before the Kennedy assassination represents a frightfully schematic screenwriting device."[46]

This discussion spends so much time on a movie that makes a sincere, albeit poor effort at drama precisely because *Dogfight* so sums up the relegation of Vietnam to the grand societal tapestry. It is a guaranteed source of pathos bulging with irony and tragedy by definition, not by on-screen evocation. The very subject has taken on a shorthand of its own that connotes government treachery and human tragedy. Obviously Vietnam is more central to the story in *Dogfight* than in *The Indian Runner*. However, these two October releases do have a number of aspects in common pertinent to the development of the Vietnam film as traced in the present work.

Both directors Sean Penn and Nancy Savoca are looking back on an era that predated their own adulthood. These post–baby-boomer filmmakers are able to attach profundity to the event without the necessity of exposition. Penn introduces his film with a song that served as the source for the entire movie, "Highway Patrolman" by Bruce Springsteen. The working-class rocker has always had a strong interest in Vietnam as a theme. Savoca utilizes the sign-of-the-times Bob Dylan tune "Don't Think Twice, It's All Right." Both cast icons of the era in their respective efforts. Dennis Hopper was the burned-out bartender in *The Indian Runner,* and folksinger Holly Near was attractive and nearly glowing as Lili's mother in *Dogfight.* Both directors use the reality orientation of media to provide elliptical accounts of the concomitant war effort. In Penn's work television reports depict helicopters and bombers lighting up the jungle. Further television footage of urban race riots join in evoking a troubled period in American society. In Savoca's film, television coverage of weekly casualties and the JFK assassination stun observers and move them to tears. Both films are concerned with the manner in which societal institutions either sanction or cultivate violence in both peace and wartime. In general both have a rather hazy sense of accurate historical chronology, preferring the poetic license of a general evocation of a troubled time.

The films depart in their lead characters. The vet in *The Indian Runner* is a very angry and dangerous man whose youth and innocence were lost years ago. He decries the hypocrisy of society when he states, "Guys over here expect their hair to stay dry in the rain." What he means is if the country sends people off to kill other people, then it cannot expect them to stay dry or "clean." Such an expectation is unfair, and he is angry about it, joining other film veterans in his inability to adjust to civilian society. His tattooed body connotes rage and angst.

Phoenix and his buddies have little bees tattooed on their skinny marine arms. They have much more innocence to lose. When he and his buddy speak to the betrayal and lies they suspect might be around them, they do so only with a modicum of insight. Phoenix will survive forever changed. His comrades will never be allowed to grow up.

Prior to the trauma of Vietnam, America grew up or, more accurately, aged a great deal with the sudden murder of its handsome young leader, John F. Kennedy. His assassination now seems to have ushered in the decade from hell. His untimely demise is now in hindsight meant to connote the personified end to "Camelot" and societal abandonment of the triumphant can-do American spirit that led us to post–World War II global preeminence.

At Christmas 1991 Oliver Stone offered up his highly controversial vision of the facts behind the assassination of the president, in the Warner Bros. release *JFK.* Stone is no stranger to controversy and in fact welcomes it as a conduit to interest and box office. The film was vilified in many corners for playing so freely with the truth and offering a plethora of crackpot conspiracy theories. In addition the medium itself was monumentally manipulated by the technical genius of the grunt-turned-filmmaker. He melded fictional re-creations with the Zapruder film and restaged home-movie type footage to blur the lines between fact and hypothesis. Most commentators rejected as irresponsible his scattershot implications of all kinds of conspirators. However, the veracity of individual theories was not Stone's concern. Rather, he wanted to debunk the Warren Commission's official version of the truth and set tongues and minds wagging anew.

The film is not about the war, but it is mentioned because it does verbally integrate the conflict into the narrative. One of the murky threads offered is the shady dealings of several characters who personify the interests of the "military-industrial complex." Perhaps they were involved in the killing in order to eliminate the president's presumed intentions to downsize the war effort.[47] This is, of course, wild and paranoid speculation, but it underscores Stone's and others' belief in the sinfulness of the Vietnam War and those who promoted its prosecution.

It is the last 1991 entry, *For the Boys*, that firmly places the Vietnam War into the rich tapestry of American history, not current events. It reflects the prevailing wisdom that war is hell and that the Vietnam War was a particular waste of lives. America lost its direction and what better way to illustrate that than in a film that stretches from World War II to the present. In covering three wars and five decades, the musical melodrama cannot help but lend an air of sentimentality and nostalgia to the bygone eras. It does not glorify the conflict; it merely underscores the new post–Gulf War status of Vietnam as no longer the United States' immediate past war.

Mark Rydell directed Bette Midler and James Caan as two USO performers and showbiz personalities who entertain the troops, sing, laugh, cry, love, and hate each other. This old-fashioned movie is replete with fine musical numbers and clichés that got to be that way because they work. In terms of production the big-budget Twentieth Century–Fox release relied on real army troops for its various crowd scenes. After the rousing show for the World War II soldiers set in North Africa was filmed, the reservist-extras had to depart for the Persian Gulf War. James Caan was struck by the fact that "we really were entertaining them before they went off."[48]

The two leads' rocky relationship commences in an airplane hangar in England in World War II. Midler loses her combat photographer husband in the war, and her son adopts Caan as a surrogate father. The film, like the nation itself, then quickly glosses over the Korean conflict with a brief sequence before arriving in the 1960s. Inculcated with Caan and his generation's notions of male heroism and gung-ho Americanism, Midler's son, played by Christopher Rydell, has gone to the Citadel and graduated a captain. His mother is deeply worried by his posting to Vietnam, but Caan is very proud of the handsome young man. Although the two professional collaborators are now estranged because of a falling out during the McCarthy anticommunist era (yet another piece of the grand, bittersweet American tale), Caan coaxes Midler out of retirement to entertain the boys in Vietnam, including her son.

The filmmakers carefully recreate an isolated fire base squeezed onto the top of a ridge in Vietnam. This is a physically and psychologically precarious place teetering toward inevitable disaster. The preview for the film prominently featured this sequence, with Midler offering an emotional rendition of "There

For the Boys **(20th Century–Fox, 1991). USO performer Bette Midler is reunited with her son, Christopher Rydell, in-country.**

Are Places I Remember" as the sad grunts' faces were shown in closeup. The trailer itself elicited a lump in the throat and by using a 1960s composition from the Beatles underscored the bygone nature of the era.

    The escort team bringing the USO troupe into the camp urges the performers to hurry because their safety cannot be guaranteed for long. Midler tearfully reunites with her son, who is sullen and distant. Nevertheless, he does muster up the energy to bluster for Caan and tell him what he wants to hear. Caan declares his pride in the young man and says, "We're gonna beat those little bastards," to which the young captain replies, "Yes, sir, as soon as we find 'em." In private his mother coaxes the truth out of him. The mythic tracks that led him and the country here have disappeared. He speaks to the recurring dichotomy of the whole genre of Vietnam films when he remarks about the great beauty of this country and the great convulsion it is undergoing. Then he reveals pieces of the truth, one anecdote reminiscent of Bruce Dern's tearful admission in *Coming Home*. He points to a handsome young soldier and says the corporal from Chicago is a sweet kid. "He collects ears!" Midler is horrified and tells her son that through Caan's connections they can get him reassigned out of Vietnam. However, the young man's sense of duty to his troops is too strong, and he refuses.

The show must go on, and trouper Midler bucks up to entertain the boys. When a comely go-go girl provocatively dances for the horny troops, it nearly provokes a riot, just like the Playmates' USO tour in *Apocalypse Now*. Then Midler comes on and sings her poignant song, moving the battle-hardened troops to tears, especially at this yuletide season. The camera lingers on the dirty faces of the boys, now heavily represented by black and Hispanic as well as white fellows. Even Vietnamese orphan children grow sad.

The moment is jarringly interrupted by the sound of incoming artillery. The men scurry to battle stations but first carefully squire the performers to the relative safety of the reinforced sandbag quarters. The movie now moves to its most heavy-handed sequence, presented in slow motion. Bodies are ripped apart as shells explode everywhere. The dancer panics and runs out of her hut as shrapnel rips through her beautiful young body. Son Danny races across the narrow boards connecting the hilltop base trying to find and protect his mother. She screams out for her son and peers out from her hiding place, only to see him hit. His back smolders as he goes down; she screams inaudibly, running to him and clutching his hemorrhaging body as he dies in her arms. Dramatically this is too much, a grandiose cliché that weakens the nature of the sacrifice and the film's ultimately antiwar messages. A telegram to her while she entertained other young men would have been more realistic.

The in-country combat sequence fades to the present day, a quarter century later. The leads have not spoken since they laid Danny to rest at Arlington National Cemetery. Now she and Caan are set to receive one of those presidential medals at an awards ceremony. She and Caan confront each other, and their love-hate relationship takes up where it left off. The glitter of the new age is shown when a huge and tacky American flag unfurls with thousands of shiny rhinestones. The ancient USO performers and television pioneers receive their accolades. This scene hints at the renewal of patriotic spirit in the post–Gulf era. This can be construed as a reflection of reality, a subtle warning, and a symbol of America's rebirth from the trauma of Vietnam.

The use of hackneyed cinematic conventions in this film is not haphazard. The medium is used to help convey the past itself. It is not just old wars that color one's view of history; it is also the movies about those wars that create the reality. *For the Boys* knows that, and when the two leads rail at each other, they underscore how our fantasy-making apparatus, the films studied herein, contribute to our mind-set.

Midler rants to Caan and to God. She understands why God took her husband in World War II, but why did he take her son, too? Implied is the especially difficult and unique aspect of waste associated with the inglorious Vietnam War. There is no answer, and a saddened Caan tries to respond by explaining that it is the price for the good times. She says we put a uniform on him. We bought into the myths and lies. The movie sidesteps the rest. The show must go on, and they put their sorrows behind them and wisecrack for the appreciative crowd. The end is both a dramatic copout from unwritable dialogue and unanswerable questions and a statement on America's capacity for rebirth and renewal. The country will go on.

Coming at Christmas in the year of the Persian Gulf War, *For the Boys* is an unlikely but appropriate example of the direction the films studied in this work have taken, and what that direction reflects. It is essential as a nation moves into the future that the lessons not be forgotten, or else it is condemned to relive the mistakes of the past.

Having difficulty overcoming his past in his presidential bid of 1992 was the former Arkansas governor, Bill Clinton, dogged on the campaign trail by his student draft deferment in 1969. His candidacy brought renewed debate about the moral issues of the war. Providing little competition was the aborted candidacy of Tom Laughlin for the presidential nomination. He of course was the writer, director, and star of the "Billy Jack" series.

Financially troubled Orion Pictures finally mustered up the funds needed for prints and advertising to release *Article 99* in March 1992. Ray Liotta, Kiefer Sutherland, and Forrest Whitaker starred. The film takes place in a Veterans Administration hospital, and its title refers to the rule requiring that vets receive full medical benefits from such institutions. One catch is that many are ill-equipped to provide the necessary services; another is that ailments must be shown to be related to military service. Financial and personnel constraints hamper the system, thereby betraying those in its care.

Permission to shoot in a VA facility in Kansas City was canceled as the particulars of the script became apparent. A hybrid of *M*A*S*H*, *Julius Vrooder*, *Heroes*, and others, the film primarily features vets from Vietnam as patients, including amputees, the mentally ill, and those suffering from a wide range of maladies. Additional tragedy is connected with the longtime internees from Korea and World War II. Liotta is a dedicated doctor who fights the inherently insane system, bureaucratic interference, and budget shortfalls. In one illustrative plot line, real-life vet Troy Evans plays a man who needs by-pass surgery. The doctors attempt to find a way to perform the operation despite red tape and budget constraints. "They hide me in a psychiatric ward, the radiation ward, the laundry closet. They substitute me for people who are supposed to be dead."[49]

Released in the summer of 1992 was the science fiction action picture *Universal Soldier*. The film manages to overcome both of the problems identified in the previous chapter as befalling action heroes in Vietnam flicks: the passage of time, which necessitates the aging of the heroes who would have served in-country, and the non–American, often accented nature of the leading men in the globalized marketplace. Here the film begins in the jungles of Southeast Asia and international stars Jean Claude Van Damme and Dolph Lundgren are shown as they are, strapping young men. They are both killed but are cryogenically preserved into the future, where they become "warrior androids." Their revitalized condition allows for their continued youthfulness and provides a cover for their limited acting ability in their automaton characters. The film goes well beyond the movie hero adventure of the *Rambo* series to a literal Vietnam soldier as killing machine in a pure fantasy apparatus.

Also released in 1992 was *Criss Cross*, a Goldie Hawn drama that featured Keith Carradine as a tangentially rendered vet character. In the comedy-drama *Hero*, it was Andy Garcia who portrayed a Vietnam vet. Even though the actor is a bit young, the dictates of star-power casting overcame his demographic unsuitability. The homeless status of the vet conveys a sense of anomie that borders on the stereotypic. In this way the character is similar to Liam Neeson's mute in *Suspect*. Underscoring the notion that there are very few new ideas, only recycled ones, is the made-for-cable *Chrome Soldiers*. Borrowing its title from the same sources discussed in Chapter 3, it depicts several Vietnam vets, led by Gary Busey, motorcycling about and avenging the death of a younger brother, this one a veteran of the recent Gulf War.

In the immensely popular action film *Under Siege*, Steven Seagal was a veteran of both the Vietnam and Persian Gulf conflicts. In *Lethal Weapon III*, stars Danny Glover and Mel Gibson reunited as vets-turned-cops. In the medium-budget exploitation realm was Triumph Releasing's *Leather Jackets*. It is about gang warfare between Vietnamese immigrants and urban whites. Lee Drysdale directs D. B. Sweeney, Bridget Fonda, and Cary Elwes. Independent Studio Three put together an interesting cast for its action entry, *1st Force*: David Carradine, Robert Loggia, and C. Thomas Howell star. It is based on the real-life adventures of marine Bill Peters. Writer-director Ted Mather shot several scenes at Camp Pendleton. Cannon had one more incidentally related action film. Entitled *50/50*, it is directed by Charles Martin Smith, "Toad" of the *American Graffiti* series, and stars Peter Weller. It concerns American mercenaries working for the CIA in the South China Sea.

The 1992 *Gold of the Samurai* was a direct to video release starring Jan Michael Vincent. The ex–Green Beret hunts renegade POW's and stolen gold in Laos amongst the Hmong tribesmen. Shot in the Philippines, this film even had Japanese soldiers from World War II running amok. *The Destroyers* was a few years old but the demand for video and cable led to the release of this tale of Vietnam vets using their skills to battle California drug dealers.

Bill Clinton was inaugurated in January 1993, becoming the first baby boomer to be president. He promised to lift the trade embargo against former enemy Vietnam if cooperation on the issue of MIA's continued. American businesses remained prohibited from investing in the quickly expanding economy of Vietnam while other countries bullishly stepped in. However, this did not stop Americans from beginning to make contacts and travel to Vietnam. Returning veterans were struck by a great sense of both melancholy and hopefulness as they saw the beautiful country begin to embrace their former enemy and the American economic lifestyle. In the context of this study, amongst the many ironies was the international surfing tournament off China Beach and the existence of the "Apocalypse Now" bar in Saigon (officially renamed Ho Chi Minh City).

Perhaps some of the foreigners relaxing at the bar were French filmmakers intent on finally returning to the actual locations of their country's colonial legacy. Several major French productions were shot in Vietnam in 1991 and 1992 and released in the United States in 1993. *Dien Bien Phu* was a $30 million epic filmed near the actual site of the 57 day battle in which 15,000 Frenchmen perished. Director Pierre Schoendoerffer, formerly an army cinematographer, was actually at the battle, and he was taken prisoner there. (Back in the 1960s he made the notable documentary *The Anderson Platoon*.) Nearly four decades later, the Vietnamese armed forces provided logistical support and set labor, as well as 100,000 extras! With a touch of irony, this required nearly 100 French "advisers" to oversee the huge undertaking.

Fascinated to have an international feature film crew nearby, many members of the diplomatic corps turned out for bit roles. The producer, Jacques Kirsner, estimated he saved more than 38 percent on production costs in Vietnam, while gaining great realism. In a process not unlike the one John Wayne undertook with the U.S. government in preparing to shoot *The Green Berets*, Kirsner, through an aide to French president François Mitterrand, began a lengthy dialogue with the authorities in Hanoi. Eventually they okayed the shoot and swore to make no script or editorial demands. Like Francis Ford Coppola and his huge financial gamble with *Apocalypse Now*, producer Kirsner had a great deal of personal money riding on the project.[50] The film cuts between Hanoi and Dien Bien Phu, beginning with a gorgeous Vietnamese sunset. An American reporter played by Donald Pleasence hustles about Hanoi meeting colorful characters and finding out about the struggle of the insurgents against the colonial power. The exciting and bloody combat scenes are in marked contrast to the elegant yet doomed Hanoi hotel lifestyle. Composer Georges Delerue provides a haunting musical score. Many of the French actions in the film are to be repeated by their American successors, here noted as the primary financial backers for the doomed colonial effort.

Dust of Life is a French-Algerian-Vietnamese small-budget coproduction.

It concerns the abandoned mixed-blood children of American GIs. It is written and directed by Algerian Rachid Bouchareb. His cowriter is Bernard Gesbert, whose father was French and mother Vietnamese. This film was shot in Saigon/ Ho Chi Minh City. Instead of telling its tale from the point of view of the pained American looking for his legacy, here the protagonist is the 15-year-old son searching for his father and an identity in a harsh environment.

Indochine is a love story starring Catherine Deneuve and directed by Regis Wargnier. This epic tale spans the French colonial period from the 1930s to the 1950s. As such it presents a beautiful prequel to much of what this book discusses. The film begins at a huge rubber plantation where the opulent lifestyle of the French is shown in marked contrast to the conditions of the indigenous workers. Labor disputes, assassinations and insurgencies threaten to disrupt the sex lives of the pampered protagonists. Eventually, Deneuve is caught up in the strife and like France itself, suffers pain, humiliation and the dissolution of her empire. As the film ends, the old rubber plantation sits in disarray, not unlike the symbolic scenes excised from the final version of *Apocalypse Now*. The film became an international sensation, with star studded premieres in Hanoi, Saigon and Paris. It received an Academy Award nomination for Best Foreign Film.

Also shot on location was another classy soap opera, French director Jean Jacques Annaud's *L'Amant (The Lover)*. This adaptation of Marguerite Duras' Indochina memoir takes place in the 1930s. It featured steamy interracial sex scenes. Jeanne Moreau provides the author's voiceover in her nostalgic reminiscence of her elicit love affair as a 15 year old with an older Chinese man. As in *Indochine*, issues of race, colonial excess, self-determination, etc., gain great meaning and poignance with hindsight. It is significant that two of France's greatest and loveliest film heroines, Deneuve and Moreau, were featured in these returns to the bygone colonial era. Subliminally this casting of the aging beauties hearkens to a lost elegance. These two pre–American war tales bring the present study full circle to the stories featured in Chapter 1.

Also examining their role in Southeast Asia are the Australians. *Turtle Beach* starred Jack Thompson along with glamorous actresses Joan Chen and Greta Scacchi. Stephen Wallace directed Ann Turner's screenplay based on Blanche d'Alpuget's novel. It takes place against the backdrop of the Vietnamese boat people crisis. Set in Malaysia, it tells the story of yet another ambitious journalist and a former Saigon bar girl.

Arts and Entertainment cable network presented the four hour Aussie production *Frankie's House*. It follows the exploits of the maverick British photojournalist Tim Page, portrayed by Iain Glen. It contains harrowing battle scenes recreated in Thailand. Most notable is its evocation of the reckless bravery of this peripatetic international group. Kevin Dillon (Bunny in *Platoon*) portrayed Sean Flynn, Michael Herr's daring colleague so often mentioned in *Dispatches*. One more example of the coming to full circle of the genre are the media protagonists in *Frankie's House*, *Turtle Beach*, and *Dien Bien Phu* and a remake of *The Quiet American*. After the intervening years with soldiers in combat, the throwback characterization actually provides a fresh perspective on the conflict.

Actually one of the era's most important pop-cultural portrayals of the war was not in film but in the international stage hit *Miss Saigon,* which premiered in London, then went to Broadway and to various touring companies. The public's access was so great as to warrant inclusion in the present work. This musical cross between "Madama Butterfly" and the Vietnam War takes place against the backdrop of the fall of Saigon and continues to the present. A young marine and the Vietnamese equivalent of a geisha fall in love. His plans to evacuate her are foiled. Unbeknownst to him, she bears a son from their liaison. Back in the United States he marries; she struggles to survive in a Bangkok brothel. Her dreams of a reunion and redemption from this life are revitalized by a Eurasian pimp known as the Engineer. He sees the woman and her mixed *bui dui* child as his ticket as well. America remains a vision of paradise for these downtrodden victims of a conflict long concluded. Part of the second act takes place in a refugee camp; other scenes are in the red light district whorehouse known as Dreamland. The Cameron Mackintosh stage show is full of black humor, pathos, and grand musical numbers.

The grandest piece of stagecraft associated with the operetta is the dramatic landing of a helicopter on stage. This bold technological stroke has become a highlight. The publicity material and logo used for *Miss Saigon* prominently employ an ingenious three-in-one image of a helicopter, stylized Chinese writing characters, and the form of Miss Saigon herself, all set over a half-moon. This extravaganza strengthens the identification of the helicopter as the preeminent inanimate leitmotif of the conflict.

On television was the made-for *When Love Kills: The Seduction of John Hearn.* The Vietnam vet played by Gary Cole is hired as a contract killer through his ad in *Soldier of Fortune* magazine. The war hero's technical ability to kill combines with an implied unmooring of his moral compass as a result of the tainted war.

Finally in the summer, the long delayed and controversial story of America's only POW to be accused of collaboration with the enemy was aired on ABC. *The Last POW?: The Bobby Garwood Story* starred Ralph Macchio and was directed by Georg Stanford Brown. It begins with the PFC's capture in 1965. Unlike most previous POW tales, Garwood is not a pilot or an older officer. He is a young draftee. The ensuing 14 years of incarceration make his survival and the conduct that allowed for it to be sympathetically portrayed. Initially, he is hog-tied, beaten and paraded about by his captors. He escapes but is recaptured and forced to sign a "soldier's appeal" for U.S. servicemen to desert. Eventually, the monotony of solitary confinement is broken by the arrival of Captain Ike Eisenbraun, played by Martin Sheen. The older officer teaches the young man survival skills and the Vietnamese language. When a third prisoner joins them, they vow that one of them will survive at all costs and bear witness. When his beloved fellow POW's perish, a bereft Garwood begins to cooperate more and more with his captors. Countless promises of release are broken.

The Last POW?: The Bobby Garwood Story (ABC Television Network, 1992). The movie of the week about the last POW to return home, suspected of collaborating with the enemy.

In 1968, Garwood is joined by other prisoners who mistrust his familiarity with the enemy and his command of the language. Years pass and the war ends but Garwood is not or chooses not to be repatriated. However, in 1979 he daringly gets the attention of a Westerner at a Saigon hotel and eventually returns stateside. The instances of defiance and cooperation with the enemy are both depicted, leading to ambiguity and thus dramatic power as the long suffering, no longer young man is court martialed. Robert Garwood served as a consultant to the filmmakers.

An interesting documentary made the rounds in the summer of 1993. Tiana Thi Thanh Nga, wife of Hollywood writer Stirling Silliphant, made the autobiographical *From Hollywood to Hanoi*. The young American actress born in Vietnam to parents who were diplomats traced her journey of self-discovery. In 1988, she had returned to her birthplace with several American veterans including Oliver Stone who encouraged her filmmaking work. The film roams throughout Vietnam, interviewing government officials, My Lai survivors, Agent Orange victims, and others, all the time examining her dual identity as an Amerasian. The film was warmly received at the American Film Institute prior to being shown as part of a cultural delegation to Vietnam. As is often the case, such interchanges are precursors to a full diplomatic rapprochement.

In the fall of 1993, *The Saint of Ft. Washington* presented Danny Glover as a kindly veteran now forced to live on the streets of New York. This quiet drama was in marked contrast to the pyrotechnics surrounding the homeless vets in *Hard Target*. They became hapless victims of wealthy scumbags who hunt them for pleasure. Vietnam films as a separate movie subgenre had reached a point where one of the unsavory druggie characters in *True Romance* was known as a "Vietnam movie producer." This tangential character makes his ill fated buy while watching rushes from his latest Vietnam epic.

In October, the inevitable miniseries adaptation of Danielle Steel's *Message from Nam* was aired. This absurd soaper featured its comely protagonist crawling around the VC tunnel system looking for her GI lover. The schmaltz started with star Jenny Robertson's graduation from that hotbed of campus antiwar protest, the University of California at Berkeley. She then becomes a war correspondent stationed in Nam. *Rescue Me* was a male coming-of-age tale starring Stephen Dorff as the adolescent who never knew his father, a Vietnam war hero. Another Vietnam vet played by Michael Dudikoff becomes his surrogate father and teaches him how to become a man. Most notable is the fact that Dudikoff goes from the previous film entries as a "B" movie grunt to the aging role of father figure, exemplifying the real life status of the vets.

Shown at art houses throughout the United States in the fall of 1993 was *The Scent of Green Papaya (Mui Du Du Xanh)*. This visually stunning film by Tran Anh Hung was shot entirely on a soundstage in Paris. It fondly recalls a forgotten lifestyle in a lovely but now forever changed place. The film opens in 1951, and follows the quiet life of a peasant girl sent to the city to serve as a household servant. Her daily routine and the joys she derives from cooking (hence the title), cleaning, and housework are shown in great detail and intimate closeup. Like the country in which she lives, however, the household she serves is a troubled place. Beauty and quietude are interrupted by domestic strife and despair. Allusions to the war are extremely subtle. Aside from the above analogy the only overt references are the far off sounds of jets screaming through the sky. Years pass and she is sent to another household where events slowly unfold with little dialogue. This beautiful film was nominated for an Academy Award for Best Foreign Language film.

Although not a war film it is most valuable as a way to examine the differences in the sense of time between the American and Vietnamese cultures. The protagonist Mui has a crush on her master's son for ten years before it is acknowledged. Another character, an old man, loves the grandmother in the film and merely gazing upon her after seven years delights him. All characters have a sense of connectedness to their ancestors and the past. This manifestation of their devout Buddhism is a cultural fact sorely lacking in all the films covered so far (but see the next, and final, film discussed). The timeless pace of life in *The Scent of Green Papaya* connotes a bygone era, almost a small townishness to Saigon. The people and the insects move slowly, the beauty and simplicity depicted literally tries the patience of the American viewer. Hence there is an inkling into the means by which the ancient Vietnamese culture was willing and able to outlast the temporary hegemony of the French and Americans. The Westerner's sense of gratification, patience and attention is totally different. This affects American films and of course the U.S. war effort.

The present examination of films about the Vietnam war comes to an end with the Christmas 1993 season release of infantryman-turned-filmmaker Oliver Stone's final installment in his Vietnam trilogy, *Heaven and Earth.* This film widened out its theatrical run around the same time as President Bill Clinton announced the end to the 19 year trade embargo against Vietnam. It is fitting that the protagonist of *Heaven and Earth* is Vietnamese, not American. It typifies the development of the genre and the recognition of the universality of human suffering which the war brought.

In *Platoon,* Stone told his most autobiographical tale. When he attempted to tell the story of his return to the United States and of the "war at home," he later admitted that Ron Kovic's autobiography was simply more compelling than his own story. Thus his adaptation of the tale *Born on the Fourth of July.* So too, Stone had planned on one more tale about Vietnam. He read Le Ly Haslip's autobiography, *When Heaven and Earth Changed Places,* and was deeply enamored of its spiritual odyssey. Nevertheless, Stone stated, "I felt there was an element missing from the story that would help to make it a fuller film, something more of the West contrasted with the East."[51] He discovered the missing element while on a trip to Vietnam with Hayslip and other filmmakers. On a flight from Hanoi to Ho Chi Minh City (Saigon) he read Hayslip's second book manuscript, *Child of War, Woman of Peace.* It was the story of her life in America. These two books became the basis of Stone's screenplay adaptation. The film was to span thirty years and two very different cultures. Stone admitted that if it were good, "It can be the Vietnamese Gone with the Wind."[52]

Once again, Stone's filmmaking platoon–creative team joined him. Robert Richardson was cinematographer. He actually filmed a number of establishing shots, landscapes, and so on, in Vietnam, although the main production took place in Thailand. Stone had wanted to film everything in Vietnam but the U.S. Treasury Department's Office of Foreign Assets Control objected because of the Trading with the Enemy Act. Also, the Vietnamese wanted some script revisions, and logistics were a nightmare.

Stone decided that the key role of Le Ly should be played by an unknown. In late 1991 open casting was held in cities that had a large Vietnamese immigrant community, such as Los Angeles, San Jose, Washington, Bangkok and elsewhere. In San Francisco, Hiep Thi Le, a 21 year old student at the University of California at Davis, tried out. She had left Vietnam in 1979 at 9 years old, as one of the "boat people." Born in Da Nang, she and her sister spent four weeks in the South China Sea and three months in a Hong Kong refugee camp before being reunited with their father. After two more years they finally joined other

Hiep Thi Le stars as Le Ly in the epic drama _Heaven and Earth_. (Courtesy Warner Bros.)

relatives in Oakland. Stone said when he saw Hiep Thi Le, he immediately knew he had his Le Ly.

Stone wanted to use as many other nonprofessionals as he could, but playing most key roles were professional actors. Tommy Lee Jones was U.S. Marine Steve Butler, and Dr. Haing S. Ngor, Academy Award winner for _The Killing Fields_ and Cambodian immigrant, played Le Ly's father. The beautiful young Chinese actress Joan Chen was aged considerably with makeup to portray Le Ly's mother. In a strange bit of casting, Debbie Reynolds returned to the screen as Le Ly's American mother-in-law.

Again continuing to typify the repetitive casting choices of the lengthy list of works studied in this book, Vietnamese actress Kieu Chinh served as a technical adviser. Marine captain turned film adviser Dale Dye once again assisted Stone. Two young men who were Saigon natives and fled to this country shortly after the fall were Dustin Nguyen and Liem Whately. They played Le Ly's brother and a Viet Cong captain respectively. Catherine Ai of _The Boys in Company C, Apocalypse Now,_ "China Beach," and _The Children of An Lac_ also appeared as a bar girl.

The film begins in the early 1950s in Ky La, a rice farming village in central Vietnam. One is immediately struck by the beauty of the soon to be despoiled landscape. The opening, with peasants working the land much as their ancestors did, introduces the film's two main themes: the connection of the agrarian Vietnamese people to their land and to their ancestors. The worship of one's forebears is at the spiritual core of Buddhism and Eastern spirituality. The film attempts to show how the war separated these people from their moorings both physically and spiritually. (In fact one of the United States' wartime programs was that of the "relocation" of the indigenous populace.) *Heaven and Earth* is more attentive to the importance of Buddhism, its centrality to the Vietnamese conciousness, than any other American film about the war.

Le Ly's family is a close knit group trying to escape the events beginning to engulf their country as it descends into rebellion against the French colonial power. In 1953, the idyllic village is burned down by the French who suspect it of harboring guerrillas. At night the Vietcong come to indoctrinate the peasants and decry the division of their country. Ho Chi Minh is portrayed as an avuncular nationalist. In addition the revolutionaries from the North appeal to the Buddhist villagers' estrangement from the predominantly Catholic leaders of their South Vietnam.

The peasants are terrorized by all the combatants. The years pass and the Americans replace the French. Le Ly's brothers go off to fight for the rebel cause. Helicopters constantly intrude on the family's quiet moments. Eventually, having witnessed much death and destruction, Le Ly joins the Vietcong. Shortly thereafter she is arrested by the South Vietnamese authorities. While imprisoned she is tortured as an American adviser watches. Her long-suffering mother uses Le Ly's dowry to bribe her way out of prison.

The Vietcong assume she was released because she cooperated with the authorities. One night as she sleeps, she dreams of her brother being tortured and killed by the ARVN and their American advisers. Shot in black and white, the dream sequence is meant as a cognitive revelation as opposed to a fantasy. When she awakens she knows he is indeed dead. Returning to the present, the viciousness continues as the Vietcong drag her into the woods for execution. There she is raped but eludes death.

In the next scene, Le Ly has escaped the bloodshed of her home for the chaos but relative peace of another world, the huge city of Saigon. There her sister and other refugees from the countryside survive as prostitutes. Le Ly is determined to avoid this fate. She goes to work as a wealthy man's servant. He impregnates her and the wife throws her out of the household. With a baby and nowhere to go, she stays with her sister. In one horrific scene (amongst many at this point) her aging father comes to the city to see his daughters. He must wait as the sister turns her tricks. The humiliation is powerful. The theme of the corruption of a society by the immoral hegemony of the burgeoning U.S. presence continues, as an MP implores Le Ly to have sex with a GI about to return stateside. Finally, she is offered so much money that she can feed her child for a year, so she relents.

Le Ly goes to work in a restaurant where she meets American sergeant Steve Butler. She assumes his attention is that of the usual horny GI. However, he treats her as a lady and eventually wins her love. Once again, in an abrupt lifestyle change similar to that which marked her leaving her village for the choking, congested city, she now goes to live in U.S. quarters as the wife and dependent of a serviceman. Akin to the gradual descent into hellishness of the boat ride in *Apocalypse Now,* is Le Ly's more benign, but no less separating and confusing immersion into an alien culture and lifestyle. Like her country, Le Ly cannot escape the war. It comes to her—this time with the fall of Saigon in 1975. She and her two sons are barely able to make it to the evacuation helicopters. Amidst the chaos, her husband finds her and gets them into the embassy gates. With him, she is a person, not just a desperate Oriental attempting to flee.

In the next scene she sits bewildered a world away in San Diego. Her friendly but brassy mother-in-law with her yapping dogs try to make her feel at home. Le Ly is overwhelmed by the plenty on display in America. The table overflows with food, the home with gadgets and appliances. Stone's penchant for a roving fluid camera captures these moments as if Le Ly were about to swoon. A scene in which she enters a modern American supermarket is comical.

An intelligent and resourceful woman, Le Ly shows great drive, and prospers within the Vietnamese immigrant business community. However, in the meantime her soldier husband suffers from classic veteran problems. His pain centers on wartime atrocities he committed. He descends into alcoholism and becomes abusive. Le Ly seeks solace from a reexamination of her Buddhist roots. Finally, in a scene of horrible domestic violence, her husband has a tearful drunk confession and then threatens to kill her. As he holds a gun to her head she thinks of the moment years before when the V.C. were about to execute her. The disintegrating man kidnaps the children, releasing them before taking his own life. He is yet another casualty of the war.

In the finale, Le Ly returns to her village to see her dying mother. The years and miles temporarily subside as she greets her family and lies down to sleep in her "father's house." Her return to her childhood home and the home of her ancestors is poignant. The circle of life and of the progression of films discussed in this book is readily apparent.

Le Ly's ("Hayslip" is her second husband's surname) suffering is meant to symbolize the travails of her country. Her life is a microcosm of the horrible war and of the human capacity to endure and go on. At some point in the 140 minute film, the viewer becomes nearly anesthetized to the parade of victimizations. While interesting, *Heaven and Earth* becomes Stone's least dramatic and emotionally resonant Vietnam film. Perhaps, it suffers from the pitfall of attempting to make an epic, or of making a real human being a symbol.

The musical score by Japanese composer Kitaro contributed to the heavy-handedness. Other background music was an amalgamation of traditional Vietnamese folk music and American pop songs of the sixties and seventies. This served the film's dialectic of creating both separation and universal sharing of the wartime experiences. On the one hand Vietnam and America are greatly different societies and cultures. On the other hand suffering and loss are shared, much like the marriage of Le Ly to her troubled first American husband.

The film's drubbing by the critics was matched by the public's almost complete apathy to the project. *Heaven and Earth* was virtually ignored at the domestic as well as international boxoffice. Perhaps, in a perverse manner, its seeming irrelevancy confirmed the evolution of the collective American consciousness beyond the urgency of embracing the opportunity for catharsis provided by Stone's much superior film of nearly a decade previous, *Platoon.*

Like any body of work the Vietnam War film collection chronicled in these pages is full of good and bad entries and everything in between.[53] Although certain individual films are quite noteworthy, it is the patterns of depiction and subject matter that are most informative. The Vietnam War represents one of the most tragic chapters in the history of the United States. Thousands gave their lives in the conflict, and many others were deeply touched by it. Its lessons remain the subject of debate, and the greatest danger is that they may recede too far into the past and become ignored.

The pop culture has provided one more monument to the past, and it must be as forthright as possible. Like any other creation, including the tragic war itself, the film depictions and interpretations of them are subject to all the foibles of human endeavor. Let us hope that truthful images continue to inform the youth of the future via the ever-important world of film.

References

1. "Vietnam Fifteen Years Later," *Time,* April 30, 1990, pp. 20–21.
2. Mac., "Film Reviews—Flashback," *Daily Variety,* January 29, 1990, p. 2.
3. Bridget Byrne, "On the Cover," *Chicago Tribune TV Week,* May 20, 1990, p. 1.
4. "Air America Hits Turbulence," *Variety,* September 10, 1990, p. 78.
5. Robert Sam Anson, "Fly the Friendly Skies," *Premiere* (September 1990), p. 73.
6. Myron Meisel, *Film Journal* 93, 6 (July 1990), p. 37.
7. "Summer Movie Preview," *Premiere* (June 1990), p. 100.
8. *Ibid.*
9. Dave Kehr, "Air America Review," *Chicago Tribune,* August 10, 1990, p. B7.
10. Dave Kehr, "Desperate Hours Review," *Chicago Tribune,* October 5, 1990, p. B7.
11. Mac., "Film Reviews—Desperate Hours," *Daily Variety,* October 4, 1990, p. 2.
12. "Cotton Club Trial Enters Penalty Phase," *Daily Variety,* September 17, 1991, p. 3.
13. Deborah Kunk, "Jacob's Ladder Review," *St. Paul Pioneer Press,* November 2, 1990, entertainment section.
14. Tim Robbins, "Leaving the Demons at the Office," *Premiere* (January 1991), p. 108.
15. *Ibid.*
16. Owen Gleiberman, "Jacob's Ladder Review," *Entertainment Weekly,* November 2, 1990, p. 45.
17. Kenneth Clark, "CBS Airs Another Tale of Betrayal in Vietnam," *Chicago Tribune,* December 28, 1990, sec. 5, p. 1.
18. *Chicago Tribune,* September 23, 1990, p. 6.
19. David Broder, "Why the Gulf War Won't Be Another Vietnam," *Washington Post,* December 16, 1990, op-ed page.
20. *New York Times,* January 13, 1991, cover and throughout.
21. Paul Greenberg, "American Will and the Test of Time," *Chicago Tribune,* January 25, 1991, op-ed page.
22. Henry Allen, "Desert Storm Troops' Conception of Combat Is Based Largely on War Movies They've Seen," *Washington Post* wire service, cited in *St. Paul Pioneer Press,* October 6, 1991, p. 10A.

23. *Ibid.*

24. *Ibid.*

25. *Ibid.*

26. Martin Grove, *Show Business Insider's Newsletter*, 11, 8 (April 30, 1991), sec. 2, p. 3.

27. Stanley W. Cloud, "Shooting the Messenger," *Time* February 18, 1991, p. 34.

28. William Pfaff, "Vietnam's Unhappy Legacy Isn't the Only Trauma to Overcome," *Chicago Tribune*, March 17, 1991, op-ed page.

29. Jenny Vogt, "Peace Talks," *Chicago Tribune*, February 15, 1991, sec. 5, p. 3.

30. Stephen Coonts, *Flight of the Intruder* (Annapolis, Md.: Naval Institute Press, 1986).

31. Ralph Rugoff, "It's Not Just an Adventure, It's a Job," *Premiere* (August 1990), p. 39.

32. Paramount Pictures, "Handbook of Production Notes," *Flight of the Intruder* (Los Angeles: Paramount Pictures, 1991), p. 2.

33. *Ibid.*

34. John Milius, "Twenty Questions," *Playboy* (June 1991), p. 159.

35. For the complete story of the production of these flight sequences, see James H. Farmer, "Making Flight of the Intruder," *Air Classics* 26, 8 (August 1990).

36. Stephen Hunter, "War from the Air," *Milwaukee Journal*, January 18, 1991, Xtra sec., p. 1.

37. Desmond Ryan, "Flight of the Intruder Review," Knight Ridder Newspaper Syndicate, January 19, 1991.

38. Lawrence Toppman, "Low Flying Intruder," *Charlotte Observer*, January 19, 1991.

39. Desmond Ryan, "Intruder Off Course," *St. Paul Pioneer Press*, January 19, 1991; Elfrieda Abbe, "Intruder Grounded," *Milwaukee Sentinel*, January 18, 1991.

40. "Film Reviews," *Daily Variety*, January 18, 1991, p. 2.

41. Hilary DeVries, "Riders on the Storm," *Los Angeles Times Magazine*, February 24, 1991, p. 10.

42. Stanley W. Cloud, "The Home Front," *Time*, March 11, 1991, p. 52.

43. Charles Fleming, "Coming Soon: Iraqi Horror Picture Show," *Daily Variety*, January 14, 1991, p. 6.

44. Randi Sue Coburn, "Marines at Their Best," *Premiere* (October 1991), pp. 29–31.

45. Dave Kehr, "Dogfight Review," *Chicago Tribune*, October 4, 1991, sec. 7, p. 2.

46. Todd McCarthy, "Film Reviews—Dogfight," *Daily Variety*, October 3, 1991, p. 2.

47. Gene Siskel, "Pick of the Week," *Chicago Tribune*, December 26, 1991, sec. 7, p. C.

48. Emily Yoffe, "Bette and the Boys," *Newsweek*, November 25, 1991, pp. 54–55.

49. "In the Works," *Premiere* (December 1991), p. 8.

50. Michael Williams, "Good Morning Vietnam, Say French Lensers," *Daily Variety*, March 25, 1991, p. 1.

51. Warner Bros., "Production Information," *Heaven and Earth* (Los Angeles: Warner Bros., 1993), p. 2.

52. Rachel Abramowitz, "In the Works," Premiere (August 1993), p. 10.

53. Additional source material is from *The Ultimate Video Catalog* (Blockbuster Video, 1991); Lee R. Bobker, *Elements of Film* (New York: Harcourt, Brace and World, 1969); Nathalie Fredrik, *Hollywood and the Academy Awards* (Los Angeles: Hollywood Awards Publications, 1970); and John Simon, *Reverse Angle* (New York: Clarkson N. Potter, 1982).

Vietnam Films
Listed Alphabetically

A-Team (1980)
Abandoned Field—Free Fire Zone (1979)
Above the Law (1989)
The Activist (1969)
Air America (1990)
Alamo Bay (1985)
Alice's Restaurant (1969)
L'Amant (a.k.a. *The Lover*) (1992)
American Commandoes (1985)
American Eagle (1992)
American Ninja (1985)
Americana (1981)
Angels from Hell (1968)
Angkor: Cambodia Express (1984)
Angry Breed (1968)
The Annihilators (1985)
Apocalypse Now (1979)
Armed Response (1986)
Article 99 (1992)
Ashes and Embers (1982)
A.W.O.L. (1972)
Backfire (1987)
Ballad of Andy Crocker (1969)
Band of the Hand (1986)
Bat 21 (1988)
The Bears and I (1974)
Behind Enemy Lines (1988)
Behind Enemy Lines Part II (1989)
Bell Diamond (1987)
Big Bounce (1968)
Big Chill (1984)
Big Wednesday (1978)
Billy Jack (1971)
Billy Jack Goes to Washington (1977)

Birdy (1984)
Black Gunn (1972)
Black Sunday (1977)
Blind Fury (1990)
Blue Thunder (1983)
Boat People (1983)
Born Losers (1967)
Born on the Fourth of July (1989)
Boys in Company C (1978)
Braddock: MIA III (1988)
Breakloose (1972)
Brothers and Relations (1986)
Brushfire (1961)
A Bullet in the Head (1990)
The 'Burbs (1989)
Captain Milkshake (1970)
Captive (1975)
Carolina Skeletons (1991)
Cartel (1992)
Casualties of War (1989)
Cease Fire (1985)
The Challenge (1970)
Charlie Bravo (1988)
Children of An Lac (1980)
China Beach (1989)
China Gate (1957)
Chrome and Hot Leather (1971)
Chrome Soldiers (1992)
Clay Pigeons (1971)
Code of Honor (1984)
Combat Shock (1986)
Coming Home (1978)
Cowards (1970)
Crazy World of Julius Vrooder (1974)

Criss Cross (1992)
Cross Fire (1988)
Cutter's Way (1981)
Dead of Night (1972)
Deadly Encounter (1982)
Deerhunter (1978)
Desert Field (1979)
Desperate Hours (1990)
The Desperate Miles (1975)
Destroyers (1992)
Dien Bien Phu (1992)
Distant Thunder (1988)
Dog Day Afternoon (1974)
Dog Soldiers (1978)
Dog Tags (1991)
Dogfight (1991)
Don't Cry It's Only Thunder (1982)
Doors (1991)
Dust of Life (1992)
Easy Rider (1969)
The Edge (1968)
84 Charlie MoPic (1989)
Electra Glide in Blue (1973)
The Expendables (1988)
Explosion (1970)
The Exterminator (1980)
Exterminator II (1984)
Extreme Prejudice (1987)
Eye for an Eye (1981)
Eye of the Eagle (1987)
Eye of the Eagle II (1988)
Eye of the Tiger (1986)
Fairy Tale for-17-Year-Olds (1986)
Fatal Mission (1990)
Fear (1988)
50/50 (1992)
Fighting Back (1980)
Fighting Mad (1972)
Final Mission (1984)
Final War of Olly Winter (1966)
First Blood (1982)
First Force (1992)
Five Gates to Hell (1959)
Flashback (1990)
Flight of the Intruder (1991)
Fly Away Home (1981)
Flying Blind (1990)
For the Boys (1991)
A Force of One (1979)
The Forgotten (1989)
Forgotten Man (1971)
Forgotten Warrior (1987)

Four Friends (1981)
Frankie's House (1993)
Free Theater Associates (FTA) (1972)
Friendly Fire (1979)
Full Metal Jacket (1987)
Gardens of Stone (1988)
Garwood (1992)
Gay Deceivers (1969)
Georgia Georgia (1972)
Getting Straight (1970)
GI Executioner (1984)
Girl on the River (1986)
Girl Who Came Between Them (1990)
Girl Who Spelled Freedom (1988)
Glory Boy (1971)
Go Tell the Spartans (1978)
Gold of the Samurai (1992)
Good Guys Wear Black (1977)
Good Morning Vietnam (1987)
Gordon's War (1973)
Graveyard Shift (1990)
The Greatest (1977)
The Green Berets (1968)
Green Eyes (1977)
Greetings (1968)
Guts and Glory: The Rise and Fall of Ollie North (1990)
Hail Hero! (1969)
Hair (1978)
Hamburger Hill (1987)
Hangfire (1991)
Hanoi Hilton (1987)
Hard Rain—The Tet (1968)
The Hard Ride (1971)
Hardcase and Fist (1988)
Head (1968)
Heart of the Warriors (1990)
Heated Vengeance (1985)
Heaven and Earth (1993)
Hero (1992)
Heroes (1977)
Hi Mom! (1970)
Hitman (1985)
Homer (1970)
House (1986)
I, the Jury (1981)
Ice (1970)
In Country (1989)
In Dangerous Company (1988)
In Love and War (1987)
Indian Runner (1991)
Indochine (1993)

Rumor of War (1980)
Running on Empty (1988)
Saigon (1948)
Saigon Commandos (1988)
Saigon—Year of the Cat (1983)
Saint Jack (1979)
The Saint of Ft. Washington (1993)
Satan's Sadists (1969)
Savage Dawn (1985)
Scent of Green Papaya (1993)
Search and Destroy (1981)
Shooter (1988)
Siege of Firebase Gloria (1988)
'68 (1988)
Slaughter (1972)
Slaughter's Big Ripoff (1973)
A Small Circle of Friends (1980)
So Cool (1992)
Soldiers Revenge (1989)
Some Kind of Hero (1982)
Special Delivery (1976)
Steele Justice (1987)
Stone Killer (1973)
Stranger on My Land (1988)
Strawberry Statement (1970)
Streamers (1983)
Street Justice (1991)
Street Trash (1987)
The Stuntman (1978)
Summertree (1971)
Surname Viet, Given Name Nam (1979)
Suspect (1987)
Swimming to Cambodia (1987)
Taggett (1991)
Taking Off (1971)
Targets (1968)
Taxi Driver (1976)
To Heal a Nation (1988)
To Kill a Clown (1972)
To the Shores of Hell (1965)
Tough Guys Don't Dance (1987)
Tour of Duty (1989)
Tracks (1976)
Trained to Kill (1973)
Trial of Billy Jack (1974)

Trial of the Catonsville 9 (1972)
Tribes (1970)
Turtle Beach (1992)
Twilight Zone—The Movie (1983)
Two (1974)
Two People (1973)
The Ugly American (1963)
UHF (1989)
Uncommon Valor (1983)
Under Siege (1992)
Universal Soldier (1992)
Unnatural Causes (1986)
Vestige of Honor (1991)
Victory at Dien Bien Phu (1964)
Vietnam, Texas (1990)
Vietnam War Story (1988)
Vietnam War Story I (1989)
Vietnam War Story II (1989)
Vietnam War Story III (1989)
Vigilante Force (1975)
The Visitors (1972)
War Bus Commandoes (1986)
Welcome Home (1989)
Welcome Home, Johnny Bristol (1972)
Welcome Home, Soldier Boys (1972)
Whatever It Takes (1986)
When Hell Was in Session (1979)
When Love Kills: The Seduction of John
   Hearn (1993)
When the Tenth Month Comes (1984)
When You Comin' Back Red Ryder (1979)
Which Way Home (1991)
White Ghost (1985)
White Knights (1985)
Who'll Stop the Rain (1978)
Wild at Heart (1990)
Windflowers (1967)
Wolf Lake (1978)
Yank in Indochina (1952)
A Yank in Vietnam (1964)
Year of the Dragon (1985)
Youngblood (1978)
Zabriskie Point (1969)
Zebra Force (1977)

Vietnam Films
Listed Chronologically

1948	Rogue's Regiment	**1970**	Captain Milkshake
1948	Saigon		The Challenge
1952	Yank in Indochina		Cowards
1955	Jump into Hell		Explosion
1957	China Gate		Getting Straight
1958	The Quiet American		Hi Mom!
1959	Five Gates to Hell		Homer
1961	Brushfire		Ice
1963	The Ugly American		Joe
1964	Victory at Dien Bien Phu		The Losers
	A Yank in Vietnam		Lost Flight
1965	Operation C.I.A.		Move
	To the Shores of Hell		Norwood
1966	Final War of Olly Winter		Ravager
	Lost Command		The Revolutionary
	Marine Battleground		R.P.M.
1967	Born Losers		Strawberry Statement
	Live for Life		Tribes
	Windflowers	**1971**	Billy Jack
1968	Angels from Hell		Chrome and Hot Leather
	Angry Breed		Clay Pigeons
	Big Bounce		Forgotten Man
	The Edge		Glory Boy
	The Green Berets		The Hard Ride
	Greetings		Jud
	Head		Prism
	Targets		Summertree
1969	The Activist		Taking Off
	Alice's Restaurant	**1972**	A.W.O.L.
	Ballad of Andy Crocker		Black Gunn
	Easy Rider		Breakloose
	Gay Deceivers		Dead of Night
	Hail Hero!		Fighting Mad
	Medium Cool		Free Theater Associates (FTA)
	The Model Shop		Georgia Georgia
	Satan's Sadists		Limbo
	Zabriskie Point		Outside In

Parades
Slaughter
To Kill a Clown
Trial of the Catonsville 9
The Visitors
Welcome Home, Johnny Bristol
Welcome Home, Soldier Boys
1973 Electra Glide in Blue
Gordon's War
The P.O.W.
Slaughter's Big Ripoff
Stone Killer
Trained to Kill
Two People
1974 The Bears and I
Crazy World of Julius Vrooder
Mixed Company
Trial of Billy Jack
Two
1975 Captive
The Desperate Miles
Milestones
Returning Home
Vigilante Force
1976 Mean Johnny Barrows
Special Delivery
Taxi Driver
Tracks
1977 Billy Jack Goes to Washington
Black Sunday
Good Guys Wear Black
The Greatest
Green Eyes
Heroes
Just a Little Inconvenience
Rolling Thunder
Zebra Force
1978 Big Wednesday
Boys in Company C
Coming Home
Deerhunter
Dog Soldiers
Go Tell the Spartans
Hair
My Husband Is Missing
Our Winning Season
The Stuntman
Who'll Stop the Rain
Wolf Lake
Youngblood
1979 Abandoned Field—Free Fire Zone
Apocalypse Now

Desert Field
A Force of One
Friendly Fire
More American Graffiti
Nightflowers
Ninth Configuration
Odd Angry Shot
Saint Jack
Surname Viet, Given Name Nam
When Hell Was in Session
When You Comin' Back Red
  Ryder?
1980 A-Team
Children of An Lac
The Exterminator
Fighting Back
Miami Vice
Octagon
Promise of Love
Return of the Secaucus Seven
Rumor of War
A Small Circle of Friends
1981 Americana
Cutter's Way
Eye for an Eye
Fly Away Home
Four Friends
I, the Jury
Kent State
Nighthawks
Search and Destroy
1982 Ashes and Embers
Deadly Encounter
Don't Cry It's Only Thunder
First Blood
Magnum P.I.
Purple Haze
Some Kind of Hero
1983 Blue Thunder
Boat People
Lone Wolf McQuade
Memorial Day
Saigon—Year of the Cat
Streamers
Twilight Zone—The Movie
Uncommon Valor
1984 Angkor: Cambodia Express
Big Chill
Birdy
Code of Honor
Exterminator II
Final Mission

GI Executioner
Karma
Killing Fields
Missing in Action
Purple Hearts
When the Tenth Month Comes
1985   Alamo Bay
American Commandoes
American Ninja
The Annihilators
Cease Fire
Heated Vengeance
Hitman
Killzone
Lady from Yesterday
Latino
M.I.A. II—The Beginning
Ordinary Heroes
The Park Is Mine
Rambo: First Blood II
Savage Dawn
White Ghost
White Knights
Year of the Dragon
1986   Armed Response
Band of the Hand
Brothers and Relations
Combat Shock
Eye of the Tiger
Fairy Tale for 17-Year-Olds
Girl on the River
House
Intimate Strangers
Left Alone
Let's Get Harry
Nam Angels
Opposing Force
Platoon
POW—The Escape
A Quiet Little Town
The Refrain of Hope
Riders of the Storm
Unnatural Causes
War Bus Commandoes
Whatever It Takes
1987   Backfire
Bell Diamond
Extreme Prejudice
Eye of the Eagle
Forgotten Warrior
Full Metal Jacket
Good Morning Vietnam

Hamburger Hill
Hanoi Hilton
In Love and War
Lethal Weapon
Long Journey Home
Malone
Moon in Scorpio
Nightforce
No Dead Heroes
O.C. & Stiggs
Off Limits
Outlaw Force
Proud Men
Steele Justice
Street Trash
Suspect
Swimming to Cambodia
Tough Guys Don't Dance
1988   Bat 21
Behind Enemy Lines
Braddock: MIA III
Charlie Bravo
Cross Fire
Distant Thunder
The Expendables
Eye of the Eagle II
Fear
Gardens of Stone
Girl Who Spelled Freedom
Hardcase and Fist
Moving
My Father, My Son
Night Wars
Nineteen Sixty-Nine (1969)
Platoon Leader
Presidio
Private War
Rambo III
Running on Empty
Saigon Commandos
Shooter
Siege of Firebase Gloria
Stranger on My Land
To Heal a Nation
Vietnam War Story
1989   Above the Law
Behind Enemy Lines Part II
Born on the Fourth of July
The 'Burbs
Casualties of War
China Beach
84 [Eight-Four] Charlie MoPic

The Forgotten
Hard Rain—The Tet 1968
In Country
Iron Triangle
Jacknife
Lethal Weapon II
No Retreat, No Surrender II
Operation War Zone
The Package
Soldiers Revenge
Tour of Duty
UHF
Vietnam War Story I
Vietnam War Story II
Vietnam War Story III
Welcome Home

1990 Air America
Blind Fury
A Bullet in the Head
Desperate Hours
Fatal Mission
Flashback
Flying Blind
Girl Who Came Between Them
Graveyard Shift
Guts and Glory: The Rise and Fall
  of Ollie North
Heart of the Warriors
Jacob's Ladder
Last Flight Out
Nightbreaker
Revenge
Vietnam, Texas
Wild at Heart

1991 Carolina Skeletons
Dog Tags
Dogfight
Doors
Flight of the Intruder
For the Boys
Hangfire

Indian Runner
Last Stand at Lang Mei
Lethal Innocence
Point Break
Quantum Leap
Street Justice
Taggett
Vestige of Honor
Which Way Home

1992 L'Amant (a.k.a. The Lover)
American Eagle
Article 99
Cartel
Chrome Soldiers
Criss Cross
Destroyers
Dien Bien Phu
50/50
First Force
Garwood
Gold of the Samurai
Hero
The Last POW?: The Bobby
  Garwood Story
Leather Jackets
Lethal Weapon III
So Cool
Turtle Beach
Under Siege
Universal Soldier

1993 Dust of Life
Frankie's House
Heaven and Earth
Indochine
Message from Nam
Rescue Me
The Saint of Ft. Washington
Scent of Green Papaya
When Love Kills: The Seduction of
  John Hearn

Vietnam War Documentaries

American Dream, American Nightmare (1979) CBS News; Perry Wolff, Executive Producer

Anderson Platoon (1967) Academy Award 1967 Best Documentary; Pierre Schoendoerffer, Director

Another Part of the Family (1971) Museum of Modern Art; Paul Ronder, Director

Battle Hell—Vietnam (1984) Ferde Grofe Films

The Bloods of Nam (1986) PBS Video; Wallace Terry, Director

Combat 'Nam (1974) Ferde Grofe Films

Dear America: Letters Home from Vietnam (1988) HBO Films; Bill Couterie, Director

A Face of War (1967) International Historic Films; Eugene S. Jones, Director

Far from Vietnam (1967) Directors: Jean Luc Godard, Claude Lelouch, Alain Resnais, Agnes Varda, etc.

From Hollywood to Hanoi (1993) Tiana Silliphant, Writer and Director

F.T.A. (1962) Free Theater Associates; Francine Parker, Director

A Good American: The Ron Kovic Story (1990) Loretta Smith, Director

Hanoi, Martes 13 Diz. (1967) Third World Newsreel; Santiago Alvarez, Director

Hearts and Minds (1974) Nelson Entertainment; Peter Davis, Director

Hearts of Darkness: A Filmmaker's Apocalypse (1991) Paramount Home Video; Fax Bahr, George Hickenlooper, Writers/Directors

In the Year of the Pig (1969) New Yorker Films; Emile deAntonio, Director

Inside North Vietnam (1968) California Newsreel; Felix Greene, Producer

Introduction to the Enemy (1974) Jane Fonda; Haskell Wexler, Director

It's a Mad War (1965) NBC News

No More Vietnams (1979) NBC News; Films Inc., Distributor

No Substitute for Victory (1971) John Wayne Productions; Chuck Keen, Director

No Sweat Blues (1990) MPI Video

No Vietnamese Ever Called Me Nigger (1968) Cinema Guild; David L. Weiss, Director

Oliver Stone Inside Out (1992) Pacific St. Producers Group; Joel Sucher, Steven Fischler, Producers and Directors

A Program for Vietnam Veterans and Everyone Else Who Should Care (1986) PBS Video; Michael Lorentz, Director

Requiem for the Vietnam Unknown (1984) CBS News

The Selling of the Pentagon (1971) CBS News; Peter Davis, Producer

The 17th Parallel (1968) Argos; Joris Ivens, Director

Sons and Daughters (1967) American Documentary Films; Jerry Stoll, Director

Starting Place (1993) Robert Kramer, Director, Writer, Editor

Street Scenes (1970) Image Film Archives; Martin Scorsese, Co-Director

Television's Vietnam (1984) Accuracy in Media; Douglas Pike, Director

Tell Me Lies (1968) Budget Films; Peter Brooks, Director

Terry Whitmore, for Example (1969) Grove; William Brodie, Director

The Uncounted Enemy: A Vietnam Deception (1982) CBS News; George Crile, Director

The Underground (1976) First Run Films;
Robert Richter, Director
Vietnam — Chronicle of a War (1981) CBS
News
Vietnam in the Year of the Pig (1968)
Knowledge Collection; Emile deAntonio,
Director
Vietnam in Turmoil (1968) American Film
Institute
Vietnam Newsreel Review (1967) Department
of Defense; International Historic Films
Vietnam Perspectives (1965) CBS News
Vietnam: Remember (1968) Knowledge
Collection; Department of Defense
Vietnam — Talking to the People (1985)
Community TV Center; John Alpert,
Director
Vietnam — The Battle of Khe Sanh (1988)
Goodtimes Home Video
Vietnam — The Bombing (1969) Interna-

tional Historic Films; U.S. Army
Vietnam: The 10,000 Day War (1985) (13
video series) Knowledge Collection; Ian
McLeod, Producer
Vietnam — The War at Home (1978) MPI
Home Video; Glen Silver, Producer
Vietnam: A TV History (1984) (13 videos)
WGBH Boston; Richard Ellison,
Producer
Vietnam! Vietnam! (1971) Department of
Defense; John Ford, Director
Vietnamese Cultures and Customs (1969)
International Historic Films; U.S.
Government
We Can Keep You Forever (1987)
Lionheart Video
Winter Soldier (1972) Third World News-
reel
Year of the Tiger (1975) Odeon Films;
David Davis, Director

Note: These titles are all at least sixty minutes, or nearly feature length. Many other "shorts" exist on this subject.

The first place to attempt to find these educational tools is in a public library. The advent of video has made many of these works much more accessible. The second place is the "documentary" section of the new video superstores such as Blockbuster.

Additional research aids include good reference books such as: *The Video Source Book* (ed. David J. Weiner, Gale Research, Inc., Detroit) or *Bowker's Complete Video Directory* (R.R. Bowker, Inc., New York).

Further information may be obtained by writing the Reference Department of the Library of Congress, Motion Picture and Recorded Sound Division, Washington, D.C. 20540.

Film Distributors

(All were in business as of January 1, 1994)

Academy Home Entertainment
1 Pine Haven Shore Road
P.O. Box 788
Shelburne, VT 05482

A.I.P. Home Video, Inc.
10726 McCune Ave.
Los Angeles, CA 90034
800-456-AIP1

Budget Films
4590 Santa Monica Blvd.
Los Angeles, CA 90029
213-660-0187

Buena Vista Home Video
500 S. Buena Vista St.
Burbank, CA 91521
818-840-1111

California Newsreel
630 Natoma Street
San Francisco, CA 94103
415-621-6196

CBS, Inc.
51 West 52nd Street
New York, NY 10019
212-765-4321

CBS/Fox Video Library
39000 Seven Mile Road
Livonia, MI 48152
313-591-1555

Cinema Guild
1697 Broadway
Room 802
New York, NY 10019
211-246-5522

Facets Multimedia
1517 W. Fullerton Ave.
Chicago, IL 60614
312-281-9075

Ferde Grofe Films
4091 Glencoe Ave.
Marina Del Rey, CA 90292
800-626-6095

Films Inc.
5547 N. Ravenswood Ave.
Chicago, IL 60646
800-323-4222

First Run Films
153 Waverly Place
New York, NY 10014
212-243-0600

Fries Home Video
6922 Hollywood Blvd.
Los Angeles, CA 90028
213-201-8800

Goodtimes Distribution Corp.
401 Fifth Ave.
New York, NY 10016
212-889-0044

HBO Home Video
1370 Avenue of the Americas
New York, NY 10019
800-648-7650

Image Associates
352 Conejo Road
P.O. Box 40106
Santa Barbara, CA 93103
805-962-6009

Indiana University A-V Center
Bloomington, IN 47405-5901
812-335-8087

International Historic Films
Box 29035
Chicago, IL 60629
312-436-8051

The Knowledge Collection
800-637-5335

MCA Home Video
70 Universal City Plaza
Universal City, CA 91608
818-777-4300

Media Home Entertainment
5730 Buckingham Parkway
Culver City, CA 90230
800-421-4509

MGM/UA Home Video
10000 W. Washington Blvd.
Culver City, CA 90232
213-280-6000

Modern Sound Pictures
1402 Howard St.
Omaha, NE 68102
402-341-8476

MPI Home Video
15825 Rob Roy Dr.
Oak Forest, IL 60452
312-687-7881

National Film Board of Canada
1251 Avenue of the Americas
New York, NY 10020
212-586-5131

Nelson Entertainment
1901 Avenue of the Stars
Los Angeles, CA 90067
213-553-3600

New World Video
1440 S. Sepulveda Blvd.
Los Angeles, CA 90025
213-444-8100

New Yorker Films
16 West 61st Street
New York, NY 10023
212-247-6110

Orion Home Video
410 Park Ave.
New York, NY 10022
212-888-4514

Paramount Home Video
5555 Melrose Ave.
Los Angeles, CA 90038
213-468-5000

PBS Video
1320 Braddock Place
Alexandria, VA 22314
703-739-5380

RKO Pictures
1900 Avenue of the Stars
Suite 1562
Los Angeles, CA 90067
213-277-3133

Swank Motion Pictures
201 South Jefferson Ave.
St. Louis, MO 63166
314-534-6300

Third World Newsreel
358 West 38th Street
Fifth Floor
New York, NY 10018
212-947-9277

University of California at Berkeley
Educational TV Office
9 Dwinelle Hall
Berkeley, CA 94720
415-642-2535

Video Home Library
75 Spring Street
New York, NY 10012
800-862-5480

Warner Bros.
4000 Warner Blvd.
Burbank, CA 91505
213-954-6000

Index

Vietnamese and Chinese names have not been inverted